The Unforgettable Sea Of Cortez

Baja California's Golden Age 1947–1977

The Life And Writings Of Ray Cannon

GENE S. KIRA

CORTEZ PUBLICATIONS • TORRANCE, CALIFORNIA

The Unforgettable Sea Of Cortez
Baja California's Golden Age 1947–1977
The Life And Writings Of Ray Cannon

ISBN 0-9632188-2-4
Copyright © 1999 by Gene Kira
Printed in the United States of America

Published by Cortez Publications
20343 Donora Avenue, Torrance, CA 90503
Telephone: 310-371-4479

First Edition
2 4 6 8 7 5 3 1

Library of Congress Cataloging in Publication Data

Kira, Gene, 1946–
The Unforgettable Sea Of Cortez : Baja California's Golden Age 1947–1977 : the life and writings of Ray
Cannon / Gene S. Kira.
p. cm.
Includes index.
ISBN 0-9632188-2-4
1. Baja California (Mexico)—History. 2. Baja California (Mexico)—Social life and customs. 3. Cannon,
Raymond, 1892-1977.
I. Title
F1246,K57 1999
972' .2—dc21 98-49533 CIP

ENDPAPERS: Front, a shark fisherman and his dugout *canoa*, Puerto Escondido, October 1, 1959, photo by
Harry Merrick; Back, the dredging of the inner harbor of Cabo San Lucas, viewed from the Hotel Finisterra,
c. 1974, photo by Ray Cannon.

BOOKS BY GENE S. KIRA

with Neil Kelly

THE BAJA CATCH
A Fishing, Travel & Remote Camping Manual For Baja California

KING OF THE MOON
A Novel Of Baja California

ACKNOWLEDGEMENTS

The generosity and trust accorded us during the creation of this book is a tribute to Ray Cannon and the lasting impression he made on the hearts of so many people.

A special debt of gratitude is owed to Harry Merrick, the photographer without whose artistry and generosity this book would not be possible in its present form. Mr. Merrick's magnificent photographic collection, including the image on the cover of this book, is a unique and precious life's accomplishment, and it has been a privilege to work with him.

Another outstanding photographer deserving special thanks is Al Tetzlaff, whose fishing action photographs grace many of these pages.

A very special note of acknowledgement is due to Robert Twilegar of Western Outdoors Publications for his invaluable help and generosity in granting permission to reprint text and artwork from the early beginnings of his 45-year-old company. The venerable weekly publication, *Western Outdoor News*, has long been an indispensable part of the tourism industry of Baja California, and it continues to fulfill that important role today. Thanks, Bob, to you and your dad, Burt Twilegar, for giving Ray Cannon a voice, and for the help your publication has given the people of Baja California.

Another special thank you and a great big abrazo goes to Dr. Gustavo Farías Noyola, State Tourism Office Coordinator for Baja California Sur, and especially to Rosa Romero Vélez and Oscar Padilla Rivera for their infinite patience and help in tracking down historical details and providing introductions to many residents of their beautiful state. We thank them also for their permission to reprint historical research from Estella Davis' important reference book, *El Alojamiento En Baja California Sur*, published by the Coordinación Estatal de Turismo in conjunction with the Colegio de Bachilleres del Estado de Baja California Sur.

With those special acknowledgements thus expressed, following is a partial list of the generous people who have aided the creation of this book. Each of these individuals, in some way, was touched by the Golden Age of Baja California, and thus became part of a special time and place that will never pass our way again: Enrique Achoy, Enrique Achoy Jr., Jesús Araiza, Bill Benziger, Jack Brown, Francisco "Paco" Bulnes, Luis Bulnes Molleda, Bob Butler, Randy Case, Bobby Castellón, Steve Chism, Charles "Shipwreck Charlie" Cohen, Luis Cóppola Bonillas, Mario Cóppola Joffroy, Jorge Enrique "Coco" Corral, Nicandro Cota León, Saul Davis, Aurora Díaz, Rafaela "Prieta" Díaz, Samuel "Sammy" Díaz, Nancy Dillman, Michael L. Farrior, Rodolfo Galindo, Mike Gallagher, Sandra Gallagher, Fanchon Gallagher, Vicente García Collins, Ricardo García Soto, Chuck Garrison, Martin Goldsmith, Sergio Gómez Cota, Gary and Yvonne Graham, Mrs. Loren Grey, Gill Gunnell, Hector Gutierrez, Donald Halliburton, Bam and Jerry Heiner, Bill Hilton, Lynn Hollingsworth, Al Hrdlicka, John Ireland, Peter Jensen, Don Johnson, Diana Johnson, Fred and Gloria Jones, Abigail Kira, Gifford Kira, Mary Kira, Mel Kirby, Mere Kress, Alix Lafontant, Mel Lane, Graham Liddy (Irish Air Accident Investigation Unit, Dublin), Jorge Limón Tejada, Dorothy Lovelady, Kit McNear, Fred Metcalf, Juan Bautista "Chi Chi" Meza, Quirino Meza, Rosario "Chayo" Meza Evans, Shirley Miller, Ramona "Mocha" Miranda Amador, Lucille Morrison, Spencer Murray, Alvaro Obregón, Sra. Doris Ortega, José Ortiz Ruiz, Michael O'Toole, Lynn Page, Mark D. Parr, Ed Pearlman, Eduardo Pickett Manríquez, Ralph Poole, Chuck Potter, Alfredo Ramírez, George W. Reiger, Tony Reyes Baca, Tony Reyes Montéz, Jan Walters Rockefeller, Abelardo L. "Rod" Rodríguez, Abelardo Nicolas "Niki" Rodríguez, Edrulfo Fiol Ruiz, Carol Sanders, Tony Schuck Jr., James Pledger "Jimmy" Smith, James L. Squire Jr., Bertha Davis Garayzar Tabor, Sonia Tabor, Ted Tetzlaff, William G. Tharpe, Rick Thompson, Felipe Jesús "Chuy" Valdéz Vásques, Tom Ward, Robert "Bobby" Van Wormer, Frank Van Wormer, Ernest Vanier, Dr. Boyd W. Walker, Mary Ev Walker, Mark Walters, Vee Webber, Whitey Whitestine, and Jack Williams.

NOTES ON THE TEXT AND PHOTOS: The stories by Ray Cannon reprinted in this book have been complied mainly from his original manuscripts, field notes and letters. In only a few cases have stories been taken directly from Ray's articles as they were printed in *Western Outdoor News* and other publications. As such, the text of this book represents more of what Ray actually wrote, rather than what may have been published under his byline after editorial cuts and changes. A number of stories appearing here have been compiled from the best of various versions that Ray wrote over the years, and one story in particular, "The Kids' Trip," is an abbreviation of a book that he wrote but never published. In all cases, "copy editing" has been kept to a minimum in order to preserve the style, tone and flavor of Ray's writing, and all composite pieces have been so noted in the text. Scientific names are as given by Ray in his original manuscripts. Place names have been updated when necessary for clarity.

Thousands of photographs from Ray's personal files, or as provided by others, are not attributable (the majority of these photos were undoubtedly taken by Ray himself). Some of these photos are faded, damaged, or of poor technical quality, but are nevertheless unique and historically significant. A sincere thank you is hereby expressed to those many unknown photographers and Baja adventurers whose work may appear here.

DEDICATION

To Carla Laemmle—born in Chicago, Illinois on October 20, 1909—whose enduring love, faith and courage have brought to life for a second time the story of Ray Cannon and the Golden Age of Baja California.

CONTENTS

The Hotel Twin Dolphin, located near Cabo San Lucas at the tip of Baja California, opened in 1977 as the last great resort of the Golden Age to be built during the career of Ray Cannon. — PHOTO BY RAY MOSS

THE LEGACY OF RAY CANNON

TWO MESSAGES FROM THE RECENT PAST

For the newcomer to Los Cabos and the other tourist centers of Baja California, some of the stories and images in this book may seem to come from another place, or at least from a time quite removed from the present. It might seem logical to assume that the thriving tourist industry of Baja California must have developed over a considerable period, and that many of the curiously quaint photographs and otherworldly fishing stories presented here must be from some epoch of the distant past.

But that is not so. *The Unforgettable Sea Of Cortez* is about a distinct and very recent period of Baja California history that spanned the years roughly from the end of World War II until the completion of the Transpeninsular Highway in 1973 and the opening of the international airport at San José del Cabo in 1977.

During that brief one-third of a century, the people of Baja California brought their desert peninsula from a world of ox carts and sailing canoes firmly into the modern age. Almost every element of Baja California's modern infrastructure has been created entirely since the end of World War II. This includes the myriad of luxury hotels and resorts, the sport fishing fleets, the international airports, the harbors and ship terminals, the communication systems, the agricultural developments, some of the towns and cities themselves, and all but a *single* paved highway—from Tijuana to Ensenada.

Those accomplishments brought many benefits to the people of Baja California, but at the cost of a gracious and traditional way of life, also rich in many ways, that was inevitably pushed into history by the pace and pressure of contemporary society.

And, there has been another cost. It may be surprising to the newcomer to learn that most of the "unbelievable fishing stories" contained in this book are actually true. Only a few decades ago, the Sea of Cortez supported a density and richness of life that is almost incomprehensible today.

The writing career of Ray Cannon, the weekly sport fishing columnist for *Western Outdoor News*, coincided almost perfectly with this era of tremendous economic, social and environmental change; Ray made his first trip to "Baja" in 1947, and he wrote about the peninsula until his death in 1977. In more than a thousand columns and magazine articles from this period, he left us with two important messages:

First, there is the story of the beautiful Golden Age of Baja California—a time of miracles and progress, but in a land still unspoiled and still heavy with the romantic perfume of old Mexico. This was a time when the people of Baja California enjoyed the best of both worlds.

And second, there is the story of how recently rich the Sea of Cortez once was, compared to its present status. In the fantastic descriptions of the chapter, "Good Fishing Everywhere!" and in the strong words of the chapter, "Storm Clouds On The Horizon," Ray documents the depletion of population after population of fish species—from the California sardine, to the totuava, the yellowtail, the yellowfin tuna, the giant bass and groupers, and many others—and he warns us of how fragile the sea really is.

Ray Cannon—through his charisma, his many articles and his bestselling book, *The Sea Of Cortez*—did more than any other single person to popularize the early tourist industry of Baja California. But now, as Baja's modernization becomes a *fait accompli* in the opening years of the 21st century, Ray's second message—of our desperate obligation to conserve the beauty and richness of the natural world—emerges as his most lasting legacy.

As the people of Baja California begin to take the first steps toward the restoration and preservation of their magnificent Sea of Cortez, they may perhaps be encouraged by the enthusiastic ghost of Ray Cannon and this vivid reminder of a beautiful past, still alive just beneath the surface of things, that happened only yesterday.

Ray's favorite and best-known portrait, taken off Rancho Buena Vista by photographer Harry Merrick on October 1, 1960.

ULISES TILLMAN CANNON

PIED PIPER OF BAJA CALIFORNIA

How SHALL WE take the measure of a writer's life? In the spanning of decades and years? If that is the case, then the man known to the world as "Ray Cannon" lived a very full measure indeed—84 active years—from September 1, 1892 until his death in Los Angeles on June 7, 1977.

He was born, he said, "Ulises Tillman Cannon," dirt poor, son of a part-time Baptist preacher, one-quarter Cherokee Indian, "on a farm near Sharps Chapel" in Union County, Tennessee. He rode the rails to California, took the stage name "Raymond Cannon," and became a successful Hollywood actor, screenwriter, and ultimately, a director.

But plagued by doubts and recurring stomach ulcers, he wrote and directed his last movie, *Samurai* in 1945, and abruptly abandoned the Hollywood scene to become a modestly-paid freelance outdoor writer. He struggled for years before he found success again, as the author of two bestselling books, and eventually he became one of the most famous outdoor writers of his time, a living legend whose published words were pivotal in the modern development of Mexico's Baja California peninsula.

Shall we measure Ray Cannon by the volume of his work? The sheer mass of it is difficult for the mind to encompass in a single thought: more than 200 movie scripts, dozens of roles played and movies directed, more than 1,200 first-person magazine and newspaper articles describing his adventures, thousands of photographs, letters and unpublished research notes, two watershed books, each of which took many years to research and write, and a third book that he wrote but never published. Much of this output has been lost, but what survives would form a stack of yellowed, crumbling manuscripts and photographs about twelve feet high.

It may be more appropriate to measure Ray Cannon by his effect on the development of modern Baja California. When Ray first visited Baja in 1947, the 800-mile-long Mexican desert-peninsula was rich in history and fish but poor in nearly everything else. It was a land fallen through the cracks of historical accident, a gorgeous wilderness still bearing only the most superficial scars of human endeavor. The mountainous spine of the peninsula was populated by the ruins of centuries-old Spanish missions, by the rusting remnants of mostly failed European mining operations, and by the hardy Californios, the goat and cattle ranchers who struggled to maintain their herds wherever water could be found in the blistering hot arroyos of the Mexican desert. The unspoiled natural panorama of the peninsula's 2,000-mile coastline was marked by only a handful of settlements that were more villages than towns, and in the entire peninsula there was only one paved highway—about 140 miles long—connecting the U.S. border at Tijuana with the port of Ensenada, and recently extended south to Arroyo Seco near the present-day town of Colonet.

For the people of Baja California, the 1950s and 1960s were decades of great opportunity and risk, an era of awakening from a long slumber that had held their land in thrall for centuries.

To their north, they watched the post-World War II economic growth of the United States, the population boom of Southern California, and the great rise in personal incomes just across the border. For most residents of the peninsula, however, there was no way to participate in this wealth. Baja California lacked water, capital, population, infrastructure, natural resources—virtually every basic requirement for economic growth.

However, Baja did possess some assets. First, it had fish, arguably more fish and more kinds of fish than any similar area of the world, and it was this bounty from the sea that would provide for two of the modern peninsula's leading industries—commercial fishing and tourism. Second, Baja had that most valuable quality of any piece of real estate—location. The romantic, wild natural beauty of the ocean-desert was separated from the wealthiest population in

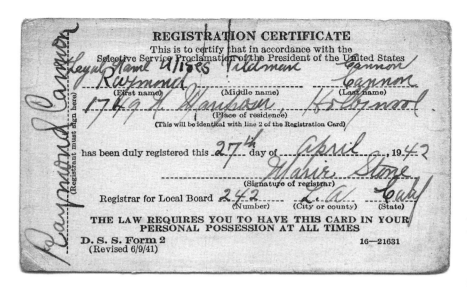

The Preacher from Long Holler

By Faye Paul

HE was just another little mountaineer dutifully "totin' a turn" of corn to the mill, but his thoughts were far from commonplace that colorful summer morning "down Long Holler" in the Cumberlands. For what lad's meditations are ordinary when ambition to be and to do in the great world outside of home, first sets his little heart throbbing in the trail of youthful imagination? That the details of his attack upon an awaiting universe were surprisingly indefinite, mattered but slightly. He was alive in a regular world, and success would "jus' natchelly" be his.

Consequently it was a bit disturbing to discover himself a very few years later half-heartedly and even rebelliously studying for the ministry in a well-known Southern theological seminary. You see the preacher idea had been purely Mother's and it did seem like a fellow ought to make his mother happy if he could! Only it was tough that when there is but one big chance, it had to come this way.

Of course the end was inevitable, and as is the case in most real stories, the climax of one chapter provided a running start for the next. Raymond Cannon, destined to be a screen hero, escaped from the stately school via a grape vine, or a waterspout, or whatever it is that striplings are wont to employ as a means of departure when they feel the call of the wanderfulst; and during the years

The young man who deserted the ministry for pictures, the cabin in which he was born and the old mill referred to in the story

that followed with a "two-a-week" stock company, the young mountaineer knew that he had at least made his final choice.

When pictures called, as they invariably do, Raymond grabbed right on, and he gives much of the credit for his success in juvenile characterizations to the camera schooling which he received while with the old Kay-Bee and Selig outfits in the romantic days of picture pioneering in California. It was during the filming of "Hearts of the World" that Griffith found the young actor and made a place for him in his stock company. After characterizing several roles under the personal direction of the master, Cannon was chosen for the lead opposite Dorothy Gish in "Battling Jane," her first picture with her own company. Here the part of Homer the country boy (he of all the usual trick clothes and embarrassed postures) was a gold mine for the lad from Tennessee.

A scene from "Nugget Nell," in which Cannon played the fascinating city chap to the complete dazzlement of the "littler" Gish

(Continued on Page 36)

Ray's given name and place of birth are mysterious. He was born, he said, Ulises Tillman Cannon, and he said that his only birth certificate was literally carved on the trunk of a tree "on a farm near Sharp's Chapel," in Union County, Tennessee. At other times he listed his birthplace as "Long Hollow, Tennessee," which is a few miles from Sharp's Chapel.

The only known physical evidence for Ray's original name is this 1942 Selective Service draft card showing in his own hand that "Ulises (the Spanish spelling of Ulysses) Tillman Cannon" was indeed his legal name. The selection of the Spanish spelling "Ulises" over the English "Ulysses," would be consistent with his parents' naming of an earlier son also with a Spanish first name; Ray's older brother was named Manuel Lee Cannon.

Ray was called "Cousin Tillmon" by at least one relation in Tennessee who wrote a letter to him in 1956, and in 1962 Ray himself wrote a letter saying that he had been named for Governor Benjamin Tillman (1847-1918) of South Carolina, although he did not know the reason why.

And the name "Ray"? It is known that he adopted the name "Raymond" to use in theater credits during his early years in California, and later shortened it to "Ray" for his bylines as a sport fishing writer. He may have taken the name from a possible old fishing spot, "Ray," that shows up in some maps on a river only a few miles from the area where he was born. But that place—and undoubtedly the old "birth certificate tree" that witnessed Ray's naming in 1892—were both subsequently inundated by the Tennessee Valley Authority in the 1930s.

Apocryphal article, "The Preacher From Long Holler," in *Screenland Magazine*, November 1920, supposedly shows the log cabin where Ray was born near Long Hollow, Tennessee. The article describes how Ray briefly attended a "well-known Southern theological seminary" to make his mother happy, but escaped after a few years "via a grape vine" (also sometimes described as a gutter drain) to find work with a "two-a-week" stock company, and eventually, the movies in California.

human history by nothing more than a barbed-wire border fence. And lastly, Baja California possessed its own wealth of energetic dreamers—from both sides of the border—who were drawn there by the raw frontier excitement, the opportunities of an empty land, the brilliance of the life-filled sea, and the fostering richness of the Mexican way of life.

In some ways, it might be said that the road to Baja California's postwar economic development was first paved not with asphalt, but with fish—both commercially-caught, and just as significantly, as part of a pioneering sport fishing industry that played a vital role in bringing much needed business and capital investment to the peninsula.

Many of the early entrepreneurs of the modern age were airplane pilots of the World War II era who established fly-in fishing resorts on the shores of the Sea of Cortez. The very first pioneers of this group included Abelardo L. "Rod" Rodríguez of Rancho Las Cruces, Ed Tabor of the Flying Sportsmen Lodge, Herb Tansey of Rancho Buena Vista, and Luis Cóppola Bonillas of the Hotel Los Arcos in La Paz. Whether by coincidence or by historical imperative, all four of these former pilots opened their businesses within a few

---

STARTING OUT IN TENNESSEE

[Ray talks of his boyhood and youth during an interview given in 1973.]

"I was born in a log cabin on the Tennessee-Kentucky border. We were about 100 years behind the rest of the United States. The kids had to go to school on mule back. You know, when I think back on how I finally came out here, it's the same old story: the kid who looked over the mountain and saw another one. I was born with a big charge of curiosity.

"All in all I stayed in eastern Tennessee long enough to get a couple of years of college. I was a student of divinity. But I started to question the discipline of the Baptist teachings, and I got kicked out for denying the faith. This didn't go over too big with my father because he was a circuit rider in the Cumberland region. He would ride on horseback to all of the churches in the area and preach.

"I got my first taste of traveling on the Southern Railroad when I was still in high school. During the summers I worked on the railroad as a news butch. That's what they called us. We would sell newspapers and candies. The train took us from Washington, D.C. to New Orleans.

"Later on in college I got a spot in a repertoire. We would learn about half-a-dozen plays and then tour the South. We'd move into a town and have a new play every night." — RAY CANNON, ARIZONA DAILY STAR

In 1960, Ray obtained this "Delayed Proof of Birth" in Los Angeles with the sworn affidavit of his older brother, Manuel Lee Cannon. It lists the name that Ray assumed for theatrical credits sometime before 1920: Raymond Cannon.

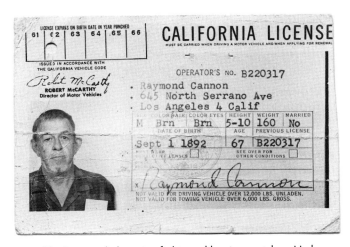

"Ray liked to watch the prize fights and boxing matches. He knew quite a lot about them from personal experience. It seems he had actually tried his hand (or his head) at boxing at one time, but gave it up after getting one of his ear drums smashed. That's why his left ear stuck out like it did." — CARLA LAEMMLE

From a grateful Mexico, Ray receives three awards for his work in promoting tourism in Baja California, at an elaborate testimonial banquet in Los Angeles, June 18, 1969. Ricardo García Soto, top center, Director of Tourism for Baja California Sur, presents a silver platter, inlaid with a map of Baja California in mother-of-pearl, from Hugo Cervantes del Río, Governor of Baja California Sur. A bronze plaque is presented by Mexicana Airlines' Juan Matute, right, President of the Los Angeles Association of Tourism. Guillermo Moreno, left, Sub-coordinator General of the Mexican National Tourist Council, presents a silver medallion—the council's highest award—from Miguel Alemán, former President of Mexico. After Ray's death in 1977, Alemán would write: "I can think of no one who has done more to acquaint the world with Baja and the Sea of Cortez than Ray Cannon. He was a great friend of Mexico and will be sorely missed by all of us who were privileged to know him."

months of each other between 1950 and 1952.

In all of Baja California, there was only one other fly-in fishing lodge that opened for business more or less concurrently with these first four. This was the legendary Casa Díaz of the Mexican prospector and miner Antero Díaz and his wife Cruz, located on the terrifyingly isolated but fantastically beautiful bay of Bahía de los Angeles. Díaz first came to Baja California from Mexico City in 1939, returned to stay in 1945, and by 1951 Casa Díaz was fairly well established in the business of serving meals to fly-in tourist anglers and providing them with boats and guides.

Over the next two decades, these and a host of other Baja entrepreneurs would build fishing lodges on virtually every suitable bay and cove of the peninsula, and these businesses would open and close with Darwinian ruthlessness whenever the vagaries of the economy, the fishing, the capital backers, or any of a dozen other factors caused the briefest interruption in cash flow. Ultimately, the survivors—such as Luis Bulnes Molleda who invested $5 million to remodel Cabo San Lucas' Hotel Solmar in 1993—became wealthy. But their colleagues went broke in droves, and close beside nearly every successful operation today can be found the weathering remnants of someone's failed endeavor, whether it is an abandoned hotel building with its windows broken out, or just a pattern of rotting palm fronds and two-by-fours lost on some lonely beach. Baja was built with dreams and guts.

In 1947, a supremely enthusiastic and jovial rogue of a man who called himself "Ray Cannon" stumbled upon this magical world of risk-taking entrepreneurs, seemingly inexhaustible natural beauty, and the emergent postwar tourism industry.

Already 55 years old and bearing the fresh emotional and physical scars of his recent Hollywood burnout, Ray had arranged with former Mexican President Abelardo L. Rodríguez (father of Abelardo L. "Rod" Rodríguez, who would open Baja's first luxury fishing lodge at Rancho Las Cruces three years later) to visit and test-fish the waters surrounding the shrimping port of San Felipe at the north end of the Sea of Cortez. The exact details of how Ray managed to obtain this assignment have been lost, but it is possible that the contacts he had already made during his research for his 1953 book, *How To Fish The Pacific Coast*, may have lead to an introduction and invitation.

Ray was accompanied on his first forays to San Felipe by his friend, Eddie Urban—also known as "Eddie Abdul" and "Eddie Abdo"—who operated charter fishing boats in Southern California and was a part-time movie actor and opera singer. What they found at the end of the 125-mile dirt road leading to San Felipe changed the course of Ray's life and greatly accelerated the speed at which resorts would be built throughout modern Baja.

The fishing at San Felipe was stunningly rich compared to Southern California, and Ray was the perfect person to appreciate the difference. He had been fishing the shoreline from Los Angeles north since about 1913, and he was already expert enough to have begun writing *How To Fish The Pacific Coast*.

In 1947, the area around San Felipe had already been somewhat reduced by commercial fishing, but by today's standards it was still far beyond what one might think of as "unbelievable." Ray and Eddie Urban camped on the beach just north of town and they fished the area out to Consag Rock on shrimp boats chartered by the former President of Mexico. They caught fantastic, unlimited numbers of many kinds of fish, some never before identified, including the legendary totuava, a gigantic member of the croaker family that grew to well over 200 pounds. Ray claimed to the end of his life that during this period he observed one specimen weighed in at 303 pounds, and there is no compelling reason to disbelieve it.

The rest—as they say—is history. Standing on the hot, sandy beach at San Felipe, Ray undoubtedly looked south and imagined the Baja peninsula stretched out seven-hundred miles beyond the horizon—a vast, unspoiled, almost completely unknown wilderness that could provide the world with unlimited adventure and exploration. He returned to Los Angeles convinced that he had discovered the Holy Grail, not only of sport fishing, but of his own life and the lives of millions of others who sought refuge from the cut-and-thrust pressures of modern-day industrialized society. He saw himself as a pied piper who would use the allure of sport fishing to lead people to happiness through a greater appreciation of nature's beauty.

Ray began writing in earnest about his newly-discovered mission in life. He completed *How To Fish The Pacific Coast* in 1953. Later that same year, when the new weekly sporting newspaper *Western Outdoor News* published its inaugural issue on December 4, 1953, the novice book author wrote an article for it that described fishing Baja's Pacific coast south to San Quintín. That was the beginning.

For the next twenty-four years, until his death in 1977, Ray spent as much time as possible fishing, exploring, and studying the Sea of Cortez and Baja's Pacific coast. Assisted by his "secretary" and companion in life, Carla Laemmle, he wrote a weekly column for *Western Outdoor News* during that entire period, and he contributed hundreds of articles to a stable of other magazines and newspapers. As he became famous, he gradually evolved into a "character" every bit as colorful as those he had created for his Hollywood movies. He grew a full beard and clapped a weather-beaten old sea captain's hat on his head that was very rarely removed in public. He traveled with a professional photographer whenever possible to ensure maximum publicity for his adventures, and he polished a repertoire of humorous stories which—with perfect timing and delivery—he used to keep audiences spellbound for hours.

People from all walks of life were instantly attracted to

CORNBREAD FOR "SEX"

[Carla explains how a young Ray accidentally offered to work for "sex" in a Greek restaurant.]

One of Ray's first jobs was working as a news butch on a commission basis.

Ray was always ready to try any new venture, so when a Greek restaurant owner advertised for a fry-cook, Ray knew just enough Greek to apply for the job. He was seventeen at the time.

When the Greek restaurant owner asked Ray what he would work for, Ray told him he would work for commission.

"Commission!" gasped the owner. He was stunned! He was flabbergasted! He couldn't believe what he was hearing!

How was Ray to know that in Greek, "commission" sounds just like the word for "sex"?

After the misunderstanding was cleared up Ray was hired for the job, but he soon learned that, in addition to being a fry-cook, he had to bake as well.

The only thing that Ray knew how to bake was cornbread. But not your ordinary, run-of-the-mill cornbread. It was cornbread like you never tasted. His secret? Eggs! Not just four, five or six eggs, but a dozen.

It was a sensation! Word got around, and Ray gained fame for his dozen-egg cornbread and the Greek restaurant gained a lot of new customers.

— CARLA LAEMMLE

Ray, not only because of his charisma and personality, but also because they sensed his essential sincerity. Ray truly *was* the colorful character he had created. Before ever setting foot in Baja, he had already experienced many facets of "modern society," found much of it lacking, and had decided to have as little to do with it as possible. When he discovered the natural beauty and pleasures of the Sea of Cortez, Ray decided instead to become a part of *it*. He saw himself as a modern-day member of the fraternity that he imagined must have existed among the *"vagabundos del mar,"* the early dugout sailing canoe fishermen who had once roamed the Sea of Cortez—gypsy-like—in their frail craft.

In his beard, hat, baggy pants, and torn checkered shirt, Ray was surely the happiest *vagabundo* that ever lived, and he poured himself into studying the Sea of Cortez and writing about it with an energy that only happiness can sustain. He jammed filing cabinets full of correspondence and scientific research, and he organized a series of full-length small boat cruises of the Cortez unmatched to the present day. It is noteworthy that during Ray's long career no rival seriously threatened his preeminence as the voice of Baja California. Ray's position was secure, for Baja was still a very difficult, challenging beat in those days, and nobody had Ray's energy except Ray.

During his career and after, wildly conflicting stories swirled around the growing legend of Ray Cannon. He was rich; he was penniless. He was a drunk; he was a teetotaler. He was a womanizer; he was a gentleman of almost Victorian propriety. He was a naive dreamer; he was sophisticated and worldly. He was an opportunist; he was an idealist-philosopher. In different ways, all of these things were quite true, and some of them simultaneously. Ray was nothing if not complex. And underlying all of these many contradictions was a fundamental *joie de vivre* and an infectious enthusiasm for everything about him that made people love him and want to be near him. Ray truly lived with a romantic "child heart" that saw wonder and beauty everywhere he looked and he had that precious, rare ability to make others do the same.

One criticism sometimes leveled at Ray by editors and fellow outdoor writers—with perhaps more than a dash of jealousy—was that he rarely wrote about any hotel or lodge that refused him at least the promise of free rooms, meals, and fishing trips. Ray was notoriously up-front in this respect. No freebies. No publicity. And that was usually that.

But while this policy may have violated the ethical standards of so-called "professional journalism," without it there would have been no publicity at all, for throughout his 24-year Baja writing career Ray earned only a very modest living from his columns and freelance magazine articles.

It was only after the runaway success of *The Sea Of Cortez* that he had any money at all. Few people knew Ray well enough to realize that his apparent freeloading was a necessary part of fulfilling his life's mission: to introduce as many people as possible to the beauty and happiness he had discovered in Baja California.

With the enthusiastic backing of Baja's fledgling airlines and impetuous hotel developers, Ray traveled, fished and wrote of his many adventures, and his readers worshiped him and hung on his every word. They came to Baja whenever and wherever he said the fishing was good, which it often actually was, although Ray never let a slow fishing day get in the way of a good story.

Ray had the power to fill hotels whenever he wished. The customers came south in a steadily rising tide, and the great resorts of Baja California were built one after another. Some of the earliest, such as Herb Tansey's Rancho Buena Vista, first opened as nothing more than humble clusters of shacks on the beach and a bumpy airstrip hacked out of the desert shrubbery. The Hotel Los Arcos opened in La Paz with twelve rooms. The Hotel Solmar at Cabo San Lucas opened with no air conditioning.

But each year, all up and down Baja California, the entrepreneurs built larger and larger hotels of ever increasing luxury, and Ray fulfilled his part of the bargain by writing a steady stream of articles to spread the word and help his friends stay in business during the lean periods. The pinnacle of Ray's writing career came in 1966 when Lane Magazine and Book Company published his masterpiece, *The Sea Of Cortez*. This magnificent, full-color volume sold over 280,000 copies at the highest price ever charged up to that point for a "fishing book," and it put "Baja" on the map forever, greatly increasing the flow of tourists to the peninsula.

RAY'S VISION OF THE GOLDEN AGE

[In this fragment, originally written as a comment about his book, *The Sea Of Cortez*, Ray expresses his hope for Baja California as an unspoiled paradise for the ages.]

Of all my discoveries in and around this enchanting Sea, I believe you will agree that the most important was in finding the illusive fountain of fun. I found it permeating the lands and the waters everywhere, over thousands of rich but unused miles. These immense, empty regions with their vast natural abundances need people to enjoy them, while in the United States, there are thousands of weary, tension-ridden people who desperately need the Cortez and the respite it offers.

While the number of Cortez *amadores* from all over the land may eventually grow to many thousands of people with kindred spirits and fun-loving minds, there need be no fear of overcrowding, for there will be plenty of room for all in the grand stretches of open spaces of water and wilderness, for generations to come. —RAY CANNON

Tirelessly, to the end of his life, Ray promoted himself, his beautiful book, and the earthly pleasures to be found south of the border. The multitude of lodges and hotels built on his watch—and the tourist boom they fueled—formed the economic basis of a true "Golden Age" for the Baja peninsula.

In 1947, when Ray and Eddie Urban made their first trip to San Felipe, there were no fly-in fishing lodges at all in Baja California. By the time of Ray's death in 1977, dozens of lodges had opened, and their names formed an honor roll of legendary establishments that have become an integral part of Baja's history, lore, and mystique: Casa Díaz, Punta Chivato, Loma Linda, Serenidad, Misión, Oasis, Flying Sportsmen, Los Cocos, Los Arcos, Hotel Perla, Las Cruces, Punta Pescadero, Palmas de Cortez, Spa Buena Vista, Rancho Buena Vista, Punta Colorada, Palmilla, Hotel Cabo San Lucas, Twin Dolphin, Hacienda, Mar de Cortez, Finisterra—and at land's end—the Hotel Solmar. There were many others besides these, but these were the stuff of which Baja's Golden Age was built.

Nevertheless—like the original fairy tale of the *Pied Piper of Hamelin*—Ray's story also had a darker side, an

THE GUIDING PHILOSOPHY OF TAOISM

[Few people who knew Ray realized that he was a follower of the teachings of Lao-tse, the sixth century B.C. Chinese philosopher who is traditionally regarded as the founder of Taoism. Shortly after Ray's death in 1977, Carla Laemmle explained how the son of a Baptist preacher came to be a disciple of Oriental philosophy.]

While doing research on *Broken Blossoms* for D. W. Griffith, Ray became interested in Buddhism and other oriental philosophies. He was particularly attracted to the mystical teachings of the ancient Chinese sage Lao-tse's philosophy called Taoism. It influenced him greatly. Later, Ray went to China and studied six months in a Buddhist monastery. It changed his whole approach to life. Taoism has been termed "The Quiet Way." It is a philosophy of "effortlessness," harmony and happiness; observing and following nature's lead as part of the forever-moving motion, everywhere present in all things; and quiet acceptance of that motion as change in our own lives; ever seeking out the good and the beautiful and adhering to the First Law: "Harm no one, especially yourself."

Ray truly lived by this quiet, gentle and happy philosophy. He enjoyed life to the fullest, and was always aware of it at the time. Through him, my own life has been greatly enriched. He taught me how to store the beauty of a sunset, a flower or work of art within my "memory bank" so it would never be lost. He made me mindful of the myriads of small lives around us, unseen, in nature's kingdom, each fulfilling its own simple and rightful destiny in the "Allness of Tao."

Ray taught me what it means to always keep the "child heart" and never lose that sense of "wonder" in the commonplace as well as in the mysteries of life. An ancient Chinese proverb that Ray sought to live by was, "make the many happy, expecting no reward."

I say from my heart, in all of the comings and goings and living and doing, Ray was the most fun to be with.

I feel the warmth of Ray's presence whenever I see a beautiful sunset or a seascape or some "way-out" island in his beloved Sea of Cortez. And because I have stored within me so much of the beauty that was Ray, he will never be lost to me. — CARLA LAEMMLE

Ray's notes to himself on the "Taoist" life of the giant sea bass: "Big sea bass lives Taoist life in own cave to fit him—no shark can get in. When hungry he just goes outside cave and when small fish passes by he inhales it down his gullet. The rest of the time he spends meditating on what not to do next..."

irony that belied his 1947 vision of an endless, unspoiled paradise where visitors from the over-industrialized north could come to renew themselves in a place of eternal natural beauty.

In Ray's idealized vision, the Baja California of the Golden Age was a quiet, idyllic place where guests would arrive at very remote, widely-separated luxury hotels in small airplanes and enjoy the pristine splendor of the life-filled Sea of Cortez. Others, he imagined, would cruise down the sea in small private boats and stop to refresh themselves at these same hotels. For one brief period during the 1960s it almost seemed that Ray's dream would come true. But the greatest irony of Ray Cannon's career was that the more he celebrated and wrote of his love for the Golden Age, the more he did to hasten its end.

If Ray was aware of these ironies, he never let on in print. In his writings he practiced a willing suspension of disbelief, refusing to acknowledge that anything but his idealized vision would ever exist. Like many things about Ray, his true feelings and awareness of the end of the Golden Age remain a mystery.

Whether or not he was aware of it, the end would surely have come anyway, its inevitability assured by public demand and government policy that had determined decades earlier that the economic development of Baja California would not be restricted to the world of private planes and remote luxury hotels. With or without Ray Cannon, there was no stopping of the commercial fishing that would reduce the Sea of Cortez to a shadow of its original richness. Nor would there be a turning away of the hordes of tourists who began arriving not just by a few thousand per year, but by tens of thousands, hundreds of thousands, and ultimately, by the millions.

For Ray, nothing symbolized the end of the Golden Age more than the completion of "Mex 1," the 1,070-mile Transpeninsular Highway that connected the U.S. border with the tip of the peninsula in 1973. Ray was correct in his assessment that the Transpeninsular Highway would shape the future of Baja more than any other single factor. Only a quarter century after the paving of Mex 1, the scale, economic diversity, and the hustle and bustle of modern Baja California make many of the relics of the Golden Age seem almost quaint by comparison.

And despite the hundreds of times that he wrote on the theme of conservation, nothing Ray did could stop the depletion of the natural richness of the Sea of Cortez that he foresaw as early as the 1950s.

So, if the writer called "Ray Cannon" cannot ultimately be measured by his effect on the environment and economic status of today's Baja California, how can we best determine his proper place in the history of the land that he loved with so much passion and devotion?

Perhaps the truest answer is found in the hearts of the many people whose lives were affected by this boundlessly enthusiastic, unflaggingly energetic old sea dog with the scruffy beard and the battered captain's hat.

In the homes of the old skiff fishermen and the owners of the great resorts of the Golden Age, Ray Cannon is remembered even today as a sprightly, inspiring vision that appeared in their midst at a time when they had little more than hopes and dreams. The older people of Baja California remember the building of the schools, and the bringing of water and electricity to the villages. They remember the building of the first humble lodges and the first great resorts, the coming of the ferries, the highway, the international airports, and they remember the man whose limitless enthusiasm made them believe it was all possible.

Ray took his final voyage on the Sea of Cortez on June 25, 1977, when his ashes were scattered upon the waters of Canal de San Lorenzo near La Paz by Carla Laemmle, the beautiful and loving woman with whom he had worked and shared the most profound intimacies of his life for the preceding forty-two years. As the solemn motorcade and police escort passed through the city that Ray had watched grow up from little more than a village, the people paused in their daily tasks and lined the roadside in a sorrowful, silent tribute to the American they had known as "Señor Cannon."

It was a tribute not only to the man they had loved for so many years—Ray Cannon, the pied piper of Baja California's Golden Age—but also to their own memories, for they knew that something beautiful had passed into history; their land would never be the same again.

*****

Here then, is the story of Ulises Tillman Cannon of Union County, Tennessee; here are his greatest and wildest fish stories; and here is the story of the land he loved, its people, its natural beauty, and its happiest time: The Golden Age of Baja California.

A DAY WITH THE "OLD MAN OF THE SEA"

[*Western Outdoor News* editor Norm Phillips writes of meeting and fishing with the energetic Ray Cannon at Rancho Buena Vista. Ray was 81 years old at the time this story was written about him.]

NOVEMBER 11, 1973—Minutes after I checked into Rancho Buena Vista and had a beer with Ted Bonney, general manager and the Chief Honcho in Colonel Walters' absence, in walked the Old Man of the Sea, Ray Cannon. I had no idea he would be dropping in, no more than he knew that I would.

Ray is without doubt one of my favorite people in the whole world and has been a dear friend for—well, decades; several of them. Nobody knows how old Ray is, but confidentially, he had his 79th birthday party at Rancho Buena Vista three years ago, in 1970. He had another 79th birthday party there in 1971 and again in '72. Preparations are now underway for another 79th birthday fiesta to be held late this year.

Ray told me he intends to stay at 79 for many years to come. The man's energy and quickness of wit is amazing. His eyesight is far keener than mine; his hearing is much better, yet I'm merely a young whippersnapper only pushing 60; really, young enough to be his son.

Take the day we spent on a Rancho Buena Vista cruiser exploring the Sea of Cannon and doing a little fishing. He was up before daylight (his room was next to mine) and in the mess hall by 6:30 a.m., impatient for breakfast. We were in our boat and away by 7:15. We cruised, fished, photographed steadily, all day long, with the hot tropical sun beating down on us. We shot action pictures of every fish caught. Ray spoke at length, knowledgeably and exhaustively, on every fish, every bird, giving its full natural history and feeding habits. He also knew the history of every house along shore and who owned it now.

And by God, on our way back home at 4 o'clock in the afternoon while I was nodding from exhaustion, Ray revealed the fact that he'd brought along a shotgun and shells because he thought I might like to wind up the day duck hunting. He said he knew a cove where we could wake up a few mallards if we did some hiking. I told him no way—forget it—you're trying to kill me.

He was still bright and cheerful at the dinner table that night and spent the evening chatting with the other guests at the ranch, all of them his admirers. When I went to bed at 10 o'clock that night, I could hear him in the room next to mine, being interviewed by another boating writer present at the lodge. Ray worked with that writer until after midnight, giving the interview requested.

The Old Man of the Sea is really sumthin', and he's for real. He really does know Mexico, and particularly the Sea of Cannon, as no other man of our time does.

God bless you, Ray, and have a happy 79th birthday! For the third or fourth time.

— NORM PHILLIPS, WESTERN OUTDOOR NEWS

Ray, left, with *Western Outdoor News* editor Norm Phillips off Rancho Buena Vista.

Raymond Cannon as a young actor, c. 1920.

WINE AND ROSES

THE HOLLYWOOD YEARS

ONE DAY, ABOUT the year 1912, a strikingly handsome young man from the mountains of Tennessee found himself on the empty beach of Santa Monica, California. Tillman Cannon—as he was known then—was 19 years old and he had come to California looking for beautiful girls. Very soon, he would find them.

He had come to the edge of the water to do some fishing, a routine he had followed for most of his life. But on that particular day, his life would take new direction when he happened to choose a beach where a movie was being shot.

Would the handsome young man from Tennessee like to fill in for a few minutes as an extra?

Why yes, he would. For the young man was not only handsome, but also almost broke.

Expelled from a Baptist preacher's college, the young man who would soon become famous as "Raymond" Cannon had ridden west out of Tennessee as a hobo, and between Knoxville and Los Angeles he had already squeezed a series of adventures into his life that included singing soprano parts as a "young girl" in vaudeville, working as a newspaper reporter in Dallas and Fort Worth, and ten days in a Chihuahua pokey as a correspondent during the Mexican Revolution.

In Santa Monica, Ray's stint as a movie extra would prove to be the beginning of a journey that would take him first into the hectic world of the Hollywood movie industry, and then beyond, into the spiritual realm of the penniless but free sea-gypsies that he called the *vagabundos del mar*. As Ray loved to tell people in later years, his was a story not only of "rags to riches," but of "rags to riches and intentionally back to rags again." He reveled in the freedom and beauty that came to him as a self-proclaimed vagabundo, once he had realized which things in life were really essential to his happiness, and which things were not.

But on that Santa Monica beach, Ray still had a long way to go before he would learn those things.

First, he would work as an actor at the Bentley Grand Theater in Long Beach, where he quickly found more girls than he had ever dreamed possible, dozens of them, a different girl every night, and he would narrowly escape being caught up in an epidemic of "social" disease that swept the city. He would launch a movie magazine called *Camera!* and work in the silent movies and later, talkies, where he would act and write screenplays for films with such luminaries as D. W. Griffith, Tom Mix, Theda Bara, Charlie Chaplin, Dorothy Gish, Buster Keaton, Clara Bow, and a host of others.

As a screenwriter, Ray churned out about 200 original scripts in about ten years, a frenetic pace in keeping with the production methods of the era, in which some films were shot in a week's time. In the late 1920s, Ray began directing films such as *Never Say Die*, *Life's Like That*, *A Slice of Life*, *Joy Street*, *Cradle Snatchers* and *Red Wine*, starring Conrad Nagle.

But clouds were already gathering over Ray's vision of Hollywood and there were signs of disenchantment with the lifestyle and make-believe world of the movies. Deep lines began to creep across the face that had been so fresh and smooth only a few years earlier.

In 1929, Ray's tax records showed an income of over $20,000 earned as a writer and director, a tidy sum for the day. He was living with his wife, Fanchon Royer, in a large, rambling house in the San Fernando Valley that they called "The Farm," and he also bought a house on the beach.

But that same year, the decade-long marriage ended in divorce, and the stress of Hollywood life began to take its toll as Ray's movie career also unraveled.

In the 1930s he took on freelance writing assignments and he did public relations work for the Chinese business community of Los Angeles and such organizations as the pre-World War II Cotton Co-Action Committee that lobbied

Ray donned a derby in *City Feller* (1936).

Clippings by the hundreds showered Ray's rising star at the height of his Hollywood career. In 1928, he had won critical acclaim for writing and directing *Life's Like That*, produced by his 26-year-old wife at that time, Fanchon Royer. By 1929, he had signed with Fox studios, and he directed two of his best-known films, *Red Wine* (also known as *Let's Make Whoopee*), starring Conrad Nagle, and *Joy Street*, featuring Nick Stuart and Lois Moran.

for the boycotting of Japanese silk products.

By 1940 Ray's once promising Hollywood career had deteriorated to the point that he was forced to declare bankruptcy.

Two years after that, the United States had entered World War II and Ray's application for a commission in the U.S. Army Motion Picture Unit was rejected by then Second Lieutenant Ronald Reagan.

By 1945, Ray had developed a severe case of stomach ulcers, and he was more than ready to heed his doctor's advice to either quit the movies or risk bleeding to death. That year, he wrote and directed his last film, *Samurai*, a war story in which he employed two of his many Chinese friends as actors; David Chow played a Japanese secret agent, and Paul Fung appeared as "Dr. Ken Morey." (It was this same Paul Fung who would reappear many years later as "a Chinese professor" in Ray's crowd-pleasing, often-told tale of translating the Chinese-like markings on the head of the chino mero fish as "two farmers, one wife—no peace!")

Casting about for a way to recover from his Hollywood experience, Ray returned to the boyhood pastime that he had loved since his carefree days in the Cumberland Mountains of Tennessee—fishing. He began visiting the California beaches where his movie career had begun more than 30 years earlier, and he began to prowl the coastline with a rod and reel. By 1948, he had decided to turn this therapeutic avocation into a second career; he began researching and writing his first book: *How To Fish The Pacific Coast*.

It would require another five years for Ray to complete that book and establish himself as a sport fishing authority, but before then, two other events occurred that would determine the course of the second half of his long life.

First came the expeditions to San Felipe with Eddie Urban during which Ray learned of the fantastic blast of natural forces that was the Sea of Cortez. It was during these trips in 1947 that he may have first become aware of how deeply he was influenced by the beauty of the sea, and it is probable that during this period he developed his vision of Baja California as a healing refuge for the human spirit.

But then, in the spring of 1949, Ray nearly died when his stomach ulcers began bleeding uncontrollably. He had no medical insurance and the $5,000 necessary for a life-saving operation could not be raised; Ray had no money in the bank, no contact with his old movie colleagues, and no collateral for a loan. Ashen and growing weaker by the day, he remained calm within the Taoist philosophy that he had studied and adopted. He waited quietly for a solution to reveal itself.

But it was clear that he would die unless the surgery was performed immediately. At the last moment, a close friend, well-known dress designer Cora Galenti, had an inspiration. She organized a fund-raising ball and raffle of some of her original designs, and she raised enough money for Ray's operation. The Taoist solution had worked.

Ray, at door, in a movie from the 1920s.

The Rejuvenation of Raymond

Raymond Cannon started his film life by playing a man of seventy. Now he is a juvenile lead, after six years of screen work in which he has been growing younger every day.

Following the suggestion of the not-over-hospitable gateman, I invaded the Hollywood Studios and found Raymond Cannon in his dressing-room. My entrance obviously interrupted the adjustment of a Western-looking spur with which he had been engaged. However, he didn't seem to mind, and I soon discovered that his was the ability to put a stranger at immediate ease, a gift which Nature had not bestowed upon the frosty gateman without.

My next impression concerned the youth of him standing there in the full cowboy "regalia" required by the rôle which he is at present playing opposite Bessie Love in *Penny*, an A. J. Callaghan production. I had long followed his work, but it had been in the old days, and my remembrance of him was not like this.

"You were thinking—?" opened the man across the table, who appeared younger at each glance. This was my opportunity, and I decided to make use of it.

"To be truthful, I was wondering if the venerable Raymond Cannon who played the Beggar in *The Garden of Allah*, and character 'heavies' in *The Adventures of Kathlyn*, and other serials, could possibly be this juvenile individual with whom I am now becoming acquainted. The personage I had in mind was scarcely young six years ago, and you—" The astonishing man was laughing heartily.

"Oh, that . . . don't tell me that they remember the pictures which were so literally 'manufactured' in those days when a man was cast for anything regardless of type, and played it regardless of experience." Then, with a reminiscent sigh, "Yes, those were great old times, and rather horrible ones, too, looking at them from the modern-studio view-point. You know," smiling now, "some way I always seemed to be particularly unfortunate when it came to acquiring those characters of which you spoke. Or perhaps it was a blessing, after all, since they gave me a training that is denied the youngster who enters pictures in this day of advanced casting directors. In any event, I was scarcely out of school when I accomplished some

of the physical atrocities just mentioned.'

"When did your luck break?" I queried.

"If you mean what occasioned my juvenile début after those years of character work, I can only say that, strange as it may appear, it was the result of a gradual growth toward youth on my part. After I joined Mr. Griffith's company three years ago, my 'heavies' became fewer and characters younger, until I found myself doing nineteen-year-olds with Dorothy Gish."

Then I remembered! The little comedienne's leading man in *Battling Jane*, *Turning the Tables*, and *Nugget Nell* had been the *Garden of Allah* Raymond Cannon all of the time.

"And your present rôle?" I asked.

"Just another enthusiastic young one with his system fuller of romance than of logic."

About here I recalled the fact that I had met Raymond Cannon for the sole purpose of conventionally interviewing him. I had been squandering his time to satisfy my personal curiosity. Could it be that, after all, our half-hour might interest my readers to whom I was under obligation for a story? And would they let the photographs tell the rest?

He had been so pleasant and serious and happy and amused by turns that it was too much to expect me to concentrate upon his favourite colour or feminine name.

Upon later consideration I doubt if Raymond Cannon has a superficial streak in his nature. All of which is going to mean much to his progress when he is starred in the near future in the unsophisticated "kid stuff" which he contemplates.

FANCHON ROYER.

From the top: Raymond as "The Beggar" in "The Garden of Allah," his first picture, made in 1915. In "The Great Love" (1917), in "Nugget Nell" (1919), and as he is to-day.

Ray with wife Fanchon Royer, c. 1920, the year they were married in Los Angeles, when she was 18 years old and Ray was 27. Royer was born in Des Moines, Iowa in 1902, moved to Los Angeles at the age of 17, and became a determined and very young actress, agent, writer, editor, and an industry pioneer as one of Hollywood's first woman movie producers. She and Ray met about 1919, when she worked for him as editor of *Camera!*, a trade publication he had founded. They were married February 9, 1920, and had three children before divorcing in 1929. She continued to work as a producer of educational films, author of hagiographical books, and as president of the Catholic Film and Radio Guild, later remarrying, having two more children, and ultimately settling in Puebla, Mexico, where she lived until her death on December 13, 1981. — COURTESY SANDRA GALLAGHER

"The Rejuvenation of Raymond Cannon," in *Picturegoer Monthly*, March 1921, supposedly describes a dressing room encounter and interview with Ray by a "reporter," who turns out to be none other than Ray's real-world wife and publicity agent, Fanchon Royer, whom he had married the year before. Royer was only 19 years old when she wrote this piece.

The article describes Ray's first credited movie role, depicted in the upper left-hand corner, as "The Beggar" in *The Garden Of Allah* (1915), then in younger and younger roles in *The Great Love* (1917) and *Nugget Nell* (1919), and "as he is to-day" (1921).

Royer's article, expertly written in the style of its time, includes the following "quotation"—so humorously pompous to the modern ear—of Ray commenting on his playing the part of an old beggar when he was actually only about 23 at the time. (Ray was all of 28 years old when he supposedly said this.) Royer writes:

"…Then, with a reminiscent sigh [Ray said], 'Yes, those were great old times, and rather horrible ones, too, looking at them from the modern-studio view-point. You know,' smiling now, 'some way I always seemed to be particularly unfortunate when it came to acquiring those characters of which you spoke. Or perhaps it was a blessing, after all, since they gave me a training that is denied the youngster who enters pictures in this day of advanced casting directors…'"

Royer concludes the "interview" with her husband:

"About here I recalled the fact that I had met Raymond Cannon for the sole purpose of conventionally interviewing him. I had been squandering his time to satisfy my own personal curiosity. Could it be that, after all, our half-hour might interest my readers to whom I was under obligation for a story?

"He (Ray) had been so pleasant and serious and happy and amused by turns that it was too much to expect me to concentrate upon his favourite color or feminine name.

"Upon later consideration I doubt if Raymond Cannon has a superficial streak in his nature. All of which is going to mean much to his progress when he is starred in the near future…"

— COURTESY MIKE GALLAGHER

"The Farm," occupied by Ray and Fanchon Royer, as it appeared about 1926. The sprawling country house located on 15 acres of land in the San Fernando Valley had a bunkhouse and pool, and was the scene of Hollywood-style gatherings. According to Ray's daughter, Sandra Gallagher, who now lives in Puebla, Mexico, "the farm" was nonworking: "The only product actually harvested and sold was walnuts, a couple of sacks at a time... as I recall."

— COURTESY SANDRA GALLAGHER

A sign of things to come. Ray, center, Fanchon Royer, her father Elwood H. Royer, and a nice stringer of fish, at Spirit Lake, Iowa, June 1922. Note frying pan and firewood. — COURTESY SANDRA GALLAGHER

Ray's three children, born of his 1920 marriage to Fanchon Royer in Los Angeles. Left to right: Elwood, born 1926; Royer, born 1922; and Sandra, born 1930. Elwood and Royer are deceased. Sandra, a resident of Mexico for over 50 years, is mother of "eight Mexican sons and daughters, fourteen grandchildren and one great-granddaughter."

— COURTESY MIKE GALLAGHER

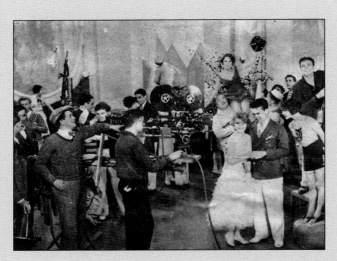

Ray, in cap, directing his "waltzing camera" invention during the filming of his second feature for Fox, *Joy Street* (1929).

NEW CAMERA SHOTS DEVELOPED
BY YOUNG DIRECTOR CANNON

[Ray's career as a movie director was marked by rapid-fire innovation in special effects and basic camera techniques in an era when they were first being discovered. In addition to the four new techniques described in this 1929 newspaper article, he is credited with inventing the "waltzing camera" on a long boom, the dollied camera, and the "living lens," that used a moving point of view that seems to have been a precursor of the hand-held effect popular in documentaries.]

FEBRUARY 16, 1929—Four innovations in camera technique have been developed by Raymond Cannon, Fox director. They are the "traveling" or "Cannon" shift, the twin-lap dissolve, the stereopticon shot and the fourth-dimensional shot.

The traveling shift is designed to avoid a choppy effect in changing from one scene to another. In this shift the continuous flow of the picture is maintained by passing from one scene to the next through camera manipulation that produces a blurred panorama during the very brief interlude between scenes. This enables the director to link two or more shots in entirely different locales without any apparent cutting of the film, and tends to make the story continuous instead of a succession of separate scenes.

The twin-lap dissolve has the result of keeping various characters in action before the camera while the background changes. Thus two players may emerge from a house, walk toward the camera, and maintain a conversation while the house melts away into a desert scene or the deck of a ship at sea.

The stereopticon shot is produced in two ways, one by a special arrangement of lights and backgrounds, and the other through the employment of a unique camera mounting and foreground setting. Both types of stereopticon shot are claimed to give an illusion of fullness and depth to the picture so that the foreground seems to stand out in relief.

The "fourth-dimensional" shot is based on the scientific hypothesis that a person asleep is really in a world where the ordinary laws of time and space do not apply. — INSIDE FACTS

On March 4, 1949, Ray had a considerable portion of his stomach removed at Cedars of Lebanon Hospital in Hollywood. He pulled through, greatly weakened, after three days of crisis in the hospital and a convalescence of several months.

While it would be hazardous to conjecture what must have gone through Ray's mind during his close brush with death and after, it is known that during this period his thoughts were strongly focused on the concept of natural beauty.

Ray slowly nursed himself back to health, with the help of Carrie Belle Laemmle—Carla's mother—at the Laemmle home in Los Angeles. For three months, Carla herself was required to be away, as she assisted Cora Galenti in a series of designer showings and meetings in Texas.

Finances, as always, were very tight; Carla took a single ten-dollar bill on the three-month trip for personal spending money.

Ray remained at home that spring and summer, doing small chores, planting a small garden, canning fruit, and starting to fish again as he regained his strength. His letters to Carla, recounting his modest daily accomplishments, are filled with references to nature and his love of it, as he learned to find beauty and meaning in a new leaf, a single butterfly, or the opening of a blossom.

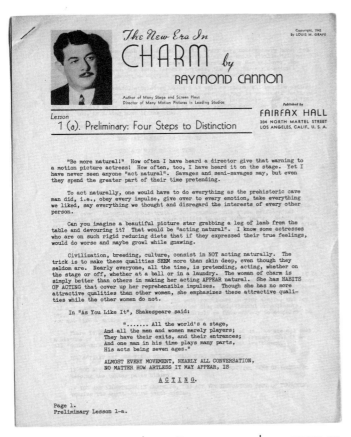

In 1942 Ray contracted to write a correspondence course on "charm" for Louis M. Grafe on a four-percent royalty basis. He had been forced to declare bankruptcy two years earlier.

In a few years, Ulises Tillman Cannon—the strikingly handsome young man from the mountains of Tennessee—would regain his vitality and capture the public eye yet again, reborn as that grizzly old salt, Ray Cannon, the legendary "author-character" of Baja California. *How To Fish The Pacific Coast* would be published in 1953, and over the next 24 years, Ray would have more than a thousand columns printed in *Western Outdoor News*. In 1966, he would publish his major work, *The Sea Of Cortez*, which would become a collector's item and his legacy to the world.

But that remarkable second career—with its exuberant celebration of life that would introduce a generation to the wonders of Baja California—had its beginnings in the small garden behind the house, in the spring of 1949, in the healing body and mind of a man who had just escaped death.

WORKING WITH D. W. GRIFFITH

Ray worked with D. W. Griffith on *Intolerance* (1916). Describing the experience of acting in the landmark film, he said, "It was the biggest picture ever made... I played over 100 parts in that one film."

Of the great director, Ray said, "Griffith always had dignity. I've even seen him shoot craps with dignity. He was the greatest thinker I've ever met, inventing a dozen things every day. He was the Shakespeare of the movie business.

"In *Birth of a Nation* [1915], Griffith gave the industry a blueprint of techniques in acting, directing and staging. Every 100 feet of film had its own dramatic value; you were either gaping or belly laughing. Every cut had an incident. Movies today have no incident; they have too much dead footage."

Ray himself was no slouch at innovative movie work. In 1929, *Hollywood Screen World* commented, "Raymond Cannon's latest directorial achievement, *Imagine My Embarrassment,* shows this young man not only knows the regular routine of screen productions but knows what to do with cameras. In the last 15 months, Cannon had given the industry the shift shot, the twin dissolve and waltzing machine (dollied cameras)." — JERRY RUHLOW, LOS ANGELES HERALD EXAMINER

DRAMATIC INTRODUCTION TO LILLIAN GISH

Ray worked at many different jobs in the movies, including stunts, lab work, camera work, and helping in the cutting room.

Always with a flair for the dramatic, he describes his introduction as a young stunt man to the famous actress, Lillian Gish:

"It was a war picture, and a three-story building was on fire. I was to jump off the top and hit the ground without a net. The scene was at night, so I rigged a black rope that hung within six feet of the ground, swung down on that, and dropped.

"Lillian was the star of the picture, but didn't know about the stunt. She saw me fall and rushed into the scene horrified and took my head in her lap. That's how we got acquainted." — JERRY RUHLOW, LOS ANGELES HERALD EXAMINER

RAY'S LUST FOR LIFE—AND THEN SOME!

[The photos are myriad: women sitting on his lap, leaning on his shoulder, with their arms around him, cradling his head in their laps. There is no doubt that Ray had a way with women that he never lost. Carla explains how he got his start.]

Ray had no trouble getting a job as an actor at the Bentley Grand Theater in Long Beach. Taking advantage of his actor status, Ray had choice pickings when it came to dating the eager and willing opposite sex.

As things transpired, this adventure was one that was to change his life. I am not sure that Ray would want me to tell it, but it happened a long time ago, and at nineteen, Ray was a virile, young Casanova with a lust for life— and then some.

For the entire summer season that Ray worked as an actor in Long Beach he had a sexual encounter with a different girl every night!

Unbridled promiscuity hit its peak in Long Beach about that time, triggering a widespread outbreak of venereal diseases. By some miracle of Fate, Ray escaped the epidemic. But not the psychological effect the events had upon his psyche. Such revulsion set in, it turned him off women and sex life like the plague and changed his whole outlook on that part of his life. For over a year

afterward Ray remained totally celibate.

Ray left Long Beach and found himself a small cabin in Malibu, where he fished and lived the life of a hermit for months. It was a period of spiritual awakening, reevaluation and finding new directions." — CARLA LAEMMLE

FISHING WITH A "BEAUTIFUL, YOUNG DOLL"

[In a masterpiece of humor and sly double entendre, Ray describes fishing with an "enthusiastic" young lady at Rancho Buena Vista, c. 1960.]

I was busy trying to develop a technique for catching needlefish and needed a helper for photographing. The only person available (I should always be so lucky) was a beautiful, young doll by the name of Sandra Kompar. Her reactions to our fishing adventure were magnified by her inexperience and lack of inhibition in expressing her feelings.

Little José, my skipper, had our skiff ready before daylight, a time that always adds a feeling of adventure to any fishing trip. Our little outboard was gliding on a platinum-plated surface until the sun rays streaked in from Sinaloa across the Sea and changed it to molten gold.

Sandra hummed like a bee settling in a rewarding blossom. Her expressions of deep satisfaction continued in response to the gentle, air conditioning breeze, the rapidly changing coastline that was now a white beach, then a rugged rock cliff broken by tropical gardens stretching up the arroyos.

Sandra's quiet droning changed to sharp gasps when we saw a dolphinfish rise for a rainbowing leap just ahead

Ray and an unidentified dance partner, c. 1970.

The old movie director hamming it up with Sandra Kompar, c. 1960.

of our bow. That was the beginning of a full day of vocalizing that would end with a voice as hoarse as a Georgia bullfrog.

As we plowed into Pescadero Cove we saw schools of yellowfin tuna and dolphinfish jumping all over the place. But I was on an assignment to get a needlefish story and must concentrate on refining the new technique I had discovered for the fathom-long species. I had already explained to Sandra that this particular needlefish was seldom hooked because of its bony mouth and small throat, and that it would grab the end of the four-inch skip-strip and wrap the bait, and sometimes the whole leader, around its beak, thus getting itself well snelled.

I gave her an outfit rigged for needlefish and a briefing on how she was to pay line at the first strike, giving the needle enough freedom to muzzle itself, then signal to José to stop the skiff.

The last bit of instruction went for naught, for as soon as she saw the first needle take to the air 50 feet from her bait and come vaulting toward it like a skipped rock, she began screeching like a skidding tire. By the time it hit and started peeling off the 200 yards of free-spooled line, you would have thought she'd tied into a two-headed dugong, or just been propositioned by an incubus.

She quit her screeching long enough to reel up the slack, but when the line came taut and the hooked needlefish again went into orbit, Sandra rejoined the networks on all her kilocycles.

A local goat herder came running from around the point and stopped astonished, wondering what kind of hanky-panky was going on in the boat. Seeing it was only a girl catching a fish, he showed signs of disgust by slamming a shillelagh he had picked up on the way against a boulder. He stalked off but stopped in a delayed

About 1930, Ray with pal and fellow actor Paul Fung, and friends. Fung, in addition to being active in the Chinese business community, was the "professor" who Ray said translated the bizarre markings on the head of the chino mero fish as "two farmers, one wife—no peace!" Fung also played the part of "Dr. Ken Morey" in Ray's last movie, *Samurai*, in 1945.

after-thought-take when he must have realized that he was about to miss an eyeful. He sat down and let his goats go.

Despite it being an undersize offspring of the king-size species, Sandra's needlefish performed some magnificent aerial stunts. Never had I seen a fish of its weight reach such jumping heights or execute such body-twisting contortions while in the air. At the apex of one of its shenanigans Sandra gasped, "Look, it's picking its teeth with its tail!"

And that was just what it appeared to be doing. By bending its body into a circle it could use its tail in an effort to flip the leader from between its teeth.

After Sandra finally decked the critter and I was snapping a picture of her holding her catch in a victory pose, the squirming needle came unlatched and started gnashing its teeth and flipped from bow to stern. At that, the doll climbed right into my beard, and I must say, that with that cuddled bundle in my lap, the thought of singing her a fatherly lullaby never once entered my head.

We got reorganized and went on catching needlefish, small yellowfin tuna and dolphinfish. I doubt that Sandra will ever again experience a day filled with more thrills unless it is spent fishing in the same place.

I learned a lot about the joy of fishing, for Sandra had clearly displayed the emotional reactions to fishing I feel but choke back to maintain a phony something called adult dignity. — RAY CANNON

HOW RAY QUIT DRINKING

[Ray was such a forceful personality, such a great storyteller and center attraction, that whenever he "took up a position" in a hotel lobby or bar, some people automatically assumed that he was drunk, or had at least been drinking a fair amount. This was not the case. A broad survey of over a hundred people from all walks of life who knew Ray could locate only four who remember him as drinking any alcohol at all, and only two who remember him as being under the influence—with both of these latter recalling a single apocryphal incident in La Paz. Whether or not that incident actually happened, most of the evidence indicates that during his Baja career, Ray drank water, sodas, and fruit juice only.

Ray clowning around with Rancho Buena Vista guides Eusebio Liborio "Laborio" Cocio Cocio, right, and Pepe Verdugo.

This is confirmed by José Ortiz Ruiz, who began working at Rancho Buena Vista in 1959 both as a skipper and as a bartender. Ortiz states categorically that Ray did not drink alcohol.

But there was a time when Ray did drink. Carla describes the youthful contretemps that caused Ray to give up alcohol for life.]

When I first met Ray he didn't drink, period. But that was not always the case. It was a certain crazy incident that took place in his younger, wild-oats days that drove him to become a teetotaler.

Ray was keeping company at the time with a very beautiful young lady. On this particular occasion they were spending a romantic evening together, sipping on peach brandy.

Everything was going beautifully. It was a perfect night for romance. Ray was feeling particularly high-spirited by then, and uninhibited, and perhaps a bit macho. He didn't intend to be boisterous or rough. It was only meant to be a gentle little love tap as Ray playfully popped the girl on the chin—and broke her jaw!

Looking a little like Clark Gable, Ray shows the stress of his movie career. He directed his last film in 1945 and left Hollywood for good. — PHOTO BY E. R. TREIBER, BEVERLY HILLS

The sight of this beautiful girl with her jaw askew, grimacing in pain, so shocked and sobered Ray, he swore on the spot he would never touch another drop of liquor again, and he never did. — CARLA LAEMMLE

HECTIC HOLLYWOOD DAYS

[Ray describes the stress of fast-paced movie making in the 1920s when the revolutionary advent of "talkies" was causing turmoil in the industry.]

I then became a director-producer for William Fox. But when talking pictures came in it almost killed me. There was too much of a great load placed on the directors.

Nobody knew what to do. The burden was placed on the shoulders of directors. We had to figure out how to hide the microphones. The director had to decide on when to have music. We had to get actors from the Broadway stage because the silent actors didn't know what to do or didn't have good voices.

But the trouble with stage actors was that they had been trained to project their voices to the third balcony. We had to train them to talk in a normal voice and not look at the camera when they said their lines. I had ulcers so bad I started to move around and make movies in Mexico, China, all over the place. They were talkies but the pressure wasn't as great at those places.

You know, I remember one time we did a movie and we needed bloodhounds. Well, bloodhounds have a low tone of voice when they start to track down their prey, but the animals we had sounded… high and shrill. We had to figure out how to control the sound and make it come out lower.

My doctor told me to give up that goddamn movie business and go fishing. — RAY CANNON

RAY'S GARDEN IN THE SUMMER OF 1949

[As he recovered from surgery, Ray wrote the following letter to Carla, who was in Texas with Cora Galenti.]

My Sweet, The garden has never before expressed itself with so much luxuriance. As I walked there for a look of the day an amorous butterfly was waiting. T'was twilight and all the tiny people had long since sought their protective shelters. It settled on my hand and I noticed that no matter how I turned my hand it would move around, always facing me.

As I surveyed the delightfulness of the growing, flowering, fruiting things, I wished my vision could be televised to you. I know how your heart would have been flooded with sheer joy. The sun-rouged cheeks of the peaches. Ming-yellow blossoms flourishing among the guava vines match the brilliance of the evening star. The wholesome redness of the ripening tomatoes, jade-green fugwa hang and sway from their bamboo trapicus, now completely covered. All a promise of goodness. Truly a garden of glory.

Quince must be canned in a day or so. Then the bushel or so of peaches. Had the first ripe one today. The second planting of beans are just beginning. I hope they last for you. I will soon plant lettuce, turnips and carrots. The broccoli is still flourishing; so is the squash, cucumbers, etc., etc. The tomatoes are just reopening. All their vines took a second growth despite the early blight and have now reached the top wire. The cactus in your window box is beginning to send out little sprouts. The sponge vines climbed all over the bamboo arbor and are now up to the porch roof.

Day by day I gain strength and endurance. The only pain is in the emptiness and mysterious vacuum in my heart, arms, and…—Ray

MYSTERY OF THE SWALLOWTAIL BUTTERFLY

[Carla describes an unexplainable event that occurred in the garden of 1949.]

Ray was an excellent gardener. He enjoyed being close to the soil and digging in the earth, and it was important to him to have a garden to work in.

When Ray first came to live with us in 1937 we lived in a house on Mariposa Avenue in Hollywood, and one of the first things he did was start digging up our large backyard in preparation for planting a flower and vegetable garden. We grew all kinds of vegetables in it and it was very productive.

For Ray however, the garden provided much more than its productivity. Physically, there was the fringe benefit of healthful exercise. Esthetically, and more importantly, the garden was a place for inspiration, a place to experience quietude—and perhaps to ponder on the mystery of it all.

Which brings me to the mystery of the swallowtail butterfly. In the months following Ray's critical ulcer operation in March of 1949, he spent much of his time while recuperating in the healing and refreshing sanctuary of the garden.

It was in that garden on one warm summer day in June of 1949, that the first of a series of most singular events occurred.

Ray and I were out surveying the luxuriant growth and beauty surrounding us when a large, brightly-colored swallowtail butterfly showed up. Butterflies were a common sight in our garden as there were numerous blossoms to attract them, but this one behaved differently. First, it circled around a few times, then came to rest on one of Ray's hands. As Ray raised his hand up and turned it, I noticed that the butterfly adjusted its position to face him. It was very odd. The butterfly remained on Ray's hand for a good moment or so, then flew off. What a charming encounter we thought—a fluke of sorts.

A day or two later Ray was out gathering some tomatoes when the butterfly returned. It fluttered around the same as before and once again settled down on Ray's raised hand, obviously facing him. It rested there for a couple of butterfly minutes, then flew off again. This was no fluke. It appeared to be deliberate. The butterfly actually seemed to have a rapport with Ray. Really strange.

Most bizarre of all, that swallowtail butterfly returned to our garden again and again during the entire summer season for its mystical tryst with Ray, each time repeating its curious and enigmatic little ritual. Ray christened it his "amorous" butterfly.

How to explain it… we had no answer. It was simply one of the inexplicable, whimsical, fey mysteries. Or, perhaps, just maybe we had an enchanted garden.

— CARLA LAEMMLE

Cora Galenti, right, saved Ray's life in 1949 when she raised $5,000 for his ulcer operation by organizing a charity ball. Shown in Los Angeles, from left, Carla's mother, Carrie Belle Laemmle, Carla, Ray, and Galenti's son Anthony Palma, on leave during World War II.

In the garden; Ray as a young actor, c. 1920.

Carla Laemmle at her home in Los Angeles, 1998. — PHOTO BY GENE KIRA

LOVE STORY

RAY & CARLA & THE SEA OF CORTEZ

TWO YEARS AFTER Ray Cannon's death, *The Sea Of Cortez* was taken out of print by Lane Magazine and Book Company. With the force of Ray's personality and charisma gone, the risk of printing such an expensive volume could no longer be justified.

Carla Laemmle, the woman who had accompanied Ray through the last forty-two years of his life, began a futile search for a new publisher. One after another, a series of prospects expressed interest in the well-known book, but then ultimately declined when it became clear how truly daunting the cost of printing such a large, full-color volume

Carla, c. 1925. — PHOTO BY MELBOURNE SPURR

would be. Like Baja California's Golden Age itself, the magnificent, bestselling *The Sea Of Cortez* became a memory.

Still slender and vivaciously attractive in her 70s, Carla remained in the house on Serrano Street that she and Ray had bought only seven months before his death; prior to that, they had always rented it. Ray's cramped study—with its glass-paneled French doors, book collection, typewriter, overflowing filing cabinets, and his photo mounted high on one wall—was kept just as he had left it.

Carla packed away the accumulated papers and small mementos of her life with Ray, his fishing tackle, the albums of Hollywood clippings and book reviews, his honorary plaques and awards, and the piles of boxes containing thousands of photographs from his career. She packed these things away securely, and she settled into the house alone, nurturing her remembrances.

Although she had allowed the public to know her only as "Ray Cannon's secretary" during his long career, in private life Carla Laemmle had been much more than that. Since their first meeting in 1935, she had been not only the love of Ray's life, but also his editor, occasional ghost writer, publicity agent, and the encouraging spirit that saw him through good times and bad.

Few people outside a close circle of friends ever knew that Carla had also once enjoyed her own glamorous Hollywood career, complete with openings, and press clippings, and movie credits that in many ways were just as noteworthy as Ray's.

Carla's uncle—Carl Laemmle—had founded Universal Studios in 1915, and six years later Carla's family moved from Chicago to the Universal City movie lot in Hollywood. Carla was eleven years old at the time. She grew up amid the sets for such classic productions as *Foolish Wives*, *The Hunchback of Notre Dame*, and *Frankenstein*, and she was trained as an actress and ballet dancer. She played the female

In Chicago, c. 1913.

Carla's parents, Joseph and
Carrie Belle Laemmle, c. 1910.

Carla, c. 1922, at play with her dog Dixie on
the lawn of the Universal City movie lot. Behind
her is the set for *New York Street*.

lead in *Romeo and Juliet* at the Carthay Circle Theater in 1933; was featured as prima ballerina in *Phantom of the Opera* (1925) with Lon Chaney; danced "Rhapsody in Blue" for George Gershwin on an enormous prop piano in *King of Jazz* (1930); and had the very first speaking part in the first "talkie" supernatural horror movie, *Dracula* (1931) with Bela Lugosi.

But it was in 1935 that Carla—then under contract to Universal—met the man who would change her life. Ray Cannon had written a short comedy which he would also direct, and the strikingly beautiful, 25-year-old Carla was assigned by the studio to play a small part.

For the next four decades, Carla and Ray maintained an extraordinary business partnership and love affair, as Ray's Hollywood career ended, and together they forged a new life for him as a sport fishing authority and author.

Money was a perennial problem. They bought an old typewriter and Carla taught herself how to use it. She drew the fish illustrations for their first book, *How To Fish The Pacific Coast*, and every week for 24 years she typed and forwarded Ray's column to *Western Outdoor News*— whether Ray had written it or not; there were many weeks when Ray would be out of touch in Baja—shipwrecked on a remote island or grounded by storms—and it was actually Carla who wrote that famous column. And there were many times when Carla would complete a column for Ray, working feverishly from sketchy notes that he had scribbled on a piece of hotel stationery and somehow gotten back to her from deep in Baja.

For 12 years, they worked together on their biggest single project, *The Sea Of Cortez*, and Carla typed, retyped and edited many drafts of that future best-seller, often using

As "Beth Laemmle" a "pretty Universal player" with Trixie, the laughing horse, a member of the Universal Studios menagerie that included lions, tigers, a giraffe, a couple of elephants, and Houdini, the escaping camel, who loved bowls of oatmeal.

— PHOTO BY RAY JONES

On the Universal City lot in the mid-1920s.

Carla, c. 1929. — PHOTO BY LANSING BROWN

scissors and Scotch tape to make Ray's paragraphs flow smoothly and compellingly.

With the immediate success of *The Sea Of Cortez* in 1966, the financial pressures were eased at last, and Ray and Carla were able to enjoy the fruits of their labors after three decades of struggling side-by-side. But to the end, Carla remained true to her role as "Ray Cannon's secretary" and she never revealed to the world the extent of her contribution to that success.

In the years that followed the end of Baja California's Golden Age, Carla continued to live in the house on Serrano Street as it grew older and the circle of fame that had once shined around the legend of Ray Cannon grew dimmer and smaller. She kept the old study intact, behind its glass doors just off the parlor, exactly as Ray had left it, and she settled into her memories of him and into the calm acceptance and

spirituality of the Taoist philosophy that had guided their long life together.

In the fall of 1993—when Carla was 84 years old—the house suddenly began to settle, and she was required to empty a back corner room so it could be demolished and reconstructed. It was the room that held the dust-covered old boxes, the fishing tackle, the manuscripts and photos, the engraved plaques, the hand-lettered parchment scrolls tightly rolled and sealed into cardboard tubes.

As she carried the boxes out to the garage, Carla came to a realization that the time had come to pass some of Ray's things on to others who might value the memories preserved in them.

But those thoughts were put aside when a series of difficulties arose to cause her one of the most trying periods of her life. First, a disastrous experience with a

"Among the rugged peaks that frown down upon the Borgo Pass are found crumbling castles of a bygone age." With this opening line, read aloud from a guidebook in a bouncing carriage, Carla, lower left, opened a new movie era, in *Dracula* (1931). Hers were the first spoken words of the first talkie "supernatural" horror film. Carla later described the experience for the magazine, *Famous Monsters of Filmland*: "I seem to have become famous because of that opening scene in *Dracula!* They gave me a booklet and the dialogue was written there. They told me, 'just read it from there.' I didn't even have to memorize it!"

— UNIVERSAL STUDIOS

With George Gershwin, left, and Billy Rose in *King Of Jazz* (1930), also featuring Bing Crosby in his movie debut as "himself," a member of "The Rhythm Boys." Carla, credited as "Beth Laemmle," danced "Rhapsody in Blue" on an enormous prop piano for the film.

— UNIVERSAL STUDIOS

Universal Pictures Corp. publicity photo, c. 1929

— PHOTO BY FREULICH

Standing, top center, on a set representing the Paris Opera, Carla was featured as prima ballerina in the Lon Chaney production of *Phantom Of The Opera* (1925). She had been studying with ballet master Ernest Belcher, who choreographed the film.

— UNIVERSAL STUDIOS

building contractor delayed the house repairs.

Then—at 4:31 a.m. on the morning of January 17, 1994—Carla was jolted awake by the magnitude 6.7 Northridge Earthquake, which caused severe additional structural damage. And finally, she suffered an acute recurrence of the near-fatal internal bleeding that had first developed just a month after Ray's death in 1977. At that time, she had been discovered unconscious by a neighbor and was rushed to the hospital just in time to save her life.

Eventually, the house repairs were completed and Carla returned from the hospital to contemplate the final period of her life. The circle of fame that had once been so large and brilliant, it seemed, had now grown so small that only she and the old house still remained within it.

Alone and distraught, Carla knelt on the floor and she prayed for guidance, for some sign that would give meaning to a life that seemed to have been drained of it during the long, lonely years since 1977. Her thoughts turned to Ray

and to the boxes of mementos that she had carried out to the garage, and she remembered her idea of passing them on to others who had known him.

On July 9, 1994 she wrote a letter to Chet Sherman, president of the Vagabundos Del Mar Boat & Travel Club— the rapidly-growing organization of adventurous small boat enthusiasts that Ray had helped found three decades before and in which he still held the perpetual office of "Commodore Eternal."

In her letter, Carla offered some of Ray's old things to the Vagabundos Del Mar club, and director Mike Bales was immediately dispatched to collect them and make arrangements for an auction to be conducted by club members. When he arrived at the house, Carla took him out to the garage. She opened the heavy wooden door to reveal what at first appeared to be nothing more than a pile of dusty old cardboard boxes, but what on closer examination proved to be a treasure trove of original Baja memorabilia. Here— some of it preserved for more than half a century—was not

Carla emerging from a giant oyster shell in *Broadway Melody* (1929), which received the 1930 Oscar for Best Picture. She described working on the film during a magazine interview: "One time, when I was under contract, MGM borrowed me for *Broadway Melody*. This was an underwater scene, and they had a huge shell, an oyster shell, I guess, and this oyster shell came up—a huge thing—and opened, and I got out, and then I did a very seductive dance and then got back into the shell and it disappeared. I worked in *Night And Day* at Warner's, and *On Your Toes... just* a whole lot of musicals." —MGM

Carla and her uncle, Carl Laemmle, during the 1928 Shrine Light Opera Season in Los Angeles, where Carla was featured as actress and prima ballerina. Uncle Carl sold Universal Studios in 1936. He died on Sept. 24, 1939—three weeks after Germany's invasion of Poland—but prior to that he had signed some 300 affidavits for $10,000 each to help get Jewish refugees out of Europe.

Carla, about 19 years old, in a publicity still by Universal Studios photographer Freulich. Uncle Carl had a fit when he saw this photo and ordered the negative destroyed, but Carla managed to save this print and a few others that she gave to close friends.

only the love story of Ray and Carla and the Sea of Cortez, but also a compelling first person account of Baja California's Golden Age, recorded week-by-week by two people who had actually lived through it.

In a singular convergence of time and place, it happened that Mike Bales was not only a director of the Vagabundos Del Mar club, but also an old Baja hand and book author and publisher as well. Standing in that dusty garage, he recognized instantly the uniqueness and importance of those old boxes. Here was a fitting tribute to the legend of Ray Cannon. And here in a thousand bits and pieces was an almost lost story that needed to be told to a whole new generation of enthusiasts who had never heard of him.

A book contract followed in short order. At last, Carla would realize her dream of seeing Ray's work continued.

A month later, Carla was gathering material together for the new book, and she happened upon a box that had been long forgotten under a dresser. In it she discovered the love letters that Ray had written to her in 1936—the year after their first meeting—while he was making a movie in Mexico City. She had not read these letters for many years, and in them she found the uplifting spirituality of Ray's Taoist philosophy, his reaching out to her across the span of time that separated them, and his frank expressions of earthly, youthful love. Somehow, she felt Ray's presence near her again, and she knew it was he who had led her to find and read those letters. She sat down and wrote a long reply to him, and she folded it and sealed it, and put it away with a renewed sense of calmness and strength. The grizzled old sea dog's Taoist solution had worked yet again.

HOW I MET RAY

[Carla looks back on the Universal Studios years and the beginnings of her love affair with Ray.]

It was in the year of 1921 when my father, Joseph Laemmle, at the urging of his brother, Carl Laemmle, founder and owner of Universal Film Studios, moved his family (my mother, grandmother and me) from Chicago out west to Universal City.

My uncle had arranged for us to live in a bungalow right on the studio grounds. In fact, the movie set of building fronts representing "Old New York Street" was situated but a short distance from the rear of our house. As you might imagine, growing up in that fantasy world of make-believe was quite an extraordinary experience.

As a child back in Chicago I had taken dancing lessons since the age of six. After moving to California I continued to study the art and eventually became a professional ballet dancer, performing in many stage and film productions.

By the 1930s I was under contract to Universal Studios, but it wasn't to be until 1935 that I was to meet my destiny. For, as fate would have it, Ray Cannon was

In the 1940s Carla, right, choreographed and danced this number for the Paris Inn in Los Angeles.

also working at Universal, both as a writer and director. He had already achieved notable success in both fields in the film industry.

It so happened, I was given an assignment to play a small part in a comedy short written by Ray and which he was to direct. Little did I know then that the course of my life would change forever through that little acting assignment and my meeting with Ray.

Inexperienced as I was as an actress, Ray put me to ease immediately. Right from the start we had a wonderful rapport. I had never met anyone as charismatic as Ray. From that very first day I fell under his spell.

As time went on and our relationship evolved, I came to know a side of Ray that few, perhaps, were aware of.

The esoteric and metaphysical religious teachings of the Far East had long held a fascination for Ray, Buddhism, especially. At one point in time, Ray took a leave of absence from the Hollywood scene and traveled to China where he spent six months at a Buddhist Monastery. He was seeking a respite from the Hollywood rat race and sought serenity of mind at the Monastery. He found just that in the quiet, gentle, non-competitive philosophy of Lao-tse, called Taoism. It profoundly affected his thinking and the way he lived and conducted his life. A strong emotional and spiritual bond developed between Ray and myself, a bond which has not diminished to this day, even though he is no longer with us on this physical plane. He was the guiding light of my life throughout our long relationship.

Serving as Ray's personal secretary over the years was very pleasurable work for me—typing and editing (Ray was a terrible speller) his *Western Outdoor News* weekly columns, his magazine articles and correspondence. But the greatest joy was my involvement and participation in the development and creation of Ray's two beautiful books, *How To Fish The Pacific Coast* and *The Sea Of Cortez*.

Ray was truly an extraordinary man—a genius in many respects. In our 42-year relationship I was privileged to have known the many unique and mystical sides of his multifaceted personality and I am happy to share the biographical vignettes I have written, as well as some of the treasured letters that Ray wrote me when he was working on a picture in Mexico in the fall of 1936.

— CARLA LAEMMLE

THE MEXICO CITY LETTERS

[In 1936, Ray traveled by train to Mexico City to work on a movie. These excerpts from his letters to Carla during that trip reveal a keen observer of the human condition and someone strongly grounded in the natural world, but with a romantic and spiritual vision that sought constantly to transcend it.]

"At last some pleasant country—green valleys, lots of cattle and wild horses—interesting mountains with grassy slopes—and much cooler. We are now 8,000 feet up. Just passed the very old city of Zacatecas. Only one person in my car speaks English, a dentist from Mexico City…"

***

"I noticed you found my message in the sunset even before I wrote you. Yes, the message told of my love…"

***

"Today I walked again in Chapultepec gardens. I saw more Aztec ruins and garden spots. You were with me—I felt the touch of your warm hand. I was enthralled with each new beauty because of your presence. At times I was sure I was living something of the past over again and that we did stroll among those same ancient trees not so many lives ago. It seemed so familiar…"

***

"I have just been to a night club. I have never seen one more beautiful.

There were three orchestras. A very cosmopolitan place with lots of rich Americans who try to flirt like Mexican girls do in pictures—they are really funny. But funnier still are the American men from Texas who go for them and are disappointed to find that the girls are also from Texas. We had a lot of laughs…"

***

"Yesterday I saw the Café San Angles and had tea there. This is the most charming spot yet. It was an old monastery—Spanish-tiled fountains almost four hundred years old—gardens—old orchards—nooks, vine-covered and jungly beds of very fragrant flowers, gardenias and orchids and the like—a glorious patio—but all the houses here have beautiful patios…"

***

"Did we do a day's work today—we made scenes in the gardens of the old palace Chapultepec. We played scenes on the very spots where Max and Carlotta actually did them. If the cameraman was any good the scenes should be beautiful…"

***

"As we returned from location we passed through the red light district. The girls are forbidden to come out on the street but are permitted to lean out of a small window

Carla, left, modeling a dress by designer Cora Galenti at the King Cotton Ball (1939) which was organized by Ray to help boycott Japanese silk prior to World War II. The ball was held in Los Angeles at the Ambassador Hotel and featured Bob Hope as master of ceremonies. Ray organized such activist groups as World Peace by Boycott and The Cotton Co-Action Committee in addition to his work for the Chinese business community. Of Ray's promotional activities during the era, Carla writes, "There wasn't much money in it, but it helped out. I also continued with my career as a professional dancer in pictures, stage and nightclubs through 1956."

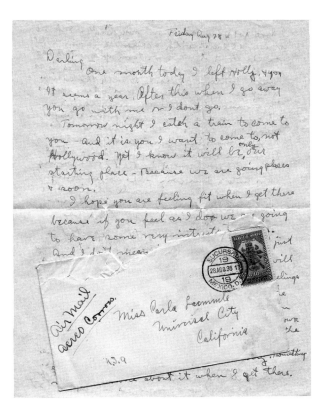

A letter from Ray's trip to Mexico City in 1936.

and say anything they wish to attract customers. The boys translated some of their cracks—they were very funny…"

***

"You would like the bull fight, that is, all except the killing. The matadors were handsome young fellows, more graceful than their best imitators among the dancers. We had an exceptionally good day. Everything happened—the traditional parade around the ring opens the show, very showy and impressive, elegant pageantry. One matador was especially good and as he took his bows, one young lady was so thrilled she took off one of her shoes and threw it. The gallant kissed it and threw it back. It is customary to throw hats and flowers but this was a new one…"

***

"As I write this it is eleven here, and if you feel the love I send you, your heart will sing I'm sure—for you have never known or heard of more—and as you close your eyes, you will see mine, and in them you will see the goodness of my love—a love that down through the centuries has tried to help you—to be fulfilled in this life…"

***

"Tomorrow we go to Xochimilco, the paradise of lagoons and flowers, to shoot some scenes. You and I were there once together—try to remember tonight—a narrow canal, water lilies, still water, flowers flowing over the bank into the water. Our boat softly gliding. I sang to you of my need of love—of a heart of loneliness. The world was filled with its glory, the flowers in full bloom. The grains and fruit swelled with ripeness but my heart was empty. I sang of the blessings of the summer night when all living things were comforted and caressed by their chosen mates…"

***

"We passed the rain storm just in time to see a glorious sunset. I wonder if you are seeing one. Look for them and I will send messages by the setting sun to you…"

***

"The lovely things you say will endure through all eternity to me. They will become indelibly impressed on my memory as songs of everlasting good. Though I be a victim of all the raging evils, with every man's hand against me—though all my senses be dead and I dwell in a dungeon—the beauty you have given me would fill the darkest hour with visions of loveliness…"

***

"I hope you are feeling fit when I get there because if you feel as I do we are going to have some very interesting times. I just noticed that my face, etc., is burning. I will be in a very exaltable mood if my feelings continue to increase. I am about the most healthy person you have ever known. I have had a few sun baths and am quite brown. I have lost two inches around the waist, the result of walking—and an accumulation of energy that is almost overwhelming. Something must be done about it when I get there. I kiss you with all of me—my love. And send a wish that you feel the full warmth of the caress. I send also my spirit to comfort you 'till I arrive. May all your thoughts be bathed in the mist of the rainbow of loveliness."

***

"I am dying to go fishing with you. These warm days drive me crazy.—Ray"

SUCCESS WASN'T MEASURED IN DOLLARS

Before I knew Ray, he was a successful motion picture writer and director, so one could say he was a fairly rich man then. But when I met him in 1935 he had very little money. He had just recently gone through a divorce.

Ray was living with a Chinese family at the time I met him. He had many friends among the Chinese people.

Although Ray was on the payroll at Universal Studios as a writer and director, he was not engaged in any major production then. He was merely on the payroll for comedy shorts, and salaries in those days were not what

Carla as Princess Quan Mui Mai in *Her Majesty The Prince* (1936). Inspired by new love, Ray wrote the play especially for her within a year after their first meeting. Carla describes their early times together:

"Ray certainly did have a stunning effect on me. I was awed by him—he was so overwhelmingly charismatic. I fell completely under his spell. It was only later when we had long and fascinating talks together and I got to know him and his philosophy that I truly fell in love with him. I just loved him.

"Ray was deeply steeped in everything Chinese at the time of our meeting, and in a matter of weeks he was inspired to write a most captivating avant-garde Chinese play for me, *Her Majesty the Prince*. I played the part of Princess Quan Mui Mai. Ray even taught me how to walk like a Chinese princess! He was exceptionally knowledgeable about everything relating to the Chinese theater. *Her Majesty the Prince* opened at the Music Box Theater in Hollywood on May 10, 1936 to excellent reviews. It was produced on a shoestring. I remember it as one of the most enchanting times of my life. The play itself was presented in the traditional Chinese manner, without use of scenery—only a huge embroidered Chinese curtain as a backdrop, the proverbial visible property man who moved props around, and a three-man string orchestra in the wings. It was way ahead of its time. A few weeks after the show closed Ray left for Mexico to work on a film there." — CARLA LAEMMLE

they are today. Money was very tight and there were still to be a good many lean years yet to come. In 1952, when Ray received an advance royalty check of $700 from Lane Publishing Company for *How To Fish The Pacific Coast,* it seemed like a fortune to us.

Not even after the publication of the enormously successful *The Sea Of Cortez*, could Ray be considered a rich man. His true riches were in his incredibly fertile and creative mind and in the wealth of beauty he had stored within him. — CARLA LAEMMLE

LIFETIMES TOGETHER

You may wonder why Ray and I never got married. Well, in the early days the timing wasn't right for it. Ray didn't have a steady job, money was scarce, and my mother was alone and she needed me. Later, marriage was not a priority. The truth is, I feel that Ray and I were united by a far more enduring bond that has brought us

together again and again, life after life, over the centuries, and will continue to do so in the eternity of things. Ray likewise believed in reincarnation and that we had shared many lifetimes together. — CARLA LAEMMLE

THE LETTER FROM CARLA

September 1, 1994—To Ray, My dearest one of all times past and yet to come. I sought your presence and counsel at this difficult and painful present life experience. I so needed your comforting words of wisdom to help ease and light my way into the days, weeks, months or perhaps years of the unknown future.

Then, yesterday, I opened a special keepsake box and found your letters to me written in 1936 when you were in Mexico working on a picture with Miguel Torrey.

As I read and reread the letters my heart burst with emotions of deepest love, loss and tears. These letters are truly now my greatest most precious possession. I never want them destroyed when I am no longer their custodian.

These letters reactivate in me a time in my life filled with love, beauty, dedication and happiness. Ray, dearest, you were, still are, and always will be the love and guiding light of my life.

Your spirit and presence is ever with me, and though we are separated by another dimension physically, there is no separation in spirit.

In some of your letters you wrote that we have had a bond together for centuries and that in this life we would find fulfillment of past dreams and aspirations.

Well, we accomplished much of that, didn't we? You wrote *Her Majesty The Prince* for me, *Yang Kwai Lai*, and *The Mongolian Emperor*; who knows, it may one day be produced.

Then you wrote "The Fishing Bible"—*How To Fish The Pacific Coast*—and I did the fish drawings for it. It was very successful. Most important of all was your (our) beautiful book—*The Sea Of Cortez*. The "Gulf of California" became "The Sea Of Cortez" and you brought the beauty, wonder and thrilling adventure to hundreds of thousands of people who discovered for themselves that land where time stands still. I feel that *Her Majesty The Prince* and my contribution toward the development of these two wonderful books fulfilled our destiny together in this life but with greater and greater partnerships to come in the Eternity ahead.

You taught me so many unforgettable things, my dearest—how to collect all the beauty in a sunset, a seascape, a flower—and store it in my memory bank where it will never be lost to me. How never to lose "the child heart"—nor the wonder and "ah-ness" of things. You taught me to seek the "good life" and be happy. Your Buddhist philosophy—"Harm no one, especially yourself"—I have aimed to live by. Unfortunately I have not always followed the latter part of it in my life, and consequently I must take responsibility for most of the bad karma I experienced.

Only the magical 42-year relationship with you, my dearest, was one of goodness, love, beauty, fun and fulfillment. You gave me your heart and I was blessed. You are and ever will be my own true love. — Carla

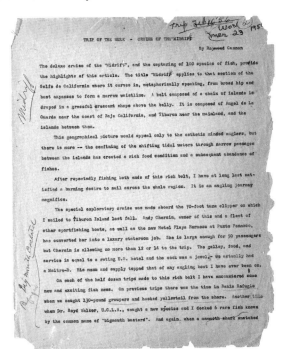

Ray did not type. All of his manuscripts—such as this one sent to *Western Outdoor News*—were typed by Carla before they were submitted. She bought her first typewriter and table for $15 and taught herself, using a book titled *The Shortest Typing Course In the World!* During the next 24 years, she typed thousands of articles, letters, and the many drafts of *How To Fish The Pacific Coast* and *The Sea Of Cortez*.

"QUESTIONS"

[Ray's poem, written to Carla, c. 1936.]

Was it only the image of her that dwells on the shore of the silver river projected by the moon's brilliant radiance to earth?

Was it the earth—or was it a lucid cloud—or was it more like a nebula floating where stars roam, floating through endless time?

Did time stop—was it hours or years?

How long are hours or years when immortals woo?

When the wells of emotions are filled—and yet streams of Olympian nectar flow in—what then?

Is there a planet of ruby or clouds of claret that moonbeams could filter through? How could a pearl at midnight retain the rubescent reflection of the setting sun?

Is there a glow in the perfume of morning honey dew that can penetrate beyond the human heart and envelop it in unendurable torridity? Is that the fire that sears sins from the soul—and gives life another birth?

Is this the immersion of the Holy Flame that begins again the beginning of things?

Tony Reyes Baca with five totuava near or over 200 pounds in weight, San Felipe, c. 1953. Reyes entered the panga mothership business in the mid-1950s and today owns the *José Andres*, skippered by son, Antonio "Tony" Reyes Montez. About 1959, the elder Reyes established the small resort called "Okie Landing" south of Puertecitos. He poured the six concrete slabs that are still there today and ferried wood from Puertecitos to build the cabañas. They had six small pangas with 10 or 15-horsepower Evinrudes on them. The original name of the place was "Miramar," and Ray Cannon wrote about it, but Tony changed the name to "Okie Landing" when some American clients kept calling each other "Okie farmers" whenever they lost a fish. — COURTESY TONY REYES BACA

SAN FELIPE DISCOVERIES

RAY'S FIRST TRIP TO BAJA

FOR REASONS THAT have been lost to the fog of time, former Mexican President Abelardo L. Rodríguez contacted Ray in Los Angeles in 1947 and hired him to test fish the waters around San Felipe at the northern end of the Cortez.

It is clear why Rodríguez would have wanted to explore the sport fishing potential of San Felipe; he and his partner Guillermo Rosas had extensive real estate holdings in the area, and they were interested in developing them. In fact, the Mexicali-San Felipe highway was paved in 1950, only three years later, repeating a pattern that Rodríguez had followed on the opposite coast of Baja, when, as Territorial Governor, he had overseen the paving of the Tijuana-Ensenada road in 1923. These two paved highways, about 65 miles long on the west coast, and about 125 miles long on the east coast, were Baja's first.

What is not clear is exactly why Rodríguez picked the 54-year-old Ray Cannon for the job. In 1947, Ray was only two years out of his Hollywood director's career and he was still a complete unknown as either an angler or an outdoor writer. In fact, he had just recently caught the "opaleye that changed his life" at Point Dume, and he had just begun the research that would not result in the publishing of *How To Fish The Pacific Coast* for another six years—in 1953. Even in that year, when the inaugural issue of *Western Outdoor News* was published on December 4th, Ray was still not well enough known to merit a byline for his feature article that appeared in it (his first column, in the same issue, did receive a byline). At the time Ray was hired to test fish San Felipe in 1947, there is no evidence that he had written or published anything at all about sport fishing.

Nevertheless, he was hired. And he did go, in the company of his friend Eddie Urban, here called Eddie Abdo, who ran a sport fishing boat out of San Diego called the *CAN-DO* and was a part-time opera singer and movie actor. That year, 1947, was the beginning of Ray's next life, and the Golden Age of Baja California as well.

EARLY DAYS AT SAN FELIPE

[From his 1966 classic, *The Sea Of Cortez*, Ray describes those magic first trips to San Felipe:]

I have a special attachment for the North End, since it was there that I experienced a single, adventure-packed day that changed the whole course of my life. It was a day so filled with excitement and enchantment that it caused me to shed my lifetime career and become a vagabundo del mar—a vagabond of the sea—a way of life that has given me many rewarding and fun-crammed years. It was a rags to riches story in reverse.

That day was my first on the bountiful and mysterious waters of the Sea of Cortez, and within a few hours I became involved in the most fantastic fishing I had ever experienced.

The fishing village of San Felipe, c. 1960.— PHOTO BY AL HRDLICKA

Downtown San Felipe, c. 1951. — COURTESY SUNSET MAGAZINE

The time was 1947, a couple of years before the first road had been graded to this sector of the Cortez. Señor Abelardo Rodríguez, former President of Mexico, and his partner, attorney Guillermo Rosas, co-owners of a large section of San Felipe, engaged me to make a survey of the area's angling potential and to help train native shrimp boat crews so they could assist stateside anglers who were anticipated as soon as the proposed paved road and accommodations were completed. Eddie Abdo, an opera singer and my fishing amigo, persuaded me to let him in on the venture. We drove down from Hollywood to Mexicali in a pickup and took a shortcut to our campsite, two miles above San Felipe. Señor Rosas had a comfortable and well-organized camp and enthusiastic crews ready for our three months of "work."

Rodríguez and partner Rosas owned a vast stretch of the beach above and below San Felipe as well as most all of the land occupied by the pueblo. They had a fine camp, two small shrimp boats and two outboard skiffs fitted out for us.

The excitement began the next morning, soon after we rounded guano-plastered, 286-foot-high Isla Consag.

From a distance the island itself seemed to be quivering, but a closer view revealed only restless activity of immense numbers of birds, sea lions, and other sea creatures.

I had heard sea lions roar, cough, and trumpet many times in the Pacific, but the hallelujahs the sea lions in this assemblage were blasting out sounded like an old-time revival meeting.

There were more than three-hundred of the tuba-throated creatures. Great, bewhiskered bulls were busy routing the younger males from their sprawling harems, which filled the tide-washed caves and spread far into the grottoes and benches. In nearby surf a younger, virginal set was performing like a corps of dancers executing a circular ballet routine. Despite the racket, the whole show was one of nature's finest circuses.

It was spring, a period when creatures on the land and in the sea are stirred by a restless agony to get mixed up in some kind of an adventure, romantic or otherwise. It was a time when that latent primitive urge to return to the wilds becomes compelling among kids and codgers, and all ages in between.

In the 1950s most anglers camped and launched at Camp 2, just north of the old ice plant. — COURTESY LOS ANGELES EXAMINER

In 1951 Augie's Riviera was the place to stay in San Felipe. Tourist business was already brisk, with reservations recommended for weekends, through Augie Sylvestre, Augie's Turf Club, Mexicali. Room rates were $6 double, $4 single. Two other motels, the Avalos and La Posada, had rooms for $3 double. — COURTESY SUNSET MAGAZINE

The full force of spring was bubbling in both of us as we glided over the velvety blue surface of the Cortez at sunrise. The voyage and the Sea were delightfully strange—it felt like we were cruising on out into the beyond. As the first rays of the rising sun beamed over the water, our reverence for that new day was expressed in Abdo's dramatic and devout Arab invocation. The six-foot-four, 250-pound singer stood atop the wheel house of our shrimper, and facing toward Mecca, gave full thunderous volume to the Mohammedan call to prayer: *"La illa la"* (There is no God but Allah)… *"Allah azime"* (Allah is great).

Jack Weed, of *Automotive News,* approaching Consag Rock, 18 miles off San Felipe, aboard an early charter fishing boat, the 42-foot *Marlin II,* in 1957. During this period, converted shrimp boats operated by Charlie Rucker and Tony Reyes Baca were taking clients from San Felipe to the Midriff islands on the first "panga mothership" trips. — COURTESY LOS ANGELES EXAMINER

Except for the young and neat skipper, our crew of five Mexicans looked like cutthroat pirates, but all assembled on the bow and were so awed by Eddie's ritual they repeatedly made the sign of the cross.

MONSTER FROM THE DEEP

Crew members had hosed the lengthy deck and were working on the opposite corner from our position on the stern, where we had settled for some fishing, when I tied into something that sent vibrations up the rod to my uppers. Whatever I had was as heavy as a log and felt like no other creature I had ever tied into.

Eddie quit fishing and set his rod aside to see what I had hooked. He was amazed when ten feet down in the water there appeared a great and vicious-looking head with beady eyes and gaping jaws set with glistening teeth. The head was followed by a huge, squirming body that seemed to extend to the depths.

Both of us froze. We were gazing right into the face of a real sea monster. As I cautiously eased it up to the surface, Eddie grabbed the shark gaff, and in one powerful swoop, caught the creature through the throat. The sting caused it to lurch upward, helping Eddie to hoist it aboard. As the slithering monster hit the deck, both hook and gaff came free, and it went skidding straight toward the bare feet of the Mexican crew, teeth snapping like castanets. As one, they gave the fearsome thing one horrified glance, and scurried up the mast pole. And who was the top man on the timber? *El Capitán.*

The ten-foot denizen proved to be a conger eel (*Muraenesox sp.*), the largest recorded to that date. We soon caught two others measuring over eight feet, which led us to the mistaken belief that they were quite common. Instead of saving the rare specimens for our collection, we committed a scientific error by cutting them into steaks and eating all we could of the white, poultry-like meat. (The

The village of San Felipe, c. 1960. — PHOTO BY AL HRDLICKA

only other king-sized conger reported to have been caught in the Cortez, to my knowledge, is an eight-footer taken at Mazatlán.)

Moving out to deeper water, we brought up several other kinds of fish, among them a 100-pound baya grouper, a 60-pound spotted pinta cabrilla, a 125-pound totuava, a large dog snapper, and a 30-pound white seabass. The seabass was the only species in the whole day's catch that was familiar from Pacific Coast fishing. It was easily identified and distinguished from its close relatives, the corvina and totuava, by the raised white cord along its belly.

Although several of the fishes that we caught around Isla Consag were closely related to some I had taken in the Gulf of Mexico and the Caribbean, most of our day's catch was completely new to me. We felt that we had been angling in an untouched Eden. Even the behavior of the birds—pelicans, goonies, terns, gulls, and frigates—and the crazy performances of the sea lions seemed different from elsewhere.

Then there were the other queer sights, such as the occurrence of thousands of coconut-sized jellyfish, most of them with one to two-inch jacks residing in their tentacles. The jellyfish were so poisonous that a mere touch

The Orozco family resort at Puertecitos, 1959, three years after Arturo Grosso opened the road from Laguna Chapala to San Felipe to collect a 10,000 peso prize offered by the state government of northern Baja California.

would have killed other small fishes or given a human a serious sting. On spotting drifting food morsels, the tiny jacks would dash out for them, then scuttle back to resume peeking from under the protective, bowl-shaped blobs. These young jellyfish (floating invertebrate colonies called Portuguese man-of-war) were being moved southward by the current. Scientific reports of six-inch-long jacks seen in residence in large jellyfish at the mouth of the Cortez caused us to speculate on the long and adventuresome voyage the little fish were embarking upon.

On our way back to port, to climax the day in the fish fantasy land, a big marlin grabbed a bone jig I was trolling and made four magnificent jumps before breaking the hook and taking off.

It was the return to San Felipe that added the final touch of sheer delight to this fullest of days. Just a mile out from the village, as we were gliding into the setting sun with a breeze at our back, Eddie climbed to the top of the housing and sang a medley of Mexican songs to express and to share his joy of that day.

Most of the town's populace, awakened from their siestas, came rushing down on the beach to find out whose highly trained voice was booming out their native melodies. At that moment they would have elected Eddie the *jefe* (mayor) of the pueblo. In fact, from that time on, every service we asked for was happily granted. — RAY CANNON

TOTUAVA: THE CROAKER BIG AS MARLIN THE GREAT BLADDER ENTERPRISE

[From that first Baja trip, to San Felipe in the spring of 1947, Ray describes several discoveries: the gigantic totuava; using live corvina as bait; the technique of "rhythmic pumping" for large fish; and the "skip-strip" bait skied over the surface of the water. While fishing for needlefish in 1958, Ray would make a second discovery about skip-strip baits; he would learn to trim and hook the bait so its forward edge curled up like a sled's, throwing up a wake to imitate a small flyingfish. In the 1960s, his work to develop live bait sport fishing in the southern Cortez would revolutionize the industry there.

The story about the totuava bladders being ground into a powder for Chinese soup is erroneous. The bladders were, in fact, shipped to Mexicali and China for a soup called *Seen Kow*, but they were not ground into a powder.

The exporting of fresh totuava to the U.S. actually began much earlier than is implied here. In 1927-28, for example, over 1.8 million pounds of totuava reached the Southern California market.]

Near our camp, two miles above the village of San Felipe, we met an old Chinese named Quan who lived in a cave. We were told that he had accumulated an immense fortune by exporting dried totuava bladders to China, where they were ground into a costly powder used to

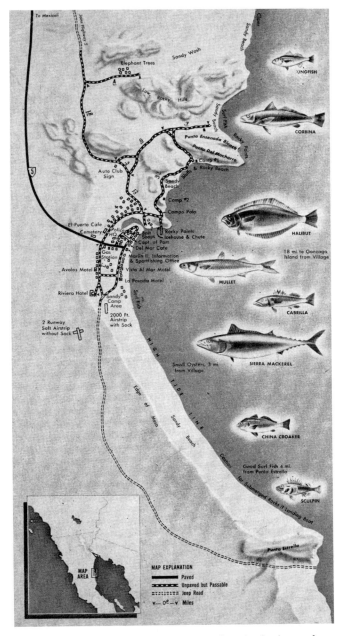

Map of San Felipe in 1951, a year after the highway from Mexicali was paved. Note lack of a road leading south toward Puertecitos (opened about 1956); the "downtown" laguna, now filled in and developed; the "Camp 1" and "Camp 2" areas north of town, now developed; the ice house already present on the hill north of the landing beach; and the old unpaved road that Ray would have followed on his first trip into town in 1947. A *Sunset Magazine* article from the period describes launching at Camps 1 and 2 with amphibious truck assist, pangas available at Carrillo's barbershop for $5 to $10 per day, and a 42-foot charter fishing boat, the *Marlin II*, leaving daily from the downtown area. One-hundred miles north of town, the fish camp now known as Campo Río Hardy was open with "16 neat, clean, cane and mesquite shelters at $1.25 per day." Or, camping without a shelter for 50 cents per day. — COURTESY SUNSET MAGAZINE

A commercial catch of enormous totuava being butchered on the beach at the site of the present day boat launching area of "Papa Fernandez" fish camp on Bahía Willard (just north of Bahía San Luis Gonzaga). From left to right, Tony Reyes Baca, Gorgonio "Papa" Fernandez, and his son, Chi Chi Fernandez, c. 1954. — COURTESY TONY REYES BACA

enrichen and thicken soups. In addition, we learned that at the end of World War II, when there was a rush on harvesting of shark livers for vitamins, Quan had salvaged the shark fins, which he also shipped to China.

Many of the villagers had been employed in Quan's fin and bladder enterprises. After removing the bladders, they discarded tons of totuava on the beach and there it waited until a high tide flushed the remains out for sharks to feast on. That's how it worked until a couple of venturesome Californians with initiative arrived, saw the waste, and started a sizable business. They hauled ice down from the States and trucked the big totuava back to the U.S. where they sold them as "sea bass." We saw the kaput body of a truck that was still being used as an ice storage house for the huge fish between trips.

One of the totuava brought in by a native weighed 303 pounds. It helped convince us that there could be a potentially enormous angler interest in this great and abundant croaker (*Cynoscion macdonaldi*). We decided to study habits and habitat of the species.

The next day we were back at Isla Consag with a new crew. One of them, José Limón, who operated a fishing fleet in San Felipe, had fished totuava commercially near the island so he directed us to their habitat. We found it to be a 20 to 22-fathom, narrow, mud-bottom trench, starting about a quarter of a mile northwest of Consag and extending westward. After fishing there with various baits

without success, we switched to very small hooks and baits and began catching foot-long corvinas—then suddenly something hit and made off with one of them.

The next corvina caught was quickly switched to my heavy outfit. The lively bait had barely reached bottom when a tug indicated that I had hooked something like a slow-moving submarine. I gave it all the pressure the heavy line would take but couldn't turn it. The contest was resolved not by sensational runs but by matching

Johnny Dunn, left, and Gordon Case, with a totuava caught at San Felipe, c. 1956. — PHOTO BY INA CASE

From Ray's files, this 1942 clipping from *National Geographic* magazine, showing "sea trout," or totuava, crashing the beach in the northern Cortez. The caption: "These voracious sea trout are so excited chasing sardines that they pay no attention to people wading among them. The man is grabbing them by the gills and throwing them out on the bank." — PHOTO BY JAKE MILLER/NGS Image Collection

endurances. Both fish and I were close to exhaustion when he gave up. The catch proved to be a hefty totuava weighing close to 200 pounds. We seemingly could have caught tons more of these huge and excellent food fish. Instead we tested different techniques for catching them. Lures and dead baits were far less effective than live 8 to 12-inch croakers and corvinas which we caught on the same mud bottoms with totuava.

To allow the baits more freedom to swim around, we used a light, 30-pound test, flexible leader as long as the fish we expected to catch, and a sinker with a hole that would allow the line to run through it freely, just heavy enough to hold against the current.

After two weeks in the Consag area refining techniques, we covered the San Felipe sector searching for totuava hangouts. We found one loaded, deep depression, seven miles southeast of the island, which we suspected was their main swimway, two fairly productive holes

nearer the village, another off Punta Diggs, and a shallow, undefined flat, 15 miles north of Punta San Felipe, over which small schools roamed.

One of the most important of all angling techniques developed was "rhythm pumping." This method worked not only for totuava but for all large fish. The art of

Easter Week 1956. Young fishing guide and future restauranteur, Jorge "George" Limón Tejada, right, with clients Lorraine Slade and her son, Steve Slade, and one of three totuava caught that day at San Felipe. They are on the ramp of "Alberto's Camp," now the Club de Pesca. Today, Limón is the owner of San Felipe's fine George's Restaurant, and is also president of the town chamber of restaurant owners.

— COURTESY JORGE LIMÓN TEJADA

Angel Angula, left, Ray, and Gene Perry on a sand bar 20 miles south of Lower Ferry on the Colorado River, 1956. The following year, Perry would lead Ray's first long-range cruise down the Sea of Cortez.

pumping a fish during retrieving has long been practiced by astute anglers. With this method, the fisherman pulls the rod upward as far as possible without cranking the reel, then cranks rapidly as he lowers the rod.

In the new method, the rhythm is achieved by making three or four half-second halts while pulling the rod up. These should not be yanks, but rather a slight lessening of the pressure on the fish in a regularly timed rhythm. This causes the fish to keep its mouth open and gills closed. Without water passing by its gill filaments, the fish smothers.

The timing of the upward strokes should be regulated according to the size of the hooked fish; the smaller the fish, the more rapid the strokes. While not difficult, this technique must be learned by practice. The strokes should be continued even when the fish stops, or takes off. When most fish begin to smother they usually get panicky and spend their energy in erratic and charging runs. Billfish tend to do more jumping.

Casting from the beaches below and above San Felipe we caught many orangemouth corvina (*Cynoscion xanthulus*) on a variety of light-colored lures by dropping them to the sand bottom and bouncing them on it when retrieving. We tried other baits and found that we did even better with strips of sierra and squid. Fresh shrimp topped both of them, especially after dark. Live bait proved best of all. For corvina, a tidal estuary toward the Colorado River on incoming tides was most effective.

Trolling from a skiff, we accidentally discovered a bait that was subsequently developed to be sensational for trolling. We were fishing about 40 feet from Punta San Felipe rocks, where we saw disk-shaped pompano jumping

and flipping on the surface like pancakes being tossed in a griddle. We tried trolling and casting almost every lure and bait without getting a single taker. That is, not until I baited a hook with a small strip of fish and peeled off a couple hundred yards of line. As I retrieved, the two-inch strip-bait began to ski on the surface. A pancake pompano (*Trachinotus paitensis*) grabbed it at once and went into flapping, four-foot-high leaping turnovers.

Monterey sierra (*Scomberomorous concolor*) is the most abundant fish available to anglers in the North End, except from December through March, when it becomes scarce. Each late afternoon, returning from Isla Consag, we watched schools of Monterey sierra jumping in a follow-the-leader pattern as far as we could see in all directions. — RAY CANNON

DOWN THE COLORADO RIVER
THE GENE PERRY EXPEDITION

[In the spring of 1956, Ray made his first attempt to cruise the Sea of Cortez in a small boat. This expedition, headed by Gene Perry, launched boats at Lower Ferry on the Colorado River, but it failed in its objective of reaching the Sea of Cortez to explore and fish for totuava. Nevertheless, much information was obtained that must have been a revelation at the time. In the following year, Gene Perry would also take Ray on his first successful small boat cruise down the Cortez—a trip from San Felipe to Isla San Lorenzo and back.]

MAY 4, 1956—An unprecedented amount of interest has been shown by deep sea anglers during the past two years in a pair of comparative newcomers to the sport fishing scene—totuava and corvina.

Anglers, literally by the thousands, have invaded the little town of San Felipe, Baja California during the current run, seeking the big gamesters. Most caught some fish but missed the big corvina runs which occurred one hour before the night high tide.

This trip dwells on a series of jaunts by a host of anglers and scientists making negative as well as positive observations, in an attempt to learn more about the theory that has to do with the calendar occurrence of the fish.

Normally the totuava and corvina ply these waters through about June 15. But unless an angler knows the fishes' habits, their coming and going, it's possible to "miss the boat" during the height of the runs. Last week, for example, comparatively few fish were boated, though natives report that they are still around en masse.

Our angler survey trip was to investigate the lower reaches of the Colorado River and the shoreline extending above San Felipe.

Twenty anglers with seven boats made up our trip to the river. To get there, we turned off the San Felipe highway at El Mayor, and drove over a fairly good dirt road to the Lower Ferry, where we pitched camp.

Next morning, with a fine 16-foot cabin job serving as flagship, we ventured 20-odd miles downstream, examining and attempting to locate corvina and totuava. We did find fresh skeletons of large totuava about 15 miles below the Ferry.

The river contained the largest population of mullet I have ever seen, but no corvina, proving that the corvina and totuava come into the river with the extreme high tides on the full and dark of the moon, and desert this stretch of water completely between moons.

The water drops from a high of fifteen or more feet to a low of one foot over some sand bars and since our cruise was during a low period, all boats had to be pushed over them. It was lucky that we engaged Angel Angula, the ferry tender, as guide and helper. Otherwise I would have floundered completely. As it was, I only had to push part of the time. There must have been eight miles of non-navigable bars.

Among the many things we learned from him was that the water begins to rise a couple of days before the moons. Then a sudden wall of water called a "bore" rolls up the river with considerable speed. It may vary from 15 or more feet at the mouth of the river to three or four feet by the time it reaches the Ferry.

Angel discounts its dangers (as mentioned by explorers who witnessed it) and says anyone who has been accustomed to launching a boat through ocean breakers can meet it head-on in a row boat.

Confirming Dr. Walker's opinion that the corvinas and totuavas spawn in the river about the time of the bores, Angel and other natives told us that they had examined the

Ray with a leopard grouper, c. 1955

eggs and conditions and found this to be true. Angel believes that the corvinas and probably the totuavas will not feed before the bore but will really go for strips of frozen sardine, sierra, mackerel and other fish as well as shrimp afterward. In the gulf they sometimes show a preference for a small chrome-head barracuda feather.

Following our negative but profitable river adventure, nine of our party took off for San Felipe. In addition to our chuck wagon staff, Perry and our first mate, Bernie Soutar, Bill Dungey teamed with Benton Jame, and Gus Poulett with Fail Wright. We hauled four boats and were joined by a couple more for the trip up the San Felipe coastline. Since this cruise was also between moons, we can testify that few fish were present, especially at this time of year.

But we learned that 16 miles above San Felipe, an estuary is formed at the extreme high tides where you can make book on a huge run of corvinas for an hour or more before high tide. The landmark for this estuary is a single-rock, cone-shaped hill about two miles north of it.

Finding the jeep trail over to it may be an experimental job and you may have to walk about a half-mile across mud and salt flats. But it is my guess that the trip will be worth it.

A special scientific study on the spawning habits in the river seems urgent, principally because of the lack of fresh water to be expected when the vast lands now being cleared for cultivation demand the water for irrigation. It may be that fresh water is necessary to the spawning success of these fishes, the lack of which may have already contributed in reducing the totuava population. — RAY CANNON

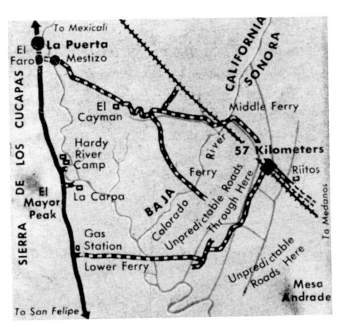

Map shows location of Lower Ferry in 1951, just south of the confluence of the Río Hardy and Colorado River, about 50 miles south of the U.S. border at Mexicali. — COURTESY SUNSET MAGAZINE

Ray promoting *How To Fish The Pacific Coast* on Cavalcade of Books, 1954. — PHOTO BY JACK CASE

On a Morro Bay party boat, c. 1957.

"HOW TO FISH THE PACIFIC COAST"

RAY'S FIRST HIT BOOK

ALTHOUGH RAY HAD written more than 200 movie scripts by the time he retired from Hollywood, he had never attempted a book, much less a fishing book. His first effort, *How To Fish The Pacific Coast*, published in 1953, was an immediate success, not only because it covered its subject with unprecedented thoroughness, but also because Ray proved to be a tireless promoter at book signings and interviews—and because Carla proved to be an excellent press agent, booking Ray for as many as eight "author events" in a week's time.

About the book writing project, Ray would later say, "I wouldn't have started it then, believe me, if I had realized how ignorant I was on the subject (after 25 years of fishing the coast, I thought I knew it all) and how I would have to spend six years, a lot of sweat and blood, and a small fortune to write a book on the subject."

From fragments written for *Western Outdoor News* and the *Los Angeles Examiner* in 1954, Ray tells how his friend Mike Haggar launched him on the writing of *How To Fish The Pacific Coast* after the catching of a mysterious fish that was eventually identified as an opaleye. This "fish that changed Ray's life" was caught about ten miles north of Malibu Beach in 1947.

AN OPALEYE CHANGED HIS LIFE

It was a seven-pound opaleye that changed my whole life, or should the metamorphosis be dated from that instant when my hook snagged a rock and came loose with a gob of moss on it?

Or, perhaps it was that split-second later when a greenback fish four times as big as the sea perch I had been casting for grabbed at that vegetation and headed seaward.

That all-important, fateful accident occurred off the rock formation at Point Dume. Although I had caught fish from most of the rocky shoreline of the Pacific Coast, I had never encountered a more stubborn and conniving trickster.

It dashed out with the receding waves and back in the rolling breakers, gaining line faster than I could reel it in, then trying to circle rocks and seaweed.

It was on one such a breaker rush a half hour later that I used the fish's momentum to slide it upon a flat rock

Ray's first big seller, *How To Fish The Pacific Coast*, was published by Lane Magazine and Book Company in 1953, became a classic, and stayed in print until 1982. Shown here is the cover of the 1964 Second Edition, with photos by Harry Merrick.

Ray with an opaleye. A seven-pounder caught in 1947 changed his life and launched his career as a sport fishing writer and author. — COURTESY LOS ANGLES EXAMINER

Shore casting, c. 1954.

surface and grab it by the throat. I brought the fish to my neighbor, Virg Nova, expert surf angler. He weighed it in at exactly seven pounds, but had no name for it.

After searching through all the literature and questioning every angler I knew, I met Dr. Francis Clark, who told me the Department of Fish & Game had just named it the "opaleye."

It was this opaleye, this confusion of names, and Mike Haggar that got me started on this crazy business of writing about ocean fish and fishing.

Years ago Mike started me angling for the opaleye and pointed out that there was no written material available to the angler on this species, or on a couple of hundred others, for that matter.

"Of all the outdoor sports surely ocean angling is tops, but how can we call ourselves sportsmen without even knowing the names of the object of our pursuit?" Mike jibed. A few years of having my ears bent by his cracks finally forced me into it. Haggar is still trying to convince me that it was the opaleye and not himself that pushed me into this business.

It was tough having to go back to school in an attempt to learn the ABCs of marine biology and to write 15,000 pages of junk for the wastepaper basket, but these years produced some of the happiest times of all, especially the last couple.

This year [1954] the hardy opaleye is to become recognized as an international game fish, a tribute to the Southern California Spinning and Gun Association, which

for the past five years has conducted the important opaleye derby.

When first caught, this fish is easily recognized by the opalescent blue eye and yellowish skin between the dorsal fin spines. The young have one or two white spots on each side, just under the skin.

Sea moss from rocks is the best bait for the real lunker. Mussel, red rock shrimp, clams and canned peas are good for the young ones. The opaleye ranges the full length of California and on halfway down the Baja California peninsula. The opaleye (*Girella nigricans*), often miscalled perch, is not even closely related to that family. It spawns and thrives in rock areas, bays, and around breakwaters. The population is increasing rapidly.

In these many years of trying I have never again come close to catching another seven-pounder. — RAY CANNON

HOW RAY LEARNED TO FISH

[Ray tells how he learned to fish the Pacific Ocean from Russian, Greek and Japanese commercial fishermen in California, and how Dr. Carl Hubbs and Dr. Boyd Walker of UCLA helped him produce the first edition of *How To Fish The Pacific Coast*.]

JANUARY 23, 1976—I was less than four years old when I was taught to bait a bent pen with an angle worm and yank an eating-size fish out of the headwaters of the

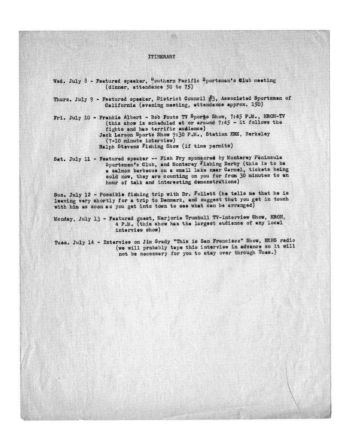

ITINERARY

Wed. July 8 - Featured speaker, Southern Pacific Sportsman's Club meeting
(dinner, attendance 50 to 75)

Thurs. July 9 - Featured speaker, District Council #3, Associated Sportsmen of
California (evening meeting, attendance approx. 150)

Fri. July 10 - Frankie Albert - Bob Fouts TV Sports Show, 7:45 P.M., KRON-TV
(this show is scheduled at or around 7:45 - it follows the
fights and has terrific audience)
Jack Larson Sports Show 9:30 P.M., Station KRE, Berkeley
(7-10 minute interview)
Ralph Stevens Fishing Show (if time permits)

Sat. July 11 - Featured speaker -- Fish Fry sponsored by Monterey Peninsula
Sportsmen's Club, and Monterey Fishing Derby (this is to be
a salmon barbecue on a small lake near Carmel, tickets being
sold now, they are counting on you for from 30 minutes to an
hour of talk and interesting demonstrations)

Sun. July 12 - Possible fishing trip with Dr. Follett (he tells me that he is
leaving very shortly for a trip to Denmark, and suggest that you get in touch
with him as soon as you get into town to see what can be arranged)

Monday, July 13 - Featured guest, Marjorie Trumbull TV-interview Show, KRON,
4 P.M. (this show has the largest audience of any local
interview show)

Tues. July 14 - Interview on Jim Grady "This is San Francisco" Show, KCBS radio
(we will probably tape this interview in advance so it will
not be necessary for you to stay over through Tues.)

A busy book promotion schedule typed by Carla, c. 1954, had Ray making eight radio, television, and personal speaking appearances—plus a fishing trip—in a single week. Ray's tireless work to help sell his book paid off as *How To Fish The Pacific Coast* sold 10,000 copies in its first year. On July 12, 1954, George Pfeiffer III, Book Division manager of Lane Publishing Co. (Sunset Books), would write to Ray: "I was delighted a few moments ago when the Accounting Department called to point out... that sales of your book have now crossed the 10,000 mark and from now on will operate in the higher royalty bracket. This is always such a nice milestone to pass that I cannot resist dropping you this brief line..."

Powells River in east Tennessee. My elation was boundless and self-confidence gained would stay with me until this day.

When we got our first length of extruded round wire to be used for shoe tacks and sprigs, replacing wooden pegs, I got my first metal fishhook fashioned by my father in our bellows (blacksmith) shop. I learned early to thong a small white duck feather on the hook for a fly-like lure.

With the exception of a few months of fishing Florida and the Caribbean, I stuck to stream and lake until about 1913 when I left the theater and city life for a six-months camping vacation near the commercial fishing village at the foot of the 1 1/2-mile long Huntington's Pier. It was called Port Los Angeles and had a railroad and later a streetcar hauling the fish from it to supply Los Angeles.

I offered my services as a fisherman free to the three groups of commercial fishermen and started from scratch to learn how each of the Russians, Greeks and Japanese caught so many large fish per day. I found that their techniques were quite different from each other.

The Russians caught small (Pacific) mackerel and large sardines for live bait and caught most of the big white seabass and got top price.

The others got very few. But the Greeks were terrific with tuna in season and switched to halibut with queenfish bait, other times. The Japanese caught numerous species and brought in the greatest poundage. I saw them weigh in a black sea bass that tipped the scales at more than 600 pounds. It was the largest any of the fishermen had ever

seen. I haven't seen its equal since.

The Japanese used a large selection of cut baits tailored to attract the particular species they were after. I found their methods highly attractive and spent most of my time fishing with them, and once they learned that I was an actor and not about to become a commercial fisherman but a vacationing angler they were very generous with their ideas on fishing methods.

I was hooked on saltwater fishing and kept at it all of the years between 1913 and 1945, whenever I found time between pictures (movies) I was working in.

When ulcers forced me to retire from show business I went fishing full time and am still at it. When eventually I was pushed into writing about angling along the Pacific Coast, a book-size manuscript with fish drawings was produced. Carla Laemmle did the drawings. When I showed it to Dr. Carl Hubbs, the great ichthyologist was very encouraging. However, when he gave me the details on a much needed revision, I went to work with him and his assistant, Dr. Boyd Walker, now head of fisheries at UCLA.

A couple of weeks and I realized that I could have committed a colossal error by not knowing the science of fish and their places in evolution. I spent a year studying and learned more than during any other five years of schooling.

A year later, in 1953, after Hubbs and Walker had checked it out, the book was published by Sunset as *How To Fish The Pacific Coast.* — RAY CANNON

Ensenada, 1953, the photo that accompanied Ray's feature article on fishing Baja's northern Pacific coast in the first issue of *Western Outdoor News*. A thriving sport fishing industry operated from the wooden pier projecting into the bay, taking clients a short distance to fish the waters of Bahía de Todos Santos and the kelp beds around Punta Banda. The Ensenada fishery benefited from an area of cold water upwelling off the point that nourished a rich population of forage fish.

A twenty-fifth anniversary facsimile cover of the first issue of *Western Outdoor News*, published December 4, 1953. Ray's weekly column would appear continuously for the next 24 years.

— COURTESY WESTERN OUTDOOR NEWS

"WESTERN OUTDOOR NEWS"

BURT TWILEGAR'S WEEKLY MAGIC CARPET

IF EVER THERE was a ménage à trois made in heaven, it was between Ray Cannon, *Western Outdoor News* and Baja California's early sport fishing industry.

In 1953 Burt Twilegar—then Outdoors Editor of the *Los Angeles Examiner*—and his business partner Earl H. "Tex" Hardage used their industry connections to put together and print the first modest edition of the weekly sporting newspaper that would ultimately grow to a circulation of over 70,000.

The launching of the "Green Sheet," as it was called then because of its green-colored outer pages, coincided perfectly with the new writing career of Ray Cannon, whose first book, *How To Fish The Pacific Coast*, had just been published.

The debut of *Western Outdoor News*, often abbreviated to *"W.O.N.,"* also coincided with the needs of the emerging tourist industry of Baja California, where the owners of the first resorts of the Golden Age were just opening their doors and were in great need of publicity.

Even before the completion of *How To Fish The Pacific Coast*, Ray had been thoroughly enchanted by the natural beauty and unspoiled fishing of Baja. He was soon successful in convincing Burt Twilegar—who would ultimately become sole owner and publisher of *Western Outdoor News*—to assign him the entire peninsula as his beat. Ray Cannon—to say the least—had arrived somewhere very near the center of "hog heaven."

Ray always considered *Western Outdoor News* his "home," and he thought of his *W.O.N.* column as "my weekly letter to all my friends." For the remaining 24 years of his life, Ray's column would appear in every single issue of *Western Outdoor News*. He would grow famous and the paper would become the largest weekly hunting and fishing publication in the United States. Within a few years, *Western Outdoor News* would purchase its main competitor, *Pacific Fish and Game News*, and in 1960 it would launch the monthly magazine, *Western Outdoors*.

Meanwhile, Baja California's modern tourist industry was being firmly established, as resort owners discovered that their advertisements in *Western Outdoor News*—and Ray's columns in that publication—were an effective form of publicity.

During the following decades, *Western Outdoor News* and *Western Outdoors* would become "home" to many widely-known outdoor writers besides Ray. These would include Ray Arnett, Oren Bates, Bill Beebe, Jack Brown, Dave Campbell, Lew Carpenter, Charlie Davis, Bill Downey, Fred Hoctor, Rich Holland, Russ Izor, Bob Ketcham, George Kramer, Pat McDonell, Tom Miller, Norm Phillips, George Ramsey, Bill Rice, Bob Rogers, Jim Ruch, and Jerry Ruhlow. After the death of Burt Twilegar in 1992, his son, Bob, assumed the reins of the company as it consolidated its position as the premier source of sporting information for Baja California and the southwestern United States.

From 1953 to 1977, it was Ray Cannon's unfailingly enthusiastic weekly column that generated the most loyal following. The popularity of Ray's column in *Western Outdoor News* was an important factor in the success of the paper and of the entrepreneurs of Baja's Golden Age. In return, *Western Outdoor News*, the owners of Baja's great resorts, and such key figures as Mayo Obregón of Trans Mar de Cortés and Carlos Gutierres of Aeroméxico, provided Ray with a magic carpet that carried him to the vast personal happiness and fulfillment that he achieved in the second half of his life.

In the following tribute, written after his death in 1977, Ray was remembered by the staff of *Western Outdoor News*, the paper that helped make his career, and that he helped to build:

"His was a fantastic vitality, and how he enjoyed communicating it! He would come in from a day's hard

Ray, center, with *Western Outdoor News* publisher Burt Twilegar, right, and another guest, at Rancho Buena Vista, 1968.

fishing under severe limitations and feel that he'd been in seventh heaven. He was a giver—a lover he would say— not a taker. Ideas for his columns came from virtually everywhere and they were done with a key sense of humor and a showbiz flair. *W.O.N.* readers went with Ray on his journeys through his weekly column. Fishing brought health and joys immeasurable to this man who walked away from the bright lights of Hollywood without even a backward cast."

SOUTH OF ENSENADA — RAY'S FIRST ARTICLE IN *WESTERN OUTDOOR NEWS*

[When *Western Outdoor News* was launched in 1953, early elements of the sport fishing industry were already in place along the 200-mile coastline from Ensenada south to El Rosario.

—In Ensenada itself, a party boat sport fishing trade of many years' standing operated from a long wooden pier projecting out from what is now the downtown area of the city. And around the shores of the bay, there were pangas and guides available near the present Estero Beach Resort and along the base of Punta Banda.

—South of Ensenada, the predecessors of the panga guide services at Puerto Santo Tomás, and Castro's Camp at Puerto San Isidro were already in operation.

—On the small semi-open bay nestled into the south side of Cabo Colonet, Adolfo Meling had a fish camp and guide service.

—Farther south, in the San Quintín area, the cannery and failed wheat-milling complex on the inner bay that would become today's Old Mill Resort had rooms to let, a restaurant, boats with live bait, and guides that took clients out to fish around Isla San Martín.

—Aponte's Sky Ranch was already open south of the bay on Laguna Santa María, as was the Johnson Ranch north of Cabo Colonet, and the fish camp on the south side of Punta Baja.

—Although not on the water, the establishments of Hamilton Ranch and the famous Espinoza family restaurant and stopping place in El Rosario were already well-established and catering to tourists.

Most of these places normally engaged in the fishing or lobster trade and took in tourists when the opportunity presented itself. Others were working cattle ranches and doubled as hunting lodges. Virtually all of them were serviced by airstrips, either on-site or nearby.

Ray's first feature article in *Western Outdoor News*, December 4, 1953, accompanied by an ad for his recently-published book, *How To Fish The Pacific Coast*, "$4.00 plus 14 cents tax."

In his first feature article for *Western Outdoor News*, combined here with a follow-up column written a short time later, Ray describes travel conditions and fishing opportunities as they existed in this part of Baja California during the early-1950s. The trip described was in the company of Dr. Carl Hubbs of the Scripps Institute of Oceanography.]

DECEMBER 4, 1953—If you find pleasure fishing Southern California waters you can double it south of the Baja California border. The element of adventure is also multiplied by the primitive and decidedly foreign atmosphere.

A trip down along the west coast is no longer a hazardous journey. Paved and surfaced roads have been extended to within 30 miles of Bahía San Quintín which is 200 miles south of the border. Hauling an oversized trailer over one of the side roads that leads down from the main El Camino to the water's edge is occasionally rough going but usually passable.

Dropping down out of the hills and onto the palisades 15 miles below Tijuana, the sea-loving visitor is struck with the grand vista of the Pacific at its best. Miles of kelp forests acting as massive breakwaters shelter the clean beaches, causing the breakers to glide ashore in gentle rhythms.

North of Rosarito no other stretch of sandy shoreline is more productive for the surf angler. Corbina and croaker are abundant about nine months out of the year, surf perch (five species) and flat fish (four species), the year round. The owner of a small boat or rubber raft can catch kelp bass, three or four species of rockfish and a like number of other fishes among the kelp beds.

This 20-mile beach extends from Rosarito down to San Miguel. The beach is accessible all along the way and there is plenty of room for the camper to spread out.

Caution: Fresh water is scarce between villages and the villages few.

The angler who is not a camp or trailer enthusiast can find excellent accommodations at Rosarito Beach. Boats and guides are available here and at four or five other spots on the way down to San Miguel. At this point the highway bends inland and about fifteen miles later you see blue again, more kelp beds, more beaches, and a greater variety of fishes. Within a few miles of Ensenada, operators of new and attractive beach cabañas (auto courts) offer friendly and accommodating welcome. Among the best are Quintas Papagayo and El Morro. On the latter, the name Hussong's

An early cartopper in the Santo Tomás valley south of Ensenada as pictured in *Western Outdoor News*, July 29, 1955. At that time, the Transpeninsular Highway was paved to Arroyo Seco, near the present day town of Colonet, and work was in progress to extend the pavement to San Quintín. — COURTESY WESTERN OUTDOOR NEWS

stands out, as it will again and again in Ensenada.

Ensenada is just about the most angling-minded town along the whole Pacific Coast and it well ought to be, for sport fishing has been going on there for a century.

Every fall the populace of Ensenada stages a big fish fiesta complete with bull fights and beautiful señoritas.

If you plan on going out on one of the many scheduled angling boats, make your reservations the night before, and if you have a preference for a stern position aboard, go to the dock half an hour early, hail a rowboat operator and he will ferry you out where your boat is docked and put you aboard before it comes to dock to load. One other tip, if you are a newcomer, is to engage a land guide for a few pesos to show you the best spots. He will also act as porter, meeting the boat when it comes in, haul your catch of big yellowtail and white seabass to the deep-freeze house and otherwise look after your interests.

The big drawing card for Ensenada is the abundance and size of the yellowtail and white seabass. The regular scheduled boats usually specialize in the two species and seldom need to leave the bay in pursuit of them. If it happens to be an "off" day, *el capitán* will take his passengers to the kelp beds for some hot kelp bed fishing.

There are probably more different kinds of fish in Bahía Todos Santos and out around Punta Banda than in any other area between it and Alaska. There are more than a hundred species, if you count everything that can be taken on angling tackle, from the topsmelt to swordfish and big game sharks.

ESTERO BEACH

Six miles south of Ensenada is just about the most perfect spot for the surf angler that could be dreamed up.

The cabañas are delightful and modern. Walk from the door across a fifty-foot beach and you can start fishing. Follow the surf a few hundred yards and you will find some of the best spotfin croaker holes we have ever come across.

The beach here borders the calm inner bay and you can step into a rowboat without getting your feet wet. Boats with or without outboards can be rented very reasonably. Competent guides are available.

SOUTH TO PUNTA BAJA

We are heading straight for Punta Baja, the northern extremity of the Bay of Sebastián Vizcaíno some 250-odd miles below the border. From this point we are to work our way back along the coastline.

Seventy miles below Ensenada along a good, paved road we observe a small sign beside the highway that spells out "EJIDO MEXICO." Another few miles and the nice, blacktop road runs out, and we find ourselves on a graded but somewhat washboardy camino.

About five miles from the switch-off that leads to Bahía San Quintín we see the last glimpse of a graded road. From there on, it's strictly for the jeeps and trucks armed with Army rubber. Here also, we lose touch with civilization, as people term it. Except for a couple of spots, there are few humans to be encountered.

A few miles short of Punta Baja we bounced down a rutty trail and suddenly arrived in a verdant, well-watered valley that mothered the early Spanish settlement of El Rosario.

From a distance, the massive, grotesque cliffs of Punta Baja appear foreboding, but all apprehension disappears when a close survey discloses a teeming sea life.

Ray's first column in *Western Outdoor News*, December 4, 1953 was a general feature on rockcod fishing. Note ad at lower right, with special subscription price, $3 (three dollars) for one year.

— COURTESY WESTERN OUTDOOR NEWS

Beginning in 1953, Ray's "look" gradually evolved during his 24 years with *Western Outdoor News*. The one constant throughout was his trademark battered sea captain's hat.

This is the southern end of the belt of very cold water which extends up to Punta Banda near Ensenada. Some warm water fishes turn back south at this cold barrier, while some cold water dwellers refuse to venture south. These waters would supply enough material for a couple of dozen volumes.

So back to our trip.

The shoreline all the way back to San Quintín is composed of a series of massive, awe-inspiring points of solid stone formations separated by small bays that time and tide have carved into some of the most beautiful of nature's sculptury, each point chiseled into a different design as if its creator abhorred symmetry.

Now and then we found a small group of hardy lobster fishermen conducting the only commercial enterprise we saw along this stretch. Approaching Bahía San Quintín however, we passed some newly-developed farm lands.

From the village of Santa María we drove down to a semiprivate lodge and rancho which includes a bass and duck-laden freshwater lake, and a sandy stretch of the bahía which has produced more big Pismo clams than any

other beach along the coast. Here the water is laden with surf perch. The vast assortment of aquatic creatures that inhabit or visit San Quintín Bay (written in Spanish as Bahía San Quintín—pronounced San Keen-teen) number in the hundreds of species. From smelt to the giant black sea bass, with all the usual in-between sizes and kinds, all are encountered in the morning calm.

Isla San Martín, a few miles off shore, provides big game fishing where yellowtail, groupers and other heavyweights abound. This island is fished from a live bait boat out of the village of San Quintín.

This newly constructed settlement is located on the site of a ghost town, a British enterprise that died a half-century ago. For lack of rain, according to William Pendleton, the last manager of the grist mill, shipping, and hotel that once flourished there. No attempt has been made by the present enterpriseurs to revive those industries. A modern fish cannery replaces the old mill and a delightful, well-equipped array of tourist cabañas surrounded by gardens occupy the old hotel grounds. The angler will find just about all the modern conveniences required. Gas station, grocery store, guides, charter, outboard and live bait boats are available the year round.

Back on the graded washboard, we skip 20 miles of sandy beach to hit the coastline where again the mountainous rock bluffs begin. Anywhere along this road for the rugged, a man with fishing tackle or mask and flippers could do very well living off the sea. These waters and submerged rocks are literally crawling with lobsters and shrimp.

As we crossed one rather wide canyon with the usual barrier thrown up across the mouth of it we counted 90 lobster shells to ten square feet of beach. The newly-shed coverings extended for about a mile.

Your map will show Cape Colonet in the shape of a nose. Our next "spot" would be the mustache under it.

You can make a short trip of it by leaving the paved highway at that aforementioned sign "EJIDO MEXICO," driving nine miles down a narrow valley over a rather rough road to a village at the foot of the Cape. Mention the name Adolfo Meling, and the natives will point out his campo.

The next turnoff from the main highway north of Ejido México is a rough ten miles to the Johnson Ranch— not a very productive fishing spot. Further north at San Vicente, a turnoff leads to the picturesque colony of San Isidro where you can follow a road along the shoreline for five miles in either direction. Boats and guides are available here and fishing is fair to good.

On 15 miles north of San Vicente is Santo Tomás. One and a half miles north is a fairly good road that leads down through a beautiful narrow valley to the most interesting and productive rocky stretch of the whole trip. Boats and guides are available here.

From the town of Santo Tomás, heading toward Ensenada, you cross a mountain which extends out to form the colorful Punta Banda. There are good camping and fishing spots on both sides of the Punta. It is reached by a road eight miles south of Ensenada.

Now all of this had been a rugged, adventurous trip. A good, sturdy car can make it, but some of the rougher roads can best be traveled in a jeep or pickup truck. Good rubber and extras are definitely advisable. — RAY CANNON

BAJA CALIFORNIA INVADED!

[Just seven months after the launching of *Western Outdoor News* and Ray's first dozen articles about fishing south of the border, American tourists arrived in numbers. It was the beginning of a tide that continues, greatly increased in size, to the present day.]

JULY 16, 1954—An estimated 100,000 Norte Americanos dashed across the border and took up positions along a 200-mile coastline that extends from Rosarito Beach to San Quintín Bay. Not since Dick Ferris led his skid row army down to capture Tijuana has there been such mass movement of Gringos pouring over into the place.

The principal culprit instigating the invasion was *Western Outdoor News*. A dozen feature articles glorifying the unspoiled and primitive fishing spots to be found in the area must have aroused the adventurous spirit of its readers.

For two days and nights there was a constant stream of trailers and boat trailers going south. Unfortunately, all of them tried to return at the same time. The border guards were swamped when the great retreat of the returning invaders reached the customs gates.

The principal objective of the grand invasion was fish—and all those with plenty of basic training came home with mucho loot—but complaints are still coming in from the rookies who went ill-prepared in know-how and equipment.

Half-a-dozen homemade trailers broke down on the washboard graded highway between the village of Ejido México and Bahía San Quintín.

A few squads turned off the main highway one and a half miles south of Andrew Bradley's gas station at Ejido México and drove over one of Baja California's best side roads to Cabo Colonet. Among them were three station wagon loads of skin divers and a party of two cars with a "Campster" trailer. Your scrivener was a guest of Ed Johnson, who manufactures this collapsible trailer.

On our way back up the coast we were surprised to find many of our readers who (following the directions given in our "Trip of the Week" article on Punta Banda) were camping on both sides of the point. Estero Beach was having its largest crowd to date. Ensenada was so jammed and in such a state of confusion the traffic cops had given up and gone fishing. We managed with a bit of conniving to get a table at the El Rey Sol, which serves some of the best food in all Mexico.

If I had even guessed that so many fishermen would converge on Ensenada for the holidays I would have warned them that advance boat reservations should be made. I suspect that some of the migrators are still down there trying to maneuver for a place on a boat. Henceforth drop a line to the Ensenada Chamber of Commerce.

— RAY CANNON

THE OUTDOOR SHOWS
PROMOTING BAJA AND *W.O.N.*

[For the public—and for the Southern California and Baja California sport fishing industries—today's "Fred Hall Western Fishing Tackle & Boat Shows" are an annual rite of spring where old friendships are renewed, contacts are made, and new products are introduced. This key event of the outdoor industry had its early roots in the years following World War II with such shows as the Werner Buck Sportsman's Show, and throughout his career, Ray attended

Standing by her man, Carla at the *Western Outdoor News* booth, Fred Hall Western Fishing Tackle & Boat Show at the Great Western Exhibit Center in Los Angeles, 1965. Ray was a perennial favorite at the show and loved to meet the crowds so he could poll them on their interests.

these functions each year as a representative of *Western Outdoor News*. In the following write-up of the 1970 show, Ray concludes, somewhat ominously in retrospect, that Baja California will not experience overcrowding "at least for the next 30 years, or the year 2001."]

APRIL 10, 1970—A day at the Werner Buck Sportsman's Show at the Pan Pacific was as interesting as ever, and I am dutifully thankful to the hundreds that dropped by the *W.O.N.* booth to ask questions about the Cortez, or to get their *Sea Of Cortez* books autographed, or just to visit and talk fishing and a few other goings-on below the border.

U.S. environment in comparison to that of the Baja California Territory, was topic No. 1. "When will it become overcrowded by visiting anglers and permanent residents from the U.S.? What about fishing pressures on the fish populations by anglers and commercials?"

These questions are all related and many of my readers think I will ruin this last of the warm and delightful frontiers by writing about its happy style of living.

You only have to fly over the vast expanses of that "forgotten peninsula" to see how little of its coastlines and wilderness and mountainous interior is occupied by humans. Some estimate that there are 7,000 miles of

coastline around the islands and Baja shores south of the Midriff and that less than 250 miles of it are being used.

A close inspection, cruising into the bays and coves, reveals that large sections of the land were cattle and goat ranches long ago. But most all have been abandoned for many years. So have the gold and silver mining shacks and the ghosts of pueblos, also the ruins of stamp mills and smelters.

When I first cruised along to study the coast from Santa Rosalía to La Paz, there were five villages and three labor camps at salt and gypsum works. From La Paz to Cabo San Lucas, only two small towns and a half-dozen ranches. Thence up the Pacific—three villages, a military port, and several temporary lobster and abalone camps south of Ensenada.

Since those early visits I have kept track of developments: down the Pacific below Ensenada some important resort and residential areas have been opened down to the tip of Punta Banda; four small auto court-like fishing camps; a couple of large agricultural areas; three canneries with workers' settlements; large salt works at Black Warrior Lagoon and a transshipping port on Cedros Island; a scattering of five or six shark fishermen's shacks, with nothing else added between Magdalena Bay and Cabo San Lucas.

On the Cortez side there are six resorts north of La Paz with 130 rooms, and south of the city five resorts at Palmas Bay accommodating about 180 persons in 120 rooms, and five larger hotel resorts across the south end with about 300 rooms, for a total of 550 rooms, not including 350 in La Paz. A 900-room hotel would be considered medium size in other resort areas. So, worry no more about overcrowding the Territory, at least for the next 30 years, or the year 2001. — RAY CANNON

CALIFORNIA LANDINGS
RAY'S FIRST BEAT AT *W.O.N.*

[It took Ray less than two years after the 1953 launching of *Western Outdoor News* to get himself assigned "full-time" to writing about Baja California. But his first beat at the paper was the Southern California party boat scene, and he would write hundreds of stories about it—off and on—for his entire career. Here are three of his best.

Notable in the following story is not only the bountiful catch described, but also the fact that the anglers involved were disappointed by it. The yellowtail derby mentioned offered $25,000 in prizes. Also featured in this piece are Capt. Eddie Urban (with whom Ray had made his first forays into Baja seven years earlier at San Felipe), and Ray's lifelong love of fishing for oddball species with light tackle. In later years, Ray would confound observers in southern Baja when his "favorite fish" turned out to be not marlin or dorado, but the lowly needlefish.]

LA JOLLA KELP BEDS
AN AMAZING DAY

SEPTEMBER 9, 1955—The enormous number of fish caught in the small area off La Jolla is astonishing. Just about all species of game fishes of Southern California waters seem to collect in and around the relatively small kelp field that lies between Scripps Institute of Oceanography and Point Loma.

On a trip there last week I counted 150 boats fishing the area at one time. Included were 12 party boats and 16 large private boats. The balance were outboard skiffs. This was not an unusual occurrence. It happens most every weekend and just about everyone aboard, with any degree of know-how, gets fish.

The official count at the end of our day's fishing as posted at the H&M and Point Loma Sport Fishing landings: yellowtail, 18; barracuda, 865; albacore, 3; white seabass, 62; bonito, 375; marlin, 1 (weighing 406 pounds); black sea bass, 1 (weighing 640 pounds); miscellaneous fishes, 640. Also a world record (for skin divers) of a 48-pound yellowtail. Among the miscellaneous were shallow water rockfish, kelp bass, sheephead, Pacific mackerel, halibut, sharks, cabezon, and numerous other species.

I checked the incoming fish and found my count tallied with the officially posted numbers. I also verified the weight of the diver record yellowtail and Frank Nassan's 406-pound marlin.

In discussions with skippers and commercial men I found a general agreement on my theory that albacore feed at night during the dark moon and are therefore not as available to anglers during these periods. My stay there was during a dark moon but we were able to take a dozen albacore principally by fishing deep. All other boats combined caught only three.

The next day most boats switched from their open sea albacore runs to the La Jolla kelp beds with the aforementioned results. The important point to be made is in regards to this switch. Despite the number of fish caught, it produced a great deal of confusion and disappointment.

In talks with a number of anglers from distant parts of California and Arizona, I found that most of them had made the trip to get yellowtail and tuna. Having read week-old stories in their local press about the great hauls and of the big yellowtail Derby, they were so frustrated they thought the whole business was a hoax. The fact that they caught sacks full of big fighting bonito, barracuda, etc., was of no consequence to them. Some of them had waited a whole year for this one fishing day.

Without attempting to run other people's business or their fishing lives, I'd like to throw out some suggestions—to wit: No. 1, if bonito and barracuda were included in a separate category of the Derby, anglers would be happy to fish for them during those in-between weeks when albacore and yellowtail are scarce. No. 2, those disappointed anglers spent an average of $50 on the trip. They could have saved $46 of it if they had spent $4 for a subscription to *W.O.N.* No. 3, most important is that anglers learn to appreciate any one of the many fine game fishes in our waters and learn to match the size and ability of the fish with tackle accordingly. The bonito rates among the top six game fishes of our coast, providing light tackle is used.

A few thousand anglers who have not become mentally equipped to enjoy the immense pleasure of catching whatever fish is available are meeting with crushing defeat and disappointment every year.

I have been crusading for angler education along these lines for two years in this column and in my book before that. I have received a gratifying number of "good work, keep it up" compliments, but that is not enough. Everyone interested in any phase of ocean angling should "get with it." There are hundreds of ways of glorifying the lesser game fishes and unless there is concerted and energetic action, people engaged in the sport fishing enterprises will have to find thousands of new converts each year or lose ground.

In complete contrast to the yellowtail-albacore-or-nothing fishermen were my well-adjusted fellow anglers

Sport fishing customers at the Balboa Pavilion in Newport Beach, c. 1960.

on Eddie Urban's boat *CAN-DO*, which makes daily runs to the La Jolla kelp. They were happy to a man. Everyone used light tackle, caught lots of fish and had a ball.

Skippers could learn a lot from Eddie. He knows how to make everyone feel proud of his catch regardless of what kind it is. He has learned to enthuse and create enthusiasm among his fares. With every hookup he creates dramatic suspense. Furthermore he always knows of another hole when fish fail to show at the regular spots. I know few skippers who get fish as consistently as Eddie.

The concentration of fish in the La Jolla area may be partially caused by the richness of the water which upwells from two very deep underwater canyons that end near shore. An enormous squid spawning ground is located near the shore end of Scripps Canyon. Squid is very important as forage for game fishes. Topsmelt, also used extensively as forage fish, inhabit the kelp beds in great abundance.

— RAY CANNON

YELLOWTAIL ON THE UMGWADI

[Written c. 1960, this article provides a good snapshot of the Southern California party boat fishing industry during that era and also of the long-range cyclic effect of ocean conditions; the year 1957—cited by Ray as the beginning of a period of "good" fishing—experienced an "El Niño" ocean warming phase. Earlier, the private boat mentioned, the *Umgwadi* of Bill Harker, had been on two of Ray's best-known Sea of Cortez cruises, the abortive "Hurricane Cruise" Midriff crossing of 1957, and his all-time favorite, the successful "Kids' Trip" crossing from Kino Bay to Caleta San Francisquito in June 1958.]

The bright new era in ocean angling that struck Southern California three years ago is now reaching the fishing bonanza stages. The "good old days" refrain has been forgotten amid runs of game fishes never before equaled. Not even the accounts of Zane Grey, glamorizing kite fishing for 100-pound tuna around Catalina Island fifty years ago come close to matching present day raves praising angling for the platinum-plated yellowtail.

The record catches now being made stand out in sharp contrast to a decade-long dearth of game fish in these waters. Fishing grew so bad the Los Angeles Chamber of Commerce and All Year Club quit mentioning the sport in their catch tourists advertising. Each year of the 1947 to 1957 period showed a decline over the previous years.

The popular California barracuda, oceanic bonito and the highly-prized California yellowtail became so scarce the owners of the twenty-million-dollar landing and party boat business were literally scraping the bottom for the less desirable rockcod in 40-fathom water. They were further alarmed by the avalanche of small, privately-owned boats that began to hit the last dwindling fishing grounds like swarms of locusts.

The influx of outboarders spilling over from overcrowded lakes brought on a feud that looked for

Bill Harker's boat, *Umgwadi*, shown with a good-sized yellowtail at gaff, was on two of Ray's Sea of Cortez expeditions, the "Hurricane Cruise" of 1957, and the "Kids' Trip" of 1958. The boat was also featured on the cover of *How To Fish The Pacific Coast.*

awhile like the Old West shooting wars were about to begin all over again. There was practically no law west of the Pedro breakwater, and no Judge Roy Bean to contrive any. All the Fish & Game officers could do was to come boring in like Bull Halseys then politely ask to see if your fishing license was up to date.

The party boat skippers had an unwritten code of rules among themselves, such as never crossing a chum line or anchoring any place near except a few hundred yards away and abreast.

The outboarders, however, violated all ethical regulations. They held to the "freedom of the seas" to practice a bit of pirate-like anarchy, and came close to driving big boat skippers and their loads of anglers nuts.

Their *modus operandi* was to hover in the background until a skipper had located a rare school of yellowtail or other top feeders, and chum bait fish were being thrown over. Then, dozens of the small crafters would make a run and come trolling right through the school, often close enough to the stern of the big boat to catch a propeller full of anglers' lines.

Party boat crews were legally allowed to carry small caliber rifles to frighten away marauding sea lions—and they were beginning to see seals in all directions. But when one skipper mounted a brass cannon on his bow…

Wide-open hostilities seemed inevitable. Old time commercial fishermen, remembering a shooting war among themselves when seven had been killed a number of years back, took off to do their trolling in far away places.

During the peak of those days of tension, I witnessed one of the provocative acts that nearly triggered a second Civil War.

I was with Bill Harker, of Hughes Aircraft Corp., and his kids Harriet and Jimmie, an ingenious nuisance, aboard their 20-foot outboard cabin cruiser, the *Umgwadi*, when the conniving youngsters cooked up the dastardly fish-napping caper.

They had already learned from fishing aboard party boats how the bait man attracts a school of game fish to the boat by throwing out small, live bait fish to establish what is termed a "chum line" for a distance of a couple of hundred yards; then, stopping the boat so their passengers could cast hooked anchovies into the school.

Bill and I were in the cabin and hardly noticed Harriet go into the head with a large bucket. Nor did we know that the young'uns had seen a school of fish being worked by a party boat and had planned to draw the school away by establishing their own chum line across the party boat's bow. If seen throwing the chum fish out, they knew the boat's crew would break out the shooting irons, so Harriet was sent to slowly flush a few chum fish at a time down the toilet bowl.

Their scheme worked too well. As their chum line drifted back alongside of the big boat, the school of yellowtail came trailing toward the *Umgwadi* like a pack of bloodhounds.

It was only then that Bill noticed a live anchovy flipping near the door to the head and guessed why Harriet had taken the big bucket in there. He dashed out onto the stern just in time to see a big fish hit a trolled feather and the entire school barreling after the boat. He quickly cut the troll line to keep the crew from seeing the fish on it and forgot about Harriet while giving Jimmie a tongue-lashing.

When the irked dad did remember, he hurried to the head to stop Harriet's flushing activity. Jimmie, realizing the *Umgwadi* was by that time out of rifle range, stopped the boat, started fishing, got a big yellowtail hookup and began yelling for the gaff. While Bill, in an utterly confused rage automatically grabbed the gaff, Harriet snatched a rod, got a bait out and was soon screeching like a banshee, with a yellow on her line.

Bill decked Jimmie's fish then slumped over the wheel in despair, muttering, "You'll get us all killed, you idiots." But when he realized they were at a safe distance and saw the two of them congratulating each other, he couldn't hold back a bit of fatherly pride. After all, he had bought the boat principally to keep Jimmie out of trouble!

Jimmie's finest moment came toward the end of that fishing day when he mounted the *Umgwadi's* stern and proudly displayed his big yellow to the teeth-gnashing envy of the anglers and crew aboard the big *Matt Walsh,* with whom he had fished so often.

I had been with Jimmie and his dad aboard the *Matt Walsh* before they had bought their own boat. From the time he conned his father out of a couple of bucks to enter the jackpot, until the *Matt Walsh* pulled into dock, the pest had generated his own magnetic field for trouble. He got sardines in the neck when the bait man threw them overboard to form a chum line. His nose invariably connected with someone's elbow when he snatched for a bait. Other anglers crossed themselves and ducked to avoid getting a hook in an ear every time he hauled back to cast. Then, when he got a hookup with his overly-light spinning tackle, the fish circled the lines of about half-a-dozen anglers and caused one helluva gooney bird's nest snarl. This unforgivable goof resulted in his getting his line cut and banishment to do his fishing on the bow of the boat.

Bill suffered through it all but his worst moment came during the lunch break when Jimmie blurted out, "I'm getting awful sick of being pushed around on these 'cattle boats!' Why don't we get our own outboard?"

What Jimmie didn't know was that the fisherman sitting next to him at the galley snack bar was Mac McClintock, owner of the *Matt Walsh* and of the largest fleets and landings on the Pacific Coast. His dad did, and was embarrassed a sickly sea-green by the thought that Mac knew the kid was just repeating that dirty word "cattle boat" he had heard at home.

Typical of the hundreds of other fathers who were going through similar experiences, Bill there and then had his mind made up for him. He would buy a boat.

Mac McClintock was already aware of the sloppy party boat conditions of that time and was the first operator to realize that he couldn't stop the small boat revolution. In the months that followed, he constructed four great hoists, floating docks and live bait receivers for the use of outboarders, bought a whole fleet of small boats for rentals, then started his own TV program, *Fishing Flashes,* to tell California about his diversified operation. He also rebuilt the *Matt Walsh* and every other party boat in his fleet with scientifically constructed live bait tanks, radar, a galley as white and sanitary as an operating room, a sonar, bottom-viewing and fish-finding scope, and a loudspeaker system to advise anglers on the depth of a school of fish and how best to hook them. The reconstituted boats were not just modernized, they were jet-aged. And Mac's example was followed by most of the other operators.

Every manner and method of attracting new anglers to replace those deserting to buy their own boats was employed, but fishing grew steadily worse. So few fish

Rare 1950s photo catches Ray in jacket and tie—and looking somewhat discomfited—as a representative of the Ocean Fish Protective Association (O.F.P.A.).

were available, the State Wildlife Federation and its affiliate anglers clubs were demanding legislative action to put bag limits on commercial catches as well as on their own.

Landing operators at San Diego were sending their fleets of boats down across the border to fish the Mexican-owned Coronado Islands, and conducting a $25,000 Yellowtail Derby in an all-out effort to attract anglers.

Most threatening of all to the business was the added pressure on the few and diminishing fish schools by the small crafters and the havoc they raised by scattering them. The great party boat fishing industry was facing disaster.

Just when everything seemed blackest—came the millennium!

A three-degree temperature change occurred in the waters of the Western Pacific Ocean. Such a small increase in ocean water temperature would have meant little elsewhere in the world, but along the coast of Baja California it was like opening the Pearly Gates to Southern California anglers.

The prevailing winds along the Pacific coast of the Baja Peninsula had normally kept the water upwelling and many degrees colder than that off Southern California, thus keeping the fish migrations running through it at a minimum.

Following the warmup, the first indication of a possible major fish movement northward was seen when small, pelagic crabs, a favored tidbit of the game fishes, appeared above the border for the first time of recent record. A few weeks later massive migrations of the warm-water species were running through the otherwise cool barrier.

Ocean bonito, missing for twenty years, arrived off Southern California in super abundance. The California barracuda, which had become about as scarce as Model T's, reappeared in schools, armies, then in galaxies. But far more sensational, was the comeback of the most popular of all local game fishes, the California yellowtail, *Seriola dorsalis*.

This up-to-60-pound, streamlined, power-driven member of the jack family is a close relative of the amberjack, with even more thrust, drive and tenacity than its slightly larger cousins.

Scientists John Fitch and John Baxter of the California Department of Fish & Game not only found the yellowtail to be more abundant than ever but discovered that they were spawning in California waters for the first time since men had been observing and keeping records of such things.

The young that were hatched here in 1957 are now catchable size and growing fast. Added to the older population, which has apparently taken up permanent residence here, the loaded waters are sending anglers into a high state of frenzy as they go after the fish in every kind of a conveyance that floats.

Yellowtail are now coming in so close to shore they are being caught from piers and dragging fishermen off of breakwaters and jetties. Only a very few old-timers can remember seeing anything resembling such a run and all admit "it was never like this." For the first time in many a

Ray's *Western Outdoor News* mug shot, c. 1961.

year the Fish & Game wardens are being kept busy checking the bag limit of ten per angler-day.

The demand for yellowtail in the fresh fish market dropped to nil when anglers started supplying their neighbors with all they could use.

The yellowtail is not an erratic, many-gaited runner. He takes off in sprint speed directly toward the nearest clump of seaweed and will circle it unless the angler is able to turn him short of the goal. This is done by gentle, rhythmic pumping, the effect of which is something like yanking on a mule's bridle. This big jack rarely ever wastes energy on bucking, jumping, or other tricks. He depends on punch, power and endurance to break the line or the angler's spirit. Even when brought close to gaff he can always be expected to make a sudden, second-wind takeoff.

No other species, unless it is the bluefin tuna, seems to have such a keen perception of lines and other bait encumbrances. An angler using something less than a 12-pound test mono line will get twice as many hookups but is apt to lose three fish to one decked, over the fellow employing a heavier line.

Commenting on the speed of a yellow he had hooked, Frank Dufresne once said, "This projectile would make a salmon look like it was going backwards."

Estimating how many small boats have taken to the ocean is next to impossible since some of them are trailered to the lakes one week and to the sea the next. Space to dock the constant seafarers has long since been jammed full. Despite a colossal program of small craft harbor building by state and county officials, there are ten boat owners demanding berths for every niche carved and dredged out.

It is fortunate that the fish schools are spread out all along the coast and island shorelines and on the banks between. Otherwise the pileup of boats on the grounds would likely present one helluva traffic problem. But once in the brine, however, there is room enough for a million more outboarders to get lost from each other out in the vast open spaces around the Channel Islands and down the primitive Baja California coastline. Then there is space for millions to come down in my wonder world of fishing—the Sea of Cortez.

As things stand now, the fishing is being called "fabulous" by sports writers and the half-dozen TV announcers, including Mac McClintock, who gives a strike-by-strike account of the hundreds of fish being brought into the landings daily.

As of 1959 there were 412 party boats sailing out of the 30 landings between Morro Bay and the California-Baja California border. They carried 436,414 passengers who caught 3,796,319 fish, of which an average of about one yellowtail, two bonito, three barracuda and two other fish were caught by each angler per day, or close to the bag limit of ten of any one species per day.

Party fleet owners and small craft builders are weeping now only when the income tax man comes around. Little Jimmie and the likes of him are yelling "Bonanza!" as they plow the sea in the most exciting Gold Rush since the days of '49.

All is love and peace now. I am going back to Mexico.

— RAY CANNON

LIGHT-TACKLE ROCKCOD REVOLUTION

[Writing for *Arizona-Wildlife Sportsman* in January 1955, Ray describes the early transition of bottom fishing from a crude "meat" harvesting operation into something more like present day sport fishing. It was the beginning of the development of spinning reels, other forms of light-tackle fishing, and eventually, the practice of catch-and-release.]

JANUARY 1955—Hear that BOOM?

That's the new boom in winter fishing on the Pacific Coast.

Maybe it ought to be called a revolution, rather than just a boom. The methods these days in what has been called "rockcodding" seems more like the results of an explosion—if that's what a boom is.

The type of tackle now being used is at the other end of the pole from the old. Even the fishermen have changed—from outright meat hunters to idealistic light-tackle sportsmen. The shuffle involves thousands of anglers, and new converts are taking to the sea in droves.

This new flipover isn't a passing craze like bat-eye

The *Umgwadi* at the San Pedro Light.

canasta or peewee golf. It has the makings of permanency and seems to be growing into some kind of new concept in the sport of ocean angling.

It all grew out of a traditional type of wintertime fishing called "rockcodding." Just about every port along California's coast sent out its quota of regular scheduled boats.

The ten to forty passengers, for a fare of $3.50 to $6.50 each, were taken out to the deep submerged reefs. Each was supplied with a big ball of trotline-like twine of about 500 feet, or assigned to a wooden winch reel on which the line was wound. A window sash weight for a sinker and a dozen No. 8/0 hooks completed the rig. For bait, each dipped into a box of chunks of salt or fresh fish or squid, hooked a dozen on and let out enough line to drift a couple of feet over the rock bottom.

The strike and fight of the fish "latching on" was barely perceptible. The weight of the big sinker held the fish as if tied to a stake and in a very short time the fish was exhausted.

To determine whether or not he had a fish hooked, the fisherman would haul up a yard or so and make his decision on the extra weight a fish might add. He would usually wait for four or five fish to get on before hauling them in.

The major rewards in "rockcodding" were plenty of manual exercise and a sack-full of excellent food fish. Interest in this kind of a food-gathering pursuit gained a lot of momentum during the wartime meat shortage.

Time and association have changed many of those fishermen to angling sportsmen, causing a considerable slump in the number going out last winter.

Light-tackle enthusiasts express the belief that the old method is on the verge of becoming history and that a wonderful era of the sport is being ushered in.

The introduction of monofilament line, strip-bait, wintertime use of live bait, and the discovery of large bottom populations over shallow and moderately deep reefs, all contributed to the change-over.

Some of the new ideas were developed three years ago when the writer (working with a crew of anglers and skin divers on research for the book *How To Fish The Pacific Coast*) located a great number of rockfish (eight different species) feeding over a shallow reef.

With the aid of the skin diver (who watched fish reaction to baits) it was discovered that these fish did not respond to the conventional baits and lures offered, and that their feeding habits were quite different from other bottom fish. Some would take strip-bait, a piece of fresh fish tailored to resemble a small bait fish. Others preferred live "pinheads" (small anchovies) or live red rock shrimp.

Although the virtues of monofilament line have been overstressed by some few enthusiastic anglers, its value in strong, deep currents can hardly be overrated. The small diameter and smooth surface allow monofilament to slice through a rapid, moving current with little resistance. Consequently a comparatively light sinker is required to hold it down.

With this light rig the angler can feel the slightest strike and get the full thrill of the fight when the fish makes long and unhindered runs.

My early experimental fishing in this style was done with a conventional 950 Ocean City reel loaded with Western's "W-40" 20-pound test monofilament line. I have recently found that I can get a great deal more satisfaction and efficiency when working with a 12-pound test line and a rod equipped with rolling guides. At present I am using a Norm Beg Rolguide rod for deep water. With these late developments an even lighter sinker is required. An improved depth-glider about to enter the market may reduce the weight still further.

All these changes in tackle and this new use of them is no trivial matter. The event has caused hibernating ocean anglers to stir as never before during the cooler season. Their enthusiasm is approaching the "albacore run" temperature or pitch, or whatever you want to call that feverish psycho condition.

At times it seems that some of them are getting as much of a bang out of trying to find the smallest line possible in catching fish.

One character has been trying a 6-pound test line for weeks but hasn't decked a fish on it yet. If this trend keeps up some gink is likely to show up with a two-strand spider web.

For that great majority of anglers who take their fun-hunting seriously—there are fish. Among the great and medium-sized (none smaller than a fair-sized bass) are a number of different species of rockfish, called, or rather miscalled, "rockcod" by natives of Los Angeles County. Some of these fish achieve a length of three feet. The ocean-whitefish and sheephead—up to 20 pounds; lingcod up to five feet long; the giant black sea bass may run from 20 to 600 pounds; and with the new method, they're being caught in great numbers.

Perhaps the most abundant in moderately deep water are the bocaccio and yellowtail rockfish. These 1 1/2 to 3-footers can be chummed up to the surface in some areas.

Finding all these fishes at lesser depths has added still another value. When a fish is brought up from a great depth the sudden change from the heavy bottom pressure kills it instantly. By the time it is brought to the surface the eyes bulge and air bladder expands. The same species taken in shallow water, not being subject to pressure change, will fight until it is decked.

With the exception of the winter months, anglers have for many years fished with live bait from Ensenada to Point Conception. This point, which is about 50 miles above Santa Barbara, California is the dividing promontory between the cold currents north of it and the warm waters of Southern California. The northern and southern fishes are more or less separated by the point.

Live bait was not used regularly to the north until Virg Moores, a skipper from Balboa, California, introduced the practice at Morro Bay. His venture has proven so successful he is likely to revolutionize the whole northern sport fishery. His winter fishing is about as productive as that of the other seasons.

The glamorous Malibu Beach landing, where movie stars sometimes act as bait hands, is also trying winter live bait fishing. Likewise a couple of landings in Santa Monica Bay, three in the San Pedro–Long Beach area, and two or three at Balboa Bay.

Some of the boats out of these ports will sail out around the Channel Islands where thresher and bonito sharks are occasionally found. Some anglers consider these 50 to 100-pound monsters the best ocean game fish next to the marlin.

Reports from San Diego suggest that their regular winter boats will try the new method. Ensenada will likely follow suit.

Wintertime surf and rock fishing from the shore and bay fishing from the outboard boats was also greatly stimulated by the introduction of a new live bait last year. This one, the red rock shrimp, was found to be abundant and fairly easy to trap around breakwaters. It can be kept alive for a couple of days in a damp cloth or in seaweed. Three species of fish thought to be rare are being caught regularly on this shrimp.

These winter innovations have not only given the California angler and the sport fishing business a boost, but the saltwater writer can now find something more than the colorless "rockcodding" to write about, without having to hash over last summer's events for angler dream material. — RAY CANNON

The original front terrace of the Hotel Los Arcos in 1954. It is now a part of the hotel's expanded dining room. Woman in dark glasses is Evangelina Joffroy, wife of Luis Cóppola Bonillas. Beside her is son, Mario Cóppola Joffroy.

— COURTESY MARIO COPPOLA JOFFROY

The four arches of the hotel in 1959. Ray's dinner with Mayo Obregón, Luis Cóppola Bonillas, and Guillermo "Bill" Escudero took place five years earlier at a table just behind the left-hand arch.

DINNER AT THE LOS ARCOS

LAUNCHING THE GOLDEN AGE

NEARLY LOST IN the hustle and bustle of the waterfront *"malecón"* of today's modern city of La Paz are four rather smallish-looking arches built into the high white facade of the Hotel Los Arcos.

Approaching the city by boat, the arches today are hard to spot in the clutter of multistory buildings along the margin of the bay.

But in the early 1950s, those arches were a major landmark that formed nearly the entire front wall of the original Hotel Los Arcos, which at that time had only 12 rooms.

The hotel's dining room was located directly behind those arches and at a corner table, just behind the left-hand arch, a dinner meeting took place in the fall of 1954 that would be a major factor in the successful launching of Baja California's Golden Age.

Present at that fateful meeting were four men who would witness and participate in the building of modern Baja: Ray Cannon, newly-published author of *How To Fish The Pacific Coast* and sport fishing columnist for the brand-new weekly, *Western Outdoor News*; Mayo Obregón, son of Mexico's former President, General Alvaro Obregón, and owner of the brand-new airline, Trans Mar de Cortés; Guillermo "Bill" Escudero, Trans Mar de Cortés' La Paz manager; and Luis Cóppola Bonillas, a pilot for Trans Mar de Cortés and the new owner of the Hotel Los Arcos.

It was one of those magic moments that occur perhaps only once in a lifetime, a night when the coming together of forces was little short of miraculous.

Luis Cóppola Bonillas, in the cockpit of his B-17 bomber in England, c. 1944. Cóppola flew 35 missions over Europe as a pilot for the U.S. Eighth Air Force and settled in Baja California after reading a copy of the novel *Journey Of The Flame* while grounded by bad weather in Greenland. He flew DC-3s for Mayo Obregón's nascent airline, Trans Mar de Cortés, and piloted the plane that brought Ray Cannon on his first trip to La Paz in 1954. With his wife, Evangelina Joffroy, he bought the Hotel Los Arcos in 1952, and later participated as a partner in many other properties and businesses in Baja California Sur, including Servicios Aéreos de La Paz, the Hotel Cabo San Lucas, and the Hotel Finisterra. — *COURTESY LUIS COPPOLA BONILLAS*

View of the future site of the Hotel Los Arcos, looking northeast, c. 1948, gives a good feel for downtown La Paz at the time. Note the windmill at top right, and at the extreme top left, the tall "pine tree" that still stands on the corner of the present-day hotel's "Cabañas" facility. — COURTESY MARIO COPPOLA JOFFROY

—The end of World War II only nine years before had unleashed a global surplus of aircraft, including the Douglas DC-3 transport plane (the legendary and almost indestructible "Gooney Bird") as well as an enormous corps of experienced pilots suddenly out of jobs.

—That war, which had begun with the U.S. Army still fielding horse-mounted cavalry, and which ended with the atomic bomb, was followed by an economic and technological boom that brought air travel and exotic vacation "resort" destinations within reach of the middle class for the first time.

—After centuries of neglect and isolation, the Baja California peninsula was being discovered not only by Americans from the north but also by Mexicans from across the Sea of Cortez. Both groups recognized Baja's tremendous potential to participate in the newfangled "industry" of tourism and they were eager to exploit it.

—In the forefront of this group were Mayo Obregón, owner of a very small airline, and Luis Cóppola Bonillas, a pilot for Obregón's war surplus DC-3s, and himself the new owner of a very small hotel in La Paz, all of which they were anxious to keep filled with clients.

—And in La Paz for the first time was the American writer—Ray Cannon—who had a new book he needed to promote, a new job at *Western Outdoor News*, and a whole new purpose in life since he had discovered the fantastic fishing of the Sea of Cortez only a few years before.

—Ray was on his first trip not only to La Paz, but to anywhere in Baja south of the Midriff Islands. He had come

as a result of a telegram sent to *Western Outdoor News* the previous spring by Ed Tabor, who was struggling to establish his Flying Sportsmen Lodge at Loreto, a hundred miles up the coast.

By the time Ray sat down to dinner with Obregón, Cóppola and Escudero at the Hotel Los Arcos, he had already decided to write a second fishing book which he planned to call *How To Fish The Sea Of Cortez*. And that night, Obregón offered Ray free air and ground transportation, boats, hotel rooms, meals, and any other support necessary to make that book possible.

It is doubtful Obregón realized that Ray's book—which was ultimately retitled *The Sea Of Cortez*—would not be published for another 12 full years. Nevertheless, Obregón stuck to his end of the bargain, and he was rewarded with the most magnificent volume on Baja ever written in the English language.

The Sea Of Cortez was published in 1966, the midpoint of Ray's career as the pied piper of the Golden Age, and it would sell over a quarter of a million copies, bringing many thousands of new tourists to the peninsula. The financial support given to Ray by Trans Mar de Cortés, the hotel and resort owners, and by Aeronaves de México (later Aeroméxico) was repaid many times over.

On that fateful trip in 1954, Ray gained not only the patron that made his Baja career possible, but also a first look at the rich offshore big game fishing of the southern Cortez that would soon become a major asset for the building of the Golden Age. Three years later, in 1957, he

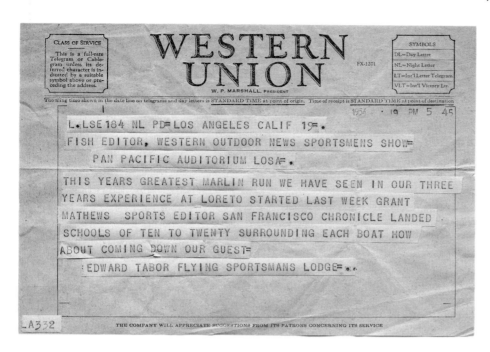

The telegram that spurred Ray's first trip to southern Baja California, from Ed Tabor, April 19, 1954, was sent not personally to Ray Cannon, but to *Western Outdoor News* at the Sportsmen's Show at the Pan Pacific Auditorium. *Western Outdoor News* was almost brand-new and still relatively unknown, since it had been launched only four months before. Tabor's Flying Sportsmen Lodge in Loreto had only been open two years, and he sent this invitation simply to "Fish Editor," praising the fishing at Loreto and offering a free trip as his guest. Later that year, Ray did visit Loreto, and he then continued south on his first trip to La Paz. He stayed at the Hotel Los Arcos and had his fateful dinner meeting with Mayo Obregón, Luis Cóppola Bonillas, and Guillermo "Bill" Escudero, at which he revealed his plan for writing the book that eventually became *The Sea Of Cortez*, and at which Mayo Obregón agreed to provide Ray with the transportation that would make that book possible.

Ray with a Trans Mar de Cortés DC-3, the airline's La Paz agent, Guillermo "Bill" Escudero, center, and an unidentified man, 1960. Escudero accompanied Ray on many excursions around the southern peninsula.

The original Fondo del Mar Bar at the Hotel Los Arcos, c. 1954, was the scene of many festive evenings during the Ray Cannon era. The bar is now part of the much-enlarged hotel's main dining facility, but traces of it can be found in the walls near the back corner of the room. Shown here are several members of the hotel's founding family. Fifth from left is Evangelina Joffroy, owner of the hotel with her husband Luis Cóppola Bonillas. At extreme left, her sister, Estella Joffroy Elias, and beside her, husband Bobby Elias, manager of the hotel. The small boy standing near the pillar in back is Mario Cóppola Joffroy (son of Luis and Evangelina) who manages the hotel today.

— COURTESY MARIO COPPOLA JOFFROY

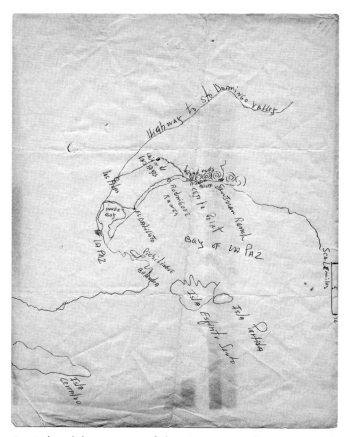

Ray's hand-drawn map of the city, surrounding area, and nearby islands of La Paz, as he found them on his first visit in 1954. At this time, no paved roads reached the area.

would make his first visit to Rancho Buena Vista and around the southern end of the peninsula, in company with Bill Escudero and Frank Dufresne of *Field & Stream*, and from that point to the end of his career Ray's attention would be focused on the southern half of Baja as the great resorts were built one after another.

LA PAZ
ANGLER'S SHANGRI-LA

[Ray looks back at his 1954 discovery of La Paz.]

JUNE 1960—The first time I took a swing around the old City of Peace (La Paz), sailed out to Espíritu Santo Island and saw the fields of basking marlin and sailfish, I made a mental note: "If I ever decide to settle down to retire, La Paz will be that final port." Nothing since that time has changed that decision.

There were many good reasons, such as the almost perfect climate and the hospitable friendliness of the gentle people, especially the señoritas. But the lure that cinched it was the fishing. For out of this port I could take a small cruiser or taxicab and get fishing unmatched any place I had heard of.

That was seven years ago and the things I have learned about the fishes and fishing in that region since then have multiplied my determination.

Each of the three or four trips annually have produced

Downtown La Paz, looking west, in 1964, just before the big boom in vehicular traffic caused by the development of agriculture in the Santo Domingo Valley area and the beginning of ferryboat service to Mazatlán. Note unpaved streets and lack of vehicles. At upper right is El Mogote, the long sand spit that forms the north side of the bay. — PHOTO BY HARRY MERRICK

some new and exciting angling adventure, with this past year topping them all, and I expect even more astonishing things to happen this summer, when fish are super-abundant.

For some reason people have been mixed up on the best fishing seasons in this region. They may have confused it with that of Mexico's mainland south of Mazatlán, where the main runs of fish occur in winter. Only across the blunt tip of the Baja California Peninsula is the fishing rated slightly above average during winter months.

Striped and some few black marlin and sailfish do remain in the waters the year round as far up as Rancho Buena Vista. They become more plentiful all up this coast throughout spring, summer and fall months.

When I first visited this area little thought was given to the teeming schools of other game fish. Today, most anglers like to catch one billfish, then spend the rest of their vacation time battling big dolphinfish, yellowfin tuna, roosterfish, amberjack, wahoo, black snook, giant groupers and snappers, all of which may weigh upwards of 50 pounds.

Many anglers prefer the lesser game, of which there are close to 300 species. Among them are the fathom-long needlefish, "the wildest thing in the sea," and other aerial acrobats like the tenpounder (ladyfish), the jumping pompanos, sierra, big-eyed snook, tenacious yellowtail, jack crevalle and a dozen other members of the dynamic jack family, *Carangidae*. To list and give techniques for catching the whole checklist would require a large volume, and I am doing just that.

If you think I am bragging about the place, you should read the opinions of other writers, anglers and scientists, especially the observations of Dr. Boyd Walker, head of fisheries studies at UCLA, with whom I fished and helped in scientific collection. He has described the black snook and bonefish spawning in La Paz Bay; the permanent habitat of needlefish, yellowfin tuna and 60 other species around Punta Pescadero; wrasses, parrotfish, morays and other eels and 80 other rock-dwellers in Las Palmas Bay and 85 species collected at Cabo Pulmo.

Corey Ford in *The Saturday Evening Post* termed the area "…the best fishing in the world," a phrase that has been used by numerous writers since then.

The old La Paz airport and a Trans Mar de Cortés DC-3, c. 1955.

When the big game fishes are less plentiful in La Paz Bay, anglers hop a taxi and drive over to Los Muertos Bay, or when time permits, on down to Rancho Buena Vista, where a deep, 500-fathom canyon comes right up close to shore with the great fish schools following it.

Before my first trip to Buena Vista I thought stories of catching 60-pound yellowtail casting from the beach, and 200-pound yellowfin tuna 100 yards from shore were outright fables. But when I actually saw larger ones caught and wrote about it, I was accused of using fishermen's measures.

Describing this region in generalities fails to convey the fascination. The enchantment is found in the individual's ability to react to surroundings, as well as to the emotional thrill or stimulation of fishing.

La Paz offers many other diversions. For the ladies, shopping for native arts and crafts and photographing quaint structures and tropical patio gardens with beautiful girls and character models.

Anyone may participate in the festive, balmy evening promenade in which a hundred or so young señoritas stroll around the Plaza counterclockwise, while an equal number of young men walk clockwise, all to the native strains of a small orchestra. There is no whistling or conversation between the sexes, but by an exchange of glances they do convey the message and proceed to decode it at the dance, which follows in a nearby hall. The old custom has not changed for a couple of centuries but the U.S. fishermen are making inroads.

For men, there are the illicit cockfights, also night clubs, but according to reports, Mrs. Murphy's Riding Academy has closed. However, another shady one has opened up at the back of the Bay. By shady, I mean it is in a palm grove.

La Paz has retained its original charm. Even the modernized hotels have preserved some of the old, Mexican-Spanish architecture. The newest, La Guaycura, is built around a flowering patio and swimming pool. The plush Los Cocos has an atmosphere of an elegant wayside inn in the tropics. The older Los Arcos has added delightful bungalows throughout a grove of India laurel trees. La Perla has added another hundred rooms, spacious veranda and open dining area. All have air conditioning and other modern facilities.

There are five fishing fleets. The three largest are owned by Enrique Ortega, International Travel Service, L.A.; The Ruffo Brothers, La Paz merchants; and Rudy Vélez, brother of the former film star Lupe Vélez.

Executive Bill Escudero, of Trans Mar de Cortés airlines, reports direct turbojet flights from L.A. to La Paz will soon be added to their regular scheduled planes from Tijuana via Santa Rosalía-Loreto, to La Paz.

Ray with waitresses at the Hotel Los Arcos, c. 1960.

It takes only a few hours to get there but brother if you are not hog-tied to your stateside job, you'll take a long time getting back, or join me in chucking everything to spend the rest of your natural days in that realm of fulfilling the good life. — RAY CANNON

ROMANTIC LA PAZ

[From a handwritten fragment, possibly never published, on the "romantic" life of La Paz, c. 1960.]

The hordes of tourists that prefer the nightlife and gambling of Las Vegas or the sights and bullfights of Mexico City are not likely to take to La Paz for many years.

It mainly attracts fishermen and hunters and those who appreciate the genuine loveliness of its people, its ancient structure, its quiet tempo of living, its very foreign but charming atmosphere with an aura of enchantment.

It is somewhat like Hawaii or Tahiti before they were transformed into artificial show places.

La Paz is still real and really romantic.

In La Paz, the ladies in general are the most affable I have ever met. Being cordial to strangers as well as to friends is fashionable and truly sincere. This could have developed a half century or so ago when men seeking employment and higher education left the town to an overbalanced female population—a ratio of six women to one man.

On my first visit to La Paz I was agreeably surprised to find the young ladies so very genial. Elsewhere in Mexico I had been accustomed to seeing them look down their sleeves when spoken to by a stranger. But when I asked a sloe-eyed beauty here where the post office was, she didn't just tell me, she took me.

From all over Baja California and much of Mexico, young men's ambition is to make a pilgrimage to La Paz.

Among a group of musicians just in from Guadalajara, playing at the La Perla cafe, a young blade looked out across the malecón and saw a shapely type to match his longings. He broke off playing and dashed out to follow a respectful ten feet behind her, strumming his guitar and singing a romantic ballad. This midday serenade did not embarrass the girl. She was delighted and flattered but played it with coy dignity. Her longings were shown only by an occasional look out across the sea.

In the song, the walking Romeo suggested she turn onto the pier. She did, knowing full well she would be cornered. She was.

The charming manners of some of the young ladies was put to good use when Mr. and Mrs. Bobby Elias took

Before the malecón was widened. — PHOTO BY HARRY MERRICK

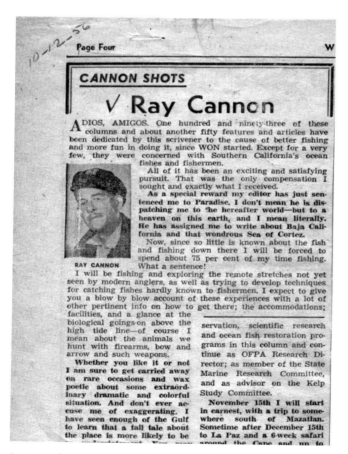

Ray's "Adios" column in *Western Outdoor News*, announcing his "sentencing" to paradise: "Whether you like it or not, I am sure to get carried away on rare occasions and wax poetic about some extraordinary, dramatic, and colorful situation. And don't ever accuse me of exaggerating." — COURTESY WESTERN OUTDOOR NEWS

management of the Hotel Los Arcos. With little training they became more like domestic hostesses than waitresses, trying to impress the boss. With their gaiety and tricks they had the visiting fishermen jumping. One flipper was when refilling a coffee cup they rarely failed to accidentally make bodily contact, and being well stacked, it wasn't difficult.

Meeting George Escudero saved me much time. He knew more about the fish and fishing than anyone I had met in La Paz. I may have spent years learning the techniques and places for catching some of the fish he showed me.

George also spent time showing me the land-side things of interest. Such as the surreptitious cock fights and the somewhat less secretive "Mrs. Murphy's Riding Academy." It was once a glamor spot, but time and lack of patronage had taken their toll.

It was the general dilapidation that made the place interesting. Remarkable also was the survival of this edifice of civilization's oldest profession in a climate that generated so much active competition. — RAY CANNON

SENTENCED TO PARADISE
ADIOS, AMIGOS!

[Given the small number of potential advertisers located south of the border in 1956, it would seem improbable that in October of that year, Ray managed to talk *Western Outdoor News* publisher Burt Twilegar into making him a full-time Baja correspondent. Undoubtedly a factor was Ray's ability to travel and fish in Baja without an expense account. In addition, he was to be paid "per article" on a freelance basis.

Whatever the reasons, Twilegar's fateful decision not only benefited the publication, but also left an indelible mark on the lives of many thousands of people as Ray used the public stage of *Western Outdoor News* to become not just a correspondent, but the pied piper who would play an important role in the building of modern Baja California.

For Ray, the Baja assignment was a dream fulfilled. He had in many ways become disenchanted with the fishery of Southern California which he had watched decline since shortly after the turn of the century. In the Baja California of 1956 he saw a new, undiscovered universe where he could start over again. Ray's joy-filled announcement of his new assignment:]

OCTOBER 12, 1956—Adiós, amigos. One hundred-ninety-three of these columns and about another fifty features and articles have been dedicated by this scrivener to the cause of better fishing and more fun in doing it, since *W.O.N.* started. Except for a very few, they were concerned with Southern California's ocean fishes and fishermen. During this period I have given more than 250 talks at sportsmen's clubs and service organizations on the same subject. Have also served as Research Director for O.F.P.A.

The Hotel Los Cocos, c. 1960.

Ray with sport fishing fleet operator, Rudy Vélez, at La Paz' beachfront Hotel Los Cocos, 1964. In 1969, the Los Cocos became the Hotel Continental, and in 1974 it was converted to workers' quarters for construction of the adjacent 250-room high-rise, the Hotel Presidente (later, Gran Baja), which closed in 1994. Both complexes are now abandoned.

(Ocean Fish Protective Association) which required scores of trips to Sacramento and to scientific institutions.

All of it has been an exciting and satisfying pursuit. That was the only compensation I sought and exactly what I received.

As a special reward my editor has just sentenced me to Paradise. I don't mean he is dispatching me to the hereafter world—but to a heaven on this earth, and I mean literally. He has assigned me to write about Baja California and that wondrous Sea of Cortez.

Now, since so little is known about the fish and fishing down there I will be forced to spend about 75 percent of my time fishing… what a sentence!

I will be fishing and exploring the remote stretches not yet seen by modern anglers, as well as trying to develop techniques for catching fishes hardly known to fishermen.

I expect to give you a blow-by-blow account of these experiences with a lot of other pertinent information on how to get there; the accommodations; facilities; and a glance at the biological goings-on above the high tide line—of course I mean about the animals we hunt with firearms, bow and arrow, and such weapons.

Whether you like it or not, I am sure to get carried away on rare occasions and wax poetic about some extraordinary, dramatic, and colorful situation. And don't ever accuse me of exaggerating. I have already seen enough of the Gulf to learn that a tall tale about the place is more likely to be an understatement. You may expect considerable bad rhetoric. I will constantly be repeating adjectives trying to describe the place and the fishing. As you may have already discovered I lean heavily on the semi-salty language of ocean anglers. However, I will try to paint the picture as I see it and give it to you straight.

You may not be thinking of fishing these Elysian fields just now but it is my guess that you will—and sooner than you think. So keep an eye on the information in this column and on an occasional "Trip of the Week" and other feature news stories in *W.O.N.*

I will keep plugging for conservation, scientific research and ocean fish restoration programs in this column and continue as O.F.P.A. Research Director; as a member of the State Marine Research Committee; and as an advisor on the Kelp Study Committee. I expect to be relieved of many other time-consuming duties so that I can plunge into that Gulf business right up to my ears.

November 15th I will start in earnest, with a trip to somewhere south of Mazatlán. Sometime after December 15th, to La Paz and a six-week safari around the Cape and up to Magdalena Bay, plus other quick trips in between.

In the meantime I must learn how to catch those giant snooks at Mulegé and get a finish for that shell fishing story I started there.

If you would like to join our team and help develop a "where and when" fishing calendar of the Gulf, please keep notes and snapshots of your trip there and send them to my address. Or, if you want information about the area don't hesitate to write me. — RAY CANNON

The Hotel Perla on the malecón of La Paz, 1960. The Perla opened in 1940 as Baja California Sur's first modern hotel. Its founding was sponsored through a semipublic corporation that sold shares to leading citizens throughout the territory. — PHOTO BY RALPH POOLE

RICHNESS OF THE CORTEZ

Somewhere in the warm waters of earth there may be a region where more kinds of game fish occur or there may be a greater number of one or two species than in the Cortez, but I have heard of no place where so many fine gamesters are so super-abundant. All who know something of the world's best fishing regions and who have given this Sea a thorough testing are unanimous in declaring that fish-wise, it adds up to the biggest and most important angling news story in the 20th Century. — RAY CANNON

THE WONDER AND MAGNITUDE

[This fragment—created many years later as the introduction for *The Sea Of Cortez*—expresses better than anything else he wrote the sense of pure joy Ray must have felt upon being "sentenced" to Baja. During nearly a quarter-century of constant exploration and writing, the enthusiasm and "wonder" of Ray's "child heart" would never wane.]

The wonder and magnitude of this sea's fishes and the world they live in can hardly be expressed in our land-bound language. New words are needed to describe this strangest of all great bodies of water, and the spell-casting illusions seen in nature's unusual displays in this region.

What land similes are there paralleling such unique occurrences as when the sea boils up like a volcanic cauldron at one end of a 1,000-fathom channel, while at the other end, 10 to 50 miles away, a crater-size whirlpool funnels down whatever gets trapped in the twirling surge of the suction?

What expressions will convey the enormity of a ten-mile-long horde of fish feeding on a still larger body of forage fish?

What on earth can compare to the fierce savagery of the bloody fish "pileups," in which massive tribes of these migrating sea creatures meet head-on in a collision of mass slaughter, with countless thousands of small and great fish running amuck, devouring, and in turn being devoured by greater denizens in the gluttonous carnage?

The water surface and air above are rent and churned when clouds of diving birds rain down to feast on the maimed, while from the depths, lurking reptiles, crabs, and octopi rise to add to the confused violence.

What phrases are there to adequately caption even the less spectacular scenes in this vitally exuberant world?

Yellowtail and jack crevalle chasing bait fish right up onto the beach. Thousands of manta rays flapjacking ten feet above the surface, looping the loop as they come down to smack it, in an effort to rid themselves of sea fleas. Hundreds of mullet taking to the air when corralled up in the head of an estuary by giant snook riding herd on them. Airborne yellowfin tuna, dolphinfish, and needlefish skipping on the surface in pursuit of little flyingfish. Bird clouds breaking and raining down from the cliffs to feast on anchovetas being pursued by ravenous groupers. Cormorants winging their flyway in miles-long, single file bread lines to the feeding grounds, or teaming up with pelicans, ascending to 1,000 feet or more, to migrate across the peninsula.

Below the surface scene are myriads of exotic fishes, pulsating, plant-like animals, swimming, crawling and attached creatures, moving and swaying in rhythms that sometimes lull and hypnotize the unwary diver beyond that point of no return.

While English is expressive of the two dimensions of upward and outward, there is little in it that defines things or conditions downward from surfaces, and nothing but abstract words to portray the changing and mixing of the dimensions we observe underwater. Here, time, age, and direction lose the meaning we apply to them. Open spaces, as we think of them, do not exist and light comes in shifting, swaying shafts instead of constant, direct vibrations. As if by magic, colors and vistas disappear and reappear in the moving reflections, creating illusions of a fourth dimension, with a feeling of being enclosed inside of it.

Even such similes as the "Kingdom of Neptune," the "submarine zone of Jules Verne," or "The Elysian Fields" cannot approach the fantasy-like realities to be seen, felt, and otherwise experienced beneath that tranquil surface of the Cortez.

The fact that the Sea of Cortez is the finest fishing region yet known to man should be enough to write about, but to me, fishing is only half the story. I have photographed the fish and the fishing, the bordering landscapes and quiet baylets, but try again and again, I have never been able to capture the mystic other half.

The Hotel Guaycura at Kilometer 3 on the Transpeninsular Highway near La Paz. Owners, Antonio and Sabino Pereda, also managed the original Hotel Los Arcos in 1950.

Because it is not the material things, but man's emotional reaction to the montage or kaleidoscope, in which many things combine to produce dreamlike substances. Mirages, sudden currents and atmospheric changes, traffic jams in fish migratory movements, and nature's twists in underwater phenomena, produce such weird goings-on they would tax the imagination of the most visionary outer space writer.

It is as if you could taste and smell the delicate and the explosive coloring of seascapes. Be witness to electric storms in which streaks of lightning, cloud formations, and the sea below turn blood red; or another nighttime phantasma, in which a formless mass of bluish-tinged, phosphorescent stuff the size of a bed sheet plunges from the face of a cliff into the water below, leaving a lingering afterglow.

You can watch whitecaps taking off from the tops of breakers, sail out around into a less turbulent cove, there to disintegrate into a parallel rain. And, strangest of all, accept as normal, mirages that lift whole islands and shorelines high above the horizon. Your eyes see these things, but your responses come from your spinal column, your adrenals, nerve centers, or marrows.

Likewise compelling are the vagaries in which time, space, and light are not separated but flow into the crucible of the mind to intermix, fume up, and be projected as daydreams, weird quirks that spin and unravel webs among the cells and dendrites of the brain.

The mind's appetite for more, and more again, is whetted by contrasting vistas, odd and grotesque, or excitingly beautiful. Some like stage settings for Dante's Inferno, were formed in nature by volcanic action—half-submerged craters have left crowns of jagged, towering pinnacles encircling baylets. In others, time, tide, and wind have sliced mountains, carved the slices into rubble isles, then excavated cavernous grottoes across the faces of solid granite cliffs just above the high tide line.

As I write these lines, tropical scenes are rerun on memory's screen—palm trees marching down a ravine to the edge of the bay; estuaries and backwaters walled around by brilliant green mangrove bushes dotted with the pure white of the egrets and cranes against a background of date and coconut palms and groves of intermingling tropical fruit trees. Superimposed on all this is the spectrum's range of colors seen in sunrise and sunset displays.

The moistureless, clear air, with its balmy temperature and mellow sea breezes, provides an atmosphere that could be termed an opiate and compared to the fictional, hop-dream slumber of the lotus-eater. Surely for the next century and on, poets, painters, writers, and others of the arts will find drama and boundless inspiration in the sights and sounds and feel of this world of new perceptions.

— RAY CANNON

Ray, third from right, on a 1956 Charlie Rucker panga mothership trip—San Felipe to the Midriff islands.

The *Galeana* at Isla Angel de la Guarda, 1956. — PHOTO BY HARRY MERRICK

AMESING MIDRIFF

EARLY "PANGA MOTHERSHIPS"

RAY'S EARLY MIDRIFF fishing discoveries were made beginning in 1954 aboard the "panga motherships" of Charlie Rucker out of San Felipe, and the charter boats of Dave Hyams and Andy Chersin out of Puerto Peñasco. These converted shrimp trawlers or small commercial tuna boats were outfitted with minimal creature comforts to take clients on one-week explorations of the new sport fishing world around Isla Angel de la Guarda, and south to Isla San Lorenzo. This type of sport fishing trip continues to the present day in the hands of such operators as Tony Reyes and Bobby Castellón of San Felipe.

ULTIMATE PARADISE DISCOVERED
ISLA ANGEL DE LA GUARDA

[Ray's first "Charlie Rucker trip" to the Midriff islands was a true revelation to someone who had already been fishing for half a century. The area described is Puerto Refugio at the north end of Isla Angel de la Guarda.]

MAY 7, 1954—At last the ultimate paradise of fishing paradises has been discovered. You have heard of them and dreamed of them, but in your wildest flights of fantasy you have never pictured anything like this one. In this retreat of the Gods, fish are counted by the billions and angling conditions are unequaled elsewhere on this planet.

Writing this article frightens me. If I tell where this place is, the new Governor of Baja California, Braulio Maldonado, is apt to think an invasion by lost Americanos is under way and the region is likely to be choked with the biggest fleet of private sport fishing boats outside of Balboa on regatta day.

Johnny Miller, angler extraordinary of the Long Beach Anglers, the Tuna Club and O.F.P.A. (Ocean Fish Protection Agency) director, may find himself admiral of

the migrating fleet. He is exploring the area now. Charlie Rucker most certainly will need to add more charter boats. Regardless of the consequences, a news story that promises as much pleasurable adventure as this one just must be published.

The place—Isla Angel de la Guarda—"Isle of the Guardian Angel," 14 hours down the coast from San Felipe and five miles off shore. This island looks as if it were once a volcano, with four craters two or three miles in diameter. Three of them form sheltered bays.

The fourth, a circular inner bay, is connected by narrow passages to the three. This inner submerged crater is protected from all sides by a precipitous rim extending up to mountainous heights.

The inter-space fantasy creator of Flash Gordon would find this island a rich spot for background material. It resembles no other place I have ever seen or heard of.

I booked on one of Charlie Rucker's trips along with a group of swell sportsmen, Al Andrews, Harry Newland, Burt Blackmore, Al Schyarz, Dwight Koonce and Ralph Armstrong. Angler-photographers George Blackmore and Vern Noller were on my shore fishing team. We fished the Enchanted Islands and Bahía de San Luis [Gonzaga] on the way down. These spots were highly productive but were soon forgotten when we pulled into the inner bay of Angel de la Guarda.

Our first glimpse revealed a half-dozen birds working on yellowtail breaks. Our outboard skiffs took off and were soon going in circles with big "yellow" hookups. A few minutes later it was monstrous gulf groupers, some weighing more than a hundred pounds.

My shore-working crew found miles of perfect rock formations for our experimental fishing. There, deep calm shore waters were as loaded as the balance of the bay and for the first time, I hooked yellowtail from shore. Every inch of the water to 50 feet out was saturated with newly-

Charlie Rucker's 65-foot *Alfredo*. A brochure from about 1954 for Rucker's panga mothership operation out of San Felipe listed among the amenities for these early trips: "...paper plates and cups, wooden forks and spoons and plastic knives; new ones each meal."

Ray on a Charlie Rucker panga mothership trip to the Midriff, 1955.

hatched 1/2-inch fishes. I judged them to be the young of groupers and cabrillas because of the abundance of these species and by the results of our examinations which showed that they were completely spent (no eggs or milt was found in them).

We found a half-dozen different fingerling game species in great abundance under our light at night, all of which suggests that this area may prove to be the most highly concentrated spawning grounds of the continent.

The fishing was so pleasant and exciting from the rocks we nearly forgot our experimental and photographic work. Among the strange specimens captured were three fishes not yet identified.

The word sensational could be applied in all of its true meaning to the yellowtail fishing in the whole region around La Guarda. The most plentiful among the various abundant species in the bays of this island is the gulf grouper, *Mycteroperca jordani*.

This fish may appear with oblong spots, small round spots or without any. It is quickly distinguished from the next most abundant fish in this area, the pinto cabrilla (in the genus *Epinephelus*) by having a slightly concave tail fin and a triangular pointed anal fin, while those of the cabrilla are rounded. The round spots of the cabrilla are comparatively larger.

While both of these species can be taken on slowly trolled (three knots) lures for the next couple months, a large strip of Monterey Spanish mackerel (sierra) will be the killer after June 1.

Strip-bait of Spanish mackerel, frozen squid and two-inch Nylure feathers proved best for shore fishing. Our Sila-flex surf and spinning rods proved faultless in this rugged work.

Just about every type of lure was used successfully in our deep water trolling, with the chrome-plated Homicide and ruby-eyed Sneve getting the edge.

— RAY CANNON

"MIRACLE" FISH AT REFUGIO

[Ray is humorously candid in telling how he accidentally caught his first large grouper in 1955. By the 1970s, his feelings of guilt in taking slow-growing species would cause him to write that such fish should not be caught at all.]

The monicker "fishing authority" hung on me by other sports writers has been difficult to live down and every group I fish with expects me to perform fishing miracles. Once, I did it and fished myself right out of business with the first bait I put out.

The incident happened on one of my earlier trips. Having read my stories of the fabulous Midriff fishing, my home organization, the Hollywood Rod & Gun Club, and the L.A. Postman's Angling Club had chartered two Rucker boats in June 1955. Both groups had planned big fish fries on their return and would need enough fish to feed about 300 people, and they expected me to repeat something like the fishes and multitude miracle.

My club's boat had arrived in Refugio before daylight and our breakfast was being spread on the deck. Thinking I could tie into one of the gigantic sharks I had seen there I broke out heavy tackle and was baiting the large 14/0 shark hook with a whole two-foot-long sierra, when the Postmen's ship pulled alongside.

No one in the two groups had ever seen anyone use a

hook and bait that size. Thinking I was putting on a phony show, which I really thought I was, they were having a smart-cracking field day, ribbing about my trying to catch whales to show off.

I was not too surprised when I got a heavy, tugboat pull as soon as the bait struck bottom, or when, after I had set the hook with all I had, the fish showed little fight as I eased it toward the surface. But I nearly shed my skin when I saw that the monstrous thing was an enormous bass of some kind.

The astonishment all around was well-expressed by Bob Jurgens when he yelled, "I guess I got up too early. I know this isn't so."

I knew I would have to sit back and be an instructor for I didn't dare put out another bait. I might fish for weeks without catching another this size so I quit while I was ahead.

I had never before seen a grouper that size (138 pounds), much less decked one. Because of the light brown or bay color (which is perhaps just a color phase) natives call it "baya."

Since that trip I have caught a dozen or more that weighed above a hundred pounds but have always felt guilty since learning that they were 80 to 100 years old.

Grouper this size are not often taken near coastal villages, indicating that they have been fished out and that their movements are restricted to within a few miles of their individual habitats. — RAY CANNON

Black sea bass caught at Ensenada Grande aboard a Charlie Rucker boat out of San Felipe in June 1956.

YELLOWTAIL A NUISANCE FISH

[Ray's vivid description of discovering the massive schools of yellowtail that once blanketed the Midriff area, sometimes from horizon to horizon.]

JULY 22, 1955—Here was a trip in which yellowtail became a nuisance fish in a one-week-long exploration trip to the southern tip of Isla Angel de la Guarda and to the fabulous fishing grounds around Isla Partida.

In the straits between these we witnessed an unforgettable surge of nature. We saw and passed through a wave of yellowtail estimated at one and one-half miles long and about one-eighth in width!

One wave followed another for the three days we were in the area. Coming up out of the southeast they plowed through the strait, turned westerly and disappeared toward Bahía de los Angeles.

At close range we could see the yellows in pursuit of the massive schools of sardines and anchovetas.

The length and breadth of each great wave was covered with diving birds working in rhythmic motions. Each would rise 20 to 30 feet above the surface, peel off in a jet-propelled dive, then repeat, again and again, the graceful maneuver as if timed by a metronome.

All hands aboard rushed for their cameras, for we

On a Charlie Rucker trip, 1956.

were already fed up catching yellowtail.

On this, my third trip as a guest of Charlie Rucker, of Entz and Rucker Hardware and Sporting Goods Store, who books these trips, I sailed with ten members of the Postman's organization.

For me this trip started when my neighborhood Post Office Supervisor, Ed Johnson, and Bob Jurgens of the Hollywood Rod and Gun Club and director of the Southern Council, invited me to join their P.O. group on this exploration safari. Johnson, who organizes the annual charter, and his fellow worker, Andy Anderson, picked me up for a leisurely drive to San Felipe.

The triple incentive—fishing, fun, food for the P.O. Club's big fish fry, and collecting specimens, spurred everyone into a fishing frenzy. But yellowtail were so abundant we were forced to use tricks to avoid them after the first two days.

Grouper and cabrilla became the main objectives and the seas were overly kind.

Ramón Comacho, the number one guide of the Gulf, who manages these trips for Charlie Rucker, never misses. He has made great improvements in the accommodations since last year. This trip is a luxurious cruise in comparison.

Following the Baja California coastline past the Enchanted Islands we found fishing good south of San Luis Bay and down past Los Angeles Bay. But all other fishing "paradises" fade into insignificance when compared to the islands.

The bays and recesses near the southern point of Angel de la Guarda are loaded with real red snappers and spotted bass. The triggerfish, a terrific fighter, is found over most rocky reefs. Cabrilla, grouper and yellowtail are everywhere.

I did not believe that any spot on earth could equal Refugio Bay which lies in the north end of La Guarda but we found a better hole around Isla Partida, some four or five miles south of Angel de la Guarda's southern tip. Fishing around this one and another half-mile-long island that lies nearby, nine of us caught more than a ton of grouper and cabrilla in one late afternoon and an early morning.

White marlin-type lures proved most effective in this area except when the sun was high. Then the darker colors became more favored.

Many large fish were lost when single wire leaders were used. A loop pulled tight snaps the single wire. No losses occurred when plastic-impregnated Sevenstrand wire was employed.

A small bay on the north side of Partida served as anchorage for the night. Here we exchanged a huge hammerhead shark for a turtle, with a crew from a commercial shark fishing boat. At night our lights attracted great schools of sardines, anchovetas and young (Pacific) mackerel. We could have brailed them.

If you can remember how your spinal column chilled and quaked and your innards danced a jig in the surprise thrill while hooking and fighting your first marlin or tarpon, you can understand what happened to me while shore rock fishing with Ed Johnson on Partida. The boys in the skiffs saw it from a distance but Johnson and I were within ten feet of one of the most exciting fish boiling occurrences I've seen. Imagine dozens of big groupers in tight formation clearing the surface at one time, followed by a like number, and another, and another.

The frantic diving birds, the panicky sardines taking to the air and the fury of the groupers running amuck created such a storm of violence that my emotions almost drove me to jump off the ledge and join the melee.

We both had seen thousands of schools of fish boil, but never before close enough to hit 'em with a shillelagh. This was also the first time we had seen such numbers jump clear out of the water en masse.

Each hundred feet around this solid rock point produced a new and thrilling experience. Looking down

A 1957 brochure of booking agent Dave J. Hyams describes a unique way of going fishing in Baja. In Mexicali, anglers boarded this deluxe Pullman train car, which took them to Puerto Peñasco and then parked on a siding. They slept and ate in the car, and fished from the boat *Galeana*.

into the deep clear water from one ledge we saw an assemblage of fishes as thickly populated as the big glass tank at Marineland. From another we saw huge groupers dash for cover and scatter in all directions just before the grand entrance of a granddaddy of all granddaddies. This gigantic gulf grouper gracefully glided in and around the ledge just under our feet.

At one point he turned and stopped to inspect my two-inch strip-bait. I still haven't figured out what I would have done if he had inhaled it. A length of five and one-half to six feet would be a conservative estimate of his size, and the 130-pounder I caught on a previous Gulf trip would have appeared as a pygmy beside him. — RAY CANNON

ISLA TIBURON
BILLFISH TO THE HORIZON

[A fantastic concentration of billfish in an area where they are not commonly seen today. Notable in this article are Ray's conjectures, later confirmed, of the general richness of the Midriff area and the role of tidal upwellings in maintaining the food chain.]

JANUARY 27, 1956—Heretofore the fishing places described in our "Trip of the Week" articles were correctly termed "fishing holes," "spots," and "areas," but this one is about a whole region in which the water is crawling with sea life and the air above it a whirling mass. Picture a vista of the sea that ends only with the horizon in convulsion during a dead calm. Stretch the imagination as far as you can and it will still fall short of the reality.

This vast expanse extends from Tiburón Island across the Canal el Infiernillo (Channel of Little Hell) that separates it from the mainland, and on northward up the coastline. Astronomical terms would be necessary to describe the abundance and numbers of living creatures that inhabit these waters.

A sampling type of count, of the jumping marlin and sailfish, estimating so many to the acre, then multiplying that number by 640 acres to a square mile, and again by the number of miles to the horizon, and the total would seem much too fantastic to publish.

No one angler or crew member aboard our boat had ever before believed that there was such an enormous population of billfish in the Gulf of California, or in our section of the Pacific, for that matter. As we stood on the deck about ten miles off shore and about the same distance north of the N.W. corner of Tiburón, we could see them leaping clear of the surface as far as we could see water—and in all directions.

Although billfish were the more spectacular, they formed only a fraction of the number of other species that churned the water into continuous eruptions. An army of thousands of dolphin (mammal) spotted us a mile away and within seconds bore down and surrounded us to give a grand display of their extrovert natures. Small, three-inch flyingfish, in an almost continuous stream, took off from both sides of the bow and skittled on out with the wake. Masses of other small fishes, perhaps round herring, and anchovy-like forms, could be seen all about our boat.

Among the most numerous of the game fishes was the big Mexican bonito which is shaped similar to, and fights like a bluefin tuna. Here we found them ravenously

The *Galeana* at Puerto Peñasco in February 1956. Dave J. Hyams' resort development in background. — PHOTO BY HARRY MERRICK

cooperative. They would latch on to whatever kind of lure was offered. But of all the gamesters of the Gulf, the dolphinfish should rate first. That is, to all who are not completely gone on billfish.

The dolphinfish has no equal in speed, color and graceful aerial activity. Furthermore, it rates among the best of food fishes. Because of its habit of taking off at an angle of 45 to 60 degrees, the angler is not always aware of the hookup. The body of the leaping dolphinfish is usually curved in perfect harmony with the semicircle of the arc. Phleuger, the noted fish taxidermist of Florida, may have captured the brilliant coloring of the dolphinfish but I have yet to see a painting or mounting that even approaches the exquisite beauty in life. An angler wishing to get his catch mounted should get a color close-up in a photo as soon as it is decked.

This first survey trip was fitted out by the hospitable Andy Chersin, owner of the delightful new Hotel Hermosillo and up-to-the-minute sport fishing fleet at Punta Peñasco. Our boat was a sizable tuna clipper now converted into a luxury fishing craft. Andy has made it into the most comfortable angling boat in the Gulf with stateroom accommodations for 14, a spic and span galley, and other liner conveniences. A refrigerated hold will allow anglers to take home as many fresh fish as they can haul.

I expect to make an extended survey trip to Tiburón shortly to locate the most productive spots of the giant gulf grouper, black sea bass, cabrilla, and red snapper, corvina, totuava, and a dozen other game fishes that seem to be abundant in this region.

This locality may prove to be the spawning ground of a great number of the Gulf fishes. Water conditions between Tiburón and the mainland are unique. The shallowness of the channel causes the water in it to be heated. When the tide changes, this warm water collides with the cold water welled up from the deep canyon off

Dave J. Hyams' boat, *Galeana*, c. 1956.

Bahía Agua Dulce, Freshwater Bay, on the north side of Isla Tiburón, looking across Canal el Infiernillo. The area north of this place is where Ray found the highest density of billfish of his career. He estimated the number of marlin ten miles off the island as "four in every 100-foot square." — PHOTO BY HARRY MERRICK

the west side of the island, producing a rich food chain and an ideal spawning condition.

If my suspicions are confirmed we may have discovered one of the world's richest angling localities. I will be able to give you a lot more information after my next trip. I must learn whether the fishes found there last fall are seasonal visitors or permanent residents. Young fish must be collected to learn which of the fishes spawn in the area.

I have been unable to find any angler who has fished this area before our trip, or scientist who has collected fishes there. It seems to be a virgin field for such activities. There are indications that a belt of rich and productive water extends across the Gulf from Tiburón to the south end of Isla Angel de la Guarda. Included would be the islands forming a chain between the larger bodies. Here the mainlands pinch the Gulf into a narrow waistline and the belt of islands forces the shifting tides of 90 miles of water to flow through the squeezed gaps between them. This action forces the fertilizing chemicals up from the deep channels stimulating plankton growth which serves as the basic food for most all small fishes, which in turn supply forage for the big game species. On subsequent trips I expect to work this whole belt.

The new shortcut road between Mexicali and Punta Peñasco has been blacktopped except for 35 miles of good graded surface. This reduces the travel time between them to four hours. Sailing time from Punta Peñasco to Cape Tepopas is about 18 hours. Between this point and Tiburón lie the fabulous El Infiernillo Straits, where we found such an abundant sea life. It is 11 miles wide. The small guano-

covered Isla Patos sits midway. Situated on a line between the cold and warm waters, this island should prove highly productive the year round. Especially the reef that projects out from the south side of it. We found it loaded with giant grouper and cabrilla last fall. — RAY CANNON

GIANT BLACK SEA BASS UNLIMITED

[Ray would eventually come to regret the catching of such fish as described in this article about Ensenada Grande.]

JUNE 15, 1956—Black sea bass in such vast numbers as I have never before seen were located on my most recent trip. I also discovered a new method of attracting these giants.

The fishing grounds—Ensenada Grande (Big Cove)—a 16-hour boat ride from San Felipe or about 105 miles, situated due west of the north end of Isla Angel de la Guarda along the shoreline of Baja California.

There are really two coves. The southern one is carved out of a mountain. The sheer cliffs vary up to 300 feet and plunge another 50 feet below the surface except where fallen rocks have filled shore spots. The northern cove is separated from the other by a narrow, jutting cliff, and curves back into the mouth of a canyon and wash. It is shallow with a boulder beach.

We hit the black sea bass concentration a half-mile off the south cove, over rock bottom in 60 to 75 feet of water. It is worth noting that there was a distinct dividing line between the rock floor and the sandy bottom. As we drifted over sand we started hooking totuava and 30-inch red snappers but no sea bass.

A small hand-lining commercial had caught three tons of black sea bass and was trying to make it five tons. We landed nine and farmed a like number. The largest one decked weighed about 250 pounds. A 600-pounder was reported taken near this spot two weeks before.

The whole trip was one of discovery. In addition to the black sea bass grounds we found areas loaded with totuava, corvinas, yellowtail, large red snappers and a gulf full of goldspotted bass, which proved a killer as live bait for black sea bass and totuava.

Our schedule was to fish the little-known 75-mile coast between the Enchanted Islands and Bahía de los Angeles.

May 20—One mile off Red Rock near the San Luis Bay, we found a large area populated with three-foot-long corvinas, mostly shortfin. Also a few 100-pound totuavas. We used fresh-dead sardines and strips of sierra for bait.

May 21—A short stop at Ensenada Grande produced three black sea bass—one was 5' 6" long. We farmed about a dozen. Red snappers were plentiful. We were about one-half mile offshore in water 60 feet deep. Later near shore we contacted totuava, grouper and a few yellowtail. We had not yet discovered the abundance of goldspotted bass or its value as a terrific bait for the big fish.

May 22—Hit yellowtail over a wide area at the entrance of Los Angeles Bay. All fish here were taken on lures, trolling, with some caught on white bone jigs and feathers.

May 23—Back at Ensenada Grande where I learned that the rocky bottom was loaded with goldspotted bass at depths of 50 to 150 feet. This species is apt to be found in abundance throughout this region of the Gulf. I was able to keep all hands supplied with goldspotted live bait and believe this will prove the top bait for black sea bass and totuava and perhaps for large groupers. In this area it was really hot. Chunks and strips of sierra were chewed up by triggers and other small fish long before attracting the attention of the large fish. The live baits were attacked only by the monsters.

For the most effective use as live bait the goldspotted bass should be transferred to the large hook and returned to deep water as soon as possible. Without the pressure of the deep water this bass will die quickly or become too lifeless to serve as good bait. The hook should be inserted under the soft-rayed section of the dorsal fin. For black sea bass, the live bait is dangled from two to four feet above the bottom. Slightly higher for totuava.

Rucker, who books these trips at his hardware store at 4275 Crenshaw Blvd., plans to run them throughout the summer and fall. Ramón Comacho acts as guide and he really knows this part of the Gulf.

From now on Ramón will be able to hit a half-dozen spots that are really loaded and each of the places will yield

a different group of fishes. The black sea bass hole would make a dramatic climax if he could schedule it for the last day. Catching red snapper and the yard-long corvina provide very exciting fishing if done before tying into yellowtail, giant grouper, totuava and black sea bass.

Little effort to improve angling technique has been practiced in fishing the Gulf. Very few anglers are able to set the big 12/0 to 14/0 hooks in common use there. The mouth of the giant sea bass is tough and while natives set the large hook on their stretchless cotton hand-lines with apparent ease, getting the hook to penetrate beyond the barb is another matter. Especially when the angler is using an elastic line or a flexible rod.

Now that the windy season is over and the surface of the Gulf like a mirror, sailing and fishing down the Ballenas should produce a new crop of poets. — RAY CANNON

HOW THE BIGMOUTH BASTARD GOT ITS NAME

[Ray adored humorous, odd names—such as the moniker "Mrs. Murphy's Riding Academy" that was attached to a house of ill-repute in La Paz—and he went out of his way to mention them in his columns. One of his favorites was the "Bigmouth Bastard" fish, a species of jawfish with the tongue-twisting scientific name of *Opisthognathus rhomalea*.

"Bigmouth Bastard" was confirmed as the fish's legitimate name during a field trip to the UCLA Life Science Department's specimen collection in Westwood, California. There, preserved in jars of alcohol since the early 1950s, were several examples of the elongated, bullet-headed fish, many carefully labeled "Bigmouth Bastard" and noted as having been collected in the Sea of Cortez by UCLA's head of ichthyology at that time—Dr. Boyd Walker—and none other than Ray Cannon. This 1998 visit was witnessed and confirmed by Pete Thomas, outdoor writer for the *Los Angeles Times*, and it was recorded for posterity in an article printed a few days later.

But, where did the name come from?

Ray, lower left, at the formation of the Bigmouth Bastard Club, *Western Outdoor News*, March 9, 1956.

— COURTESY WESTERN OUTDOOR NEWS

Dr. Boyd Walker with a well-preserved Bigmouth Bastard at the UCLA Department of Life Sciences, 1998. — PHOTO BY GENE KIRA

Ray and Dr. Boyd Walker with a collecting net at Puerto Escondido, 1959. — PHOTO BY HARRY MERRICK

That mystery is explained in the following *Western Outdoor News* column, probably written in 1954, which describes Ray and Dr. Walker on a research/fishing trip to Bahía Refugio at the north end of Isla Angel de la Guarda in the Midriff area. Perhaps it was the same trip on which the fish in the accompanying photograph was collected.

Although he does not say so in the column, Ray had undoubtedly reached Bahía Refugio aboard one of the "panga motherships" pioneered by Charlie Rucker of out San Felipe.

Notable in this story is the fact that Ray's brother, Manuel Lee Cannon, was along on this trip. Also, the detailed description of collecting fish by stunning them with rotenone, which Ray and Dr. Walker did on many trips to the Midriff, Loreto, La Paz, and Los Cabos areas, as well as Bahía Magdalena.]

On another cruise to Refugio with Dr. Boyd Walker, I assisted him collecting fish specimens from a couple of coves within the bay.

Rotenone, a powdered South American plant, is generally used as a fish "mickey" by scientists. Walker selected a spot where the bottom was part sand and part rock and had a considerable growth of sea weeds. A five-gallon can of the material saturated a 75-by-50-foot area.

Within 20 minutes just about every creature in the place turned belly up. Less than half of the stupefied fish rose to the surface. The others had to be ferreted out from between rocks and weeds.

We found sardines down to larva size, suggesting that a Gulf race of the species spawns in bays or close to shore, differing from the Pacific-raised sardines which broadcast their eggs a hundred miles or more from shore.

Walker wore a face plate and flippers and dived for the non-floater fishes, while I dip netted those showing on and near the surface. Before we could gather all of them, large triggerfish, groupers and a number of sizable wrasse the natives call "vieja" (old lady) came dashing in to help harvest. The rotenone had become too diluted to affect them. I grabbed a fishing rod and beat the surface while Walker finished collecting.

Meanwhile, my brother Lee Cannon of Santa Monica, California was catching a number of species casting from a ledge. Included was a two-foot-long vieja taken on a fresh strip-bait. It proved a lively gamester on his spinning outfit. Later we caught them on shrimp and frozen squid. The brilliant red, black and yellow colors trimmed with neon blue gives this "old lady" a showy appearance in the water.

Our total catch numbered 97 species taken in areas of less than 150 feet square. Many were rare or not known to inhabit the region. One, a goby, was a new species.

BIGMOUTH BASTARD NAMED

Dr. Walker was very anxious to get more specimens of a small, deep-water fish so rare that only three had ever been recorded as taken. One of these had been caught in a drag net just off the entrance to Refugio Bay. He told me that no common name had been selected but when one of his students was trying to find their first specimens he had misplaced he asked, "Have any of you seen that strange fish?" Then when another student asked, "What fish?" the first replied, "That bigmouth bastard."

Walker agreed with my suggestion that whenever reasonable, a thing should be known by the first name ever applied to it. But I had trouble convincing my editor when he spotted the name. He really hit the ceiling when he read how we had taken the angler ship out to deep water and with the use of two-inch strip-baits on No. 1 hooks I had decked a half-dozen and that Dr. Walker had said, "You are the world champion. You have caught more bigmouth bastards than anyone."

He finally agreed to publish the column, then to fire me if authorities objected. To our surprise, the only comment was in letters suggesting that, since *Western Outdoor News* was of interest only to fishermen and hunters, why not use more of the salty language they were accustomed to hearing. — RAY CANNON

WITH DR. WALKER AT PUERTO ESCONDIDO

[Another bigmouth bastard is caught, this time by Dr. Walker himself at Puerto Escondido, just south of Loreto. Professional photographer Harry Merrick happened to be along on this collecting trip, resulting in some excellent photos. Merrick was filming footage for the Mac McClintock television show, *Fishing Flashes*. Walker accompanied Ray as often as possible on these trips to Baja because of the transportation on Trans Mar de Cortés and Aeronaves de México that Ray could arrange for them and their bulky collecting equipment.]

PUERTO ESCONDIDO, NOVEMBER 20, 1959—"Hey, Ray! I've got a bigmouth bastard!"

It was Dr. Boyd Walker doing the yelling, and by his surprised tone you would have thought he'd just nabbed an illegitimate offspring of a dugong. He wasn't being humorous but expressing true excitement at finding this rare fish. (Bigmouth bastard is the accepted common name of this species.) Only 21 men are known to have ever caught one on rod and reel and they have an exclusive B.M.B. Club. To qualify, a candidate must take one by angling.

Before the day's work was finished we had 24 of the strange fish preserved in formalin, the largest scientific collection ever before made in a single area. These and an additional number of other rare specimens were being retrieved in Puerto Escondido (Hidden Port), one of the most enchanting spots to be found anywhere.

Up to our arrival in Puerto Escondido our journey had been a lux deal. We had excellence of service and a plush bungalow at the Los Arcos Hotel in La Paz and at Gene Walters' Casa Arriba at Rancho Buena Vista, and had traveled up and down the coast in spacious cruisers,

Ray and Dr. Boyd Walker preparing rotenone used to stun fish specimens at Puerto Escondido, 1959. — PHOTO BY HARRY MERRICK

Dr. Boyd Walker collecting specimens in the Midriff islands.
— PHOTO BY HARRY MERRICK

including one kindly sent up to Loreto from the Ruffo Brother's La Paz fleet. Here in wild and primitive Escondido, which is destined to become the site of the most luxurious resort around El Golfo, we would be roughing it.

To be near the chow house we spread our sleeping bags under a shading tree, and without knowing it, were sleeping within three feet of a varmint freeway. It was 2 a.m. when

Roca Vela, or Sail Rock, stands off the western entrance to Puerto Refugio at the north end of Isla Angel de la Guarda. Ray's caption for this photo taken in February 1956: "The small white (guano-covered) rock is 100 feet high. It is the "Guardian Angel" of Isla Angel de la Guarda."

— PHOTO BY HARRY MERRICK

we realized our mistake. We heard the farm house pack of five big dogs get underway about half a mile up the valley. Down they came, closer and closer, sounding off with each leap. Except for the clamor and flying of rocks, the chase resembled a greyhound race as they made a shortcut across the foot of my bed. There was one other difference, instead of pursuing a stuffed rabbit, it was a huge bobcat in the lead.

I would have considered the charge an exciting pleasure if they hadn't repeated the exact same kind of ruckus an hour later, then again just before daylight. Each time following the same trail right across the foot of my bed. Hunters would have loved it but romping varmints are not my specialty. I am strictly a below-the-high-tide-line man. As for sleeping, we may as well have spent that night in the city pound.

We were also annoyed by small worms that kept dropping from the tree. At first I thought we were under a bird roost but learned better when Walker yelled that one of them had crawled right on into his ear. I got a flashlight and chummed it up where I was able to grab it by the head and yank it out.

These incidents were forgotten next day when we took the boat out to survey the rugged coast around to Punta Coyote and across the 1 1/2-mile channel to examine the hewn and escarped coves along the 3 1/2-mile-long Isla Danzante, then down the chain of small islands that all but fence in the outer Bay.

Back in through the narrow neck of the inner Escondido we circled its shoreline of mangrove bushes, beaches and cliffs, where Walker selected a couple of small esteros. In these he would spread rotenone to knock out all the small fish, collect them for identification and study, and add them to his large UCLA collection of Gulf and Pacific fishes.

When not assisting Dr. Walker, photographer Harry Merrick and I spent most of our time trolling. In the deep, clear water at Punta Coyote we saw enough grouper, cabrilla, snappers and other rock dwellers to stock another Marineland. At Danzante Island, Harry tied into a dolphinfish and got some good pics of its jumping. In and around the bay we caught roosterfish (one so small we believe it spawned there), sierra, jack crevalle and grouper. We could have caught a whole checklist of game and good food fishes, as I had taken on previous trips to this fabulous spot, if I had not insisted on spending most of our time in pursuit of needlefish.

We found my favorite giant needles, *Strongylura fodiator*, and the yard-long, slender needlefish, *S. pacificus*, abundant. Dr. Walker says our catch of the latter extended its range (in scientific records). Heretofore it was not recorded as being in the Gulf at all. We did not have live mullet, the essential bait for the big snook, but saw a dozen that had been netted there by a shark fisherman while seining for bait. Now about those varmints. We learned that this region is crawling with them as well as with mountain lion, deer, bighorn sheep and a lot of game fowls. We saw doves and ducks on and around the freshwater lakes on a neighboring ranch.

Javelina, antelope, pheasant and some other fowls have been introduced from the mainland and appear to be thriving here. It was exciting watching one of the dogs chase a javelina into the brush, but none so when the little boar turned and chased the dog right back into the house and under the bed.

From atop of a knoll overlooking the bay, the south and east coastline of precipitous cliffs and coves and the string of small offshore isles resemble the floating islands in a Chinese painting in fantasy. The westerly vista is even more awe-inspiring. Looking back across the emerald bay that almost became a lake, and past the little, tropical valley to the abrupt end of the Sierra de la Giganta, the mountain backdrop extending upward for 4,700 feet gives one the impression of seeing an enlarged side of the Grand Canyon, or a crater wall of the moon. This whole area seems anyplace but on this earth.

The bay is four to seven fathoms deep. The narrow, 75-foot-wide entrance spreads out to a quarter-of-a-mile and extends back for slightly more than a mile. It is the best protected puerto in the Gulf.

Escondido was the climactic finish to a highly dramatic series of scientific collections made by Dr. Walker on an extended trip. We started at Cabo Pulmo near the tip of the Peninsula. Diver Bobby Van Wormer of the Bahía de Palmas Lodge, joined us to help collect around Rancho Buena Vista, where 150 species were taken in three small areas. At La Paz the discovery of month-old snook in the very back of the Bay was of great importance to anglers.

Summing up the whole, Walker said this was the finest and richest individual collecting trip he had ever made and it has given me a world of new material to write about. Furthermore, I learned more in those two weeks than during any of the extended expeditions I have made into the Gulf area. — RAY CANNON

NAMING THE MYSTERIOUS MIDRIFF

[Ray's first use of the name "Midriff" for the middle portion of the Sea of Cortez was made in some unpublished field notes probably written in 1954, and if he did not actually coin the term at that time, he was the first to popularize it. (The earliest confirmed use of the name was in a column written in March 1956.) Here, in combined fragments, Ray describes the spectacular tidal effects that he says inspired the term "Midriff."]

The word "midriff" is defined as "belly," also as "swift-turbulent water." Both fit this region. The deep (down to 800 fathoms) channels receive and digest the rich chemicals which have poured into the mouth of the Gulf from the Colorado River for millions of years.

Upwelled from those deep bowels to the surface, the nitrates, phosphates, potash and other nutriments fertilize

In 1969 Ray suggested the name "Hotel Midriff" for this resort project at San Francisquito that was never built.

the phytoplankton (microscopic vegetation) which is eaten by the zooplankton (minute animal organisms). This mass of plankton (450 million to the cubic foot) provides the basic foodstuff for most all living creatures of the sea. In this respect the Midriff is among the richest areas on earth.

The turbulence in the channels occurs when the high lunar tides dash up the Gulf from the Pacific and are funneled into the narrows. They are seen as great maelstrom-like whirlpools and erupting upwelled water which reaches a height of 12 feet above the surface.

At a point one-quarter of a mile off San Esteban Island we saw the strangest phenomenon we had encountered in this or any sea.

A wall of water five or six feet high stood before us. I climbed up on the bow to where I was able to see that the breaking waves were not one behind the other but flowing down like a staircase cataract from a smooth top about 200 yards across and that the whole violent upheaval was circular.

I had seen turbulent stretches in an otherwise calm sea across the north end of Canal de Ballenas and in discussion with Dr. Carl Hubbs had learned that they were caused by upwelling resulting from the strong lunar currents.

In area, the belt composing the Midriff is about 80 miles wide. Centered by the 29th Parallel, it extends from a line between Punta Bluff on the Baja California Peninsula (100 sea miles below San Felipe) and Punta Lobos on the Sonora or Mexican mainland side, southward to a line between Kino Bay and Bahía San Francisquito.

Within these bounds are 21 islands, including Tiburón, the largest, and Angel de la Guarda, the longest in the Gulf. None are inhabited except Tiburón which is occupied by Seri Indians seasonally.

Canal de las Ballenas and Canal Salsipuedes stretching along the Baja coast and bordered on the sea side by the islands Angel de la Guarda, Partida, Raza, Salsipuedes and San Lorenzo, reach depths of 800 fathoms or more. It is in these channels that the maelstrom-like whirlpools and explosive upwellings occur. Only one paved highway leads to the region. It terminates at the village of Kino Bay. Bahía de los Angeles and Puerto Lobos, population about 100 each, are the only other villages. They can be reached by very rough truck and jeep roads.

In 14 exploration trips I have seriously examined all of the 500 miles of the Baja and Sonora shores and the coastlines of all the islands, giving special attention to fish and fishing as well as observing the strange phenomena. I have been unable to find any more than sketchy accounts in modern or old literature on the region. — RAY CANNON

The Midriff "panga mothership" sport fishing concept pioneered in the early 1950s by Charlie Rucker out of San Felipe, and Andy Chersin and Dave Hyams out of Puerto Peñasco, is still thriving nearly half a century later, with modern operators such as San Felipe's Tony Reyes, and Bobby Castellón, whose boat the *Celia Angelina* is shown here in 1997.

MONSTROUS MAELSTROMS OF HORROR

[In combined descriptions, c. 1957, Ray's best accounts of the tidal whirlpools of the Midriff area.]

At the south end of the Canal de las Ballenas, great swirling eddies two or three-hundred feet in diameter can be seen. While at the north end the upwelling can be seen in like-sized boils, belching up four to five feet above the surrounding surface level. This process is reversed when the tide shifts southward.

At the south end I saw a three-mile circle with mirror-like surface—at the center, a strange moving turbulence. Beyond the rim of the calm circle, six monstrous finback whales were obviously avoiding the area. An enormous shoal of boiling yellowtail accompanying diving birds detoured in a semi-circle. Sea lions, porpoises, and a sea teeming with marine life churned all the water within view except for that within the abhorrent area. Just how all these creatures were able to sense and fear the danger at such distance was indeed mystifying.

When we approached the center turbulence we saw it was caused by great hungry whirlpools which trapped and swallowed all transient sea life. Hosts of jellyfish and a massive strew of sargassum seaweed circled toward the center and then zipped down the maw and disappeared. According to natives and some early day explorers, the power and size of these whirlpools become sights of horror during storms. They tell of sizable ships being whirled around and sometimes swallowed.

On one of my early exploration expeditions on an Andy Chersin shrimper out of Punta Peñasco I saw two of the immense, whirling funnels sucking slabs and chunks of sargassum seaweed down into the vacuum of their vortexes, and I feel that a sizable skiff would have gone down like a match.

I had a chance to witness the phenomenon again with Eugene Perry in his 18-foot outboard and on several small boat voyages. On another larger shrimper I held the wheel and plowed through a moderately strong whirler and felt the pull. — RAY CANNON

FISH PILEUPS—OUT OF THIS WORLD

[Over the years, the spectacular fish "pileups" of the Midriff islands were described by Ray more often than any other natural phenomenon he observed in the Sea of Cortez. From combined manuscripts:]

The words "schools" or "shoals" fall far short of describing the mass movements of fish populations in and around these islands. They must be visualized as hosts, armies or clouds when seen churning the surface from horizon to horizon in all directions.

Enormous and awesome "fish pileups" occur each spring along the south rim of the Midriff. They are triggered when up-to-ten-mile-long schools of migrating yellowtail first hit the line of cool water, boiling up from the deep channels.

The herring-like fishes, such as sardine and anchovies, preferring the cool temperature and the massive food supply, build up water-saturating populations. The hungry yellowtail, suddenly running into such a flourishing meadow, forget their manners and start grazing like a powered lawn mower. They become so hoggishly competitive they gorge themselves then disgorge and start over again.

Thousands of sea birds that have been following overhead, join the fiesta. Their squawking broadcasts from roost to rookery bring more thousands winging in from near and distant islands. Sea lions get the message and relay it as they come barreling in. All of the fish-eating carnivores of the deep use their own telegraphic methods of inviting all and sundry to get in on the bacchanal binge. They come and run amuck, devouring whatever is smaller than themselves, and disembowel or behead the larger, even their own kind, in their slaughtering frenzy.

Both man and beast become totally oblivious of danger or threat from one another. A bonito in pursuit of a sardine will chase it right through the open jaws of a mammoth shark. I have seen a sea lion surface alongside of our boat and chomp up a big, flailing yellowtail. One time a huge bottlenose dolphin, about to collide with a speeding skiff, vaulted right over the bow, drenching the occupants and causing them to doubt their sanity for ever getting mixed up in such goings-on.

One of the skiff-long mammals chased a skipjack right up into the boat. Next, a 15-foot shark came up to snatch a gaffed yellowtail from the native boy's hand as he lifted it out of the water, leaving the boy the fish head and his hands, by a couple of inches.

But the final nerve-shattering payoff came when a diving pelican got a bead on a maimed sardine and peeled off for a 30-foot dive. A shark spotted the same morsel a split second ahead. The pelican got the sardine, but it was already between the shark's jaws. The shark clamped! I still shudder every time I see a pelican using his head for an upside-down periscope when he shoves it underwater to watch for fish.

I am unable to think of any other kind of adventure that builds a bigger head of suspense steam among anglers. I have seen oldsters champ their store uppers to the point of crushing them, and young'uns squint wild bug-eyes, like a Western gun shooter, as they get ready to plunge into the berserk rumpus. And I have seen newcomers shiver and wish they had stayed in bed—in Denver. — RAY CANNON

"Mama and Papa Díaz," Cruz Rosas Ortiz and Antero Díaz Alvabera, of Bahía de los Angeles. Photo taken in Ensenada, c. 1939. — COURTESY DIAZ FAMILY

Bahía de los Angeles, 1960.

MAMA & PAPA DIAZ

PIONEERS OF BAHIA DE LOS ANGELES

OF THE FIRST four great resorts of the Golden Age—
Las Cruces, Los Arcos, Buena Vista, and Flying
Sportsmen—none was built by a native-born Mexican.

Abelardo L. "Rod" Rodríguez of Rancho Las Cruces
was born in Berkeley, California. Luis Cóppola Bonillas of
the Hotel Los Arcos was born in Tucson, Arizona. Herb
Tansey of Rancho Buena Vista was born in San Diego. And
Ed Tabor of the Flying Sportsmen Lodge was born in Salt
Lake City. The fifth early pioneer-builder of the Golden Age,

Ray with captured sea turtles at Bahía de los Angeles, c. 1960.

Bud Parr, was also an American, born in Roscoe, Texas.

The honor of being the first native Mexicans to build a
fly-in fishing lodge in Baja California belongs to Antero and
Cruz Díaz, who moved from Mexico City to the very remote
mine of Calmallí, in central Baja California, in 1939.

The robustness, courage, and strength of this couple and
the other early residents of Bahía de los Angeles are almost
beyond imagining when one considers the difficult
conditions they must have endured in those early years.

Antero Díaz Alvabera was born in Zaqualpan, Mexico
in 1914, and he worked in the mines near Mexico City,
eventually becoming an assayer.

Cruz Rosas Ortiz—who became universally known by
generations of Baja aficionados as "Mama Díaz"—was born
about the same time in Zimapán Hidalgo, near Mexico City.
She was raised by friends of her birth parents, and became
a stage performer and singer, catching the eye of young
Antero, but refusing to speak to him, and thus earning the
nickname of "La Abajeñita"—the aloof one.

In 1939, Antero was offered a job working at the mine
of Calmallí—located in the center of the peninsula east of
Guererro Negro—by a company headquartered in San
Francisco. Cruz decided to cast her lot with the miner that
she had previously spurned, and they were married and left
together for the remote desert of Baja California, where the
fashionable young woman of Mexico City was shocked by
the isolation and harsh conditions.

Work at the mines of Calmallí, and later, Bahía de los
Angeles, was sporadic, and Antero and Cruz moved back
to Mexico City at least three times between 1939 and 1945,
always returning to Baja California where Antero worked
at mining, pearl diving, shark fishing, turtle fishing, and
finally, sport fishing, as the family settled permanently in
Bahía de los Angeles about 1945, and title to the land was
perfected in Mexico City.

In the early years, the only contact with the outside

Díaz family portrait, c. 1955, in front of the original house, now completely obliterated, which stood near the entrance to the mine just south of the village. Left to right: Cruz; Rosa María "Rosita," born in Calmallí, 1939; Elvira, "Licha," born in Mexico City, 1939; Ana María "Anita" (on shoulders), born Bahía de los Angeles, 1953; Antero; Samuel "Sammy" born in Mexico City, 1942; Aurora, "Bolita," born in Bahía de los Angeles, 1944; Rafaela "Prieta," born in Mexico City, 1945. The other children of Antero and Cruz Díaz were: María del Carmen Díaz, born in Mexico City, 1937; Antero "Chubasco" born, Bahía de los Angeles, 1952.

— COURTESY DIAZ FAMILY

Cruz and Antero Díaz with Paul Jacot, left, the man who brought them to work at the Calmallí mine in 1939. Antero also worked at the mine of Deseñano y Luz, in addition to Bahía de los Angeles. All three mining sites are now abandoned. — COURTESY DIAZ FAMILY

Antero Díaz, right, with his brother, Arturo Díaz, and their mother, Rafaela Alvabera, at Bahía de los Angeles, c. 1953. The two brothers made their first trip to Baja together in 1939, but Arturo later returned to Mexico City. — COURTESY DIAZ FAMILY

The Casa Díaz boat landing, November 1966. — PHOTO BY MARTIN GOLDSMITH

The original buildings of Casa Díaz, c. 1960. The section on the left was incorporated into the present complex. The building on the right was the Díaz home and also served as a "gas station" for aircraft that were refueled from drums. — COURTESY DIAZ FAMILY

The expanded guest facility, dining room, kitchen and chapel of Casa Díaz, substantially completed by 1963. — COURTESY DIAZ FAMILY

Cruz Díaz, right, with niece Alejandra, in the kitchen of Casa Díaz, c. 1980. — COURTESY DIAZ FAMILY

world came when the DC-3 arrived from San Francisco, bringing supplies and taking away the tumbler-sized ingots of gold that had been melted down from nuggets dug out of the earth.

In the tiny village of Bahía de los Angeles, the early population consisted of the Díaz family, Dick Dagget's family with two daughters, Tilongo Smith's with 14 children, Vasilio Navarro's with five children, and Juan "Pincheda" Ostriaco, an Austrian national who lived alone in a shack above the village.

Eight Díaz children survived, from a total of 14, and their birthplaces reflect the itinerant life of the family as it moved from place to place before settling permanently in the village:

María del Carmen, Mexico City, 1937; Rosa María, Calmallí, 1939; Elvira, Mexico City, 1939; Samuel, Mexico City, 1942; Aurora, Bahía de los Angeles, 1944; Rafaela, Mexico City, 1945; Ana María, Bahía de los Angeles, 1953; and Antero Jr., Bahía de los Angeles, 1952.

Even before World War II, fly-in sport fishing anglers had been landing at Bahía de los Angeles; John Steinbeck describes a 1940 encounter with some of them in *Sea Of Cortez: A Leisurely Journal of Travel and Research.*

As the gold, pearls, shark oil market, and turtles gave out, one after another, the family gradually developed a fly-in sport fishing business during the early 1950s, using their profits to build a stone lodge—the legendary Casa Díaz—that was substantially completed by 1963.

In the early days, life was never easy at Bahía de los Angeles. Daughter, Aurora, was born beneath a tree near the site of the old village school. Son, Antero Jr. acquired his nickname, "Chubasco," when, on the night he was born, the roof of the house blew off and landed on nearby Punta Arena. Antero Sr., the village midwife, was very busy that night, trying to deliver his son, while running around the house, tying ropes over it in order to hold it down in a howling "westerly" windstorm.

But the family prevailed, under the harshest of conditions, and they made a profit in all five of the businesses they entered over the decades. In 1989, Antero Sr. died in Escondido, California. Cruz, today, is cared for by family in Ensenada, and Casa Díaz endures in the village, operated by the family much as it was when first completed in the 1960s.

Although the great Midriff fish schools discovered by Ray Cannon are now gone, at Bahía de los Angeles the harsh natural beauty of the ages remains intact. The small, dusty village, caught between desert and sea, seems frozen in time, a living reminder of the old Baja California and of the hardy, resolute people who lived there.

Antero Díaz' 80-foot charter boat, *San Augustín II*, returns to Bahía de los Angeles, c. 1963, fresh from a refurbishing in Kino Bay. Díaz had bought the boat from a Spaniard the previous year and he sold it in 1982, when he figured he had taken enough chances on the sea. — COURTESY DIAZ FAMILY

Rancho Las Cruces as it appears today, little changed from its beginnings in 1950. — PHOTO BY GENE KIRA

An evening with generals and presidents. Former U.S. President Dwight D. Eisenhower, left, and former Mexican President Abelardo L. Rodríguez at Rancho Las Cruces, 1963. Both presidents were also five-star generals in their respective armies. At right is the resort's builder, son of the elder Rodríguez, Abelardo L. "Rod" Rodríguez.

— COURTESY ABELARDO L. "ROD" RODRIGUEZ

RANCHO LAS CRUCES

THE FIRST OF THE FIRST

SEVERAL SINGULAR COINCIDENCES have conspired to make the private resort of Rancho Las Cruces (Ranch Of The Crosses) near La Paz the historical nexus of Baja California's Golden Age. When Hernán Cortés first set foot upon the Baja peninsula in 1535, it may have been at this very spot. Cortés called his landing place "Santa Cruz," supposedly naming it for three crosses placed on a hill in memory of crewmen who were killed by hostile Indians.

Whether or not Cortés landed at the exact location of today's resort of Rancho Las Cruces, the ranch's cattle brand, three crosses, is said to be the oldest in either North or South America, and there is reason to believe that this may actually have been the place.

Although Rancho Las Cruces lacks protection from rough seas, in 1535 it reportedly made a favorable landing place because it did have plenty of water, a running stream of it that came down an arroyo and flowed out to sea.

By 1889, this water was the basis of a substantial fruit orchard planted by Juan and Gaston J. Vives, who also owned the pearl diving concession for nearby Isla Cerralvo and launched sailing canoes across the channel for the harvest that sent pearls to stiffen the robes and vestments of European royalty and clergy.

But by about 1912, the flowing stream that once may have attracted Cortés had gone underground. Then, in the 1930s, the pearl oysters were wiped out by disease.

By 1948, Rancho Las Cruces was virtually abandoned, with only a few trees and small buildings remaining on the

The ranch's three crosses commemorate the first Baja landing of Hernán Cortés in 1535.

— PHOTO BY GENE KIRA

Former Royal Air Force pilot and North American Aviation test pilot Abelardo L. "Rod" Rodríguez in a P-51D Mustang. It was this model plane that he used to set the speed record from Los Angeles to Mexico City in 1948, and it was there that he met General Agustín Olachea, Governor of the Territory of Baja California Sur, who invited him to visit La Paz on his way home. Rodríguez landed on a dirt airstrip outside the city, later joined Olachea in developing some farm land at San Juan de los Planes, and soon thereafter bought the abandoned fruit orchard that would open as Baja California's first luxury fishing resort.

— COURTESY ABELARDO L. "ROD" RODRIGUEZ

Abelardo L. "Rod" Rodríguez, builder of Rancho Las Cruces, with his son, Abelardo Nicolas "Niki" Rodríguez, who operates the private resort today. Photo taken in Todos Santos, c. 1960.

— COURTESY ABELARDO L. "ROD" RODRIGUEZ

Rodríguez' wife in 1948 was Hollywood celebrity Lucille Bremer, with whom he developed the Rancho Las Cruces property. — COURTESY ABELARDO L. "ROD" RODRIGUEZ

Baja's first fishing resort, Rancho Las Cruces, c. 1952. Rodríguez and his family lived in the building on the right.

— COURTESY ABELARDO L. "ROD" RODRIGUEZ

Ramona "Mocha" Miranda Amador has cooked for princes and presidents at Rancho Las Cruces since 1948. — PHOTO BY GENE KIRA

Bing Crosby aboard his boat *Dorado*, with guide Antonio Virgen at Rancho Las Cruces.

property. In that year it was purchased by Abelardo L. "Rod" Rodríguez, a former World War II fighter test pilot who had been developing the farms of nearby San Juan de los Planes in partnership with the Territorial Governor, General Agustín Olachea.

Rodríguez' wife at that time, and the mother of his four children, was Lucille Bremer, a Hollywood actress and dancer. Bremer rejected a lucrative contract with MGM in order to join her husband at Las Cruces, and they worked together to develop the old world charm and ambience of the property.

On that abandoned fruit orchard, the Rodríguezes built something that had never existed before in Baja California— a luxury fishing resort.

The construction and opening of Rancho Las Cruces in 1950 as a fly-in private club catering to such personalities as Desi Arnaz and Bing Crosby was the first such event of the Golden Age, and it was the beginning of Baja California's modern tourist industry. In 1951, the resort was opened to the public as the Hotel Rancho Las Cruces, but later it reverted to a private club. (In 1952, fellow Baja pioneer, William Matt "Bud" Parr, would briefly become a partner in Rancho Las Cruces; Parr would later go on to develop the Hotel Cabo San Lucas in 1961, as well as other important properties.)

Sport anglers had been flying to Baja California in private planes well before 1950, but Rancho Las Cruces was the first resort built specifically for them.

About the time when "Rod" Rodríguez was buying Rancho Las Cruces, his father, former Baja California Territorial Governor Abelardo L. Rodríguez, was engaged seven-hundred miles north in another defining event of the Golden Age. The elder Rodríguez—who had also been President of Mexico from 1932 to 1934—had hired a former Hollywood director named Ray Cannon to test fish the waters around San Felipe with the idea of developing a considerable amount of real estate that he owned in the area.

As the resort buildings of Rancho Las Cruces were being constructed near La Paz, Ray was making his first camping trips to the beaches just north of San Felipe, and he was making the sport fishing discoveries that would lead to a bestselling book, 24 years of weekly columns in *Western Outdoor News*, and his remarkable career as the pied piper of Baja California.

Within a few months after the opening of Rancho Las Cruces and Ray's first trips to San Felipe, Baja California's Golden Age would be launched in earnest by Ed Tabor of the Flying Sportsmen Lodge in Loreto, Luis Cóppola Bonillas of the Hotel Los Arcos in La Paz, and Herb Tansey of Rancho Buena Vista to the south.

That was just the beginning of a multitude of resorts that would soon follow all up and down the Sea of Cortez, but Rancho Las Cruces was the first of them all, and it would be fitting and somehow very satisfying if the legends were true and the first resort of the Golden Age really is located on the spot where Hernán Cortés landed in 1535.

Mulegé, 1961, looking east over the Sea of Cortez. Note prison to left of river and mission on the near side of the dam. The presently-existing highway and bridge across the river would not be built until 1973. — PHOTO BY AL HRDLICKA

Setting a small mesh net for mullet in the river at Mulegé, c. 1957. On right, is guide Juan Bautista "Chi Chi" Meza. Small mixed species of other fish, including young snook, were also caught by this method. Large snook were harpooned in the river at night using very quietly paddled boats and carbide lamps.

GIANT SNOOK OF MULEGE

RAY'S QUEST FOR A WORLD RECORD

CENTROPOMUS NIGRESCENS—THE legendary giant black snook that once inhabited the Santa Rosalía River of Mulegé—was the most elusive and frustrating quarry of Ray's fishing career. From 1956 to about 1962 Ray made perhaps a dozen trips to Mulegé for the specific purpose of landing a record-sized giant snook. But the available records seem to indicate that he never caught a *Centropomus nigrescens* that could have qualified legally for a record.

He did report catching several of a smaller species, *Centropomus pactinatus*, around the mouth of the river, and his field notes include those fish. But the only available record of Ray's catching a record-sized snook is of an incident that ended in disaster when a mix-up in his Spanish caused his guide to harpoon the fish rather than gaff it, thus disqualifying it as a sport-caught fish and a world record.

That guide, Juan Bautista "Chi Chi" Meza, born in 1935, still lives in Mulegé and he vividly remembers Ray's determined efforts to catch a record snook. "He hooked some big fish on live bait," Meza recalls, "but he always lost them when they got tangled up in the mangrove roots."

Meza, his brother Quirino, and his sister Rosario "Chayo" Meza Evans, often took their boat, *Rafael*, on the river on winter nights to harpoon snook, using carbide lamps to spot the large fish in the darkness. Chi Chi recalls catching one about 1946 using live mullet as bait, but harpooning was the preferred method since it could result in a harvest of perhaps ten or twelve fish in a night. The darkest nights of the deep winter months were the best times, especially if storms were blowing outside the river mouth, and it was very important to be completely silent, never even letting the paddle rub against the side of the boat.

It is Chi Chi Meza who is pictured with Ray and two large snook on page 119 of *The Sea Of Cortez*. (He is also shown with a lobster on page 128.) Those two large fish,

Rosario "Chayo" Meza Evans and her brother, Juan Bautista "Chi Chi" Meza, at the river in Mulegé, with a copy of *The Sea Of Cortez* opened to the photograph on page 119 of Ray and Chi Chi dragging two large snook into a boat. Chayo, Chi Chi, and their brother Quirino, had harpooned the fish the preceding night.

— PHOTO BY GENE KIRA

Setting up a posed shot. Ray and Mulegé panguero, Quirino Meza, with a large harpooned snook in the river at Mulegé.

Possibly in an actual action sequence, Meza aims his harpoon at a fish in the river, surprisingly close to the boat.

The "harpooned fish" thrashes immediately…

…and is pulled into the boat.

which appear stiff and dead in the photo, were harpooned in the river the night before by Chi Chi and Chayo from their paddled boat. The famous photo was taken against the south side of the river, directly across from the Huerta La Fortuna RV Park.

According to Meza, there are still a few small snook in the river, but they were pretty much gone by about 1975. The sensitive fish were driven away by boat noise, pollution and spraying for mosquitoes, and the dredging of the river bottom which altered their habitat.

Ray's experience with Mulegé's giant snook began on February 6, 1956 after he had been contacted by Sal Salazar, operator of the Club Mulegé, who said there were large "tarpon" in the river. Ray arrived at Santa Rosalía on a Trans Mar de Cortés DC-3, was driven to Mulegé, and witnessed the seining of enormous fish from the river. He reports seining five locations on this trip and seeing hundreds of fingerlings and "a ton or more of snook above record size" in each hole. On this trip he also saw snook that had been harpooned in the river, and he wrote the hilarious story of the "Snook That Shook Mulegé," reprinted later in this chapter, about his own nighttime harpooning experience. But the fish steadfastly refused to be caught with hook and line.

After several unsuccessful trips, Ray convinced writer Frank Dufresne of *Field & Stream* to give it a try, but Dufresne's trip also ended without catching a snook. On Dufresne's recommendation, Ray wrote letters to Sal Salazar urging him to develop a method of catching and holding mullet for live bait.

Salazar did eventually develop a method of providing live "lisa" baits, and finally, in January 1959, Ray hooked a large snook in the river, only to yell "harpoon" instead of "gaff" in his fractured Spanish, and then watch as his guide Chi Chi Meza drilled the fish with an iron shaft, thus disqualifying it as a legal catch.

That, apparently, was Ray's last opportunity to land a giant snook at Mulegé. By then, the fish had already begun to thin out, and although he probably hooked several large fish, there is no available record of him landing one legally. The technique Ray developed of baiting snook with very long lines undoubtedly resulted in more hookups, but with the high probability of losing fish in the mangrove roots. Chi Chi Meza confirms this hypothesis with his stories of being with Ray when large snook were lost.

Following are three of Ray's best articles about his quest for Mulegé's giant snook. In the first, he writes of discovering the fish in 1956. The second story is about the hilarious "Snook That Shook Mulegé" by waking up the entire town in the middle of the night. And last is Ray's story of the world record snook that he "ordered" harpooned by mistake.

RECORD SNOOK DISCOVERED AT MULEGE

[In this story, assembled from various fragments written in February 1956, Ray tells of how he was first called to Mulegé by Octavio "Sal" Salazar and how large fish were netted in the river. This was also the trip of the harpooned "Snook That Shook Mulegé," the story of which follows. There is little fishing information in this story, but it describes the beginning of Ray's quest to catch a giant snook, and it gives an excellent portrait of the large village of Mulegé during the early part of the Golden Age.]

FEBRUARY 1956—The big news story from the Gulf of California is snook which run well above world record sizes, at Mulegé (pronounced Mool-a-hay).

If you are at all interested in becoming immortalized by establishing a new world's record, your chances were never better. For here at Mulegé a small river runs right through the town and it is loaded from one end to the other with snook (called *robalos* in Mexico) much larger than any yet recorded. One 60-pounder we speared night fishing was considered small by natives.

Dr. Earl Hershman and counselor Harry Goza, of the Long Beach Spinning Club, who accompanied me on the trip, landed snook and ate them without knowing they were feasting on world spinning records.

We didn't learn of the enormous population and giant-sized snooks in the river until our last day. Since our trip was one of survey we were compelled to spend the last day seining in an effort to estimate the number of different species in the stream. Among the 15 landed, were snappers, groupers, grunts, two-foot-long pompano, and the largest giant snook I've ever seen.

The drama got going in January when Sal Salazar, owner of Club Mulegé Lodge, quoting natives, insisted that the tropical, mangrove-fringed river down there was loaded with tarpon. His story was baffling to me, since there was no scientific record of tarpon being in the Pacific except near the mouth of the Panama Canal.

Choking with curiosity, I stopped in at Mulegé on my way to La Paz. We drove to Tijuana, flew Trans Mar de Cortés Airline to Santa Rosalía on the east side of the Baja Peninsula, where we were met by Club Mulegé's station wagon and driven the 42 miles to Mulegé.

This is an ancient pueblo situated in the middle of a small, tropical valley. A perfect picture-town for poets, painters and photographers, with ruins, adobe and stone houses and a hundred extraordinary character types. Palm and mangrove-bordered lagoons and streams, flowering

Frank Dufresne of *Field & Stream*, looking a bit chagrined on the Mulegé river, 1956. He had made the trip especially to catch giant snook, but didn't connect by using the artificial lures and dead baits available at the time. Later, his recommendation of live mullet baits would prove to be correct.

jungle-like thickets and overgrown tropical fruit trees. Mulegé is a place where you don't require a sunset to give color.

Standard price for workers (such as helped with our operation) from the federal "pen" located on a hill nearby, is 90 cents per day. The gates are opened at 7 a.m. and prisoners go fishing or whatever until 4:30 p.m. lock up time. When asked why none escaped, one prisoner said, "We never before had it so good—the only people who ever leave Mulegé go by way of the other hill." (The cemetery.)

Señor Francisco Gutierres is a shortcut for information on these and on all the expressions of nature, found in great abundance, in this singular area. No matter what your pursuit, the native wisdom of this old self-taught naturalist will astonish you. To me, he is the most important man in all Mulegé and is recorded in my log as the top unforgettable character of these parts. For a living, Francisco fixes anything from watches to trucks, and builds native-type skiffs as a sideline.

Mulegé Lodge is not a plush deal at present; it's more like a U.S. hunting lodge. Our host, Octavio "Sal" Salazar, was the most hospitable and thoughtful I have encountered in Baja. The food (especially the game) was splendid. The late evening clambakes made a hit with everyone. Good spring water, U.S. coffee and ample soft drinks and other beverages kept healthy thirsts satisfied.

One of the owners, Jack Sartor, El Monte, California, showed me blueprints for a new modern motel-type lodge to be constructed within the next few months. I saw their 23-acre tropical garden spot situated about a city block from their boat docks at the mouth of the river. Jack has just bought a 104-foot army hospital boat and is now converting it into a luxury cabin liner. It will make weekly runs from San Felipe to Mulegé.

This combination of boat and hotel service should provide the most ideal family fishing trip in the Gulf. Al Zapanta of Mexican Big Game Fishing Service will handle the reservations.

We spent considerable time fishing around the "Sombrero," the hat-shaped rock that guards the little bay and river mouth. Most of the fish common to the shore waters of the Gulf are abundant here. A boat ride into the

Sal Salazar's Club Mulegé, c. 1959.

Rosario "Chayo" Meza Evans at the Club Mulegé, c. 1960. She and her brothers Juan "Chi Chi" Meza and Quirino Meza were three of Ray's main snook fishing guides. They harpooned the two big snook shown on page 119 of *The Sea Of Cortez*.

great bay of Concepción, three miles to the south, will produce giant grouper, roosterfish, dolphinfish and yellowtail, with marlin and sailfish showing up in summer and fall. A checklist of all the different species would fill a book.

Three well-qualified adventurers popped in out of nowhere in a jeep—and I mean NOWHERE. They had driven down past San Quintín Bay over the mountains to Santa Rosalía and on to Mulegé, a region as rough, rugged and arid as can be found. The party included Burr and Howard Pentoney of San Diego and Ham Skelly, Riverside.

A special bid is being made to owners of private planes to land at the Mulegé air strip and spend the weekend at the Club. The distance is 650 air miles from L.A. In addition to the fame to be gained catching a world record snook, the owners are discussing adding a valuable prize such as a fabulous trip on their boat. As soon as they decide I'll let you know. — RAY CANNON

THE SNOOK THAT SHOOK MULEGE

[The events of this wild story actually took place during Ray's first trip to Mulegé in 1956, although he didn't write about it until later. The following version is assembled from early fragments and from the tale as told in *The Sea Of Cortez*. It was this chapter on snook that convinced Sunset to publish the book.]

To appreciate the fantastic developments of the episode which is about to unfold, it is necessary to first get a mental picture of the scene of action.

You must understand that Mulegé has an enormous population, but only 800 are people. There are an equal number of burros and about 400 dogs. Also, quantities of turkeys and chickens, some cattle, pigs, and mules. Wild creatures, such as coyotes, bobcats and the like have also crowded in on a co-existence plan.

An old mission crowns one hill, and the Territorial Penitentiary occupies the top of another which projects up 100 feet overlooking the burg.

Being a frugal people by necessity and not wanting to waste kerosene, comes nightfall, the town, like a big turtle, pulls everything in and goes into a complete hush.

The dead silence and eerie blackness had me in a weird state of mind.

I sat in the middle of the dugout between my crew of two. The oarsman paddled quietly in the stern, without a ripple of water to break the silence. Only the far off chirps of a katydid could be heard. It was like moving in a vacuum as we slowly glided past overhanging palms and mangrove branches. The spearman stood on a small board across the bow with a lightweight, iron harpoon in one hand and a miner's carbide lamp in the other. We had reached a stretch in front of the sleeping fishing camp when the spearman's scanning light beam came to rest on what first appeared to be a submerged log. As it shifted forward, a great forked tail fin disclosed it to be an enormous fish.

Cautiously and quietly, in rapid, whispered commands to the paddler, the spearman got the boat into flanking position. He took careful aim, drew the harpoon back the full reach of his arm, and with a mighty heave drilled the denizen just under the dorsal fin without hitting any vital organ.

In a split second the little river was ripped asunder. Mangrove bushes thrashed as violently as in a chubasco. A sheet of water geysered over the dugout as the fish exploded up and just past the spearman's head, the impaled harpoon whipping past within inches. The man emitted a screaming stream of Mexican profanity.

The oarsman on the stern began bellowing commands to the spearman, who had all he could do to keep vertical while holding the straining harpoon line. The line suddenly zipped under the boat and nearly tipped us all into the river, and I found myself yelling louder than either of them.

The still night was shattered by the splashing, our yelling, and the echoes bounding from hill to hill. Fishermen and their families came pouring out of the nearby camp to the river bank to join in the uproar. They boomed their advice, out-cussing the spearman in razzing, hog-calling tones. This hullabaloo in the middle of the night triggered a chain reaction among the town's dogs, which were quick to join in. Their yelps and howls caused other creatures to sound off. Pigs squealed, turkeys gobbled, chickens cackled, all in frantic alarm. Jackasses and burros brayed, horses whinnied, and a multitude of coyotes and wild birds added their bit.

An army soldier at Mulegé's hilltop penitentiary, c. 1959.

Dufresne with a nice snapper on the south side of the river mouth.

On penitentiary hill, the single night guard was awakened by the terrifying clamor. He switched on all the prison floodlights and grabbed his conch horn to bugle out the full guard.

That did it! The citizenry panicked! Not since the revolution had such a night disturbance occurred. Having no phones to call the police, and no police to call—there was only one thing to do—head for the hills! And that's exactly what they did. If the hard-of-hearing padre had awakened and started pealing the bells, I might have high-tailed it for high ground myself.

Throughout the fracas I had seen no more than flashes of the huge, jumping fish and could think of no aquatic creature except a tarpon that would trigger such a ruckus. After considerably more thrashing and churning the waters of the river in a desperate effort to free itself of the spear, the great fish was finally subdued and dragged to shore. The native kibitzers crowded around.

By the light of the carbide lamp I could now see a turned-up snout and black stripe along the body. No tarpon this, but the largest black snook I had ever laid eyes on! It measured 5 feet 7 inches from snout to tail fork, a whole foot longer than the world record snook.

It couldn't be considered, of course, because of the way it was caught. I was still looking the black monster over when the spearman and his helper took off in the darkness again. They shouted something back to me, and the village mayor interpreted. "They are unhappy," he said, "they promised you a six-footer and this one is five inches short. They're going out to keep their promise by catching a bigger one." It took me an hour to convince them that I was satisfied with the snook in hand.

I asked the boys to keep the fish wrapped in damp

gunnysacks so we could weigh it on the storekeeper's scales in the morning. Either they misunderstood me or wanted to throw in some extra service, for when they did bring it in they had done a par excellent job of cleaning, beheading, and gutting it. We could only guess that the whole, uneviscerated fish must have weighed above 65 pounds.

The important thing was that this little river had in it one of the most extraordinary of all game fishes. And it was no ordinary snook. This was the giant black snook (*Centropomus nigrescens*), called robalo prieto in Spanish, largest of all the snooks inhabiting the tropical waters of America, attaining a length of six feet and a weight of at least 80 pounds! — RAY CANNON

A "GIANT" MISTAKE IN SPANISH!

[Ray hooks a giant snook, but it is harpooned by mistake and disqualified as a world record. The main events of the story occurred in January 1959.]

The world record for snook on spin tackle would be mine today if I hadn't made a mistake in Spanish grammar. At the crucial moment of truth when the scoop-faced monster was stretched alongside the dugout ready for landing, I yelled *"arpon"* instead of *"gancho."* Instantly, my Mexican guide picked up his long iron harpoon and let fly with deadly aim. He killed the fish, all right, but he also disqualified it for entry in the record books. If I'd called out "gancho," Juan would have wielded the gaff-hook and I would be the new spin snook champ.

But maybe I wasn't really entitled to that big snook, because it was through no skill of mine that it struck in the first place. It was pure accident. I was surrounded by these giant black robalos in a jungle stream in Baja California. I'd seen their great swirls at the mangrove edges all day, and knew they were in there by the hundreds. But

Bill Lloyd's Mulegé Beach Lodge at Playa Equipalito just south of the river mouth, c. 1961.

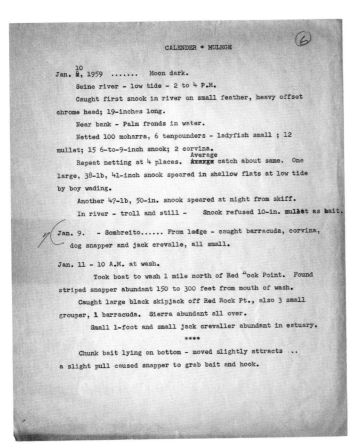

```
                    CALENDER * MULEGE                    ⑥

         10
Jan.  9, 1959 ......   Moon dark.

      Seine river - low tide - 2 to 4 P.M.

      Caught first snook in river on small feather, heavy offset
chrome head; 19-inches long.

      Near bank - Palm fronds in water.

      Netted 100 moharra, 6 tenpounders - ladyfish small ; 12
mullet; 15 6-to-9-inch snook; 2 corvina.
                              Average
      Repeat netting at 4 places.  Average catch about same.  One
large, 38-lb, 41-inch snook speared in shallow flats at low tide
by boy wading.

      Another 47-lb, 50-in. snook speared at night from skiff.

      In river - troll and still -   Snook refused 10-in. mullet as bait.

  Jan. 9.  - Sombrerito...... From ledge - caught barracuda, corvina,
      dog snapper and jack crevalle, all small.

  Jan. 11 - 10 A.M. at wash.

      Took boat to wash 1 mile north of Red Rock Point.  Found
striped snapper abundant 150 to 300 feet from mouth of wash.

      Caught large black skipjack off Red Rock Pt., also 3 small
grouper, 1 barracuda.  Sierra abundant all over.

      Small 1-foot and small jack crevaller abundant in estuary.

                         ****

      Chunk bait lying on bottom - moved slightly attracts ...
a slight pull caused snapper to grab bait and hook.
```

Ray's personal trip log from his January 1959 trip to Mulegé documents the seining, harpooning, and catching of snook in the river. Ray indicates he caught a 19-inch fish and witnessed the netting or harpooning of a few dozen others, mostly small, but two weighing 38 and 47 pounds.

Jan. 10, 1959... moon dark.

Seine river—low tide—2 to 4 p.m.

Caught first snook in river on small feather, heavy offset chrome head; 19-inches long.

Near bank—palm fronds in water.

Netted 100 moharra, six tenpounders—ladyfish small; 12 mullet; 15 6-to-9-inch snook; two corvina.

Repeat netting at four places. Average catch about the same. One large, 38-lb, 41-inch snook speared in shallow flats at low tide by boy wading.

Another 47-lb, 50-in. snook speared at night from skiff.

In river—troll and still—Snook refused 10-in. mullet as bait.

Jan. 9—Sombrerito... From ledge—caught barracuda, corvina, dog snapper and jack crevalle, all small.

Jan. 11—10 a.m. at wash.

Took boat to wash one mile north of Red Rock Point. Found striped snapper abundant 150 to 300 feet from mouth of wash.

Caught large black skipjack off Red Rock Point, also three small grouper, one barracuda. Sierra abundant all over.

Small 1-foot and small jack crevalle abundant in estuary.

* * *

Chunk bait lying on bottom—moved slightly attracts... a slight pull caused snapper to grab bait and hook.

Shore casting south of El Sombrerito at the mouth of the river at Mulegé, c. 1959. Ray's handwritten note on the back of this photo says the fish is a snook. Ray caught several small ones at this spot.

On the north side of the river, c. 1960.

I hadn't been smart enough to coax a rise. It took a lousy cast and a monofilament bird's nest to turn the trick. As I picked and loosened one strand after another, the live mullet bait drifted far downstream. It was almost around a bend when something that looked as big as a hippopotamus started doing push-ups under it. Suddenly, there was a boiling belch. The mullet vanished in a great flurry of water, turned right angles to the slow current and headed steadily for the overhanging mangroves. Hastily, I untangled the last snarl and struck back hard against something that seemed to be as solid as a sunken palm-log. Juan ripped off a stream of Mexican talk. "Robalo prieto! Robalo prieto!"

He didn't have to tell me what it was. I already knew. It couldn't be anything but one of the fabulous black snook giants of the Cortez Sea. And it was about time I connected, I thought. Behind this strike lay three years of trying, wild experimenting, errors and hard luck.

It had all started when Sal Salazar who runs a lodging house in the dreamy little village of Mulegé (Mool-a-hay) told me about a mysterious, huge fish that lurked in the dark river which runs through the center of town.

In the four-mile river and tidal estuary which ran alongside his angler headquarters he had, in truth, one of the most extraordinary game fishes of the continent.

All I had to do was catch one on tackle and I'd be the world champion snook-catcher. So I hired two Mexican lads to paddle me up and down the Mulegé River while I cast and trolled every kind of plug, feathered lure and spoon-hook in my tackle box. I didn't get a strike. I switched to cut baits. Nothing happened, and that's when I called on my good friend Frank Dufresne, *Field & Stream's* pacific coast editor. Frank had fished snook in Florida waters. He'd write me how to do it.

Frank didn't bother to write. He landed in a Trans Mar de Cortés airplane with an assortment of plugs and streamer flies which had done the trick for him in the Florida Everglades. We fished morning, noon, sundown and midnight and we didn't catch anything except boat loads of mangrove snapper, corvinas, crevalles, triggerfishes and groupers. All we got from the snook was a royal snooking.

In desperation, Frank begged the Mexicans, "Get us some live mullets. Big snook go for them like bears to honey."

But there wasn't a mullet seine in the village, and even a reward of 25 pesos for a single, live mullet went unclaimed. We hook-and-lined other small fish and strung them on our snook rigs, but they wouldn't work. When Frank headed back to Olympia, Washington the mystery was still unsolved. It remained so during two more years of experimenting. I was about to give the whole project up as hopeless when Sal Salazar called on me again. The Mulegé Mexicans had found a way to impound some live mullet. On the next dark of the moon on January 9, when signs in the sky pointed to favorable conditions for snook to be in the river, I was there with my heaviest spin-reel loaded with 200 yards of 15-pound test monofilament. This time we'd do it.

That morning I caught my first snook, though one look at it told me it was the wrong kind. It was a *Centropomus pactinatus* which is a smaller species with larger eyes, smaller anal fin and shorter spines. My boatman, Juan, shook his head as he tossed the fish back into the river, then reached into the live-box we were towing astern to hand me an outside mullet at least 18 inches in length. It was big enough for a shark-bait but I ran a short-shanked hook through its back and turned it loose to go find a giant snook. It scuttled under the dugout to hide, and when I lifted it clear and tried to make a cast it sailed off the hook and into the mangroves. I tried another, and let it wiggle around the edge of the bushes. Nothing happened, so I put on a weight and sunk the struggling mullet down into a deep hole or two. Then I trolled it awhile with no results. In late afternoon and into the dark hours, I cast my mullet baits into the mangrove pockets. I fished the rapids and shallows. I spit on my bait. I tried hooking it by the tail. When Sal Salazar led me back to the Mulegé Club that night, I was about ready to give up on snook and send Frank Dufresne a nasty letter about his mullet baits. Sal made it even worse. He had his cook serve me fried mullet for dinner.

Sal Salazar, whose Club Mulegé is right among the greatest concentrations of black snook along the Sea of Cortez, came in to hand me a belt of tequila liquid-lightning for a nightcap. He felt sorry for me, and tried to coax me into going out after something he could guarantee: sailfish, striped marlin, roosterfish and giant sea bass up to 700 pounds. I shook my head, and then Sal laid a sympathetic hand on my shoulder.

"Mañana, amigo," he consoled, "mañana, maybe you will do it."

And then, quite casually, he dropped a morsel of information which was hotter stuff than even the tequila. In the stomachs of all the great black snook brought into the village by harpoon fishermen they had never found a mullet more than seven inches long!

Neither Juan nor Rodríguez, my Mexican guides, approved the small mullet I baited the next morning. "Little bait, little fish," they told me. After a half-day of dunking,

casting and trolling, they changed it to "little bait, no fish." Time after time we saw the huge swirls in the mangrove shadows, and once our canoe floated over what I believe to be one of the largest snook ever seen by an American. But it wouldn't bite and neither would the dozens of other robalo prietos as I changed to an assortment of artificial lures from almost every manufacturer between Tampa and Tokyo. If it hadn't been for that careless cast and that bucket-sized bird's nest of monofilament which permitted my live mullet bait to drift almost a hundred yards away from the boat, I don't think I'd have caught a single snook.

After that, it was much easier. Once I'd gotten onto the hang of letting the bait trail a long distance away, I began picking up snook. They weren't all big ones, and they weren't all of the black giant species, and in the extremely large sizes the snook proved to be both wary and slow to strike. But I do think I made some real progress in tapping this new kind of Baja California fishing, and I am positive that better snook fishermen than I am can go down there and upset all existing records for this slashing game fish.

When bigger snook are caught, I'm betting it will be done at Mulegé. And when the black giant has been brought alongside your boat ready for landing, I hope you won't yell "arpon!" and see your prize-winner clobbered with a spear like mine was. Point to the gaff-hook and say "gancho!" — RAY CANNON

Mulegé's Saul Davis at his downtown market. — PHOTO BY GENE KIRA

WESTERN OUTDOOR NEWS TRIP OF THE WEEK

EXCLUSIVE!
To Western Outdoor News

Four Hardy Small Boat Devotees In Historic 'Felipe-La Paz Trip

In a recent issue of Western Outdoor News, columnist Joe Mears revealed that a quartet of Southland small boat enthusiasts were to make an unprecedented 1,400 mile trip from San Felipe to La Paz in the Gulf of California. The story aroused a great deal of interest among our readers. The story, we're happy to say, had a — *happy ending. In the interim, we've received a great many inquiries as to the outcome.*

In response to these inquiries, we present herewith an exclusive account of the trip as told by Bob Francis to Joe Mears. We feel that it's one of the most unusual "Trips" we've ever published.

By BOB FRANCIS
(As told to Joe Mears)

Fourteen hundred miles in two 16-foot outboard motor boats from San Felipe to La Paz and back in less than three weeks, fighting rough water, winds of near-gale velocity which several times forced us to seek safety on shore or in protected coves. The first time boats of that size ever had attempted—and completed—this hazardous, exciting voyage in the fabulous Gulf of California.

"Putt-putt trail blazers," an American called me and my three companions. "Loco gringos," muttered an unbelieving Mexican who helped re-fuel us at Loreto, far down the peninsula and the first capital of the Californias.

San Felipe—Ready to Go

This thrilling adventure for me and my friends, Martin Rothschild of Pasadena; Roy Francis, my uncle, and Kenneth Anderson, the latter two from Pomona, began at San Felipe Nov. 4, 1956. We'd trailered our two Crown Craft open utility boats from Pasadena. Each boat was powered by two new Johnson 35 horsepower motors, which we'd broken in on test runs at Salton Sea and in the ocean. Martin and I were to use his boat, Bloody Mary II; Roy and Ken in the San Francisco Babe.

Each boat was equipped with special parts, safety equipment including rollers which could be blown up if we had to beach the boats; our boat carried 88 gallons of fuel; the other 92 gallons. Each had fire extinguishers, emergency food and five gallons of drinking water. We'd made prior arrangements to refuel at overnight stops at the Bay of Los Angeles, Santa Rosalia, and Loreto.

We'd expected good weather. It didn't take us long to find that you can't sign up Mother Nature. We spent the night at Augie's Riveria Hotel. Raymond Vasquez, manager, had read all about our projected and was a fine host.

Next morning at 5:26 o'clock the wind was blowing about 25 miles an hour but we figured it would be o.k. to take off with the sea on our stern. We hadn't cleared the Sandy Point below San Felipe when the sea began to break over the bow and over our convertible top. We decided it was too rough to try to make the Bay of Los Angeles so we put in at San Luis Gonzales Bay, 104 miles south of San Felipe. It took us six hours.

Nov. 5 at 5 a.m. the wind was blowing 37 miles an hour. Sea still rough. Weather clear. Sure hated to start. But we shoved off with the turn of the tide—it was running about 25 feet—and made it safely through treacherous Ballenas channel. Arrived without too much trouble at the Bay of Los Angeles. Time, 11:30 a.m. Our good friend Antero Diaz met us. Too rough to refuel so we spent the night. Antero told us the fishing was good; he runs a camp there catering to airborne anglers. Has a good landing strip. About 100 people there; 37 children and they have a school.

We stayed over an extra day on account of the wind and left

Nov. 7 in clear weather and calm seas for Santa Rosalia. All went well until we got to Cape Virgenes about 15 miles from Santa Rosalia where the swells were 20 feet high topped by whitecaps. Our motors were still running o.k. on the Mexican fuel. By 2 p.m. we sighted the tall smokestack of the copper smelter, started more than 50 years ago by a French company, but now run by Mexicans.

We beached our boats, walked toward the town. There we were met by a taxi driver, Arturo Pearce, who told us our friends, Allan McAlister and Chris Peterson of Pasadena, had flown into town the weekend before but couldn't stay to meet us on account of our delayed schedule.

Nov. 8 at 7 a.m. we started for Mulege. No wind. Cloudy weather. Made it to Mulege without incident and docked at a landing on the Rosalia River. It cost us two props but we made it up the river, in a beautiful tropical setting of coconut palms, dates, grapefruit and other fruits. At Club Mulege we were entertained royally by Gregory Hirales. And we had a duck dinner. Fishing was excellent but we were behind schedule.

From Mulege to Loreto we hit rough seas and had a few anxious minutes trying to avoid the reefs but we made it by 12:10. That night we spent at the Flying Sportsman's Lodge run by Mr. and Mrs. Ed Tabor. Best of all was a swim in the pool. Again our coming had been anticipated by Mrs. Tabor and guests who'd read WON.

Nov. 10 at 9 a.m. we left for La Paz. No wind and cloudy skies. Found a nasty reef at San Marcio point but we arrived at 5 p.m. in front of the Los Arcos Hotel. As the next day was Sunday we made arrangements to refuel. We were quite a curiosity at the hotel. No one dreamed we could make it that far in small boats. We stayed a couple of days in the dreamy, pleasant resort to rest up and check our motors which had put on 600 miles of hard going.

Nov. 12 we left La Paz at 6 a.m. The wind was about 25 miles an hour and the sea was rough. It took us an hour to get out of La Paz harbor. For the first time we had the seas in front of us. The swells were
(Continued on Page 9)

Lashed by Heavy Seas at Los Angeles Bay

Adventurers Rest at Mulege Harbor

No Place to Land for Three Days

La Paz—the Destination

The story of the "Bob Francis Cruise"—*Western Outdoor News*, January 11, 1957.

DARING 16-FOOT OUTBOARDS

BIRTH OF CORTEZ SMALL BOAT CRUISING

THE HISTORIC 1956 "Bob Francis" full-length cruise of the Cortez by two 16-foot outboard boats may have been the first trip of its kind made by tourists. Notable in this story is the month of the year chosen—November—which reflects the lack of seasonal weather information available at the time.

OTHER EARLY CORTEZ CRUISES OF NOTE

—Five months after the "Bob Francis Cruise," Ray took his first long trailer boat trip down the Cortez, reaching Isla San Lorenzo with Gene Perry in April 1957.

—Mike Farrior, historian of the Tuna Club of Avalon, reports that in 1958, Tuna Club member Philip Clock and two companions cruised in a 15-foot outboard from San Felipe to Cabo San Lucas. This is the earliest documented Baja trip of that distance in a small outboard.

—In the following year, on April 28, 1959, Ray departed San Felipe with "Shipwreck Charlie" Cohen in a 24-foot outboard boat and reached La Paz, his first full-length cruise of the Cortez.

—Their trip was mirrored by another outboard boat sponsored by Glasspar, the 17-foot *Searcher*, of Milt Farney and Larry Foglino, which came down the Pacific side and met Ray at Rancho Buena Vista. The Farney/Foglino trip was the earliest documented cruise down the Pacific Coast of Baja in a small open outboard.

—In late 1960, Spencer Murray and Ralph Poole cruised from San Felipe to Cabo San Lucas in the 22-foot cabin cruiser, the *Peggy Sue*, resulting in Murray's 1963 book, *Cruising The Sea Of Cortez*. Ray also happened to meet that boat, at the still under construction Hotel Cabo San Lucas.

The following account of the "Bob Francis Cruise"—as told by Francis to *Western Outdoor News* columnist Joe Mears—appeared on January 11, 1957.

Notable in this story is the early description of Antero Díaz of Bahía de los Angeles, who had been catering to fly-in anglers, off and on, since about 1940.

THE BOB FRANCIS CRUISE

Fourteen-hundred miles in two 16-foot outboard motor boats from San Felipe to La Paz and back in less than three weeks, fighting rough water, winds of near-gale velocity which at several times forced us to seek safety on shore or in protected coves. The first time boats of that size ever had attempted—and completed—this hazardous, exciting voyage in the fabulous Gulf of California.

"Putt-putt trail blazers," an American called me and my three companions. "Loco gringos," muttered an unbelieving Mexican who helped refuel us at Loreto, far down the peninsula and the first capital of the Californias.

The thrilling adventure for me and my friends, Martin Rothschild of Pasadena; Roy Francis, my uncle; and Kenneth Anderson; the latter two from Pomona; began at San Felipe, Nov. 4, 1956. We'd trailered our two Crown Craft open utility boats from Pasadena. Each boat was powered by two new Johnson 35-horsepower motors, which we'd broken in on test runs at the Salton Sea and in the ocean. Martin and I were to use his boat, *Bloody Mary II*; Roy and Ken in the *San Francisco Babe*.

Each boat was equipped with special parts, safety equipment including rollers which could be blown up if we had to beach the boats; our boat carried 88 gallons of fuel; the other 92 gallons. Each had fire extinguishers, emergency food and five gallons of drinking water. We'd made prior arrangements to refuel at overnight stops at the Bay of Los Angeles, Santa Rosalía, and Loreto.

We'd expected good weather. It didn't take us long to find that you can't sign up Mother Nature. We spent the night at Augie's Riviera Hotel. Raymond Vásques, manager, had read all about our projected trip in *Western Outdoor News* and was a fine host.

Next morning at 5:26 o'clock the wind was blowing about 25 miles-an-hour but we figured it would be okay to take off with the sea on our stern. We hadn't cleared the sandy point below San Felipe when the sea began to break over the bow and over our convertible top. We decided it was too rough to try to make the Bay of Los Angeles so we put in at San Luis Gonzaga Bay, 104 miles south of San Felipe. It took us six hours.

—Nov. 5 at 5 a.m. the wind was blowing 37 miles-an-hour. Sea still rough. Weather clear. Sure hated to start. But we shoved off with the turn of the tide—it was running about 25 feet—and made it safely through treacherous Ballenas channel. Arrived without too much trouble at the Bay of Los Angeles. Time, 11:30 a.m. Our good friend Antero Díaz met us. Too rough to refuel so we spent the night. Antero told us the fishing was good; he runs a camp there catering to airborne anglers. Has a good landing strip. About 100 people there; 37 children and they have a school.

—We stayed over an extra day on account of the wind and left Nov. 7 in clear weather and calm seas for Santa Rosalía. All went well until we got to Cape Vírgenes about 15 miles from Santa Rosalía where the swells were 20 feet high topped by whitecaps. Our motors were still running okay on the Mexican fuel. By 2 p.m. we sighted the tall smokestack of the copper smelter, started more than 50 years ago by a French company, but now run by Mexicans.

We beached our boats, walked toward the town. There we were met by a taxi driver, Arturo Pearce, who told us our friends, Allan McAlister and Chris Peterson of Pasadena, had flown into town the weekend before but couldn't stay to meet us on account of our delayed schedule.

—Nov. 8 at 7 a.m. we started for Mulegé. No wind. Cloudy weather. Made it to Mulegé without incident and docked at a landing on the Rosalía River. It cost us two props but we made it up the river, in a beautiful tropical setting of coconut palms, dates, grapefruit and other fruits. At Club Mulegé we were entertained royally by Gregory Hirales. And we had a duck dinner. Fishing was excellent but we were behind schedule.

From Mulegé to Loreto we hit rough seas and had a few anxious minutes trying to avoid the reefs but we made it by 12:10. That night we spent at the Flying Sportsmen Lodge run by Mr. and Mrs. Ed Tabor. Best of all was a swim in the pool. Again our coming had been anticipated by Mrs. Tabor and guests who'd read *W.O.N.*

—Nov. 10 at 9 a.m. we left for La Paz. No wind and cloudy skies. Found a nasty reef at San Marcio point but

we arrived at 5 p.m. in front of the Los Arcos Hotel. As the next day was Sunday we made arrangements to refuel. We were quite a curiosity at the hotel. No one dreamed we could make it that far in small boats. We stayed a couple of days in the dreamy, pleasant resort to rest up and check our motors which had put on 600 miles of hard going.

—Nov. 12 we left La Paz at 6 a.m. The wind was about 25 miles-an-hour and the sea was rough. It took us an hour to get out of La Paz harbor. For the first time we had the seas in front of us. The swells were sharp and close together. I was glad to see Mechudo Head go by our stern. I had changed plugs ten times. I blamed the gas; it must have had water in it. Martin and I had a regular routine, one at the wheel, the other cleaning plugs. Roy's motors seemed okay. I wished I'd taken our mechanic's advice and got some "dry power" or alcohol to put in the tanks to burn the water.

We arrived at Loreto soaking wet. We took three hours longer than on the way down, due to changing plugs. We refueled, got some new plugs. A nice chicken dinner at the lodge and life seemed okay. Fishermen were still doing fine, especially on roosterfish.

—Nov. 13 we left Loreto for Santa Rosalía at 6:30 a.m. with an oily sea, clear sky. We arrived at 12:30 p.m. at Santa Rosalía. Nice thing about traveling in two boats, same motors and same speed, you keep together. We left for San Carlos Bay at 3:30 p.m. and as we pushed through Santa Ana Bay the westerlies began and I could see we were in for it. But we found a bay out of the wind.

—Next day, Nov. 14, we left for Los Angeles Bay at 6 a.m. The wind blew hard, then seemed to break up. But after an hour of smooth weather all hell broke loose! I felt we had to make San Francisquito as there's a nice bay there. We were getting low on fuel so I felt if we battled the seas we'd run out before we reached the Bay of Los Angeles. At last, about 20 miles from the bay, we found a cove behind a rocky formation. We stayed there four hours and got most of our clothes dry again. But when we started out it was still rougher. So we spent the next day behind the rock.

—At last we decided to push on to Los Angeles Bay. The first half hour wasn't so bad although we were drenched. The waves were 20 to 25 feet high. With both motors open we were only doing five miles-an-hour! The wind must have been 45 miles-an-hour. Several times I was afraid we'd be carried backwards onto the rocks.

Half the time we couldn't see the other boat. At last Roy's boat appeared in the trough of a huge wave. They apparently were going ahead. The next few hours were a nightmare; at times it seemed the stinging salt spray would suffocate me. Just about dark we made it to Las Animas Bay. We didn't see the other boat. Had they gone on to Los Angeles Bay?

—Nov. 16, at 5:50 a.m., we peeked around the corner of the bay, found it still rough, came back to the bay and threw out our storm anchor. At 7:35 a.m. a plane came over, made a couple of passes at us. We were relieved because we felt Roy and Ken had made it and had sent the plane to look for us.

We sweat it out until 10 p.m. that night, then decided to make a run for it in the full moon. We had a rough, wet time of it but finally made the beach at the bay at 11:20 p.m. Who was waiting? Good old Antero Díaz! Roy and Ken were awakened. They looked at us like we'd risen from the dead!

—By 4 a.m. Nov. 18 we were off for San Felipe. We had a little trouble with rough seas and spark plugs but after the ordeal of Las Animas Bay it was anti-climactic.

It took us nine hours. Believe me, San Felipe may not be Palm Springs but it seemed like heaven to us!

Lots of people have asked if the trip we made is safe for the average boatman. Yes, with 16-foot boats at least as sturdy as ours, with motors as powerful and in good working order. You should take ample reserve food, water and fuel to carry you between stops. Make the trip in April if possible when the gulf's usually calm.

It's a wonderful trip for small boats and good motors if the boaters have common sense and knowledge of their boats. I wouldn't trade this experience for any I ever had.

Would I do it again? You bet! I'm planning another trip already! — BOB FRANCIS AS TOLD TO JOE MEARS, COURTESY WESTERN OUTDOOR NEWS

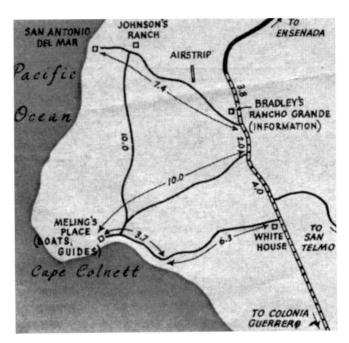

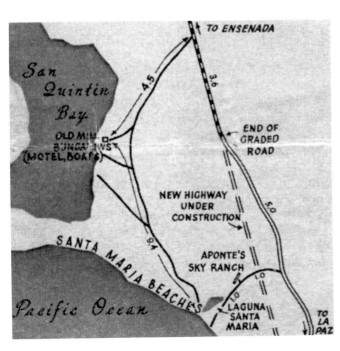

A series of maps from *Sunset Magazine*, November 1955, documents Baja roads and tourist accommodations at the beginning of the Golden Age.

"Ensenada Area," top left, shows the old immigration checkpoint where tourist cards were issued—off and on—for many years. The original small concrete block building just west of the highway was once an isolated landmark, but it is now hidden amid the extensive commercial development of the town of Maneadero.

"Arroyo Seco Area," top right, shows where the pavement ended near the present day town of Colonet until the building of the Transpeninsular Highway, 18 years later. The Tijuana-Ensenada road—Baja's first improved highway—was originally paved beginning in 1923 by then Territorial Governor Abelardo L. Rodríguez. The Mexicali-San Felipe highway was paved in 1950.

"San Quintín Area," lower left, shows the Old Mill doing business on the shore of Bahía San Quintín, and the place where the graded road ended and became a Jeep trail.

— COURTESY SUNSET MAGAZINE

On the Gene Perry Cruise with a Fairships 21 and twin Mercury outboards.

Gene Perry with black sea bass caught at Isla San Lorenzo.

GENE PERRY EXPEDITION

RAY'S FIRST CRUISE DOWN THE CORTEZ

UNDOUBTEDLY SPURRED ON by the historic "Bob Francis Cruise" to La Paz only a few months before, and by the other long Baja trips then being taken in small outboards, Ray departed San Felipe on April 19, 1957, with Eugene Perry, on his first trailer boat trip down the Sea of Cortez. (The month chosen, April, had been recommended by Bob Francis at the end of his cruise log published in *Western Outdoor News*.)

The "Perry Cruise" group consisted of two 21-foot boats powered by twin Mercury outboards. It successfully reached Isla San Lorenzo in the Midriff area before returning safely to San Felipe on April 27th.

Ray had already covered this route several times aboard the panga motherships of Charlie Rucker, but on this trip he discovered the joys of long-distance cruising in a small trailerable boat.

Despite the relatively rough weather encountered on this cruise, once it was over, Ray formed the mistaken and temporary opinion that the route from San Felipe south to Bahía de los Angeles was a good one for small outboard boats trying to reach the southern Sea of Cortez.

That opinion would be reversed by the disasters of the storm-wracked "Shipwreck Charlie" Cohen Cruise along the same route in 1959, which convinced Ray that the safest and most pleasant way for a small boat to reach southern Baja was not to launch at San Felipe, but at Kino Bay on the eastern side of Cortez. From Kino Bay, boats could more easily island-hop across the Midriff archipelago, and then cruise down the peninsula.

That seaway would become the standard route for small boats cruising down the Sea of Cortez until the opening of the Transpeninsular Highway in 1973 made it possible to trailer boats directly to Bahía de los Angeles or other launch points farther south on the Baja peninsula.

Notable in the first of this three-part series from *Western Outdoor News* is Ray's description of the turtle steak dinners served by Cruz Díaz at Bahía de los Angeles. Those famous dinners at Casa Díaz were a rite of passage for anyone exploring the Midriff during the era.

SAN FELIPE TO THE MIDRIFF

"HOOK-UP!" This exclamation keeps bouncing around between my ears like a haunting tune riding on thunder, as I try to write about one of the most exciting adventures I've ever had. If this column comes out slightly incoherent, blame it on the guy who started yelling that palpitating phrase.

If I can clear my head of it for a few minutes I'll try to give you a few of the hundreds of highlights of our success in exploring Isla San Lorenzo and its three satellite islands, together with a bit of info on our trip there in two outboard cabin cruisers.

Our ships were good, sturdy 21-foot vessels and we needed all that was built into these Fairships Cruisemasters to buck the wind, wave and tide of the Canal de las Ballenas. We didn't realize how daring we were until we had a few hours of that churning sea. The storm that swept Southern California Easter week caught up with us a few miles south of Diggs Point, a sand promontory seen from San Felipe, our starting point. Smaller craft would have been in serious trouble, especially along the shallow beach that continues to within 15 miles of Puertecitos and the 25-mile series of cliffs midway down the Channel of the Whales.

Although our trip down to Bahía de los Angeles was rugged, we had a mirror-like surface most all the time from there across to Islas Partida and Raza and down to Isla San Lorenzo. The latter is an island surrounded by great and abundant beauty. The sea life there is stacked up. In one 200-hundred-yard-square section we caught giant black

Isla Partida: "...Next morning we crossed the Channel, circled Isla Partida, caught a few grouper and sailed on down to the flat, bird-plastered Isla Raza... Spent our first quiet night at sea and dashed down to Isla San Lorenzo, the real objective of our expedition."

sea bass on the 200-foot level, giant grouper above that, then snappers, near the surface, 10 to 25-pound groupers and cabrilla, with big bonito and yellowtail milling under forage fish. Even the air was filled with diving birds.

This island is on the southern rim of the Midriff. It seems to be something of a dividing line between the cool, rich currents of the Midriff and the warmer waters below it. This may account for the pile of migrating forage and game fishes.

Our planned timing was perfect, in that we met the massive yellowtail movement head-on. This was one month ahead of the regular schedule.

Our boat, owned and skippered by Eugene Perry, O.F.P.A. Board Chairman, carried his father-in-law Fred Smith, insurance man Lee Wakefield, and me. The other boat had aboard owner Verne Chambers and wife Jean, of Reseda, and skin divers Bob Love Jr., from Inglewood, and his brother George, who flew up from Houston, Texas just to make this trip. Every last one of them is making plans for a return trip just as soon as they can arrange it. I never saw a group get more pleasure on such a long cruise. Each thinks the journey the greatest of all fishing adventures. I would say the same, but since I have used the expression for the last half-dozen trips, repeating may sound monotonous. Anyway I still say it was the top trip yet. The last of June or late September should be twice as exciting.

On our way down we had a happy evening at Bahía de los Angeles as guests of Antero Díaz, owner of the lodge. His wife supervises the "out-of-this-world" cooking. Her turtle steaks, butter clams and the "works" will long be remembered. Antero has added a six to eight-passenger, converted shrimp boat to his fleet of a dozen outboard skiffs and cabin jobs. His fairly modern cabañas accommodate more than 30 people. Heretofore all his guests have come in by private plane.

That lingering, tom-tom beat of "hook-up" is a carry-over from the fishing at San Lorenzo, where the weight of a sinker and boat speed determine the type of fish you catch. More on this next week. — RAY CANNON

SERIOUS CONCERNS ABOUT THE SAN FELIPE ROUTE

[In another telling of the run to Bahía de los Angeles, Ray anticipates his future concerns about rough weather along the unprotected coast south of San Felipe. He also describes encountering tourists at Puertecitos, which had just been established on the road south of town opened by Arturo Grosso of Rancho Laguna Chapala.

Ray's description in this story of an overnight stay at "hidden San Francisquito" is a reference to an obscure inlet at the south end of Bahía San Luis Gonzaga, not the well-known weather-protected small bay on the Baja coast opposite Isla San Lorenzo in the Midriff area.

The "Whale Cove" described as "ten miles past Puertecitos" is most likely the small semi-open indentation on the coast known today as Campo La Costilla.

The "airstrip house between upper and lower bays" at Gonzaga Bay where fuel was found was undoubtedly the early beginnings of the long row of houses known today as "Alfonsina's."]

Reads like a Class-A Movie—a drama filled with breathless suspense, fearful conflict, intense struggle, magnificent adventure, humor, color, and cheer—rousing victory—all of it in a once-in-a-lifetime production.

My notes mention—my doubts in shoving off from San Felipe in a heavier than light offshore breeze; facing a choppy sea just past Diggs Point; crosswind building up to a stiff blow, with no refuge along the whole 50-mile stretch of dangerous shallow beach. The sea piles up and we chance a full throttle run to Whale Cove about ten miles past Puertecitos and make it with all hands and equipment still aboard our two 21-foot cruisers.

Found half-a-dozen other cabin jobs ready for beach launching in this cove. They had been trailered, truck-pulled by a Pasadena group headed by Dick Hunt, destination Bahía de los Angeles and Angel de la Guarda.

Second day: Wind increases as we sail past Red Rock. Run into still another blow off Isla San Luis and make run for San Luis Gonzaga Bay. Pick up only five gallons of gas from airstrip house between upper and lower bays; get like amount from chartered shrimp boat. Sail across lower bay to hidden San Francisquito baylet 1 1/2 miles out from end of sand beach.

We cuddled in comfort in this completely protected bay through a stormy night, sailed out with the dawn and into the wind-swept Canal de las Ballenas; plowed through the heavy sea, hoping, holding our breath, hoping our gas would get us to Los Angeles Bay. Our small craft were subjected to the heaviest pounding of all, five miles off the entrance to the Bay. As we cut in just before the high dome island that guards the entrance, all hands sounded off with great jubilance, for a moderately calm bay stretched out past the second row of islands and on to the village and good lodge of Antero Díaz.

Winds died and the sea flattened like a vast sheet of chrome. Apprehensions remained with us but fears were gone for we were now Vikings—we had "had it," and could "take it" again. But for the rest of the journey we glided across a surface of glass. Even the Channel of the Whales lay as motionless and as blue as the sky. — RAY CANNON

REMOTE REFUELING RENDEZVOUS

[Refueling from a larger boat at Isla la Raza, a precursor of the standard procedure Ray developed for small boat cruises down the Cortez in which fuel would be pre-positioned somewhere on the west side of the Midriff, usually Caleta San Francisquito, or weather permitting, Rancho el Barril, a few miles south.

The gathering of bird eggs, described at Isla La Raza, is no longer permitted.]

Next morning we crossed the Channel, circled Isla Partida, caught a few grouper and sailed on down to the flat, bird-plastered Isla Raza, for a rendezvous with the large converted shrimp boat chartered by a group of physicians headed by Dr. Mark L. Beauchamp, North Hollywood. By prearrangement they carried enough gas to last us for the next three days. Their crew gathered about four bushels of sea pigeon eggs (considered a delicacy by natives) and the doctors loaded the boat with grouper, yellowtail and bonito.

Our genial and efficient guide, Ignacio, whom we picked up at Los Angeles Bay, was at first unable to grasp the idea of chasing diving birds and made some humorous remarks about our running out to catch pajaro (birds) when the pez (fish) along the shore were trying to catch up with us. Few native fishermen understand our desperate eagerness to catch yellowtail (which they seldom eat) instead of the abundant grouper and cabrilla (a favored food fish) caught slowly trolling near shore.

We found ocean whitefish and goldspotted bass plentiful in deep water but were unable to contact black sea bass or giant grouper. Spent our first quiet night at sea and dashed down to Isla San Lorenzo, the real objective of our expedition.

We had heard of no other anglers exploring this wondrous island but found evidence of native shark and turtle fishermen's rare visits to the place. None of the people at Los Angeles Bay were able to give us info on it. We were on our own—and what a glorious couple of days we had.

I am almost ready to conclude that the geographical position of this island makes it a sort of a Grand Central Station for fish migrations. They seem to funnel in from all southerly directions to the rich waters surrounding the three satellite islands at the west end, for a simple breakfast, then fan out into three distinct swimways, leading northward.

The flourishing marine flora on the south side of San Lorenzo differs greatly from the sparse short seaweeds on the north. It seems possible that there are wide water temperature variations because of the island's cross-wise position to the Gulf's surging north and south currents. The cold upwelling waters from the deep channel boil up along the north side while the south receives the warmer current. All of which suggests a great variation and bountiful food supply. The number of species and abundance in the resident fish populations provide some of the evidence for these theories. I hope to get more info next trip.

Whatever the cause, my last week's crack about the fish being "stacked" here was no exaggeration. Actually they were layers—each species to its favored strata. One gigantic grouper got out of bounds, followed a Spoofer-hooked snapper to the surface, and rammed his broad head right on above the surface as he inhaled the two-footer. Pop Smith's bulging eyes almost equaled the groupers at the sight of the steam shovel gulp.

He was on the other end of the line but wished he wasn't after battling the stern and side-wheeler for 25 minutes, mostly on the surface.

We caught all the yellowtail we wanted and could have decked tons of black sea bass, giant and small grouper and other species, but two days of fabulous fishing was enough.

All that was needed for this happy ending to that epic drama was a rollicking seafaring song to match our exuberance and sheer joy. — RAY CANNON

Herb Tansey, founder of East Cape's legendary Rancho Buena Vista, with crutches at left; Ray, center; and Trans Mar de Cortés' La Paz agent, Guillermo "Bill" Escudero, c. 1957.

Loading clients at the "Ranch."

RANCHO BUENA VISTA

RAY'S "HOME" IN BAJA

THROUGHOUT HIS CAREER at *Western Outdoor News*, Ray wrote more columns about the East Cape Area's Rancho Buena Vista than any other place in Baja. It wasn't only the wonderful fishing and the quiet, tropical setting that attracted him; a trip to Buena Vista offered many other pleasures, including a stopover at his favorite city of La Paz and the opportunity to visit the "Ranch's" owner, his close friend, retired U.S. Army Colonel Eugene Walters.

These two men from different backgrounds shared an intense love for the Sea of Cortez. They grew old together after meeting at the Ranch in 1957, and they would die within a few months of each other in 1977.

Sometime about 1966, it was decided that Colonel Walters would build a permanent house for Ray on the grounds of the resort. A choice spot was chosen at the edge of the water just north of the main buildings, a small cabaña

was demolished to clear the area, and construction was begun on the "Round House." The architect of the semi-circular, single-story building was Dale Frederich, who had accompanied Ray on two of his best-remembered early Cortez cruises: the 1957 "Hurricane Cruise," and the 1958 "Kids' Trip." A special circular bed was constructed by San Diego furniture manufacturer and Vagabundos Del Mar club member Roy Wickline.

In January 1969, the Round House was completed and a lease was executed that entitled Ray to occupy it for life at the rate of about $21 per month. For the remainder of his career, Ray would return to the Round House as often as possible, and he would consider Rancho Buena Vista his "home" in Baja.

Following is the story of how Rancho Buena Vista was founded by Herb Tansey and then taken over by Colonel Walters after Tansey's untimely death in 1959.

THE FOUNDING OF RANCHO BUENA VISTA

In the years following World War II, Herb Tansey lived in San Diego, and he had two sources of income that seemingly were somewhat at odds with each other: he owned a bar on University Avenue, and he also gave flying lessons at Kenny Friedken's School of Aeronautics.

In 1951, Tansey had two students who were receiving flying lessons for free. These two—Frank Van Wormer (brother of East Cape legend Bobby Van Wormer) and Olen Burger—were partners in a San Diego autobody and paint shop, and they had accepted free lessons as payment for restoring an old car belonging to school owner Kenny Friedken.

Another Tansey student at the time was a young man named Enrique García, and one day, Enrique's father, José "Joe" García, came to the school and started talking about

Frank Van Wormer, left, and Olen Burger, with the Navion plane that took Burger, Herb Tansey, and José García on their first trip to Rancho Buena Vista in 1951. — PHOTO COURTESY BOBBY VAN WORMER

a place he knew way down in Baja California where there were "more fish than anywhere else in the entire world." This place was an old goat ranch called "Buena Vista," and Joe García said that if anyone ever wanted to start a fishing resort, Buena Vista was the best possible place.

Soon thereafter, Tansey, Burger, and Joe García, flew down to Buena Vista in Burger's Navion airplane. They landed on what is now the soccer field of the small town of La Ribera and caught a ride to the goat ranch.

The fishing was very good. A partnership was formed, with Herb Tansey putting up cash and Joe García putting up sweat equity as on-site manager of the planned fishing resort of Rancho Buena Vista.

Tansey returned to San Diego to run his bar, and García began construction of the first resort buildings. They started off with two 19-foot outboard cruisers, which they bought used from Ed Tabor, who was just opening the Flying Sportsmen Lodge in Loreto.

In May 1952, a group of planes flew down for the grand opening of Rancho Buena Vista, but business turned out to be slow, and a few years later Joe García sold his share of the company and Tansey moved to the Ranch to take over operations himself.

Business continued to be very slow. By January 1957, Tansey's money had just about run out and he was ready to give Rancho Buena Vista back to the goats.

But in the final week of that month, an American writer, Ray Cannon, arrived by taxi on the long dirt road from La Paz, in the company of another writer, Frank Dufresne of *Field & Stream*. They were on their first trip around the southern tip of Baja, and they had stopped at Rancho Buena Vista to test the fishing, and in particular to fish for the "albacore" they had heard about in La Paz.

Pulling boats at Rancho Buena Vista, c. 1959.

The "albacore" turned out to be yellowfin tuna, a disappointment for Cannon and Dufresne, but otherwise the fishing was a spectacular success, and the two writers advised Tansey to hold on a little longer; they promised him they would help to publicize Rancho Buena Vista and save the business.

Over the course of the next two years, widespread publicity in *Western Outdoor News* and in such national publications as *Saturday Evening Post* and *Field & Stream* caused business to skyrocket, and Rancho Buena Vista became the most popular resort in Baja California.

But tragedy struck on January 5, 1959, when Herb Tansey and employee Arthur Young were killed in a crash of Tansey's Ercoupe plane near the town of El Triunfo.

Beginning sometime earlier, Ray Cannon had accompanied former U.S. Army Colonel Eugene Walters on fishing trips to Rancho Buena Vista and the two had talked

Early afternoon at Rancho Buena Vista, September 25, 1964. — PHOTO BY HARRY MERRICK

about how the colonel wished he could find a place just like it to buy and operate during his retirement.

Shortly after the tragic plane crash, Ray contacted Colonel Walters and advised him that Herb Tansey's widow wished to sell out. In March 1959, Colonel Walters took over as the new owner of Rancho Buena Vista, and a new era—complete with a storybook of future legends of its own—was just beginning.

RAY & FRANK DUFRESNE
DISCOVER RANCHO BUENA VISTA

By the end of 1956, Ray had fished all of Baja California except for the southern tip—from La Paz, around Cabo San Lucas, and up the Pacific side to Bahía Magdalena.

On New Year's Eve of that year, he wrote a letter to *Field & Stream* editor Frank Dufresne about an elaborate trip the two had planned to explore and test fish that entire stretch of coastline, and on January 19, 1957 Ray and Dufresne began that trip around the southern end, escorted by Trans Mar de Cortés' La Paz office manager, Guillermo "Bill" Escudero.

The discoveries they made would inspire the writing of hundreds of columns and magazine articles as the great resorts of Baja California Sur were built over the next two decades. Indeed, for the remainder of his career, the extraordinary fishing, beauty and boomtown atmosphere of southern Baja would overshadow Ray's earlier discoveries in the Northern Cortez and Midriff areas. After 1957, the majority of Ray's writing was about Loreto and southern Baja.

Combined from articles and fragments written during the period and after, Ray tells the story of that magic first trip around the southern tip:

THE LETTER TO DUFRESNE

[Ray writes Frank Dufresne about the free accommodations he had arranged for them. Rancho Buena Vista was on the original itinerary, but considered a "side trip." In this letter, "Cóppola" is Luis Cóppola Bonillas, owner of the Hotel Los Arcos in La Paz.]

Dec. 31, 1956
Dear Frank, They will roll out the carpet for our trip…
Cóppola is wide awake to publicizing Baja and will really do things to help us. His La Paz Mgr.—Mr. Guillermo Escudero Luján is the most helpful person I've met in Mexico. Mr. Elias, Mgr. of the Los Arcos Hotel, and Rudy Vélez who operates the boats, are very enthusiastic about your joining me for the January 19 trip.

All of the above facilities and accommodations will cost us nothing. We spend little except for liquor and

women—of course I mean the tips we give the lady waitresses and the drinks we buy for our devoted readers we meet there…

There may be some expense connected with a side trip across Baja to Magdalena Bay. We will need sleeping bags for that one, it's rough. Mr. Luján will organize it and supply us with a guide and truck. He says the lagoons of this bay are loaded with super giant snook and plenty of bonefish, tenpounder, milkfish and numerous other game fish…

On the trip I have just made [to Mulegé]… I learned a lot, had wonderful fishing and explored some islands, bays and shores seldom, if ever before, fished by anglers. This leaves me a couple of islands and a stretch of coastline above La Paz and the coast below Las Cruces around the Cape and back up to Magdalena Bay to finish the whole of Baja California…

Within the next week I will work out a detailed schedule for our trip with Trans Mar's local agent. It will include January 20, 21, 22, fishing at La Paz; 24, 25, 26 or more, at the Cape; with open dates for Magdalena Bay, Rancho Buena Vista and other side trips, up to February 2 or longer, if you like…— Ray

"ALBACORE" AT THE LOS ARCOS

[Most native speakers in today's Baja use the Spanish word "atún" to refer to the yellowfin tuna, but that was not always the case, as Ray discovers in this story, which begins when he and Frank Dufresne arrived at the Hotel Los Arcos in La Paz.

The tip-off about this "albacore" fishing location by George Escudero—brother of their escort Guillermo—seems to be what spurred Ray and Dufresne to visit Rancho Buena

Guillermo "Bill" Escudero and his Chevy Bel Air station wagon on a camping trip to Bahía Magdalena, c. 1957. As La Paz manager for Trans Mar de Cortés, Escudero often provided ground transportation for Ray's travels around the south end of the peninsula.

Vista first on this trip. Perhaps they otherwise would not have discovered Herb Tansey's resort at all.

In this version, Ray identifies his skipper as "Fiol" (Edrulfo Fiol Ruiz), but in others, it is "Laborio" (Eusebio Liborio Cocio Cocio), who would later become Ray's favorite guide at Rancho Buena Vista.]

Seated on the veranda of the elegant Hotel Los Arcos, 75 feet from the shore of the La Paz Bay, Dufresne and I were listening to George Escudero, owner of a fleet of marlin cruisers, tell of the numerous game fishes in the region.

We were buying every word until he pulled this shocker—"There is an area 75 miles south of La Paz where 200-pound *albacora* are plentiful."

We didn't doubt that by "albacora" he was referring to the Pacific albacore, the gamester Californians dash out 100 miles to sea to catch. But we did know according to all scientific records that no albacore above 96 pounds had ever been recorded. And furthermore, none had ever been officially observed anywhere near the Sea of Cortez.

Bill Escudero offered to drive us to Rancho Buena Vista where the albacora hangs out the year round.

Our first big surprise was to find an elegant and well-conducted lodge and fleet of boats instead of an old weather-warped farm shack and stable, as we had expected of a Mexican "rancho."

We questioned all of the dozen or more boat skippers and all agreed that the north end of their bay was loaded with "albacora," and that "they weighed up to 250 pounds," and that "they came within 20 feet of the shoreline."

Fiol, my skipper, and his mate made up the most cheerful and optimistic crew I had ever fished with. While the mate was rigging my heaviest outfit, I broke out spinning gear, thinking I could snag some small but interesting oddball.

We had skirted the shore for less than three miles when Fiol turned toward some diving pelicans churning the water about 50 feet out from a cliff. "Está aquí, la albacora (it is here, the albacore)."

I saw a six-inch flyingfish take to the air. Right on its tail the sea blew up and out of the exploding bulge came an albacore-like fish as big around as a yearling steer. I saw the fish quite clearly. In shape it was exactly that of an albacore, color resemblance and all. The long pectoral fin, by which the albacore is identified, was in use and the length could not be estimated. In this startled condition I started doubting everything I had ever learned.

Next, there was one snappy yank on my spinning rod and all went limp. I didn't have to retrieve the little lure; there wasn't even any line to reel in.

I grabbed for heavy equipment rigged with an eight-inch white Compac feather and payed out a hundred yards of line. The skipper was clipping off an eight-knot trolling speed, far too fast I thought, but I figured he knew something.

East Cape sage, James "Jimmy" Pledger Smith, left, with Edrulfo Fiol Ruiz, who in 1951 became the first sport fishing skipper at Rancho Buena Vista, working for Joe García, then Herb Tansey and Colonel Eugene Walters. Fiol was born at Rancho Tintoreras near Buena Vista in 1923. — PHOTO BY GENE KIRA

Ray's favorite Rancho Buena Vista guide, Eusebio Liborio Cocio Cocio. Ray always called him "Laborio."

East Cape sport fishing skipper Jesús Araiza, 1998.

— PHOTO BY GENE KIRA

Rancho Buena Vista skipper José Ortiz "Little José" Ruiz in October 1959. Ortiz was born in Buena Vista in 1941 and is still a skipper at "Rancho." — PHOTO BY HARRY MERRICK

Ray and Ortiz, c. 1975. — PHOTO BY ALIX LAFONTANT

Ortiz at his home in Buena Vista, 1998, with a float "liberated" from illegal fishing boats in the 1960s. — PHOTO BY GENE KIRA

The strike was for keeps. It was just like hooking a discharged torpedo going in the opposite direction. If Fiol hadn't changed ends of the boat in less than 20 seconds and had her roaring at full bore, my line would have been completely peeled off. The line on my reel spool was down to no more than two or three wraps when the boat gained enough speed to equal that of the fish.

Gaining a few yards of line while the fish ran tangents restored my confidence but that was shaken when the skipper gulped a hopeless—"The albacora will soon be in deep water and he will go down 500 fathoms."

I had already tightened the star drag for all the pressure the line would take, but in the excitement had forgotten my own technique of applying "rhythmic pumping."

Seeing me pump the rod, the skipper thought I was trying to get shed of the fish. He throttled the motors down to idle and beat his fist against the boat in utter disgust. But he nearly wrenched himself and the motors apart when he saw that the pumping had caused the tuna to turn and start circling the boat.

Under the magnifying surface water the tuna looked as big around as a yearling steer and too large to be gaffed.

I yelled for the spear and Fiol drew the slender rod back and sent it straight as a bullet.

I was almost sure our specimen was the largest albacore ever heard of until I stretched the long pectoral fin back along the fish's side and saw it did not reach past the anal fin. This and other distinguishing characteristics proved the fish to be a yellowfin tuna.

We made a forced run to show the magnificent results to Dufresne. He took one look and scoffed, "This fish doesn't weigh near 250 pounds."

Following a few smoky, obscene phrases, I told him that I didn't even want to catch a 250-pounder and I meant every word I said, including the salty ones. (My large tuna weighed 82 pounds and would have been a world record for 48-pound line.) — RAY CANNON

RANCHO BUENA VISTA
1957 BOOKING INFORMATION

[Ray was instantly enchanted with Herb Tansey's Rancho Buena Vista, as described in a "Trip Of The Week" article in *Western Outdoor News* a few months later. The booking details at the end of the article give prevailing rates for the day as well as information on Enrique Ortega's International Travel Service, the first travel agency to book fishing trips to Baja California.]

If you would like to surf cast for yellowtail (up to 50 pounds), roosterfish, tenpounder, sierra, jack crevalle or a dozen other first-class game fishes; or like to boat a hundred-pound yellowfin tuna, record-size sailfish or marlin, or fight it out with my favorite of all, the jumping dolphinfish, then it's Rancho Buena Vista—where they say weather is mild and fishing is hot all the time.

Although Herb Tansey, owner of the Lodge, may not realize it, he has a diamond mine in that place, and it is safe to predict that he will be needing a couple of dozen more cabañas as soon as word gets around.

I had somehow a complete previous mistaken idea of the Lodge. I had expected a typical thatched and dingy ranch house but was surprised to find it on a par with the U.S. hunting lodge—showers, toilets, hot and cold water in every cabin, a very large dining clubroom, with bar and spacious veranda facing the Gulf. But more important, a happy, congenial atmosphere and delicious food.

Rancho Buena Vista Lodge on Bahía de Palmas; 76 miles good road, from La Paz. Taxi for five people or less, $25. Lodge: meals and room $10 per person. Weekly and family rates. Manned boats: $5 to $35 per day.

Heavy tackle, guns, horses, guides available.

For reservations or additional info contact Enrique Ortega, International Travel Service, 510 W. Sixth St.; Phone MA. 9-2666. — RAY CANNON

CONFIRMING A BAJA LEGEND
HOW HERB TANSEY LOST HIS LEG

Herb Tansey, the founder of Rancho Buena Vista, was missing the lower portion of his right leg from about six inches below the knee.

The legend of how Tansey lost his leg—as the pilot of an airliner that "crashed into a river in Ireland"—is one well-known "Baja story" that turns out to have a basis in fact.

From contemporary newspaper accounts, the Irish Air Accident Investigation Unit in Dublin, and from aircraft historian and writer Michael O'Toole, here is the story of how Herb Tansey lost his leg:

On the night of December 27, 1946, Tansey was a senior TWA pilot assigned to fly from Paris to New York with a stop at Shannon Airport, Ireland. He took off from Paris about midnight with 23 people aboard his L-49 Constellation, "Star of Cairo," and as he neared Shannon Airport about 2 a.m. on the morning of December 28th, he made a practice instrument approach to the field. He was making a turn back toward the runway in light rain when one wing of the airliner struck the ground on a marshy island named *Inishmacnaghtan* at the confluence of the Shannon and Fergus Rivers, about a mile from the airport. The resulting horrendous crash and fire tore the airliner to pieces, killing 12 people and spilling the survivors into a nightmarish swamp which took rescue workers nearly two hours to penetrate.

Tansey was thrown from the plane, still strapped in his seat, and his right leg was crushed under a piece of wreckage thought to have been a motor or piece of one. He remained in critical condition at County Hospital in Ennis, about 15 miles from the airport as TWA ground staff members donated blood to save his life. His severely injured right leg was amputated at the hospital.

An official investigation concluded that Tansey was not at fault in the crash. It was determined that both of the Constellation's altimeters had been improperly installed, making them indicate higher than true altitude.

The rest of Tansey's story is pieced together from details that he gave to various people during his years at Rancho Buena Vista. According to these accounts, he subsequently sued TWA and won an award, which is sometimes said to have been $40,000 in cash, and it was this money that he used to form the partnership with Joe García that purchased the goat ranch known as "Buena Vista" and founded one of Baja California's first fishing resorts.

News accounts of the Shannon Airport crash tell of a stewardess who saved a baby that was thrown from the plane, and its mother, an 18-year-old French war bride who was coming to the U.S. to join her American husband in New Jersey. The stewardess, Ms. Vina Ferguson, 22, was officially commended for her heroism in aiding survivors of the crash. The mother, Mrs. Edith Delaby Waterbury, was critically injured, but survived, and the baby, four-month-old, Charles Bruce Waterbury, also survived after recovering from a broken leg.

RANCHO BUENA VISTA
SAVED FROM THE GOATS

[In this remarkable fragment, found scrawled on the back of a 1958 manuscript on how to catch needlefish, Ray candidly recalls the moment at the end of his first trip to Rancho Buena Vista when he, Frank Dufresne and Bill Escudero promised to help Herb Tansey save the financially struggling resort from bankruptcy. Corey Ford, mentioned here, and Frank Dufresne were both associate editors of *Field & Stream*.]

This was the beginning of the most pleasant, exciting and rewarding weeks and months and years of my life to date.

Before we left, we found that the skippers could put us on most any big game species we could name. Within four minutes after Fiol had taken us to a roosterfish spot, Frank and I had hookups.

"What fish you wish next?" he would say. Whether it was marlin, amberjack, wahoo, or huge dolphinfish, he would set a straight course to a piece of sea and say, "Está aquí," and we would be into them.

Both of us knew we had discovered the finest big game fishing spot we had ever heard of. But when we were ready to leave, Tansey confided that his little lodge was ten thousand in the red and was about ready to be returned to the goats. Both of us, and Escudero, promised ourselves, even more than to him, that we would save the place.

We did. Before Tansey smashed up in a plane wreck

within two years, Corey Ford joined us on a subsequent trip and in writing about the place. Feature articles in the *Saturday Evening Post*, *Field & Stream* and *Western Outdoor News* turned Buena Vista into the most popular resort on the peninsula. — RAY CANNON

LEARNING TO FISH AT THE RANCH

[Many years later, in 1976, Ray recalls his early days of learning big game fishing at Rancho Buena Vista.]

JANUARY 28, 1976—My best chance for learning and developing techniques came at Rancho Buena Vista where a long list of people spent much time and energy fishing, diving, and assisting me in testing every wild theory we could get from angling guests… or whatever fishing ideas we could dream up. Among the contributors were the late Herb Tansey, the first operator, and his assistant Bobby Van Wormer, enthusiastic diver. All skippers, especially José (Little José) Cota, Jesús Araiza Ruiz, and the most knowledgeable of all, Laborio, spent much overtime freely, testing new ideas. — RAY CANNON

OLD WORLD CHARM OF SANTIAGO

[After visiting Rancho Buena Vista, Ray and Frank Dufresne loaded themselves into Guillermo "Bill" Escudero's almost brand new 1956 Chevy Bel Air station wagon for the trip to San José del Cabo. The road in those days was a rustic, ungraded dirt trail with more hoofed animals using it than motor vehicles. This was probably Ray's first introduction to the "old Baja" that was almost untouched by the modern age, and he was instantly enchanted by it. For the remainder of his life, Ray would remember this car trip into the past, and he would write about it again and again.

Here, Ray's descriptions of the quiet town of Santiago are combined from several fragments he wrote as late as 1967.

Cirilo Gómez and his wife Virginia were owners of the Hotel Palomar. Gómez worked for Herb Tansey and Colonel Eugene Walters in the early days of Rancho Buena Vista. The Hotel Palomar was reportedly built at the urging of Bing Crosby, who felt it would be ideally located as a hunting lodge for the Santiago area. The original buildings were damaged by Hurricane Liza in 1976 and reopened by Gómez' son Sergio and his wife Gloria in 1981. Today, the hotel still offers excellent seafood and some of the quietest hideaway accommodations in Baja California Sur.]

Leaving Buena Vista is always painful.

We halted on a hilltop overlooking the valley farms, sugar cane fields, and the quaint pueblo of Santiago, where we would stop for coffee and a visit with my good friend

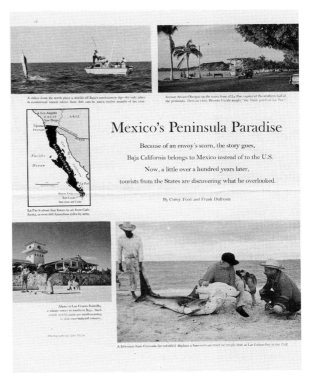

Mexico's Peninsula Paradise

Because of an envoy's scorn, the story goes, Baja California belongs to Mexico instead of to the U.S. Now, a little over a hundred years later, tourists from the States are discovering what he overlooked.

By Corey Ford and Frank Dufresne

The four-page article by Corey Ford and Frank Dufresne in *Saturday Evening Post*, 1958, that "put Baja on the map" by calling the Sea of Cortez "the world's greatest year-round sport fishing" spot. The story ran with color photos and 2,500 words and was the first major national publicity ever given to Baja California's still almost unknown sport fishing resorts. (Note: on the article's first-page map, Buena Vista is incorrectly located on Baja's Pacific coast.) — COURTESY SATURDAY EVENING POST

the Mayor. Santiago is actually two hilltop villages joined by a tree-shaded lane across a wide arroyo. A photo of the homes, stores, primitive sugar mill and pastoral vistas could be mistaken for a California scene in 1849. The same could be said of little Miraflores, where several families are engaged in making fancy leather saddles, purses, belts, and other objects.

Several years ago Santiago made a bold attempt to go modern by establishing one telephone in its city plaza, and another in the plaza of the other half of the town, which is on another hilltop a mile away. They are separated by an arroyo which floods about every 50 years.

The phone proved a failure because whoever answered a call would have to spend an hour or so locating the guy being called. So no one would stick a neck out to answer.

I got to know the mayor-store-owner, Señor Cirilo Gómez, English-speaking retired army officer, and his very charming wife, Virginia, and a beautiful niece. Also, the pistol-packing marshal-barber, who wore a .45 while cutting hair on the courthouse porch.

Everything except autos and a gas pump looks ancient, and from the crown of the hill you can see patch farms that were laid out two centuries ago, as was the sprawling sugar mill, which is made mostly of wood, the only modern instrument being a diesel motor sitting beside its predecessor, an old wood-burning steam engine.

The walking haystack you'll see coming in, will be a driverless burro literally obliterated from all view by the sugar cane latched on.

There are some spectacular marine fossil deposits nearby. Also, Indian pictographs and burial grounds, and about the best dove hunting ever heard of, and the only organized hunting for mountain lion in Baja.

On another hilltop, a break in the flowering forest of small trees and cacti is called "La Ventana" (The Window). Through it the view of the lofty, 6,500-foot-high Sierra de la Laguna and the intermediate valleys is magnificent.

— RAY CANNON

SAN JOSE DEL CABO

[At the time of this 1957 trip, the only lodging facilities from Rancho Buena Vista all the way around the southern tip of Baja California were the Fisher House of Carmen Fisher in San José del Cabo, and the Hotel Palmilla (then called Las Cruces Palmilla) which had just been opened by Abelardo L. "Rod" Rodríguez, with Bud Parr as an early partner.

The promised new resort referred to in this story was most likely the one opened four years later, in 1961, by Bud Parr. This was the Hotel Cabo San Lucas, which was built not on Playa el Blendito, but on the low, rocky bluffs of Chileno Bay. Parr's amazing resort set a new standard of luxury for Baja California and was a forerunner of things to come.]

As we rolled on down past several rustic but less attractive villages we could see the beginning of the tropical fruit orchards which extend down a valley watered by the Río San José to a large tidal lagoon at San José del Cabo, a prosperous town but still reluctant to enter the 20th Century.

Mule, horse and burro transportation continues to compete with motored vehicles. One of the three ancient sugar mills has recently replaced its horse-driven machinery with a diesel motor.

Carmen Fisher, owner of the Fisher House hotel at San José del Cabo, is opening another small inn at the Cape. Her son is remodeling and expanding the old house.

The palm bordered lagoon here fills so rapidly, manual labor is required every two weeks or so to drain it. Snook, snappers and other fish dash in and out from the sea while it is open.

Except for the few primitive ranches and the villages and towns mentioned and those at Cabo San Lucas and Todos Santos, this vast region south of La Paz is a wilderness covered for the most part with a jungle

Carla admiring a papaya tree with Cirilo Gómez, owner, with his wife Virginia, of the Hotel Palomar in Santiago, c. 1968.

profusion of blooming vines, small trees and numerous fruiting cacti.

We need a new set of words to describe San José del Cabo and the blunt end of the Baja peninsula.

The climate is like that of Java, the people gentle and sweet, and the fishing like no place else on earth. The place is the same Old Mexico it was a century ago—it's the town of Gordo, Miss Ruiz, Pelón, burros and Halley's Comet. Great orchards and forests of tropical fruit trees extend from the flowering patios to the humidless bushland.

The populace find keen delight in simple, humorous incidents. Like the one when a loose, playful mule chased our 300-pound landlady across the plaza and up onto her porch. She made a grand show of the chase, screeching like a puma all the way, to add to the comedy value. I am sure she was not frightened at all but she certainly gave the couple of hundred citizens a convincing and agile performance and provided them a day of laughter.

We found a dozen places on down around the tip of Baja where fish ignore the seasons and move in by thousands of tons instead of schools, where rock formations were inhabited by hosts of vicious-striking gamesters and wondrously colored exotics. Places that would be a credit in a Walt Disney fantasy in Technicolor.

It is across the fairly straight stretch between the point of San José and that at San Lucas that the warm waters of the Gulf meet the upwelled Pacific water to produce an ideal year-round habitat for a whole list of southern fishes, as well as a rich feeding ground for the hosts of migrators.

Very common all winter are the billfish, dolphin, sierra, amberjacks, yellowfin tuna, yellowtail, jack crevalle and roosterfish, but these are also halfway up the Gulf at

Near San José del Cabo, about the time of Ray's 1957 trip to Rancho Buena Vista and around the south end of Baja California with Frank Dufresne and Guillermo "Bill" Escudero. — PHOTO BY HARRY MERRICK

this date. It is the abundance of shore-dwelling species that seems most exciting to me and most all light-tackle enthusiasts.

Tidal rock formations are scattered most all along this southern end. Narrow passages provide fish runways from the sea to deeply hewn pools. Most any kind of a lure drawn through the crystal clear water will be followed by an assortment of jewel colored fishes, together with some of the best game fishes to be found on any shoreline. I can think of no other type of fishing, no other place, no other time, that would compare with a day spent fishing such a rock tide pool as at El Blendito, halfway between San José and San Lucas.

A modern popular priced fishing resort will be under construction near this spot within a short time.

Mayo Obregón, head of Trans Mar de Cortés, assured me that their line flights will be extended on down to this area from La Paz soon. At present a charter plane flies to San José and a low fare taxi takes you anywhere along the coast.

But full and complete facilities for the angler on a budget have not yet been completed. The exceptions are the Fisher House at San José del Cabo and the new Las Cruces Hotel at Palmilla, which I will describe in future articles. — RAY CANNON

A HOPHEAD'S DREAM

[On the road between San José del Cabo and Cabo San Lucas, Ray, Frank Dufresne and Guillermo "Bill" Escudero stopped to test the shore fishing in the rocky tide pools between Shipwreck Beach and the coastal hill called Cabeza de Ballena. Once again, they ran into a natural spectacle that would sustain Ray through a lifetime of columns.]

This is about a scene which three men will carry in their mind's eye as long as they live and not one will ever be able to fully describe it. Frank Dufresne came close with his classic phrase—"It looks like something swimming through a hophead's dream."

For everyone, there must be one vista or view that stands out above all others—each according to his own pursuit of the joyful thing to behold. What we saw at Rancho El Tule would doubtless be to any angler the ultimate piece of living art in Nature's handicraft.

We three, including Bill Escudero, not only saw it, we got right into it and gave full feeling to the immense pleasure it produced.

Bill had pointed out this promising shoreline while trolling for marlin the day before, but not until we looked

A vaquero near Punta Palmilla, c. 1964. — PHOTO BY AL TETZLAFF

Carmen Fisher de Ortiz, c. 1960. When she opened her guesthouse, "Casa Fisher," at San José del Cabo in 1951, it was the only organized lodging place on the entire south end of Baja California. Her facilities were used as temporary quarters during the construction of the Hotel Las Cruces Palmilla, opened in 1956, and the Hotel Cabo San Lucas, opened in 1961. The family relocated the business to Cabo San Lucas in 1962. Ed Tabor's canoe-fishing clients also stayed there until Tabor built his own bungalow facilities.

down from the vertical palisades could we appreciate the frilled and scalloped tidal pools, filigreed in stone by the sea's mighty chisels.

There were circular, oblong and angular pools in the shelf that extended one-hundred yards to sea and stretched for miles along the shoreline. In some, the water was 40 feet deep but so perfectly clear a pebble on the bottom was magnified to boulder size.

We selected a 100-foot-diameter basin and circled down to it.

It was after I had cast a lure down the full length of the pool and started a fast retrieve that the "stuff" broke out. A whole roster of multicolored game and exotic fishes rainbowed out from the honeycombed walls in pursuit of the lure.

It seemed that every crevice, crag and tunnel was jammed as a beehive. It was at this point that Frank let go with the very appropriate "hophead's dream" remark, and the usually quiet and composed Bill Escudero shook us up with a loud and emotional blast in Spanish— "MAGNIFICO!"

It seemed that everything in sight was bent on getting that lure. The moving mass assembled into a romping Mardi Gras, weaving and waving like flags in a United Nations parade.

Into the array came the yard-long blue crevalle, the lineal-striped, blue-and-gold snapper, red Colorado snapper, and grass-green and brown-spotted leopard grouper and golden grouper—tackle wreckers all of them.

Then there were triggerfish with a broad slash of orange, brilliant bejeweled parrotfish and wrasses, and a magnitude of smaller fishes glowing in unearthly radiance.

We awakened from our wild-eyed astonishment and the hypnotic state to realize that these were fish. The gentle, esthetic side of our natures was suddenly given the heave-ho to make room for three barbaric predators with a charge of greed to equal that of the predators we were after.

The glorious coloring was but a front for villains that could sink their teeth into a lead sinker. One of them (the Chino) had a face like an evil Chinese mask; another could grind clam shells like a grist mill—and a close-up view disclosed that the big blue crevalle had a look so mean it would likely frighten the sharks.

The fishing we had will make many more pages in our memory book than ever will be written on ordinary paper.

We cast every type and kind of lure and each seemed to serve as a preferred target for some one of the species. Our catch went into a small tidal pond where the fish could be kept alive for photographing and a fish dinner. This larder grew to look like an animated crazy quilt, and our appetites increased with it. The blue crevalle was the last one hooked. He created such a commotion everything fled

the basin, including the crevalle, and with my last white Spoofer, yet.

Out beyond the El Tule tide pools, in an extensive submerged shelf, a list of fishes almost equaling that of the basins moves in and out of the stone labyrinth. Among these are the heavyweight broomtail and Gulf groupers, jewfish (called "mero") and three kinds of huge snappers. Above them, roosterfish, yellowtail, amberjack and a number of other jacks, crevalles, sierra, and bonitos, move across the blunt end of the Peninsula with the tidal shift.

From three miles offshore and on out, marlin can be taken throughout most of the year, also dolphinfish, wahoo (called kingfish in some other parts of the country), skipjack, Mexican bonito and sailfish. Yellowfin tuna move by in large schools but are rarely taken in the deep waters on rod and reel. The reason being in their habit of sounding to such depths that angling lines are not long enough to stop the descent. Out near Punta San José some few are caught when they come into shallow water.

Our ideas for the dinner, having expanded to a feast, by now had swelled on up to a fiesta—and that evening Señora Fisher, owner of the Fisher House Inn produced a fish banquet fit for a king, but even more fitting for three starved anglers and an appreciative group of Mexican officials.

Ray and Guillermo "Bill" Escudero fishing about ten kilometers east of Cabo San Lucas, near the coastal hill, Cabeza de Ballena, visible in background. — PHOTO BY HARRY MERRICK

Entering Cabo San Lucas, 1961, during Ray's "El Dorado camper trip" with manufacturers Everett and Don Hamel. They had crossed the Cortez by loading the camper aboard a freighter, and were on a fishing and hunting tour of the peninsula's south end. The Cabo San Lucas cannery, just visible against the far shoreline, is the only significant structure. There is no harbor, just a salt flat that would be dredged in 1975.

San José del Cabo is a place for fisherman and family. It has retained a lot of the charm of Old Mexico. Mule mounted vaqueros and laden burros add to the picturesqueness. Tropical patio gardens can be seen back of most all old buildings. Pastoral meadows surrounded by tropical fruit orchards provide a source of delight to the photographers, as do the many other strange and beautiful vistas about the town.

Rancho El Tule is but one of a number of rocky places along the blunt end of the Baja California Peninsula between San José del Cabo and Cabo San Lucas. A good dirt road runs close to the shoreline to connect the two towns. There is no cafe nor are rooms available in San Lucas at present. — RAY CANNON

CABO SAN LUCAS CANNERY
GOATFISH—A ROMAN DELIGHT

[When this 1957 trip was taken, Cabo San Lucas was a fish camp of about 300 people who made a living either by working in the cannery described by John Steinbeck on his 1940 trip around the peninsula, or by catching fish to be canned in it.

The first "cannery" at Cabo San Lucas arrived about 1913 in the form of a factory ship that was kept anchored in the semi-exposed outer harbor; the present-day "inner harbor" did not exist at that time. There was only an occasionally-flooded salt flat that was not dredged out to create the present harbor until 1974-1975.

In 1932 a permanent cannery building was constructed, along with the small landing and fueling dock mentioned in the following story.

When Ray, Frank Dufresne and Guillermo "Bill" Escudero arrived at this cannery pier in early 1957, they did not happen to meet the facility's plant manager, a native of Ribadesella, Spain, who had arrived from Mexico City just the previous year to take over his new post with Impresas Pando.

That young man was Luis Bulnes Molleda, and he and Ray would later become good friends as Bulnes built the Hotel Finisterra in partnership with Luis Cóppola Bonillas, and later the Hotel Solmar on the rocky point at the very tip of Baja California.

In 1957, the fish population around the cannery pier of Cabo San Lucas had benefited from decades of feeding on dumped offal refuse from the canning operation. An enormous density of resident fish had built up beneath the pier, and migratory predators moved in daily to feed on them. Given the natural richness of the surrounding area— with or without a cannery—the underwater scene beneath the pier must have been fantastic indeed.]

Three-thousand tons of fish within sight is what we saw at Cape San Lucas. Among them were such vast numbers of goatfish as would have sent the citizenry of ancient Rome diving off the wharf.

The productivity of food supply for the fishes in this area is supplemented or enhanced by the enormous amount of fish scraps discharged into the water from a tuna cannery. Just how so many fish can make a living in such a compact mass taxes the imagination.

Here they come in layers, each species according to its preferred depth. On the bottom we found a solid-appearing blanket of mullet, so thick as to obliterate the white, sandy floor. I was surprised to find the goatfish (usually considered a bottom-feeder) forming a surface layer. Three other distinct species occupied intermediate depths.

When we looked down into this sardine-like pack for more than 30 seconds we would see avenues appear in lightning-like streaks. A split-second later a rampaging big game fish would rocket down the middle of the clearing. Once I saw a straggler or confused goatfish fail to get the message in time. Although I know it must have gone down the gullet of the big fish, it appeared to disappear like a sleight of hand trick.

Just why a goatfish is so greatly prized, I'm not up to as yet. The Romans, especially around Nero's time, went overboard for this little fish with the two beard-like barbels. They called it "mulla" (meaning a stylish red shoe), from which we get the scientific name *Mullidae* for the goatfish family.

Rome's top brass raised goatfish artificially. One big-shot had a tunnel cut through a mountain to divert sea water into a low basin for the sole purpose of raising goatfish. In keeping with the popular cultural pastime of the period of watching Christians and gladiators get killed, the most elegant of the citizenry took great delight (or pretended to) in watching the goatfish die on the table before having it cooked. During the death throes it goes through a series of prismatic color spasms from silver to crimson red, gradually becoming pale after the demise. They always had the goatfish in sauce made of its own entrails. It may be the lack of this sauce is why the cooked goatfish doesn't "send" me.

We viewed the great field of fish from a pier projecting out from the cannery. On the end of the structure a gang of young boys were fishing especially for their favorite food fish, the sierra—the largest I had seen anywhere. They would first snag a smaller fish, then cut it into strip-bait, using a method employed all around Mexico's Pacific Coast, a hook on a hand-line which they would twirl cowboy fashion and cast out. They would then begin a series of short jerks keeping the baited hook near the surface until it was retrieved or until a fierce slashing sierra latched on.

I joined them and the spinning tackle I used created quite a sensation. When I cast a lure out and hooked a sizable sierra and allowed it to run, they started an uproar cheering me on like an Oklahoma U. rooting section. They couldn't believe that a sierra could be landed on such a small line (12-pound test monofilament).

One little muchacho hooked a fish too big to handle.

Spence Murray's boat, *Peggy Sue*, at the old Cabo cannery pier, 1960. — PHOTO BY RALPH POOLE

He tried to get leverage by holding the line across his fanny and leaning back on it with all his weight. Nevertheless he was being dragged toward the end of the rail-less wharf. He showed no thought of letting the fish go. Then just as he was about to be plunged into the water 20 feet below, another lad about his own size grabbed him by the back of his shirt collar. A strange and exciting tug-o'-war contest followed as they repeatedly gained a few feet then were pulled to the edge again. The little guy in the middle was getting a royal stretching both from the fish end and from his amigo who was having to choke him to save him.

When the little fellow finally got the big fish on deck he not only clubbed his catch with a vengeance but hurled abusive oaths at it in the process. He blamed the spotted diablo for all the pain he had suffered in his neck—and butt. — RAY CANNON

SALLY LIGHTFOOT
THE INFAMOUS BAJA GUILLOTINE CRAB

[The comic frustration of trying to catch these wary, quick-footed Sally Lightfoot crabs was also recounted in detail by John Steinbeck.

Of note is the description of year-round fish densities—keeping in mind that this visit took place in the month of January—and also the annual spring yellowtail migration from the area outside Bahía Magdalena into the Cortez.

The Sally Lightfoot crab incident occurred along the sandy beaches on the outside of the rocky point that forms the extreme tip of Baja California. This area is just south of today's Hotel Solmar.]

From the top of the knoll near the cannery you can look out to your right across the Pacific and see surging schools of migrating fishes. Turn to your left and look beyond the massive concentration in the bay and you will see white geysers shoot high above the surface. That would be jumping billfish, manta rays, dolphinfish, or blowing whales; more often all of them working the rich feeding grounds at the same time.

There seems to be an endless chain of billfish moving in and out of this area. They are just about as plentiful in July as in December. Although yellowtail move down from Magdalena Bay, around the Cape and on up the Gulf to the Midriff during the summer, most of the other 350 fishes of special interest to anglers are regular boarders.

It was here at Cabo (Cape) San Lucas that the forces of the earth-shaking upheavals creating the arm and hand of the Baja California Peninsula weakened. The index finger, pointing out toward the equatorial Galapagos, stood out in bold relief. The mighty currents of the Pacific surged back and forth and with the aid of chubascos, tore at the mountainous index finger. After 40-million years, the dissected joints of the finger still hold.

Fishing in the narrow passages between these "joints"

The Sally Lightfoot crab.

is an awe-inspiring experience. Especially in a small outboard skiff. When close in, the enormous height and breadth of the sea-chiseled obelisks make man and boat look the size of ants floating on an oat husk. My fishing partner, *Field & Stream's* Frank Dufresne remarked that we seemed small enough to get lost in the sea foam.

On the "knuckle" not yet detached we went ashore to try casting from a narrow, sandy beach. After trying our lures with little success, we thought of making bait of some small crabs we saw romping across the sand.

Nothing—but nothing—on the entire trip plagued us more than these ornery, satanic creatures. Both of us had collected, trapped, and gathered crabs around two oceans and two continents and had been clawed and bitten by them, but none equaled this razor-packin', ink-spittin', Devil's spawn of the beach. We added a long and unprintable checklist of invective before we admitted complete and total defeat.

Frank was the first to suggest we try a crab as bait and casually started to pick one up, but as he bent over, the thing evaded him like a bullfighter, moving to one side in a split second as Frank snatched a handful of sand. He made pass after pass at the darting crustacean. He tried his cap and failed, but when he finally started to use his jacket as a flailing blanket, the crab took off and actually out-ran Frank across the soft sand. He tried sneaking tactics, but when he peeked over the concealing sand mound, the dastardly, bastardly object of his frantic pursuit had vanished. The voodoo-hoodoo caused him to turn to me with—"That infernal cangrejo is a son-of-a-bitch witch."

I joined in and launched a campaign on another one. I noticed that it seemed to look me right in the eye and that when I shifted my head ever so slightly to one side the crab would move in the opposite direction. It was most versatile. It could move forward, backward or to either side with equal speed. I allowed time to escape behind a mound and tracked it down. The spoor was quite distinct and led me to a circle that was hardly distinguishable in the sand. I scooped it out and quickly grabbed it by the back end (the conventional way of grabbing crabs), but this one was a contortionist. It reached over with a double-jointed claw leg and performed a neat biopsy on my thumb as clean and deep as if using a new Gillette blade.

Frank now had finally brought one to bay, smacked it with a club, picked it up in his cap and shoved it into his coat pocket. When he was ready to use it as a bait, he reached in for it and got his hand clawed and sliced as if a bobcat had worked on it.

We eventually learned to handle the crabs with pliers.

We were keeping them in handkerchiefs in our pants pockets to avoid their finger-slicing claws. We didn't know then that they could also discharge an indelible red "ink."

As I was baiting up, Frank noticed that my light tan colored pants were soaked and running with "blood" from my crotch down. He yelled that the crabs were about to turn me into a eunuch!

I then saw that his clean white jacket and slacks were streaked also.

We took inventory and discovered that the crabs we had laboriously captured had evened their score of revenge by discharging quantities of red indelible ink over us. My fishing jacket has gone through three laundries and still looks blood-stained.

Frank and I voted this crab the vilest creature of its size on this planet. The bait payoff was—not a single nibble. Frank said: "Fish may be dumb but they are not as stupid as some people." — RAY CANNON

From the hills the road runs close along the shore. At the mouth of a small arroyo we saw a herd of wild ass digging holes three to four feet deep to get fresh water.

The pitahaya cactus was in full fruit, the most delicious of Baja's wild fruits. We stuffed ourselves on them. The giant pipe organ cardón and barrel cactus were just blooming, as were most every other plant in this interesting wilderness.

The town site of Todos Santos is glamorized by contrast to the vast wilderness of the surrounding territory, where wild vegetation is limited by lack of rainfall. Here the cacti and thorn-bearing shrubs grow 15 or 20 feet high, thrive and mat up to form a jungle. Sugar cane, bananas, coconuts and all sorts of tropical fruits and flowers all but smother this ancient, rustic town. The night mists carry the scintillating aromas from millions of blooming things to perfume the countryside.

We found an outdoor dance pavilion and cantina crowded with the local younger set, whooping it up. It was a romantic play place engulfed in towering mango trees, date, cocoa palms, and surrounded with flourishing vegetation.

Our only regret in making this detour was in not scheduling enough time for Todos Santos and its very important citizen Señor Carlos Gil Hinojosa, operator of the Planta Piloto "Santa Anita," a commercial fish processing plant.

The bulk of the product is a superior "salt codfish" for the South American market. "Codfish?" you ask. But there are no codfish within a couple of thousand miles of the place.

One taste of Señor Hinojosa's "salt cod" and everyone agrees that it is the best ever. The fact that the clean, transparent fillets were cut from shark is one of the reasons

EARLY TODOS SANTOS

[After visiting Cabo San Lucas, Ray, Dufresne and Escudero drove up the winding dirt road to the Pacific coastal town of Todos Santos. It would be another 30 years before the Todos Santos road was paved and linked to La Paz. In these combined fragments, Ray gives a good early portrait of the Pacific coastal town long before it was "discovered" by its present-day expatriate community.]

This is a preview, a peak into the future at a place yet to be discovered… Check back on this prediction a year or so hence, for it is inevitable that any place in Baja California with all the potentials to be found in Todos Santos is sure to attract thousands just as soon as the word gets out.

The dirt road from Cabo San Lucas to Todos Santos (56 miles) has been kept in fairly good shape. It runs through tall thickets of cacti, mesquite, and flowering thorn bushes, passing an occasional century-old ranch house.

Ray fishing at Todos Santos with a tarp over his shoulders to ward off the Pacific mists. — PHOTO BY HERB BERSIN

Rancho Buena Vista skipper Nicandro "Nico" Cota León with Ray's Penn 349 reel and Sila-Flex rod in 1966. Cota was born in San Bartolo in 1931. When he first arrived at the Rancho Buena Vista resort looking for work, Eugene Walters refused to hire him because of the big bushy beard he had grown while fishing with his family at Bahía Magdalena. The recently retired Army colonel said he wasn't going to hire anyone that looked like Fidel Castro. On the advice of young Bobby Van Wormer, Cota shaved the beard off, and was hired. Cota's first client as a skipper was Ray Cannon. He remembers that Ray offered him half of a ham and cheese sandwich for lunch, and not being familiar with such "gringo" food, he threw it overboard when Ray wasn't looking. Cota recalls that Ray liked to fish twice a day, always near shore, trolling small white feathers or small strip-baits, and he liked to catch different types of small fish. Ray was "always chatting" in the boat, and they fished for two or three hours at a time, from Punta Pescadero to Cabo Pulmo. Cota is the man gaffing the marlin in the photograph on page 191 of *The Sea Of Cortez*.

for its goodness but the prime factor is found in the processing.

The firm's fleet of skiffs are kept busy fishing shark and there is no waste.

The skin is made into a super-fine leather; internals into fertilizer; the flesh into "codfish"; the teeth are made use of as ornaments; and even the liquids serve as a chum when they are washed down and emptied into the ocean, attracting fish right up close to shore.

Planta Santa Anita's smoked sierra department is supplied with fish in a most astonishing manner. Three teenage boys standing on a shore rock just above the high tide line catch enough fish with hand-lines to supply and keep busy the entire factory with its assembly line of 30 workers.

These boys use a strip-bait cut from the belly of a sierra to catch sierra. They cast it out about 30 or 40 feet and start a fast retrieve. At the first strike they give line for about a second and a half, then set the hook.

Although there is no unison of action, it is not unusual to see three sierras performing their exciting leaps at one and the same time.

Even though these lads work at this from daylight 'till mid-afternoon, day after day, they seem to lose none of their enthusiasm, which is expressed in yips and yells as if they were catching the first fish of their lives.

As soon as the sierra is hauled in, it is tossed back to the bank of a stream where seven old men work feverishly cleaning the fish. Carriers then rush cordwood-like bundles of them to the factory in a hundred-yard dash.

Frank and I joined the boys on the rock with our spinning equipment and got into some of the fastest fishing either of us had ever experienced. Every now and then a 30-pound yellowtail would get mixed up with the sierra and almost drag us off the rock before we could realize what we had on.

About 2 p.m. when the prevailing wind came up, we saw the dugout shark fleet coming in. — RAY CANNON

PUTTING IT ALL TOGETHER

[Ray returned from his first exploration around the southern tip of Baja knowing that he had discovered something really "big" that would fill his columns and dreams for the rest of his life. Shortly after his return to Los Angeles, he put it all together in the following column.]

MARCH 15, 1957—Having finally assembled all the notes on my recent trip around the lower end of the Baja Peninsula I find myself sitting on the biggest fishing news story ever reported.

Now that I have been able to bring the whole coastal waters of Baja into focus, the picture overshadows all other regions by far. With the exception of some northern forms just about every saltwater species found around this continent has a counterpart here—with more than a hundred others found no place else in the world. Many found elsewhere grow larger in these waters and seem more ferocious with strange and different habits. But most astonishing is the abundance of them that surge up and down the Gulf, along its shores and into its bays and coves.

Space in this or any other publication will not permit giving the whole story at once but I will attempt to give you the high and low-lights a piece at a time.

Don't get the idea that I think I've seen everything. I haven't even got the lay of the coastline yet, much less the jolting surprises I'm apt to find in some of the weird and awesome places.

Except for a few sport boat operators, the natives are unaware of the magnitude of the fishing potential. They catch a select few favorite food and marketable fishes and ignore or despise others as nuisances. Therefore little or no technique for catching many of the favored game fishes has been developed, much less estimates of their abundance or habitats.

I am making considerable progress in appraising and learning to catch this long checklist of game fishes but I need additional helpers to meet the challenge, the greatest yet to face the angler.

With all the new developments planned below the border there are vast areas and opportunities for adventure and discovery. And these begin just outside of the cities and towns. We hardly stopped at a spot that didn't provide a storybook episode of a never-before-reported occurrence. Some staggering in scope, numbers or sizes; others—the little things like the crabs at San Lucas that defeated us in hand-to-claw battle when we tried desperately to catch them for bait; or the 12-year-old who talked like a sage but guided us halfway up a mountain for trout that turned

Nicandro "Nico" Cota León at his home in Los Barriles, 1998.
— PHOTO BY GENE KIRA

out to be "water dogs" (salamanders).

It seemed that wherever we turned we ran smack into new or exciting adventure. Even the wild animals were different—bobcats' legs were too long, old deer too small, and the wild and vicious boar was a razorback that took to the bush a hundred years ago. No question about it, we were in a foreign country a century and a world away from the one we have known.

If all this seems exaggerated, wait 'till you read some of the detail coming in future columns and see the pictures. Better yet, wait 'till you see it yourself and you will be telling me. — RAY CANNON

ON THE DEATH OF HERB TANSEY

[Suddenly, Herb Tansey was gone, killed in the crash of his Ercoupe airplane while trying to fly from La Paz to Rancho Buena Vista. Following is the text of the initial press release written by Guillermo "Bill" Escudero on the plane crash that killed both Tansey and Arthur Young, an employee of the resort. In the months immediately following the tragedy, a chain of events was put into motion that would eventually result in the purchase of Rancho Buena Vista by Colonel Eugene Walters.]

LA PAZ, BAJA CALIFORNIA JANUARY 13, 1959—On January the 5th, at around 8 p.m., Herb Tansey, Manager and operator of Rancho Buena Vista, and his Assistant,

Mr. Arthur Young, were instantly killed when their small Ercoupe crashed into the "Quien Sabe" (Who Knows) mountain 1 1/2 miles west of El Triunfo, ghost mining town, population 503, elevation 1850 ft., after they had been flying around apparently lost since shortly after their takeoff from the La Paz Airport at 05:35 p.m. bound for Buena Vista which is only 35 minutes flying distance.

It is believed that fog enveloped them soon after their departure and that for that reason they flew 2:25 (two hours and twenty-five minutes) trying to find their bearings. It is also understood that before taking off they were seen drinking, but the situation did not seem serious enough to prevent them from flying.

This loss has been deeply felt around here as Herb Tansey was very well liked and known for his generosity. The details are as follows:

Takeoff time was at 05:35 p.m.

Crash occurred at 08:00 p.m.

Plane was reported heard between 05:35 and 08:00 p.m. at La Ribera and later heard over San Bartolo heading for La Paz.

Rescue crew of 25 men selected and organized by acting Delegado de Gobierno at El Triunfo (Mayor) Second Lieutenant Fernado Ramírez immediately after crash was reported 1 1/2 miles west of El Triunfo worked their way in search of plane using improvised "hachones" made of dry pitahaya shoots.

Search ended at 01:00 a.m. January 6 when wrecked plane was found with the two mutilated bodies in it.

A careful search around the area produced 1900.00 pesos in five and ten peso bills, golden bridge of Tansey's teeth, watch belonging to Tansey, watch belonging to Arthur, a toilet set, one electric razor and a cigarette lighter.

Bodies were removed from wreckage and carried in improvised stretchers down the mountainside to the Village's Mayor's office and there a wake was set up, candles lighted and flowers deposited over the bodies.

Upon arrival of the investigating officials from La Paz and Herb's Staff Manager at Buena Vista, Robert Van Wormer, the bodies were searched for papers and personal items and all of these items were turned over to Robert Van Wormer and bodies transferred to La Paz for Official examination and embalmment at the request of Van Wormer representing next of kin.

On January 10 and in the presence of Mrs. Herb Tansey and no kin representing Arthur Young, burial rites (Protestant for Tansey and Catholic for Young) were performed on a hill overlooking Buena Vista Ranch in compliance with Tansey's wish in life to be buried there if he died in Buena Vista.

The local press gave the people of El Triunfo a very high praise and recommendation for their cooperative spirit and honesty plus their kindness, mentioning the fact that nowadays when plane accidents occur in isolated areas it is common to read of the dishonesty of some natives. [Signed] Bill Escudero

BOBBY VAN WORMER RETURNS TO MANAGE RANCHO BUENA VISTA

[During the early days at Rancho Buena Vista, Herb Tansey's young assistant was enthusiastic skin diver, Robert "Bobby" Van Wormer, who helped Ray's research by making underwater observations.

Bobby was born in Craig, Missouri in 1925, and he made his first trip to Rancho Buena Vista on December 31, 1956 at the instigation of his brother Frank. By March 1958, he been captivated by the area, and he went to work for Colonel Walters at a salary of $100 per week.

Bobby also had a boat at that time, a 21-foot cruiser that he had shipped to La Paz in kit form and assembled on the beach at Rancho Buena Vista with help from his father. But money at the Ranch was tight, and when Colonel Walters needed to lay off some help, Bobby laid himself off instead and went to work for Johnny Mitre, who had just built the Bahía de Palmas. After Herb Tansey died in 1959, Bobby was hired back to manage Rancho Buena Vista for Colonel Walters, which he did until he and his wife Rosa María "Cha Cha" Ruiz Gonzales opened the Hotel Punta Colorada in 1966. In 1973, he and Cha Cha took over the Bahía de Palmas when Johnny Mitre's lease ran out, and they renamed it the Hotel Palmas de Cortez. Then, in 1994, they bought the Hotel Playa del Sol and renamed *it* the Hotel Playa Hermosa.]

Robert "Bobby" Van Wormer. As a young diver at Rancho Buena Vista in the early 1950s, he helped Ray take photographs and research fishing methods for the area.

FEBRUARY 1959—In response to the flood of inquiries on the La Paz area, more especially on conditions at Rancho Buena Vista since the passing of Herb Tansey, I

Noontime shade at Rancho Buena Vista, February 1964.

have just checked with Bobby Van Wormer, now managing the Buena Vista Lodge.

His report on the crazy fishing in the Bay sent my blood pressure missiling. The most staggering was his account of six big wahoo being caught, and only a few hundred yards from shore.

Bobby also told of a black marlin battle that even tops the Herb Jenks tussle. It seems a neighboring rancher, fishing a couple of hundred yards offshore for small fish for a family dinner, tied into a huge black. His family and neighbors watched from the beach as he fought the contest of his life in a small dugout canoe, using a 100-yard-long hand-line. His victory in beaching the monster was acclaimed only because his fish weighed more than 650 pounds!

Roberto, as the natives call him, is the only person I have ever known who could fill the vast emptiness left by Tansey. The two personalities were quite similar, especially in their love of humor and warm and sincere friendliness.

Bobby, 32 years old, is an educated Missouri farmer. He seems a lot more Irish than the name Van Wormer suggests. He was making great strides in the electronics and missile field, but when he saw Buena Vista he forgot to go back.

Tansey not only took him on as his assistant but made a brother of him. The native workers, without an exception, transferred their deep love for Tansey to Bobby and are making his job a very pleasant and easy one.

On a visit to see me last week, Bobby assured me that the policy of fun and freedom will continue and that he will carry out all of the elaborate improvements scheduled

for completion within a month. He further reports that the neighboring Bahía de Palmas to be managed by Johnny Mitre will be opened by April 1, and that the two lodges will be cooperating very closely. — RAY CANNON

COLONEL WALTERS TAKES COMMAND

[Ray announces the change of command as Colonel Eugene Walters assumes ownership of Rancho Buena Vista. In later years, management of the Ranch would pass first into the hands of Colonel Walters' son, Charles "Chuck" Walters, then to his grandson, Mark Walters.]

MAY 1959—The purchase of the Lodge by Walters from Herb Tansey's widow is official. Anglers who know Herb and loved the place will be happy that it is in such good hands. I have spent many happy weeks fishing and traveling around the whole south end of the Baja Peninsula with Gene and can think of no better personality, sportsman and genial host for Buena Vista than this happy-go-lucky friend. What's more, he is keeping Bobby Van Wormer as manager, assisted by Joe Benales and all the skippers, crews and hands anglers liked so well. — RAY CANNON

GOOD DAYS AT RANCHO BUENA VISTA

[By the time this article was written in 1961, Rancho Buena Vista was a leading resort of the Golden Age, with a clientele that included movie stars and even former presidents. Here, former President Eisenhower just misses a hot marlin bite in March 1961, at a time when fishing seasons throughout Baja were generally longer than they are today.

Also mentioned in this column are Burt Twilegar and Lou Kicker of *Western Outdoor News* and Dr. Boyd Walker of UCLA, with whom Ray had just made an unsuccessful trip to Isla Cerralvo in an effort to get scientific confirmation of Ray's observation of the "intelligent" prey-herding behavior of the golden grouper.]

MARCH 1961—The largest spring run of marlin in the history of this resort blitzkrieged this bay the day Dr. Walker and I arrived back from our expedition to Cerralvo Island.

The fish crowded the water from Punta Pescadero to Cabo Pulmo, from 3 1/2 miles off shore to the horizon beyond. As many as eight marlin were seen at a time working a small school of sardines.

Every cruiser at the lodge, plus a couple of skiffs, were out after them. Most of the anglers aboard them had all the big game fishing they wanted for the day and were back at the lodge in time for lunch.

All but four of the 28 guests were catching their first marlin in this region. Most of them the first ever. You can

In 1974, Rancho Buena Vista's top tag and release skippers with awards presented by National Marine Fisheries biologist James L. Squire Jr. From left: Jesús Araiza, Lino Perez, Manuel Araiza, hotel owner Colonel Eugene Walters, and hotel manager, Ted Bonney.

— COURTESY MARK WALTERS

Charles Milton "Chuck" Walters working on his sculpture of Ray, at Rancho Buena Vista, c. 1979. Walters was a Navy fighter pilot in World War II, and operated the resort in conjunction with his father, Colonel Eugene Walters. He died of cancer at his home in nearby La Capilla in May 1981, and is buried beside Herb Tansey and Arthur Young on the hill above the Ranch. — COURTESY WESTERN OUTDOOR NEWS

Mark Walters, with hotel guest Nina Hazard at Rancho Buena Vista in July 1971. Walters became the third generation of his family to manage Rancho Buena Vista when he assumed responsibility for day-to-day operations after the death of his father, Chuck.

— COURTESY NINA HAZARD

Ray's famous "Round House" shown under construction at Rancho Buena Vista, October 1968. When the building was completed the following year, Ray paid Colonel Eugene Walters $3,000 for a 9-year 11-month lease, renewable for life.

imagine the whooping-it-up ruckus as they exchanged exciting experiences. As for the host of native workers at the lodge, they were gay as the guests.

To make the festive spirit complete, lodge operator Gene Walters ordered a "roast goat" fiesta. This is actually a barbecued kid and is one of the most delectable foods ever, the way natives prepare it.

Many of the guests who planned a three-day stopover here are staying on for two or three weeks. Having caught their marlin, most of them are now going out for the other big game fishes.

In addition to the super-abundant roosterfish, yellowfin tuna, skipjack, giant needlefish and jack crevalle, amberjack and dolphinfish are showing. Wahoo and black marlin should be appearing by May 1.

The water is crawling with lesser game such as tenpounder (ladyfish), green jack, cabrilla, grouper, mero de Chino, and triggerfish, with sierra and the whole checklist due in soon. Most of these can be caught within two or three-hundred feet from the cabaña doors.

It was unfortunate that a number of notables visiting here got away just before the big marlin run.

Ex-President Eisenhower did get some out-of-this-world dove hunting while here and my bosses, Burt Twilegar and Lou Kicker, did tie into a few marlin and farm 'em. — RAY CANNON

RAY'S RBV "ROUND HOUSE"

[Ray's first known record of the "Round House," under construction by Colonel Eugene Walters at Rancho Buena Vista. The residence was completed in 1969.]

SEPTEMBER 23, 1966—Col. Eugene Walters, operator of Rancho Buena Vista, has just returned from a short vacation visiting old friends in Germany, where he served as U.S. Provincial Governor after the war.

One of the reasons for his stopover in L.A. was to discuss plans for building my house at the resort.

He says he has the resort running automatically (I claim it has always run by itself), and that he will retire as soon as I move there; and that we'll take his best boat, a couple of good skippers, and take off for long voyages, spending our time visiting people at forgotten ranch houses, unique coves, bays, islands, and study land and sea life. He will paint them (he is a real fine artist) while I compose prose of the quaint, beautiful, and exciting things.

And do you know what? These delightful dreams will most likely come true. Soon. — RAY CANNON

A Flying Sportsmen Lodge DC-3, c. 1969, with copilot Guillermo "Memo" Chávez, left, and Bertha and Ed Tabor. Bertha, in stewardess uniform, flew while expecting the Tabor's first daughter, Susan, who also flew along in a bassinet after she was born in 1967. A second daughter, Sonia, would be born in 1978. — COURTESY BERTHA TABOR

The Flying Sportsmen Lodge, December 1972. — PHOTO BY HARRY MERRICK

AIRLINE FOR LORETO

ED TABOR'S FLYING SPORTSMEN LODGE

ED TABOR LOVED to tease the children of Loreto.

In the early 1950s, as he descended in his "PBY" amphibious seaplane over the quiet Mexican town on the Sea of Cortez, he would fly low over the beach, making the children think he intended to land on the water. They would come running over the hot sand in their bare feet to meet the American's plane. But then, Ed would climb up again and descend over the flats behind the town, and the children would have to run that way. Back and forth, he made them run, over and over, until he decided to let them off the hook and allow them to meet his plane.

What Ed didn't know at the time was that within that crowd of blister-footed children was his future wife, little 12-year-old Bertha Davis Verdugo, whom he would marry 15 years later in 1965, and with whom he would operate one of the most famous fishing resorts of Baja California—the legendary Flying Sportsmen Lodge.

Tabor was used to people running to meet his plane.

Born a Catholic in Salt Lake City in 1917, he moved with his family to California, and at only 17 years old, he was already a young businessman who bought a biplane without his parents' knowledge, using money that he had made by installing the first car radios for the police force of Woodland, California, near Sacramento.

He took flying lessons on the sly, and—apparently quite confident of his new skills—he took off on his first flight in the new plane with his grandmother as a cockpit passenger.

The first knowledge Ed Tabor's parents had of his flying activities was the sight of Ed and grandma in the biplane as they buzzed the house. According to future wife, Bertha, Ed kept telling his grandmother to wave so his parents would know everything was all right.

Unfortunately, the plane ran out of gas, and Ed and his grandmother were forced to crash-land in a tomato field owned by some Chinese farmers who lived nearby. The farmers came running and screaming, and made Ed pay for the tomatoes he had flattened.

By the time he was 23 years old, Ed was living in a hotel in San Francisco and was making good money as a radio broadcaster with his own show, "Tabor Topics," on which he interviewed famous movie stars and other celebrities.

During World War II, he was a civilian contractor, flying cargo and ferrying aircraft for the military, and after the war, he moved to New York and—still only about 30 years old— he used his radio money to start Tabor Luxury Airlines, with six war surplus DC-3s running between New York and Puerto Rico.

About 1950, Ed sold his airline business and discovered Baja California by chance, and in Loreto he fell in love with

Ray and Ed Tabor at the Flying Sportsmen Lodge, in 1966.

Sleepy downtown Loreto, 1959. — PHOTO BY HARRY MERRICK

both the Sea of Cortez and the woman who would be his wife from 1965 until his death in 1987.

Bertha Davis Verdugo was one of the famous "Davis Girls" of Loreto, whose names seem to appear in nearly every old story about the town. She began working for the Flying Sportsmen Lodge as a secretary, and after she and Ed were married, she helped run the revolutionary fly-in fishing resort that used its own mini-airline to bring clients from Southern California. She flew as a stewardess on their airplanes, even when she was pregnant with their first daughter, Susan, who also flew along in a bassinet after she was born.

After its gradual opening in late 1951 and early 1952, the Flying Sportsmen Lodge quickly grew famous, as Ed Tabor used a biplane at first, then his PBY seaplane, a converted B-25 bomber, and finally, DC-3s to bring anglers not only to Loreto, but also to Magdalena Bay at San Carlos, where he built a six-bungalow complex to house them, and even to San José del Cabo, where he would land the PBY on the water and rent canoes to fish on the open Pacific. (The B-25 bomber eventually ended its career in a spectacular way when it was sold as a movie prop and shot down in flames for the 1970 production of *Catch-22*, which was filmed on location near Guaymas).

About 1973, Aeroméxico began direct flights to Loreto, and the Tabors sold the DC-3s—which they had bought in partnership with Enrique Ortega's International Travel Service—to Raúl Aréchiga of Aerocalifornia. Ed and Bertha moved to San Diego and began promoting the business with

travelogue films, leaving on-site manager Fidencio Pérpuli to run day-to-day operations in Loreto.

The Flying Sportsmen Lodge became very successful, with eight telephone operators filling planes for Aeroméxico, but in 1980 a series of unresolvable legal disputes began with the local ejido, and the property was liquidated in 1982.

Ed and Bertha Tabor continued to produce travelogue films and operate a travel agency in San Diego, specializing in Hawaii, Mazatlán and Baja California. But the famous lodge on the beach, with its small concrete and stone pier, and its pioneering role in the history of Baja California's Golden Age, was sold off in two separate parcels and ceased to operate as a sport fishing business.

Following here are some of Ray's best columns—of the many that he wrote—about the historic mission town of Loreto and Ed Tabor's Flying Sportsmen Lodge.

GOTTA MARRY A "DAVIS GIRL"

[Ray's humorous piece on the ubiquitous "Davis" family name of Loreto. Ed Tabor's "Davis" bride was Bertha Davis Verdugo, whom he married on October 11, 1965.]

JUNE 19, 1969—Having a Loreto "Davis" girl for a wife may not be absolutely necessary to owning a hotel in this oldest of pueblos in all of the Californias, but so far the proof is in their favor.

The two established resorts, and one uptown inn now

Looking west from the Loreto mission bell tower, October 1959. — PHOTO BY HARRY MERRICK

operating, and two hotels within three or four months of completion, plus another planned resort, have all got "Davis" women as first mates, or skippers.

Ed Tabor, pioneer resort operator of the Baja California Territory, tried getting along without a Davis, but after years of struggle, cleared the decks, married a beautiful member of the clan, and prospered greatly. They will close August 1 to renovate the whole place and try to make their Flying Sportsmen Lodge the most up-to-date in the region.

Gloria Davis was among my first friends in Loreto. She married Bill Benziger, my Tambobiche shipwreck

The Flying Sportsmen Lodge, 1966. — PHOTO BY MARTIN GOLDSMITH

companion. They own and personally manage the delightful Hotel Oasis. They are talking of adding more rooms and more boats.

Stella Davis (divorced) has the uptown Posada, a neat little inn of five, spic-and-span rooms. Prices are held to the old rates of $7.50 per day, meals included. Al Green's angling cruisers are available for her guests.

I took the very merry and young divorcée to the Flying Sportsmen's and had the houseful of fishermen gaping when I pretended Stella was my local girlfriend. She played the part so well I became almost convinced and am not exactly sure now.

A visit with Dr. Enoch Arias and his Señora Davis Arias, proved highly informative. Their big, deluxe Hotel Misión de Loreto, now being rushed to completion, will have 65 elegant rooms and suites. It is close to the new pier and dock where small boats take on gas and other supplies.

Hearing that there would likely be a shortage of rooms in the Loreto region, the Dr. (a swell guy) proceeded to build a second resort and dock, Hotel Baja, about seven miles above town, or parallel with Isla Coronado. We took a picnic lunch to the new rustic resort and passed it up for a bushel of clams baked on an open fire. We also cruised to and went ashore on the very grotesque north end of Isla Coronado. Light-tackle shore casters would have gone bug-eyed at the swarms of game fishes seen almost underfoot from the tide-high ledges around the island.

The next resort will be built at Nopoló, according to

owner Al Green, also married to a "Davis" girl.

Spaces for seaside hotels are getting scarce in Loreto, but there are several more "Davis" cousins, all charming, so if you hurry, who knows? — RAY CANNON

THE GREAT CHUBASCO OF '59

[Ray puts as positive a spin as possible on the damage caused by the great chubasco of 1959. The destruction from this storm would not be exceeded until Hurricane Liza of 1976.]

LORETO—This town is in the throes of rebirth. Floods resulting from the recent chubasco gave it the most violent baptism for more than half a century. Most of the palm-thatched and some of the old adobe dwellings were wrecked. Stone and brick structures were little damaged. However, half the cabañas of the very popular Flying Sportsmen Lodge were hit. All boats were beached but five have already been recommissioned, as are the damaged bungalows, with capacity for 30 people. During reconstruction everything around the place is being painted and smartened up.

The lodge and boats are already more attractive than ever and everything is being readied for the fall run of big game fishes. Dolphinfish, needlefish, jacks and numerous small game fishes are back in the channel now, with billfish showing just off Isla Carmen. Ed Tabor is making favorable changes in management and staff.

With all the rebuilding and general cleanup job now in progress, the town looks far more attractive to me than ever.

Mulegé took an even worse beating. Club Mulegé Lodge lost its ugly adobe front. In rebuilding, Salazar is adding ten new units, complete with modern facilities. Improvements that have long been needed. Sal has set a deadline for November 15 for reopening, just in time for the host of anglers going after the world record size snook that choke the river from now 'till June.

The sombrero-shaped point at the mouth of the Mulegé River is now an island but the washed out gap will likely be refilled by high tide wave action within a month or so.

Except for the destruction of outlying palm-thatched shacks, washed out roads and toppled trees, La Paz suffered little damage. Half of the great spreading India laurel trees along the waterfront and streets were blown down but most all of them have been trimmed back and reset. About a fourth of the towering coconut palms were broken off.

Numerous crews are busy repairing the old road which runs the length of the Baja California peninsula. At present it is impassible in the central sector. All main roads leading south from La Paz are now passable. Damage to lodges in the south end was slight. A few boats were given

Ed, daughter Susan, and Bertha Tabor aboard their boat, the *Pescador*, c. 1974. — COURTESY BERTHA TABOR

Damaged cruisers at the Flying Sportsmen Lodge, 1959.

— PHOTO BY HARRY MERRICK

Ray and Flying Sportsmen guide Ricardo "Caldillo" Romero.

This small cove, now the 14th hole of the Nopoló golf course south of Loreto, was one of Ray's favorite places for both fishing and photography. This photo was a candidate to be used on the front cover of *The Sea Of Cortez*.

— PHOTO BY HARRY MERRICK

a beating but most of them have been repaired.

The central sector seemed to have taken the brunt of the chubasco. Thirty-seven people were reported dead or missing among the inland villages and ranches. Very few of the domestic fowls and animals caught in the flooded arroyos were killed but they were scattered all over and are collecting around the hundreds of new lakes left by the largest rainfall in memory of the oldest natives.

Ducks are arriving on the lakes and the prolific growth of vegetation is proving an abundant forage for wild animals. I have never seen the countryside so green and flower-covered or so alive with bird life and small creatures. — RAY CANNON

ROOSTERFISH—BARRELERS OF THE SEA

[A description of the roosterfish "barreling" phenomenon. The 114-pound world record described stands to the present day.]

NOVEMBER 20, 1974—Roosterfish run. That is the big story this week, and according to Ed and Bertha Tabor, owners of the Flying Sportsmen Lodge, "big schools of huge roosterfish are in Loreto waters and they are right on time and hungry and mean. The channel all the way from our pier to Isla Carmen is really jammed with several kinds of herrings, which gives us a guarantee of plenty of big gamesters all winter and spring."

This is the time of year for roosterfish action from the Midriff to Peru. Short migrations seem to occur twice annually. The other, in April or May, is seen more often. In both seasons, schools of large, 20 to 50-pounders can be observed "barreling," *i.e.*, moving in an abreast formation. As they break through and leapfrog to three or four feet above the surface, the mass movement can be mistaken for a breaking tidal wave.

Such displays are not apt to happen this season, as the great quantity of forage fish will make striving for it unnecessary. Baja Californians believe that the "barreling" is a method of thrashing a school of herring or other small forage animals when food is scarce.

The roosterfish, called "pez gallo" in Spanish, is known in the scientific language as *Nematistius pectoralis*. It ranges throughout the Sea of Cortez, from Bahía Vizcaíno to Peru, and at some islands of our eastern Pacific coast. It was first described by Gill of the Academy of Natural Sciences in 1862, from a specimen taken at Cabo San Lucas.

The most striking characteristic for identification is the cock's tail-like appearance of the first dorsal fin. All of the eight spines except the first are greatly pronounced, with feathery filaments. In the young the colors of this fin are alternating yellow and black bars, the yellow fading with age or when a specimen is preserved. The dark bands, used otherwise in describing the rooster, are very black and photograph so when alive and still underwater. The black bars around the head and the one resembling heavy eyebrows give this cock a violent angry appearance, especially when a big one comes dashing straight at you.

The 1960 I.G.F.A. record catch at La Paz by Abe Sackheim of San Diego of a 114-pounder still stands. Several above 135 pounds have been caught, however. I have seen three of them weighed.

The habitat of the roosterfish is seldom crowded by other large species. Its most consistent visitor (above forage size) is the sierra (also good bait for record-size fish). Both species choose a checkerboard mixture of large or solid rock with an equally wide corridor of sand between them—more ideal when near a freshwater seepage. Jack crevalle, a cousin of the roosterfish, is an occasional visitor.

The seepage usually supports a large population of minute food items for the very young rooster, also a host of larger invertebrates eaten by growing and grown roosters. Small schools of the various age groups often move over sand stretches on long distance food forays.

New techniques for taking big roosterfish change from year to year, so don't hesitate to ask residents the latest. There was a time when a white Spoofer and Pflueger-5 spoon were the hot baits, and they are still very good except in hot weather when everyone switches to ten-inch live bait. More and more anglers are turning to live bait for most large fish.

When this ferocious looking fish cracks the surface in a boil that looks like a sea belch, then rips and slashes the upheaval with his monstrous dorsal fin, some greenhorn fishermen wish they had stuck to catfish.

— RAY CANNON

LIVE BAIT EXPERIMENTS

[In the summer of 1963, Ray cruised down the Sea of Cortez with Herb and Douglas Holland in a Rolls Ryan boat specially equipped with a live bait well. The long trip, from Kino Bay to Rancho Buena Vista and back, was made for the purpose of testing the effectiveness of live bait, especially during the hot summer months, and especially on roosterfish in the southern Cortez. These and other live bait experiments were part of a gradual evolution in a Baja sport fishing industry that had previously relied mainly on whole dead baits, cut baits, and artificial lures. Colonel Eugene Walters of Rancho Buena Vista and Ed Tabor of Loreto's Flying Sportsmen Lodge were among the first to realize the importance of fishing with live bait. Within ten years after Ray's "Holland Live Bait Expedition," tanks had been installed in virtually every sport fishing cruiser in Baja. Even pangas began using live bait, and the practice is almost universal today.]

RANCHO BUENA VISTA, AUGUST 20, 1963—We lost little time in getting to Colorada and Arena Points where acres of roosterfish had been seen constantly but very few

caught. And in other areas, we could see a half-dozen follow a lure close to the boat, but no takers. As soon as the live bait was presented, however, they latched on.

When we returned with the report of our success with the roosterfish, Colonel Walters ordered the purchase of bait tanks for the fleet and the construction of a receiver.

— RAY CANNON

LIVE BAIT COMES TO LORETO

[In Loreto, Ed Tabor became equally convinced of the effectiveness of live bait. Also notable in this story is the description of illegal fishing with dynamite.]

APRIL 6, 1970—In all the years I have known Ed Tabor and all of the time I have spent with him, I have never known him to get so excited as he was on the phone today.

Ed is the operator of the Flying Sportsmen Lodge at Loreto. His exclaiming was due to the results of a big live bait test, in which skippers had to quit fishing a couple of hours early, to keep game fish counts down to legal levels. He says he will get a tagging program going so that anglers can get limits, then fish-for-science by tagging and releasing all above the legal bag allowance.

Tabor reminded me that I had been urging him to get with a live bait operation ever since I made the Cortez-length Live Bait Expedition several years ago. Said he had not expected to catch so many game fish species, some so rare they were unknown to Loreto natives.

Bill Collins, an old hand at Cortez fishing, his son Mark, and brother Chet, took one of the resort's new 36-foot cabin cruisers to Isla Catalán and ran into that school of up to 200-pound yellowfin tuna which appear to be

The Hotel Misión de Loreto in what is now downtown Loreto. The hotel, shown here in December 1972, had been opened in June 1969 by Dr. Enoch Arias Gudiño. — PHOTO BY HARRY MERRICK

Doña Blanca Verdugo Garayzar at her guesthouse near the mission of Loreto in 1964. In 1946, she and her husband, Juan "Juanito" José Garayzar, opened the first lodging facility in town and catered to distinguished professionals, scholars, and visiting dignitaries such as Territorial Governor, General Augustín Olachea. Every Christmas, Doña Blanca made a big dinner for guests and family, with pork tamales, chicken soup, and refried beans. The family also distilled a special Brandy Garayzar— known as *"leche de tigre"*— from grapes grown at the family's Rancho el Zacatal. The business closed in 1988 with the death of her daughter, Luz María "Lucha" Garayzar, who was a famous cook in her own right and winner of a *premio nacional de gastronomía* for her famous *aletas de cahuama rellenas* (stuffed turtle flippers). The building has now been demolished. — PHOTO BY HARRY MERRICK

permanent residents of Juanaloa. I have run into the school twice at Catalán and again in Puerto Gatos, near Bahía Tambobiche. The Collins family spent two days fishing Catalán and confirm everything I have written about the fishing there.

Tabor has apparently gone all-out in the live bait equipment, with a large and very expensive net, and plans to operate a big Southern California-style party boat with a live bait well. The fare will be about $12.50 per angler.

I'll get all of the details soon, as I expect to be there next week, looking over and testing everything at the other resorts as well as Tabor's place.

Last June when I was on a small boat voyage, several people on the trip saw some small commercial boats with no nets nor large quantity of hand-lines aboard, near Santa Rosalía.

Mulegé and Loreto skippers told us that those mainland commercials were using dynamite. We relayed the info to the very alert Governor Hugo Cervantes del Río. Within a week, a naval contingent with a fast boat was established at Loreto on a permanent basis. Their orders were to confiscate any boat other than a sizable freighter and throw the whole crew in jail, with a promise of stiff fines and sentences.

No one has reported a fish blasting case in the Territory's waters since. — RAY CANNON

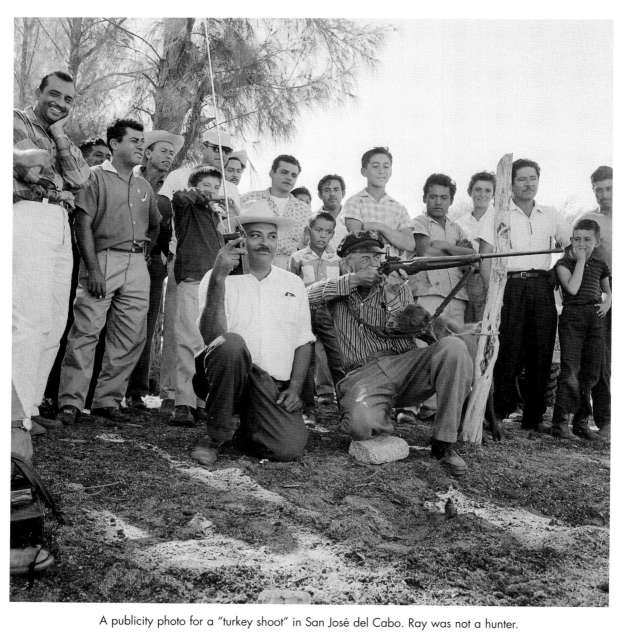

A publicity photo for a "turkey shoot" in San José del Cabo. Ray was not a hunter.

SOFT-HEARTED RAY

HUNTING IN BAJA

DESPITE HIS TENNESSEE backwoods origins, Ray was no fan of guns or hunting. Nevertheless, he dutifully wrote a few pieces on hunting in Baja for *Western Outdoor News* and other publications. There was a time in the early 1960s when it seemed that bird and big game hunting on the Baja peninsula might become an important part of the tourism industry. But regulatory restrictions and concerns about damage to the environment would eventually all but eliminate hunting as a significant income-producing business.

HAPPY HUNTING GROUNDS

[A good description of hunting opportunities on both sides of the Cortez at the height of the Golden Age. This was written after Ray's exploratory 1961 "El Dorado camper trip" across the Cortez on a freighter and around the south end of the peninsula with company owners Everett and Don Hamel. The brief mention of *W.O.N.* editor Tom Siatos shooting doves in downtown Loreto is elaborated in more humorous form in the fragment that follows this column.]

NOVEMBER, 1962—The Cortez area is in reality the Indian's dream come true with a game potential that is almost unlimited.

Many U.S. Indian tribes called the "Hereafter" the "Happy Hunting Grounds," and thought of it as a land with pleasant weather and where there would be such abundances that man would have no reason to contest with man.

If those tribes had communicated with the tribes of Western Mexico and the Baja California Peninsula, they would have learned that such a hunting heaven could be reached while in the mortal body.

Recent discoveries of virginal areas abounding in game, south of the border, suggest that modern nimrods can still find whole territories of peace and plenty. At present these are little known, but you can bet a buck that outdoor writers will soon be headlining Mexico features with phrases like: "Ducks Unlimited for Real"; "More Canadian Geese than in Canada"; "Primeval Panther Population"; "Mule-deer Multitudes"; "Too many Doves"; and "Virgin Region for Varmints."

Serious plans have been made to organize guide and transportation systems for the mountainous big game, such as mountain lion, tiger (jaguar), javelina (Mexican wild boar), bighorn sheep, mule deer, and antelope.

Arrangements for fowling in easy-to-reach areas have already been well established in a few localities, but this phase of hunting is wide open and the field game is almost continuous.

Doves are over-abundant on the Baja Peninsula south, and in farming areas from Hermosillo to Mazatlán. Quail and rabbits are also teeming in these same areas. On the mainland, geese are hunted in the rice fields south of Obregón, more especially at Los Mochis. Ducks are found wherever there are freshwater ponds and in some brackish lagoons.

On a recent trip along this stretch we started the shooting along the road between Hermosillo and Kino Bay and found ducks, dove, quail and rabbits most everywhere. The "we" included Everett and Don Hamel, builders of the "El Dorado" camper, in which we traveled.

At the new San Carlos Bay resort we found some few ducks and an abundance of quail and dove, with plans being pushed enthusiastically for a big 1962-'63 season for deer and javelina in nearby mountains.

We ran into excellent duck shooting at the Tom Jamison ranch lake a few miles out of Guaymas. Jamison and César Gandara, General Manager of the Hotel Playa de Cortés, Guaymas, were planning to get the hunting in

Bird shooting in the mangrove channels of Bahía Magdalena during Ray's 1961 "El Dorado Camper trip" across the Cortez on a freighter and then around the southern tip of Baja. Note Bill Escudero's Bel Air station wagon beside camper.

this area on an organized basis.

The late summer and fall rains leave small ponds along the highway from Guaymas south. Many of them attract ducks and serve as watering places for doves and varmints.

The local citizenry at Obregón and Navajoa showed little interest in exploiting their great hunting potential. But at the booming and sports-minded city of Los Mochis, enthusiasm was boiling for all kinds of outdooring, with facilities for hunting and fishing well organized. Guides with conveyances take parties out to the rice fields for ducks and geese; others to the mouth of Río Fuerte for both fish and game; still others to Topolobampo Bay for shooting around the freshwater lagoons and for the exceptionally fine fishing in the Bay.

The headquarters for all this activity is the Santa Anita Hotel, Los Mochis. Its manager, and the organizer, were planning big-game trips up the new railroad to Mexico's Barrancas Tarahumara.

At Mazatlán, an established hunting service is operated by Bob and Gil Aviles, for big game safaris as well as for the local duck and dove shooting.

In the southern end of the Baja California Peninsula, except for the great, 150-mile-long, inland waters of Magdalena Bay, water fowl occur only in a few specific areas and hunting in general is mostly on a primitive basis.

Good rains for the past few years have created such a favorable environment, the dove, and perhaps other game populations, have exploded. I have heard that doves, feeling the congested condition, take off in suicidal migrations into the sea. It is a fact that marlin have been caught with doves in their stomachs.

Natives seldom waste precious ammunition on quail, which have crowded down into the villages. At the Club Aereo Mulegé, I saw coveys of quail repeatedly trying to crash into an aviary to join a flock that had been

domesticated. Doves are even more abundant around this town. Ducks are shot as they shuttle between the river mouth and a reservoir at its source.

The three Mulegé lodges maintain hunting facilities. Louis Frederico, manager of the Aereo Mulegé resort, is a big game enthusiast and can arrange for guides to the back country.

Ed Tabor, operator of the Flying Sportsmen Lodge at Loreto, has been fitting out hunting parties for a go at the big stuff in the nearby mountains, for a number of years. Tom Siatos, former editor of *W.O.N.*, on a trip there, found doves swarming in the quiet old town's central plaza. It was during siesta time when he started blasting them out of the trees and the citizenry got so shook up they headed for the hills. Tom joined when he saw the town cop charging toward him.

Rancho Buena Vista features hunting in its area and keeps a good stock of guns and supplies, as well as guides and transportation. Doves are super-abundant and quail numerous as are ducks and brant on nearby freshwater lagoons. Trips for mountain lion and deer, with dogs and guides, are arranged.

The San José del Cabo lagoon attracts numerous geese and ducks. The shooting there is done principally by hunters from Hotel Palmilla and the new Cabo San Lucas Resort. The businessmen of the town have a unique hunting club. We joined them for a domestic turkey shoot. Some fowls were shot but the big deal of the day came when they broke out goats as targets. Roast goat is a favorite dish of the natives, and mine.

Bud Parr and Luis Cóppola, operators of the Cabo San Lucas, and Dale Jeffries, who runs the marlin fleet, are all such ardent nimrods, we can expect the hunting phase of the resort to be one of its main attractions.

La Paz, the center of all kinds of outdooring activities, is making strides in catering to hunting parties. George

Pickett, assistant manager of the Hotel Los Cocos, is in the process of building a hunting and fishing lodge on Almejas Bay, which is the south end of Magdalena Bay.

Writers are already saying that this area has the greatest concentration of water fowl to be found on the North American Continent during winter months. Many of them thought to be close to extinction are plentiful, especially in the curlew and snipe order of birds.

Canadian geese and brant are seen in astonishing numbers along the full 150-mile length of Magdalena. I had already heard and read of flights of geese blocking out the sun and thought the expressions were exaggerations, but at Almejas we actually saw such an eclipse.

The clouds of winging wild fowl darkening the sky, jumping fish, wading shore birds in the water, bright green mangrove trees, and the brighter, white egrets and cranes, created a most pleasant but eerie feeling, as if we had really been transported to the Indian paradise, the "Happy Hunting Grounds." — RAY CANNON

DOVES IN DOWNTOWN LORETO

[This elaboration of the Tom Siatos downtown Loreto dove hunting story is one of Ray's most humorous pieces on any subject.]

During the dry season, which is most of the time, game fowls and varmints crowd in on the town. Doves actually become over-abundant.

Hearing of this, Tom Siatos, an ardent hunter and writer, then editor of *Western Outdoor News*, took a companion to Loreto.

Arriving at the Lodge, Tom explained to manager Al Green that their time was limited. Al at once had them in a car with their equipment and they were off for the hunt.

It was siesta time when they reached the Plaza in the center of town and Al told the hunters to get out and get their guns ready for the doves.

They did, but chickened out when the first flight came winging in over the stores and mission to the overhead trees. "It would be like necking with a new girlfriend right in front of her parents," said Tom.

Al berated them, and seeing another swarm heading over their way started yelling—"Shoot! Shoot!" They did, and littered the street.

Before their first shot, not one person could be seen, but by the time they finished, the startled population had dashed into the open. Most prominent was the town sheriff who was running toward them. Al yelled, "Hurry! Hurry! Pick up the evidence before he gets here!"

Tom and partner, feeling great guilt, visualized languishing in a Mexican jail. They quickly gathered the doves, while Al diverted the officer's attention. He then quickly jumped into the car with the hunters and drove off, leaving the officer shaking a threatening fist.

Knowing there was no way to get out of town, Tom asked, "Isn't he sure to catch us?" Al answered, "Yes, but he has no evidence. Besides, he is my cousin." — RAY CANNON

WHY RAY DIDN'T LIKE TO HUNT

One day I asked Ray if he had done much hunting in his life. He said he had gone deer hunting once. He had tracked down the deer for some distance and finally got a good shot at it.

The bullet hit its mark and the deer fell to the ground mortally wounded. As Ray moved in toward it, the deer raised its head—its large, gentle, soft brown eyes gazed directly into Ray's.

Ray was so shaken and remorseful for what he had done he could never bring himself to go hunting again." — CARLA LAEMMLE

Soft-hearted Ray, a fisherman, not a hunter.

The objective of the "Hurricane Cruise" was Caleta San Francisquito, shown here, looking north from an altitude of 9,000 feet, as the small wedge-shaped inlet on the north side of the peninsula in center photo. During the 1960s, this protected bay was one of the principle anchorages and refueling points for small boats crossing the Midriff archipelago from Kino Bay on the Mexican mainland. In the extreme upper right-hand corner is Isla San Lorenzo. — PHOTO BY PALOMAR PICTURES

HURRICANE CRUISE

FIRST ATTEMPT TO CROSS THE CORTEZ

RAY'S FIRST ATTEMPT to cross the Sea of Cortez in a trailerable boat ended in near disaster as a November 1957 storm of hurricane-force winds struck a fleet of four small outboards at Isla San Esteban—halfway across the Midriff from their Kino Bay launch point.

The ultimate goal of the trip, Bahía San Francisquito on the Baja Coast, would not be reached until Ray's next attempt—the "Kids' Trip" of the following year. The four boats from this "Hurricane Cruise" would return for that successful crossing, plus two new boats and nine teenagers.

Ironically, after the series of mishaps during the "Shipwreck Charlie" Cohen cruise from San Felipe in 1959, Ray would decide that the original Kino Bay route of the "Hurricane Cruise" was the best one after all. However, he would always recommend that seasons and tides be taken into consideration when planning trips of this kind.

In combined columns and fragments written in 1957, Ray describes the worst weather he would encounter during his quarter-century career on the Sea of Cortez.

PLANNING THE MIDRIFF CROSSING

On November 15, another unique exploration trip across the Midriff of the Gulf of California should make angling history. Owners of three outboard cabin jobs headed by Dale Frederich and including this vagabundo, will take off from Kino Bay and out across a shallow bank to Turner Island where the bottom drops abruptly from 16 to 100 fathoms.

Then on to study the south end of Isla San Esteban and the fishes of its rugged shoreline. The next stop, the south end of Isla San Lorenzo. You will remember my trip to the north end of this Grand Central Station of migrating fishes with Gene Perry and company last spring.

It is not likely that any angling explorations have

occurred along the southern extremities of these islands or at the next stop, Punta San Francisquito, with its magnificent little bay. I have flown over this point a dozen times and from the air it looks like a fishing Shangri-la. It is here that the cold upwelled waters from the deep, 700-fathom channels began. At this point the cold and warm waters from the south meet and no doubt form barrier

The always sunny-tempered Ray, shown here in a photo taken by Chuck Garrison about 1970, was known for his calm demeanor during bad weather at sea. But after the 1957 "Hurricane Cruise," he wrote his friend, *Field & Stream* editor Frank Dufresne: "...My desire to experience a storm in the Gulf is completely and forever satisfied and saturated. I've had it..."

pileups of great migrating schools from the south. I have seen thousands of birds diving near the point when our plane flew at a low altitude over it.

When there, we will investigate the possibility of building a lodge somewhere around the little bay.

Recently, divers discovered a new and highly productive bed of pearl-bearing oysters a few miles south of the point. This particular species of oysters, from which millions worth of colored pearls were taken, was thought to have been exterminated.

From San Francisquito Point we will set a northwesterly course across San Rafael and Las Animas Bays, up around the broken coastline and on into Bahía de los Angeles and enjoy Señor Antero Díaz' comfortable lodge and his wife's famous victuals.

Our return trip to Kino is scheduled to work the northerly shores of the islands mentioned, beginning at Isla Salsipuedes, a satellite of Isla San Lorenzo, and ending by skirting the broad southern end of Isla Tiburón, and perhaps a visit with its Seri Indians.

This safari should provide a lot of fishing news. This will be my first trip along the southern extremities of the Midriff, often referred to as the richest waters of this continent.

Having recently learned that some of the big game migratory fishes establish permanent habitats elsewhere in the Gulf, we will be on the lookout for signs of such hangouts in this area. — RAY CANNON

THE HURRICANE STRIKES

HURRICANE! And we were caught in it—right in the middle of the Gulf—November 24, 2:30 a.m. Our second boat had lost an anchor and was drifting helplessly toward the channel where a 100 mile-an-hour wind and a 20-foot tide combined to convulse the sea into waves the like of which I had never before seen. Not in the big blows off Florida or the China Sea did I see the like.

Our flotilla had consisted of four 17-to-21-footers, all with twin outboards, and a small, single outboard open job now resting in Davey's Locker. Heading the party were Dale and Eve Frederich, owners of the *Eve-D*, the only boat to sit out the storm without losing or dragging anchor; also Harold and Jerry Swenson, Chuck "Pinky" and Betsy Lundy, and Bill and Virginia Harker, and a native guide, Pancho. We sailed from Kino Bay, surveyed the shoreline up to the narrows, crossed the roughish straight to Tiburón, fished down and around its south end past Turner Island and pitched camp in a protected baylet. Here we spent a couple of days, then sailed out toward Isla San Esteban. Halfway across this 17-mile stretch, a heavy wind bore down and we changed course to the nearest point of land and made the lee without event.

There was one possible anchorage (not recommended by any navigation book or chart) at the southeast corner.

Here we accidentally met Dave Hyams' big converted tuna clipper, the *Galeana*, with a party of eight members of the Crenshaw Rotary Club.

We had arranged a rendezvous with this boat at another island, Isla San Lorenzo, but were certainly happy to find it and its load of gasoline for us. We felt a margin of safety when Hyams decided to keep his ship mothering us throughout the night. Later we had cause to bless him for that decision.

All boats, with two hooks out, anchored as close to shore as possible. Lines connected them but proved a hazard when the crazy wind exploded down a canyon to strike from another direction.

There was a buildup in the tormented sea and above it; 300 yards off our port, 45-foot waves Niagraed the channel to meet a like convulsion from the channel we had crossed. At midnight my watch had finished and I hit the sack. At 2:00 a.m., Harold Swenson, owner of our craft the *Jerry II*, had been on watch two hours when the wind changed and came down a ravine pockmarked with caves. The hundred-mile-an-hour flow turned all the caves into screaming whistles. The sounds were louder than air raid sirens, combined to produce a piercing, eerie pipe organ effect.

Harold yelled—"We are in trouble!" and I hit the deck to find the 20-foot tidal change had dislodged one of our anchors and started the other slipping. A wind shift gave us a broadside and we headed for the maelstrom.

Still half-asleep, I thought San Esteban was blowing her volcanic top. I couldn't imagine anything in nature making such an unearthly sound.

Our boat was bucking like a mad bronco. Great breakers were splashing against the rocks 20 feet away. Jerry was trying to start water-soaked motors. Harold was heaving on an anchor line. It was pandemonium! Jerry finally managed to get the motor going, and Harold swung us right out of the cascading breakers.

The change in wind had snapped an anchor line on every boat in our group. We were dragging. Harold managed to throw a line to Chuck "Pinky" Lundy's boat, *Pot-O-Gold*, as we passed him.

"Pinky" latched onto the line thrown and secured us to his stern. Our dragging anchor line fouled his and we all spent the night dreading the moment when both boats would be adrift. Only then did I learn that the *Pot's* towed outboard skiff had flipped and sunk.

The chill of the storm started me back to the sack but I had no sooner crawled into the warm folds when all hell broke loose. Every disaster horn in the fleet was sounding off. Bill Harker's *Umgwadi*, with motors out, had broken off her last anchor and was on her way. Bill's wife, Virginia, bailed out of her Asiatic flu bunk, crawled to the bow and heaved a line toward the *Galeana*.

Having heard the sudden clamor of horns, all the Crenshaw anglers hit the big ship's deck without benefit of britches. One of them made a fingertip catch of the thrown rope, the one last hope for the *Umgwadi* and its gallant crew. Other lines were thrown and the 21-footer was made fast to the *Galeana's* stern where we rode out the storm.

The night was one of real horror, with one such terrifying incident following another.

This was the beginning. Next week the balance.

— RAY CANNON

TEN-FOOT-HIGH UPWELLINGS

As soon as the daybreak provided enough light, Pinky and Harold decided to disengage our entangled boats. All of us were astonished to find that the *Pot-O-Gold* had held both boats throughout that wild night with one small anchor—the other was found to be without any bite at all.

Toward noon Harold and I took the *Jerry II* for a cautious look-see cruise across the lee south end of San Esteban.

Around a small point a few hundred yards from our anchorage we found that we had had company—half-a-dozen 70-foot finback whales which had apparently sought refuge from the storm, moved along against the shore at a pace resembling slow motion. They showed little concern for our presence.

The most exciting moment of the whole trip to me was in our being caught in the middle of a 200-yard-wide boil, in which our boat was suddenly lifted 10 or 12 feet above the surface beyond the boil.

I have seen, on a number of occasions, this mighty upwelling occur at the north end of Isla Angel de la Guarda, where the upheaval of water is caused by the rushing lunar tide being sucked down into the 1000-fathom canyon at one end of the channel and up at the other. These boiled up to five feet above the surrounding surface and spread out as much as a mile or so across. But this one, perhaps because of the combined high lunar tide and the storm action, exploded up to about 15 feet and not more than a hundred yards from shore.

The sea was otherwise flat along this lee side and we had no warning that we were about to straddle a volcanic-like eruption. Our boat shot up as if on an elevator, then flowed out with the boil in the crazy wave action. Harold did a magnificent job of quartering into waves that came from all directions. I was so interested in observing the overwhelming phenomenon I forgot to get frightened until we were out of it, when I was suddenly stricken by reoccurrence of ague and Montezuma's Revenge.

Shepherded by Hyams' *Galeana*, we managed a safe crossing back to our quiet bay on Tiburón, pitched camp ashore and enjoyed three delightful days exploring cave kitchens of an ancient race, and fishing out around Turner Island, where there was an almost continuous run of surface-feeding yellowtail.

All of our party saw and fished in the middle of some of the exciting pileups of diving birds, yellowtail, sardines, sea lions, porpoises and other sea creatures I have often described as dog-eat-dog occurrences unparalleled elsewhere.

Turner Island is among the best of the Midriff but I cannot say as much for the shores of Tiburón. Great numbers of fishes do move in and out of the big island's bays and coves but not to compare with the consistency of its satellite which lies a half-mile off its southeastern tip.

On our way home we ran up into the narrow El Infiernillo Strait to visit the Seri Indians. Long before we located their camp we saw flashes from a beckoning mirror. Although some members of this southern group speak Spanish and have learned to make baskets, they have failed otherwise to bend to our way of living. Their supposedly stoic dignity was shattered in the scramble when presents were passed out by the ladies of our crews. Those on the north end of Tiburón still remain aloof. The population of the tribe is declining rapidly. It is presently estimated at about 200.

Back in Hermosillo we were entertained royally at an appropriate Thanksgiving dinner and a Cuba Libre party at the State Fair by one of the city's most distinguished and hospitable citizens, Señor Nito Lucero. While this trip may sound like a cruise of doom to outboard enthusiasts, it is certain to become a frequented course for fishing the islands of the Midriff, one of the richest regions to be found. Hurricanes can strike anywhere and none like this one has hit this area for 20 years. Every member of our party plans to go again next May—and I'll be with them.

— RAY CANNON

Ray and all nine kids of the "Kids' Trip."

KIDS' TRIP

RAY'S ALL-TIME FAVORITE CRUISE

THE "KIDS' TRIP" was Ray's all-time favorite small boat cruise, and it was one of his earlier ones, leaving Kino Bay in June 1958 for a voyage across the Midriff islands and south to Caleta San Francisquito. This trip followed the same route of the terrible "Hurricane Cruise" seven months earlier, and many of the same people participated.

Ray wrote more stories about the "Kids' Trip" than any other single event of his long Baja career. He even wrote a book about it that he never published. The following account is adapted from that recently-discovered manuscript and several other versions.

The "Kids' Trip" is Ray's best and most complete record of what it was like to cruise the Sea of Cortez in a small boat in the days when this new pastime was just being invented and discovered. It would be another eight years before the Vagabundos Del Mar Boat & Travel Club organized its first cruise in 1966.

Notable in this story is the wide range of discoveries Ray makes that are personal in nature and not related to fishing, and the degree to which he allows his imagination to conjure up visions of human remains, Aztec treasures, prehistoric civilizations, and the like.

In the first part of this story, Ray refers to a movie-making experience that he says happened "not long ago" but which had actually occurred 30 years earlier. This was during the 1928 filming of his second movie for Fox Film Company, *Joy Street*, in which he built on the success of the "wild youth" party scenes used for *Red Wine*, also known as *Let's Make Whoopee*.

TEENAGERS IN PARADISE

Here, from the log book of the cruise across the Sea of Cortez, is an account of a true adventure. It was the craziest. There were more than a hundred "first-time-evers"

in which violent, ghoulish, humorous, and frightening events overlapped each other in a sea and land wilderness almost as weird as a region on the moon.

For years I had tried to get to the area around San Francisquito Bay, at the southwest corner of the Midriff. Six previous trips fell short of the goal because of gas shortage, motor troubles, storms, or for lack of knowledge on convulsing lunar tides. Only seven months before, I attempted this same crossing in company with operators of four of the boats engaged in this voyage. We got caught right in the middle of the Gulf in the worst hurricane ever recorded in the region.

The four couples who had gone through the hurricane had developed Viking determination to conquer that plaguing sea.

The phone rang!

It was a good thing I was sitting, for the message that came from the receiver just about gassed me. My friend Dale Frederich was on the other end. He had just said, "Ray, the gang and I have decided to take all nine of our kids along with us."

What the devil could they be thinking of? Especially those parents who had gone through the horrors of the rampaging sea. The very thought of taking kids into such treacherous waters seemed the height of unthinkable.

Originally I was not a hater of precocious teeners. I had actually admired their revolt against conventions. But not long ago I got a bellyful and became sick of the ilk.

While directing motion pictures for the Fox Film Company, now Twentieth Century Fox, I made the horrible mistake of doing a flaming youth picture called *Joy Street*, with a cast of 60 Hollywood teenagers. On a shortened, three-week location trip to Santa Barbara, California, my assistant directors and chaperons lost control. But completely.

Some of the town's rich kids started throwing over-

All six rigs lined up on the highway at Kinsley, Arizona.

lively parties for my gang and the otherwise quiet citizenry was thrown into panic. During one fracas the police were forced to rope off a city block when the gang threw all the furniture out of the upper floor windows of a hotel.

I was given a 12-hour notice to clear my troupe out of the town. Needless to say, I developed an allergy for the whole teenage segment of our society.

But now—a three-week-togetherness with nine teenagers. "Easy old boy," I said to myself while stroking the back of my neck, "remember your Tao." I was trapped and I knew it. Since I was to be a guest of these fine people, it would be stupid to offer any objection to their youngsters.

The hope came to me that I could keep the brats at a distance by employing a mum strategy. I never made a worse guess, for I was to learn that keeping that radioactive bunch off would be like brushing away your shadow in the middle of Death Valley.

SIX-BOAT CARAVAN DEPARTS LOS ANGELES

JUNE 21, 1958—All boats arrived at rendezvous in Pomona, California aboard heavy trailers pulled by station wagons in the following order:

—Harold and Jerry Swenson's *Jerry Two*; 21-foot Glasspar; with Carolyn, 15, and Warren "Unc," 13.

—Harp and Agnes Brubaker's *Blue Breakers*; 19-foot Glasspar; with Dave, 13, and Tommy, 9.

—Chuck and Betsy Lundy's *Rock N' Roll*; 19-foot Glasspar; with Chris, 15.

—Bill and Virginia Harker's *Umgwadi*; 21-foot Trojan; with Rich, 16, Harriet, 14, and Jimmy, 12.

—Dale and Eve Frederich's *Eve-D*; 18-foot Merlin; with Michael, 13.

—George and Aggie Elias' *Moja Decla*; 18-foot Performer; children too young for trip.

At 2:10 a.m., the boat-trailered station wagons peeled off in a long single-file and swung out onto the fine freeway running out of the Los Angeles basin, up across a mountain pass and on down through the Imperial Valley to El Centro, California.

Attention was diverted from the sweltering heat when skippers, turned comedians, made use of the boat-to-boat radios which had been transferred to the cars.

"*Umgwadi* to fleet! There is a cow on our port side. Correction, it is a bull. Correction, it was once a bull… over."

An answer comes, "*Eve-D* to *Umgwadi*, did I understand that you hit the brute, thus causing the transformation, or was it neuterized at an earlier period of life?"

Arrived at Blythe, California, gassed, lunched, and crossed the Colorado River to arrive at Phoenix, Arizona at 5:10 p.m. Our caravan caused quite a sensation. A number of wealthy citizens expressed desires to get boats and follow up. Some even offered to buy our boats on our return.

When our caravan maneuvered into a plush motel parking lot, all kids dashed for the swimming pool. This was the first time I had seen the gang in mass action. Thinking of things to come, it was frightening.

SECOND DAY—CROSSING THE BORDER

On our way again. Stopped by a lake at the "Half Way Place." When asked what the place was halfway to, some wag, noting the 110-degree temperature, said, "It feels like it's halfway to hell-and-gone."

Arrived at Nogales. We cleared the border and headed south on Mexico's west coast El Camino. Five hours of this, then we saw the fine city of Hermosillo. We were greeted by our good friend Señor Nito Lucero. He had made all the arrangements for our stopover and took us to the elegant Granada Motel. Once again the kids made a beeline for the swimming pool.

CULTURE SHOCK IN HERMOSILLO

The day began quiet enough. Because of the hot weather the ladies started hurrying from shop to shop dressed in shorts. A near-panic ensued at the central market when a farmer, seeing the "half-dressed" women, was so shocked he let go a door to his chicken truck and all the fowls flew out.

I asked a policeman if the women's costumes were unusual in his city. He answered with restrained emotions, "Sí, señor, they are very unusual and very illegal. I shame to speak. You, por favor, tell them to quit our streets quick."

The ladies, red-faced, rushed to buy skirts and then continued their tour of the town.

The cars had by now become scattered and the kids were yacking in their offbeat language on the radios. By some freak coincidence, our intercom system was on the same wavelength as that of the local Police Department.

The Department's whole radio system suddenly became jammed with messages flying over the airwaves from half-a-dozen stations, and all of them in a "language" unknown at City Hall. The broadcasters seemed to be shifting rapidly from one section to another.

The kids mummed up fast when they heard the voice of an English-speaking officer sound off with: "This is the Police Department! Do you speak English? It is illegal to speak on this wavelength! It is illegal to own this kind of a machine!"

It is doubtful that the youngsters were any more shaken up than the Hermosillo Police Department, and to this day the case remains on their blotter as a major unsolved mystery.

After the shopping, mothers were rounded up—and after a suspenseful dash back to hook up the boats—our caravan silently stole away.

KINO BAY—LAUNCHING THE BOATS

Kino Bay, 65 miles off the main El Camino, is the end of the road leading down from Hermosillo to the sea.

If our teeners had expected to find glittering, fiesta-clad natives, as shown in the movies, they were totally and

In convoy off Isla Tiburón.

completely disillusioned. Instead of lush, tropical jungle, there was only dry barrenness. Even the sea here looked strange. Their dream of spending a lazy vacation sipping coconut milk on a South Sea island-type of beach was dashed.

They took solace in drinking pop in the town's only store, owned by Art Dawson and José Jiménez. José was to manage our launching and accompany us on the voyage as guide. We had engaged a couple of native fishermen to haul a thousand gallons of gas across the gulf to San Francisquito Bay for us. Two trips would be necessary in the little open boat.

By 3:00 p.m., the last of our boats had been launched by the simple method of backing them down the beach. We were off on course 252, for the southern tip of Isla Tiburón, a distance of 22 nautical miles.

Once more I was about to experience the familiar spell of El Golfo, ready to slough off the old and become again the "young man of the sea," in harmony with its rhythms, coloring, and mystic power, and taking keen delight in the view and feeling of all about me. Getting back to the sea was like quenching a mighty thirst. The crossing was uneventful. We sailed into Dog's Bay, anchored for the night and went ashore.

In this waveless, placid Sea, the outboard motors were just tilted up and the boats backed up to the beach for unloading our equipment.

FIRST NIGHT AT ISLA TIBURON
RAW FISH DINNER

For the flooring of our camp pavilion, a large tarpaulin was spread out on a level spot between the top of the clean, sandy beach and a mangrove-rimmed lagoon. A war surplus parachute was stretched over bamboo poles for a shading canopy. (Tents are not required in this arid, dewless climate.)

Boat seats, chairs, cushions, collapsible tables, Coleman lanterns, cooking utensils, aluminum foil, paper cups and dishes and other typical camp paraphernalia were brought ashore. Some Coleman cartridge galley stoves were set up for coffee making and boiling water. The rest of the cooking would be done on a grate-covered fireplace we constructed some distance downwind from the pavilion.

All of the youngsters had taken swimming and diving lessons in preparation for this trip, and they lost no time in getting into the cooling water to collect shellfish and lobsters for a live-off-the-land dinner.

Taking advantage of this preoccupation I grabbed a spinning outfit and headed for some quiet shore fishing around a rocky point. I had no sooner gotten out of sight when up popped little Jimmy Harker, a smart-cracking nuisance, trailing me like a bloodhound.

I taught him to cast, and between the two of us, four,

At camp on Isla Tiburón.

$2^1/2$-foot-long sierras (Spanish mackerel) were landed. Added to a like number brought in by Jimmy's parents, Bill and Virginia, who had been trolling from their boat, we had enough to make a huge raw fish dish called *"ceviche,"* in which the sierra is filleted out and diced, marinated in lemon juice for a couple of hours, then mixed with chopped onions, tomatoes, bell peppers, salt, and a dash of chili pepper sauce.

All parents expected the youngsters to start gagging at the very thought of eating raw fish, but something had come over them since arriving on Tiburón and all were anxious to prove their hardiness. There were some Tarzanish breast beatings, yelps and cries of—"Bring on the raw meat!" But the first bits were taken like a dose of quinine. Once the samples were down, however, every last barbarian demanded full plates for their second helping of the "cannibal gupe," as they called it. The delicious shellfish and lobster dishes prepared by the mothers were left entirely to the grown-ups.

ACROSS THE GULF!
BAHIA SAN FRANCISQUITO

This was to be an historical day. Never before had such a large fleet of outboard boats made a successful Midriff crossing.

Our flotilla sailed out through the narrow channel between Tiburón and its satellite, Turner Island, and on past Bahía Las Cruces. All the Midriff islands came into view.

Directly across the first channel was the cube-shaped Isla San Esteban. Beyond it was San Lorenzo and its satellite, Salsipuedes. Then to the north came the flat bird island, Raza. Next the smallish twin rocks called Isla

A "late model" canoa under sail. Note rudder and planked construction. — PHOTO BY RALPH POOLE

Partida, beyond which began the longest of the gulf's islands, Isla Angel de la Guarda.

The day was so clear we could see the coastline of Baja California and the point which enclosed our destination, San Francisquito Bay.

As we came abreast of Isla San Esteban we shuddered at the very sight of this area, for it was here that we had gone through the worst experience of our lives. The "shaker-upper" had occurred just seven months earlier. It was hard to believe that the placid waters around this island were in the same sea as when we ran into the worst hurricane to strike the region in 30 years.

As per plans and schedule, we were once again sailing this sea of many faces as we headed on toward Isla San Lorenzo. All the convulsive agonies of the Midriff were like vague dreams as we skimmed across the smooth channel. Never had any of us seen a millpond more calm. The boat's movement was so smooth it seemed airborne. One adult skipper after another slumped over the wheel, sound asleep.

With the aid of binoculars, a small sail was seen projecting above the southern horizon. It remained motionless in the doldrums, awaiting a breeze to bear its owners to whatever direction it blew. They were made out to be a couple of the seafaring vagabundos of El Golfo. I have encountered a number of these sea-rovers on various trips to the gulf and have been fascinated with their philosophy of total freedom. They sail with the tide and wind, crossing and recrossing the gulf, migrating up and down it in search of nothing more than pleasant temperatures.

Suddenly the mountainous backdrop of the Baja California shore seemed to move right out to meet us. As our fleet moved in near shore, some coves could be made out. We saw the deep, curved Bahía San Francisquito, but nowhere could we spot an opening to the hidden inner baylet.

Harp and Harold sailed their boats in to get a closer view. Suddenly they disappeared as if swallowed up by the sea. Even as we came abreast of a high, solid pyramid, we could see nothing more than a recessed cove behind it. Then we saw that this rock stood ajar like an open door.

The inner beach of Caleta San Francisquito in November 1966, showing the remains of the old rock pier and the oyster shell mounds.

— PHOTO BY MARTIN GOLDSMITH

We looked right into the gullet of the least-known bay in the Gulf.

At last we saw the object of months of planning, hundreds of hours of work, tests and failures, and an enormous amount of energy and finance by each of the boat owners. For me, after having tried by every means to reach this place over a period of many years, it was even more satisfying.

It looked exactly the opposite to everything we had imagined.

STRANGE DISCOVERIES
AT CALETA SAN FRANCISQUITO

The beach resembled a prehistoric boneyard. Piles of sun-bleached pearl oyster shells, eight to ten feet high, were stacked to occupy most every foot above the high tide line. Clumps of dried thorn bushes and cacti added to the evil, splotched landscape. A few adobe ruins lay crumbling.

One look sent imaginations soaring. We knew practically nothing about the place and were totally unprepared for the all-astonishing events and discoveries that awaited us.

The boat engaged to haul our extra gasoline supply

from Kino was a welcome sight. This we had expected, but to everyone's surprise, a large pearl diving craft lay at anchor near the beach, with its half-dozen skiffs high and dry near an active camp.

We dropped anchors and the kids scampered over to the pearlers' camp. For the first time since they had crossed into Mexico, the kids found their friendly greetings being answered by hostile grunts. I explained that the pearlers probably thought we were about to raid their oyster beds. I suggested we could send José over as our ambassador after they had had a chance to give us a thorough once-over, and then we would probably find them just as friendly as other natives.

OPERATION "PRIVY"
HISTORICAL SPECULATIONS

Among the many other questions to ponder over was the problem of toilets.

It was during "operation privy" that some of the most important discoveries were made—the very key to proving this bay was the Baja California port of the Aztecs, and a source of Montezuma's black pearl treasure.

While our boats were all equipped with heads (toilets), in San Francisquito Bay, being almost completely

A huge shell midden at Caleta San Francisquito, photographed during the "Jurgens Cruise" in the summer of 1961.

landlocked, we found it necessary to decommission them.

To me the solution was simple enough, for there were numerous concealing clumps of cactus, shell mounds and bushes to provide individual privacy.

The distance from camp and from each other spread the privies over a considerable territory. This provided time to observe and give a thorough investigation of the whole section. Some of the most interesting discoveries of the entire trip were made during periods of enforced contemplation.

The first significant discovery was made by Dale. He had staked out a large horseshoe-shaped pile of oyster shells a couple of hundred yards from the beach. We decided that the water of the bay must have extended back a few centuries ago and that the shells had been stacked on what was at that time the beach. The old shells had undoubtedly been collected in pearling operations centuries ago.

Dale's son Michael discovered the first piece of old pottery to have been found on the east side of the gulf. With this new evidence, a picture of Aztec operations at this port began shaping up. Crossing the gulf at this point in the flimsy, reed boats used by Aztecs seemed logical, since it was the only place they could have done it in short, island-hopping stretches.

Stones, mineral ores, strange cacti, odd shrubs and rare shells were brought in from the vicinity of the privies. The difference in age showed the middens to have been occupied in prehistoric times. The ruins and remains of the dwellings of various types suggested that many different kinds of people of modern times had set up housekeeping in the area.

It appeared as if sizable villages had been formed at various periods, each flourishing for a time, each dying, as the place became cursed.

MEETING THE PEARLERS

Having become acquainted with the pearling operators, José soon worked out friendly relations by explaining that we were not there to raid their oyster beds.

The kids approached close enough to look over the workers' shoulders and see pearls being taken from the oysters. The small and knotty pearls were dropped in the sand around their feet. The kids started prospecting in the centers of deserted mounds and began finding pearls. A big mining deal was on.

Harriet found a lucrative mound and was furiously working it when she discovered that it also housed a rattlesnake. She called for an assist from her mother, who helped kill it, then calmly went on with her project.

Meeting the pearlers of Caleta San Francisquito.
Note shell middens in background.

Tommy caught the biggest yellowtail.

Tommy and Jimmy, mining another hole, got mixed up with a nest of scorpions, mashed them all, and resumed operations.

Lesser incidents occurred involving biting bugs, lizards, and other creepers, all of which were ignored in the wild clamor. Each sizable pearl found was cause for loud acclaim. The noise reached such a pitch all adults, including the pearlers, halted whatever they were doing to watch.

FISHING BAHIA SAN FRANCISQUITO WHOOPIN' & HOLLERIN'

In one glaring flash the sun missiled up out o' Sonora across the Gulf and exploded in our faces.

I took off with the Swenson family. We crisscrossed the bay to catch black skipjack for bait. Both Carolyn and her mom Jerry gave their lungs a full workout every time they got a hookup. Later, when Carolyn tied into a 60-pound grouper you'd have thought it was air raid siren testing time.

Now this may seem strange to the uninitiated, but that whoopin' and hollerin' is music to my ears. I sound off myself. It not only lets off steam but I think it adds to the pleasure.

Carolyn's very next hookup was an enormous shark. She fought it until fish and girl were all but exhausted, then the shark broke loose—the girl in tears at having lost it.

I hadn't realized that getting a monster on deck was so important to anyone but me.

As we passed near the inner bay entrance on our way to camp, we slowed to allow Warren and Carolyn a chance to troll through an interesting stretch. Warren had hardly payed out a feather when he came near getting jerked off the boat. He had nailed a big yellowtail. Carolyn brought her even bigger yellow to gaff in half-an-hour and was ready to call it quits.

Before that grand day of fishing was over, every youngster, including little Tommy, had caught a yellowtail, and each grew up a little and swelled out with well-earned pride. Tommy didn't weigh much more than the big jack on the other end of his line, and there were moments when this contest was in doubt. Harper and I stood close by to grab if the fish started jerking him overboard. Tommy handled his tackle very well—the smallest angler I had ever seen handle a big yellow.

I had had little or no previous experience fishing with youngsters and was agreeably surprised to find the sport so excitingly interesting to them. I had forgotten the joyful madness that engulfed me every time there was a chance to get to the river with pole and worms when I was a kid.

REDISCOVERING THE "WILD CHILD RUCKUS"

There were two reasons for selecting the reef that extended out from a bluff near the bay entrance for the day's activity. First, it appeared to be an excellent place to do some experimental fishing. And of equal importance, rock fishing is to me more enjoyable than any other form of outdoor sport.

It wasn't my intention to sneak away from the kids but they were still asleep, and knowing how irritating rock fishing is for beginners, I wasn't about to encourage them to try it. I felt a bit guilty for not mentioning my plans to

Rediscovering the "wild child ruckus" at Caleta San Francisquito.

the youngsters. A couple of minutes later I regretted the thoughts, for looking back toward camp, there they came, bloodhounding after me.

Chris was the first of the gang to join me. It was surprising to find that he was an experienced rock angler. When his lure got fouled, he would swim out, dive down, and retrieve it without a grumble.

After the others caught up I briefed them on the various hazards of rock fishing, but it was six or seven bruised fannies later before they learned to heed the "watch your step" warning. Other aggravations, such as getting lines caught on rocks and losing lures were pretty discouraging, but when Chris landed a couple of hefty ten-pound groupers their spirits revived and they sportingly accepted the challenge with renewed determination.

I decided it was time for serious lab work. Inspecting the food particles in the stomachs of fish was a very important part of my study.

I settled down to record the data of the first fish, carefully separating the food particles, when Jimmy broke me up with his drollery, "Gallstones, Dr. Kildare?"

To shake the incorrigible Jimmy out of my hair, I knocked off for a few minutes. Little Tommy had launched

an investigation in one of the numerous tide pools. As I walked over, he turned to me and simply said, "Look!" One glance at his eager, young eyes and I was hooked.

I quickly switched the subject to a sea snail shell that was being occupied by a hermit crab, on how the crabs gang up to play a sort of musical chairs game in which the largest crab finds a roomier shell and this starts a scramble by slightly smaller hermits to get the bigger guy's house. As each leaves his shell vacant, a smaller brother makes a dash to homestead it, and so on down to shells no bigger than peas...

"What am I doing?" I said, catching myself. This was exactly the disturbing, time-consuming thing that I'd been doing my best to avoid, and here I was letting myself get all wound up voluntarily. "I must be losing my grip," I thought. I kicked myself in the fanny and stomped back to work.

I was getting along okay until Harriet got a strike, set her hook and started emitting the usual caterwauls. Everyone else was too busy to lend a hand, so I reluctantly left my examining and advised her.

Then David landed an oddball known by the scientific name *Cirrhichthys rivulatus*. The few natives who have

Refueling at Caleta San Francisquito.

ever seen one call it "Chino actor" because the markings on its body and face resemble a Chinese actor's makeup or mask.

All activity came to a halt. I told the gang how I had once caught one and had taken it to a Chinese friend of mine, to have him read it. He took one look and accused me of having the characters painted on the fish by a scholarly Chinese. "The writing," he said, "is early Ming and tells an old joke. It very clearly says: 'two farmers, one wife—no peace.'"

To the kids, the "chino" suddenly became the most important fish in the Sea of Cortez.

The morning sun poured down on the over-energetic fishermen. Its rays bounced up from the mirrored surface to fry them once-over without turning.

Despite all their plans for a lazy vacation, the kids just couldn't really relax. Frolicking in the surf provided variety enough to keep the youngsters busy for a couple of hours. Here they could be kids without being accused of doing "kid stuff," the most despised accusation in the English language to them.

As I watched, I was struck with the enthusiasm they showed for whatever they tackled. I wondered what had happened to most modern teeners, as well as adults, back in the States, where spirited enthusiasm seemed to be a thing of the past. What had happened to that child heart

which awakened so readily? Here, once again, I saw inhibitions and pseudo-sophistication forgotten in a frolic of sheer joy.

Two minutes later, I found myself the center of "the wild child ruckus" as Jimmy called it. I became so involved I never once wondered what the parents would think of my cavorting and carrying on in such an undignified manner.

GASOLINE-FIRED PRIVATES

During a refueling operation we lifted a large drum of gasoline up on top of others so as to drain it into five-gallon cans. The heat had created a lot of pressure in the drum and when José tried to ease the cap out just far enough, it blew out of his hand and the gas squirted all over me from head to foot. I wheeled and dashed into the surf. Some of the kids saw me dive in with all my clothes on and thought the gas had burned my eyes. My eyes weren't hurt but some other part of my anatomy felt as if they were blazing. The more I washed them with salt water, the worse they burned.

The boys soon got the idea but the two girls and a couple of mothers who rushed on deck of a nearby boat were mystified. Someone produced a cake of saltwater soap and I didn't hesitate to drop my pants so I could apply it. When the soap didn't work the girls and women produced a drug counter of cures. One of the first, "Johnson's Baby Oil," stopped the burning at once.

The girls were so concerned with my suffering they forgot to get embarrassed until I declared myself off of the casualty list. No one laughed in front of me but the predicament was certainly a humorous situation. No one except Jimmy mentioned the incident again (and the sly cracks he pulled to rib me were not repeatable in print).

NEAR TRAGEDY FOR TOMMY

We had experienced our days of striving, our days of rejoicing, but this was to be the day for weeping.

Tragedy struck our expedition when little Tommy was stricken to a state of unconsciousness by the poisonous stings of a scorpion fish. He had suffered unbearable agony for two hours and he slipped into a coma.

Tommy's father and I had gone out looking for billfish. We returned to find nothing but trouble. In addition to Tommy's infection, Carolyn had been hit by near sunstroke, a leg injury had put Bill Harker out of commission, and Dale Frederich was limping around on an injured foot. Added to all this mess of horror, a motor of Chuck Lundy's boat had three vital parts busted.

Some of the kids explained how they had been flipping small fish out on the beach with their hands, and how Tommy had carried a five-inch sculpin ashore before it drove five, needle-sharp spines into his hands.

Eve Frederich, a former nurse, had immediately applied spirits of ammonia and hot water but the pain continued until she administered a second sedative.

Tommy awakened without pain but was suffering from nausea. Stimulated vomiting failed to help. At a conference of the fathers, every emergency was considered. If the lad became worse he would have to be taken back across the gulf and to an Hermosillo hospital.

A crossing in a boat was ruled out as too risky. The only safe method would be to fly him over; and the only means of communicating with an airport would be to send a boat across to Kino Bay. The lunar tides were running higher than at any other period of the month. Such a trip would be the most hazardous ever known to have been attempted in the region. It was decided that two boats would be safer; if one broke down the other could tow it to the nearest protected cove and go on.

All night a close watch was kept. Late the next afternoon severe cramps in Tommy's midsection set in. The emergency was at hand.

Harold Swenson and George Elias volunteered for the dangerous crossing. Chuck would go with Harold. José would go with George.

Both boats were stripped down to bare necessities. The increasing wind would be ignored. The course was laid out to Kino.

Eve confided to me that getting Tommy to a hospital for a glucose shot within a few hours was a matter of life and death. At 10:25 p.m. the two boats pulled out for a desperate race against time, wind, and tide. Morale at camp dropped to zero and we hit the sack with little conversation.

We had hardly bedded down when a stiff wind came tearing up out of the south. We could well imagine the awful sea the boats were running into.

At daybreak our hearts were in our throats. Some of

The boat that ferried gas from Kino Bay to Caleta San Francisquito.

Fishing the shore of the inner caleta.

the mothers had spent most of the night sewing a large piece of cloth to be put up as a wind direction sock. By 8 a.m. the airfield was made ready. Keeping a straight upper lip in front of their children required real courage of the mothers.

I took the kids out on a point where we could look down from a cliff. They knew very well that they were being diverted and I suspected that each one of them was trying to help by pretending cheerfulness.

By noon, glances toward the eastern horizon became more frequent and less concealed. By 1:30 p.m. just about everyone in camp was about ready to flip, when the sound of a motor was heard.

Then, the twin-motor plane came roaring around the point, across the bay and over our camp. The relief was so great some of the mothers ran into the boat cabins and had a good cry.

The plane made an easy landing. Tommy was placed aboard together with his mom, Agnes Brubaker, and Aggie Elias. The plane took off at once.

Chuck related how the boats were hit by the full force of the blow and tide, how a motor on George's boat was flooded, forcing them into the lee of Turner Island. Once in quiet water the motor was put in order and they sailed on to Kino Bay.

Chuck went on to tell us they'd been unable to get official clearance for a Mexican plane, and in final desperation, succeeded in contacting a flyer by phone in Nogales, Arizona and persuaded him to undertake the life and death mission. He also told us that Tommy's

symptoms were discussed with the doctors at Hermosillo and that Eve's diagnosis had been correct—dehydration. Tommy would likely snap out of it as soon as he could get the glucose shot. This good news sent the kids to cheering as if their side had won a football game.

Little Tommy, having recovered completely, was brought back from Hermosillo to join us for a few wonderful days on Tiburón. Once again he joined the other youngsters in swimming, fishing, skin diving and exploring.

RETURN TO ISLA TIBURON

We arrived back at Las Cruces Bay.

All parents had decided to sleep in the very comfortable bunks aboard their boats and their offspring had planned to do likewise, that is, until they saw me get my bed roll and spread it on a level spot atop a beach sand hill. Then there was a wild scramble to see who could get bed rolls from the boats and spread them next to mine.

At first I resented the invasion of my privacy by the horde and should have kept my big mouth shut, but I allowed myself to get hooked by their subtle chumming. They caught me by an exchange of wild speculations among themselves on and about the stories they had heard and read about Tiburón.

Thinking I could send them shivering under the covers, I let go with the worst of the horror events I had heard of and experienced on previous trips to the island. Among the stories I told was one about a friend of mine who had gotten a couple of old Seris stoned and had tricked them into saying that their tribe had once practiced cannibalism, until the Mexican Government clamped down, and how they caught shipwrecked sailors, or whoever they could during famine periods, and barbecued them just like they would sea turtles.

Then I told them how I had personally found the charred "jaw bone" of a "human" in a cave which may have served as one of their rotisserie ovens. That's where I goofed, for I would have to prove that one.

Instead of being frightened by the macabre tales, they yelled for more.

They got it when a chorus of coyotes a couple of hundred feet back of our camp took over and started vocalizing in ear-splitting howls.

I was surprised that the whole gang didn't bolt for the boats. But if they had, they would have scrambled right back again, for from the water-side came a gargantuan bellowing followed by an equally stentorian hissing. Six, 80-foot-long finback whales had become bedfellows to our boats and were snoring as they oscillated up and down. The steam pop-off when the Moby Dicks expelled air, and the roaring, guttural noise as they inhaled, were like winds of a hurricane colliding with a thunderstorm.

You would have thought that such an inexperienced

Ray and Jerry Swenson at cave entrance.

group would have "had it" after that, but no, before the night was half over, they had tricked me into a promise to take them to the cave of bones.

THE CAVE OF BONES

Just before daybreak I hollered, "Time to get up!" hoping that the gang would not respond and we could forget the whole idea, but they popped up like a colony of Oklahoma gophers, dashed into the surf for a wash-down then made for the camp pavilion and started scrounging for fruit and sandwiches to take along for breakfast.

The food and half of the water was gone before we crossed the last razorback hill, five miles from camp. The first-aid kit had also taken a beating for the many repairs caused by hooked spine cactus and barbed thorns.

Back away from the water, we missed the cooling sea breeze and welcomed the partial shade of a clump of pipe organ cactus halfway down the steep side of the last ravine. Across on the opposite side, about 300-feet away, we could see right into "Barbecue Cave" as the gang called it.

At the first sight of our main objective I had expected to hear some victorious whoopin' and hollerin', but if the kids felt such uninhibited reaction, the urge died in their throats.

Strewing corpses around in TV Westerns was one thing, but facing stark reality was another, especially when the real thing was the breakfast-nook of "people-eaters."

Suddenly Jimmy shattered the silence with, "Hey, look! There are eyes in there, way back where it's dark! Maybe they're ghosts!" His sister, Harriet, was the next to see them. "They're moving!" she gasped.

We all saw the glowing eyes, a half-dozen pairs of them and they were moving. I knew there were no cattle on the island and the eyes seemed too large to be those of local varmints.

Carolyn, less shaky than the others, scoffed, "Who ever heard of ghosts in broad daylight? They're only mountain lions or something."

"Mountain lions!" came from a whole chorus.

The thought of that many loose lions so close caused muscles to tighten and a general shift to take-off positions. No one started to run because none wanted to be the first to chicken out in front of the others.

The next reaction was one of defense. Hunting knives were whipped out and grips on shovel handles were tightened. Blood rushed back to pale faces and jaws quit quivering to clamp down in determination.

My silence was puzzling to the kids and I could see they expected me to give out with a plan equal to the emergency. Although I had quickly discarded the idea of mountain lions, I had no intention of robbing them of the dramatic suspense. I was about to suggest gathering a battery of stones together for defense, when eagle-eyed David spoiled the little melodrama with, "Aw they aren't lions, they're only elks or deer, or something with horns."

I got a glimpse of pronged horns and shushed everyone to silence.

A few seconds later we heard the buck blow a loud hiss. As if cued by his command, a female mule deer, the largest I had ever seen, bolted out of the cave and into a series of graceful leaps over ten-foot bushes. Four others followed, then the buck. I whistled, and the majestic creature stopped on a rise and lifted his antlered head in a high, kingly pose. Again spreading his nostrils, he gave out with a signal apparently intended to notify a skittish doe to make her entrance. She bounced straight up and over the eight-foot bush near the cave entrance and all but changed ends while in the air. Unlike the others which followed a beeline, she chose to clown it up by zigzagging and making high, twisting leaps, whether there was anything to jump over or not. The buck stood patiently by without a motion until she finished her performance, then followed her off in long, gliding jetés.

We watched and stood entranced as the herd danced down the slope, across a little valley and on up a distant hillside to another cave.

Suddenly we remembered that we were sweltering, and when someone remarked that the deer's cave must be a very cool one to have been chosen as their shelter, we lost no time in scrambling across to it, to soak up some of its coolness and allow ourselves a double ration of water.

Everything about the cave seemed foul with the imaginary effluvia of burned bodies, but in reality, the stench was left by the animals. The solid rock part of the ceiling was still black from the great fires that once burned there. The back of the cave was soft like decomposed granite. It had crumbled down, filling the back floor with eight or ten tons of moldering earth. The cavern that had appeared so beautiful from a distance was now a dank and repulsive place.

We shoveled along the walls and came up with "arm" and "hand" bones. Only the smaller "finger" bones were charred.

The kids' reactions were mixed. The two younger ones hesitated to touch the "human" remains, drawing back as if they feared being contaminated by unclean things. To the older members, the roasting had somehow removed the stigma. Having been through fire, these bones had been returned to the earth and were no longer sacred objects to them.

While the others were busy digging up bits of pottery and some ancient artifacts, but hoping for treasure, Warren and David were seized with a weird impulse to reenact a "cannibalistic" fiesta. The gruesome climax came when David, pretending to be carving a barbecued cadaver asked Warren if he preferred light or dark meat and handed him an "arm bone" saying, "Be my guest."

At this point the actors became sickened at their own revolting make-believe and followed the others, whom they had already sent bolting for fresh air.

Harriet had been first to get to the cave and was the leader in bolting out of it. She was heading for the clean sea water seen in another bay a couple of miles down the slope.

Treasure hunting had lost much of its glamour by the time we reached some grave mounds halfway down, but avariciousness revived when I explained that the occupants could possibly have been pirates.

Despite weariness, all hands set to work removing boulders that covered the selected graves, and the digging was going at a good clip until Warren's shovel struck something hollow enough to sound like a bass drum. He dropped the spade as if he had received a 220-volt charge.

We carefully removed the dirt from what appeared to be a coffin but found it was a layer of large sea turtle shells. Removing these we saw a large, clean skeleton with a two-century-old bottle lying close to the head. Its cork and contents had long since disappeared. Little Jimmy opined that the "character must have been an alcoholic."

When I lifted the skull out and tried to explain why it was so thin, my thumb accidentally crushed a hole in it. That did it! Our treasure hunt was ended and we hurriedly replaced everything as we found it and headed for purifying water.

THE SECRET RITUAL GROUNDS

Half a mile back of the bay we came to an almost impassible thorn bush jungle and decided to follow an animal path tunneling through it. The trail veered off to a high bluff instead of straight to the beach. We emerged to find ourselves in a clearing, completely hidden by the jungle on one side, and sheer cliffs on the other. There were no indications that the place had been visited by humans in a great many years.

A wide avenue up the center was marked by rows of large boulders that must have been brought from a mile away. On either side of the walkway were rows of ancient, ten-foot symbol characters carefully marked out by the large stones. An altar rock stood up at the end of the walk.

This proved to be the secret ritual grounds of the Seris, hidden from explorers by its isolation.

Imaginations ran riot on what diabolical practices were once performed and treasures offered as sacrifice. Although sure we could find many strange objects by digging around the altar, weariness tempted us to postpone any further investigation for a later day. Seeing one of our boats coming around the point cinched it.

We scaled down a split in the cliff much too dangerous for anyone to climb, then ran along the beach where we could swim out to meet the boat.

For the next few days everyone was contented with the happy pursuits of fishing, skin diving, rare shell collecting, and helping me examine and photograph sea creatures.

A MIDRIFF FISH PILEUP

At Las Cruces Bay we ran into a fish pileup. I have never heard of any mass slaughter on land or sea to compare with these mile-long, dog-eat-dog-or-die-young mix-ups which occur certain times of the year here in the Midriff.

It starts when army-size schools of migrating fish hit

Betsy Lundy, left, and Jerry Swenson with a Seri woman.

the rich feeding grounds and tear into the abundant sardine schools. Tens of thousands of sea birds gather to dive for the small, wounded fish. Sea lions from nearby rookeries grab the big yellowtail and bonito and are seen chomping them up. They, in turn, are disemboweled by huge sharks.

Then, as if triggered by some mysterious signal, all the meat-eating denizens of the deep come plowing into the fray—porpoise, bottlenose dolphin, giant squid, octopi and killer whales. All run amuck in a grand distortion of the slow processes of evolution.

I knew the fearful sight caused brave men to shiver as if the ague had set in and was afraid the kids would "flip their buttons" when the parents took the boats plunging right into the middle of the sea-convulsing pileup.

There were a few minutes of horror-stricken yells and screams. Then to my utter astonishment the kids turned as savage as the sea predators, catching big fish as fast as they could reel them in. They gave full freedom to the latent caveman instincts within them, vocalizing in hyena laughs and yells.

They caught enough fish to supply the whole population of Kino. To keep the catch from spoiling we made a forced, top-speed run to Kino Bay to distribute them.

TRADING WITH THE SERIS

Word reached the Seri camp a short ways below the town and the whole tribe came hurrying up the beach.

The youngsters' high eagerness to get a close look dropped to a new low when from 50 feet away they saw the brilliantly-colored face paint carefully designed in zigzag patterns across the nose and cheeks of all the

unmarried Seri maidens. It looked like Apache war paint to them and it took a bit of explaining to overcome cautiousness. Once fear was somewhat cooled, the kids had a ball trading for baskets and native-made trinkets.

The girls on our side cornered the basket market. Carolyn had a habit of applying lipstick when she got nervous about anything. The Indian women were held spellbound when they saw her whip out a stick and start applying it. Their standard of living would be upped a notch if they could get the canned paint instead of having to make it out of weeds and bird droppings.

Noting the interest, Carolyn offered the lipstick for one of three baskets a squaw held but the woman insisted she take all three in exchange. That triggered a swapping binge that lasted as long as lipsticks and baskets held out. Both Carolyn and Harriet cleaned up on the resale market when they made the boys shell out a lot of U.S. folding money for each basket they bought.

During all the bartering our youngsters moved about as if they were in a cage of lions and expecting an overly hungry one to run berserk at any moment.

The payoff came after the Indians had depleted all their stock and kids had raided all boats for clothes and leftover food items to give as goodwill presents.

When we had broken camp, someone had dumped a dozen lemons in a shopping bag still half-full of biscuit-size charcoal briquettes. Harriet had given it to the Chief. He distributed most of the lemons and when he pulled out a briquette he proceeded to chomp it up as if it were a delicacy. In doing so he got a big black smudge all around his mouth, as if he had been smoking an exploding cigar.

Not being able to see the clownish makeup on his face he became enraged when all his tribe started laughing and pointing at him. His storming at them panicked our teeners. They realized this was real trouble and not just imaginary scare stuff they had experienced on Tiburón. Some of them wished they were back on that peaceful island.

With the thought that the dignified Chief would turn his vengeance on them the moment he realized his face was black, the kids panicked and ran for the cars, urging their parents to get out of town and pronto.

Parents agreed that strategic retreat was not without merit. They had not yet learned that close surveillance by Mexican officials had tamed the Seris and they were not about to lay a hand on any visitor.

It was only after we were installed in a plush auto court in Hermosillo, had showers and a change of clothing, that relaxed conversation resumed. Then it broke loose with an exchange of the things to be told to classmates. Harriet summed it up with, "We'll give those kids enough daydream and nightmare material to last them for the rest of their lives." — RAY CANNON

The *Cory-Jo* and *Yorba Lady II* at Bahía Willard.

The "Shipwreck Charlie" Cohen boats in the windswept panorama of Bahía Willard.

"SHIPWRECK CHARLIE" COHEN CRUISE

SERIOUS LEARNING EXPERIENCE

BASKING IN THE easy success of his 1957 "Gene Perry" cruise, from San Felipe to the Midriff islands, and the wonderful adventures of the "Kids' Trip" from Kino Bay to Bahía San Francisquito in 1958, Ray felt ready by the spring of 1959 to tackle his first small boat trip down the full length of the Sea of Cortez.

In April of that year, he joined a flotilla of four trailer boats organized by "Shipwreck Charlie" Cohen that did in fact make it from San Felipe to La Paz and back, but only after having one boat drop out and enduring the worst series of mishaps that Ray would suffer during his entire quarter-century career in Baja.

(At the conclusion of the southward leg of the cruise, the members of the expedition continued by car to Rancho Buena Vista before rejoining their boats at La Paz and returning to San Felipe.)

In later years, Ray would often refer to the "Shipwreck Charlie" Cohen Cruise as an example of things gone wrong. From combined manuscripts written in 1959, he describes the many mistakes they made and the hard lessons learned.

After this trip—and until the opening of the Transpeninsular Highway (1973) and the side road to Bahía de los Angeles (1974)—Ray would advise against the San Felipe route in favor of the crossing from Kino Bay.

The "Shipwreck Charlie" Cohen Cruise was only one of three expeditions that were timed to rendezvous at La Paz. On the Pacific side of Baja California, Milt Farney and Larry Foglino were simultaneously cruising down the coast in their 17-foot outboard, *Searcher*. And crossing the gulf from Topolobampo was Dr. Philip Savage Jr. in his 22-foot outboard, *El Regalo*.

The "Shipwreck Charlie" Cohen Cruise is also notable because at its conclusion Ray met Jack Whelan at Rancho Buena Vista. This was the spotter plane pilot who guided a fleet of purse seiners to the "100-mile-long" school of yellowfin tuna that entered the gulf that spring. For the remainder of his career, Ray would credit that fleet of over 50 commercial fishing boats with "breaking the back" of the Cortez tuna population.

The "Rucker trips" Ray refers to in the opening paragraph of this story were aboard the panga motherships out of San Felipe that he had been fishing on since 1954.

Note: Ray left the "Shipwreck Charlie" Cohen group at Rancho Buena Vista. Cohen eventually made it back to San Felipe in *Yorba Lady II*, but says he was barely running at the end because of the bad gas he was forced to burn. He used 55 spark plugs on the trip.

From combined fragments, the story of the 1959 "Shipwreck Charlie" Cohen Cruise from San Felipe to La Paz, and on to Rancho Buena Vista by car:

"SHIPWRECK CHARLIE" COHEN CRUISE
ALL THE WAY DOWN THE CORTEZ

Although we had been forced to hightail it for shelter on some Rucker trips, it was not until my second small boat voyage in the north end that I came to realize the immense danger of cruising in this region.

My first expedition along this stretch with Eugene Perry met with sheer luck along every step of it. With very little knowledge of what we were doing, our timing was perfect, with all of the elements working in our favor. I was on the verge of writing that small craft could run down this west coast of the Cortez in a breeze, but fortunately, with another expedition planned, I held off.

This second cruise, organized by Charles Cohen, Santa Ana, California, and Harold Nash, Los Angeles, California, was scheduled for six boats to launch at San Felipe and to go all the way to La Paz.

One boat didn't even get to San Felipe.

Ten of us met at Santa Ana, California, April 27 to

The "Shipwreck Charlie" Cohen boat caravan crossing the border at Mexicali. Note sign at upper right: "End U.S. 99." This point was the terminus of the main north-south highway through the Western states from Mexico to Canada prior to the opening of Interstate 5.

trail four small boats to San Felipe.

Our fleet consisted of Phil O'Brien's 21-ft. inboard *Jainy*, with Bob Paulson; Harold Nash's 22-ft. inboard *Hallu*, with Jack Jeffers; Charles Cohen's 24-ft. outboard *Yorba Lady II*, with Milt Beral and me; and the 20-ft. inboard *Cory-Jo* belonging to Corydon Bernett.

We were to be escorted by Paul Jenkins with his 52-ft. Stephens cruiser, *Wild Goose*.

During the final shakedown the *Cory-Jo* developed a crack in her manifold, so we left her in San Felipe to wait for additional parts to be flown down from California.

Three of the craft took off and planed down with the swift current for the 50 miles of shallow coveless beaches to Puertecitos.

We remained offshore to stay in the favorable swift current. Later we swung in behind Isla Huerfanito, first in the Enchanted Island Chain, because of a tidal change. The water behind the islands was soon running as a countercurrent in our direction.

Charles Cohen aboard *Yorba Lady II* followed a course outside the islands, however, and was caught in the full reverse tide. Although his instruments showed they were making 20 miles-an-hour, a check with the shoreline indicated they were almost standing still.

Two boats arrived safely in Willard's Bay, where gas had been trucked down for us. Cohen missed the Bay and ran out of gas. Learning of it, Nash ran down and towed him back to Gorgonio Romero's camp at Willard Bay, where we gassed up.

A change in the wind forced us to quit Willard's. We sailed across four-and-a-half-mile wide San Luis Gonzaga

to a hidden cove called Ensenada San Francisquito (not to be confused with the large Bahía San Francisquito 115 miles to the south), where we caught all the grouper we could use. The entrance to this cove is "S"-shaped and located just in from two of the four small beaches.

That evening the repaired *Cory-Jo* arrived from San Felipe, running against the current after dark. Nash chanced going after it, and on their way back both craft got shipwrecked on a reef.

From the Nash radio came the message, "We have run aground at Willard's Point," then no more until Paul Jenkins' big, 52-foot *Wild Goose*, the only boat able to go to the rescue, radioed that both hulls were okay but that the mechanism of both were wrecked.

The next night, before the first two casualties could be repaired, Charles Cohen's outboard *Yorba Lady II* was pounding on the rocks as the result of another hell-raising blow. A 20-foot rise in the tide had lifted the anchor.

I was asleep on this one when Charles broke out the disaster horn. The sound-off brought a dozen native turtle fishermen swarming over our boat and the *Cory-Jo* along side. Despite the rampaging squall they scrambled over us like a bunch of underwear-clad monkeys and had us netted in the dozens of crisscross lines being hurled by their leader, Gorgonio Romero.

With a sizable hole in its bottom the *Yorba Lady II* would have sunk in a short time, but for the rescue. Fortunately, it was repairable. Cohen's navigator, however, hitched a ride back on a truck.

The *Cory-Jo*, unable to go on, limped back to San Felipe. With the three remaining boats back in shape, we went on, learning valuable lessons the hard way.

On May 3 we plowed around Punta Final and into more foul weather. It was a "Pilgrims's Progress" journey, with problems around most every bend.

Having the current with us we could avoid heavy swells and offshore winds by running close to the lee provided by the cliffs.

Whenever we could find a bay or quiet water between points we found favorable countercurrents and much less wave action.

This held good until we ran out of the mountainous walls and came down to lower lands stretching up from Bahía de los Angeles. Here we were not only plagued by the fury of a headwind, but were forced to steer offshore and into the face of the turbulent channel to avoid crashing into uncharted reefs and rocks reaching out from the shoreline. We got in after dark.

We found Los Angeles Bay to be a wind-maker. A large freighter had pulled her anchor and been thrown astride the sand bar the day before. It was pulled off the next day.

Cohen dropped out to wait for motor parts. He arranged to have mechanic Bob Hall from Scott Outboards fly down.

Later, off Bahía de las Mujeres, the most northerly cove in Bahía San Francisquito, we encountered a mild upwelling and were forced to run to the coves to avoid being pushed backwards. We found quartering up to the flat plateau upwellings difficult, but not overly dangerous. Small boats can make it by quartering up the upwelling, but not by plowing straight into it.

We cruised down to San Francisquito to pick up fuel and went ashore to have a look at the airstrip, shell mounds and ancient dwelling places.

At Santa Rosalía we were met by the mayor and port captain and other officials who offered every assistance. We learned that Bill Escudero of Trans Mar de Cortés Airlines had alerted all officials along our route, as well as the company's local managers who rushed gas to us because of a shortage in the towns.

We headed for Mulegé.

Nash cracked up again barreling into the Mulegé River and had to be towed into port.

Cohen caught up. "Sal" Salazar, the lodge owner, was most hospitable. A dance and party proved a welcome relief. We had our best day so far, cruising to El Coyote, halfway back into Concepción Bay, for clam digging and fishing an enormous school of jack crevalle.

Leaving Mulegé in excellent weather, we examined coves along the way, noting that most of them were encircled by dangerous rocks.

We were again met by city and Trans Mar officials at Loreto. They drove us around to see the town and made our visit very pleasant. To find good anchorage we sailed on to Puerto Escondido.

The rugged shoreline and offshore rocks seemed

Refueling the *Jainy*, possibly at Isla San José.

strange, but once past Candeleros Point the coast straightens out until Bahía Agua Verde is reached.

We learned that our gas supply had been diverted from Agua Verde to Isla San José. (It would have been safer to have supplies boated down the 37 miles from Loreto.) We were caught in a strong current and high headwind as we crossed Canal de San José, but found good going by running up close to the island shore. There was little protection from the southerly wind when we met our fuel boat off the salt works at Isla San José's southern tip, but thanks to the electric pump which Nash had brought we were able to transfer the gas.

We headed for the lee on the west side of San José's satellite Isla San Francisco and fought heavy seas on down to Isla Partida, attached to the north end of Isla Espíritu Santo. Halfway along, the wind dropped a little and skin divers Phil O'Brien and Bob Paulson on the *Jainy* decided to troll for marlin. They ran between us and the sun and we lost sight of them.

Cohen's *Yorba Lady II* dropped behind because of bad gas. We slowed to wait for her and took a terrible drenching as the storm let go its full fury. Seeing the *Yorba Lady II* was able to make it at creeping speed, we made a run so I could show Cohen the baylet by flashing a light.

Darkness had settled down and the sea was raging. We got Cohen's boat safely in and learned that the *Jainy* had drifted out to sea, driven by the offshore wind. Cohen could not help because of his own trouble.

The Harold Nash boat, *Hallu*, spent half the night searching but failed to make contact. We all feared the *Jainy* was lost.

"Shipwreck Charlie" Cohen attending to the *Yorba Lady II*.

Cohen with a nice pompano caught near Mulegé. Note the "white Compac feather," Ray's favorite lure, and the tandem wire leader setup he used most of the time.

Shortly after daybreak we tried to make radio contact to get a plane to search but could not receive an answer.

We decided to run the rough sea (30 miles) to La Paz to get a plane.

After fighting an awfully rough sea halfway to La Paz, we saw a boat pull out of a cove and were really elated to discover it was O'Brien's boat, the *Jainy*.

It seems they had refiltered the gas and adjusted the motors and had found the cove long after dark.

Pilots flying the Trans Mar de Cortés Airline planes which had been following our ill-charted progress, radioed a report that one of our craft was lost and presumed down at sea. Our message had been picked up in La Paz but they could not be certain where any of us were.

On our arrival, everyone was relieved and happy. Bill Escudero of Trans Mar de Cortés Airlines met us. Paul Jenkins' *Wild Goose* got in a day ahead of us and told of our progress but lost radio contact. The Los Arcos hotel gave us the royal treatment with a celebration dinner.

Another boat in our expedition, the 22-foot outboard *El Regalo*, skippered by Dr. Philip Savage Jr., of San Bernardino, California, met us at Rancho Buena Vista after a most hazardous trip across the Gulf from Topolobampo, but only after running out of gas many miles off Isla Cerralvo's southern tip. Its radio distress signal was picked up by a yacht that had 15 gallons of gas aboard, enough to get the *El Regalo* to Las Cruces where it refueled and sailed on down for the rendezvous.

The other three boats, the *Hallu*, *Yorba Lady II*, and *Jainy*, were made ready for the trip north in La Paz. All participants in the Cannon Expedition were driven overland to Rancho Buena Vista for a two-week fiesta at the lodge given by owner Colonel Gene Walters.

We stayed at Rancho Buena Vista where a fiesta was held in our honor.

Another 17-foot outboard manned by Milt Farney and Larry Foglino sailed down the Pacific side of the Baja California peninsula and made Rancho Buena Vista two days late for the elaborate fiesta.

On May 19, Jack Whelan, air spotter for tuna movements, flew in and reported seeing a compact school of fish, principally tuna and bottlenose dolphin (mammal), at least 100 miles long racing into the mouth of the gulf and heading across toward Rancho Buena Vista. Although he had been keeping tabs on such migrations for a number of years, he said this was the largest single group he had ever seen.

*****

No voyage in all my life had taught me more, and my log showed that every unpleasant incident could have been avoided, all being the result of human errors or ignorance of the odd quirks of this strange Sea. — RAY CANNON

At the conclusion of his cruise down the Cortez with "Shipwreck Charlie" Cohen in late May 1959, Ray traveled by car to Rancho Buena Vista and met Milt Farney and Larry Foglino. Farney and Foglino's boat *Searcher*, just visible over Ray's left shoulder, had just made it down Baja's Pacific coast and around Cabo San Lucas in an effort to "top" Ray's cruise, according to Cohen. The *Searcher* was sponsored by Glaspar and had air support for fuel, supplies, and even spare engines, Cohen says. However, it was damaged and sank at Mulegé, and Farney and Foglino flew back to San Diego. On the beach with the group is Ray's pal, the Rancho Buena Vista dog, Matador.

Searcher at anchor off Rancho Buena Vista.

The Hotel Los Arcos in La Paz, 1959, at the end of the Cohen Cruise. — PHOTO BY CHARLES COHEN

Ray, driving the *Peggy Sue* on its way to the discoveries of Isla Cerralvo. — PHOTO BY RALPH POOLE

INCIDENT AT CHILENO BAY

SERENDIPITY & THE "PEGGY SUE"

TWO OF RAY'S greatest tales—the "'Intelligent' Golden Grouper" and the "Vagabundo Graveyard"—had their beginnings in a chance November 1960 meeting with Baja adventurers Spencer Murray and Ralph Poole at the Hotel Cabo San Lucas, which was still under construction on Chileno Bay just a few miles from the tip of the Baja California peninsula.

Murray and Poole had launched their 22-foot cabin cruiser, *Peggy Sue*, at San Felipe on September 28th of that year, and they were on the final leg of a full-length cruise

of Baja that would result in Murray's classic book, *Cruising The Sea Of Cortez* (1963).

(These two would also win fame in July 1967, when they set a pre-Baja 1000 speed record by driving a virtually stock AMC Rambler American from Tijuana to La Paz in 31 hours flat.)

Ray happened to be at the hotel—still a year from being fully operational—as a guest of its owner, Baja pioneer, William Matt "Bud" Parr.

The *Peggy Sue's* owner, Spencer Murray, had returned

Hotel Cabo San Lucas statuary carved at the Chileno Bay site by Guadalajara sculptor Carlos Gonzales.

The Hotel Cabo San Lucas' first "dining room," still under construction, 1960. Seated left to right: An unidentified construction staff member; Ray Cannon; hotel staff member, "Doc Ross"; hotel staff member, Carlos Ungson; boat builder, Dale Jeffries; and Spence Murray, owner of the *Peggy Sue.* — PHOTO BY RALPH POOLE

to the U.S. by plane because his wife was about to give birth to a child, and he had left Poole at the Hotel Cabo San Lucas with instructions to put the boat in storage in La Paz and also fly home. Somehow, it was decided that Ray would ride along on the *Peggy Sue*, and furthermore, that he and Poole would stop at Isla Cerralvo on their way back to La Paz.

They anchored the *Peggy Sue* just south of a small hook of sand at the extreme southwest corner of the island, and they decided to go ashore. There, Ray discovered a school of brilliant orange-colored golden grouper—an uncommon form of the normally drab leopard grouper—swimming near the rocks.

And on shore nearby, he and Poole found some rough wooden crosses and a place beside them where candles had been burned. Ray imagined that this place was the graveyard of the "vagabundos del mar" (vagabonds of the sea), the fishermen he had observed wandering the Sea of Cortez in their sail-driven dugout canoes.

As Ray later described this "vagabundo graveyard":

"On my first trip to Cerralvo, with photographer Ralph Poole, we found dried flowers and recently burned candles by the graves, indicating the reverence held for members of their very detached fraternity. Yet this burial ground seems to be the only place where they assemble.

"The decaying conditions of some of the crosses and

rusted out cans, still filled with wax from melted candles, gives mute evidence of the great age of the oldest of the graves, suggesting that these freedom-loving gypsies have been plying the waters of El Cortez for a century or more."

From these encounters with the golden groupers and the simple graves found on Isla Cerralvo sprang two of Ray's all-time favorite stories.

The first was the fable of the "intelligent" prey-herding behavior of the brilliantly-colored golden groupers, which he saw as a cooperative hunting effort. He would write versions of this story many times in *Western Outdoor News*, in magazine articles, and in his book, *The Sea Of Cortez*.

The second story was of the "Vagabundo Graveyard" of the gypsy-like canoe fishermen who Ray said roamed the Sea of Cortez in blissful freedom and were brought after death only to this corner of Isla Cerralvo for burial. Ray had been interested in these itinerant sailors since his first trips to Baja and he had written about them as early as 1957, but on this visit to Isla Cerralvo, he and Ralph Poole speculated together on their origins and social organization, and it is probable that the story of the "Vagabundo Graveyard" formed in Ray's mind at this time.

Although Ray also wrote of observing the "intelligent" behavior of the golden grouper in the Los Cabos area and on Isla Catalán as well, no less an authority than Dr. Boyd

Walker, head of ichthyology at UCLA and Ray's companion on some of these trips, says unequivocally that he is not convinced that he ever saw it happen. Nevertheless, this is one of Ray's most memorable stories. Surely, anyone who has ever heard it will always give golden groupers a second look wherever they are encountered, in hopes of observing the "intelligent" herding behavior that Ray described.

And the "Vagabundo Graveyard"? Ralph Poole, later publisher of *Trailer Boats Magazine*, recalls seeing perhaps three crosses on the island during that 1960 trip aboard the *Peggy Sue*. And James Pledger "Jimmy" Smith of Los Barriles, arguably Baja California's foremost folk historian, says that he sees no evidence for the idea. Nevertheless, it too, will forever be remembered as one of Ray's greatest Baja stories, and one that has taken on a life of its own. Today's large and successful Vagabundos Del Mar Boat & Travel Club takes its name from Ray's vision of those roaming canoe sailors, and whether or not they really were brought to Isla Cerralvo for burial, the story of those eponymous old vagabundos has become an essential part of the mystique and lore associated with the Sea of Cortez. Because of Ray's imaginative inspiration, that body of water could almost be thought of as the "Sea of the Vagabundos."

The following columns and fragments tell the story of Ray's fateful encounter with the *Peggy Sue* at the still-building Hotel Cabo San Lucas, and of his subsequent trip to Isla Cerralvo. Separate sections, combined from fragments dating from 1957 to about 1961, give Ray's best versions of the golden grouper story and the colorful legends of the vagabundos del mar.

BUILDING THE HOTEL CABO SAN LUCAS

When it opened its main buildings in 1961, William Matthew "Bud" Parr's palatial Hotel Cabo San Lucas was the most spectacular resort ever built in Baja California Sur.

Parr and his business partner, Luis Cóppola Bonillas, bought the 2,500-acre Rancho El Tule, surrounding the beautiful, rocky cove of Chileno Bay ten miles outside of Cabo San Lucas, and with virtually nothing available at the site that could be called "infrastructure," they built a luxurious fly-in resort capable of catering to presidents and movie stars.

Reportedly, buying the land from its five women owners required a month of negotiations. One of the first

Ray, holding hose, helps refuel the *Peggy Sue* at the Hotel Cabo San Lucas. — PHOTO BY RALPH POOLE

improvements was the grading of a 3,600-foot airstrip that would allow supplies to be flown in.

Diesel generating equipment followed, and a small army of workers was brought in to build virtually everything on site, including milled wooden parts, concrete block, roof tiles, drain pipe, decorative floor tiles, and even hand-carved furniture.

Water was piped in from a mountain spring. Rubber trees came from Mexico City, bougainvillea from California, banana plants from San José del Cabo.

Renowned architect Cliff May designed the stone and concrete buildings, and on-site technical installations were supervised by Carlos Ungson and Simón Yee. Noted Guadalajara sculptor, Carlos Gonzales, was hired to carve 300 pieces of monumental statuary for the grounds. Los Angeles boat builder Dale Jeffries constructed the resort's fleet of state-of-the-art sport fishing cruisers in a boat yard built beside the hotel.

It was near this place on Chileno Bay that Ray and Frank Dufresne had their "hophead's dream" shore fishing experience, and it was also here that Ray met Ralph Poole and Spencer Murray who had just cruised south from San Felipe in the *Peggy Sue*.

In columns from the summer of 1961, Ray describes the magnificent new hotel and the Dale Jeffries boat works.

ELABORATE RESORT PLANNED NEAR CABO SAN LUCAS

[At the time this report was written, 1960, Ray, apparently, was still not aware that Bud Parr was the principal partner in the Hotel Cabo San Lucas, together with Ray's old friend, Luis Cóppola Bonillas, owner of the Hotel Los Arcos in La Paz.]

The big news break coming from Baja California Sur is a release just received on the ground-breaking for an elaborate resort at Puerto Chileno. The company to operate the tropical spa is headed by Luis Cóppola, former manager of Trans Mar de Cortés airlines.

Included in the enterprise are three ranches comprising thousands of acres. These lands situated between San José del Cabo and Cape San Lucas, extend from the coastline to the mountains.

The area selected for the lodge-hotel and bungalows is atop a rock palisade overlooking white sand coves and a half-mile-wide reef with dozens of tide-washed rocks extending along the shore for miles. This is the stretch where I found tide pools the size of Marineland tanks, and almost as loaded with brilliant colored fishes of all sizes and many kinds.

Construction has started on the clubhouse, the first 50 dwelling units, and elaborate tropical gardens. A private plane airstrip has been completed near the lodge. The federal government is now grading a mile-long landing

Construction of the Hotel Cabo San Lucas on Chileno Bay, 1960. Concrete blocks, lower left, and most other materials were fabricated on site. At upper right, Carlos Ungson in a war surplus truck rebuilt by Bud Parr's son, Mark. Dale Jeffries at window. At lower right, the hotel's original guest rooms.

— UPPER LEFT PHOTO BY HARRY MERRICK. OTHER PHOTOS BY RALPH POOLE

strip on nearby Mesa Colorada. Trans Mar expects to extend its flights to include this airport in the near future.

According to Cóppola the resort will include numerous entertainment attractions for guests in addition to fishing, hunting and water sports. — RAY CANNON

DALE JEFFRIES BOAT WORKS

[The Dale Jeffries-built sport fishing fleet of the Hotel Cabo San Lucas—like everything else about the hotel—set new standards of luxury and comfort for Baja California. Ray describes Jeffries and his operation.]

JUNE 1, 1961—With the event of the opening of the Cabo San Lucas resort [Hotel Cabo San Lucas], anglers will be fishing from a new and revolutionary-type angling craft. Twenty of these 30-foot, high-speed cruisers, designed by Dale Jeffries especially for angling in this region, are being constructed on the spot.

Among the many interesting features are the big, 6-71 Diesel Jim motors, good for 22 knots, and the comfortable roominess of a stern 12 feet across.

Jeffries, former head of the famed sports-boat builders firm, Jeffries Boats, Inc., of L.A., is noted for originating the waterproof plywood in 1938. Also, the stress-skin plywood, wide-transom craft, and numerous innovations which launched the plywood boat industry.

Of equal interest to me was the discovery that Dale was my kind of guy and just as "far gone" on experimental fishing as I am. And I have a hunch that as soon as he gets his new boats in operation, he'll knock if off and join my cult of doing nothing but fishing and telling and laughing about it. He is already hooked on the region and is building a home right on the end of a high point and has suggested a couple of months' cruise up El Cortez with me early next summer.

If he isn't a confirmed initiate by the start of that voyage, he will be before it's finished.

Among Dale's latest plans for experimental angling is the use of live bait for billfish. There are times when both marlin and sailfish (so plentiful in the area the year round) refuse all frozen baits. Jeffries will install live bait tanks and a receiver. He will never have a shortage. He can net all he wants at any time at the [Cabo] San Lucas Pier.

You may have read of the fish around the San Lucas Pier in this column, in which I wrote that they form layer blankets, one species above another, in such tight formations any one blanket would completely black out the white sand bottom. Photog Harry Merrick nearly flipped trying to get pix of them. Earl "Salty" Bacon, aircraft executive and Gulf comber, flew in and joined me in test fishing from the pier. With a triple hook we could snag most of the half-dozen species in the constant layers and catch an equal number on strip-bait or small lures.

Jeffries could have netted tons of mullet, goatfish,

Boat builder, Dale Jeffries, and his boat works at the Hotel Cabo San Lucas, 1960. — PHOTOS BY RALPH POOLE

bigeye jack, striped grunt and corbina, all of which make excellent bait for billfish.

I had another strange encounter with that demonic double-jointed crab called Sally Lightfoot that sliced Frank Dufresne's fingers, and mine as well, when we tried to catch one for bait on a previous trip. They also ruined our clothes by spitting indelible ink on them. Last night I had a signal fire going on the beach when I noticed a dozen or so dash up to inspect it. They showed little fear until within scorching distance. A half-inch live coal popped out and was immediately grabbed by a "Sally," who juggled and spit on it until cooled, then ate it.

I flipped half a cigarette to another one who quickly shucked it by splitting the paper with her Gillette-edged pinchers, then ate the tobacco, got crocked and chased all the other "Lightfoots" into their holes. — RAY CANNON

BUD PARR'S ULTRA-LIGHT-TACKLE WORLD RECORD MARLIN

[William Matthew "Bud" Parr, owner of the Hotel Cabo San Lucas, was not only a visionary and pioneer of the Golden Age, but also a consummate light-tackle angler at a time when heavy reels and roller-guide rods were still coming into general use. Ray's story tells of Parr catching two marlin in a single afternoon on four-pound test line. On April 3, 1972, Parr would set an IGFA six-pound test world record for striped marlin (205 pounds) that stands to the present day.]

JUNE 22, 1967—Somehow I feel that this column should be suppressed, for fear that my other angler readers might get discouraged. On the other hand, it may give courage and hope to those who are too timid to go forth to battle the mighty marlins.

Now, I was right there, standing on the deck beside Bud Parr, operator of the Hotel Cabo San Lucas, when he caught two striped marlin on four-pound test line, on a reel not much larger than a spool of thread and a rod in the buggy whip class.

Working with Stan LoPresto on what I believe will be the wildest fishing movie ever made, I had been involved in a sea full of marlin all the way from La Paz to the Cape and had completed the billfish phase of the documentary film, "The Sea of Cortez," (which may be available to clubs in a few months). But when Parr said he could go straight out and catch marlin on four-pound test, we reopened the case.

People going to this resort expect the best of everything and Parr most often provides it, but when he promised to get a Goliath with a slingshot, I started thinking up alibis for him to use when he failed.

We didn't start out until after 3:00 p.m., an hour when sensible billfish anglers have returned and are slurp-gunning their third beer. We were about 20 minutes out

With William Matthew "Bud" Parr of the Hotel Cabo San Lucas, c. 1962.

from the puerto when the first tail fin appeared. To keep the sizable flyingfish skiing on the surface, Parr held the rod as high as possible. The fragile line would have been snapped quickly if attached to the outrigger.

Our skipper brought the bait across in front of the marlin which wasted little time in beaming in on the trail, and less in latching on to the bait. From this instant on, the skipper must handle the boat with a delicate touch and go. He is guided by keeping his eye on the bend in the very flexible rod. If it starts to straighten, the boat is moved forward—when too much bent, it is moved backwards.

Parr popped the first fish when he applied more muscle than the line would take in setting the hook. With a gentle hair-trigger technique he brought the next two to the boat, to be tagged and released.

****

One of the big success stories of the Cortez-Baja country is that of Carlos Ungson, now manager of this magnificent hotel. He not only engineered its construction but supervised every part of the building. Just now, in addition to his hotel duties, he is constructing a new 16-unit wing facing the sea and sunrise, plus some of my favorite tide pools. The several super-deluxe

features of this resort make it highly desirable for the ladies. Here they can go out for the rough stuff or remain as fastidious as they like in a tropical garden and housing splendor. — RAY CANNON

ISLA CERALBO
EXPLORING EL GOLFO'S LAST ISLAND

[The *Peggy Sue's* cruise to Isla Cerralvo, and the final run to La Paz with Ralph Poole. The discoveries of the golden grouper and the vagabundo crosses are described briefly here, and in more detail in the following sections.]

JANUARY 13, 1961—Some day when fresh water can be extracted from the ocean economically, Isla Ceralbo (Spanish spelling) will become another Catalina Island. But today, this 18 by 4 1/2-mile mountain projecting up from water depths of 300 to 850 fathoms, is inhabited principally by goats, birds, and prehistoric lizards that seem to live in tidal caves.

I also saw signs of ringtail cats. The only human visitors are a group of shark fishermen and an occasional pair of vagabundos del mar who sail the Sea with the wind.

Ray's "Trip Of The Week" article in *Western Outdoor News*, January 13, 1961, in which he introduced the legends of the "'intelligent' golden grouper" and the "vagabundos del mar's only graveyard" on Isla Cerralvo. Note Ray's early usages, "Isla Ceralbo" and "El Golfo."

— COURTESY WESTERN OUTDOOR NEWS

But fish populations and numbers of species of big game fishes choke the waters, especially at the south end.

Many times I had fished the north end of the island for sailfish, marlin and dolphinfish and had worked the cliffed shoreline for giant grouper, but this was my first visit to the highly exciting south end.

This trip started at the new Cabo San Lucas resort when photographer Ralph Poole and Spencer Murray arrived in their 22-foot cabin cruiser *Peggy Sue* from a voyage down the whole length of El Cortez.

After a few days celebrating the occasion, Spencer and I changed places. Bud Parr flew him back to La Paz and I took his place on the *Peggy Sue*.

Poole and I kept radio contact with the resort, reporting the tuna schools and billfish we saw over the Gordo Reefs, but were blacked out as soon as we rounded Punta Gorda.

For both of us, the cruise up the strange coast was delightful and it gave me a chance to reexamine the coves and protective points around Los Frailes, Cabo Pulmo, and the bay between it and Punta Arena. I was reminded of the emptiness of this vast region when we saw no more than a half-dozen ranch houses, half of them deserted.

As soon as we reached Punta Arena, the lower perimeter of Las Palmas Bay, we plowed into sea-ripping schools of tuna, dolphinfish, jacks and billfish. Although we were anxious to make Rancho Buena Vista before dark we couldn't resist a few passes for the big yellowfin tuna and dolphinfish. With each contact with a school we boated one, but the time it took to deck a 38-pound yellowfin forced us to reluctantly move on.

As we passed the freshwater lagoons six miles below Buena Vista we were surprised to see Parr and Luis

Cóppola, owners of the Cabo San Lucas resort, shooting ducks and brant. They had flown in an hour or so before. Plane travel in this region is about to take the meaning out of the word "mañana."

Following a two-day fiesta with tables laden with turtle, dolphinfish, brant, doves and ducks at the Buena Vista Lodge, Poole and I took off. We glided up past Punta Pescadero, across Muertos Bay to the long, sandy Punta Arena de la Ventana, then due north to Isla Ceralbo. Billfish were seen jumping all along the course.

We examined and fished all the reefs and coves across the whole south end of the Island and found them crawling with many species. We ran into surface-working schools of jacks, rarely seen elsewhere in the region. We also went ashore to examine ancient Indian middens and the burial grounds of the sea-roving natives.

While examining tracks and spoor of goats, ringtail cats and crawling creatures on the Island, we saw a couple of very large lizards (not as big as an iguana) dash to the water and slosh through it to get into caves. The first I have seen that liked a watery hangout.

Most interesting of all we saw was a troupe of golden grouper working a school of anchovetas in an inlet about 40 feet across. I had a box seat atop a sheer cliff directly above the arena.

We spent the quiet night aboard the boat on the south side of a sandy point at the extreme southwest corner of the Island.

Following a daybreak breakfast and a look at another land-side section, I noticed some goat trails and was reminded of a story told of this spot by Bill Escudero, Trans Mar de Cortés executive. It was his first hunting trip after arriving in Baja California. A couple of friends had

Ray and Ralph Poole at their anchorage on Isla Cerralvo, 1960. — PHOTO BY RALPH POOLE

persuaded him to go for a wild goat shoot on Ceralbo Island. "Halfway up a 2,000-foot mountain," he said, "they stationed me below a big rock, explaining that they would climb on up and flush out the goats, and that the wild animals would come tearing down one or the other of the two paths that straddled the rock, giving me a clean shot no matter which route was followed."

"In less than half an hour," he went on, "I was jolted to my feet by a thunderous roar. Looking up the steep slope I could see a great cloud of dust rising above the bush tops and it was coming down the mountain at such speed I was sure a rock avalanche was about to come down on me. I crouched in a hole in the rock, waiting for the first boulders to come whizzing overhead. When none came, but the noise came close, I peeked out. What I saw was 200 goats! I grabbed my gun but couldn't pull the trigger."

Bill gave us a Buster Keaton stare and continued with, "Can you imagine? Those were billy goats, the kind that we had for pets when we were kids. It would have been like shooting my cousins."

There were tugging aches when we felt forced to tear away from this blessed wilderness. We looked back at the jumping fish, diving birds and glorious landscape and wondered how long it would take for people worn and tired of the big-city rat race to learn of the exultation and happiness to be found in such way-out places.

Knowing we would find no climax to top our Ceralbo experiences, we sailed a straight course to Punta Coyote, thence to La Paz and the Los Arcos Hotel where we would trim our beards and slick up for the first time in six weeks. I really do this once in a great while but hate myself afterwards when I look in a mirror. — RAY CANNON

An "intelligent" golden grouper, this one caught by trolling an albacore feather (visible under Ray's right hand).

"INTELLIGENT" GOLDEN GROUPER

RAY'S WILDEST BAJA YARN

THE STORY OF the "intelligent" prey-herding behavior of the golden grouper, as told by Ray, following his 1960 cruise to Isla Cerralvo on the *Peggy Sue* with Ralph Poole:

"THE WEIRDEST SIGHT IN ALL MY FISHING EXPERIENCE"

It was the weirdest sight in all my fishing experience. I'm still shaken by it. I can't make myself believe that fishes could display intelligence far above that of mere instinct; actual ability to make plans and to carry them out with deadly precision. It occurred among a family of groupers classified as *Mycteroperca rosacea*, in which about two or three out of a hundred are not olive-drab in color but brilliant luminescent orange or gold. I often wondered why Nature spotted the schools with these flame-bright individuals. One day, down on the Sea of Cortez, I found out.

Ralph and I had arrived at the southern tip of Cerralvo in late afternoon. Seeing a flock of sea birds diving at the back of a triangular cove, a sure sign that game fish were working small forage fish, we hurriedly dropped anchor, grabbed our spinning outfits and dashed over to a ledge above the area. There was a roaring splash as 100 or more leopard groupers leaped into the air in close-to-unison precision.

We knew they had been waiting in ambush for the fingerlings to pass over them, to vault up and come thrashing down maiming as many as possible, then to vacuum them down grouper gullets in a free-for-all.

I had often seen a gang of leopards work over a hemmed-in ball of bait fish by blasting up through the surface en masse and come crashing down on the small fry like an avalanche, but I never was able to observe how the little fish were corralled, or by what means the groupers knew which area the forage school would move through.

Within a few minutes, I was to get a clear picture and discover a completely new twist in fish behavior.

As we were about to cast some white feather lures into the action we noticed a line of golden groupers emerge from the melee, move into the shadow of the bluff and proceed in single file just below us. We counted 14, the most I had ever seen in one place.

Each individual came to the outer corner of the bluff and made a sharp right turn in military order until they were spaced across the mouth of the cove. Then, with a "squad right," they proceeded abreast, slowly herding the scattered forage fish right over the reef where the unseen leopard brigade awaited them.

As the bait fish passed overhead, the hidden predators exploded up to come smacking down on the dazed small fry to repeat the crippling strategy. At this cue, the gold demolition squad broke ranks and plunged in to help gobble up the spoils.

The survivors fled out to sea through the narrow escape, chopped and flailed by the golden ones, and I thought to myself, "I will never, never see the like of this again."

But I was wrong. We watched this exact procedure reenacted twelve times and were so awed we forgot all about trying to catch one to photograph until it was so dark we could not distinguish the golden from the leopards.

The next morning we found that the whole grouper army had moved out.

We had clearly seen something new and exciting in fish behavior, and as soon as I returned to Los Angeles I called Dr. Boyd Walker of UCLA to tell him about it. I had hopes of chumming him on another trip to Cerralvo with me. Sure enough, he couldn't resist, and canceled his classes for ten days.

Our special friend, Colonel Eugene Walters, operator

Anchoring the *Peggy Sue*, just south of a sand spit at the southwest corner of the island. Ray's fateful observation of the "intelligent" prey-herding behavior of the golden grouper occurred near this spot. — PHOTO BY RALPH POOLE

of the fabulous Rancho Buena Vista Lodge, fitted out an expedition for us, including his largest boat, and assigned my favorite skippers, Laborio and Fiol, as guides.

Each day on Cerralvo proved more delightful than the last. Dr. Walker collected over 1,000 specimens of fish. Included were 100 species, some of them rare. It was wonderful, but the golden groupers seemingly had business elsewhere.

We regretfully left for Cape San Lucas, where I had previously seen leopard groupers jumping in unison on many occasions. As we cruised down across Muertos Bay the sea was seen crawling with game fish great and small; sea birds were diving for wounded fish; whales and porpoise pods rolled and blew across our course; dolphinfish and yellowfin tuna ripped the flat, glistening surface in pursuit of flyingfish; gigantic manta rays and marlin pushed up geysers of water as they leapt to rid themselves of parasites, or for the pure fun of it.

Watching this expression of the sea's magnificent abundances all around us, Walker's only comment was, "You know, Ray, this is the best day of my life."

At the Cape we again spent our waiting time

collecting, found a couple of new species, and filled half-a-dozen cans with rare exotics. Then, on the afternoon of the third day, it happened.

From the top of the cliff we saw four golden groupers surround a forage school and herd them through a narrow passage and into a tide pool right below us. As they reached the center, about a couple of dozen leopards shot up out of the water and started flailing before they hit the surface. The goldies then rushed in for the fiesta.

Twice more we watched the routine repeated, then saw the whole grouper school move out and on around the point, with the four golden guardians leading and swimming near the top, while the leopards hugged the dark rock bottom.

All Dr. Walker would say about the performance was that it "appears to indicate that the rosacea in the golden phase has a special function within the colony," but that we should see it repeated in many other areas to draw final conclusions.

None of the several dozen other species of groupers or sea bass in the tepid Sea of Cortez are known to possess either the brain power or radical color separation of *M. rosacea*. Though this feature baffles the scientists, they have managed to scrimp together a few odd facts on its life history.

Strangely enough, this fish, when hatched, is just like all the other leopard groupers in the spawn—drab brownish-green with light brown spots. But when about ten inches long, as if by some secret alchemy, golden blotches begin appearing on its body, which turns gradually to a color of brilliant, molten gold. They remain much smaller in size than the drab members of the family who are big dumbbells by comparison. They are much more alert, faster and brighter in every way, and specialized for their work among the other groupers.

Shortly thereafter, the golden leopard begins performing specialized functions within the colony, showing unusual intelligence in providing food, directing the school movements, and serving as decoy, drawing predators away from its complacent relatives. Only three or four out of a hundred leopard groupers turn gold and become smart; the others remain spotted and stupid. The mystery is—where does this intelligence come from?

According to Dr. Walker, the color transformation is destined by genetic processes, suggesting the possibility that the gene that carries the gold color destiny also provides a matrix for its high I.Q.

When there are no tide pools into which to herd prey for the big groupers, the golden ones do a fair job of surrounding a school of bait fish on the open sea. And they are just as quick to defend their big relatives from enemies. Does a hungry sea lion show up, he is met by flashing gold-plate jobs and decoyed away. Hammerhead sharks get the same treatment. I watched a hammerhead wear itself out chasing a little goldie while the rest of the grouper school practically yawned in boredom. They seem to know when there's a job to be done, and they go out and do it.

I tried using an unscaled side of a goldie as bait, and got all confused with another puzzler. The other trolled bait, a similar size and cut from a leopard, went unnoticed by the host of fishes that viciously slashed the gold strip. Half of them could have swallowed it. At least 50 violent attacks were made before an 85-pound gulf grouper got it nailed. It was as if the attackers were getting revenge for having been tricked so many times by the gold villain, rather than trying to eat it.

Future studies of the strange behavior pattern of *M. rosacea* and deviation from the uniform actions in the fish school may help to disclose the mystery of how hundreds of fish in a single group move and shift as if they were a single body responding to a single brain. Some scholars have suggested that the porous lateral line of a fish acts as sort of a radar apparatus and that in a tightly grouped school it may serve as a wireless nerve system compelling the individual members to react as if they were parts of the single body.

However, the golden members of a *rosacea* school appear to have their own shortwave intercom and can work independently from mass thought control.

I have since discussed the golden grouper with native fishermen, who call it *"La Reina de la Cabrilla"* (Queen of the Basses) and claim it dictates the movements of its school in audible orders that can be heard underwater.

The Seri Indians go them one better with the name *"Mitano"* (Goddess of the Fishes), and claim she has super being intelligence. — RAY CANNON

In the "Vagabundo graveyard." Ray would gain a lifetime of personally inspirational stories from these moments on Isla Cerralvo in 1960. — PHOTO BY RALPH POOLE

"Vagabundo" canoa. Patched sail and paddle steering were characteristic.

LEGENDS OF THE VAGABUNDOS

SEA GYPSIES OF THE CORTEZ

THE SECOND GREAT Cannon yarn that originated on the 1960 Isla Cerralvo trip aboard the *Peggy Sue* was the tale of the "Vagabundo Graveyard" at the southwest corner of the island, which Ray envisioned as a place where the wandering canoe gypsies of the Cortez were brought after death. Ray remained fascinated to the end of his life by the concept of the penniless but free-living vagabundos and he loved to tell people that he had become a vagabundo himself by renouncing the physical trappings of modern society. After Ray died in 1977, his ashes were scattered on the Sea

of Cortez near La Paz, where the outgoing tides would carry them toward this very spot at the southwest corner of Isla Cerralvo.

Here, from *The Sea Of Cortez*, is Ray's retelling of the story, and his fanciful attribution of the "Vagabundo Graveyard" legend to Eusebio "Laborio" Liborio Cocio Cocio, his favorite guide from Rancho Buena Vista.

DISCOVERY OF
THE VAGABUNDO GRAVEYARD

Not far from our camp we came upon a graveyard with a couple of dozen crosses, some with candles freshly burned. Laborio, one of our Mexican skippers, who had spent several years as a sea rover, explained that this southernmost point of Cerralvo, the last island in the Cortez, was the only place the vagabundos ever congregated, and then only after they were dead. Laborio was unable to give us more than a sketchy history of the vagabundos and nothing more than a guess as to their numbers in the Cortez—which he estimated at somewhere between 100 and 300.

The name vagabundos is a title and a way of life that sea drifters apply to themselves. Their origin, according to one version, was with some Yaqui Indians around Bahía Adair in the north end of the Cortez who learned to use sailing canoes a century ago and deserted the land for a pleasanter life on the warm and abounding Sea. Happy-go-lucky Mexicans who disliked working for others and being subjected to the rules and laws of land-side society imitated the Indians.

Since then they have been joined by an assortment of other men, from peons to college professors, who preferred complete freedom, breaking off land ties to follow a life without tensions or concerns.

A casual sketch, "Back To Eden, Vagabundos of the Sea of Cortez," c. 1960, seems to have been a rough design for a book cover. In 1966, Ray said of his self-proclaimed conversion to the life of the vagabundo: "With strenuous effort I have succeeded in evolving from a position of fame and wealth to the enviable status of *vagabundo del mar* and I wouldn't swap jobs with any man on earth."

During the shark liver boom several years ago, their numbers increased. Every able-bodied man around the Cortez who could get a canoe or skiff joined in the vitamin gold rush. Fishermen sailed to distant islands and isolated shores for long periods, building little brush-covered shelters, some no larger than pup tents, at the back of almost every good cove. These deserted camps are occasionally occupied by vagabundos and also serve as landmarks for small boaters looking for a safe port.

Many of the original shark liver fishermen, having enjoyed voyages to distant places and the freedom of it all, joined the vagabundo brotherhood. However, a few of them settled down to permanent residences and continued to fish for sharks as a market developed for salt shark meat.

In many personal contacts with vagabundos, I have found this strange group eager to talk and always ready to be of service. On three occasions my companions and I have been saved from possible shipwreck by vagabundos, and at no time would they accept rewards. Our offers of cigarettes or wine were received socially as gifts but never as payment. The more I see and hear of these happy wanderers, the more I envy them. — RAY CANNON

"GLORIOUS, IMAGINATIVE BUMS"

[In the following letter, written September 10, 1957 to *Field & Stream* editor Frank Dufresne, Ray comments on a recent trip to Rancho Buena Vista and his first discovery of the canoe "bums" whom he would later call "vagabundos."

Ray also mentions Rancho Buena Vista's legendary fish-catching dog Matador (who owned his own cat, according to Jimmy Smith), and Erle Stanley Gardner, whom he and Dufresne were apparently keeping track of.]

Dear Frank, When I left Buena Vista the other day I really thought I had the greatest action pics ever, but when they got processed I was somewhat let down…

I had every opportunity—we caught two-dozen or more dolphinfish in a single hundred-yard spot and all of them jumped—some as many as 12 times. We trolled into the sun so as to get a direct light on the fish but I still didn't seem to get the brilliant colors…

I'm getting a new Rollei and will test various color films until I can get the greens and gold I'd like to see…

I saw that bait-catching dog Matador actually catch a ten-inch fish in the surf. He ate it—head, tail and all…

Tansey has just completed his spacious house on the hill in which he expects us to occupy guest rooms next February. Says he'll really roll out the carpet and make our stop there as complete as possible.

Haven't learned anything about Erle Stanley Gardner doing anything down Baja way or in the Gulf at all, but will keep the grapevine hot on his trail. Anyway, no one will be getting near the abundance of original material

The "vagabundo graveyard" at the southwest corner of Isla Cerralvo. — PHOTO BY RALPH POOLE

available to you in our pet region.

I have run into a dozen new stories since I saw you. One of them is a dilly—mentioned it in my column of August 9. It is about the glorious, imaginative bums who have no ties on land but live as near to complete freedom as any human I have ever heard of. They sail with the wind in dugouts that turn into flying carpets…

Nothing is apt to stop me from that February trip with you guys, only I don't like that two-week limit you mentioned.

Try your best to keep it elastic. You never can tell what exciting interest might develop. I have just learned that three weeks at Buena Vista can happen between a couple of sunsets and two señoritas. —Ray

FIRST VAGABUNDO ENCOUNTER

[Combined from *The Sea Of Cortez* and the August 9, 1957 *Western Outdoor News* column referred to in the preceding letter, this is the story of what may have been Ray's first encounter with a vagabundo sea-gypsy. In this column, Ray uses the word "vagabonds" which soon evolved into "vagabundo."]

The romantic and endearing halos bestowed on vagabonds by Anglo-Saxon poets as expressions of envy of the carefree life enjoyed by such characters would go

Rare close-up view of a "vagabundo" canoa. Note narrow beam and double ends; plank construction rather than traditional dugout tree trunk; shape of paddle blade and handle; mast; harpoon and running line; all-white garb of man in stern.

double for the roaming pescadores in the Sea of Cortez. For if ever anyone in modern times has come close to achieving the ultimate state in human freedom, it is the meandering fishing vagabonds of El Golfo.

Sail anywhere around the shoreline and you will see them. There are places where you may move along the coast of the Baja Peninsula for a hundred miles without finding any other sign of human inhabitancy, then suddenly see a dugout canoe in full sail, bearing a couple of our heroes bound for a better cove or wherever the wind blows them.

A frightening experience occurred when I was returning from one of my early cruises into Bahía de Concepción with Dr. Earl Hershman of Long Beach, California. We were aboard an old tub of an outboard, totally unseaworthy, when we met a stiff blow near the mouth of the bay, which is usually flat. In those days, our native skipper knew very little about outboards, Hershman less, I nothing.

We were making almost no headway against the wind and the 12-foot waves that threatened to flip over our 16-footer. Suddenly we were shoved down the face of a roller, the stern plunging under until the outboard and transom were completely swamped. There wasn't a cough, not even a death rattle from the old coffee grinder. We may as well have been cruising in an iron bathtub with the plug open. What's more, we were being pushed straight toward the flat face of a perpendicular bluff.

We urged the skipper to drop the anchor. He did, but it didn't help. There wasn't enough line to reach halfway to the bottom.

Each wave added more water; there was no use bailing. All we could do was peel off and swim for a niche of a nearby gravel beach. Even then, there was but a small chance of avoiding getting our brains bashed out on the bluff.

We were just about to hit the water when a couple of vagabundos appeared out of nowhere on shore and shoved a little dugout down the beach into the face of the fury. How they got to us, took us aboard, and landed us ashore in that raging blow, I still don't know. The anchor of our abandoned boat somehow connected 50 yards from the bluff, and a change of wind direction left it floating in the lee.

Since that day these nomads have been my favorite heroes. In talks with them I have been able to get something of an understanding of their philosophy by piecing together phrases they commonly use. The number-one qualification is zest—not just desire—for such a life. Meeting the challenge of hardship with a modern wrestler's sense of humor—to grunt and groan and laugh at it at the same time; to dramatize and enjoy all conflicts with nature with an eagerness to participate in all it has to offer, in the imaginative as well as the realities.

Only when you have experienced some of the extra-mundane visual phenomena of the Gulf can you understand that the tall tales told by these vagabundos make about as much sense as some of the strange

"Vagabundo" canoa under sail off Isla Coyote, between Isla San Francisco and Isla San José north of La Paz. Note early stage of development of the island's dry fish camp.

occurrences you have witnessed.

One of the most farfetched "believe-it-or-nots" I have ever heard was told by a genial drifter. He insisted that his boat was once caught in a chubasco that lifted it far above the surface and sent it soaring from the middle of the Gulf to the shoreline where he and his partner could look down and see the island tops zipping by beneath them; after which they made a three-point landing on the beach and were none the worse for wear. Once, after witnessing a scene where the shoreline and islands disappeared beyond the horizon, when sailing a direct course across the Gulf, a dozen anglers, including myself, saw the islands reappear a half-hour later. Furthermore, they raised well above the surface and we could see the breakers at the base of them. At nightfall we all experienced a feeling of taking off, and we had nothing more than a few beers. — RAY CANNON

THE CAREFREE LIFE

[From *Western Outdoor News,* Ray's most complete version of the legend of the vagabundos.]

JANUARY 27, 1961—Readers of this column have often noticed a mention of the vagabundos of the Sea of Cortez and wondered who they are. First of all they are not to be compared to our U.S. vagrants, bindle-stiffs or drifters, for they ask favors of no man, and of very few women.

They are the kind of vagabonds poets would envy and make immortal verse about. Their glowing lyrics would describe the unfettered life of the vagabundos in idyllic terms.

Just what caused them to take to the sea, none will tell but if they were seeking boundless freedom, they found

it. Not only have they escaped all the laws, regulations and rules imposed by today's society, they have found total release from worries and apprehensions that keep modern men gyrating like addled mice.

To my repeated question—"How many of these rovers are there?" I get answers of "50, 100, 200." For taking a census would be as difficult as counting wild geese, and like the wild fowls, they migrate up and down the Cortez with the winds, according to seasons. They never flock but always travel in pairs. No women except when a couple are taken for a short boat ride.

The magic carpet for travel is a weather and water-beaten dugout "canoa," hewn from a single tree and propelled by a triangular sail, or oars that are seldom used.

The only other earthly possessions usually seen are heavy hand-lines and hooks for fishing; an *"arpon"* for spearing sharks, turtles and fish; an oil can bucket; a couple of pots for cooking; machete knives; wine bottles for water; a blanket each and a coil of rope and a few odds and ends.

The store foods are usually limited to small amounts of beans, tortilla meal, dried chili peppers, and salt. Oregano and other wild condiments are gathered ashore. But all major foodstuffs come from the sea. Once every few months when supplies are needed, live turtles or salted shark meat are taken to the nearest town and traded in.

Days and nights and weeks and years without concern relieve brain cells and provide leisure to create thoughts in abstract, giving the sea-gypsies stocks of stories as far-out as Chinese fantasies. Most of these tall tales begin with fishing or sailing but wind clear out of this world. I have been collecting and hope to one day publish these flights into the wanderer's wonderland.

What would you give for a couple of months respite

from the pangs of ambition, ulcer-producing tensions and demands to fill obligations—to be beholden only to this bountiful Sea that gives so freely, and to the Creator of big and little fishes? — RAY CANNON

BLACK MARLIN FROM A NATIVE CANOE

[This column from *Western Outdoor News* is remarkable on several counts: first, for its vivid description of catching an enormous, dangerous black marlin from a vagabundo canoe; second, because the battle described took place off Isla Tiburón in the Midriff area; and third, because it was a black marlin, rather than a striped or blue marlin. Although black marlin are rare in Baja today, in the early 1960s they were sometimes more frequently caught than blue marlin. Neither species has ever been as common as the striped marlin. In the early years of the Golden Age, Ray described Isla Tiburón as having fantastic "pileups" of billfish and other species. These have faded into history, and although billfish still occur in the Midriff, they are no longer a targeted species in that area.]

AUGUST 3, 1967—A story that would come close to topping Hemingway's highly dramatized *Old Man of the Sea*, was related to me by a small boat skipper, Charles Mason of Los Angeles, who had just returned from a cruise in the Midriff. He told of seeing a couple of native shark fishermen, "vagabundos del mar," in a typical dugout skiff, fight an enormous black marlin off the southwest tip of Tiburón.

It seems that one of the natives had accidentally hooked a two-foot dolphinfish while hand-lining for sharks. But before he could boat the dorado, the gigantic black, reckoned to weigh more than 1,000 pounds, grabbed the jumping dorado and swallowed it.

One of the most amusing incidents was when a spear was thrown at the marlin's head but hit the fish instead in the back of the neck or just ahead of the dorsal fin and the monster charged the boat, got his beak under the bow and would have flipped everything if the pescador hadn't turned picador and held the marlin off, just like the bullring scene when the bull tries to upset the picador's horse.

Mason and his son were in a big hot school of dolphinfish, and kept on fishing right around the marlin battle for several hours. They used small dolphinfish for marlin bait on their large rigs and lost a couple but couldn't get a big marlin hooked.

When the big black was finally conquered the two natives did a remarkably fast job of slicing huge slabs off it. These were to be salted and used as bait for sharks. (Fillets sliced from sharks are salt-treated, packed in wooden boxes, and labeled "Bacalao" (codfish), a fine and popular fish product.)

Each year we learn a little more about the blue and black marlin migrations into the Cortez (June 15 through November). Our lack of knowledge of the size of these populations is due to the few anglers going after them, most of whom are contented to work on the less riotous striped marlin and sailfish, with flyingfish or lesser size baits.

The big marlins show a decided preference for 10 to 15-pound live bait caught in the same area as they are fished.

Down this tropical side of the Pacific, barrilete skipjack and sierra are usually available along the 100 to 300-fathom lines, which the large marlins seem to use as a swimway. No other surface fish will attack such lively, sizable baits.

The bait fish are easily hooked on a trolled, 1/4-ounce

Big payday. Fishermen with a good-sized grouper they have managed to wrestle into their canoe. Note harpoon and heavy hand-line passing over gunnel. Many canoas had strips of tire tread nailed to the gunnels to prevent wear when pulling in fish.

A canoa loaded with 20 people.

Compac feather, the kind that slides up on the leader. The large hook is inserted just ahead of the bait's dorsal fin, then payed out for a couple of hundred feet from a drifting boat. — RAY CANNON

"ME ALWAYS TELL TRUE STORY—SOMETIME"

[Ray retells a vagabundo "bedtime story" to a group of teenagers during the 1958 "Kids' Trip" cruise of the Midriff islands.]

My vagabundo stories were not having the bedtime effect I had expected. Instead of producing sleep, the kids were even more jumpy at the end of the third tale. I was just about exhausted and decided that the next should ring down the curtains. Remembering one I thought would be scary enough to send them under the covers, I dramatized it to the limit.

I started off telling of running into a couple of vagabundos camped on Isla San Pedro Mártir, a small island seen ten miles south of our course as we came across.

One of the sea nomads looked like a Yaqui Indian cutthroat. The stare in his fierce eagle eyes suggested that he was mentally around the bend. However, after we had given him a bottle of wine and he had poured it down his gullet, he mellowed and became rational enough to tell why he and his partner were camping on this isolated, Godforsaken bit of land.

He said it was his first trip back to the island since an earthquake shook the region three years before.

Pointing to the flat-top cliff above our heads, he explained that he had been up there looking for tern eggs near the edge when the earth began to tremble, twisted, and dropped. He said he rode it safely down into the water but that his partner, boat, food, drinking water and everything were buried under tons of rock at the bottom of the sea.

The water was still boiling up from the fallen cliff when he swam ashore. In it he saw something flopping and floundering around. The object turned out to be a mangled sea lion, large enough for many good meals. He brought it ashore and was about to bash its head in with a boulder when it lifted its head and looked him straight in the eye.

"The eye very sweet and sad—round, brown eyes like baby. The leetle lobo cry and say 'mama, mama,' same as baby," he went on. "If I starve to death I could not kill such a sad little theeng."

His explanation of survival on this barren island with nothing more than his machete (hunting knife) and strips of cloth cut from his pants was quite logical.

He fashioned the knife to the end of a fairly straight driftwood stick and was able to spear as many fish as he wanted and plenty for the sea lion, which he nursed back to health.

Although he could build a driftwood fire by using the knife as a flint spark striker, he learned that eating fish raw gave him both water and food.

Some days later he dared climb the cliff again for eggs, ventured near the edge of the broken bluff and was astonished to see a human skeleton had been exposed by the slicing off. Under the stretched-out bones he noticed a shiny object. Climbing down to it he uncovered a large deposit of old Spanish coins.

At first he was maddened with joy, but after some sober thought, realized that the treasure could not be

Trolling past a dugout canoa in El Salvador, 1967. Ray was fascinated by the apparently carefree lifestyle he imagined among the early fishing people of the Cortez. — PHOTO BY AL TETZLAFF

eaten and therefore was of little value.

The sea lion grew fast and became a real companion, even helping to catch fish for their meals.

Half a year later the marooned vagabundo, having seen one boat pass in the distance, carried wood to the summit so he could build a smoky fire to attract the next. Finally one day a couple of turtle fishermen saw the smoke and came to his rescue.

He offered to divide the treasure and took them to see it. Being almost dark they decided to remove it the next morning.

During the night the turtlers tried to kill our hero. He dived into the water and when they followed, the sea lion pulled one of them under. Then, just as the other was about to knife the vagabundo, he was grabbed by the throat, taken under by the sea lion and drowned.

"My lobo compadre very proud," our storyteller said, then continued sadly, "I scold him. I say to kill man is sin."

He went on telling how the guilty animal went out into the darkness and when daylight came, his friend was nowhere to be seen.

Suddenly he realized that he had possession of the turtle men's boat and could escape. Then, just as he dashed up the cliff to get the treasure, another quake came and it was carried down into the sea with the sliced cliff. He hurried back down to the boat and escaped. He continued, "I came back now to see—you not believe my story? Come look."

We followed him around a jutting cliff and there sunning himself on a flat rock was a large bull sea lion. As our hero approached and gave a guttural grunt, the beast deserted a harem collected around him and came lumbering to meet his friend.

After giving the lobo a few friendly slaps our hero turned with an outspread arm gesture and said, "You see, me always tell true story—sometime." — RAY CANNON

Juanaloa, looking south over Puerto Escondido, December 1986. — PHOTO BY HARRY MERRICK

JUANALOA

NAMING AN EARTHLY PARADISE

BY 1954, RAY had begun using the term "Midriff" to refer to the narrow midsection of the Sea of Cortez. In 1961, he announced his coining of a second name, "Juanaloa," which he defined variously as the area roughly between Loreto and either Bahía Agua Verde, or Punta Mechudo at the north end of Bahía de la Paz. The concept of "Juanaloa"—which Ray claimed came originally from old Spanish documents—

— PHOTO BY HARRY MERRICK

came as a big surprise to residents of Loreto, since they had never heard of the idea, but like "Midriff," Ray made it stick by referring to it many times in his columns and magazine articles. In a letter to fishing pal and *Field & Stream* editor Frank Dufresne, Ray makes the "Juanaloa" announcement:

"I AM CALLING IT JUANALOA"

OCTOBER 24, 1961—I am on the verge of throwing imaginary boundaries around another region and naming it as I did with the Midriff section. I am calling it "Juanaloa." The area was originally described to the Cortez conquistadors by Indians as a Utopia with Amazons and all. It includes Escondido and Agua Verde bays and about two-dozen islands, including my recently described Catalán.

While the Midriff was described as grotesquely beautiful, Juanaloa can be pictured in esthetic terms. Encompassing an area of 1,200 miles, it has a population of no more than 35 people, including the visiting vagabundos, who sing many songs about this paradise.

— RAY CANNON

ENCHANTING VIEW
FROM PUERTO ESCONDIDO

[In 1962, Ray describes his first good view of Juanaloa with photographer Harry Merrick.]

There is a narrow peninsula that comes close to making a lake of Puerto Escondido. When Harry Merrick and I walked to the top of it and looked out southward we froze in our tracks. We were happily paralyzed by the unearthly vista. Our attention was not centered on one

A beautiful moment, caught in time. Five boats speeding toward Bahía Agua Verde in the heart of Juanaloa. The inner bay and Roca Solitaria are just visible in the upper right-hand corner.

single object; our view of astonishment included all before us. Beyond a sea as placid as a pan of bluing we saw a new dimension in visual perspective.

Two chains of small islands converging in the distance appeared to be floating above the water surface like hovering flying saucers. We opened our mouths to exclaim but choked the words, each fearing the other was not seeing the same illusion and would think some hallucinating had set in. Only when we regained our composures and unscrambled our cameras were we able to let go and blurt out our praises of the mystic beauty. I exclaimed—"A Chinese painting of Nirvana!" Harry whispered as if it were about to vanish—"A materialized fantasy right in front of us."

The scene was like that, only more so. Down between and around the islands, hundreds of sea birds were wheeling, plunging and diving into a silvery blanket formed by small fish jumping a couple of feet into the air to avoid their game fish predators.

These, and multitudes of sea creatures moving quietly in the tequila-clear water nearby gave us an extra charge of the dynamic reality of the Sea.

We snapped many pictures but knew that the magnificence would be lost in distance. When we finally turned and raised our eyes, our cameras came up and were aimed as fast as shotguns, for there to the west, was a picture we could shoot.

Mountains that had been sliced off in the catastrophic faulting of a few million years ago, had been reshaped by the handiwork of nature's rains and winds to resemble Tibetan temples. The wooded bench sloping down from the mountain base was aglow and aflush with yellows and greens. All this was superimposed on the blue reflected from the sky to the Bay, and all this we did capture in our little Rolleis, and in our vaults of lasting memory.

The place was worthy of pages of esthetic description, and chapters more if I included the exciting fishing and hunting and the sheer joy we found in soaking up the balmy, tropical climate. But this is just one notch in a whole region filled with such glorious vistas and exhilarating things to do in them.

The Cathedral mountain back of Puerto Escondido

Approaching Bahía Agua Verde, 1964. — PHOTO BY HARRY MERRICK

Gifford Kira near the same area on the shore of the bay, 1995. — PHOTO BY GENE KIRA

forms the northwest corner of the region to be described and renamed here. The crescented mountain behind Aqua Verde Bay, 23 miles to the south forms the southwest corner. The eastward extremities include Catalán, the last sizable island in the Cortez to be described.

Just as I found a need to establish imaginary boundaries and create a title for the section I named the "Midriff," I now find an equal need to propose a title and bounds defining this very different kind of an area.

The name I have selected, "Juanaloa," was suggested in the private reminiscences of one of the Cortez conquistadors. He wrote of seeing a huge but beautiful and shapely Indian woman in La Paz, who had been rechristened "Juana." According to the legendary account she had been kidnapped from a Utopian paradise inhabited only by statuesque Amazons and the few men they captured for breeding purposes. The only clothing worn in this Utopia was a small apron made of strings of pearls. They lived on wild honey, wild fruits and fish they caught from wind-blown rafts on which they sailed out to the islands.

Except for the giant women, the recorder's description of the isolated realm and its distance from La Paz fit that of our "Juanaloa," a name he used for the place, meaning a "toast (praise) to Juana," a "reino de felicidad ultimo" (a realm of ultimate happiness).

How can I tell you about a place when I have never seen another to compare it with? There are no waterfalls or large trees like Yosemite, no parched deserts like Death Valley, and no people to stumble over.

There are only about 30 persons, including a number of seagoing, freedom-loving vagabundos, within the imaginary bounds of more than 750-square-miles. There are two of the finest bays in the Cortez; 16 sizable islands; a broken shoreline of coves, beaches and prominent headlands, and a bench covered with vegetation extending back one-half mile to three miles to the foot of sheer-faced mountains that poke up to more than 4,000 feet.

But this is only the lay of the land, which abounds in game: deer, bighorn sheep, mountain lion, ducks, geese, doves, quail, and numerous varmints, by a sea pulsating with great and small fishes, shellfish, and lobsters. The enormous abundances of these should provide enough incentive to stir the average outdoorsman. But there is far more to attract those who seek adventure in far-out places. Here, within a few hours from the border, is a new world to explore and to satisfy the deep longing to see the indescribable. I can give you no more than the impressions I gained on four expeditions that covered the region.

At Puerto Escondido, Merrick and I were assisting ichthyologist Dr. Boyd Walker of UCLA. A boat sent up from La Paz by Bill Callahan of Ruffo Brothers had picked us up at Loreto for a cruise to some of the islands and to collect fish specimens in the Bay.

On the Nash-Cohen Expedition, I learned something of the reefs and the shoreline recesses. It was the only calm stretch we found between San Felipe and La Paz in three weeks of raging winds.

On the Nash-Jeffries, and the more recent Mike Ryan Expeditions, I was able to complete the survey, see the picture as a whole, and came to realize that the area differed so greatly from all others.

On this voyage I got a more thorough look at Agua Verde Bay, its lush, tropical background, the spreading

"Juanaloa" near Punta San Telmo, 1964. — PHOTO BY HARRY MERRICK

palm grove next to it, the two exquisite coves that provide protection from all winds, the large, spreading trees that march down close to the water's edge, the beach and prominent rock headlands, and the little settlement, housing four families of gentle and friendly people—all nestled in a crescent of the extended arm of the precipitous Sierra Giganta mountains.

The Ryan Expedition, planned and well fitted-out to chart the most interesting, safest, and most pleasant seaway for small craft, started at Kino Bay, proceeded across, then down the coastline to Escondido. From there we worked the north rim of "Juanaloa," including the 3 1/2-mile-long Isla Danzante, and the smaller, flat-topped bird islands, Las Galeras, which may be called satellites to the four-mile-long Monserrate, an island with many points and recesses on its west side, a small beach in a cove on the north, and many projecting reefs, caved and honeycombed and housing armies of fishes, including the giant basses,

shellfish, lobsters, eels and clouds of small, exotic fishes.

This cruise continued on to complete the exploration of Catalán's land-side hills and green valleys, strangely covered with enormous pipe organ and barrel cactus and trees that grow parallel to the ground instead of upward from it—a natural preserve for tropical birds with no animal predators.

We found shore casting just as productive as the fantastic trolling done on the previous trip. The ferocious green jacks kept a couple of hundred pelicans stuffed with anchovetas they chased right up onto the beach. A few casts showed that we could have caught jacks by the ton.

If ever there was a place where the term "fabulous" could be applied, Catalán is it. The greatest.

The nearest comparison I can think of is to say that "Juanaloa" could be considered exactly opposite in many ways to the Midriff sector. Readers of *W.O.N.* will remember my picturing the Midriff as beautiful in the awesome grotesqueness of its islands and lands; with currents that surge through the deep channels, creating whirling maelstroms and great upwelling boils; massive fish "pileups" in which most all kinds of monstrous sea creatures, fowls, and fish collide and run amuck in a carnage of slaughter; Tiburón Island with a history of the Seri Indians and of civilizations that were built, and died, on the ghostly ruins of other dead and forgotten cities.

None of these are encountered in the celestial realm of tranquil "Juanaloa." As the name "Juana" suggests the feminine of "John the Beloved," this most idyllic sector of the Cortez produces a quiet, caressing contentment. The hurricane-like chubasco of a couple of years ago that raged up the Baja Peninsula, flattening trees in La Paz and houses in Loreto, hardly broke a twig in the mountain-protected "Juanaloa." Rain storms hit only the mountain tops to form three-mile-long lakes. It is the seepage from these that keeps the shore lands well watered, leaving the atmosphere strangely dry, with no fog or dew. Tides seldom reach the maximum of four feet, and the flow of near-shore currents is barely noticeable.

"Juanaloa" is the safest area of its size in the Cortez for small craft and for large yachts with instruments to keep clear of rocks and reefs. There are lees and coves with fair to good anchorage around the islands and along shores.

"Juanaloa" is an arena for a week's exciting fishing, a month-long period of exploration, or a half-century of peaceful contemplation, if you love the complete freedom as found here by the self-sufficient "vagabundos del mar," who have no land ties or obligations and are not affected by man's laws, regulations, or rules, adhering only to those of God and nature. — RAY CANNON

Just south of Juanaloa, Isla Espíritu Santo near La Paz. — PHOTO BY HARRY MERRICK

Sailfish at Rancho Buena Vista, 1964. — PHOTO BY HARRY MERRICK

GOOD FISHING EVERYWHERE!

RAY'S GREATEST "FISH STORIES"

WHEN PEOPLE WHO knew Ray reminisce about him, the word that recurs most frequently in their descriptions is "enthusiastic"—especially when they talk about his absolute love of fishing. For Ray, there was no such thing as a manta ray swimming just beneath the surface with the two tips of its wings showing. No, that was two marlin tails, probably big black marlin weighing at least a thousand pounds. Roosterfish didn't just swim in schools; they "barreled" over the surface of the water, lined up like chorus girls. Grouper were as big as water buffalo. Dorado "rainbowed" out of the water in sheets of color. Needlefish tied themselves into knots, trying to pick their teeth with their own tails.

Down to the soles of his often bare feet, Ray consistently reveled in every aspect of his life as a sport fishing writer. Even in his letters to Carla and in his personal notes, he very rarely mentions the inevitable sore spots of the outdoor experience. In thousands of pages, representing hundreds of trips, he complains of "bugs" only once, and only once does he mention being bothered by heat and sun.

Ray truly loved what he did and he literally immersed himself in his passionate quest to experience intimately the beauty of the Cortez and to learn as much as possible about it. Bill Benziger of Loreto's Hotel Oasis tells of people being amazed when Ray would walk out into the water, fully clothed, and then return to sit at a table as though nothing had happened. Ray saw nothing unusual in that.

There was, of course, a kernel of truth in all of Ray's "fishing stories," but that kernel was magnified and turned into a rainbow-hued vision as it was refracted through the prism of his love for the beauty he saw everywhere. This most deeply-seated enthusiasm bubbled through all of Ray's writing, and it sustained him through 24 years of weekly deadlines in which he never missed a beat—a truly remarkable record.

Of the many hundreds of columns he wrote, the following selection of "greatest fishing stories" gives a small sampling of Ray's humor, his curiosity and love for the natural world, and his boundless enthusiasm for "fishing" as a splendid way to celebrate the beauty of life.

Note: A few of these stories aren't exactly "fishing" stories—but they're good ones.

TOTUAVA
PESCA GRANDE NOT HUNGRY!

[An early and rare encounter with a massive, non-feeding school of totuava in the Midriff area. This account was written about 1956, after a trip aboard the Dave J. Hyams panga mothership, *Galeana*, which operated out of Puerto Peñasco.]

Ten anglers' jaws quivered like a starved hound suddenly spotting a ton of fresh meat, when they saw it. They did remain civilized enough to swallow instead of drool. I know exactly how they reacted—I was one of them. The "it" was a school of totuava—a host, an army—no, you'd have to count 'em by the thousands of tons.

We were heading back to port at Punta Peñasco from a fishing trip to Tiburón Island, when "it" happened. An experience that will provide enough daydream material to last us for the rest of our lives.

The Sea of Cortez was dead calm until we suddenly found ourselves in a five-mile stretch of water being churned as if in an active volcano's crater. It could have been just that, since most of that mountainous region was molded by volcanic upheavals. The thoughts, "earthquake and tidal bore and other phenomena" were soon erased when we saw foot-long tail fin exposures. Then clear outlines of fathom-long fish. The native Mexican skipper of our converted tuna clipper threw her into reverse so fast the cook skidded out of the galley and clear onto the stern rail, still holding on to a basket of shrimp he was peeling.

It was every man for himself as the outboard skiffs were all but thrown over the rails.

No one would ever be lost at sea if they could equal our time in getting from the big boat to those skiffs. Ten, foot-long baits were in the water and being trolled at three knots before the captain could get down from the wheelhouse to tell us that we were wasting our time. In fact, he never did get a chance to tell us. All of his yelling (in Spanish) was drowned out by the blood pressure pounding in our ears. Our lack of knowledge of the language may also have added to our switching him off. We had to learn the hard way.

We struggled, changed trolling speeds, and threw every plug and jig in the catalog at the quarter-ton fish. We circled the edges of the boiling mass, plowed through the middle, fished them from the bottom to the surface and, except for one that got snagged accidentally, not a hookup.

We learned that totuava, like salmon, seldom feed during their migrations to the spawning ground.

We returned to the mothership, hoisted the hook, pulled out and into port just in time to see 22 tons of the mighty fish being landed from small commercial vessels. Their crews were only able to gill net those with heads small enough to be stuck in the 12-inch mesh! We watched and made resolves to learn just when, where and how to catch the pesca grande by angling.

For years, I have studied techniques for angling for the totuava and something of its habits. Yet this no-feeding during northward migrations was one more big hole in my education. It seems that the more you learn about a fish, the more holes you find in your knowledge of it.

There is a century-old history of this fish being caught at San Felipe but not until last summer could we say, with a degree of certainty, where it lived when not on a spawning journey. Our discovery of its habitat was an absolute accident. — RAY CANNON

REALLY, REALLY BIG TUNA
ZANE GREY'S 318-POUND CARROT

RAY STRUGGLED THROUGHOUT his long Baja fishing career to catch a yellowfin tuna larger than his 88-pound personal best. As late as 1969—when Ray was already 77 years old—the largest sport fishing tuna recorded at Rancho Buena Vista was the 99-pounder caught in October or November of that year by Ted Uben. By then, the ebbing of sheer physical strength would in all likelihood have prevented Ray from achieving his dream. But he was always spurred on by the local pangueros' stories of harpooning tuna well over 100 kilos (220 pounds) near Punta Pescadero, and by his sure knowledge—although he never said so in print—that the 318-pound world record for yellowfin tuna on rod and reel had been set in 1925 at Cabo San Lucas by none other than Zane Grey. (Mike Farrior, historian of the Tuna Club of Avalon, reports that sport fishing expeditions to the Cabo San Lucas area, and even into the Sea of Cortez, occurred as early as 1908.)

HUNTING TUNA WITH "THE RIFLEMAN"

[This story about chasing yellowfin tuna with actor Chuck "The Rifleman" Conners at Rancho Buena Vista gives a good description of fishing without live bait. Photographer Harry Merrick accompanied Ray on many Baja trips to film action footage for the Mac McClintock television program "Fishing Flashes."]

NOVEMBER 11, 1960—Our job: Get a sizable yellowfin tuna or bust! For two days we scoured the Sea looking for the school of big yellowfin everyone at the lodge was talking about. We caught everything but, including wahoo, dolphinfish, giant needlefish, and a whole checklist of smaller game. Mr. and Mrs. Chuck Conners flew in and joined the search. We thought we saw a couple of jumps, but no contact.

The third day started off with very few fish of any kind being sighted up until 10:30 a.m. We had made half-a-dozen passes up Tuna Canyon when Laborio, my longtime skipper, spotted some terns working off Punta Pescadero,

Two young totuava caught on spinning gear at San Felipe, May 1956. Totuava are now protected and may not be taken.

Pectoral fins held rigidly outwards, a formidable black marlin comes out of the water beside the boat, c. 1964. Note proximity to shore. This photo appears on the title page of *The Sea Of Cortez.* — PHOTO BY AL TETZLAFF

whipped our skiff about and gave the outboard the gun.

Harry Merrick checked his battery of TV and still cameras and started rearing like Silky Sullivan at the gate when Laborio and I began yelling—"*A-tún! A-tún!*" We could see the shoals of sardine taking to the air as the big fish hit them, then the foot-long tail fins sliced the surface, throwing a sheet of spray a couple of yards high.

We had no bait fish large enough from which to cut skip-strip bait, so must rely on large white feathers, trolled at full speed a hundred yards back of the boat. The school was breezing by so fast we had one hell-of-a-time keeping near it. The fish zigzagged in every direction and by the time we would catch up with them, they would sound and reappear a quarter-of-a-mile away.

For a number of years I have been trying to get a yellowfin large enough to make interesting photos; spent weeks and months trying to get a big one on deck, but of the dozens hooked, something always happened. It was as if jinxed.

We thought we had it made when Merrick hooked a 20-pounder and Laborio whipped the skiff about for the expected long chase. This one gave little trouble and we were off again. Then it happened! Anticipating the direction the school was about to take, Laborio cut across ahead of the leaders. With cameras hanging on all sides, Merrick's reel clicked, hummed, then started screaming before he could get it out of the socket. By the time he got the rod butt seated in his belt there were no more than three

or four wrappers of line on the spool and Laborio was gunning the motor full bore.

Merrick was yelling, "I'm running out of line!" I was blasting out with—"*Línea no más!*" and Laborio was

Actor Chuck "The Rifleman" Conners with a yellowfin tuna at Rancho Buena Vista.

trying to out-shout us, but I could make nothing of his machine-gun chatter.

The straight-away race lasted for an estimated quarter-mile before the fish started running in tangents and Merrick was able to gain a few yards of line, then lose them again when the torpedo changed its course. The direction could be seen, not by the curving line, but by the wake the fish made as it missiled along a couple of feet under the surface.

After a number of sounds and shenanigans, Harry had the fish pooped. He gave me the rod so he could get pictures and TV shots of the action. Once, while he was shooting, the fish took off for a wake-making run, and if that scene turns out as it looked, viewers of the "Fishing Flashes" program are going to get a real thrill. He also got the still pictures I have needed. The tuna weighed slightly less than 40 pounds but it performed like one three times the size.

We spent the next couple of days working sailfish and dolphinfish, then packed for the next leg of our journey to San José del Cabo. — RAY CANNON

CHALLENGING BIG YELLOWFIN TUNA

RANCHO BUENA VISTA, 1960—The few yellowfin decked by anglers has little to do with the number of fish available.

Anglers hooked hundreds of the monstrous tuna and not only lost the fish but whole spools of line with them.

To handle a hooked heavyweight in shallow water, a fisherman needs to be mentally prepared, have good tackle, a fast boat, and a skipper as alert as a flyweight boxer. In 500-fathom water a couple of miles off shore, stopping one, where it always heads for the bottom, is about like trying to halt a diving torpedo.

Anglers new to the region rarely know what kind of a bolt struck. The few split seconds from the time the tuna strikes and the reel end of the line pops gives the newcomer no time at all to adjust his scattered brain cells. It wouldn't help anyway. If Zane Grey's 14/0 reel, loaded with 800 yards of 100-pound test line wouldn't stop a sounding yellowfin, what would?

According to the tackle builder at the lodge, such fishing cost Gene Walters, the owner, more than $200 for line last season alone.

I boarded one of the large pursers at anchor near a deep basin we call Tuna Canyon in the Buena Vista region. Its captain told me he was quitting the business and turning his ship into an angler carrier. The reason: he had made the mistake of netting a school of tuna so big they tore up a $20,000 nylon net. He weighed one of the half-dozen that did not escape. Its weight—252 pounds.

In this area we catch the abundant 250-pound striped marlin, 200-pound sailfish, 82-pound dolphinfish, and six foot-long needlefish, throughout the year. Also an

Zane Grey aboard his yacht *Fisherman*, off Cabo San Lucas with his world record 318-pound yellowfin tuna caught in 1925.

— PHOTO COURTESY LOREN GREY

occasional black marlin up to 825 pounds. All are great spectacular game fishes, but none can develop the power, drive and speed to match the first long run of the yellowfin tuna.

Except for the black marlin, more large yellowfin are hooked and lost than any fish I know of. The percentage decked by expert anglers in shallow water is about one in two-hundred. In deep 800-fathom water, it is nil, for the simple reason that those above 45 pounds head straight down at full speed and keep right on going after all the angler's line is payed out and snapped off.

Although the Pacific yellowfin tuna, *Neothunnus macropterus*, is in the true tuna family, *Thunnidae*, with the Atlantic yellowfin or Allison tuna, *Thunnus subulatus*, the two are not in the same genus. The anal and soft dorsal fins of the Allison are especially long, while those of the Pacific yellowfin are noticeably shorter. Otherwise there is a marked resemblance.

The Pacific species are found in most of its warm

waters. Those migrating up the Mexican coast move all the way from Panama and perhaps from Peru. A yellowfin tagged off El Salvador, Central America was recovered off Manzanillo, Mexico, and air scouts and boats have followed migrations on into the Cortez Sea.

For the past three years, at least, a sizable population has remained around Buena Vista. The life span of this tuna is believed to be five or six years. Otherwise little is known of the life history. — RAY CANNON

RAY'S HUMOROUS "FISHING STORIES"

[One of the great set-pieces of Baja's Golden Age was the spectacle of Ray Cannon ensconced in a hotel lobby, bar or dining room, autographing books and keeping guests spellbound for hours with his dramatic and colorful stories. Mark Walters of Rancho Buena Vista recalls Ray's exquisite sense of timing—undoubtedly honed during his career as a movie director and actor. Ray would carefully build up to the punch line of a story and then take a long, slow drink of water, leaving his listeners gasping for air until he decided to let them off the hook. The performance was extemporaneous, but perfected by many repetitions. Following is a list of humorous stories that Ray made for himself, perhaps in preparation for one of his many book-signing appearances:

White Horse Story
Al Green Cockroach Story
His Foster Father's Trial For Moonshining
Wild Cat On Head Of Juan José Riva Gonzalez
Drunk Guide
Woman On Shrimp Boat
Small Fish Pose For Photo
Whale Shark Courts Our Boat
Chickens & Pigs Swept Into…
Big Mouth At Finisterra
Grandma Story
Camping On Mulegé Air Strip]

GRANDMA IS *STILL* MISSING!

[Not a fishing story, but a classic nevertheless, *"Grandma Is Missing"* has long been one of the more macabre Baja tales told—with infinite variations—by *norteamericanos* since the early dawn of time. In this fantastic version written in 1965 and included in his standard list of funny stories, Ray adds another twist, to make it *"Grandma Is STILL Missing!"*]

Driving down Baja California's primitive roads can be strange. My roving correspondent, Al Hrdlicka of Redondo Beach, California, who drives it often, reports on a follow-up story that "grandma is still missing."

It seems that about a year ago this granny from L.A.

was camping with her daughter's family at isolated Cabo Pulmo, when she had a fatal heart attack. Having heard about the days of red tape required to get a body prepared and out of Mexico, the son-in-law decided to zip grandma up neatly in her bedroll then roll it in a tarpaulin, strap the bundle on top of the station wagon and make a dash for the U.S. side. While the family was having a quick breakfast in Ensenada, the station wagon was stolen, and grandma with it.

Last week Hrdlicka picked up the story again in Mulegé Prison where he interviewed the two natives who had taken the station wagon—"but only to get transportation to Santa Rosalía," they said. After stealing it they had decided to camp on the desert for the night. But when they unstrapped the bedroll they discovered its contents and panicked. More especially, when a lost driver of a camper from the U.S. insisted on following the station wagon as guide to Santa Rosalía, where they were seen by friends.

In their efforts to rid themselves of the car, the culprits deliberately left it out on the highway. But instead of it being stolen, it was stripped of everything—including grandma!

Grandma is still missing. — RAY CANNON

THE 130-YEAR-OLD WOMAN

[Also written in 1965—when Ray was 73 years old himself—was this inspirational tale of Rancho Buena Vista owner Colonel Eugene Walters' encounter with the mother of a 100-year-old woman.]

Stop at most any of the backcountry ranch houses around the Cortez and you will likely find one or two people of great ages. I have often mentioned such special qualities as the calmness of the Sea; its warm midwinter temperature; the world's finest fishing in it; the unmatched climate; balmy nights; the friendly, mild-mannered and happy people; and the lack of illness.

A briefing by Buena Vista's Colonel Eugene Walters was case in point. He wrote that "a small colony living up in the hills back of the resort make all of the hammocks used and sold at the lodge. Among the best of the workers is a woman 100 years old."

With his report the colonel enclosed a photo of this woman spending her spare time taking care of her mother, who was 130! — RAY CANNON

RAY FROLICS DURING HOSPITAL STAY

[Never-say-die Ray somehow manages to get a humorous column even out of his hospitalization for prostate surgery in 1972.
Mike Ryan—the coughing critic in this story—was a

Los Angeles boat builder and companion on several cruises. It was on a Ryan boat that the big grouper pictured on Page 125 of *The Sea Of Cortez* was photographed while at dock at the Hotel Serenidad in Mulegé.]

AUGUST 15, 1972—There has been a slight gap in plans for my greatest of all pleasant years. But now that the three weeks I got sidetracked are past, I am not sure that it wasn't mostly a fun time. Since all plans I make are for highly pleasurable endeavors, you may wonder about how much fun I found in a hospital after I had been plugged like a watermelon.

After a temporary catheter plumbing job my doctors had discussed a kind of a "Roto-Rooter" operation. But when they explained that it may have to be repeated about every five years they seemed relieved and happy when I decided to go for a real opening, which proved to be the easy way to take it.

The gentle and thoughtful treatment I was getting the second and third days had me thinking I was in a very weakened condition. Then when I began to notice how good looking and attentive the nurses were, I thoroughly enjoyed playing possum.

By the fourth day I had begun to understand why some oriental potentates had large harems. By this time I had a private room and could tell stories, and I think the

A small "football" tuna off the Hotel Cabo San Lucas, 1960.

girls appreciated the break from serious work to get a laugh.

The first two nights I was in a room with a guy who had a cigarette problem. He would start coughing at about 3 a.m. and go on and on until the coughs became brays— the Mexican wild ass kind of vocalizing. Eventually the whoops seemed to come all the way up from the lower bowels, and each aggravated my nerves and stitches so much I arrived close to the splitting point, or at least to the point where my fellow explorer, Mike Ryan, had enriched the English language with his classic expression.

It was at Mulegé and Ryan was sleeping with his bed next to a partition of a single layer of palm leaves, without knowing that another of our explorers had his bed just on the other side of the thin wall. And he had the same kind of a cigarette cough as my roommate. After Mike had suffered through 10 minutes—20 minutes—a half-hour— three quarters—and on into a full hour of hacking and barking, Mike expressed his deep sympathy by yelling— "Die, you son-of-a-bitch!" In the two weeks that followed I never heard that explorer smoker cough again. —RAY CANNON

GOOD FISHING EVERYWHERE!

MARCH 29, 1960—The array of game fish schools now migrating up the Sea of Cortez can be counted only as in galaxies.

On March 26, commercial fish spotters reported sighting continuous yellowfin tuna schools, from the Tres Marías Islands off Puerto Vallarta to Isla Catalán off Agua Verde, or about one-quarter of the way up the Baja California Peninsula. This is six weeks earlier than the movement of last year.

Many of the 100-mile-long school that entered El Cortez last May remained in the south end, and catches of foot-long (one month old) tuna at Buena Vista suggest that they were spawned in the vicinity. All of which indicates a pileup of yellowfin to top all previous records, and chances seem good that they will move on above the Midriff. It seems certain that they will soon be abundant around Isla San Pedro Nolasco above Guaymas, and along the south rim of the Midriff.

An explosion in the yellowtail population is also noted all around the south end of the Peninsula. A report from Todos Santos opposite Buena Vista on the Pacific side, says the water is loaded from Cape San Lucas to Magdalena Bay. Word from Palmilla says enormous schools are still seen between the Cape and San José del Cabo, a full month after their usual departure time. Bulletins continue pouring in reporting that yellows are swarming the bays and around offshore islands, halfway up the Sea of Cortez. The sizes range from ten inches long to monsters weighing 60 pounds. There is an increasing number of amberjack mixing with the yellowtail schools.

Two years of warm water and enormous rains seem to have produced an extra abundance of forage fishes and other food creatures throughout the Sea. This condition may have caused large numbers of game fish to remain and spawn along this region and may stimulate a massive migration into the north end of El Cortez. If no protracted windstorms blow up, it seems safe to predict that the big game fishes will reach Punta Peñasco and Consag Rock off San Felipe by June 15. — RAY CANNON

ROYAL DORADO
GREATEST FISH OF ALL

[In fragments written from 1957 to about 1960, Ray reflects on the magnificent game fish that in Baja California is today universally called "dorado"—*Coryphaena hippurus*. By about 1972 in Baja California, the confusing names "dolphin" and "dolphinfish" were supplanted by the Spanish "dorado" (golden). In Hawaii, the fish is known as mahimahi. Although Ray acknowledged the dorado as the "greatest game fish of them all," his *favorite* game fish was unquestionably the giant needlefish or agujón.]

"The most enthralling thing I have seen in the Sea of Cortez." Ray with a dorado, 1960. — PHOTO BY RALPH POOLE

"THE MOST ENTHRALLING THING I HAVE SEEN IN THE SEA OF CORTEZ"

If asked what was the most enthralling thing I have seen in the Sea of Cortez, I would have to sift through a thousand exciting incidents. But if I were to choose the one that stimulated the greatest number of head-to-heel emotions, I would select the time at Ensenada Cove when I saw a school of a hundred or more dolphinfish rainbowing up in unison for a leap of 50 feet.

Throughout the warm waters of the earth's seas the glamourous dolphinfish is held in high esteem.

Down through the ages and pages of historical writing and illustrating, man has pictured this fish as an object worthy of great praise and in some instances, a symbol of worship. In the profound opinion of most saltwater angling authorities, no other creature of the oceans can match the many qualities of El Dorado, the finest game fish of them all.

What other fish takes off from a distance of 200 yards, hurtles through the air in 40-foot skipping jumps to nail the bait? Then, when hooked, missiles up through the next dimension to a height of 15 feet, performing all the loops, twists and turns of an Olympic champion, and like the graceful diver, reenters the water without creating more than a ripple?

What 50 to 75-pound swimming thing will hit a lure at ten knots and pass the boat before the angler can feel the strike, then keep the fishing rod in the shape of a "?" for 1 1/2 hours?

Search your memory for any single member of the animal kingdom that can match, or be used as an example, in describing the coloring of the dolphinfish. Not butterflies, birds, nor even flowers will do—the vivid brilliance and rapid change must be compared to the spectrum as viewed through a kaleidoscope.

The changing hues and shades of a captured dolphinfish are just not equaled elsewhere. Add to all these the hocus-pocus tricks this magician among the fishes uses to flamboozle the fisherman, such as a hundred-yard peel-off straight away, then a sudden reverse right at the boat; quick and unexpected slips under the craft, across its bow then under and up near the outboard prop; twisting, gyrating jumps, never repeating a pattern or maneuver. Then, if failing to dislodge the hook, playing possum until the overconfident angler relaxes the line, then spitting the hook out right in front of the gloating, premature victor.

Sure, the black marlin, mammoth bluefin tuna, and some sharks can dog it for a longer period; the sailfish and lesser marlins can jump and perform a tail dance; the yellowfin tuna can sustain a longer first run; and other lighter game fishes may cavort and fight a good battle. Some are sharp and tricky and many have colors like the rainbow. But even if all their attributes were combined into one, it would still fall far short of the magnificent Dorado.

Too often the average fisherman is so beguiled by the grace and color glory he forgets that he is dealing with one of the most vicious creatures of the deep, a Satan dressed in angel splendor.

The sentimental behavior attributed to the dolphinfish in which other friendly members of the school would follow the hooked fish and attempt to free it, as observed by old-time writers, was somewhat imaginative. The real purpose they follow is to snatch the bait away from the dope that got hooked, or if he is small enough, to eat him.

There seems to be no limit to their ravenous appetites. On one occasion a pelican got a bead on a sardine, peeled off in a beeline bomber dive. A big bull tried to beat the bird to it but was a split second late. When he clamped down, instead of having just the sardine he had the whole beak and head of the pelican. The bull disregarded the bulk and feathers and attempted to swallow what he still thought to be a sardine. The wrestling match threw geysers into the air which in turn attracted another skiff load of anglers who thought I was connected to the battle. The fury ceased and ended in a draw when the contestants crashed into the skiff. Neither seemed the worse for wear except that the curve of the pelican's neck appeared to have straightened somewhat—in flight it resembled a migrating goose.

This particular breed of the common dolphinfish, called dorado by natives, seems to differ from other members of the species *Coryphaena hippurus* throughout the warm seas, in both habit and size. No one, it seems, has determined whether or not the dolphinfish of El Golfo is a different breed or race from those of the Atlantic, but certainly the tenacity, endurance and mad fighting ability of this one makes all the others seem anemic.

According to fairly reliable native fishermen reports, 90-pounders are common. One weighing 82 1/2 pounds was the largest I have seen.

A 50-pounder along the Baja coast is twice as difficult and requires double the amount of time to bring to gaff as a billfish weighing three times more, on equally heavy or light tackle.

I tied into one bull-size bull that almost took me—in fact he did and had me yelling uncle 1 1/2 hours later. I passed the rod to Laborio, my skipper-comrade, with the flimsy excuse that I wanted to get photos of the fish coming to gaff. Even when the great gold boar came alongside I was sure he was a 90-pounder. The weight was only 62 pounds.

When a bull decides to sound for a hundred yards or so and sulk for half an hour, he does just that. It seems as if nothing short of block and tackle will hoist him. At least until he decides to surface and give the angler another beating.

I can't remember having any of the Atlantic breed making these straight down, hell-bent-for-China runs and remaining down there with such jackass stubbornness. Nor have I seen other dolphinfish jump five feet above the surface to grab the bait in midair.

The latter performance occurred three times, each when I tried to avoid sailfish by jerking the bait away from it. As out of a magician's basket, a dolphinfish would leap up to take the bait on the fly. This special trick may result from their habit of chasing the Gulf's abundant flyingfish, in which they seem to make a game of nailing the highly desirable morsel while airborne.

To get action shots, a camera-wielder needs two heads. One dignified photographer representing a big national journal was loaded like a pack mule, with cameras and equipment hanging from his neck, belt and pockets. Trying to follow a sprinting dolphinfish around the skiff he got tangled up in his gear, plunked overboard, went straight to the bottom and lay there like a chunk of lead. He didn't even come up once, much less for the usual third time.

Afterwards he admitted that if the skipper had not been an expert at diving to great depths, he may have become a Friday "blue plate special" for fish.

There may be many places in the world of dolphinfish where they have set up permanent housekeeping in a shallow-water hole but I know of one only, and of another suspected as being inhabited on a year-round basis. The latter at Espíritu Santo Island at the mouth of La Paz Bay. The sure one is just two miles north of the Rancho Buena Vista Lodge where most of my dolphinfish concentration occurred. Natives call the exact cove Ensenada Las Palmas.

The dolphinfish will go for any bait that moves, including trolled lures, spoons, feathers, or plugs, and sometimes even a bare hook that is jigged. Skip-strip is first choice, unless a live bait is handy. Second choice— white feather. They are often found lurking under clumps of seaweed or anything else that floats. Also where cool and warm waters converge, as along the line where the outgoing current from the Cortez collides with incoming tides of the Pacific around the lower end.

Dolphinfish roam the warm waters of all the open seas.

Up to recent years the name "dolphin," applied to the dolphinfish, was terribly confusing. The dolphin is a mammal and is a member of the whale order, beloved by sailors from ancient days for its high degree of intelligence and extrovert personality. Aristotle called the fish *Koruphaina,* from which its scientific name *Coryphaena* is derived and by which it is known in all languages.

The smaller *C. equisetis* is distinguished from the *C. hippurus* by having a larger eye, a less vertical head and shorter pectoral fin. Although thought to achieve a length of 30 inches, I have seen none over 22. I have taken a great number on 1/4-ounce white feathers.

The two dolphinfish are recognized by the dorsal fin extending from the top of the head to the caudal peduncle (tail base), low, set eye and spectacular color.

The big news in scientific circles is the astonishing growth rate of the dolphinfish. A recent test showed a gain of 44 pounds in eight months, or about 60 pounds for the first year, suggesting that those 90-pounders at Rancho Buena Vista would be not more than three years old.

On top of this news comes word that the yellowfin tuna in this same area also gain 60 pounds per year and that the huge sailfish seldom live past five years.

It's no wonder the dolphinfish is so ravenous and

Expert photographer and fisherman Al Tetzlaff of Downey, California accompanied Ray on many expeditions. — COURTESY TED TETZLAFF

daring. On numerous occasions I have seen them snatch bait a few inches from the nose of big sharks and billfish.

One was placed in one of the Marineland (California) glass tanks with a pygmy whale. When the slow-motion whale was given his ration of squid the dolphinfish would dash right into its mouth and grab one. This went on for months but a few days ago the dolphinfish slipped up on his timing and the whale clamped. Curator Dr. Kenneth Norris is now on his way to Rancho Buena Vista— objective—another dolphinfish. — RAY CANNON

GIANT BLUE STEALS 20-POUND DORADO
BARFS IT ON SCALES!

JULY 21, 1972—Of all the 32 members of the Outdoor Writers Association of America who came to Baja California following their Mazatlán convention, surely Bob Dennie of the *New Orleans Clarion Herald* and Halton Henderson, *American Outdoors*, fishing with 40-pound test line, got mixed up in the most spectacular action of all.

They drew skipper Pepe Verdugo, out of Rancho Buena Vista, and he proceeded to get Dennie tied onto a

blue marlin that weighed out at 472 pounds, and that was after the monster had grown gaunt and thin from a battle that lasted 17 hours. The decision came at 1 a.m., with other boats of writers including our own Jim Potter, editor of *Western Outdoors*, and Don Johnson of the *Milwaukee Sentinel* bringing food and drink. They also got night action pictures of the man-fish contest, perhaps the first night photos of a big blue being captured.

Even more unique was the strange way another big, 506-pound blue came to be captured, according to boat dispatcher, Pancho. It was brought in and weighed by angler Bob Ronne of Rolling Hills, California.

From the beginning to the final weighing-in, the whole thing was a cliffhanger suspense drama. A dolphinfish was hooked as soon as skipper Plutasco Marklis got his boat on the fishing grounds and the outriggered bait skiing properly. Bob was enjoying the rhythmic jumps of the 20-pound dolphinfish, but when the time came for its fifth jump, a huge blue marlin took over the trampolining, coming up exactly where the dorado was supposed to.

Bob was utterly confused until he felt something more than the tug of a dolphinfish. Only then did he realize that the enormous blue had managed to gulp in his hooked dorado. Bob being a heavy-pressure angler, laid it on. In less than two hours he had the enormous mule-like fish within 20 feet of the boat, when it suddenly turned belly-up and died as if by heart failure, and before the good angler could gain a yard of line, it sank to the bottom like a half-ton of steel.

To get the dead weight moving upward, the boat had to do part of the pulling from an angle. One hour and a half of the big tugging and the fish was lashed alongside.

At the scales, with the usual gallery of spectators watching and betting some beer on the weight, an astonishing weight change occurred. Ronne may have had a record fish if the weighing had not been delayed a couple of minutes while an extra steelyard weight was brought. Twenty pounds may have made the difference. But before the big marlin could be hoisted to get its beak above the ground, out came the 20-pound dorado with the hook still deep in its belly. The marlin had never been hooked at all. He had most likely died when the dorado was pulled up from inside the stomach to choke off the heart pump and the blood's circulatory system.

The second day OWAA president "Buck" Rogers; Homer Circle, *Sports Afield* editor; George Bolton, KTBC; Wally Taber, *Outdooring Publicist*; Ed Zern of *Field & Stream* fame; and TV man Hal Sharp all took to the skiffs with extra light tackle such as fly and bass casting rods. All came in as excited as Bill Escudero and I were when we first fished the tide pools between the Japanese long-liner and Cabeza de Ballena. Our shore and skiff fishing started there 18 years ago [1957]. Dr. Boyd Walker of UCLA collected specimens there, close to 100 different species which included numerous exotics in almost as many jewel-like colors.

Bill and I caught nearly half as many kinds on rod and reel. I expect that the writers will be saying that the freshwater fly caster can get some astonishing action down here. — RAY CANNON

Surf fishing near the site of Cabo San Lucas' Hotel Solmar.

BONEFISH DISCOVERED IN LA PAZ BAY

[In 1957, Ray describes a plentiful catch of bonefish inside Bahía de la Paz. Dredging, increased human population, and the destruction of habitat would later reduce the fishery of the inner bay, which at that time also included a significant population of snook.]

JUNE 8, 1957—Bonefish at La Paz a certainty! Its capture by rod and reel was demonstrated when George Escudero of the Los Cocos Hotel, acting as our guide, personally put us right on the fish. We caught 17.

For three years this fish has plagued me and more than a score of anglers. Although we were unable to catch them previously, we knew of their presence all up and down the Baja side of the Gulf. Dr. Boyd Walker, UCLA, and a

number of his students collected young bonefish up near the mouth of the Colorado River. George Barlow, just now completing his doctorate under Dr. Walker, recently discovered that the river at Mulegé was loaded with young and larvae and could be considered a spawning ground.

Escudero has from time to time found small bonefish among his mullet bait catches. He noted one large nine-pounder caught last year. (Elsewhere bonefish have been recorded up to 15 pounds.)

The group of anglers reporting to me on their attempts in Baja have been unable to get responses when employing Florida techniques, and although I have caught some few on the Pacific side, this is the first I have taken on the gulf side of the peninsula. I am not at all satisfied with the methods I used in landing these. I was able to catch any number on the soft parts of the large scallop found in the same area, but persuaded only one to take a lure, a small 1 1/2-inch white jig. We found a channel 12 feet deep loaded with them.

It is quite possible that bonefish feed on the tidal flats in other inlets and may respond to other methods. Since the giant scallop does not seem to be very plentiful elsewhere, other baits and lures should be tried.

Some coast defenders will wonder just why catching a few fish less than a foot-and-a-half long should be such a big news story in gulf fishing; especially when billfish and a score of other great game species are being caught off every port and point south of the Midriff. Every angler east of Texas could write a sizable volume on the merits and glories of catching a bonefish. Included are some of the most noted sportsmen of our time.

Ex-President Herbert Hoover, an ardent bonefish enthusiast, is one of the many anglers to make inquiries about bonefish possibilities in El Golfo. He will fly down to La Paz on hearing of this news.

Scientist-angler William Follet, curator of fishes at Steinhert Museum, San Francisco, has been pushing me for the info for three or four years. He is trying to learn whether or not this bonefish is the exact same species as the *Albula vulpes* found in Florida and elsewhere. He will probably catch the next plane south.

Escudero believes that the local bonefish population does all their shifting around within the La Paz Bay and can be captured the year round.

Two years ago I saw a 37-pound snook caught at almost the exact spot where we caught the bonefish, and I have just received a report of eight smaller robalos being taken in the mouth of one of the many mangrove-bordered estuaries near the place. — RAY CANNON

SKIFF FISHING FOR MARLIN

[Catching a 178-pound marlin from a 14-foot skiff would be an accomplishment for any angler. Ray was 65 years old when he wrote the following column about fishing at Rancho Buena Vista.]

FEBRUARY 14, 1958—After 30 years of catching billfish in the conventional manner, only yesterday did I learn how to get the maximum amount of fun defeating a marlin. It all happened by accident, or rather, by a mistake. If described in detail you would think this was a rewrite of Hemingway's *Old Man and the Sea* or one of Zane Grey's spectacular accounts of his marlin fights, and I assure you that the battle had all the ingredients except I did it the easy way. A 30-pound test line forced me to keep energy at a minimum.

I had no intention of fishing a marlin. My program for the day was catching and photographing the abundant dolphinfish about 100 yards or so from shore. I was being helped by my favorite skipper, Laborio, and his young son,

Battling a striped marlin. — PHOTO BY AL TETZLAFF

José. Our craft was a 14-foot open skiff with a 25-horsepower outboard. It was just about ideal for my photographing work and proved equally efficient in working the billfish.

Having finally succeeded in getting the special pictures of jumping dolphinfish I had spent many weeks striving for, we were all in a high state of victorious elation and on our way back to the lodge, when we saw fins of what appeared to be an exceptionally small marlin near shore. Our mistake was in misjudging the distance between the dorsal and tail fins which seemed short with the fish headed toward us.

Thinking such a little fellow would make a prized mount and that taking it would be a breeze, I decided to offer it a seven-inch strip-bait which I had prepared for dolphinfish. Laborio cut the motor to a crawl, allowing barely enough speed to skip the bait 50 feet astern. He didn't even bother to change course as the fish made for the bait before it was abreast. I payed line at the first pass, counted 20, then some extra time for the marlin to get the bait all the way down the hatch and on into his bowels. Even then the hook somehow slipped up to be sunk into his mouth, which was to cause me a lot of extra time.

I gave Laborio the signal—"*listo*"—and he gunned the motor. When I got the feel of taut line and weight, I sunk the almost barbless, needle-sharp 6/0 salmon hook and we were in business. Three seconds later I regretted the whole thing, for when the water rose to a head, busted and splattered, it was no creeping infant but a monster that blasted off and missiled up to its full length into the air.

After a series of half-a-dozen leaps, one of which was near the stern, we all got a baptismal. The 178-pounder seemed longer than our skiff as we looked skyward. For some reason unknown to me Laborio tipped and tied the motor and from then on for the next 2 1/2 hours he worked the oars with skill and speed. He knew that the fragile line would pop if it touched the boat or if he allowed the fish to peel off any beyond the 200-yard capacity. His was the real race in keeping within distance; mine was in retrieving fast enough to keep the line taut when the denizen plunged toward us. Any slack would have permitted the fish to throw the undersized hook. Our greatest problem was in keeping the line away from the raspy tail, as the five-foot dolphinfish leader was less than half long enough.

With Laborio's swift oars and my desperate application of rhythmic pumping, we succeeded in keeping an angle to all runs. Once we thought we had "had it" when the fish torpedoed down to within a half-dozen wraps of line on the spool and my oarsman was forced to ease up, losing all but a fraction of our angle.

There were a hundred close squeaks, incidents that caused us to turn almost blue-in-the-face from holding our breaths. Especially when a stiff breeze came up, darkness settled in and we were unable to see the line. For the life of me I couldn't remember the few Spanish words to direct Laborio, so he kept up a continuous flow

so I could answer with a "si" or "no."

The three of us succeeded by using all the strength and skill we could muster in getting the belly-up fish up and across the skiff. Between each stroke of the merciful clubbing Laborio muttered in Mex jargon something that sounded like—"Bless your soul you son-of-a-b…" Only at the end of that ritual did we all give full voice to our success, and only then did I learn the reason for killing the motor in the midst of a marlin battle. It was lack of gas and Laborio was forced to make a quick decision on whether to fight the fish by rowing or row all the way home against a headwind.

At the lodge, Laborio was the hero and I was merely the guy who held the rod, and rightly so. He had expended energy and shown great skill, while I was enjoying to the fullest catching a magnificent fighting marlin from a skiff.

— RAY CANNON

SEA GULLS' GRAVEYARD AND MYSTERIOUS TOY SHIPS

[Ray describes two strange phenomena discovered at Isla Catalán with fellow adventurer Mike Ryan.]

The story of all elephants traveling miles to a certain valley to die may not be true but we did find the last resting place for many seagulls in a cove on Isla Catalán.

Pelicans and some other sea birds, too old or weak to find food, allow themselves to be eaten by varmints. But

Two Mike Ryan boats in Jeffries Cove, Isla Catalán. Note boom on left-hand boat, used to photograph the large grouper pictured on page 125 of *The Sea Of Cortez*.

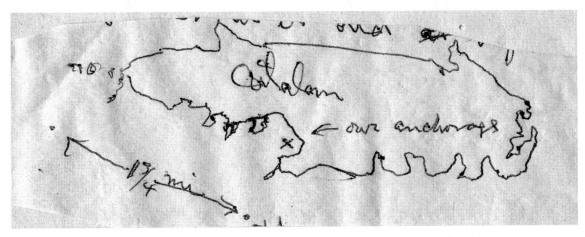

Ray's sketch of Isla Catalán, made during a Mike Ryan Expedition, July 1961.

not so with seagulls. They go to Jeffries Cove on Isla Catalán where there are no predators and spend their last days in a sunny, protected cove where they can subsist on the abundant amphibian bugs, awaiting peacefully that final day.

This observation was made by Ryan after a careful study of an enormous number of gull skeletons and half-a-dozen weak gulls awaiting death in the back of Jeffries Cove.

This cove on Catalán Island is strange in many ways. For some reason, hand-carved, toy ships have sailed in here from distant shores. We found half-a-dozen up on the beach but were unable to estimate their age. The sails were gone but otherwise they were well preserved. — RAY CANNON

RECORD-BUSTING BLACK SEA BASS

[The current official IGFA all-tackle record for black sea bass—563 pounds 8 ounces—was set August 20, 1968 at Anacapa Island off the California coast. The fish described in the following story would exceed that record by almost a hundred pounds. The Charlie Rucker charter fishing boat described operated out of San Felipe and was a precursor to the "panga mothership" boats still run today by such operators as Tony Reyes and Bobby Castellón.]

JULY 2, 1967—The big fish news story of the week is about a 660-pound black sea bass, *Stereolepis gigas*, the largest of all records I have ever heard of. This cow-size monster was taken by Robert Bennett of Garden Grove, California on Charlie Rucker's 67-foot *Rudy*, a sport fishing boat on its cruise to the Midriff.

The largest *gigas* I have seen weighed, tipped a reliable scale at 603 pounds. It was netted by Japanese commercials fishing out of an isolated village a couple of miles above Santa Monica, in 1914.

A big black estimated at something over 600 pounds was decked on a previous Rucker trip but it had been butchered before weighing. I had fished this same, deep hole at Ensenada Grande (northwest corner of the Midriff) on two occasions. The first, on Rucker's boat, was chartered by nine doctors. None of them had ever caught a large fish before. All of us caught one each, none less than 200 pounds.

We located the giants on a 30 to 35-fathom shelf of a submerged canyon 700 or 800 fathoms deep. We caught them on foot-long goldspotted bass, caught at the same spot and same depth.

Although the black sea bass may spend most of its life in a single cave, much of its time is spent foraging around some distance from home.

The interest in the blacks has been revived since the *Red Rooster* and other angling boats have been working them on the reefs several miles out from the Pacific side of the Baja California peninsula. There are still a few off Southern California where they were once taken 100 yards off of piers.

In the Cortez they remain very deep, except on feeding runs or perhaps to spawn.

Black sea bass is often miscalled "jewfish," a common name used for the gigantic bass, *Promicrops sp.*, (we are not yet sure of the scientific name of the species) as shown with a recent column on El Salvador. I have not seen this Pacific jewfish north of Bahía Magdalena on the Pacific, and Isla Georges in the Cortez.

The black sea bass seems to prefer deep cool waters in a more temperate zone and the young are rarely caught—while the juvenile jewfish (20 pounds) are plentiful in most tropical bays.

According to Bennett's report, the fishing grounds at Ensenada Grande were located as per description in *The Sea Of Cortez* book, and he made use of the black sea bass technique, including "rhythm pumping," also described in the volume. The hook was a 10/0 Mustad, the line 80-pound test Gudebrod dacron.

Whatever the method, real skill was needed to master such an enormous fish, which towed the skiff for one hour and five minutes before running out of gas.

The fishing on these Rucker trips to the Midriff is done from an outboard skiff lowered from the *Rudy* deck and occupied by a guide and two anglers. I have gone on several of these six-day cruises and I recommend them for the great fun and adventure. — RAY CANNON

LIVE BAIT ROOSTERFISH REVOLUTION

[The widespread introduction of live bait fishing in the Cortez during the 1960s resulted in increased catches of many types of fish, including the roosterfish described here. However, depletion of resident species such as snappers and bass soon followed.]

AUGUST 25, 1967—Throughout the Cortez, wherever there is a suitable environment south of the Midriff and on down the tropical Pacific Coast to Peru, the roosterfish,

Nematistius pectoralis, called "pez gallo" in Spanish, is quite abundant. In shallow water where a seepage of fresh water comes up in a mixture of large rocks and sand, mullet are apt to be flourishing, with a permanent population of roosters most always present.

Sierra, in pursuit of young mullet, barge in to the rooster's hangout and often wind up in rooster gullets. Several record-size *pectoralis* (up to 111 pounds) have been taken on sierra.

Throughout the summer beginning in early June and lasting 'til winter, the usual lures, such as large chrome spoons or white flattish lures, are shunned in favor of live bait. A large ten-inch striped salema grunt seems best. In some areas a long ski-bait will get equal attention.

Catching large live bait and holding them is a major problem in the Cortez. So far a beach seine has proven fairly efficient but natives would rather use a *tarraya*, the native casting net, which flares out when thrown. Until more efficient seining is developed, resorts will have to

Two gigantic fish, either giant black sea bass, or gulf grouper at the limit of their size range, at the Flying Sportsmen Lodge in Loreto. Ray would eventually come to regret the catching of such fish because of their enormous spawning capability and because of their very slow growth rate which makes them impossible to replace even if all fishing were to stop for half a century.

Seining live bait at Rancho Buena Vista, 1971. The live bait experiments encouraged by Ray helped revolutionize sport fishing techniques throughout Baja at a time when lures were becoming less effective. — PHOTO BY ANN PATULLO

expect a profit loss in supplying the bait, but being able to attract anglers during summer months and assuring them of getting roosterfish is worth the small loss.

The sudden avid pursuit of the roosterfish started off like a gold rush and seems to be getting more attention than any other Cortez species, including billfish.

The full story of the roosterfish size and numbers at the many resorts will be revealed only when live bait fishing has been developed at each of them.

Prior to our live bait expedition a few years ago, very few natives or U.S. visitors had any idea of the vast numbers of roosters in the Cortez, but our discoveries showed large colonies every few miles, from the Midriff to Cabo San Lucas. Since then I have had a go at 'em with ski-bait all down the mainland side and also made a test along the shores of El Salvador, where they shot through the surface for 50 feet, with that cock-tail fin leaving a trail of spray.

The small 1 to 1 1/2-foot young roosterfish is highly prized for mounting. As a food fish the rooster is out-rated by many species and is of little or no value as a competitive market fish. — RAY CANNON

WORLD RECORD ROOSTERFISH AT LA PAZ

[The 114-pound roosterfish record described, set on June 1, 1960, still stands as the IGFA all-tackle record.]

LA PAZ, 1960—The catch, made by our friend Abe Sackheim of San Diego, of a rooster weighing 114 pounds, tops all previous records by 38 pounds, and it may prove a tough one to top, since he used a 27-pound test line. The fish was taken near Pichilingüe Island, right in La Paz Bay. Previous IGFA record was 76 pounds.

Word comes that the vast number of large roosterfish in the region is diverting angler attention from the abundant billfish now swarming up El Cortez. — RAY CANNON

71-YEAR-OLD MAN BATTLES GIANT BLACK MARLIN

SEPTEMBER 15, 1967—Except for the three-day period of the big rain storm that turned into a chubasco by the time it reached San Felipe and wrecked the town,

In a separate incident, photographer, Al Tetzlaff's father, O. H. Tetzlaff, 89, whips a 151-pound marlin on 12-pound test line off Cabo San Lucas, 1966. — COURTESY TED TETZLAFF

and for some few days after, fishing in the Cortez has been the best ever.

So many monstrous blue and black marlin have been taken, anglers catching 400 or 500-pounders no longer make headlines, but a 71-year-old professor from Oklahoma State College, came close to it recently at Buena Vista.

According to my roving photographer and fishing buddy, Harry Merrick of Long Beach, the salty old angler caught a big billfish a day for three weeks, one of them a black that weighed in at 425 pounds. But he topped this when he tied into the largest black ever seen by the crews of two boats.

The leviathan, thought to weigh over 1,300 to 1,400 pounds, was hooked about noon. Long before dark the fish had come close to the boat and surfaced as if to give up, but a close view of the craft, or its occupants, or both, sent the great black on a power drive toward Topolobampo. Neither the well-preserved muscles nor the full weight of the old man was enough to hinder the marlin's progress.

The skipper revved the motor full-bore in the hell-bent race. It was a dead heat. But the boat had run beyond its gas limit. There was not half enough to get back to port, and it was pitch dark.

Despite empty bellies, the crew continued to yell encouraging words to the hardy and determined angler.

After an hour of trying to get the broken radio in order, the skipper finally fixed it and got contact with a boat that had been sent out from the resort with food and an extra gas supply. This was close to 10 p.m., but professor Bill Leake was still fighting, steaming, and nearly floating off of the fighting chair in his own sweat.

The skippers, afraid the professor would wreck his stout and durable heart, threatened to cut the fish free to make him give up. He did, and returned on the rescue boat. His crew fought the marvelously strong marlin until 2:20 a.m., when it finally broke free. And then, as if to prove its victory, gave a couple of full length leaps and plunged on toward the dark depths of the Cortez. — RAY CANNON

FISHING PREDICTIONS HAZARDOUS

[Ray describes a learning experience and a fantastic day of fishing that took place at the Hotel Los Arcos, December 1955. From combined columns dating from 1961 to 1967:]

From several sources I have been asked to give the exact locality of the best fishing on a weekly or monthly basis.

One of the main reasons for my hesitating to forecast

exact times for fish occurrences was the prize boo-boo I pulled the first time I fished La Paz. Having caught marlin throughout most of the winter in Mazatlán, I expected La Paz waters would be the same, especially when on my first trip there I saw a sea full of marlin and sails in mid-October, and wrote about it.

By the time my readers could get foot-loose and get there, it was late December. Returning, I found the La Paz hotels full, and not a single billfish had been seen for a week or more.

I sat in the Los Arcos dining room. About 30 anglers were crying in their coffee. They had taken off for their winter vacation week to catch marlin, and none were to be found. They were a dejected lot. The thought that the La Paz bay could be loaded at that time of year with other gamesters had not struck them. Nor did boat operators, crews, and others consider it important enough to tell them.

I was about ready to leave the country. I thought it best to avoid bringing up the subject of lesser game fishing until I could show proof. I discussed it with fleet owner, Rudy Vélez, and Bill Escudero.

Next morning I was off at daybreak in a skiff. Running behind the islands beyond the oil docks we picked up three 35-pound grouper and a large needlefish. Swinging out into the outer bay we followed diving birds and decked a big dolphinfish and a half-dozen black skipjack. We then crossed to the outer bay beach and ran up to a spot about equal to the back end of the inner bay. There we found a huge school of roosterfish and decked a 50-pounder.

Returning, we found the inner bay loaded with yard-long sierra. With a desire to make a staggering impression, we worked the sierra schools with all the muscle and know-how we had, and literally loaded the boat. We accidentally caught a 34-pound snook, one of many.

Before we got to the shore in front of the hotel, the skipper had tied all the sierra by the tail in two huge bundles. He swung the bundles on the ends of an oar, shouldered the load and paraded right through the hotel entrance and on to the kitchen, so everyone could see. I waited in the skiff until the anglers had come out to see where the fish were coming from. Then I started flinging and carrying other fish ashore.

As they gathered around and started hurling questions I knew my message had gotten through without saying a word.

The chef did a swell job of cooking the sierra and everyone got a plateful, whether he ordered it or not. Every last angler was out after them the next morning and my face was somewhat less colored.

— PHOTO BY AL TETZLAFF

Gaffing a black marlin. — PHOTO BY AL TETZLAFF

From that day on, Bill Escudero and I have exploited the lesser game fishes as being equally important as the marlin and sailfish, with the result that thousands of people fishing the Gulf have found great pleasure instead of going home disappointed when billfish are scarce.

Incidentally, I did not go fishing the next day. I quit while I was ahead. — RAY CANNON

into the Cortez enter it in early spring, depending upon water temperatures, with exception of the more tropical forms such as blue and black marlin and wahoo, which enter in mid-summer. Several native species move to deep water when the surface gets too cool in late winter or when mid-summer surface gets too warm. Violent storms may also send them to the depths. — RAY CANNON

UNPREDICTABLE "FISH CALENDARS"

[A reliable and accurate "fishing calendar" is the dream of every angler. In this fragment, written toward the end of his career, Ray describes his struggles to calculate a precise fishing timetable for the Sea of Cortez.]

For nine years, in collaboration with Cortez resorts, I kept a calendar on all game fishes around the Cortez. Each resort maintained a reliable record of arrival dates of the species and quantity caught, and I thought we had a firm seasonal calendar for each worked out. Then, change in the seasonal weather scrambled the whole thing. Finding as much as two months delay in fish seasons, I dropped the idea of the reliability of any kind of calendar, other than to suggest that most fish migrating

ELEVEN BLUES & BLACKS IN ONE DAY AT RANCHO BUENA VISTA

[Two remarkable big marlin fishing stories, a year apart and both in November, which remains a peak month for really large fish in the waters of southern Baja. Black marlin, once as common as blue marlin, are now relatively rare in Baja. This report also contains an early reference to problems with drug trafficking.]

NOVEMBER 20, 1969—Eleven blue and black marlin were caught in one day (November 11) at Rancho Buena Vista. Most of them were tagged and released. Four to six are the daily averages. This, according to Col. Gene Walters, who came up to L.A. for a couple of days.

A few years ago that number of blue and blacks for

the entire season was big news. The colonel also reported that while the U.S. border snafu had hit the ordinary tourist business, fishermen came in droves and kept the resorts filled above the fall averages.

While there is no question that the U.S. government must halt the smuggling of harmful drugs and narcotics, the method employed, under the present administration, showed little profound thought. A little common sense planning could have saved millions in legitimate tourist dollars for both countries as well as millions in Mexican purchases in the U.S. Tourist spending in Mexico produces multiple profits to the U.S. — RAY CANNON

COUNTESS PAULA CLARY

[The Countess Paula Clary of Austria was a close personal friend of Colonel Eugene Walters. They met while he was serving in Europe with the U.S. Army, and they were later married.]

NOVEMBER 6, 1968—Two black marlin, one weighing 880 pounds and another of more than 1,000 pounds, were taken within a week's time by Leon Tact, of Oxnard, California. Also, an estimated 550-pounder, after a four-hour battle, by Countess Paula Clary of Vienna, Austria, in the Buena Vista-Bahía de Palmas area. A fourth black over 900 pounds was taken in the Cabo San Lucas region—and this is the time of year when they enter the Cortez in the largest numbers.

One of the blacks was said to have been caught on a ten-pound dolphinfish which had just swallowed the trolled flyingfish. There are several places in the South Seas where that size dolphinfish (live) is considered the favorite bait.

Elsewhere, tuna or tuna-like fishes found in the same area as the gigantic billfish are used.

Skipjack, dolphinfish, sierra and small yellowfin tuna are taken fast-trolled on 1/4-ounce white Compac feathers, then transferred to the marlin rig. These lively baits are less apt to be taken by the more sluggish sharks. Also, because of the bait's large size, other big game fish, including striped marlin and sailfish, will seldom try to take them.

Most of the blue and black marlin in the Cortez are usually taken accidentally on frozen flyingfish by anglers in pursuit of the smaller billfish.

There is a general belief that the Cortez would produce more black and perhaps blue marlin than any other comparable place if enough mentally and physically prepared anglers would go after them and have enough patience to do a lot of experimenting. — RAY CANNON

SIXTY-POUND BAITS FOR BLUE MARLIN!

OCTOBER 10, 1973—One of the questions frequently asked me in the mails is: "What does a big marlin eat?" The general reply is: "Whatever he wants."

In a 1972 scientific study of billfish stomach contents,

biologists Bob Iversen and John Naughton reported finding a 63-pound bigeye tuna, *Thunnus obesus*, in the stomach of a 748-pound blue marlin, *Makaira nigricans!* And I have had to urge and urge anglers to catch and use 10 to 15-pound skipjack or tuna as live bait for the large blues and blacks. This 748-pounder also had a deep water species of lancetfish in its stomach, showing that blues feed deep as well as near the surface.

The striped marlin enter the Sea of Cortez two or three months earlier, when the water is cooler, than when blues, blacks and sailfish come in.

This preference of the striper for cool water suggests that it may also feed deeper than we suspected. The great quantity of deep water squid found in striped marlin during a scientific study made over a period of several years at Rancho Buena Vista should strengthen the deep, cool water feeding theory. Most all marlin and sails examined in this area feed more consistently on the foot-long frigate mackerel, *Auxis thazard*, and the smaller bullet mackerel, *A. eudorax*, a lesser number of the common Pacific mackerel, *Pneumatophorus sp.*, and a mixture of whatever is plentiful or in compact schools at intervals, including very small foot-long dolphinfish, yellowfin tuna, and a conglomerate of rock or bottom dwellers. — RAY CANNON

CRABS AND RED SNAPPERS COME UP FROM THE DEEP

[A rare occurrence of the normally deep-dwelling huachinango, or true red snapper, boiling on the surface in pursuit of pelagic red crabs.]

MAY 6, 1970—This is the time of year for the pelagic red crab, *Pleuroncodes planipes*, to leave its 500-fathom habitat and float up into surface waters. There are so many at times that vast stretches of the Baja California side of the Cortez seem to be flowing blood-red paint.

The body of this little crab may average one-inch long, with the tail section curled tightly under the head end. The slender legs may spread out to three inches. At the Baja south end they surface at about half that size. On the Pacific side, in warm years, great quantities are current-borne as far north as Southern California waters.

Wherever this fat-filled morsel occurs, fish of many kinds gorge themselves, thus sparing the young game fry and other forage fishes to gain much growth.

Last week while fishing with Carlos Ungson, resident manager of the Hotel Cabo San Lucas, we saw a large "birdwork" and thinking the goonies were diving into a school of yellowfin tuna, we rushed to the spot and found the feeding fish to be huachinango—red snapper. We started dip netting crabs and using them for bait.

That evening the hotel advised ordering "Huachinango á la Ray Cannon" and a dozen or more diners did. The dish was a masterpiece of culinary art. The whole fish, with highly colorful goodies all around it, was baked. At the head end, an alcohol-filled, orange peel cup flamed like a large torch. When the row of waiters marched in and around the tables bearing the spectacular platters, the sight created a sensation.

Huachinango are super-abundant in a great many spots in and south of the Midriff, but seem to stay in tight schools and on specific rock or mud bottoms varying from ten fathoms in the Midriff to 60 fathoms at Cabo Pulmo.

— RAY CANNON

VERMILION SEA NAMED FOR RED CRABS?

[Ray describes a pelagic red crab bloom in Southern California, a phenomenon that occurs periodically, sometimes resulting in windrows of dying animals left on the beach. Ray suggests that pelagic red crabs may have been responsible for the old Spanish name for the Sea of Cortez: *Mar Bermejo,* or Vermilion Sea. Other proposed sources for the name include red tide plankton blooms, sunsets and sunrises, and the silt-laden runoff from the mouth of the Colorado (Spanish for red) River that once accompanied the spring thaw in the Rocky Mountains.]

JUNE 6, 1973—The red crab seen dead and dying in Southern California shore waters and blanketing most of the beaches appear like one of the plagues of Pharaoh to our fastidious sand-sprawling people, but to anglers the occurrence means better fishing and more game fish migrating up from tropical waters.

About this time of year, this pelagic crab rises up to the surface water, where it drifts with the current for great distances.

If the movement continues for another month, Southern California should have a large run of dolphinfish and perhaps a return of Pacific (green) mackerel with noticeable increases in runs of several other species. But the greater value is the escapement this crustacean provides for the weak anchovy population and other forage items, especially the young of large fishes. In the Sea of Cortez I learned that the *Pleuroncodes planipes* is favored by many kinds of sea creatures. I examined hundreds of fish stomachs and found them loaded with little else during the seasonal blooms; also noted that game fish are apt to refuse all other baits offered during the period, thus proving the crab's unique food value.

Starting as early as February during warm years, the bloom spreads vermilion blankets from the outer La Paz bay all along the Baja California coast to the Midriff and continues for weeks. For more than a century the Cortez was called the Vermilion Sea, and according to historical accounts from the archives of Spain, the sea was made red by *cambaro*—crustaceans, without reference to dinoflagellates—red tide, credited by some modern writers as the reason for the title "Vermilion." Patches of red tide

are seen in the Cortez, but in all the years I have cruised and flown over it I have seen none to compare with the Southern California occurrences. — RAY CANNON

MARLIN RECORD ON SPINNING TACKLE

[In 1971, Ray wrote this entertaining feature as a promotion for spinning reels.]

The idea has been bouncing around for several years and a few lucky fishermen have done it. But recently the challenge has caught on and is being met with some confidence. Among astute anglers, and no few rank amateurs, this lighter-than-light-tackle craze is becoming the "in thing" to get with.

The fervor set in by a simple accident. I had just advised a newcomer to the Sea of Cortez that he would

Millions of dead and dying pelagic red crabs form a solid blanket on the inner beach of Caleta San Francisquito, 1963.

— PHOTO BY AL HRDLICKA

The pelagic red crab, *Pleuroncodes planipes.* — PHOTO BY AL HRDLICKA

December 26, 1956—Early spin fishermen, identified as Chick Bradley, left, and March Robinson of Los Angeles, with dorado caught at La Paz. The scene is on the beach in front of the original Hotel Los Arcos.

do better attracting marlin with a fresh-dead rather than the refrozen flyingfish being used. It was just about sunup and about three-dozen marlin fishermen were about to board the 18 boats lying 50 to 100 feet from the beach in front of the Rancho Buena Vista resort, when Costa Aronis, a member of the Westchester Rod and Gun Club, California, in a skiff with a native boy at the outboard, started racing around among the marlin cruisers and passed a large yacht anchored 200 feet out. Within a minute or so of trolling, Costa's 1/4-ounce feather was nailed by a foot-long bigeye jack.

On medium spinning outfit and 12-pound test mono line, the jack proved a fighter. Costa said he was wondering why he should leave such good fishing for a … when suddenly—zoommmmmm—zoommmmmm—zoommmmmmm—he nearly got jerked overboard, and after peeling off half of his line, Costa was sure he had caught a dynamite fish.

What he didn't suspect, nor did any of the fishermen on the beach, nor the boat crews, nor the 30 people aboard the yacht, was that a 152-pound marlin had come in from deep water usually five miles out and swallowed the hooked jack, feather and all. But a few seconds later everyone for miles around knew that wild-jumping, tail-walking marlin was tearing up the surf and everyone was yelling advice to Costa.

The crazy goings-on kept going on for over 1 1/2 hours before Costa's native boy got a gaff into the pooped fish and lashed it alongside.

The fish was properly landed, weighed, and proved a world record for 12-pound test line (International Game Fish Association) and for the U.S. spinning record.

Every man, woman and small boy who saw that magnificent battle got the fever to use spinning gear for marlin instead of the conventional heavy-duty trolling rigs.

The tackle business must have been great that season, judging by the amount of spinning gear in use.

In fact it has become quite the sport in lower Baja and the Sea of Cortez. The lightweight spinning gear in general use seems to satisfy anglers in pursuit of medium to small game fish, but for the big gamesters, sturdy spinning tackle is needed. — RAY CANNON

FIVE SPINNING RECORDS CLAIMED ON ONE TRIP

[A trip to Rancho Buena Vista results in an impressive mixed bag of fish on spinning tackle. Ray himself preferred to fish with spinning tackle most of the time.]

SEPTEMBER 7, 1960—A letter from fishing pal and correspondent Earl "Doc" Hershman of Artesia reports setting five new world spinning records on two to six-pound test lines while fishing in Bahía de Palmas. Altogether, 14 species were caught by his party, including a 58 3/4-inch-long needlefish, topping my largest catch by more than three inches.

He went on: "I got 12 varieties, including three yellowfin tuna weighing 38 to 45 pounds. Roosters were thicker than mosquitoes all over. We had to troll a lure 150 feet back to get strikes, but we learned and got them.

"I was amazed when we gaffed the giant needlefish midriff and had him snap at my hand and follow it like a snake when I tried to take the lure out. He reached up and grabbed the handle on the gaff, and then let go and grabbed his tail and hung on. It was uncanny, as I had never seen a fish carry on this way.

"While we were surf fishing one afternoon, a school of yellowfins came barging in to within 50 feet of the shore and chased hundreds of 15-inch-long squid up on the beach. We had the Mexican kids pick them up and sack them for us. Each one took a fish the next day. It is the most excellent bait of all."

*****

Chuck Walters of Rancho Buena Vista reports more record-size yellowfin and billfish in the bay than ever. He also told of Matador, the famous fishing and clown dog at the resort, being shot but recovering completely.

— RAY CANNON

URGE TO JUMP AT ISLA SAN JOSE

[Recollections of the beautiful small bays and islands at the south end of Isla San José, near La Paz. The remote area Ray describes remains relatively unchanged to the present day.]

FEBRUARY 3, 1975—The most impressive spot I have ever seen along Baja's fantasy-world inner coastline is the south end of Isla San José. Here nature's landscaping designed a beautiful labyrinth of sapling-size mangrove bushes in broad rows that curve and angle between 10 to 15-foot channels of clear water so calm that reflections of bright green mangrove and blue sky appeared almost too inviting.

There was a split-thousandth of an instant when I thought of jumping in, but I was 400-feet high in a DC-3. It was July, the end of the dry season, and the 16 1/2-nautical-mile-long island was so parched it looked like a well-baked yam, until I suddenly arrived over Bahía Amortejada and its adjoining mangrove sweep. (The contrast of colors is not as pronounced during and for a few months after the rains come to bring new life to the dormant vegetation up canyons and northern slopes of Isla San José.)

Trans Mar de Cortés Airlines (now Aeroméxico) was flying me down the Cortez coast for pictures and mapping for my *The Sea Of Cortez* book.

I had flown over and passed close by this delightful spot on dozens of trips but never had a chance to spend enough time to really get at the fishing and clamming until last year when one of the young men (Manuel) of the shark fishing family living on nearby Islote Partida [Isla Coyote] guided us through and around the mangrove area.

Amongst three of us the 14 species of fish caught included large dog and mangrove snappers, yellowtail, crevalle, and other jacks such as greenjacks, threadfin and gaff-topsail pompanos.

Manuel told of enormous jewfish (mero) spawning there in May and June, and robalo snook spending the winter and spring spawning in the brackish water. He showed us where there had been a spring back of some green shore chaparral. Its fresh water is believed to run underground enough to keep the mangrove footing brackish.

We had no problem finding enough two to three-inch chocolate clams and smaller cockles, and under a night light we were able to dip net halfbeak for baits and as many large gaff-topsail pompano as we could use.

With no good roads running near this place, and being 50 nautical miles from La Paz and 80 miles from Loreto, angling boats will leave the place to the trailerable boat people with an occasional yacht and a small boat that hauls salt to La Paz from a salt works five miles above the mangrove area, and from another small salt operation across the San José channel. — RAY CANNON

THE GREAT SPRING YELLOWTAIL MIGRATION

[In 1975, Ray describes the spectacular, beach-crashing migration of yellowtail into the Sea of Cortez that arrived at Cabo San Lucas and East Cape each spring.]

MARCH 12, 1975—Not one of the skippers operating angling boats out of the resorts across the Cabo San Lucas end of the peninsula had ever seen so many yellowtail taken in any season prior to the one just passed.

Here in the cape region the big (up to 50 or 60 pounds) yellows arrive suddenly in early December. We will have to await an extensive tagging program to learn whether they come south from the cooling Midriff sector of the Cortez, or down the Pacific from the Bahía Magdalena area, to winter in these mild waters—or up out of some yet unknown tropical habitat to escape extra warm water.

By mid-January, large numbers of yellowtail show up in the Rancho Buena Vista region. In February I have seen almost endless schools rise up to slowly cross over the Pulmo reef and head northward toward Bahía de Palmas and its four resorts.

There seems to be no way to retard the frantic aggressive competition and the added excitement among groups of boat crews and their anglers when fishing a wild and ravenous feeding school of yellows.

Anglers out of Rancho Buena Vista could have started a tagging program with a smash. The whole fleet was headed for the Tuna Canyon (submerged) when the crews spotted a cloud of diving sea birds and a boiling sea under the diving fowls, and recognized that the commotion was caused by a raiding army of hundreds of yellowtail.

I was with Chuck Walters driving on the new highway up above the Bahía de Palmas resort and its fleet of 15 or more boats at anchor when the yellows came barreling straight in between the boats, chasing a shoal of anchovies right up on the resort's beach.

Anglers aboard the Buena Vista fleet were baffled when their crews chased the yellows around and around in a threading the needle pattern and going at full bore (yellows take a fast troll). With "Hookup! Hookup!" yells coming from half of the anglers, the picture turned into a Keystone Comedy.

It was sunup and one person—a night watchman I think—was running up and down the beach screaming for the invading skippers to get out of his front yard. But no one gave him the slightest attention. Chuck did sound his horn. It only added one more note to the clamor. — RAY CANNON

SAILFISH SPAWN IN THE CORTEZ

[In 1962, Ray gives observations on billfish densities and life cycles, and argues against the concept of the Sea of Cortez as a "fish trap."]

GUAYMAS—Although billfish are found throughout the warm waters of the world, by far the greatest concentrations occur in the Gulf, according to all of the scientific and laymen reports I have received or heard of. During late summer the Cortez is crowded with them. I could not estimate the number fanning out from the swimway but in one area with a 20-mile diameter I believe there were four in every 100-foot square. This at Tiburón, but at the same time the waters of other resort places along the Baja Peninsula were crowded.

Comparing my notes over a period of ten years with a recent survey chart by Scripps, I am convinced that marlin, sailfish, and yellowfin tuna follow the 200 to 400-fathom lines, especially on their spring migrations, spreading into shallow water a month or so later because the narrow swimway becomes crowded, and to reach additional food supplies.

These fishes were not on their way up the Pacific and got diverted and trapped in the Gulf; they know exactly where they are going and why. The Cortez is one of the greatest forage pastures known.

For the past three years juvenile sailfish as small as 18 ounces and 31 inches have been caught by anglers out of this port. The most recent, a fifth-size, 32 1/2-ounce *Istiophorus grevi*, was taken aboard a Tommy Jamison marlin cruiser by Dick Curries of Tucson, Arizona. It measured 37 inches.

Because of the fast growth rate of young sailfish, the small sizes suggest that they were no more than a few months or perhaps weeks old and too young to have made the long migration trip up from the tropics.

The first juvenile of record here was caught in 1959, the first of the three warm water years. This was also the first year adults, caught at Guaymas, were noticed to be in ripe spawning condition. During these years a vast concentration of sails has been observed off the northern end of Tiburón Island in late September. If this area proves to be the spawning grounds (heretofore unknown) of the Pacific sailfish, it will be of great interest to scientists as well as anglers.

Kit McNear with a 72-pound roosterfish caught near the Hotel Punta Colorada, July 29, 1966. — COURTESY KIT MCNEAR

Marlin have not been known to spawn in the Gulf.

Both billfish have short lives. May not exceed five years. A 100-pound marlin in this species is about one year old.

There are a few broadbill swordfish in the Cortez. I have seen only two. Both caught in Ventana Bay below Las Cruces.

The striped marlin does use its spear as a weapon against enemies. I have seen four attack boats and have seen six others with spears in them. I also saw two broken-off spears in a palm log. Miami University reported finding four spears in a chunk of foam rubber. — RAY CANNON

TIDAL WAVE OF ROOSTERFISH

[This "barreling" abreast behavior of roosterfish, described by Ray in 1960, is still observed at times on a much smaller scale in southern Baja.]

When Bill Lloyd, Frank Dufresne and I sailed out of Mulegé and across the mouth of the dead-calm Concepción Bay, we found our boat plunging head-on toward a strange, quarter-mile-long wave. It was white-capped like a Pacific shore breaker. At first we thought it a tidal wave and were about to make a dash for a cove.

Then we got a glimpse of a large fish vaulting above it. As it came barreling in closer we saw it was alive with fish and that the apparent wave action was being made by a whole army of roosterfish in an abreast charge instead of being strung out in a long single file, as we are accustomed to seeing migrating schools on the move. Although we had observed small groups of skipjack and young jack crevalle execute such a maneuver we had never before seen roosterfish behave in this manner.

Once aware of the goings-on we plowed into them with spoons and feathers but failed to get a hook into a single one. Only after we resorted to skip-strips of bait were we successful.

When I got home I found a dozen letters reporting roosterfish being seen by the acre all around the Sea of Cortez, with the same complaint, that my recommended lures were getting none of the roosters. One guy wrote of having caught a 60-pounder on a small sierra he had just hooked. A couple of others had made good with skip-strips. — RAY CANNON

RECORD ROOSTER
AND A STRANGE COINCIDENCE

[From the second Sea Of Cortez Fishing Tournament Internacional, Patti McClane's record roosterfish (photo, page 256), and another rooster that wouldn't take "no" for an answer.]

JULY 28, 1969—In a sea crawling with all kinds of big billfish, including blue and black marlin, would you believe a couple of roosterfish stole the show!

The headliner of the tournament meet was a world record rooster, 70.6 pounds, taken on 20-pound test line, by a lovely lady who was not in the contest at all. Furthermore, she was the wife of one of the tournament judges. Moreover, it was her first roosterfish and her first big game fish record after having fished up and down the four corners of the world. Her name—Patti McClane, Palm Beach, Florida, wife of the noted A. J. McClane, fishing editor of *Field & Stream*.

Carla, my secretary, and I were fishing with the McClanes while at Buena Vista and witnessed the whole show, including the weighing-in by a scientist from the U.S. Tiburon Lab, California, Paul Wates, who is stationed at the Rancho doing a marlin feeding habit study.

The other headliner, a real believe-it-or-not, happened to another angler not in the contest who was not supposed to be down here fishing and made me promise not to divulge his name. His skipper, deckhand, and two companions confirmed the event.

While fishing out near the Buena Vista lighthouse, after catching one roosterfish each, the three anglers tagged and released all others caught. Among them was a whopper taken by my amigo.

The fishing was so good, next morning they got their allotment of live bait (now plentiful at Rancho Buena

Vista) and returned to the same area. You guessed it! The fisherman (who was properly credited for tagging the largest rooster) recaught the same fish bearing the hook, short leader, and tag implanted the day before.

The point of this piece is that fish do not run away when tagged, and do not seem to be overly concerned. After carefully examining the tag and hook-insertion area, the angler noted that there was no sign of infection or extra injury, thus adding to the evidence already known to marine biology scientists. — RAY CANNON

RECORD-BEATING RAINBOW RUNNER
AT RANCHO LEONERO

[Gil Powell, mentioned in this article about a relatively rare rainbow runner catch, established a private guesthouse in the mid-1960s on the south shore of East Cape's Bahía de Palmas. Powell was called "El Leonero" because of his love of hunting in Africa, and ironically, after a mountain lion hunting expedition with *Field & Stream* editor Frank Dufresne to the Sierra de la Laguna came up empty-handed. (The distinctly lion-like shape of the coastal hill near the present-day hotel is a coincidence.) Powell died of a stroke

At Rancho Buena Vista with a yellowfin tuna.

East Cape's modern Rancho Leonero fishing resort. — COURTESY RICK THOMPSON

in 1974 while on safari in Africa and the land remained vacant until it was bought by John Ireland and developed into today's modern hotel and fishing resort.]

DECEMBER 1, 1967—There are places throughout the world's tropical waters where the rainbow runner, *Elagatis bipinnulatus*, is not uncommon but generally this is considered a rare species.

Last week, in a letter from my longtime friend, Gil Powell, who has a fine house several miles down shore from Buena Vista, was a report of a 35-pound runner being caught by Joe Stuard, another resident of the area, also, of his fishing partner, Ray Fansher, decking a 25-pounder.

The I.G.F.A. world record for this species is 30 pounds.

Stuard's big 35-pounder will be mounted by George Lee, of Long Beach, and displayed at Rancho Buena Vista. I hope to get a photo of it for *W.O.N.*

This rainbow rates very high in the light-tackle game fish list, not only because of its endurance, long runs and occasional spectacular jumps, but also for its exciting color (sometimes seen hitting a ball of forage fish off Cabo Pulmo, where I have seen several schools of runners estimated at as many as 50).

In the Cortez the *Elagatis* seems to go hunting in the swift currents off of points and in narrow channels between islands and the Peninsula. Otherwise remaining a good distance off shore.

A small (three or four-inch) live bait would likely be best, judging from stomach contents of those few examined. The first caught from a school would likely be taken trolling a small white lure, then a switch to drifting with live bait on a small short shank hook should be productive.

In those years when the water temperatures remain warm through October and November, as it has for the past two years, several tropical forms can be expected in the lower reaches of the Cortez.

There is some belief that the Eastern Pacific rainbow runner is a different species from the smaller Atlantic kind. However, both are easily recognized by the distinct horizontal blue and yellow stripes; long, rounded, slender body; long pointed snout; small mouth and single finlet following dorsal, and another matching it following anal fin. Caudal fin deeply forked. The runner, like the yellowtail, crevalles, and the pompanos, is a member of the true jack family *Carangidae*, but rates above the yellowtail and amberjack as a finer food fish. — RAY CANNON

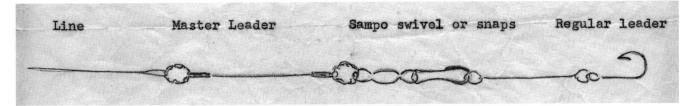

Line   Master Leader   Sampo swivel or snaps   Regular leader

From his field notes, Ray's detachable double leader rig. Ray usually fished with a lightweight version of this setup.

RAY'S TACKLE BOX

[The following tackle and technique recommendations give a good idea of how Ray actually fished. The specific products mentioned can be reproduced by similar items and materials available in the modern inventory. Little of basic importance has changed, with the exception of the widespread use of live bait, which became popular after these guidelines were written in about 1959.

Contrary to his reputation—Ray was primarily a light-tackle angler who almost always targeted mixed inshore species, not offshore big game. A saltwater angler far ahead of his time in this respect, he quickly grew bored of catching many of the same fish over and over again, and would sometimes exasperate charter boat skippers when he insisted that they move away from a good bite so he could try for another species.

Ray's favorite setup was a 12-pound test spinning rod and reel that he would use for casting from shore or from a boat. He would also troll with this rig, using a small white feather, until he caught a sierra or black skipjack suitable for cutting a six-inch skip-strip bait from the belly. Then, he trolled or cast the skip-strip bait.

For big fish, he usually trolled a larger skip-strip bait, using a heavier roller-guide rod and a medium-sized conventional reel, such as the Penn No. 349, spooling 30 to 50-pound test line. Nowhere in Ray's manuscripts does he mention personally fishing with really heavy equipment, nor is there any known photo of him doing so. The tackle items owned by Ray that have been preserved—rods, reels, lures, etc.—are exactly as he described.

In Ray's discussion of the advantages of dacron fishing line, he mentions not having to wash and dry it. This is a reference to the care required for early linen lines.]

In answer to the many questions on what tackle to use in fishing the Golfo I will give a one-man opinion as of today. Since I am continuously testing new and improved equipment I can recommend only the kinds of tackle that I have thoroughly tested and found the most efficient. Continuous experimentation will no doubt provide new favored products and I will be ready to change over as soon as they prove an advantage.

Start every day's fishing trolling 1/4-ounce feathers. Cut colored feathers out, leaving nothing but white ones. Good also for many species casting from shore.

After you have caught a couple of sierras or black skipjack, called "barrilete," for strip-bait, switch to a very large feather (same kind) and a six-inch skip-strip bait for dolphinfish, wahoo, tuna, and big oceanic skipjack. If needlefish start hitting, change to three-inch skip-strip.

A muddy or dirty spot at mouth of wash or arroyo good for tenpounder, small, mounting-size roosters and a number of pompanos and other jacks.

LEADERS

Use blue Sevenstrand (Sevalon) leader material at all times. There are very few places and times when a hook can be attached directly to mono line without having it snapped off by sierra, needlefish, small sharks, triggerfish, and several other scissor-toothed fishes.

I have found blue, plastic-covered multiple-wire leader efficient in fishing the Cortez (a single wire often forms a loop and snaps in two).

Several years ago I tested experimental leaders of this kind. I tried every other type and color, trolling each along side the Sevalon for periods of six months. None came closer than 25 percent of it. This from daily catch figures. This should not suggest that blue is a better color elsewhere. Backgrounds would in some instances indicate the most favorable color for the area.

I prefer jointed leaders for all fishing, except for giant needlefish and some species caught from shore. The upper section is connected directly to the line. The sections are connected by a McMahon snap or snap-and-swivel.

The Sampo swivel people are experimenting with a shineless substance to get away from chrome brightness (which attracts sierra and sharks to cut line). I have just given their dull-colored swivels a thorough testing and found them perfect.

LINE

The new mono is less springy (fewer pileups), less elasticity (easier to set hook) and less visible to many kinds of fishes. For heavy fish, dacron line seems to be tops for many reasons. Among them—its size, limpness, and lack of elasticity which makes setting the hook easy—and no washing or drying required—no swelling.

REELS

I have dropped my reel size from a Penn 6/0 to their new No. 349, loaded with 50-pound test dacron, and the

Penn 49-M with 30-pound test of same. Spinning equipment is much more satisfying for shore casting. For all casting: a 2080 F.B. Shakespeare, loaded with 12-pound test mono line for big fish; and a 450 Ted Williams arm pickup, loaded with 8-pound test mono for light fish.

RODS

For trolling, I take one light and one heavy Sila-flex Magnum rod, mounted with all Aftco roller guides cemented on rods. For all casting, a 66 R.A.F. and 71 R.A.F. Sila-flex Majestic spinning rod.

BAIT HOOKS

Hooks for very large jewfish and sharks, 13/0 Mustad "Tuna" hook. For less size monsters, 8/0 to 10/0 Mustad "Gultarp," and 6/0 to 8/0 "Salmon" hooks for dolphinfish to large grouper. For smaller game, Wright and McGill round-wire, short-shank hooks, No. 318 for sand bottom and 118 among rocks have proven superior after many years of personal testing.

LURES

Pure white, chrome-head feathers (brand name "Compac") that slide up on the leaders are best lures for greatest number of species. Use 1/4-ounce for small game;

2-ounce for medium; 4-ounce for large yellowfin tuna.

Other most efficient lures: Chrome-plated Spoofer during bright sunlight, and white ones otherwise, have the best batting average. Seven-inch Pflueger chrome spoon for roosterfish. Large Martin plugs for some grouper, amberjack and yellowtail. Spoofers and small feathers also excellent for shore casting, spinning, on 12-pound test mono.

BAIT

Frozen or fresh squid make good bait for a number of rocky-bottom dwellers such as small grouper, cabrilla, snapper, porgy, triggerfish and others. Small fish, strip-bait, clams and crabs better for some few species.

Whole sierra or other fish up to ten pounds used as baits for giant grouper and other huge bottom fishes. Black sea bass and other deep fish prefer foot-long live baits caught at the same place and depth.

Live mullet for black snook. Fresh-dead mullet or flyingfish for marlin and sailfish. When billfish follow but refuse mullet bait, switch to fresh, foot-long skip-strip.

Skip-strip baits for surface, cut from sierra or black skipjack, are often most productive for fish such as marlin, sailfish, dolphinfish, giant needlefish, yellowfin tuna, etc. This bait is tailored to sled along on the surface. [See drawing, page 297.]

When using fresh baits give free spool and time for fish to swallow hook. Not so with lures. — RAY CANNON

LIVE ANCHOVY CHUM FORMULA

Grind live anchovies (must be alive when placed in grinder). Grind directly into half a bucket of ocean water (two parts water to one of anchovies), keep at even (ocean) temperature until used.

There is a chemical affinity between ocean water and live anchovy blood, not effective, even a few minutes after anchovy is dead.

A cup of this mixture is dropped overboard at intervals of 50 feet or less, with two or three squeezed live or dead anchovies. — RAY CANNON

Always on the lookout for a good "fishing story" and a dramatic shot, Ray traveled with a camera, and often fished with a light meter around his neck.

Safe at Puerto Escondido, after drifting all night on a stormy sea. — PHOTO BY HARRY MERRICK

DISCOVERING BEAUTIFUL TAMBOBICHE

THE BENZIGER SHIPWRECK

RAY ALWAYS GOT a good story from his shipwrecks in Baja. This one from his beloved Juanaloa region is probably the best of the lot, and it was made all the better because professional photographer Harry Merrick happened to be on the trip and recorded it with some of the best photos of Ray's career. Even luckier was the fact that Bill Benziger—owner with his wife, Gloria, of Loreto's Hotel Oasis—also happened to be on the boat. Ray always seemed to stumble into good stories wherever he went, but for this one, he couldn't have planned it much better if he had tried.

In this article, Ray describes Tambobiche as "just south" of Juanaloa, an area he initially defined as ending at Bahía Agua Verde. Later, he extended the boundaries of Juanaloa southward to include Punta Mechudo near La Paz.

Not described in this account is what happened subsequent to the initial shipwreck. After the boat was relaunched through the surf, Ray, Harry Merrick, Bill Benziger and skipper Carlos Davis attempted to return to Loreto, only to discover the weather was still too rough to make passage. They were unable to anchor, and spent a harrowing night under pouring rain, adrift and unaware of their position, with the motor shut down in order to conserve fuel. In the morning, they were able to radio Gloria Benziger at the Hotel Oasis, who sent a boat to refuel them at Puerto Escondido. According to Benziger, that second night adrift was much worse than the shipwreck itself.

The final paragraph of this story, which was actually written two years after the shipwreck, announces a small

Roast kid at Tambobiche. "When the kindly folks learned that our food supply was ruined, and since no fish or shellfish could be brought in with storm and rain still raging, they gave us a fat kid, which we took back and barbecued. None of us could remember ever having more delicious food." — PHOTO BY HARRY MERRICK

The Hotel Oasis boat on the beach. Against the far shore, the mysterious house of Tambobiche. — PHOTO BY HARRY MERRICK

boat cruise through the Juanaloa area, and on to La Paz. That group of boats departed Kino Bay on December 4th, 1966 on what would become the first cruise of the future Vagabundos Del Mar Boat & Travel Club.

Although Ray states in the following story that the Tambobiche shipwreck occurred in the month of October, it actually took place in late September 1964:

THE BEAUTY OF TAMBOBICHE

There is no way for me to describe the waters and lands of the Rancho and Bahía called Tambobiche so that you can get the full impact of this sector's enthralling charge. I could make word pictures and show photos of the strange land side and beautiful sea, but you will have to go there to experience the exciting inner elation the place provides.

The county-size wilderness territory, 60 miles south of Loreto, is just south of the magnificent Region of Juanaloa, which is cupped in the crescent-shaped hand of the Sierra Gigantas, an impassable range of high mountains.

Tambobiche is just inside of the lower point of the crescent. During the catastrophic faulting that opened a chasm two miles or more deep and allowed the Pacific waters to flow in and form the Cortez, the lofty Gigantas were sliced off and tumbled into the gaping canyon. The near-shore islands and reefs are the peaks and tops of these drowned mountain slices. This also explains why the Sierras have such high, precipitous and flat faces facing east. They form a fantasy-land background for one of nature's finest living stage plays.

The vast Rancho Tambobiche encompasses miles of mountains and shoreline. Included is an excellent cove named Puerto Gatos (Port of the Cats), an enchanting baylet with close-to-shore big game fishing unmatched anywhere that I have ever been. And this is the pinpointed spot where you must pinch yourself repeatedly to make sure you are awake and not dreaming. Wrestling great sea fishes right inside of weirdly beautiful backwaters, where the climate, temperature, and everything else is close to a state of perfection, is the kind of an outdooring thrill every man should experience once in a lifetime at least.

At Puerto Gatos there is a short period just before sunup that would make a heathen infidel pour out all of the blessings left in his wizened soul. It is like the dawn of a day of resurrection.

At first the sea lies prone and pulseless in the great hush. Then the silence is shattered by the whine of a gnat, as loud as a siren in this vacuum. In the distance a single sardine breaks the levigated surface and starts a wave action that appears to build up to barreling ground swells. This insignificant movement is enough to trigger this whole world of creatures into living, dynamic action.

You guess that a shoal of big game fish are starting to feed when a lightning like flash above the surface follows a hundred-yard water eruption by a school of escaping sardines. You know it for sure when the enormous splashes occur as far in all directions as such things can be seen.

Even before the searching sun rays shift down from clouds to light the water drama, hordes of sea birds, in silhouette, wing in and dive in to add to the pulse-jingling excitement.

At the very sight of one of nature's most violent extravaganzas you get buck fever, but the old primitive fishing pox soon sets in, and you are revving the motor, pulling anchor, and planing hell-bent into the middle of the fray.

You choose your fish by the kind of birds hovering and diving—the elegant terns and some magnificent frigates over tuna; frigates and boobies over dolphinfish; pelicans and gulls over amberjack and surfacing leopard groupers.

When you couldn't care less which species you tie into, you let out one large white jig and one feather. Then you go as berserk as the blood-crazed fish.

Stopping overnight in Gatos on two recent expeditions, I was fortunate in experiencing these exciting expressions of nature. Both were in June.

Up to then the fishing at Gatos was the best-kept secret in the whole Sea of Cortez. No more than a dozen anglers had ever seen a close-up of this Shangri-la by the sea, much less fished it.

Now, you are almost sure to be hearing stories that will dwarf all of the tall fishing tales you have ever heard, from the few small boat adventurers who have cruised down this most remote, most isolated area in the whole Cortez.

Here is a land and a water which are even further removed in character and time, for both are of the first age of this sea. The mystic name they bear, "Tambobiche," applied by aborigines, was interpreted by early Spanish to mean a place halfway between heaven and earth—or as we would say, "Out of this world."

While the land side will be described as weirdly beautiful, it will be only the backdrop to the gargantuan tales of the mighty fishing. If you hear of 60-pound pompano and snapper, 100-pound amberjack and roosterfish, 200-pound sailfish, yellowfin tuna, grouper, and striped marlin, 1,000-pound black marlin and jewfish,

Waiting for the tide with Bill Benziger, left. — PHOTO BY HARRY MERRICK

and all close to shore, don't discount it. They are there, or at least spend the summer and fall seasons feeding in the rich waters.

The blood red bluffs of Punta San Telmo form the southern perimeter and landmark of Puerto Gatos. A mile below the point is a squarish cliff and the beginning of Bahía Tambobiche. About half a mile in from this corner the cliff ends like the lower end of the letter "J." Well hidden behind this tip end is a narrow entrance to the extensive Laguna Benziger.

From the entrance break, the bay's shore is a sand beach but with cobblestones at about eight to ten feet or less at low tide. Up to last year the most mysterious object around the Cortez, to me, was a large, two-story house at the back of the Bahía. I had seen it at a distance when flying over and when on small boat cruises to La Paz. But it took a chubasco and a shipwreck for me to get ashore and to examine the ghostly structure.

If you have read down to here, chances are good that you are thinking either of trailering your boat to Kino Bay, buying a new one, or chartering one at Loreto, for the voyage to Tambobiche. But I must warn you that while sailing like on a millpond is par for this course, it can get rough, and you can get roughed up if you ignore the rules and etiquette of Madame Cortez. I learned them the hard way.

Cruising aboard small craft on several trips past Tambobiche, I had always been forced to rush on because of our limited gas supply. I did get to spend a night and few morning hours fishing on the live bait expedition and a subsequent voyage. But when I discussed with Bill Benziger, owner of Hotel Oasis at Loreto, the need to learn something more about the land side of the little known

Ray and Hotel Oasis owner Bill Benziger, right, dine on barbecued goat as hotel skipper Carlos Davis doubles as chef.

— PHOTO BY HARRY MERRICK

Trenching to bring high tide to the boat. — PHOTO BY HARRY MERRICK

sector, he enthusiastically grabbed a few things, called a crew, and loaded us all, including photog Harry Merrick of Long Beach, Calif., in his best 22-foot inboard stern-drive, and we were off.

We skimmed down on the silk-like surface through the incomparable Region of Juanaloa, past the tranquil bays of Escondido and Agua Verde and on toward the Region's south end, as if gliding on a magic carpet.

As we approached our goal we saw but ignored a glaring white thunderhead that billowed up beyond the near mountains like an atomic bomb mushroom. This was October but only the native skipper and I were reminded that this was still chubasco season. The first storm warning signs are generally seen in large groundswell waves that precede the tornado-like hurricanes by an hour or more. But this was a sneaker from inland.

We were midway in the big bay when the first storm-like gust suddenly hit us. Thinking we could ride out the blow, two bow anchors were dropped, but one of the lines parted when the next blast belted us. It came in and carried a cloud full of water, parallel to the surface, which shot across our deck like a dozen active fire hoses.

Having been in five prior shipwrecks, I had learned a method of beaching a stern-drive craft and put it to work. We started the motor, cut the remaining anchor line, headed downwind for shore, full bore astern, even when riding the face of a ten-foot wave. Arriving in shallow water the motor was cut, the prop flipped up, everyone jumped overboard to grasp the ship and keep it straight with its bow into the breakers. We caught a big wind wave and made a perfect landing high on the beach.

The combination of high tide and wind tide had dropped our boat three feet above normal high which meant that we would have to dig a four-foot trench beside our keel and tip the boat into the high tide water.

Once you have done these things, they seem like unimportant problems, but to my companions, every step had been nerve shattering. They would be able to relax only when we took off the following day. Except for our can of coffee, our food had gotten soaked.

Shortly after we landed, the crew of a disabled shrimper abandoned ship and used a skiff or swam to get ashore. They were almost as curious as we were to examine the mystery house and joined us in the 2 1/2-mile hike to it.

Nearing the aged structure, we were met by a dozen husky young men and an equal number of old men and youngish teenagers. From two typical ranch houses nearby some few women emerged and looked on. We learned that most all of these people were descendants or married to members of the De la Toba family and that the big house had once been a prosperous hacienda. But just why it had been empty for the past 70 years, no one knew, or cared to discuss it.

When the kindly folks learned that our food supply was ruined, and since no fish or shellfish could be brought in with storm and rain still raging, they gave us a fat kid, which we took back and barbecued. None of us could remember ever having more delicious food.

While digging to level out my bedroll section, I hit dry sand and found all the dry wood we needed for our campfire.

The temperature of the rain, wind, and sea were all about 80 degrees, day and night, so getting wet and sleeping in it didn't matter.

At sunup the next morning the rain let up slightly, and the wind was less ferocious. The high tide barely reached our boat but was about three feet below the high crest that carried us high on the beach. We would have to dig a trench along the keel and tip the boat into it at the next high tide.

The day was spent examining the immense lagoon. The De la Tobas told us that many ducks and some geese

The greatly-expanded Hotel Oasis as it appears today. The hotel opened in 1963 with two (2) rooms. — PHOTO BY GENE KIRA

In 1998, Bill Benziger proudly displays the "scar"—actually very hard to see—that he received when the cruiser's outdrive scratched him, 34 years before during the Tambobiche shipwreck. — PHOTO BY GENE KIRA

and other water birds visited the lagoon throughout the winter and that snook, corvina, snapper, and many other fishes swarmed in and out of the shallowish water.

There are several patches of mangrove and other shore bushes that suggested freshwater seepages. Since the natives had never heard of a name of this backwater except "La Laguna," we christened it "Laguna Benziger," for our expedition sponsor, as is customary.

When the high tide flooded our trench, good use was made of all the extra hands from the rancho and shrimp boat in getting our boat afloat. With a bit more digging, three men could have done the launching.

Although I had been in several storms and on the fringes of a few chubascos, I considered myself most fortunate in getting right into the eye of this one. Otherwise I would not have been able to advise other boaters on how to get along in one, or to cruise in those seasons when none occur (*i.e.*, December through July). Fairly strong spring winds are not nearly as dangerous.

I like repeating this chubasco account to discourage timid sailors, for they are usually so worried about imaginary dangers, they have no fun anyway. But the major reason for my report of the worst to be expected is to stimulate interest and get disillusioned boaters into a water that can furnish about everything a daydreaming adventurer can think of.

Everything about charting a course here and cruising it is good fun, and when well planned and executed with a bit of common sense, there never need be the slightest bit of tension or concern.

Boating on the Cortez has developed into a new and unique sport. Because of its great size, its variation and contrasts, its 100 uninhabited islands and hundreds of miles of fantastic wilderness shorelines, and its excellent resorts at intervals, cruising this tranquil sea is like exploring in the South Sea when done in a small boat.

This coming December 1 [1966], I expect to be piloting a free-for-all fleet of 16' to 26' outboards and outboard stern-drive boats for a trip to Tambobiche and on to La Paz. Anyone with some boating experience and seaworthy craft can join the cruise by giving advance notice. This so that gas and supplies can be reserved at Kino, Mulegé, and Loreto. It will be a combination fishing, diving, hunting, exploring, photographing, and general outdooring fun voyage. Those interested can contact me at my home address. — RAY CANNON

Cabo San Lucas prior to the creation of the inner harbor. Note landing strip, narrow entrance to tidal flats where present harbor and marina are located, and buildings of the Hotel Hacienda. Photo taken c. 1966. — COURTESY MARK PARR AND MERE KRESS

GREAT DAYS IN BAJA

THE HEIGHT OF THE GOLDEN AGE

ON SEPTEMBER 1, 1966, Ray celebrated his 74th birthday, and as the song says, "it was a very good year." Three weeks after his birthday, *The Sea Of Cortez* made its long-awaited debut, culminating a 12-year research and writing effort and bringing him instant celebrity. Ray was at the peak of his career, still physically vigorous, basking in the popularity brought by over a decade of weekly columns in *Western Outdoor News*; and with the validation of those columns and a bestselling book to his credit, he enjoyed *carte blanche* to travel and fish in Baja virtually anywhere and anytime he wished. At long last, Ray had truly arrived at that shimmering paradise he had envisioned on the beaches of San Felipe some 20 years earlier.

In 1966 at Rancho Buena Vista, Ray's close friend, Colonel Eugene Walters, began construction of the Round House on a perfect little cove just the right distance from the resort's main buildings, with the promise that Ray would be able to live in it for the rest of his life.

And in Baja California Sur, the Golden Age was in many ways also reaching its own peak, a fulfillment of Ray's idyllic vision of a remote paradise of luxury fishing resorts reachable by airplane or boat, where refugees from an over-industrialized society could come to relax and renew themselves in a slow-paced world suffused with unspoiled natural beauty.

Work was well underway on the Transterritorial Highway linking the southern population centers of Cabo San Lucas, San José del Cabo, La Paz, Loreto, Mulegé, Santa Rosalía and San Ignacio. Grading had already begun on all of these sections and paving would be completed by

1972. Although this southern highway system was intended to serve agriculture and general business as much as tourism, it greatly furthered Ray's purposes by providing an easy way for visitors to move about and enjoy camping and fishing in places previously difficult to reach.

East Cape's Bobby Van Wormer at the Hotel Palmas de Cortez, originally opened by Johnny Mitre in 1959 as the Bahía de Palmas.
— PHOTO BY GENE KIRA

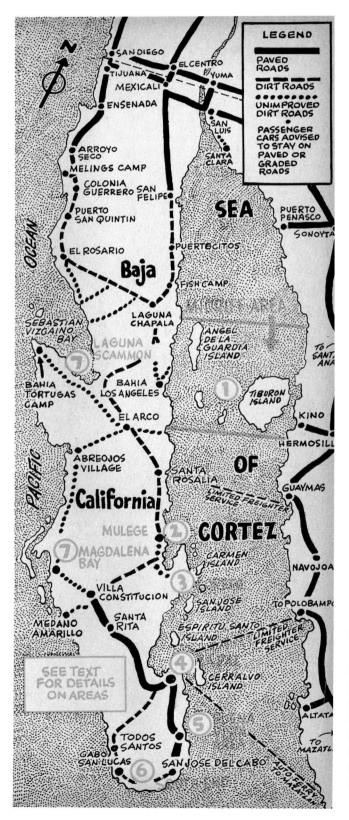

LEGEND

PAVED ROADS

DIRT ROADS

UNIMPROVED DIRT ROADS

PASSENGER CARS ADVISED TO STAY ON PAVED OR GRADED ROADS

This road system was also ideal, in Ray's judgment, for the very important reason that it continued no further north than San Ignacio. The difficult, rough section of dirt road between that point and the northern pavement, which ended near San Quintín, prevented the arrival of what Ray saw as hordes of "hippie" tourists who would spoil the gracious, jet-set atmosphere of the Golden Age. Ray was strongly opposed to the idea of the Transpeninsular Highway that would connect Baja California Sur with the U.S. border, and he wrote many columns against it, from about 1970 onwards, after it became apparent that the highway would actually be built. But in 1966, the road system of Baja California Sur was still separated from the northern section, allowing easy movement around the shores of the southern peninsula without letting in hordes of vehicles.

By 1966, access to Baja California Sur had reached a state of near-perfection for Ray's vision of the Golden Age: easy, but not too easy. In that year, the old propeller-driven DC-3s and DC-6s were replaced with the modern DC-8 jet airliners of Aeronaves de México, flying the direct Los Angeles–La Paz route which had been opened in 1962, and bringing the great resorts of the Golden Age within three flight hours of the U.S.

For those wishing to tour the peninsula in cars and campers, ferryboat service had opened from La Paz to the mainland city of Mazatlán in May 1965, giving access to Baja California Sur for those few motorists willing to drive down the Mexican mainland.

And by 1966 the people of Baja California Sur—at least those living near the main population centers—had begun to benefit from the greatly increased income created by tourism, as standards of living were raised, schools were built, water and electricity were brought to remote villages, and larger and larger resorts were built in very rapid succession.

This explosive resort building boom included—in addition to many others—such watershed projects as the Hotel Cabo San Lucas in Los Cabos, 1961; Oasis in Loreto, 1963; Hacienda Cabo San Lucas in Cabo San Lucas, 1963; the Serenidad in Mulegé, 1964; Punta Colorada in East Cape, 1966; and Borrego de Oro (Punta Chivato) near Mulegé, 1966.

Reprinted from *Western Outdoors Magazine*, November 1969, map shows a Baja California close to Ray's idealized vision of it as a remote but accessible outdoor paradise. The roads to Colonet and San Felipe have been paved. The Transterritorial Highway from Cabo San Lucas to Santa Rosalía is nearing completion, and the La Paz—Mazatlán ferry has begun service. Airline services were available to virtually all the resorts on the Sea of Cortez using DC-3s and smaller planes. Aeronaves de México had begun jet airline service to La Paz in 1966.

— COURTESY WESTERN OUTDOOR NEWS

Land's end in the summer of 1965. The Hotel Solmar would open just north of these rocks in 1974.

From its beginnings at Abelardo L. "Rod" Rodríguez' Rancho Las Cruces in 1950, until the opening of jet airliner service in 1966, the tourist industry of Baja California was characterized by experimentation, daring entrepreneurship, and in many cases, blind hope. From 1966 onwards, the guidelines and infrastructure had been largely established, and as rapidly as the industry has grown since then, its progress has been more incremental than revolutionary.

For the people of Baja California, the very brief period of no more than perhaps a dozen years, centered on the year 1966, is remembered as a time of startling progress and change, some for the better, some not, that carried them inevitably and irreversibly into the modern era.

Following here are some of Ray's impressions of those great days in Baja—the height of the Golden Age.

WELCOME MAT OUT FOR ANGLERS—1957

[The Golden Age is launched in earnest. Ray describes busy activity all around southern Baja as many builders recognized the business potential of tourism. But the risks of the era were great, and several of the projects described were soon abandoned or eventually failed. These included the development at San Lucas Cove, the Mulegé Beach Lodge, Ed Tabor's Flying Sportsmen Lodge, and the Hotel Los Cocos.]

JANUARY 25, 1957—The greatest surprise I've run into south of the border occurred on my recent trip which included Mulegé, Loreto and La Paz. It was in the sudden wakening of the businessmen, officials and the majority of the local populations in these places.

The changes made during the past year are almost astonishing. Boats and motors are kept in tip-top shape; guides are keenly alert to every requirement; lodge and hotel reception and services are now on a par with our stateside best; English-speaking hosts have been added; and chefs that could qualify for the best in the U.S. In the sweeping change over, new boats are being added, hotels and lodges remodeled and expanded, and new luxury resorts are being constructed in new localities.

A syndicate (U.S. and Mexican) has bought a 50-acre, shore-side hacienda with tropical fruit trees, just 12 miles south of Santa Rosalía on the Bahía San Lucas. They expect to have a cabaña-type hotel, private airplane strip, fleet of boats and other modern conveniences going within a few months.

Congenial Octavio "Sal" Salazar at Mulegé Lodge has bought a large beach tract and palm-covered island in the river at Mulegé. His blueprints for the new resort show real imagination in combining modern and native architecture. His new English-speaking host is a good example of the new hospitality.

Ed Tabor and very charming wife have made the Flying Sportsmen's Lodge at Loreto into a delightful and gay resort for sportsman and family as well. Little is left to wish for since they engaged manager-maitre d' Don Peppy, whose French-U.S. cuisine will more than please any appetite.

La Paz is on its toes building, expanding and dressing up for big things to come. The Los Arcos Hotel has enlarged to include another block for cottages half-finished and being occupied by angler parties or families. La Perla is remodeling and spreading out to include more spacious lounge and dining room, and 100 rooms. The new, quiet Guaycura, enlarged Misión and the new, spacious Los Cocos, managed by U.S.-trained George Escudero, are all very modern.

Will report later on the plush hotel Rod Rodríguez, owner of Las Cruces, is building at Palmilla, near San José del Cabo.

A quiet evening in La Paz, 1964. The sand spit, El Mogote, is just visible on the horizon.

I'm not sure whether or not this whole sudden change to the new tempo and modernization in services was sparked by Luis Cóppola, manager for Trans Mar de Cortés Airlines, but I am convinced that he is the most progressive and civic-minded builder I have met in Baja.

He seems quite sure and determined to develop the potentials of the peninsula to its full capabilities. Everywhere you can see the stimulating influence of the airline's policy, especially in La Paz, where their local office is managed by Guillermo Escudero Luján, highly regarded by all local officials and businessmen.

Their L.A. office arranged every detail of my trip. Although there were a series of very complicated side trips, everything clicked as planned without any delays.

— RAY CANNON

LA PAZ IN THE GOLDEN AGE

[Ray, in a relaxed swing through La Paz with his Sunset Books editor, Jack McDowell and McDowell's wife Liz, about a year before the publishing of *The Sea Of Cortez*, and just before the big building boom of the Golden Age. Ray recalls his first impressions of La Paz 11 years earlier, and he describes the social promenades that were still in fashion during the era, but have since faded from the local scene.

He also mentions the waterfront Hotel Los Cocos, originally built in 1957 and once the leading hotel of the city. In 1974, it would be converted to workers' quarters for the building of the multistory Hotel Presidente, which would close its doors permanently in 1994. Both structures are now abandoned.

This column concludes with gossip about Mulegé during a time when several resorts there were opening, closing, and reopening under different names. Business was undoubtedly brisk for Mulegé's sign painters during the mid-1960s.]

SEPTEMBER 10, 1965—La Paz means "The Peace," and during all of the great amount of time I have spent there for the past decade, I have seldom if ever, heard a sound of violence or agony. The name fits the place, but to call it a "city of romance" would be even more fitting and I have seen no letup in the pursuit of l'amour since I first witnessed the traditional promenade, in which a hundred or so señoritas stroll around the Plaza counterclockwise, and an equal number of señors (several U.S. fishermen included) saunter around clockwise.

These Sunday and Thursday evening promenades continue, but new events have been added. I have not seen nor heard of a social affair in the U.S. to compare in charm and gentle demeanor to a real ball given to a hundred graduating lady secretaries at Los Cocos Hotel's spacious outdoor dining room. This, in a flower-scented garden with coconut trees forming a massive canopy.

Although the balmy evening was kept air-conditioned

Upper photo, sport fishing boats loading clients in La Paz. Lower photo, Carlos Riva Palacio, with clipboard, managed the Hotel Los Cocos during the 1960s, and later headed the state office of tourism in La Paz.

which are completely surrounded with a tropical garden, shaded like a greenhouse by towering, spreading India laurel trees. Over its decorative garden wall you can see the bay's pleasure craft at anchor or slowly moving by.

With this new bungalow annex and other innovations, the splendid old Los Arcos has more than regained its former popularity, especially among anglers with wives who wish to do the town while the fishing is going on.

****

There is some good news from Mulegé and some that is confusing. Word from Bill Lloyd, operator of Playa de Mulegé, suggests he has won a legal battle and is operating full blast. News also of Dick Stockton selling his interest in the Club Aero Mulegé, with some questions about the reopening of Serenidad and Hacienda de Mulegé this fall. Nothing new on the big resort planned for Punta Chivato.

— RAY CANNON

FEDERAL GOVERNMENT TURNS ATTENTION TO BAJA CALIFORNIA SUR

[In 1962, Ray describes federal interest in the economic development of Baja California during the administration (1958-64) of President Adolfo López Mateos. The highway mentioned here, from Cabo San Lucas to Santa Rosalía, would not be completed until 1971.]

The Federal Territory of Baja California Sur (South), is being given a lot of serious consideration by Mexican Commissions under President Mateos. A rash of government projects are breaking out around La Paz. The harbor channel is to be dredged to a safe depth of 50 feet, the residue to be used to widen the Mogote (the sand spit enclosing the north side of the bay). The highway around the south end is to be paved and extended up to Santa Rosalía. Funds for these have awaited the activating of the Punta del Este Agreement.

According to Bill Escudero, the "tuna pirating" purse seiners will be brought under complete observation by two new helicopters, two new cutters, and a fleet of speed boats operated by the Mexican Navy. If caught netting in bays, nets and ships will be confiscated, and Mexican laws do not have all of the technical loopholes as those of California. — RAY CANNON

CITY OF LA PAZ ASTIR-1966

[Ray describes La Paz in 1966 as an energized city of astonishing change, rapidly entering the modern era.]

There was never before such a stir among the La Paz citizenry as is in progress now, at least not since the great whale smog nearly choked them a few years ago. That was

by gentle sea breezes, the dancers moved slowly, as if to aggravate their well contained emotions. The restraint was remarkable.

As I remember back to 11 years ago and my first fishing trip out of La Paz when I wrote that I would likely retire there, I must have been influenced by more than the excellent big game fishing. I now believe that the balmy nights and that ratio of seven women to one man, may have contributed to my decision.

In those days I was charmed by everything about the Los Arcos Hotel. On this trip I took Jack and Liz McDowell of Sunset Book Company there with me and we were housed in one of the Hotel's delightful cottages

Salvador Morales' taxi passing through El Triunfo in May 1965. He was the driver hired by Enrique and Doris Ortega's International Travel Service to take Ray around La Paz and down to Rancho Buena Vista. This road from La Paz to Cabo San Lucas was first graded about 1960. — PHOTO BY MARTIN GOLDSMITH

when a large pod of big whales ran aground and died in the town's front yard. The excitable stir was in hurrying up to render out the fat before the blubber issued a world record stink. That was a real gasser.

For the first time in all of the years I have been coming to La Paz I sense a quickening of the heartbeat of the City. It is as if a giant sleeping Gulliver were about to awaken and shake off the restraints of tradition. There is actually a snap to the stride of some few pedestrians. Long ago I remember writing that the pace was so slow that "the dogs walked instead of trotting." And that only Rudy Vélez strode fast enough to catch ulcers.

Today the more realistic businessmen are searching for methods of exchanging natural pleasure for finances coming to the area, not only from anglers, nimrods, and other outdooring men but more especially their wives and offspring.

People who are brought up in an area and accustomed to all of the odd features that are strange to others, rarely see the value of publicizing an ancient sugar mill or such quaint native attractions. With the profound thought and energy now being given the subject, you can bet that your non-fishing family will have plenty to do by next spring.

With Aeronaves stepping up its flights with the big new jets, the boom in private plane and small boat travel, and the number coming across from Mazatlán on the big ferry ship, one tight bottleneck is appearing, *i.e.*, accommodations at hotels and resorts.

In addition to the five popular hotels, there are a few

small inexpensive inn-type places and a few extra rooms for let. Alfredo Escobedo, with offices in the front of the old Hotel Misión, keeps track of such available quarters. You always dine at the larger hotels.

I will try to get more dope on the big modern hotel being talked about. What a profitable investment it would be, especially if the income were spent in Mexico.

— RAY CANNON

LA PAZ-CABO SAN LUCAS ROAD GRADED

[From Rancho Buena Vista, Ray records the beginning of the Transterritorial Highway that by 1972 linked the major population centers from Cabo San Lucas to San Ignacio. The southern section described, from Cabo San Lucas to La Paz, would not actually be paved until 1971.

Also mentioned is the new jet service to La Paz, and Bobby and Cha Cha Van Wormer's newly-opened Hotel Punta Colorada, one of many resorts recently completed or under construction.]

NOVEMBER 25, 1966—The new highway (to be paved next year) from La Paz to Cabo San Lucas has been well graded, and except for a couple of short stretches and a bridge to span the San Bartolo wash, fairly good speed can be made to Buena Vista and on past Santiago.

Taxi drivers say that an hour in driving time has already been cut and that Buena Vista should be within an easy 1 1/4 hours from La Paz when the paving is finished. The drivers are already talking of lowering fares from $25.00 to $20.00 for four people, between the points.

Anyone planning to drive down to Mazatlán, take the ferry to La Paz, then drive around the southern tip of Baja would be better off if traveling in a camper, especially after the middle of March, when finding a room at resorts will not be easy.

The number of black marlin in the Buena Vista Region is reaching the astonishing level. Beginning in August, the run has exceeded all previous years by far. The three or four, 200 to 500-pounders being decked per week tell only a tenth of the story. The reason so many are making off with the tackle is that anglers are not expecting the fury and energy the big blacks put into a fight.

The hunting season is on and you can get into the game by a jeep or by boat. The freshwater lagoons are swarming with ducks and brant, and doves (three species) are all over in great abundance.

Age is adding grandeur to the Rancho. Palms, tropical trees, shrubs, and other flowering greenery have had the time and care to flourish, and in this arid climate vegetation is really appreciated.

Bobby Van Wormer has his new resort, "Hotel Punta Colorada," going full-bore. Says he expects to have live

bait operational within a few weeks. This will make fishing at Cabo Pulmo quite convenient.

The prompt air service from La Paz to this area and the paving of the new highway will add more popularity to the resorts, if that is possible. — RAY CANNON

FERRYBOAT ERA
A LINK TO THE MAINLAND

The first fishing lodges of the Golden Age were based on fly-in traffic, either in war surplus DC-3s or in small private planes that could land on the rough strips that were cleared near every facility. But as the Territory of Baja California Sur rapidly expanded in the late 1960s, with more tourist accommodations, business activity, and extensive agricultural development in the Santo Domingo Valley area (today's Ciudad Constitución and Ciudad Insurgentes), the need arose for a system of ferryboats to create a vehicular link to the mainland. Dredging and construction plans were laid out for ferry terminals at Puerto Escondido (near Loreto), La Paz, Santa Rosalía, and Cabo San Lucas, and service was actually opened at the latter three of those locations: La Paz-Mazatlán in 1965, La Paz-Topolobampo in 1970, Santa Rosalía-Guaymas in 1973, and Cabo San

Crossing the Cortez before the first ferry opened in 1965 was by freighter. This photo is from Ray's 1961 "El Dorado camper trip" across the Cortez and around the south end of the Baja peninsula with manufacturers Everett and Don Hamel.

Ferryboat LA PAZ

... a highway over the sea

a service offered by

CAMINOS Y PUENTES

Federales de Ingresos y Servicios Conexos

Original brochure, c. 1965. Baja's first ferry connection to the mainland—La Paz to Mazatlán—opened a new era of tourism and business possibilities for the southern territory in early 1965 with departures twice per week from each terminal. The 350-foot *Transbordador La Paz* carried up to 114 automobiles and 370 passengers. Ferry service—also eventually opened at Santa Rosalía and Cabo San Lucas—would be the principal way for vehicles to reach the southern half of Baja until the completion of the 1,070-mile Transpeninsular Highway in late 1973.

Lucas-Puerto Vallarta in 1974 (this service was discontinued in 1986). The terminal at Puerto Escondido was partially built but never put into operation. Instead, several ambitious marina and resort projects were begun in the small bay, but none has been completed to the present day.

The "ferryboat era" from 1965 until the opening of the Transpeninsular Highway in 1973 typified the Golden Age, for during that period Baja California Sur benefited from economic links to the mainland while at the same time the existing "bad" road to the border kept out the advancing hordes that would soon bring the peninsula, willy-nilly, into the modern age.

The ferryboat era was a quiet time when the old ways still dominated life in Baja California, but when the groundwork was already being laid for the economic explosion of the 1980s and 1990s. In the following columns, Ray documents some major events of the period and gives a good feel for its pervading sense of being poised on the cusp of a rapidly approaching future.

LA PAZ FERRY SERVICE BEGINS

[Opened in 1965, the La Paz-Mazatlán ferry was Baja's first vehicular link to the mainland. Until then, the only way to transport a motor vehicle across the Sea of Cortez was to strap it on the deck of a freighter. Ray saw the ferry as a way for tourists—but not too many of them— to explore the quaint and beautiful dirt road then passable from La Paz down the coast to Cabo San Lucas, up the Pacific side to Todos Santos, and back to La Paz again. In 1971 that drive would become easier when the link between La Paz and Cabo San Lucas was paved. Only three years after that, a crash program headed by President Luis Echeverría Alvarez would complete the paving of the entire 1,070-mile length of the Transpeninsular Highway.]

FEBRUARY 5, 1965—At long last we can now report that the Mazatlán-La Paz ferry ship has provided "a road across the Sea," and that touring visitors from the U.S. can drive down all-paved highways, cross on the deluxe ferry, and drive around the Peninsula's south-end-loop over fairly good dirt roads.

The big, 260-mile circle passes through Baja California's most interesting region. Along the way are semi-ghost towns, primitive ranches, tropical oases, the resorts of Bahía de Palmas and the famed Rancho Buena Vista, the quaint and ancient towns of Santiago, Miraflores, and San José del Cabo, then past the Peninsula's most elegant resorts—Hotel Las Cruces Palmilla, Hotel Cabo San Lucas, and Hacienda Cabo San Lucas. Returning by a drive up the Pacific side to the town of Todos Santos, half hidden in tropical fruit orchards, thence back across on a level road to La Paz. Then, if time allows, take the recently repaved highway which runs northward to within ten miles of the highly interesting and productive Almejas

Everyone who was anyone turned out for the maiden voyage of the new ferryboat *Salvatierra*, which opened service between La Paz and Topolobampo in the summer of 1970. Left to right: Raúl Aréchiga, partner in Servicios Aéreos de la Paz (later, Aerocalifornia); Luis Cóppola Bonillas, owner of the Hotel Los Arcos; Gill Gunnell, Gunnell Aviation; César Gandara, Lieutenant Governor of the State of Sonora; and Ricardo García Soto, Director of the Office of Tourism, Baja California Sur. The La Paz-Mazatlán ferry, Baja's first, had opened service five years earlier.

Bay, the southern extremity of Magdalena Bay.

The accommodations aboard the *Transbordador La Paz* are as elegant as those of a modern ocean liner and it is just as seaworthy as most of them. It is scheduled to sail from Mazatlán on Saturdays and Tuesdays at 5 p.m. and from La Paz, Sundays and Thursdays at 9 a.m. One-way rates for small, compact cars, $32. Larger but less than 19 feet, $40; 22 feet, $56. Campers also according to length.

For passengers' fares, four classes are quoted as: Salon, $4; Tourist, $16; Cabin, $28, and Special, $50. These are figures and schedules from first reports received and may be adjusted. I will publish changes if they are made. It is thought that some of the top rates will be scaled down. The first trips have been so successful, reservations are necessary to get passage and vehicle space.

****

An interesting and spectacular survey of the deep, submerged canyon walls that drop off sharply to 9,000 feet just off Cabo San Lucas is now in progress. According to Bill Escudero, oceanographers, biologists, and geologists working out of the Hacienda Cabo San Lucas are using a new "jet propelled Diving Saucer" for their explorations, charting, and explorations. Involved are scientists from the University of Mexico, the U.S. Navy, and Scripps Institute of Oceanography. — RAY CANNON

CARLA GETS KICKED OFF LA PAZ-TOPOLOBAMPO FERRY!

[This story takes place near the end of the Vagabundos Del Mar Boat & Travel Club annual cruise of 1970, just as the second La Paz ferry line—to Topolobampo—was making its maiden run and just two months after the new La Paz airport had gone into operation at its present location.

The list of dignitaries present for the opening of the new ferry and airport indicates the significance laid to these events.

Bob and Gill Gunnell, operated the Gunnell Aviation air service and were active in promoting Baja fishing tournaments and fly-in tourism through their organization,

Fly-For-Funsters and their pioneering small airline, Mexico Air Service.

As a follow-up to the story of women being barred from the ferryboat's maiden run because they were "bad luck," Gill Gunnell reports that the captain of the ship strongly objected to women boarding even for the return trip from Topolobampo. Nevertheless, she, daughter Bobbye, Carla, and associate Dorothy Furman did manage to get aboard for the festive return voyage to La Paz.

However, as the ferryboat approached the La Paz terminal at Pichilingüe, it lost its reverse gear and with a tremendous crash it rammed the dock with enough force to put a hole in its hull. The ladies hid in a bathroom aboard the ship until everyone else had gotten off.

That night, the ladies were taken to a restaurant by Luis Cóppola of the Hotel Los Arcos, and they encountered not only the ferryboat captain, but his crew as well.

According to Gunnell, the captain and his entire crew stood and left the restaurant without saying a word.]

JULY 9, 1970—Carla and our friend Gene Babbitt and I left the [Vagabundo club] fleet cruising in Juanaloa.

We caught an Aeronaves DC-9 for La Paz and arrived at the new La Paz airport in time to meet Lic. Ricardo García Soto, head of tourism and alert assistant to Lic. Hugo Cervantes del Río, Governor of the Territory.

We were included on the passenger list to make the first trip—La Paz-Topolobampo—aboard the Ruffo Brothers' big, new ferry ship, the *Transbordador Salvatierra*, with a capacity of 70 standard-size autos and 350 passengers. Reservations are made on the mainland side by Roberto Balderrama, Hotel Santa Anita, Los Mochis, Sinaloa, Mexico, and at their La Paz office, Terminal San Antonio. Eduardo Ruffo manages the enterprise. His brothers, Antonio and Augustine, participate in ownership. The lounge, bar, and dining areas of the big ship are air-conditioned. Crossing is made in 10 hours, cruising at 12 knots.

One of the first things we learned when going aboard was that no women would be on this first voyage (an old sea superstition still adhered to by many skippers).

Not to be outdone, Bob Gunnell, of the newly formed Mexico Advisory Service, Santa Monica, California, flew all of the ladies to Los Mochis. Included were Carla, Mrs. Gill Gunnell, daughter "Bobbye," and their business associate, Dorothy Furman, Los Angeles—all our close friends.

Just about all of the Territory's officials and business leaders and several reps of Federal Government offices joined the Territorial Governor and the rest of us in an ocean-going fiesta that didn't quit for two days aboard and three nights ashore. The ladies helped whoop it up on the return trip. We had picked up two more governors and officials from four states in Mexico, and all were as gay as youngsters.

The Governor's invitational dinner, opening an elegant new cafe occupying the second floor of the new airport, was a fitting climax for Carla, Gene, and me, to a no-ending fiesta which started at Mulegé, June 14, and lasted through June 22. Gene and Carla returned affirming that they had had the fastest, best fun vacation ever.

Luis Cóppola flew me down to see the progress being made on his immense and spectacular enterprise, the Hotel Finisterra, right on the saddle ridge of Cabo San Lucas at the tip of the peninsula. — RAY CANNON

BAJA SUR'S EARLY MOTELS & TRAILER PARKS

[The coming of vehicular traffic to southern Baja touched off a flurry of motel and trailer court development, including such facilities as the El Cardón Motel and Trailer Park in La Paz and the Hotel Palomar, opened in Santiago in 1965 by Cirilo Gómez and his wife Virginia. Another result of the increase in motor vehicle traffic down the Baja peninsula was the advent of the great series of dirt road racing events generically referred to as the "Baja 1000."]

SEPTEMBER 17, 1965—Businessmen of the city were optimistic about possible success of the Mazatlán-La Paz ferry ship, but hotel owners were agreeably surprised at their large volume of business from it.

Ed Pearlman's original Mexican 1000 Rally brochure. Six-hundred copies were printed and mailed out to promote the race in 1967. — COURTESY ED PEARLMAN

Upper left: Bruce Meyers and Ted Mangles won the premiere 1967 race in a Meyers Manx with a time of 27 hours 38 minutes. Lower left: Ralph Poole, left, and Spencer Murray in the standard Rambler American they used to set a pre-race series production car record of 31 hours flat in July 1967.

— JOHN LAWLOR PHOTO COURTESY OF ED PEARLMAN

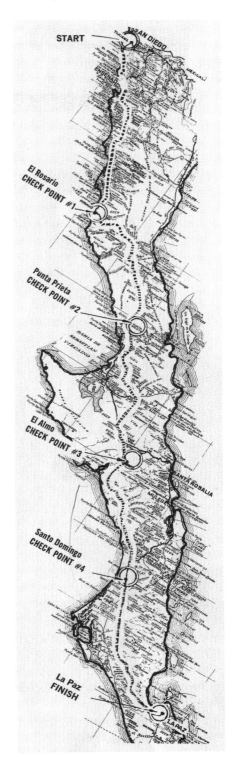

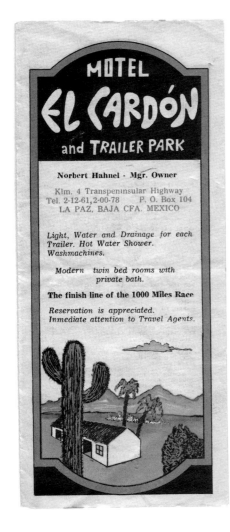

A 1960s brochure of the historic El Cardón Trailer Park, on the Transpeninsular Highway just north of La Paz. This was the finish line for the first running of Pete Condos' and Ed Pearlman's NORRA Mexican 1000 Rally which was staged in November 1967. That event was prefaced by a number of "timed runs" down the peninsula beginning in 1962. The idea for a full-length Baja race evolved into the SCORE Baja 1000 in 1975, and the El Cardón Trailer Park—relatively unchanged to the present day—is still a favorite stopping place for Baja old-timers.

The original route map, showing checkpoints. — COURTESY ED PEARLMAN

Up until the ferry began pouring car-driving visitors into the south end of Baja California, no one ever thought of building auto-courts in the small inland towns. In fact, the term "auto-court" or "motel" was new to the natives. Now, two quite modern motels are being constructed, one at Santiago below Buena Vista, and another at Todos Santos on the Pacific. Both are on the circle trip around this south end.

Heretofore there has been a slack season in mid-summer, just when big and small game fishing is at its best. No one seems to know why. But the slack will be taken up as soon as the ferry visitors learn that it is the early summer rains that change an otherwise parched land side into a green and flowering wilderness garden, with tropical birds swarming all over.

Can you remember when the Southern California Auto Club's motto "Open Road" helped sell us all on buying a jalopy and getting in on some of the exciting adventure the phrase suggested? If you wish to recapture it, this ferryboat has opened the gate to the distant past for you. — RAY CANNON

TAKE-HOME SOME HAPPINESS

[Ray sees "joyful memories" as Baja California's most important export product.]

DECEMBER 1, 1965—Joyful memories will soon become Baja California's most profitable export. This is not as abstract as it may sound, for included in this load of take-home happiness is health, inspiration, a rested and revived spirit, and mental stability. Even though there are no materials involved, efficiency in the production of substance depends upon these phases of well-being, and Baja California provides the close-to-perfect fields for getting the failing body coils recharged.

Now if you have absorbed all that, we'll get earthy. The resorts around the southern half, or the Territory of Baja California Sur, will have larger gross income than the grain or cattle growers or the recently revived copper business at Santa Rosalía. Furthermore, the products of the territory will not be drained off, nor will any of its resources be depleted.

The wealth is not the only gain for Baja Californians. They are also made happy by the fun-loving anglers and other outdooring people and the almost continuous fiestas they inspire, most always acting as equals even with the poorest native. This in contrast to the regular border town tourist who appears to be an overbearing snob and creating an atmosphere of unhappiness.

So far the Territory has developed almost without planning. Every resort established was a pioneering job mostly by people with no previous experience. This was the reason why they became such good fun places, instead of the phony and stiff atmosphere found at well established

Patti McClane's record roosterfish on 20-pound test line weighed 70.6 pounds. Story, page 234.

lodges, where customers put on airs to match that of the management.

There are few exercises to compare to fishing for giving the mind, body, and soul respite from the agonizing apprehensions felt most every day in modern city living. And there are fewer still that provide rich and happy hours that stay for years in memory's treasure chest.

To Mexico, and more especially to Baja California, there is a value far greater than the money involved and that is in the enduring public relations good. All nations should export more of this commodity. — RAY CANNON

SEA OF CORTEZ FISHING TOURNAMENT INTERNACIONAL

[The complex and unwieldy Sea Of Cortez Fishing Tournament Internacional was held twice—in the fall of 1968, and again in the summer of 1969.

The tournament featured six days of fishing, two days each from La Paz, Rancho Buena Vista, and Cabo San Lucas, with most anglers flown in and rotated from hotel to hotel. All fishing was from hotel boats.

The degree of official support given to this event indicates the importance attributed to the sport fishing

Frank Hedge, left, receives trophy from Lic. Rafael Castillo, Secretary General of Baja California, and Sra. Castillo, at the awards banquet for the first Sea Of Cortez Fishing Tournament Internacional. Hedge caught a 308-pound black marlin on 30-pound dacron line to take the top prize in the tournament, with a landing time of 15 minutes. Beside Ray is Lic. Ricardo García Soto, director of the Office of Tourism in La Paz and Secretary General of the Commission of the Californias.

— PHOTO BY AL TETZLAFF

industry by the government of Baja California Sur during the late 1960s. A highlight of the 1969 event was the breaking of the world record for roosterfish on 20-pound test line—70.6 pounds—by Patti McClane, wife of A. J. McClane, saltwater fishing editor for *Field & Stream* and author of the massive reference book, *McClane's Standard Fishing Encyclopedia and International Angling Guide.*

Ray's announcement for the first year's event, which was later postponed to November 16-22:]

FEBRUARY 21, 1968—Never before in the history of big game angling tournaments have I heard of such a fine and elaborate contest as the splendid "Sea Of Cortez Fishing Tournament Internacional" and Fiesta Grande, to be held June 29 through July 7, in Baja California's three regions of La Paz, Rancho Buena Vista, and Cabo San Lucas.

This elaborate affair is being produced by Lic. Hugo Cervantes del Río, Governor of the Territory of Baja California Sur, and other government and civil officials. Tentative rules suggest that angler contestants will fish two days in each of the regions, climaxed with a magnificent fiesta and the presentation of awards at the Governor's Palace.

Contestants for this first annual derby will be limited to 120 contestants, fishing two to a boat.

So far the game fish categories are: black marlin, blue marlin, striped marlin, sailfish, roosterfish, yellowfin tuna, and dolphinfish. Fishing editors and other important outdoor writers from the U.S. and Mexico will be invited to judge the weighing-in.

Official photographers and TV cameramen may accompany anglers, or have separate boats.

A large flotilla of small boats from Kino Bay is expected to participate as observer and cameramen craft.

Among the most coveted of the many prizes will be the cups presented by Lic. Gustavo Díaz Ordaz, President of Mexico, and the Governor of Baja, and there is talk of a Ray Cannon cup.

The citizenry are really keyed up for the great occasion. Some say it will be the biggest happening since Hernando Cortés and his conquistadors landed in La Paz on a pearling tournament in 1535.

Every participating angler, judge, and other members of the news media, will get red carpet treatment right through the great final fiesta, which will likely be given by the Governor and Señora Cervantes del Río at the Casa de Gobierno.

This whole tournament will most likely develop into the grandest fun assemblage of a lifetime, and everyone in the south end of the peninsula will be helping to make it so.

I would like to urge my readers who can take the time to make application for enrollment as soon as possible. Application blanks and rules and other info will be available at the Los Angeles offices of Carlos Gutierrez, Western Director of Aeronaves de México Airlines; Enrique Ortega, stateside contest coordinator; Carlos Riva Palacio, Mexican Coordinator; also through the office of Lic. Ricardo García Soto, Director General of Tourism and Secretary General of the Commission of the Californias.

I'll be seeing you down there. — RAY CANNON

IT'S OFFICIAL
"THE SEA OF CORTEZ"

[Ray did not favor the name "Gulf of California," and during his early years with *Western Outdoor News*, he usually referred to that body of water as "El Golfo." In 1956 he first used the term "Sea of Cortez," citing its use by early explorers, and he was pleased when that name was endorsed by former President Miguel Alemán in 1965. A year later, the publishing of his bestselling book *The Sea Of Cortez* would establish that name permanently in modern usage. Miguel Alemán's announcement, as cited by Ray:]

APRIL 23, 1965—At a recent luncheon honoring Mexico's famed former President, Lic. Miguel Alemán, now filling the important Cabinet post as head of the National Tourist Council, I was greatly impressed with his plans for the Baja California Territory and the "Sea of Cortez."

Especially encouraging was his determination to speed up the paving of the La Paz to Cabo San Lucas Highway and his sincere interest in extending it from the Santo Domingo Valley to Puerto Escondido, Loreto, and Mulegé.

In 1962 Aeronaves de México initiated direct flights from Los Angeles to La Paz, using 62-passenger DC-6s to replace the older DC-3s formerly operated by Trans Mar de Cortés. Aeronaves de México (later Aeroméxico) continued to provide Ray's transportation throughout Baja California in the same manner that had been begun by Mayo Obregón's Trans Mar de Cortés in 1954. In photo, left to right: María Luisa Cervantes del Río, wife of Governor Hugo Cervantes del Río, beside her; Jorge Pérez Bouras, Director General of Aeronaves de México; Manuel Muñoz, Western Regional Director, Consejo Nacional de Turismo; and Carlos Mario Gutierrez, Los Angeles Manager of Aeronaves de México. DC-8 jet service to La Paz would begin only four years later in 1966.

I liked his repeated use of "El Mar de Cortés" and his translation giving it as "The Sea of Cortez," for the benefit of the working newsmen assembled at the L.A. Press Club. This should once and for all eliminate the use of "Gulf of California" in the local news media.

In a private conversation with the greatly respected Alemán I was most agreeably surprised to hear him comment on details in my columns, books, and articles, and in saying he was a constant reader of them. His keen interest in the small-boat Cortez cruising I had publicized, was especially gratifying to me.

The Mexican Tourist Council activities are vital to the orderly development of the Cortez and Baja California, to all future visitors to that region, and we could say, to all U.S. outdooring people.

As stateside recreational opportunities become less and less we must look to these vast unspoiled lands and Sea and cooperate in every way with the council in maintaining the attractiveness and in keeping the happiness and goodwill we have started.

On the other hand we will help greatly in advancing the economy and standard of living where they are most needed.

We will not be depleting any of the country's natural resources but returning from our visits with little more than happy memories and aching desires to get back to the wondrous play land and Sea. — RAY CANNON

1966—THE TERRITORY COMES OF AGE

[In combined manuscripts written during the mid-1960s, Ray describes the advanced state of the tourist industry that had suddenly sprung up all around the Sea Of Cortez. Virtually all of the Baja California facilities listed in this excellent snapshot of the Golden Age had been built since 1950.

Some of the resorts and facilities described here as "nearly finished" or in the planning stages were never completed. Nevertheless, the general trend of development has continued and accelerated to the present day.

The emphasis placed here on Baja California Sur reflects the slower development of tourist resorts north of Mulegé.]

The year 1966 will be recorded in the history books of Baja California Sur as the date the Territory came of age.

The vast wilderness stretches of beautiful shorelines with elegant resorts in the southern half of the Baja California Peninsula can now be reached by all kinds of conveyances. A few years ago this forgotten region could be approached only by yachts or ships and very few ever bothered to stop and examine the land side. Some daring adventurers driving trucks, scratched their way down the Peninsula over rugged, iguana-back trails, but very few

Seventeen-year-old Bobbye Gunnell with a 130-pound sailfish caught after a two-hour battle on 20-pound line at the Hotel Cabo San Lucas. Her parents, Gill and Robert Gunnell were early pioneers in organizing fly-in trips to Baja California and mainland Mexico through their organization, the Fly-For-Funsters.

drove back for the return trip.

It was not until Señor Mayo Obregón started the Trans Mar de Cortés Airlines flying to La Paz that outside people began to hear about the soft, mild climate and a little of the fishing. Resorts were started and private plane owners flew to their strips at Las Cruces (now a private Club) and to the Flying Sportsmen Lodge at Loreto.

In time and expense, the whole region has been brought within reach with extended and improved transportation. Most important are the direct flights of Aeronaves de México, Aereo Servicios "Baja," and other airlines, from Los Angeles and border cities straight to the resorts; the exploding interest in trailering small boats for exciting cruises down the Cortez; the new, ship-size ferryboat from Mazatlán to La Paz; the improved roads that encircle the south end, and a paved highway from La Paz to Santo Domingo Valley and Almejas and Magdalena Bays. All have brought next door a playground the size of the whole State of California.

From western Arizona and points west, vehicles cross the Mexican border at the town of San Luis, due south of Yuma. Since I made this trip a few years ago aboard an El Dorado camper and shipped across on a freighter, I have strongly advocated a ferryboat and have advised my readers to go by camper.

There are many advantages in taking an overland voyage aboard a camper but most satisfying is getting into such a virgin wilderness as the fish and clam-laden coves and the abounding wild game fowl around Almejas. In every respect it is like crossing into a new kind of a world.

The big, new demand by U.S. citizens for winter homes in the enchanting region is being met by resort owners with offers to give long ground leases and build homes at figures astonishingly below U.S. costs. In some cases these homes are to be operated as lodge rooms during the owner's absence and should return good profits to the owner. All resorts are seasonally overcrowded.

MIDRIFF AND NORTH

Across the narrows (65 nautical miles) between Bahía Kino and Bahía San Francisquito, along the lower rim of the Midriff, runs the course advised for small boats. Gas is now available at San Francisquito.

One of the best Cortez party boat deals is the large 65-footer booked out of the Entz & Rucker Hardware store, L.A. Boarding at San Felipe, Baja California, the 12 anglers fish five days in the Midriff, where six skiffs are lowered and manned by a crew member and two fishermen.

A few small cruisers with crews for two to four anglers are available at Kino Bay. Guides for cruising the Midriff islands are also for hire. The same is true at Bahía de los Angeles on the Baja California side. It has a private plane fly-in resort.

At Bahía Kino, the fine, new and very modern "Posada Del Mar," now open, 42 rooms, excellent foods, a fleet of seaworthy cruisers.

At Bahía San Francisquito, "Hotel Midriff," a name that will attract thousands of boaters and several hundred private plane owners, starts this spring with army tents while 30-room hotel is being constructed. Will have gas, cold bottled goods, and temporary snack bar.

MULEGE

The Mulegé Beach Lodge (South Sea island thatched type) is building a new club house and additional units and has enlarged its fishing fleet. It is right on the beach with the best shore fishing anywhere a hundred feet from your cabaña door.

Hacienda de Mulegé (in town) has added one boat and is constructing new bungalows. A grand old Mexican-type inn, it has a native charm but keeps the food and services up to date. Hotel Las Casitas is modern in appearance and in accommodations.

The deluxe lodge of this area is the new Club Aereo Mulegé. It is expanding rapidly, with new bungalows, club house, a fleet of inboard marlin cruisers, and a fleet of jet boats, to become one of the most complete and elegant resorts around the Cortez.

An excellent popular priced resort, the Serenidad is near the river mouth where all kinds of small craft are available for whatever purpose. Cruisers, accommodating two-to-five anglers and crew of two, fish Concepción Point and Bay, and Isla Santa Ines, and run south to Isla Ildefonso for big game fishing.

The Mulegé region includes the elegant resort called Punta Chivato, with nearby Santa Ines Islands. The new Punta Chivato Hotel has a fine little port, splendid seascape view and is the most expensive of Mulegé's lodges.

Commercial flights arrive here from Tijuana by Servicios Aereo "Baja" Airline. Mulegé will have a standard airstrip with scheduled service by Aeronaves West.

A large marina and resort is planned for Puerto Coyote in Bahía Concepción. This most tropical town will likely go into an orbital boom when the big ferry from Guaymas to Santa Rosalía goes into operation. The new road from Santa Rosalía via Mulegé, Loreto, and Magdalena, to La Paz has only a few miles to complete the grand Territorial highway.

LORETO

Ed Tabor has already expanded his whole Flying Sportsmen's operation with accommodations, boats, and new buildings. He is flying a lot of San Diego anglers and families direct to the Lodge at a special rate.

Bill and Gloria Benziger have likewise enlarged their Hotel Oasis and fleet of boats.

A third beach-side hotel, the new, deluxe, 60-room Hotel Misión de Loreto, will be open, as will its Hotel Baja

Original building of the Hotel Mar de Cortés, opened in 1972 in what would become "downtown" Cabo San Lucas, by Simón Yee and Carlos Ungson, with Bud Parr participating.

(20 rooms) opposite Isla Coronado. Another centrally located resort near the dock, should be nearly finished by year's end; so will the first-rate lodge at Ensenada Blanca, a few miles south of Escondido, which is slated to become a National Park.

For the past year, Loreto has had a boom going among locals. With the completion of the new highway to Puerto Escondido, gas can be easily hauled to the big dock there for small craft. This opens up the calm and enchanting region of Juanaloa, including its 16 islands, and its especially fine big and little game fishing. Dozens of boaters this next spring, and hundreds a year later, will be making Escondido their main vacationing port, and the Loreto fleets can be expected to work out of it.

LA PAZ

La Paz is bursting at the seams with large subdivisions. Many U.S. citizens have already retired there to live like kings, on small incomes.

Most all of the five major hotels of La Paz are adding new units or otherwise improving. Each of the hotels has its individual character.

The finest expansion just completed is at the already popular Hotel Los Arcos. The management has built the most deluxe suites in La Paz. They overlook a tropical garden and swimming pool under enormous spreading India laurel trees.

The Perla, like the Los Arcos, is in town and on the waterfront malecón, but has an open sidewalk-like dining area.

Two miles farther back in the bay is the Los Cocos, situated in a coconut grove, on the waterfront, and it has its own pier for small craft. Next door is the charming Hotel La Posada on the beach and almost choked with a lush, flowering, tropical garden.

The Guaycura is several blocks back from the bay in a tropical orchard and farming area.

Two large and speedy fishing fleets operated by Rudy Vélez and Bill Callahan run out to Espíritu Santo and Cerralvo Islands and down to Los Muertos Bay for the late fall and winter runs of big game.

In planning the future of the Territorial center of La Paz, there are opposing opinions held by the planners. One group advocates high-rise hotels. The other prefers bungalow and garden resort developments. One thing is certain: there will be more places for accommodations constructed to meet the ever-increasing demand.

There is still much talk about a large hotel and yacht marina on the Mogote (sand peninsula) forming the inner bay, but a 100-room hotel projecting out over the bay from the malecón (waterfront boulevard) is already being constructed.

BUENA VISTA REGION

I know of plans to construct two resort hotels of 100 rooms or more each, and a third with half a hundred, all close to Rancho Buena Vista.

There are also plans drawn for resorts in the Cabo Pulmo-Los Frailes area, said by many to have the best big game fishing in the world, and in a region rated the most comfortable, year round. All accommodations at the four present resorts are popular priced (American Plan). Resort hotel names in this region: Rancho Buena Vista, Bahía de Palmas, Punta Colorada, and Punta Pescadero.

Their marlin cruisers accommodate two to four anglers and cost $50 to $65 per day, tackle and live bait extra. All have Southern California representatives.

The newly-paved highway from La Paz (67 miles) and improved airstrips (accommodate DC-3s) have increased fishing tourism so much that reservations several months in advance are a must.

The main reason this region is rated tops for certain game fish is actually due to its early development of live bait, and the crews' quick learning of methods of using it. Capturing live bait and maintaining it has proven a considerable loss to the few resorts having it, this above a small charge to the angler. But as a drawing card it is highly profitable.

There is considerable unorganized sight-seeing for the non-fishing members of the family. There is the 3,000-foot-high mountain with a couple of lush "Shangri-las" near the top. The town of Santiago, with a huge, wooden sugar mill a century or so old, and a pueblo that looks like California of the '49 Gold Rush days. There are bat caves, freshwater lagoons, thriving patch farms, and lots more places to go in a 4X4, some of them on horseback, at the Rancho. My Round House there is a good showplace.

THE SOUTH END

The long anticipated big boom across the southern tip of the Baja California Peninsula is in full swing, with a number of U.S. tycoons entering the picture. Bing Crosby, who has already built a winter home at Las Cruces, now a private club, is said to be an interested party in some of the south-end developments.

There are three deluxe resorts in this sector, another under construction and two more planned. They are all along the shifting Cortez and Pacific waterfront, which moves in and out with each shift in the tide. And for some reason, fishing is usually very good along convergencies.

The largest resort, the Hotel Cabo San Lucas, rated one of the most elegant in all Mexico, is situated in the middle, on Puerto Chileno. Of the Hotel Cabo San Lucas, visitors are saying that it is "the ultimate in splendor." The noted boat builder, Dale Jeffries, constructed and now operates a marlin cruiser fleet there, said to be the last word in angling craft. The onyx, Roman baths with each complete and isolated suite, terraced, tropical gardens with pools and waterfalls, super-elegant club and dining rooms and verandas projecting out over the sea, are unmatched in U.S. resorts. Engineers are blocking out estate home building sites, to be leased to selected people with means, along the miles of waterfront.

Five miles east is Las Cruces Palmilla, with all-around splendid accommodations, services, and foods.

Nine-and-a-half miles beyond Hotel Cabo San Lucas

is the Hacienda Cabo San Lucas, fairly close to the rock-cliffed Cape. Like the other two, this smaller resort has a fine beach, large fishing fleet ($55 to $70) but with slightly less rates.

Experiments made with live bait are proving sensational in catching broadbill swordfish as well as big blue and black marlin and about every other big mouth gamester in these waters, such as roosterfish, amberjack, dolphinfish, crevalles, yellowfin tuna, and others.

BAHIA MAGDALENA

Almejas Bay (south end of Magdalena) will likely be the area for the next big and important development. There is no human population around Almejas. Carlos Riva Palacio books overnight hunting and fishing trips.

As soon as the Transterritorial Highway is completed and the ferry from Guaymas gets operating to Almejas and other access places along Magdalena Bay, camper travelers will find this region a kind of an ultimate way-out frontier.

THE MAINLAND SHORE: SAN CARLOS BAY

At San Carlos Bay, half-a-dozen estates have spacious dwellings up and occupied, and another area of many acres opening. There are actually two resorts and two cafes at this perfect bay, plus a yacht club and trailer park, with every convenience and facility for the vacationist, fisherman or hunter.

BOCOCHIBAMPO BAY (MIRAMAR BEACH)

Miramar Beach, on Bocochibampo Bay near Guaymas, had a real estate boom a few years back. Mostly for wealthy Mexicans. But it was the elegant and charming Hotel Playa de Cortés that first called attention to the area. Now, with new owners, it is becoming even more renowned as "the place to go" for relaxation as well as the fishing. There are two trailer parks and another hotel (the Miramar Beach), and a large fishing fleet operated by Tom Jamison.

GUAYMAS

A large fleet fishing same area and for same fish as Miramar Beach and San Carlos. No modern hotels.

TOPOLOBAMPO BAY NEAR LOS MOCHIS

Topolobampo Bay and its nearby city, Los Mochis, is in the feverish stages of expanding facilities for visitors. My good friends, Roberto Balderrama, manager of the Hotel Santa Anita, and Gilberto Limón, head of the Los Mochis Bureau of Tourism, are sparking the elaborate drive. It is safe to predict that Topolobampo will someday become a Riviera.

MAZATLAN

Mazatlán continues to attract the greatest number of billfish anglers, fine hotels and fishing fleets. In addition to the fabulous big and small game fishing there are many interesting and exciting things to see and do, for every member of the family, day and night, the year round, in a city that has preserved its ancient charm. There are many recommendable hotels, with exceptionally fine foods and delightful atmosphere. Among them, the Eldorado, Belmar, De Cima, Freeman, Las Arenas, and the newest, the elegant La Siesta, which provides complete and free services for all of the area's outdoor and indoor diversions, such as golf, tennis, diving, and entertainment, with direct connections with the small and big game hunting enterprises run by the Aviles Brothers and their Flota Marlin for diving and fishing. Also with marlin fleet and charter boats for the Tres Marías Islands, skippered by the capable Captain Bill Heimpel, owner of the Star Fleet. Other fleets—Luis Patron's Indian Fleet, Ernesto Coppel's Bi Bi Fleet, and Mike Maxemin's Flota Faro. — RAY CANNON

BOBBY AND CHA CHA

The marriage of Robert Van Wormer to Rosa María "Cha Cha" Ruiz Gonzales on June 27, 1965 was one of the key events of Baja California's Golden Age—especially for what today is known as the "East Cape" area, which extends roughly from Punta Los Frailes in the south to Punta Pescadero in the north. To the present day, "Bobby" and "Cha Cha," as they are universally known throughout Baja California, serve not only as living links to the beginnings of Baja tourism, but also as symbols of successful dreams fulfilled through their leadership in the business community as owners of three major resorts: Punta Colorada, Palmas de Cortez, and Playa del Sol.

One of the memorable events of their wedding ceremony was the loud explosion of a large flashbulb in the camera of Bobby's brother, Frank. There are many conflicting versions of that story—probably more of them than the number of guests who were present. Ray Cannon was at the church in Santiago that day. Following is his version of what happened.

(Note: Bobby Van Wormer flatly denies that he "sank to his knees" when the flash bulb exploded, as this column states. "How *could* I sink to my knees?" he says. "I was *already* down on my knees at the altar! This is just another example of a Ray Cannon story that got out of hand!" Van Wormer says that he did turn suddenly when the flash bulb exploded, but it was only to get a look at brother Frank, who was beating a hasty retreat out the side door of the church.)

THE EXPLODING FLASH BULB

There would be no problem writing a column a day about the newsworthy activities at Buena Vista. The fishing would provide enough material, but there are a lot of unique land-side goings-on also. The wildest swinging affair was the wedding and fiesta of Bobby Van Wormer,

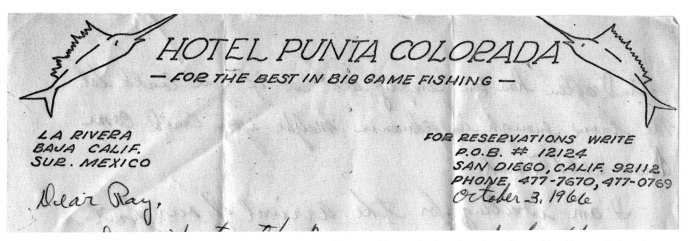

A letter to Ray dated October 3, 1966, on fancy letterhead from Bobby and Cha Cha's brand new Hotel Punta Colorada.

former assistant manager of Buena Vista and my fellow worker for many years.

The number of guests overwhelmed all facilities in the church and town of Santiago, ten miles south from Buena Vista. Among the more than 50 U.S. guests, were half-a-dozen photographers, including Bobby's brother, who had a large Graflex and a powerful flashlight attachment. We were patiently waiting for the bride and groom to emerge, when a local tipster suggested that we go to the back door, slip in behind the altar and back of the priest and get a face-on shot of Bobby saying, "I do."

We made a rush and Bobby's brother led the sneak. Bobby and the audience could make out his brother's form sneaking in the darkness, but when the camera flash was snapped, it exploded like a gun shot. The shock was profound. Bobby sank to his knees but recovered and quickly covered with a loud, "I do." So Bobby's marriage really went off with a bang and set a key for a humorous

Bobby Van Wormer and Rosa María "Cha Cha" Ruiz Gonzales, Santiago, Baja California Sur, at their wedding on June 27, 1965.

and exciting reception at the bride's home.

I had some very pleasant conversation with several happy families from the U.S. who have built homes nearby. About the only complaint I heard from them was of their fear that my writing would bring too many people and somehow spoil their wilderness. It will take a thousand other writers a century to harm this vast area and it will never be done by anglers.

If you plan on getting in on the combination of fishing and hunting, this is a good time to get everything reserved. There is the jeep, guide, and guns that should be arranged for now, for the duck, brant, dove, and quail shooting this fall and winter. If you can't get the jeep, there is always the Sea. The freshwater lagoons separated from the Sea by a low sand hill can be approached by boat. If the Sea is calm, getting ashore is easy and a hundred-yard walk will get you behind a good tule blind.

The summer and early fall rains bring on the period of great beauty and much activity at the primitive ranches and farms extending down the coast from Buena Vista to Cabo Pulmo. The Buena Vista resort has opened another half-dozen units and now has the largest fleet of fast marlin cruisers in the Cortez. Colonel Walters says that there will be no further expansion. He thinks that more people would crowd out the relaxed fun enjoyed there now, and turn the place into a business enterprise with accompanying headaches. — RAY CANNON

A FINE-FLOWERING DAY AT THE RANCH

[Ray celebrates a beautiful, flower-filled day at Rancho Buena Vista spent not in fishing, but in exploring the verdant hills with photographer Harry Merrick.]

OCTOBER 30, 1964—Harry Merrick had me holding on to the bushes, climbing up steep mountainsides to get landscape shots.

Heavy rains for the past four years have turned the

land side into a jungle of splendor. I have never before seen such massive blankets of brilliant yellow, red, and blue blossoms spreading over verdant green vines and trees, from the roadside to distant horizons.

As we drove over crests and looked down on semi-ghost towns engulfed in tropical fruit trees with doves and quail and a hundred kinds of colorful wild birds stirring the air with their massive flights, the picture was like a primitive Eden.

Merrick got so carried away he came close to using up all of our color film. All along the way, the native people and their fattened domestic animals and fowls were as cheerful as the flowing garden they lived in. Youngsters helped us gather tropical fruits from their trees and urged us to take as many as we wished.

Everyone at the gay and muy simpatico Rancho Buena Vista was especially happy. Colonel Walters was recovering from an operation and the place had had a most prosperous season, with visitors getting whatever fish they liked to catch, on live bait. All kinds of improvements, new construction of more units, more boats to add to their fleet of a dozen inboard-outdrive cruisers, and general expansions. Nearby Bahía de Palmas Lodge has added new units and a delightful clubhouse on the beach.

Everywhere south from Buena Vista to the Cabo Pulmo-Los Frailes area we saw evidence of new resorts and homes being constructed or planned, as we jeeped down this stretch. A branch road was being carved to Punta Colorada, where Bobby Van Wormer and Joe Benales are building a lodge and some elegant new homes. Close up to Pulmo two lodges have been blueprinted. Several of my friends have winter homes along the shore.

The second day with my favorite skipper Laborio we cruised down to the freshwater lagoons, went ashore and found them swarming with ducks and some brant, with doves almost as thick as flies at a Griffith Park picnic.

Anxious to photograph more sailfish jumps, we had one working in less than ten minutes out from the lagoons, and a second one on five minutes after we released the first sail. While fishing the two, we saw at least a dozen other fins.

We saw acres of roosterfish all along this coastline. The Rancho has established a bag limit on roosters because of their greedy appetite for live bait. I doubt that any resort operating with live bait will ever again close for the summer, as some have done. — RAY CANNON

CABO NOTES: "DORADO" REPLACES "DOLPHINFISH"

[This column was written in late 1971, four years before the creation of the Cabo San Lucas inner harbor and six years before the opening of the international airport of San José del Cabo.

On this trip, Ray lands at the airstrip of Cabo's Hotel Camino Real de Cabo San Lucas, which was then being operated by Western International Hotels and would be bought by Bud Parr as the Hotel Hacienda in 1977.

The "Hotel Sea of Cortés" referred to is the Hotel Mar de Cortés, opened in downtown Cabo San Lucas by Carlos Ungson and Simón Yee, with Bud Parr in partnership, in 1973.

Ray also mentions the Bajo Colorado resort, which had opened in 1970 on Bahía Santa María about 12 kilometers east of Cabo San Lucas. In 1977, it would become the Hotel Twin Dolphin of David Halliburton—the final great resort to be built during the Golden Age.

The condominium "caves" described as under construction at the Camino Real Cabo San Lucas (later Hotel Hacienda) were among the first of their kind and a precursor of today's booming real estate market of the Los Cabos corridor.

In a parenthetical note, Ray records the period—early 1970s—when the Spanish name "dorado" (golden) for the great game fish, *Coryphaena hippurus*, supplanted the English term, "dolphinfish," in Baja California.]

When I left L.A. (December 26) the temperature was in the low 50s. One hour and a half later aboard an Aeronaves jet, I arrived at the La Paz airport and found the temperature above 80. The time for the last hop by Gil Kimball's single engine job—La Paz to the Camino Cabo San Lucas airstrip—was exactly 45 minutes. I got a shot of a glorious horizon as the sun plunged behind some thin layers of brighter than molten gold clouds.

The next a.m. Kimball and I were out around the cape and up the Pacific past Cabo Falso after wahoo. But before we could make contact, two marlin and a dolphinfish had gotten nailed on our two, four-ounce feathers, in tandem, being trolled at a speed of nine knots.

The dolphinfish (most everyone has started using the Spanish name "dorado" down here) gave a splendid display of his color-changing and exciting acrobatics. One of the marlin also put on a good exhibition of tail-walking and aerial tumbling, but somehow the sea-splitting, hundred-yard dashes by the wahoo stole the show, especially with the early morning sunlight beaming through the sheets of water and spray blasted up by the great gamester's torpedoing speed. The word "streamlined" must have been created with a wahoo in mind. I can't think of a seagoing creature with a more efficiently shaped body for zooming through water resistance.

One day I fished with Sr. José Brockman, president of the Mexican branch of the Western International Hotel chain (which includes the Camino Real), along with some other Mexico City businessmen. I found them highly enthusiastic. This confidence in the future of the Territory is being shown by all of the big resort owners by the expansion programs now going full bore. When we anchored at Palmilla for lunch we found a spacious bar and cocktail area being added. Then the next day when we drove up to the fantastic Finisterra, we heard of additions and landscape plans.

At the Bajo Colorado resort, there were half-a-dozen cottages completed, with a dozen more plus an expansive clubhouse-dining building foundation being finished. Then at the Hotel Cabo San Lucas at Puerto Chileno, new developments included an enormous additional dining and bar extension, a new group of bungalows, new administrative offices, and an elaborate arched entrance. All are getting finishing touches now, and operator Bud Parr says that the additions will add to the elegance this largest of all the Territory's resorts is noted for.

The Hotel Sea of Cortez [Mar de Cortés] in the town of Cabo San Lucas is also close to being finished. But the most exciting is the opening of the underground condominiums at the Camino Real, with several finished and occupied before the garden landscaping is completed. I continue to call them "caves" but the title is not so easy to apply since I saw the super-deluxe effect the furnishings have added. Incidentally, if you are one of the clan who is eager to get back to the caveman status and get you one of these, the price is around eighty-thousand clams (U.S. dollars in the civilized language). — RAY CANNON

MILESTONES OF PROGRESS

[Ray cites the astonishing improvements made to the infrastructure of Baja California Sur during the mid-1960s. The Puerto Escondido ferry mentioned was never opened, although new lines were added at Santa Rosalía and briefly at Cabo San Lucas.]

SEPTEMBER 7, 1970—The Territorial Governor, Hugo Cervantes del Río, assisted by other public-spirited citizens, has done magnificent things for this forgotten wilderness in the past six years. Among the achievements are: an elaborate airport at La Paz and another under way at Cabo San Lucas; a fine graded and mostly paved highway the full length of the Territory; new schools have been completed in every town and pueblo; electric plants finished and operating in all towns, with their lines stretching to many villages; ferryboats from Mazatlán and Topolobampo to La Paz, and soon to Puerto Escondido; a modern sewage treatment plant in La Paz; new city and government public buildings in La Paz; radio and radiotelephone extended to cover the peninsula and outside world; local telephone service expanded in La Paz, and numerous minor innovations. — RAY CANNON

José Brockman, president of the Mexican branch of the Western International Hotel chain, at the Hotel Camino Real de Cabo San Lucas, c. 1972.

Construction of the semi-underground condo units Ray called "caves" or "bunkers" at the Hotel Hacienda, 1972. The hotel was originally built by Abelardo L. "Rod" Rodríguez as the Hacienda Cabo San Lucas, was renamed the Camino Real de Cabo San Lucas, and is owned today by the family of William Matthew "Bud" Parr as the Hotel Hacienda Beach Resort.

A dream fulfilled. Ray trolling under a full moon in 1967, just after publication of *The Sea Of Cortez.* — PHOTO BY AL TETZLAFF

"THE SEA OF CORTEZ"

RAY'S BESTSELLING MASTERPIECE

FOR TWELVE FULL years before it was published, Ray talked about a big new book he was working on, with the title: *How To Fish The Sea Of Cortez*. He envisioned this book as a greatly-expanded follow-up to his successful West Coast fishing manual, *How To Fish The Pacific Coast*—and he amassed an enormous amount of research on the fish species of the Sea of Cortez, fishing seasons, fishing locations, and detailed fishing techniques that he developed with the logistical support of Baja California's resort owners and the two airlines: Trans Mar de Cortés and Aeronaves de México.

But, as the book's 1966 publication date approached, Ray's editor at Sunset Books, Jack McDowell, very wisely scrapped some parts of the original manuscript and dropped

"How To Fish..." from the title. Much of the information related to fishing technique was cut, along with some of the detailed resort listing information that Ray had laboriously compiled as an essential part of an instructional "fishing book."

Sunset saw in Ray's extensive, unique knowledge and colorful anecdotes, something much larger than Ray himself had seen. It was decided that Ray's rich and voluminous manuscript justified the creation of a "coffee table book" that would appeal not only to hard-core Baja anglers, but to a much wider audience of armchair travelers.

Sunset poured money and time into the project, sparing no expense in providing illustrations, maps, extensive copy editing, and spectacular color photography. The result was a watershed book for sport fishing, and for Baja California as well. Ray's long-awaited, magnificent *The Sea Of Cortez* sold over a quarter-of-a-million copies, and it remains the most sought-after collector's book among Baja aficionados to the present day.

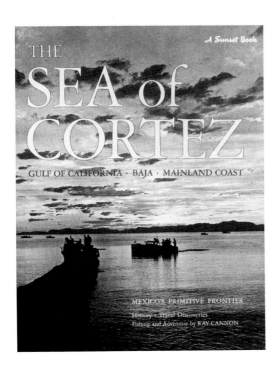

A DREAM HAS COME TRUE

[The initial book announcement in *Western Outdoor News*, written by editor Bill Rice.]

SEPTEMBER 23, 1966—A dream has come true for *Western Outdoor News* columnist Ray Cannon with the release this week of the magnificent volume, *Sea of Cortez*.

Destined to become the "bible" to all who venture to the fabulous recreation areas of Baja California, the mainland coast of Mexico, and the Gulf of California (Sea of Cortez), the 285-page masterpiece is the most complete, useful and entertaining work ever done on the primitive region, which has become known as one of the

The 1966 launch of *The Sea Of Cortez* was accompanied by full-page magazine ads and a direct mail campaign of over a million pieces by Lane Magazine and Book Company.

— COURTESY SUNSET BOOKS

world's greatest fishing areas.

Ray describes the Sea of Cortez as only he knows how, as years and years of traveling, studying and researching all combine to make the unique book possible. Ray's vast knowledge of the gulf regions, probably superior to that of any other individual, has made the book more than just a travel guide.

His captivating style of writing weaves all the romance, history, customs, solitude and excitement of life below the border into the most complete and authoritative work ever done on the region.

Cannon gives much of the credit for the book to his secretary, Carla Laemmle, who, says Ray, "researched, assembled and cataloged the thousands of notes which I made on the Sea of Cortez over the years."

The whole book is beautifully done, and as Tom Lipton, vice president of Penn Reels, said last week, it is "…the finest publishing job ever done on a fishing book."

Besides Ray's warm, exciting description of the gulf region, the book is superbly complemented by magnificent photographs, many in full color; special maps of the 12 key recreation areas; drawings; diagrams; and items of special historical or human interest.

Twelve chapters of the book deal with the 12 regions, types and methods of fishing, customs, accommodations, facilities, terrain, hunting, etc., all presented in Ray's inimitable style.

A special section deals with travel throughout the region. Airlines, airport and private airplane facilities, tips for driving your own car and/or trailering a boat are all included.

Another special section deals with fish identification, and includes 13 pages of drawings of fish; and full particulars on bait and tackle.

Cannon is also an authority on small boat cruising the Sea of Cortez, having made several trips down the sea in "little ships." His experience and expert advice are expertly told in a section dealing with this.

The man who began his career in Hollywood, first as an actor and stuntman, then later as writer, director and producer of motion pictures, and who has been a featured writer in *Western Outdoor News* for 13 years, has created a true masterpiece in the *Sea of Cortez* and it should be included in the library of all outdoorsmen.

— BILL RICE, WESTERN OUTDOOR NEWS

THE DAY RAY BLEW HIS TOP

[The long-awaited arrival of the first shipment of *The Sea Of Cortez* books from Sunset also brought a big surprise to the house on Serrano Avenue. Carla tells the story of the day Ray discovered that his name had been inadvertently left off the cover of the book.]

Ray seldom lost his cool. But when he did, you didn't want to be there.

I will never forget the terrible day that Ray got so angry with Mel Lane, publisher of Sunset Books, that he almost blew it. It was the day when *The Sea Of Cortez* arrived—an unbelievably euphoric moment for us, a day for jubilation. Our beautiful book was now in print—it was a reality. But the euphoria didn't last very long.

All hell broke loose when Ray discovered that his name wasn't on the spine of the book nor the front cover as the author. Ray was outraged. He was furious. He was ready to explode. He called Mel and threatened to pull out of the contract and sue Sunset.

He wasn't kidding and I knew it. I cried and I pleaded. I was in tears—absolutely devastated. I feared that Ray would really do this. I kept pleading with him to let it go—to please not do anything rash. It was a heart-stopping moment.

Mel kept apologizing to Ray and tried to explain that heretofore Sunset books had always been staff-produced, that Ray was the first author contracted by Sunset and that it was an unfortunate oversight but entirely unintentional. Mel assured Ray that the omission would be corrected with the next printing and that all future editions would have Ray's name on them as author.

It was a very tense moment. Everything was hanging in the balance. Sunset made a terrible goof and Ray had a right to blow his top. Ray was not happy, but in the end he accepted Mel's apology and explanation.

The crisis was over, but it was a real close call.

No, there was no party, no celebration that day. I was a basket case and Ray's blood pressure was higher than a kite. It was quite a while before Ray's anger finally subsided and he regained his composure and his Taoist serenity of mind. But I was a total wreck.

Ray was overjoyed with the book. I think it exceeded all his expectations. The design and layout by Sunset was superb, as were the fine maps and delightful art illustrations bordering many of the pages and adding so much to the beauty of the book.

No doubt about it, they had a winner there.

As far as I was concerned the book was a knockout!

There was so much activity and excitement going on. Ray was an instant celebrity. There were interviews, book signings, club appearances and a zillion book orders to fill. The fruit of success was sweet. Happiness was *The Sea Of Cortez*. It was the most wonderful time of our lives. I wish we could do it all over again. Perhaps we will someday in some timeless, faraway galaxy… (I think Ray had me write that…) — CARLA LAEMMLE

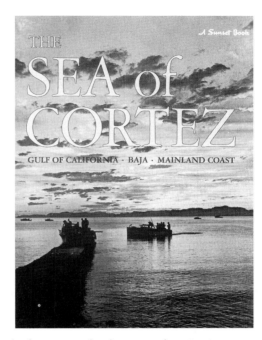

The first printing book cover without Ray's name on it. Ray blew his top when he saw it.

INTIMATE ACCOUNT OF A VAST AND RICH SEA

[In a passionately-rendered, unused introduction, intended for *The Sea Of Cortez*, Ray celebrates the body of water that inspired the book and his life's work.]

Here is an intimate account of a vast and rich Sea with 100 strange islands, and a 750-mile-long Peninsula, bypassed by history and geography for more than a century. Together they form a region the size of the State of California, and join on to it.

This Sea, youngest of all the seas of the earth, is calm, fish-crowded, and enchanting; her islands uninhabited, unexplored, and fantastic. The mountainous peninsula which walls in the Sea from the Pacific Ocean is sparsely populated with gentle, fun loving native people in the isolated villages and very few towns and resort places; otherwise, all is wilderness.

Here, then is the Sea of Cortez (Gulf of California on most maps), and the Baja California Peninsula (previously called "Lower California"), a whole new outdooring world for real adventure and enthrallment, a vacation land supreme, where the climate is called the best on earth, and where the big game fishing definitely is.

While the angling in the Cortez has now been accredited as being the finest in any area yet known, the fishing and the teeming number of species are but a part of the attractions of this seductive Sea. "Adventure," in the true meaning of the word, tops everything for all those who have the energy for it, especially if they take to sea in small boats. But all who wish can get in on the pleasant and exciting goings-on, whether they fly, drive, or sail down to the tropical resorts, where the fun and action starts only a stone's throw from the cabañas.

Here is a special kind of a place to fit the desires of all who enjoy most any single form of outdooring, whether in strenuous exertion, lolling in the shade of a ramada sipping cool pulque, or just to escape the mind-sickening clamor and violence of our jittery environment we call "progress."

If there were other vacation lands that could be used as comparisons, describing the many enjoyable features of this extensive slice of Mexico would be easy. But where else can there be found the likes of the little beach shack of a sea vagabundo made of driftwood and palm leaves, 100 miles from the nearest village, or an isolated resort with Roman baths made of onyx, with a private, tropical garden included in each suite?

Where else are there hundreds of miles of roads like the "El Camino Real," once well traveled by the Padres, Indians, and conquistadors, but left to be obliterated by jungle growth for two centuries?

Where else are there such grotesque masses of thorned shrubs, vines, and trees that become transformed by the first rains into brilliant seas of blossoms, all aglow with reds, yellows, and blues? These are on the mountains and slopes, while between them are tropical valleys perpetually green except when blanketed with exotic fruits and flowers.

There are extreme contrasts in land-side vistas. From

sand-swept deserts to tropical jungles, awesome, cave-pocked cliffs to Edenic gardens, lofty, jagged mountains, and valleys of swaying wheat and sugar cane, vast stretches of primeval wilderness, and quaint and pretty villages, primitive ranch houses, and deluxe resorts. Between these opposites are the many facets of grotesque as well as esthetic beauty, not arranged on symmetrical forms but rambling like a batik pattern, all remaining in the memory of the most casual observer as an enduring and rewarding experience. But it is the Sea that ensnares the mind and casts a hypnotic but joyful spell on all who experience its enchantment.

As recreational demands become more acute in the U.S. and area space dwindles to look more and more like overcrowded ant hills, we can be grateful that this wondrous body of water and land were overlooked. We can also be especially thankful to U.S. diplomat, Nicholas Trist, for his historical boo-boo in returning Baja California and the Cortez Sea back to Mexico in the Guadalupe Hidalgo Treaty. Were it not for that fortunate diplomatic blunder, American purse seiners would probably have already destroyed the Sea's fishery, as they wiped out the sardines in California, and the spoilers would have laid waste to the land and contaminated the air.

Now, as our distraught and drooping city dwellers grope for a place to breathe freely and to find happy and healthy recreation, comes the rediscovery of a whole new world of immense enjoyment. — RAY CANNON

FULL CIRCLE—HOW SUNSET MAGAZINE BROUGHT RAY TO CALIFORNIA

[In a case of symmetrical "karma," it turns out that Ray was first lured to California in 1912 by the same company that would—half a century later and after his movie career had come and gone—end up publishing his two books: "Sunset Books."

Mel Lane, owner of Sunset (official name, Lane Magazine and Book Company), confirms that the original Sunset Magazine referred to in the following column was launched by the Southern Pacific Railroad in 1898. In 1914, the railroad divested itself of the publication by selling it to its own employees. Lawrence Lane, Mel's father, bought it in 1928.

Lane also confirms that the *Sea Of Cortez* sold 280,000 copies and was the first "authored" book ever published by Sunset. A promotional mailing of over one million pieces was used for the launch, in addition to extensive magazine and newspaper advertising.]

SEPTEMBER 16, 1963—*W.O.N.*'s publisher, Burt Twilegar, has provided a truly great service to the regions around the Cortez and to anglers, boaters, recreational fliers who have gone, and the millions yet to go there, by allowing me the space to tell of my enthralling

explorations of this exciting new world.

Our mission will soon be augmented by the force, energy, and foresight of Aeronaves de México Airlines. Spark-plugged by their alert Regional Director, Señor Carlos M. Gutierrez, an ambitious campaign to acquaint U.S. anglers, nimrods, and other recreational seekers with the region is about to be launched.

The present situation and time of the Baja California Territory, southern half of the Peninsula, resembles that of Southern California shortly after 1912, when the Southern Pacific Railroad, with its *Sunset Magazine*, now published by Lane's, brought pleasure-living people, including your scrivener, to California's fine climate and good fishing, by the hundreds of thousands.

Whatever California had in those days, Baja California has more of it and better, and Aeronaves expects to make people aware of it.

W.O.N. will have reason to take pride in being the first and only publication to pioneer and continuously publicize this new frontier.

To those who have some ideas of getting a piece of it or getting in on the ground floor, I would advise doing it now or they will likely miss the boat. There are all kinds of opportunities. Some new resorts would welcome partners, and old ones need expansion financing. There are fifty Shangri-la wilderness areas that need opening with lodges. Hundreds of miles of private beach property can be leased for homes, some adjoining resorts with water, electricity and other facilities available. Some of them real dream spots, with the best year-round climate and best fishing on earth. — RAY CANNON

RAY'S GRATITUDE TO TRANS MAR DE CORTES AND AERONAVES DE MEXICO

[Just before publication date, Ray acknowledges his debt of gratitude not only to Mayo Obregón's original Trans Mar de Cortés airline, but also to Carlos Gutierrez, regional director of its successor, Aeronaves de México (later, Aeroméxico), and to Enrique Ortega, whose International Travel Service was an early pioneer in introducing U.S. anglers to Baja California.]

DECEMBER 8, 1965—For close to 12 years this column has been covering the Sea of Cortez and the Baja California Peninsula. From the very beginning I intended to learn to catch most of the more than 300 game species and to explore islands and shorelines that had been forgotten for a century.

Now that I have done it, you can't imagine what a wonderful time I have had and expect to continue having.

Last week at a dinner at the Los Angeles Club honoring Señor Mayo Obregón, former President of the Trans Mar de Cortés Airlines, now Aeronaves de México, I had a chance to recount a conversation we had in La Paz

One of the best-known photographs in *The Sea Of Cortez*—this shot of Ray with a big "baya" grouper on page 125—was printed "flopped," or reversed from left to right. The photo was taken with the use of a special boom installed on a Rolls Ryan boat of designer/builder Mike Ryan of Los Angeles. At right, the uncropped original photo.

in 1953 [actually 1954], in which he gave an inspired and inspiring prediction on Baja California's future. For Obregón envisioned it as a vast recreational region for people of the southwest U.S., especially California, with some stretches to be developed like the Riviera. When I told him I would like to write a book on fishing the Cortez, Obregón offered me every facility.

At the L.A. Club dinner I prefaced the talk I gave by recalling the incident and added that the book was finished and would be out next summer, but that it could not have been done in two lifetimes without the direct help of Señor Obregón in furnishing rapid transportation and other facilities, as well as encouragement.

In his reply, Obregón recalled that when he turned Trans Mar over to Aeronaves—"Ray Cannon was in the inventory."

Within a year or so, most of Obregón's vision of the Territory will have been materialized.

Among the 50 guests at the testimonial dinner were several who had a hand in Baja's development. Carlos Gutierrez, Regional Director for Aeronaves, and Enrique Ortega, President of the Western Travel Agents Association, gave talks honoring Obregón as a truly great

The photo shoot at the dock of Mulegé's Hotel Serenidad. The fish, weighing 178 pounds, was photographed with the help of Ryan (standing on dock), Harrison Evans (below, in boat) and Bill Lloyd (above, in boat). The fish was caught at the nearby Islas Santa Ines, most likely in 1961.

pioneer in opening inaccessible Baja California Sur with air transportation. Their speeches were very impressive.

Obregón's Baja California accomplishments were so important, no one thought to mention that he was the son of the illustrious, martyred President of Mexico, Alvaro Obregón, or that Mayo is now head of Mexico's Bureau

Enrique Ortega, second from right, as owner of International Travel Services with his wife, Doris, was a pioneer in the development of tourism in Baja California during the 1960s. Here, he is feted at a testimonial dinner in Los Angeles, in February 1970. From left to right, Ray Cannon; Mayo Obregón, owner of Trans Mar de Cortés Airlines; Ortega; and Los Angeles television reporter Clete Roberts. Ortega was presented with awards from Baja California Sur Territorial Governor Hugo Cervantes del Río and former President of Mexico Miguel Alemán by Ricardo García Soto, Director of the Office of Tourism of Baja California Sur. Of the event Ray wrote: "Ortega's altruistic service to Mexico, and more especially to Baja California, were greatly appreciated... For many years Enrique and I have traveled around the Territory... Enrique and his very charming wife, Doris, are muy simpatico. Everyone at the Testimonial affair seemed to feel the same kind of warm and sincere friendship for this very simpatico couple." — PHOTO BY AL TETZLAFF

of Fisheries, with offices in San Diego, California.

If you have in any way benefited from or enjoyed this column, you, too, are indebted to Mayo Obregón.

— RAY CANNON

DINNER AT THE LOS ARCOS RECALLED

[Three years after the publishing of *The Sea Of Cortez*, Ray attends a conference of government officials in Baja California Sur, and he recalls the evening—15 years earlier—when Mayo Obregón made the publishing of that book possible. Of note in this column is Ray's dream for a national park in the Juanaloa area and his ideas for the building of marinas at places that remain relatively undeveloped to the present day.]

JULY 2, 1969—In a flying conference with several Mexican Government officials and U.S. reps of various institutions, I was impressed by the intense desire of

Mexico's Department of Tourism to pitch in and help develop the Baja California Territory for the greatly increasing numbers of U.S. vacationists.

Adolfo de la Huerta, Secretary General of the Department of Tourism, expressed his division's enthusiasm for plans to establish small boat and yacht harbors around the Baja California peninsula.

My prime interest was in getting permanent fuel stores installed at Bahía San Francisquito–Rancho el Barril, another at Isla San José, with storage at the new dock in outer Puerto Escondido.

I also suggested that Puerto Escondido, the mountain back of it, and Isla Danzante be set aside as a national park, with no hotels or other buildings allowed. The park idea originated with Susie Mahieux, who owns a large part of the land around this most enchanting of all Sea of Cortez bays. It already serves as the sea's finest port of refuge for sizable yachts as well as small craft. It is also the spawning ground of numerous game fish species, including giant black snook, roosterfish, mangrove and dog snappers, and perhaps jewfish and sierra.

Our party of about 60 people was especially well organized and directed by Lic. Ricardo García Soto, Director General of Turismo for the territory. He is setting a splendid example of how an alert young man can develop a small office into a dynamic and influential one. He had us flying in large planes from a La Paz meeting to a visit to Hotel Las Cruces Palmilla, then on to dine and spend the night at the lux Hotel Cabo San Lucas.

Next a.m. we boarded a yacht for a cruise to the cape and to breakfast with Bernie Berrera, manager of the Hacienda Cabo San Lucas. From the cape we flew up the Cortez coast to the resort of Hotel Punta Chivato. Its operator, Dixon Collins, and his charming mother, made our visit a most pleasant one.

Nostalgia is not one of my favorite indulgences but when Mayo Obregón, former president of the Trans Mar de Cortés airlines, flew in from his San Diego post (to represent the Mexican Secretary of the Treasury) and joined Luis Cóppola, Bill Escudero and me for breakfast at the Los Arcos, we recounted the years since that three had started and backed me with every possible assistance in getting the big story of the Sea Of Cortez on paper.

Retold too, were the many belly-laugh accounts of my pioneering travels with Escudero into the wilderness back lands and shores.

It was at that same table location, 15 years ago, that Obregón decided to provide all facilities needed to get material and photos for this *W.O.N.* column, and for my book, *The Sea Of Cortez*. — RAY CANNON

A LETTER FROM MAYO OBREGON

[A congratulatory letter from Mayo Obregón, owner of Trans Mar de Cortés airlines, mentions the all-important meeting 12 years earlier at the Hotel Los Arcos in which Obregón offered Ray transportation and logistical support in exchange for help in publicizing tourism in Baja California. Translation of the original Spanish provided by Carlos Gutierrez of Aeronaves de México:]

October 18, 1966—My dear friend, I am writing you in Spanish to express myself better, being sure that there will be, among your numerous friends, one who can translate this letter.

I received your wonderful book, *The Sea Of Cortez*, with a note of yours, so nice, and which I don't feel I deserve, that made me feel very thankful.

All the merit of the book, which is quite a lot, is due to all the sunburns, effort, and courage with which you performed your laborious work. I wonder how many times you didn't have your three meals a day, how many nights you slept on the bottom of a canoe, or on a road, or some beach, without more roof than just the sky of Baja California.

Ray and Carla at Enrique Ortega's testimonial dinner in Los Angeles, February 1970. — PHOTO BY AL TETZLAFF

In your acknowledgments you express your deep appreciation to my company, Trans Mar de Cortés, and to me personally. You don't have any reason to do so. It was agreed. I ordered all the personnel in T.M.C. to give you all facilities in our organization, to provide you transportation all through the peninsula, and to carry all your equipment and the specimens you found from time to time. So you were lost in the great roads of Baja California, becoming a part of the scenery. As time went by, the radio let us know that you were aboard with lots of uncovered bottles, conchas, caracoles and quite a lot of the dust of the peninsula.

You, on the other hand, offered to write about Baja California and to promote tourism, and you have done it quite well in your continuous articles in the newspapers, in numerous reviews, and now with this wonderful book, magnificent in its presentation, in its photographs, maps, illustrations, flowers, and above all, its content—plenty of knowledge and experience gained by so many years of walking the roads and beaches of Baja California. You have given more publicity to this country than anyone has ever done before, showing the truth to the hunter, the angler, the traveler, so that I have heard from many people who have your book and are eager to know these places.

With this book you do a great service to our country and especially to our peninsula. Your book will bring many people to Baja California and will show them step-by-step how to find spectacular views, tie a fishhook, eat pitahaya or harden olives.

Among your friends in Mexico your presence has left a deep impression, which your book makes stronger. I vividly recall your offer, made the first time we met, when you said… "I am going to write a book about Baja California."

Te abraza con afecto, tu amigo de siempre, [signed] Mayo Obregón

El Salvador "laundry maids."

In a Salvadorian traditional canoa. — PHOTO BY AL TETZLAFF

OTHER EDENS

EL SALVADOR & PUERTO VALLARTA

THE SUCCESS OF *The Sea Of Cortez* made Ray a celebrity overnight and resulted in invitations to go on trips such as this 1967 junket with photographer Al Tetzlaff to investigate and promote sport fishing opportunities in El Salvador.

TO EL SALVADOR WITH AL TETZLAFF

When the government of El Salvador asked me to come and examine the fishes and fishing of their Republic, with the hope of attracting U.S. anglers, it took me a full five seconds to make up my mind and give an answer.

Having seen and heard less of El Salvador than of any of the other Central American countries, I was well prepared for one thing—surprise—and I got it at every turn. A mile from the very modern airport, half of the vehicles on the road were ox carts; a few miles from the elegant and luxurious Hotel El Salvador was a small sugar mill, with all machinery and molds made of wood, and about two centuries old; its cane transportation and juicer were powered by oxen. A lesser distance from the architectural-masterpiece homes of the wealthy were the typical thatched cabañas of middle class farmers, with their primitive tools, bake-ovens and kitchens that much resembled household equipment of the aborigine.

Except for the quaint and rustic, which has its own kind of beauty, all else was like being in the Garden of Allah, alive with the colors and calls of tropical songbirds.

Such a place was the large crater lake, Coatepeque, where Al Tetzlaff, who had shipped along as my photographer, and I were taken to angle for largemouth bass.

Cascading from the lofty rim of the crater was a forest aflame with red and orange blossoms and multicolor fruits against lacy fronds and leaves in bright green—all flowing down to the sweet water lake and hanging their boughs out over it in a landscape so colorful it might aptly be described as "the painted tropics."

Incidentally, we also discovered that Lake Coatepeque had considerable bigmouth bass.

Mr. Luis Drake, field director for the Madison Avenue office of El Salvador's Department of Tourism, selected as our hosts two of the best sportsmen and finest people I ever expect to meet, Alphonso and Sonia Alvarez, operators of a coffee plantation and a very large shrimping business.

Eons of centuries ago Bahía Jiquilisco was a vast body of water, but today the area is only half water for it has been deltaed by heavy rains into fingerlike peninsulas, separated by narrow channels of brackish water. Mangrove trees growing to 60 feet high dominate the vegetation, with stretches of tropical fruit orchards and small clearings occupied by a primitive house, or a group of them, all thatched with palm fronds and poles.

Our photographs showing the dugout skiffs, unpenned pigs and chickens, and nude children, could just as well have been scenes in a remote island of Indonesia.

With each rising tide, the bay gets oxygenated by 20-foot-high breakers tumbling in over sand bars across the bay's entrance and extending into it. These charged waters get jammed with big fish.

In one narrow channel we fished right in the front yard of a native house and caught sizable black snook, and we could have loaded the boat with enormous orangemouth corvina and another species that achieve a weight of 100 pounds, according to natives.

Fishing between the tall, green mangrove trees gave me a strange new charge, especially when our boat turned around a point and headed up a flat-surfaced channel that was almost choked by the mangroves.

We spent ten exciting days of fishing, including the

With Sonia Alvarez in boat *Dinga II*. — PHOTO BY AL TETZLAFF

open sea for big game, up two rivers for snook, and into dozens of channels.

Examining the sport fishing potential and recommending spots for resorts, as I had done around the Sea of Cortez, was the best assignment job I have ever had. Finding that most of the game fishes of El Salvador are the same species as those of the Cortez made the task a breeze. The fishing techniques and various methods of sampling fish populations I had learned in my 12 years' work on the Cortez, came in handy in estimating similar conditions here. Yet every day brought new and exciting experiences.

On the way to Bahía Jiquilisco we found half-a-dozen shrimp boats just pulling in. Each had saved all of the edible fish that got netted with the shrimp haul a few miles offshore in the open ocean. Among the 19 game species I examined were a great number of the giant black snook, *Centropomus nigrescens*. Nowhere in the Pacific have I ever been able to catch snook in the open sea. Now, with live shrimp as bait, I believe it will be easy to hook this great fighter offshore, as well as in bays and river estuaries.

Also netted by the shrimpers were a few juvenile jewfish up to 30 pounds, a few large dog snappers, small grouper, and jacks, including a small roosterfish and other prized game fishes.

By checking the catches of illicit bay blasters using an explosive chemical for killing young fish wholesale, by looking at catches taken illegally in weirs stretched across esteros, also by observing our own live bait netters' assortment, I was able to record a sizable checklist of fish in Jiquilisco. Employing a 200-yard-long beach seine and a host of netters, 28 game fish species, most of them the young of game fish, were hauled ashore and checked there. This gave me some assurance that the outer ocean water along the coast would be good fishing grounds.

We went out in a small boat and kept two miles offshore to avoid shallow water and large breakers. I showed the crew how to tailor a ski-bait and then how to present it. No one aboard was more astonished than I when I let the bait out. As soon as it started skiing, a fish riot broke out. In an instant the whole surface around it was boiling.

There was a clear vision of huge amberjack and crevalle. Three roosterfish fins sliced the surface, sending up fountains of spray. Before any of them got a chance, a giant needlefish came vaulting in on the surface from a hundred feet away. With bull's-eye aim, he hit the target, scooped up the bait, held it and sailed on through the air for another 15 feet.

I played the enormous 5' 5" needle almost as I play a billfish, and decked it. I had learned to catch giant needlefish in the Cortez, but the others aboard had only seen them taken by accident. That five-footer got fried for the best sea food of our trip.

Because of this state of coexistence among the game species, and the area's close proximity to ports, I must say that this is one of the world's best game angling arenas, and may prove a super place for the greater billfish. Also, there is a nine or ten months' occurrence of very weighty sailfish; nowhere else have I seen a greater number of them. Black marlin may also be abundant.

If finding the other fishes was easy, locating sailfish was a cinch. There was nothing to do but head straight out to sea for about 18 miles where rich water is encountered. I mean rich in sea life such as numerous species of sea birds, whales, dolphins (mammals), barrilete skipjack, and schools of small forage fishes. Dolphinfish were in schools that seemed boundless. We could have jackpoled tons of them, and this was our cue to start looking for sailfish fins. Two miles more and we reached the swimway or zone of the sails. Sails are usually closer in than marlin.

On this trip we were aboard the 45-foot marlin cruiser of Victor Safie and about to catch the first billfish any of the crew of three had ever seen taken on rod and reel.

I am not sure that any other Salvadorian had seen an angler-caught sail. Safie caught two that weighed above 150 pounds each. The heads were removed, kept overnight in a deep-freeze, then taken to the capital city of San Salvador, where the Tourist Bureau called a press conference to hear the important story and see the proof.

— RAY CANNON

TOPLESS CLUB A BUST

SAN SALVADOR, MAY 5, 1967—In this city of much gaiety there are four, high-standard and successful night clubs. Then there is a topless, which for some strange reason that we couldn't understand, was not drawing crowds. There seemed to be every reason why the fun loving and sexy Salvadorians should be jamming the well-stocked Corral de las Potrancas—and beautiful fillies they were.

Next day, after our peek at this den of immodesty, we set out to fish a lake. Our guide met us with a skiff and live bait towed in a sled.

As we glided along the shore our cameras ran temperatures trying to capture the immense beauty of the rain forests of tall and spreading trees that marched down to the water-edge to shade brilliant-colored tropical flowers and ripening fruits, whose passion-rousing perfumes would cause a celibate to pray for deliverance from temptation. The water was sweet and celestial sapphire.

None of the paintings glorifying the South Sea island garden spots equaled this Elysium on earth.

As we trolled around a point we saw that some grass-covered clearings along the shore were spread with vivid colored and pure white clothing. A little closer and we could see that it was laundry being washed and dried by several young ladies.

Only then did we learn why the topless club was a bust. Half of the well-stacked laundry maids were beautiful and bare from the waist up.

While our distant view of the women at work settled the question of the lack of patrons at the nightclub, there was more to our adventure. We had our guide quickly put us ashore behind a concealing point of land from which we could sneak up and get close-up photos. When we had crept to the top and were focusing our cameras we were astonished to a point just shy of getting lockjaw, when a group of topless maidens who had been concealed by the knoll we were on, called out and motioned for us to come and get their pictures too!

Our embarrassment was colossal. But we did recoup to do some fishing and found the lake full of largemouth bass. — RAY CANNON

GIGANTIC JEWFISH CAUGHT FROM DOCK

SAN SALVADOR, APRIL 28, 1967—To give a story proper form, the small things should come first, with a gradual buildup to the monsters for a climax, but this one got screwed up when one of our party started fishing right off from a 36-foot-long pier and about 100 yards from our tree-shaded rooms.

At the end of the pier the water was ten feet deep where Jaime Mongsia started catching foot-long jacks, a corvina, and a young black snook. Thinking he might contact a big (up to 80 pounds) snook, he baited a heavy rig with a ten-inch corvina.

It was a quiet and lazy afternoon. A half-dozen guests of the Alvarezes, Tetzlaff and myself included, were lapping up some refreshing liquids in the shade of the large ramada pavilion, when all hell broke out. I missed the Spanish words and by the excited running in all directions, I thought someone was drowning. One fellow had grabbed a diver's spear gun. Tetzlaff dashed for a shark gaff with a ten-inch curve. Others got ropes.

Rushing to the pier I finally got a glimpse of the object of all the frenzied activity. It was a huge fish, and it was threatening to slap the piling from supporting the pier. Everyone with a fishing weapon or rope got a connection. I was reminded of the classic picture of Gulliver being restrained by the Lilliputians. With the help (really not required) of several neighbors, the great fish was beached.

The yelling had attracted just about everyone living in this exclusive beach area called "Corral de las Mulas" (Corral of the Mules). The fish was easy to identify by the combination of small eyes and rounded tail fin and back part of the anal and soft dorsal fins as a (southern) jewfish, *Promicrops sp.* (not yet sure of the scientific name of this species). Groupers have larger eyes, and they and the black sea bass have a squarish or straight back edge of the anal, dorsal, and tail fins.

The jewfish, called "mero" or "June fish" by natives,

is the largest of the basses, reaching perhaps 1,000 pounds. I saw one weighed at Mulegé scaling 858 pounds. One reported from Java was over 12 feet long. Frank Dufresne and I saw a ten-foot skeleton of one at Almejas Bay.

By comparison, our Corral de las Mulas fish was a small fry. She weighed only 205 kilos, or about 450 pounds. The "she"—because it was pregnant with a couple of 20-pound pokes of eggs, due to ripen in two to four weeks. They are believed to spawn in this Bahía Jiquilisco in late April or May.

This Bay is enormous and has several kinds of environments, each suited to a special group of species. One near the opening to the ocean (Pacific) is favored by an extra-large race of orangemouth corvina which have a small head and high shoulders and are said to weigh up to 100 pounds. We caught a boat load but none over 28 pounds—all taken on popper lures. So also were some sizable black snook, same species as Mulegé river giants.

— RAY CANNON

EX-LAX ROMANCE IN PUERTO VALLARTA

[From an earlier trip to the Mexican mainland. If the conclusion of this story is just half-true, it gives new meanings to the term "Montezuma's Revenge."]

PUERTO VALLARTA, FEBRUARY 28, 1958—How would you describe it? As a place where the atmosphere is so balmy a person would go "balmy" trying to raise a sweat or get chill; where clouds of orchids and fruit-laden palms engulf the mountains and sweep down to the edge of the sea; where muscles and brain cells quit twitching to enjoy the luxury of being lazy; where a man's castle can be made of sticks and palm leaves! Would there be gold-cheeked, gold-bellied, gold-skinned dolls to entice you? Would you prefer a swim in water as refreshing as the lazy conditioning breeze, or sip nectar of the coconut, or a Cuba Libre—and when the mood and spirit urged—go fishing!

This then, would be the region of San Blás–Puerto Vallarta, and places between, some 2,000 miles south of the Tropic of Cancer and Mazatlán, where a plentiful rainfall and moderate, warm climate combine to produce a dreamland.

Dr. Boyd Walker of UCLA captured six new species including a couple of cabrillas (basses), a flapjack-type of manta ray and other oddballs.

Walker told of a poisonous tree sap called *leche del mar* used allegedly by natives to kill fish. And how the law-abiding citizens took a dim view of his scientific work since he too was laying out gobs of rotenone, killing more fish than the local grown dope. Reported also was good bonefish, catfish (about ten species), snapper, and snook fishing in the estuaries but more especially in the Río San Diego. Dr. Walker advises taking a quantity of insect repellent labeled "Off," a Johnson's Wax product.

Clowning around at Puerto Vallarta during a 1969 trip with Carlos Gutierrez of Aeronaves de México. For a visit to some local waterfalls, Ray picked a wheezing saddle mule he described as "an aging, cantankerous, son-of-a-jackass out of a mustang mare… the most perverse creature I have ever mounted."

Bugs are the one bad feature of this area.

My own trip there was last spring.

You will doubtless remember accounts of the yellowfin tuna I caught at Rancho Buena Vista and how I searched the whole Gulf without finding other close to shore habitats until I reached the islands off Puerto Vallarta.

A thorough survey revealed very few fish along the shore but fairly numerous in the estuaries, while the islands produced many game species. Sailfish enter the bay throughout most of the year which swarms with black skipjack, sierra and jack crevalle.

On the way out to the islands I noticed miles of white dots along the horizon. A closer view revealed them to be dove-sized terns standing upright on the surface, spaced 50 to 60 feet apart. When we plowed through we found that each bird was standing on the back of a huge turtle. If all these turtles with the white markers moved up close to the turtle fishermen in the Gulf, I doubt that many would celebrate their 200th birthday.

Around the islands we were centering attention on jumping wahoo and tuna. Otherwise we could have loaded the boat with giant snapper, grouper and other bottom feeding fishes. This we learned when the boat slowed for a turn and they would rise to latch on to our baits. A brief period of bottom fishing was very productive.

On our way in, our skipper spotted a couple of natives diving for oysters. He gave them an emotional shake-up

Caught from a 36-foot dock. — PHOTO BY AL TETZLAFF

when he changed course and bore down on them. We learned that they had just been released from the pokey for catching lobsters out of season and that the officer had used our boat for the pinch. Not being sure of oyster season, the culprits thought they had "had it" again. Their expressions of relief were something to witness when they learned that we only wanted to buy a couple of dozen oysters for lunch. They insisted on giving us half a skiff load and all the blessings of the Sea Gods.

Those oysters, mixed with chopped tomatoes, onions, peppers and some herbs, by our deckhand, was about the best dish a bunch of hungry fishermen ever gulped.

The delightful little town is a blend of the old and the older. Progress has yet to smear its quaint charm or spoil the sweet gentle dispositions of the citizenry.

There are many land-side points of interest. Six miles south of the town a group of U.S. nature boys have "got it made." They have established a thatched hut colony and live on the fruits and nuts of the land. My photographer, Bill, nearly moved in when he got a close-up view of some of the briefly-clad nature gals in the colony.

In a coconut grove on the beach, a couple of miles north, a dance pavilion provides anglers and other visitors with social contact. Bill used our last box of chocolates to make quick acquaintance. He did well until the candy ran out. He then went back to the hotel and returned with the box partially filled. He was "in" again and had a swarm of native dolls around. I recognized, by the size and shape of the chocolate-covered pellets, that he was passing out our supply of Ex-Lax. Quite an evening. — RAY CANNON

Launching at Kino Bay. After his rough weather experiences on the sea route south from San Felipe, Ray became convinced that the safest and most enjoyable way for a small boat to cruise the southern Sea of Cortez was to launch at Kino Bay on the east side, cross the Midriff islands, and then cruise south along the Baja shore. This seaway remained the standard for Vagabundo club cruises until the paving of the Transpeninsular Highway made it possible to trailer a boat down the Baja peninsula to launch points at Bahía de los Angeles or farther south.

VAGABUNDOS DEL MAR CLUB

DOWN TO THE SEA IN LITTLE SHIPS

THE FORMATION OF the pioneering Vagabundos Del Mar Boat & Travel Club greatly facilitated Ray's dream of finding fun and adventure while cruising down the Sea of Cortez in small boats, and he mentioned the club in dozens of *Western Outdoor News* columns dating from its first activities in 1966, until his last "Vag" cruise in 1976.

The Vagabundo club had its earliest beginnings as an informal group of Southern California telephone company employees who hunted deer together in the Sierra Nevada mountains.

In 1966, they became caught up in Ray's *Western Outdoor News* columns about the fabulous fishing in the Sea of Cortez, and they sought Ray out and persuaded him to lead a group of 13 small trailer boats on a cruise from Kino Bay to La Paz (Ray, undoubtedly, allowed himself to be persuaded with a minimum of arm-twisting). That first flotilla was launched on December 4, 1966, and—as might be expected of that inauspicious season—it was beset by severe winds that had many of the participants crying, "Never again!"

"It was the biggest adventure of my life," said future club founder and president Chet Sherman, "even including my time in the war in the Navy when they were shooting at me." However, the fishing was good. Sherman's first catch in Baja was a sierra which he then used as bait to catch his second fish—a grouper, variously remembered as weighing from 159 to "over 200 pounds." Whatever the actual weight, that first cruise was the beginning of many more to follow as adventurous trailer boat owners flocked to Sherman's garage in Los Angeles for a series of rollicking "fiestas" held in the late 1960s.

In March 1968, Ray made his first known published use of the name "Vagabundos" in referring to the group that was still not officially a club. He used his column in *Western Outdoor News* to help publicize Vagabundo cruises, and he would continue to lead these events as official club

"Commodore" for the remainder of his life.

In 1970, club dues of $5 a year were levied. In 1971, the Vagabundos were legally incorporated as a nonprofit social club, and an official monthly newsletter, the *Chubasco*, was launched. Membership expanded rapidly as the Transpeninsular Highway was opened in 1973 and the club began selling low-cost vehicle insurance in addition to boat insurance.

By 1988, membership had exploded to almost 6,000 and a full-time staff headed by General Manager Fred Jones was running day-to-day operations.

Chet Sherman's backyard fiestas had grown into a series of annual blowouts that took over hotels and RV parks, and the club had begun organizing RV caravans in addition to small boat cruises.

Sherman continued to serve as club president until his death in 1996, thoroughly enjoying himself and bemoaning the "hobby that definitely got out of hand." Today's president is Tony Schuck.

Ray Cannon is honored in perpetuity as the Vagabundo's "Commodore Eternal"—the enthusiastic spiritual inspiration of those first early adventurers who "went down to the sea in little ships."

In columns and fragments dating from 1959, Ray's story of how the Vagabundos Del Mar Boat & Travel Club got its start:

EARLY PRECURSORS
HUGHES-FULLERTON BOAT CLUB

[Following World War II, the rapid development of outboard motors and cheap, efficient fiberglass hulls led to the popularity of "trailer boats" that could be hauled to remote locations and launched nearly anywhere. By the time the Vagabundos Del Mar club was launched in 1966, many small boat clubs such as the one described here were being formed. The "Club Commodore" of the Hughes-Fullerton Boat Club mentioned in this story is Harold Swenson, who along with other club members Bill Harker, Chuck Lundy and George Elias, had been with Ray on the "Hurricane Cruise" of November 1957 and the "Kids' Trip" of June 1958.]

JANUARY 9, 1959—The wildfire-like boom in boating interest is exemplified in the vast number of boat clubs mushrooming up all over this State. Fairly typical of the rapid growth is the Hughes-Fullerton Boat Club. It was launched last April with eight members, and within eight months had a membership of 60.

I asked the club's Commodore, Harold Swensen, the reason for forming the organization.

He told me the idea was conceived in that hurricane we were caught in last November, and how later, in discussing the great need for general safety knowledge, with the other members of the expedition, they decided to form a study group and take Coast Guard and U.S. Power Squadron courses.

Then, as a result of our second and highly pleasurable cruise across the Gulf with family participation, the organization plans to include many other facets.

Elected to other offices were W.A. Harker, vice-commodore; C. R. Lundy and George Elias, fleet captains; all participants in the Gulf expeditions.

Commodore Swenson has offered to assist groups planning to organize. He also invites organizers to visit one of his Club's meetings. — RAY CANNON

"KIDS' TRIP" REUNION

[Later in 1959, Ray describes a reunion of "Kids' Trip" participants, and a proposal for a "Cortez Adventure Club."]

"The greatest and most pleasant adventure to be found around the hemisphere," was the opinion of the six families who made the first cruising-camping trip across the Cortez. This get-together topped all meetings I have attended for years. It set a good example for the Cortez Adventure Club, mentioned a few columns back, which is to be a loosely-formed organization of all who have crossed the Cortez or taken long voyages in it aboard small boats. Everyone I have seen or heard from is enthusiastic about the plan.

We ran movies of our first attempt to cross in four boats, when we got caught about midway in the worst hurricane to hit the region in 40 years. It showed man and wife teams struggling in the fury.

Also shown was the expedition made seven months later. This time they took nine of their teenage youngsters for three weeks of camping, fishing and exploring.

About 50 other members of the Hughes Boating Club, which started as a result of that voyage, joined us to view the pictures and were enthralled. All of which gave proof positive that an Association of all such adventurers would be a whale of a success. — RAY CANNON

THE RYAN-BURKE PROPOSAL

[In 1962, Ray again promotes the idea of a Cortez boating club, this time with Bill Burke, and boat builder Mike Ryan, with whom he had been cruising for several years.]

In answer to the half-a-dozen letters received recently suggesting that an exclusive club be organized to include small boat adventurers who have cruised across the Midriff or on lengthy trips down the Cortez, I vote "Yes."

Both Mike Ryan of Gardena and Bill Burke of Hollywood have suggested a locally formed organization with some sort of a clearinghouse for exchanging information that would be of benefit to members, as well as to newcomers desiring to make the trip.

These voyages are making history.

I will assist however I can with establishing an organization of exploring, seafaring sailors of the Cortez, but only if I am encouraged by a lot of letters of advice and ideas.

What shall we make it? A club—a clan—an institute—or go all-out and make it a cult? — RAY CANNON

THE JOYS OF SMALL BOAT CRUISING

[Three years after his first full-length cruise of the Cortez, Ray celebrates the small boat experience.]

APRIL 4, 1962—For the most completely satisfying and exciting adventure to be found around this hemisphere, many claim a small boat voyage in the Sea of Cortez rates first, and I agree.

The cruise is even more enthralling when either fishing, diving, or exploring are included, and better yet when all three are pursued with enthusiasm and a desire to observe the strange things to be seen and experienced in this youngest and most unique of all the seas.

Although I have cruised and explored the fishing around all of the 100 islands and the shorelines of the Cortez and the Baja California Peninsula, and charted and studied water conditions, another pleasant lifetime could be spent examining the lands back of the visible shorelines and looking at the wonder world below the water surface.

There are numerous reasons for small craft expeditions. First of all, an outboard, inboard-outboard or jet, can get into places that could not be approached by larger craft.

In addition to the pleasure to be found snuggling up in a tight little cove, is the protection against a sudden

A "Vags raft-up" at Caleta San Francisquito in the summer of 1996. The occasion was a special cruise to celebrate the 30th anniversary of the club's first crossing of the Midriff in 1966. — PHOTOS BY GENE KIRA

An early Vagabundos del Mar club cruise, refueling at Caleta San Francisquito, c. 1976. The boat *Vagabundo del Mar*, right, was a 26-foot Reinell owned by longtime club member Whitey Whitestine.

storm. Havens for large vessels are far between but coves and lees providing good refuge for outboards are always easy to get to, along recommended sea lanes. There are also advantages in being able to beach by using inflated rubber rollers, in case of emergency or for the purpose of camping ashore at the desirable spot.

Among other benefits are—trolling or diving over shallow reefs and close up to rock shores; running back into shallow lagoons and inlets; backing up to shore for unloading; and anchoring in shallow water.

But most pleasant of all is the exhilaration of feeling the sea glide under you, so close you can reach down and touch it and feeling the refreshing spray misting up from the wake. There is real fun in quartering to the top of an upwelling or roller-coasting over waves in the swift Midriff current. To me there was a special "charge" in conquering this new world aboard a convenience as light as a reasonable degree of safety would allow. It was something like challenging a big game fish with extra-light tackle but multiplied hundreds of times over.

Even if you discount the possibility that I have gone overboard, or a bit loco, for this kind of venturous enterprise, I still am unable to understand why any guy with a sliver of courage and adventure in his craw can hold out from getting with it, in this, the last of the pleasant seas to be thoroughly explored. — RAY CANNON

JIMENEZ' LETTER

[February 23, 1966. A letter from José Andrés "Shorty" Jiménez of Kino Bay informs Ray that there will be gas service available at Caleta San Francisquito by March of that year.]

Mr. Ray Cannon, dear friend, I got your letter three days ago. Just got back from Mexico City. I was gone for a month to see my old man. Pretty old, 87 years. Yes we have gas. We will have it in San Francisquito next month

around the 25th of March. Tell them to write to me to know the amount they want. The first haul will be 20 drums at 60 cents a gallon so we can have more people. The government of Sonora is going to start a resort in Tiburón Island for tourists in April. There will be a gas station at the airport and at the estero at Kino here, a launching ramp. A big dock to tie boats. A yacht club. Highway down to the estero. I'm going to work with them for the tourists here at Kino in information for the boats and guides. Let me know if you're coming down this year. Your friend, Shorty J. Andrés Jiménez.

FIRST VAG CRUISE ANNOUNCEMENT
BEGINNING A BAJA TRADITION

[Ray's tentative first announcement of the December 1966 cruise that would launch the Vagabundo club.]

JULY 1, 1966—I have been asked to head up a fleet of a couple of dozen 16 to 26-foot inboard/outdrive boats for a slow cruise from Kino to La Paz, about Dec. 1st. Anyone with the equipment and qualifications could join in the loosely formed group. There would be big fiestas all along, with a big splurge at the destination. There would be TV and press coverage and a repair boat with mechanics and spare parts. Nothing is set yet so I am anxious for suggestions. — RAY CANNON

RAY TO LEAD TRIP

[By the following month, Ray has assumed responsibility for planning the trip.]

AUGUST 5, 1966—My personally conducted cruise this coming December 1, or thereabouts, may have to be limited to a number not yet determined. If you wish in, drop me a line as soon as you can be sure of the time. So far there are no rules or restrictions, except that I must advise places where we expect to get gas, to stock the amount.

The kind of boat and its gas range will automatically determine the destination point. A number of small outboards will remain within the Midriff. Others will go to Mulegé. Still others will go to Juanaloa or on to La Paz and Buena Vista. The latter with powerful outboards or inboard stern-drives. — RAY CANNON

LAUNCH DATE IS SET—DECEMBER 4, 1966

[The launch date of December 4th is finalized. The "supplies" Ray mentions consist mainly of gasoline to be stockpiled for the fleet.]

SEPTEMBER 2, 1966—Our Dec. 4 Cortez voyage is shaping up. Now I need to know more details on the sizes and kinds of boats and motors, fuel range, desired destinations, time to spend. Definite decisions will soon be required to get supplies earmarked along the course.

— RAY CANNON

CREW LIST—FIRST VAG CRUISE

1. Jack Arnold (captain), Dannie Arnold, John Forbis.
2. Merle Bird (captain), Bill Metz.
3. Martin Fillet (captain), Elsie Fillet, Ray Cannon.
4. Ray Hornbeck (captain), Don Evans.
5. Howard Hugo (captain), James Otis Johnson.
6. Mel Kirby (captain), Joe Corrigan.
7. John Ollila (captain, *Seri*), Don Groves.
8. Gil Reed (captain), Gary Reed, Gene Babbitt.
9. Mike Ryan (captain), Al Routhier.
10. Chet Sherman (captain), El Klingman, Bill Matz.
11. Stan Symanski (captain), Jorace Ferguson.
12. Roy Wickline (captain), Colonel McKinstry.
13. Ray Williams (captain), Jennie Williams.

VAGABUNDO CRUISE—FINAL CALL

[Soliciting more participants two months before departure. Thirteen boats eventually went on the trip.]

OCTOBER 7, 1966—A great many boaters have made inquiries but only a dozen have declared themselves in. Most are no doubt waiting for more info, and since all are readers of *W.O.N.*, here is as much info as will be needed, except for a little on-course navigation details, which I'll give at Kino.

You pay for nothing more than if you were going alone. Take proof of citizenship and vehicle ownership slip, or note from owner, to get all papers at border, except

fishing license at Kino. Gun permit and hunting license at your nearest Mexican Consul. Read boating and study maps in *The Sea Of Cortez* book. For added navigating pleasure, get chart and chart course, and check mileage on it for your fuel range. Outboards will likely need fuel shipped across to Bahía San Francisquito and operators must write to José Jiménez, Box 605, Hermosillo, Sonora, Mexico for this, far in advance. I must get names, kinds of boats and motors, gas range, time allowed, and destination, so I can alert stations and resorts of your coming, and get supplies, etc., reserved.

I will do this and pilot the fleet south. It will be split into squads of two or three stick-together boats. Squads will reform for return, according to time allotted for trip. One week—Mulegé; two weeks—Loreto and Juanaloa Region. Over two weeks—La Paz and Buena Vista.

November 1st is the deadline for being counted in.

— RAY CANNON

DECEMBER 1—DEPARTING LOS ANGELES

I was driven down by John Ollila of Compton, skipper of the 22' outboard *Seri*, and his mate, Don Groves of Whittier, via Yuma and San Luis to Sonoyta.

We spent the night at Sonoyta in the second very modern and comfortable and inexpensive motel. We liked the meals in the adjoining No. 1 motel.

Being a day ahead at Hermosillo, we stopped, as always, at the modern Gandara Hotel (especially good food). It is still personally managed by owner Raúl Gandara.

Next day we fitted out and drove to Kino where we found several of our boats awaiting and eager. Drove over a new graded road to site of planned yacht club, small craft haven and port. A cement ramp to fit any tide and weather condition was already finished.

We spent that night (December 3rd) at the delightful new and modern Motel Kino Bay about 4 1/2 miles above old Kino, along the beach over a paved road. — RAY CANNON

DECEMBER 4TH LAUNCH AT KINO BAY

The drama of the highly significant voyage started before daybreak with breakfast aboard high and dry boats. The aroma of coffee permeating the breezeless air was perfume of ambrosia and almost as stimulating as a big belt of bourbon. Some sneaked over to "Shorty" Jiménez' cantina and got one, or maybe two.

I have never seen more efficiency than was shown by our old friend Tiburcio Saucedo in dunking boats. He had us all in the water in record time. Because of the heavy load on the *Seri*, I crossed on the 22' Catamaran *Kitty Queen*, owned and operated by Martin and Elsie Fillet, pet food producers of Whittier, California.

All boats, after matching cruising speeds, teamed up in squads of two or three. Seeing so many craft strung out ahead and back of us was a memorable sight.

At sunrise, the sea was so calm we altered course from close up to Tiburón to south of its satellite, Isla Turner. And as we rounded its tip, a 16-foot open outboard was weighted almost to the water level by a cord of yellowtail, with its two anglers fighting a couple of 40-pounders.

— RAY CANNON

BAHIA SAN FRANCISQUITO

Bahía [Caleta] San Francisquito is a place with a strange and mysterious past. In the books, the pages describing this bay are blank, but the evidence of ghost towns built on the foundations of ghost towns is there, spelling out the ebb and flow of human tides in skeletonous monuments.

The Villavicencio family, owners of Rancho el Barril, seven miles south of the bay, now keep a store of gas on hand.

If this gas supply is to be maintained, giving confidence to boaters, San Francisquito will become the most popular sport fishing port in the whole Cortez.

— RAY CANNON

SANTA ROSALIA

For boats with ample gas supply, following the outer course from Punta Vírgenes outside of Isla San Marcos to Punta Chivato saves eight or ten miles, and if the current is favorable much fuel is saved. All of our boats took this course except a couple of small outboards which put in at Santa Rosalía for gas.

Rounding Punta Vírgenes the Sea was misty and I had to go a long way before realizing that Isla Tortuga, which I could barely make out, was not Isla San Marcos. A chart would have revealed that I would have to go halfway across the Cortez to get outside of Tortuga. Fortunately I was able to see that San Marcos appeared to move against the more distant background of Punta Chivato.

If some simple facilities for small boats were constructed in the harbor at Santa Rosalía, boaters would not be so anxious to pass up this good supply port.

Two of our boats ran inside of San Marcos, visited the lagoon and Kaiser gypsum works on the island and had a slow trip through the channel avoiding reefs projecting from the island and the huge rocks scattered over the south side of the passage. The rest of the fleet went outside at full-bore. Seeing the dozen boats blasting up white water in a long line toward Punta Chivato was quite a spectacle.

It was at Punta Chivato that I once saw a couple of vagabundos wrestling an 820-pound jewfish which they lashed to their dugout and took the seven miles to the

Mulegé river and two miles up it to sell it to the late Sal Salazar, then owner of Hacienda Mulegé, where it was weighed.

It was also near Chivato at the Santa Ines Islands where I have caught several big grouper, including the one in *The Sea Of Cortez* book. This has proven to be Mulegé's most productive fishing grounds, and was selected as the site for the new deluxe resort, Borrego de Oro. Two of our boats pulled in to the resort's fine baylet for the night. All others went on to Mulegé. — RAY CANNON

BORREGO DE ORO (HOTEL PUNTA CHIVATO)

Except for the Borrego de Oro's port and the baylets near El Coyote back in Bahía Concepción, there is no other good landlocked yacht harbor between Puerto Escondido and the man-made port at Santa Rosalía.

The Hotel Borrego de Oro is truly elegant with its spacious suites and sun areas facing the Sea from atop of a low cliff. The food, service, and hospitality without the Acupulco-type disciplines, are quite deluxe. Furthermore this grand resort is situated in the heart of one of the most exciting big and small game fishing areas in the Cortez.

Our stay at the hotel was made especially delightful by our hostess, Mrs. Barbara Collins, and Marty Price, who came visiting from her power yacht, *La Orchilla*. This 65-foot, completely staffed casa afloat provides every conceivable convenience for a sizable charter party wishing to cruise the Cortez for days, or weeks, of fishing, diving, exploring, or whatever.

Arriving at the Serenidad resort, a short way in from the Mulegé river entrance, and docking at their small, gas-loading pier, we learned that Bill Lloyd's lodge, Playa de Mulegé, was closed and our fleet had no pilot until a boat from Serenidad led the boats through the winding, narrow channel to the pier, without incident.

We were greeted by my old friend Don Johnson, who now operates a half-dozen angling cruisers, several skiffs and some entertaining peddle boats. He says he'll have live bait in operation by spring. He tipped us off to a rousing fiesta that the town had planned for us at the old Hacienda Mulegé Hotel. — RAY CANNON

MULEGE & THE HOTEL SERENIDAD

Seeing a dozen of our boats clustered around the little Serenidad Hotel pier, against the bright green backyard of the palms and mangrove bushes that mask the banks of Mulegé's brackish but beautiful river was a most pleasing sight.

Taking a taxi from Serenidad to Mulegé you are driven over a slow dirt road between the mangroved river edge and a chain of patch farms and tropical fruit orchards with large clumps of date producing palms that go unattended, except for the harvesting.

Every time I go up this river I get a lot of real charges seeing places where I had been involved in exciting goings-on: The spot where my guide speared and landed a river-ripping, hell-raising, 5' 7" snook that panicked the town and made it a resort; saw also the several holes where I had caught giant blacks; where we had found the river choked with the monsters when we tested with a beach seine; where I had been challenged by a big fat raccoon, and where we had repeatedly shot pintail and red-head ducks.

There were also a hundred flashes of fond memories of those few short years ago when Mulegé was still a half-ghost town and where enthusiasm and gaiety almost would get out of hand every time Señor Tobaco threw a fiesta that was always a rouser.

Reminiscing is supposed to prove aging, but just about everything that happened to me in previous times could be repeated, and was, including a fiesta at each of the uptown lodges—the Hacienda de Mulegé and Las Casitas.

Most all boat crews lived at the more convenient Serenidad. Since Fernando del Moral took charge as manager of the place it has been greatly improved and updated and really modernized in accommodations, food, and neatness. Despite our group's sudden overcrowding, the service was excellent. I heard nothing but happy raves from our group.

The local angling boat operator Don Johnson and Moral have planned to place markers to guide small craft into and through the river channel to the Serenidad pier where gas and services will be available for the great number of boats launching at Bahía Kino next May, June, and July (the most favorable season for long voyages in the Cortez.) — RAY CANNON

Tony Schuck, Vagabundos del Mar club president, helps launch director Mike Bales' *Getaway* during a club cruise from Bahía de los Angeles to San Carlos in 1996. — PHOTO BY GENE KIRA

BAHIA CONCEPCION

As a whole, Bahía Concepción is no more attractive than the outer shorelines of the Cortez. There are, however, a couple of enchanting spots, and a visit to them is considered a must by new resort guests. They are Bahía Coyote with its several surrounding islands, mountainside caves, and tree-shaded beach, and Santispac, a beautiful, clam-crammed cove encircled by bright green mangroves and immaculate beach, at the back of a protected inlet.

When most of our fleet nosed up on the beach, a group from Hotel Borrego de Oro was already there. One of them was heard to say—"You fly all the way down from Seattle, cruise way back here for a little quiet and get trampled on by a thundering herd."

Our crews were raising an enthusiastic ruckus when they began finding bushels of cockle-size clams. Half of them found the place so inviting they stayed from one to three nights, spending their days exploring the rich underwater sea life, the storm-carved islands, and the fantastic volcanic mountains. On December 9, despite a fairly stiff breeze, four boats took off for Loreto. Included were skippers Gil Reed, Stan Symanski, Ray Williams, and the Martin Fillets in their catamaran with me aboard. One had gone on a few days earlier, the others were contented to remain in the Mulegé region.

Our boats were getting a mighty heave when the north winds and waves built up to storm strength and kept our skippers working throttles with a hair-trigger touch. We were halfway to Loreto and hell-bent for Punta Púlpito, the nearest protected cove. Despite our eagerness to get on the lee (south) side of this 500-foot-high headland, hidden rocks forced us to give it a wide berth. (Note: Cruising northward, Púlpito can be mistaken for Ildefonso Island.)

The blow reached its full fury as the last of our boats was fighting to avoid surfboarding down the face of some of the larger waves, as it turned the corner into flat water.

Actually, the water was no rougher than the afternoon chop coming in from Santa Catalina island, but because it was strange to our crews it most likely seemed like a raging typhoon in the China Sea.

Everyone was so happy to find such a calm haven, they forgot to "chew me out" for leading them into such a mess. — RAY CANNON

ON TO LORETO

Outside of our calm cove well back in the lee of Punta Púlpito, we could see a heavy sea plunging down the winds, and felt quite snug and contented, nestled in our sanctuary.

We spent a second night, and I must admit that the deck was getting a little hard, with no air mattress. I decided that such newfangled gimmicks were making me soft or something.

The Martin Fillets were as determined as I was to get on toward Loreto, but all occupants of the other three boats were for waiting out the blow, then heading back to the more interesting and calm waters of Mulegé. I was not about to urge them on, even though I knew that they could run to the cover of one of the many coves all along our route.

We got started at daybreak, found the sea choppy, but with the wind at our back, we ran on to Loreto without incident.

The tide was too low and the water too rough to chance approaching the little pier at the Flying Sportsmen Lodge, so we went on two miles south to an indentation protected from north winds, called Bahía La Conocita. We anchored, left a watchman for the night, and took a car that Ed Tabor (the Lodge operator) sent down for us.

Later we learned that we had selected our watchman from the only group that had been pinched for theft in Loreto for several years. (Our confidence must have revived that spark of honesty, for nothing was touched.)

While the Fillets were seeing the first of all of the missions of the Californias, I visited my good friends Gloria and Bill Benziger, the very hospitable and efficient operators of the Hotel Oasis, which is situated among towering date palms and on the beach.

This is the Benziger who made up the expedition to Bahía Tambobiche where we got shipwrecked a couple of years ago, and where we explored and described a vast, hidden lagoon, now named Laguna Benziger.

I had a look through the new deluxe units recently added to the Oasis and saw its boat factory (the first boat, a 23-footer, was finished last week). This place, with Rancho Buena Vista, was one of the first to have live bait.

— RAY CANNON

REACHING LA PAZ

Word came to us at Loreto that the three boats that turned back at Punta Púlpito had returned to Mulegé. Also that they were seen by Aeronaves planes which had been keeping tabs on us. But because our boat was anchored with Loreto's boats in Bahía Conocita, it was overlooked. When they learned that our boat had gone on alone and when they couldn't find us the next day, we were thought to be lost.

We pulled out at daybreak, had pleasant cruising through most all of Juanaloa but hit a roughish sea after rounding Punta San Marcial. We were too far around the point to face the north wind waves for a retreat to Bahía Agua Verde, so we skidded down the face of the rollers and on for 1 1/2 miles more to a good cove with a sand beach at the back of Bahía Santa Marta.

After lunch and a rest we chanced the less turbulent sea and cautiously edged out. But within a few minutes we were hit by the worst chop of the trip. Fillet showed a lot of steel nerves in holding the catamaran in glide after glide down the face of powerful waves. I was the first to yell "uncle," something I seldom do. Anyway we were within a half-mile of Puerto Gatos, which is no more than a mile from Bahía Tambobiche, the spot where I was shipwrecked just a couple of years before.

Later I was told that a Mexican military plane scouted the coast but was unable to locate us. So the word got out that I was lost at sea, with no trace, a report that Carla (my secretary) had become accustomed to hearing.

The wind and waves eased up but the current in our favor was racing through the San José Channel. To take advantage of it, we rode down the middle and stayed there 'til we passed Isla San Francisco (a couple of bad reefs run west and north from the north end a bit.)

There was a brief threat of another blow but we chanced getting to the fine shelters in the deep baylets on the island. However, a calm set in, which gave us a free sea lane to La Paz. I ran past a marker and got on top of shallow rocks but got off soon enough. From there on to the Hotel Los Cocos was smooth sailing and we lost no time tying into some of the luxury provided there.

— RAY CANNON

MIX-UP AT THE AIRPORT

The Martin Fillets were joined by their two sons for a ten-day's stay at the Hotel Los Cocos.

The next day after our arrival I planed out aboard an Aeronaves plane which had come in from Mexico City with Baja's best-to-date Governor, Lic. Hugo Cervantes del Río, aboard.

There was a mix-up in which I became the center of acclaim. It seems that none of the passengers from Mexico knew that the Governor was one of them. I was about to board the plane just as he got off. He started greeting a throng of La Paz citizens who were gathered there with a Mariachi band especially to meet him.

When the Governor saw me and came over to express his favorable opinion of my *Sea Of Cortez* book, the crowd and band moved with him, and Fillet hurried to shoot movies of us. A couple of fellows on the plane saw the scene, recognized the cap and beard, and called the other passengers' attention to it.

When I got aboard I was flabbergasted to suddenly find myself a great celebrity with everyone asking for introductions. The reason was finally revealed when one lady said—"Judging by the number of people and the band coming out to the airport to see you off, you must be the most popular man in all Baja California." I never told her nor the others why all the people were there.

Martin Fillet engaged a native skipper so that he and his family could give over to fishing on the leisurely trip back up the Cortez. Most all other boats took off from Mulegé a couple of days after we left there. They ran into more bad winds. Some of them got into a lot of trouble but all got back with boats intact and no serious injuries.

Chet Sherman, who managed to get a full measure of everything going, including catching the biggest fish—a 159-pound grouper—is reorganizing the group for a voyage to Loreto–Juanaloa, in May or June. The gang is having a get-together in Las Vegas to discuss it and swap stories. — RAY CANNON

CHET SHERMAN PLANS ANOTHER VAG CRUISE

NOVEMBER 17, 1967—This is the exact time to draft plans and charts for the spring voyage down the Cortez. Whatever kind of a 16 to 30-foot trailered boat you have, or expect to get, you can get in on one of the finest and most exciting sporting events on this continent.

There will be several organizers of flotillas and unattached boat operators will be glad to have you join in. I strongly advise cruising with a companion boat, for several reasons.

The first to announce the organizing of a small craft flotilla for launching at Kino Bay in late May or early June, is Chet Sherman.

Chet learned to navigate the Cortez the hard way and is not about to take a party into the kind of December weather I took him into. He will henceforth sail the sea in months when she lies flat, calm, and happy.

Anyone interested in the venture can contact Chet. He is having a get-together fiesta and cruise-planning discussion at his home, December 2. If I am in California I may be there. — RAY CANNON

FIRST VAG FIESTA

DECEMBER 8, 1967—If you have a trailered 16 to 30-foot boat, some rough water boating experience (just in case), and a happy disposition, you can, likely, get in on this:

The Chet Sherman party held December 2 was the first annual get-together of real hardy sailors who earned the title the hard way. They were the crews of the 13 small boats which I led a year ago in a "chancy" December voyage, scheduled to cruise from Kino Bay to La Paz.

After five happy days of running across and down to Mulegé in good weather, and after a couple of rousing fiestas given us by the townspeople, and some clam digging and fishing in Concepción Bay, strong winds set in.

I went on to La Paz, aboard Mr. and Mrs. Martin Fillet's catamaran, riding down the wind for a slow but fairly easy trip, barring a couple of rough afternoons when we found holing up in a cove more comfortable.

All of the others headed back right into the teeth of the wind and spent two to three days fighting it.

Al Hrdlicka on a boat-launching rig at Cholla Bay, near Puerto Peñasco, where the extreme tidal range and flat beach require special measures. This photo was taken in the summer of 1963 when interest was rapidly growing in trailer boating and camping. Three years later, 1966, the Vagabundo club would launch its first trailer boat cruise down the Cortez from Kino Bay.

— PHOTO BY AL HRDLICKA

I doubt that I could have won a popularity prize shortly after that, but, to my surprise, I was greeted at the party with much warmth and friendliness. One of the group explained it as—"We learned more about boating in those few days than we could have gotten in two years of study from textbooks." They proved to me that there are still a lot of people with charged blood and lion guts.

A loosely organized club of Cortez sailors, especially those who have good experiences to tell about, will likely be formed by the group. It will no doubt be limited to a certain number but at present it is open. So is the flotilla, for those who know boating, love adventure, and who can discuss without griping.

This should be one of the best fun cruises ever, and if I can get loose, I'll be in on it. — RAY CANNON

VAGABUNDOS GET A NAME

MARCH 1968—There will be two notable occasions in the Cortez. One, the big "Sea of Cortez Fishing Tournament" (July 11-19), in which contestants in three groups of 30 each, fish two days in La Paz, two days in Buena Vista, and two days in the Cabo San Lucas area, and then are shifted to fish the next place, repeating for a total of six days fishing.

The other big happening is the grand, small (trailered) boat voyage down the Cortez from Kino Bay in June. The fleet of about 30 members of the "Vagabundos Del Mar Sea of Cortez" Club consists of 16-foot to 28-foot craft. Most of them outdrive, with a few outboard powered. They cruise in squads of two or three buddy-boats and assemble at rendezvous places. Boat owners wishing to join the fleet (some of which will go all the way to Buena Vista) would get assurance of gas, etc., if they would make wishes known to Chet Sherman soon. — RAY CANNON

VAG JACKET PATCH DESIGNED

NOVEMBER 23, 1968—I have just received a letter from Chet Sherman, who has made several Cortez trips with groups. He is heading up a group known as "Vagabundos Del Mar—Sea of Cortez." A beautiful jacket patch has been designed and made available to members.

— RAY CANNON

FIRST FORMAL CLUB MEETING HELD

NOVEMBER 29, 1968—The fame of the Cortez will be greatly extended among owners of small trailerable boats and the news media of that field.

A letter from "Cap'n Jack" Arnold announces the first formal meeting of the newly organized "Vagabundos Del Mar Sea of Cortez" Club, to be held on Saturday, December 7 at 7:30 p.m., at the home of the organizer, Chet Sherman, Sepulveda, California.

The Club of Cortez adventurers is free from all attachments, encumbrances, or sponsorship, and with a minimum of cruising and other restrictions for each pair of boats.

Someday a limit on the membership number will need to be imposed, with other affiliated chapters getting organized.

The expansion will follow the boat buying craze now sweeping the country, and with the already crowded lakes, streams and bays of the U.S., the Sea of Cortez offers a world of room for cruising voyages, exploring, fishing, and a long list of outdooring activities. — RAY CANNON

EARLY MEMBERSHIP REQUIREMENTS

JULY 11, 1969—This year appears to be a big one for small boats launching at Puerto Kino.

Returning to Kino, our fleet met the problem of high waves rolling into the launching ramp, and some few skippers, Don Gordon and Whitey Whitestine, with his partner, Don Newton, included, chose to run down to zigzag through the sand bars at the mouth of Laguna de la Cruz, and into its calm waters.

As usual, Kino launching operator, Tiburcio Saucedo, took the boat trailers down and hauled the boats ashore on a fine, new ramp.

All three men earned my enthusiastic endorsement for full membership in that exclusive Club, the "Vagabundos

Issue No. 1 of the Vagabundos Del Mar club newsletter, *Chubasco*, March 1971. Chet Sherman's lead story begins: "Hola Amigo, big things are taking place within the Vagabundo Organization. As you can see by the current trip list many new cruises have been added. RAY CANNON'S June 1st Safari is growing and should be nothing but fun and adventure."

— COURTESY VAGABUNDOS DEL MAR

Del Mar de Cortez." To qualify for a membership in the "Vagabundos Del Mar de Cortez," the small boat skipper and crew must cruise across from Kino and down as far as Mulegé, and back. — RAY CANNON

SERENIDAD PIG ROAST

[From the 1970 Vag cruise, Ray's first reference to the now-famous Saturday night pig roast at Mulegé's Hotel Serenidad. Don Johnson, formerly the hotel's boat manager, had become an owner in 1968 with partners Fernando del Morel and Chester Mason.]

At Mulegé we visited all resorts, saw the water line being laid into the fine, newly expanded Hotel Punta Chivato, visited our old friend, Saul Davis, manager of the always delightful Hotel Mulegé; got a big embrace when we visited Cuca Woodworth, owner of the little spic-and-span Hotel Las Casitas. Had a drink and long visit with

Chet Sherman, founder and first president of the Vagabundos Del Mar Boat & Travel Club, with his trailer tongue extender at Puerto Escondido, c. 1974.

the Manager of Hacienda Mulegé, the charming old Mexican inn, or posada type of hotel.

Most of our group stayed at the Hotel Serenidad, where another old friend, Don Johnson, is co-operator and where he sees to supplying gas and supplies to the boats at his pier. Don had a whole pig barbecued for us on an old style spit beside the outdoor dining veranda. The evening was a gay one despite the day's slow fishing, due to the previous two days' wind. — RAY CANNON

FIRST "CHUBASCO" NEWSLETTER PUBLISHED

MARCH 31, 1971—The Vagabundos Del Mar Club's Vol. 1 No. 1 Bulletin, or flier, called the *Chubasco,* is now available to members and candidates for membership (annual dues $5.00). A schedule for about a dozen safari voyages is given in it. Included is the Sailfish Rodeo held at Guaymas, July 8, 9, 10, 11, and details of other exciting goings-on. This year the big trophies (including a Ray Cannon Cup) will be presented to the angler tagging and releasing the most sails. — RAY CANNON

CHET SHERMAN'S TONGUE EXTENDER

AUGUST 9, 1974—Chet Sherman, Vagabundos' President, created a lot of interest with a device he engineered for launching boats without getting his camper stuck in the soft beach mud or sand, or getting the camper's wheel bearings salt water-soaked. It is a 12-foot or more pipe fashioned as an extension of the trailer-car connection. Chet calls it a "wagon-tongue." At Santa Rosalía he pulled a heavy, loaded, 27-foot cabin cruiser out over mud when all other facilities had failed. — RAY CANNON

THE GUAYMAS BILLFISH TOURNAMENT

[The mid-July "Guaymas Tournament," officially called the Guaymas Sailfish Rodeo, was first held in 1948. One of the original organizers was Enrique Murillo, whose father, Fernando Murillo, according to Ray, caught the first sport fishing marlin on Mexico's west coast in 1929. (The first sport-caught marlin ever was landed by Tuna Club of Avalon member Edward Llewellen in 1903.)

Until the opening of Baja's Transpeninsular Highway in 1973, the majority of Vagabundos Del Mar club events and cruises launched boats at Kino Bay, on the Mexican mainland side of the Cortez, and there was more activity in the Guaymas/San Carlos area among club members than there is today. Participation in the Guaymas Sailfish Rodeo was heavy, and the club sponsored the annual Ray Cannon Conservation Award for the most billfish tagged and released. Club activities in the tournament continue to be coordinated by longtime member, Fred Harleman.

The Las Playitas Hotel and Trailer Park owned by Josefina Daniels was always "club headquarters" during the tournament, although many members also stayed at the San Carlos Marina owned by Eddie and Terri Ceroggman.

Ray concludes this column by mentioning a ride home from the tournament with Tony Schuck, who would become president of the Vagabundos Del Mar club after the death of Chet Sherman in 1996.]

AUGUST 21, 1974—Several of the Vagabundos Del Mar boats entered in the Guaymas Fishing Tournament anchored just in front of the Las Playitas Hotel and Trailer Park a few days before the big contest was to start.

Others stayed in San Carlos Bay where I had promised to revisit my friend of many years, Rafael Caballeros, organizer-builder and overall operator of the vast San Carlos resort complex. There were exciting parties going on every night and we were expected to attend all of them, and did.

After July 15, this side of the Cortez is thought to be too hot, but due to its close proximity to the mountains the area gets in on the cooling rains and breezes from mountain storms.

During a swell party at the splendid hillside home of Pete and Josefina Daniels we had veranda box seats for one of nature's finest fireworks. At the crescendo of the roaring "Donder and Blitzen," came the downpour to bring new life to backcountry deserts and general seasonal dryness.

Everyone was sure that fishing would be greatly improved by the heavy rain and it really was. And, as in previous years, the Vagabundos got a large share of the trophies.

The nightly cocktail fiestas excelled other years and each was held at the right place and time. The Yacht Club's shebang was a weigh-in and dockside *saluds,*

Vagabundos launching at the Guaymas Sailfish Rodeo. Below, Ray, in July 1971, with Enrique Murillo, one of the original organizers of the tournament.

moving to their clubhouse for dinner.

At a gourmet buffet given by and at the La Posada de San Carlos, Señor Caballeros was host. Dinner was served on the roof overlooking Bocochibampo Bay just at sunset. Clouds just above the Cortez horizon provided a couple of extra sunsets. Each like the whole Sea was ablaze. The native orchestra reacted with that sweet sad song about the final moments of a beautiful day.

The award dinner, dance, and ceremony for this 27th Guaymas Fishing Rodeo was most fittingly held on the spacious estate terrace of the Guaymas Fishing and Gun Club. I arrived early enough to see tournament director, Ernesto Zaragoza and his army of workers produce the fiesta. It looked like he was directing a movie spectacle. Some of the special foods were brought up from his fine new Restaurant del Mar.

The participation of the Vagabundos in this contest for the past few years had done much to enliven the holiday spirit, not only of the Tournament Committees but of the whole town. The big spring season for visiting tourists has been extended for two to three weeks.

A lot of credit is due to the Vagabundos Del Mar club officials and workers for arousing a kind of an old-time Fourth-of-July hoopla. All along the line, everyone in each of the several groups reported having rousing parties wherever they stopped for the night, on land or sea.

Returning home I joined up with Cap. Jack and Punkin, the Walt Webers, and Tony Schuck for a fun visit to Tucson. I rode back home with Tony, a real sportsman, with a refreshing sense of humor—thus ending the long and exciting trip in time and space on a fitting note.

— RAY CANNON

DOWN TO THE SEA IN LITTLE SHIPS

[This unpublished fragment, apparently intended for *The Sea Of Cortez*, but never used, expresses Ray's passion for small boat cruising, and might well have served as a founding credo for the adventurous band of small boat owners that formed the Vagabundos Del Mar Boat & Travel Club.]

To the young in spirit, no matter the years, to those with an inner ache to thrill once again with wild and true adventure, or who long to capture the storybook romance of cruising out in search of hidden treasure on an island, to explore painted caves for Indian artifacts, and like a primitive, live off of the fat of the land and waters, for all this and more, I say "go down to the sea in little ships."

Go for a voyage searching among the baylets, coves, and lagoons.

Go ashore, build a camp and spend a night in the wilds and hear the plaintive mating calls of creatures of the wilderness, the yowls and caterwauls of coyotes and cats challenging for your food, the thunderous gurgles of

The *Bella Donna*, owned by Vagabundos Del Mar Boat & Travel Club members, Marissa Divito and Larry Young, at speed off Isla la Raza during the club's 30th anniversary 1996 cruise to San Carlos. — PHOTO BY GENE KIRA

snoring whales making bedfellows of your boats, and the courting cries of the nocturnal birds and katydids, all accompanied with the background music of little waves breaking on the beach and the even more gentle winds.

Sleep, and breathe deeply of the primeval and tangy perfume wafted down on the balmy night breeze from blossoms of the wild hillside chaparral.

Wake up by the chuckles of sea fowls announcing the dawn, to swim in warm, clear water or dive into strange and beautiful marine gardens of flowering animals, succulent sea foods, and rare sea shells.

There are thousands of things to do, never before done by modern man in these vast and uninhabited places that once supported tens of thousands of Indians. You can cast for fish where no angler has dropped a hook, or cruise out to troll or bottom-fish, with complete assurance of success. You can sail on to new areas, each seeming more inspiring than the last.

Although this Sea is vast, its smooth surface, almost waveless beaches, bizarre islands, baroque shorelines and its wilderness character and abundant sea life make it ideal as a small craft wonder water-world. Not only for those who still cherish that precious inner spark for adventure, but for all of all ages who wish to rekindle it.

After spending half a lifetime in search of adventure in many of the remote places of the earth, I can now say with all truth, that small boat cruising in the Cortez provides the most exciting, most pleasurable, and most satisfying method of fulfilling that craving to experience the strange and unique in nature in the raw.

But I learned the hard way that these voyages can be enjoyed to the fullest only when they are well planned and carefully executed, and there are no shortcuts to thoroughness.

The Sea of Cortez is no place for the thoughtless. Beautiful, calm mornings may bewitch the careless outboarder to disaster; running down a favorable tide or breeze may speed him beyond the range of his fuel supply; a lack of knowledge of weather reports and seasonal storm conditions can prove hazardous. Much space in this volume is devoted to discussing the many aspects of boating. — RAY CANNON

Getting the perfect shot of a jumping needlefish during this 1959 shooting session at Rancho Buena Vista required a lot of film.

GIANT NEEDLEFISH

THE CRAZIEST THING IN THE SEA

RAY'S OLD MEXICAN skippers—people such as Jesús Araiza and Nicandro Cota of the East Cape Area, and Juan "Chi Chi" Meza of Mulegé—say that he loved to catch giant needlefish above all other species, and it seems fitting that the old movie director would find a kindred spirit in that spectacular, show-stopping leaper.

Ray discovered the effectiveness of trolling strips of bait over the water's surface during his first trip to Baja in 1947. While targeting needlefish in 1958, he refined the method into his "strip-skip" technique by tailoring the bait to make it throw up a wake, imitating a flyingfish skimming the surface of the water.

In these columns dating from 1958, Ray describes how he discovered the needlefish's "crazy" antics and how he learned to hook them, first by fouling them with slack line, and later by tailoring very small "skip-strip" baits.

AN ASTONISHING SIGHT

It was an astonishing sight. I'd been trolling a skip-bait for dolphin in the tropical Gulf of Lower California when a living missile burst out of the blue water and came vaulting across the surface as though shot from a torpedo tube. A long beak full of shiny green teeth opened wide as the weirdest-looking fish I'd seen in many a day came hurtling toward me in ten-foot leaps. Just when it seemed as if the awl-shaped snout of the mad thing would drive clear through the sides of the boat, it veered and smashed hell-bent into the skip-bait.

There wasn't time to think. Without conscious direction, my finger released the reel-brake and let line freespool into the sea—billowing yards of it. Through clouds of spray I saw the jaws of a beanpole-built fish clamp onto my bait, and saw its slim body spinning over and over in the wake. José yelled and revved the motor. I slammed on the brakes and when the line straightened I gripped the rod butt, yanked hard, and the thing shot ten feet up into the air.

Down it came, and its landing was even more spectacular than its leap because it bounced off the ocean surface as if it were a trampoline. Up it went again, its springy body twisting itself into figure-eights and its tail batting wildly at the line fastened around its beak. It bounded along the water, then shot higher than ever, stiff as a rake-handle, and hung there long enough for me to see that the hook had been flailed loose, but in its mad gyrations the thing had wound a dozen coils of line around its horny bill. It twisted downward, smacked the water again, and then caromed upward in four different directions and six shapes on the same take-off. On its final thrust for the moon, the thing suddenly ran out of rocket fluid and collapsed like a jointed tent pole. José reached out with his gaff and hauled it aboard.

"Agujón chico," he spluttered excitedly.

But that was only its Mexican folk name. I'd been studying the 300 and more kinds of game fish in the Gulf to do a book on the subject, so I knew this jumping string bean was a species Latin-named *Strongylura fodiator*, a rare oddball found only in the warm blue waters from Baja California to Peru. Other anglers had reported its streaking attack as they fished off Rancho Buena Vista south of La Paz. They had seen their trolled baits clipped in two, but had not been able to set a hook because the sharpest barb slid harmlessly off its bone-hard beak. A pure fluke on my part—the freespooling of loose line—had caused the whirling sixty-inch fish to weave a bird's nest around its bill.

The same technique continued to work for me. All thoughts of catching dolphin and other conventional game fishes of the Gulf were forgotten as José and I tied into the streamlined blue streaks. Mostly, the finned projectiles

Ray and a good-sized giant needlefish, or agujón, his favorite quarry of all.

came skipping with furious speed top-water. Then suddenly, one rocketed straight up from the deep blue; its toothed jaws snapped like a steel trap on the bait and carried it a dozen feet into the air as it twisted and turned and tied its limber length into every knot in the Boy Scout Manual.

The "thing" is not even classed as a game fish (except by José and me) but it belongs, brother, it belongs! In addition, we found its translucent white flesh so delicately flavored that the next time we troll a skip-bait off Baja California I'll be all set to feed gobs of free line to another one of these Giant Needlefish; in my book the craziest thing in the sea. — RAY CANNON

TAILERING A SKIP-BAIT

[Ray discovers how to tailor the bait to make it skip like a small flyingfish.]

FEBRUARY 15, 1958—The giant four-foot-long needlefish, *Strongylura fodiator*, seems destined to become one of the most popular game fishes in the Gulf and up the outer coastline of Baja California.

Learning to catch this surf-skipping arrow which travels as if shot from a bow or bazooka has been an aggravating task. For years I have thrown everything in the book at it and was unable to get any consistent cooperation. Once in a great while one would make a daring pass at my lure or bait and get itself snagged but getting it to swallow something seemed impossible until a couple of weeks ago.

I knew the needle would have a go at a strip-bait,

especially sierra, but rarely get hooked. An accident gave me the clue to the effective technique.

While trolling for dolphinfish, by skipping the bait, I let out extra line to avoid tangling with the line of my fishing partner when the boat was turning for retracing our course. This slowed the trolled bait to about two or three knots. A big needlefish struck but clipped only half of the seven-inch strip. I replaced the stub with a well tailored strip about three inches long and nailed a wild jumper but he flipped the hook. On my next try I presented the same size bait but on a No. 2. short-shank hook instead of the large 6/0 Siwash used for dolphinfish.

I had often seen a large needlefish chasing the small flyingfish and decided to create the illusion by cutting the bait so it would throw up a winglike wake. Back over the same stretch at about three knots and it happened! My attention was attracted by a splashing break 200 feet to port of our stern. Here came the most streamlined of the sea's missiles zipping above the surface and glancing off it like a bullet or a thrown flat rock. Each bounce and it was airborne for another 20 feet until it struck.

This four-footer was on no romp. He had a bead on that bait and aimed a perfectly timed takeoff for a bull's-eye hit. I payed freewheeling line to give the small-throated fish time to swallow the hook. I eased up to a taut line and set the hook—somewhere in the vicinity of his gall.

That baby executed half-a-dozen leaps which were spectacular enough to qualify it as a rating game fish if for no other reason. But the aerial activity was to be repeated with twirls in which he used his dragon-toothed beak as a spindle, in a contest trying to wind more of my leader and line around it than I could on my reel spool— and he nearly won.

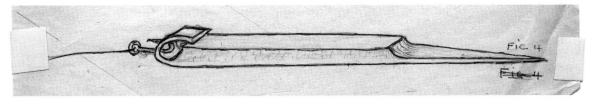

An early drawing from Ray's notes of how to rig the skip-strip bait. About 1959, Ray wrote: "Skip-strip is first cut as strip-bait… then thinned at head and tail ends. The hook is inserted back of the broader head end, giving it a toboggan shape when trolled at about four or five knots, or fast enough (depending on the wind) so it will throw up wake sprays as it sleds along on the surface…"

My skipper, Laborio, lived up to his name as he labored to deck the critter without a gaff. Whether by superstition or some unfortunate past experience, Laborio was not about to get his hands near those needle-sharp rows of bright green canines, even when they were battened down with wraps of my line.

Using the skip-strip technique, we were able to repeat the procedure again and again, keeping the Lodge larder well stocked with the top food fish of them all. People who are unable to down a single morsel of fish, go overboard for the frog-leg flavor of the needlefish.

No, the needlefish is not related to garfish, barracuda or marlin but is a member of the needlefish family *Belonidae*. It is sometimes called "little marlin" by natives of the area. Some say the young have large spreading pectoral fins and can fly. I have seen a halfbeak, which resembles a needlefish, outdo a flyingfish by gliding a couple of hundred yards without touching water. — RAY CANNON

NEEDLEFISH TECHNIQUE CONFIRMED COLONEL WALTERS VISITS THE RANCH

[Ray describes fishing with retired U.S. Army Colonel Eugene Walters, recently returned from Europe, who Ray said was ready to move to Baja and "give all the Mediterranean Sea back to the Romans." In less than a year—on January 5, 1959—Herb Tansey would be killed in a plane crash, and a few months after that, Colonel Walters would begin a second career, as the new owner of Rancho Buena Vista.]

LORETO, MAY 2, 1958—The giant 50-inch needlefish is abundant here and I am happy to report that "skip-strip" bait sends them into the vaulting jitters, just as it did at Buena Vista.

What's so important about a needlefish in a fishing world of marlin, dolphinfish, roosterfish, and a hundred other game species, you wonder? It is that this one has been elevated from just another uncommon and ignored creature, to the status of game fish first-class, in the past four months.

Discovering the spectacular jumping qualities and technique for catching this one with any degree of consistency was something like finding a new planet. In a recent column I exploded with enthusiasm describing how the needle would get a bead on a skip-strip, take to the air and come skipping across the surface in ten-foot leaps to nail the bait; then go into a series of leaps, finishing up in a Whirling Dervish spin in which he used his eight-inch beak like a cotton spindle, winding leader and line around it. Even more important is finding this fish taking the same bait and performing in the same manner in yet another area and at a different season. The find here at Loreto approaches proof that I have unveiled a real glamour fish. Add to this the quite general opinion that it is the very best food fish of El Golfo and you can begin to see why I am raving. Here also I learned that a half-yardstick-size needle can be caught on a smaller skip-bait.

After fishing a couple of quiet hours off Nopoló Cove this morning I noticed a needle make a pass at a sierra feather. I started cutting bait. As soon as the first strip started sledding on the surface and resembling a small Gulf flyingfish about to take off, a sizable needle got a bead on it from 50 feet away. He arrowed up above the water for a series of four or five vaults, barely touching the surface between the rock-skipping leaps. At the end of the last he made a perfect bull's-eye as he nailed the bait. After paying a hundred yards of line, freewheeling, I set the hook and "shook up" members of the crew by yelling "MARLIN!" There is quite a resemblance to the billfish in the first few leaps of a hooked needle.

Just about every angler fishing the Gulf may have at one time or another accidentally snagged a few needlefish on various types of lures, but not until the introduction of the skip-strip bait have I heard of any consistent degree of success in catching them.

I expect that a majority of the 20 anglers joining my June 7 fishing safari down here will also join me in singing the praises of the newest "Leaping Lena." Enrique Ortega of International Travel Service reports the list of participants in the event is about full. At present I am doing some advance work checking new fish holes and facilities for the June trip. Colonel Eugene Walters cut short a trip through Europe to join me on this one. Two days of fishing and a feel of the climate and he is ready to move down here. Says he is ready to give all the Mediterranean Sea back to the Romans. — RAY CANNON

"Shipwreck Beach"—located about ten kilometers up the Transpeninsular Highway from Cabo San Lucas—was a longtime camping and small boat launching place for area locals, and one of its main attractions was its eponymous "shipwreck," the huge, rusting hulk of the Japanese long-liner, *Inari Maru No. 10*, which went aground in the surf there in 1965. The hulk has now been greatly reduced by the elements. A broken steering mechanism is the most commonly given reason for the wreck, but a popular legend tells of a moored radio beacon that was rowed ashore by local fishermen in a successful attempt to sabotage foreign fishing for marlin and sailfish within Mexican coastal waters. Baja shipwreck historian Peter Jensen reports that the *Inari Maru No. 10* simply went aground for reasons that have not been determined, at night, in a southeast wind, with no loss of life. Whatever the reasons, the wreck of the *Inari Maru No. 10* became a symbol of foreign commercial fishing in the waters of Baja California. — PHOTO BY AL TETZLAFF

STORM CLOUDS ON THE HORIZON

RAY'S LIFELONG CONSERVATION EFFORTS

WHEN RAY CANNON was born in 1892, there were still a small number of passenger pigeons in the wild, reduced to a few scattered flocks from the billions that had once darkened the skies of the United States. (The last known wild bird was shot in 1910 in Pike County, Ohio.)

Amazingly, there were also a few wild buffalo still roaming the remnants of the Great Plains; in 1893 the wild herd was estimated at 300, down from about 60 million originally.

It is perhaps logical that a man born into the aftermath of such destruction would become the dedicated conservationist that he was. Although he is generally remembered today simply as a "sport fishing writer" and, unfairly, as a "meat fisherman," Ray was actually much more complex than that. What is not generally known about him is that while he tolerated the excesses of ignorant early "sport" anglers as a temporary evil necessary to promote the industry, he himself had evolved quite early into a dedicated proponent of light-tackle, catch-and-release fishing for mixed species.

Ray's favorite fish to catch was the unglamorous, acrobatic needlefish, and he wrote of it as often as possible. But he knew that in order to popularize the sport fishing industry—which he saw as a vital economic partner of the nascent conservation movement—he would have to tolerate and even encourage the taking of large numbers of fish by the resorts.

Nevertheless, Ray wrote tirelessly—from the beginning of his career until a few weeks before his death—about the dangers of pollution and the importance of protecting the sea and its fish. He wrote more columns on conservation than on any other theme, and as the public gradually became better informed about the dangers of overfishing, he became more and more outspoken in his published work.

Ray was also a lifelong foe of commercial fishing in any form other than individual skiff fishermen using hand-lines. Throughout his outdoor writing career, it is unknown if he ever addressed the question of how the world's supply of consumable protein foods would be affected if commercial fishing were actually banned, as he sometimes suggested should happen. Nevertheless, he consistently advocated the development of sport fishing and what today would be called "ecotourism" as alternate, less damaging, and ultimately, more profitable means of making economic use of the sea's resources.

In this respect, Ray's thinking was far ahead of his time. His theories anticipated by many decades today's growing worldwide trend toward "aquaculture," in which farmed seafoods seem destined ultimately to displace wild-caught products from the marketplace. The present escalation of market prices for seafood—set against the spectre of a global catch that continues to decline, despite greatly-increased effort—seems to indicate that farmed seafoods will come to dominate the consumer market, just as farmed red meats and poultry products do today.

By the time *Western Outdoor News* was launched in 1953, Ray had already developed his theories—later confirmed—that the removal of basic forage species such as sardine and anchovy was the worst possible practice in the management of any fishery, because all other fish would then be required to leave the area or starve. He had been fishing the California coast since about 1912, and he had witnessed the destruction not only of the sardine population, but also of mackerel, halibut, white seabass, croaker, and other easily-caught commercially valuable species.

Only three months after the launching of *Western Outdoor News*, Ray wrote a column about the anchovy decimation then occurring off the California coast. It was the beginning of hundreds of columns that would expound on the theme of conservation—and the politics of conservation—for the next 24 years.

In 1953, the anchovy had just come under greatly

increased commercial fishing pressure, after the collapse of the sardine fishery during the preceding 1952-53 season.

Sardines had been netted off the West Coast of the United States and British Columbia since the early 1900s, but commercial pressure was greatly increased when the fish began to be used not only for direct human consumption, but also for fertilizer and animal feed. For example, the catch increased from 16,000 to 70,000 tons in the course of a single year, 1917-18.

The sardine industry peaked in 1936-37, when 790,000 tons were taken from the West Coast (663,000 tons from California). During this period, scientific studies published by the California Fish & Game Commission recommended maximum sustainable catches of between 200,000 and 250,000 tons per year. This advice was ignored by a state legislature that—for political reasons—continued to allow virtually unrestricted sardine harvesting.

Following the record season of 1936-37, the catch fell steadily. In the 1951-52 season, only 145,000 tons were caught. Then—in the following year—the bottom dropped out, with a catch of only 14,873 tons in 1952-53. The sardine industry never recovered and most boats were redirected to the catching of anchovy and other species.

It was against the backdrop of this sad story that *Western Outdoor News* was launched in December 1953, and Ray Cannon began his career of promoting sport fishing, not only as a means of finding personal enjoyment and fulfillment, but also as a foundation for political and economic forces that would work to protect the environment.

It was too late to save the sardines and other fish of the U.S. West Coast, but in Baja California and the Sea of Cortez, Ray undoubtedly imagined that the force of his writing might yet help to preserve what he saw as the richest, most beautiful, and most valuable fishery of all. As he helplessly witnessed the destruction of Baja California's great totuava runs, horizon-stretching yellowtail and yellowfin tuna schools, and even the seemingly limitless masses of forage fish, Ray meanwhile worked to the limits of his strength for the building of the great resorts of the Golden Age and the founding of the modern tourist industry that has at last—in the closing years of this century—begun seriously to protect the precious natural gifts that make this miraculous Mexican peninsula unique in the world.

Following are Ray's best columns and writings on the important subject of conservation—and the devastation of the fisheries of Southern California and Baja California— written as he witnessed it from 1954 to 1976:

U.S. ANCHOVY ENDANGERED

MARCH 19, 1954—Life and death of the $15 million sport fishing industry hangs in the balance.

Here is the reason; it is the story of the northern anchovy and its present condition, developed from recent scientific data.

In 1955 Ray was appointed to the California Marine Research Committee by Governor Goodwin Knight. In photo, Ray, left, is congratulated by Manning Moore, center, president of the Ocean Fish Protective Association (O.F.P.A.), and Andy Kelly, a member of the State Fish & Game Commission. Ray's appointment to the Marine Research Committee was hailed by O.F.P.A. as "a tremendous boost for the sportsman because it marks the first time a member of the sportsmen's group has had a representative on the committee. Cannon received overwhelming support from all clubs in the area and has expressed his appreciation and has dedicated his actions to the furtherance of sport fishing protection." — COURTESY WESTERN OUTDOOR NEWS

Predator fishes must eat, and along our Southern California coast they have depended, for the bulk of their supply, upon six forage animals: the sardine, young Pacific mackerel, saury, squid, shrimp, and anchovy. All other forms must be considered of minor importance.

The sardine and young mackerel have ceased to serve as forage. The saury is not a shore fish; it serves only the tunas, marlin and other deep sea species. Squid occur only in pockets many miles apart. Little is known about the abundance of shrimp. This leaves us with the anchovy, the one forage fish capable of supplying a consistent food trail along our coast.

The great purse seine fleet, no longer able to find mackerel and sardines, have spent the past year concentrating upon the mackerel jack (Spanish mackerel) and the anchovy. The mackerel jack will be cleaned up within a year or so, according to reports. The anchovy population between Point Conception and Point Reyes was all but wiped out by the intense netting in 1952 when 22,000 tons were taken. Less than 9,000 tons were caught in 1953. Then for ten months none could be located.

This depletion may prove disastrous to the whole saltwater angling sport north of Point Conception, and Southern California is apt to be next. And now the seiners have moved south of Point Conception.

Compared to the sardine and mackerel, which withstood the onslaught for many years, the anchovy is very weak. It is preyed upon by almost every ocean fish, crustacean, and other animal, from egg to maturity; and it is doubtful if any anchovy ever had a chance to die of old age. The moment he weakened and dropped out of the school, hundreds of creatures were there to get him.

It is in this great forage demand that we see the story unfolding that looks so frightening. Nature's balances were maintained before man started to break into the picture, but when he began to take 22,000 tons of anchovy, the great host of the predators all but captured the last of them and may well complete the job in another year or so.

Another weakness of the anchovy is in its movements. It moves slowly and is believed to remain in the locality of a few miles range with little or no intermingling with neighboring populations. This was indicated when eight-inch anchovies were plentiful above Point Magu years after they were reduced to a six-inch maximum south of the point. When fish do not migrate, the destruction of a local population could prove the end of them in that area.

Fossilized skeletons of fishes now extinct prove that an ocean species can be totally wiped out. These extinct fishes were no doubt exterminated by their enemies when disease or lack of food reduced their numbers below that certain survival point, as man is doing today.

All concern about the great decline in the number of game fish available to the angler fades into insignificance compared to the havoc that would be wrought if the anchovy were wiped out. If that should happen, as it now appears likely, would not the game fishes prey upon the young of each other until many species would become depleted? — RAY CANNON

ENSENADA ANCHOVY DECIMATION

JULY 2, 1965—A large new anchovy packing plant has been added to Ensenada's Cannery Row and construction is about to start on another even larger processor.

It seems easy to predict that with modern methods of locating fish schools, the anchovy population in northern Baja California waters will be depleted within two years.

Anchovy, canned and labeled "Sardines," will likely get a quick brush-off in the Mexican market. The product is too soft and mushy and it is watery. The plants have considered this and have already bought large machinery for processing the anchovy to fish meal.

These attempts to develop a huge anchovy fishery by Mexicans was no doubt stimulated by U.S. commercials demanding legislative action to lift the ban on reducing anchovy and permit them to make fish meal, 200-thousand tons which would be caught below the border. This according to the U.S. purse seiners, would be only an experiment.

Very few legislators, marine scientists, and practically no angler or others engaged in sport fishing believe that the anchovy population could withstand a commercial onslaught.

One of the first results to be expected from devastation of anchovy below the border will be a halting of yellowtail and perhaps white seabass migrations up into Southern California. A break in the food supply along the migration swimway could hold back recruitment into Southern California for many years, or until some food item builds up to take the depleted anchovy's place, and it is not all likely to be sardine.

The threat to Ensenada's sport fishery is imminent and it could be wiped out this year if the seiners have a successful anchovy season. — RAY CANNON

STATE-SANCTIONED GRAB

NOVEMBER 19, 1965—Mexico, like most every other country on earth, is having a fantastic population explosion. If it keeps doubling as it has in the past few years, Mexico will be looking to the sea for food, and find it depleted. Not by anglers but by nets.

The netting of anchovy for the fish meal grinders at Ensenada is one of the quickest methods of eliminating their immense populations of large food fish.

The most important limiting factors of fish population quantities are food supply and predators. The netters being the most destructive predators of all.

The destruction of the sardine factory fishery by purse seiners is the classic example of man's predatory greed and bribe-taking politicians who allowed it. In the U.S., payoffs and graft, called "campaign contributions" solicited by state law makers, tax assessors and departments, are creating such a disrespect for law, widespread rebellion against the "system" seems imminent, if the swelling popularity of demonstrating is a sign.

Several years ago 30,000 tons of anchovy were netted in Monterey Bay, wiping out the local anchovy population and with it went a fine salmon fishery. The place was almost like a desert for three years when a few young anchovy that drifted in on a current made a partial comeback, but some game fish gave the bay a wide berth for several years. The anchovy does not go for long migrations like the sardine. Once depleted in a large area,

ls **Fishermen bemoan vanishing sardine**

DR. FRANCES CLARK SAYS OCEAN OVER-FISHED
State marine biologist warns nature can't keep up with hauls

Definite air of compromise develops in UN sessions

LAKE SUCCESS, N. Y., Oct. 30.-(P)-A definite air of conciliation spread through the United Nations today, with many little country delegates expressing cautious optimism that a trend may be developing.

Observers saw at least a temporary victory for middle-of-the-road influences which have persuaded both the United States and Russia to yield a little in their extreme positions, usually poles apart.

During the last 24 hours, the eastern or western blocs compromised on warmongering, Palestine and the Little Assembly. Only on the Korean problem did the United States and Russia stand un-

American Delegate John Foster Dulles said the move would delay Korean independence at least a year. He urged instead, in an amendment to the Russian motion, that consultation of Korean spokesmen be left to the temporary UN commission proposed in the overall United States plan to save the way for Korean independence with elections next March 31.

In a radio broadcast last night

California's $60,000,000 fishing industry was biting its fingernails today over the awful truth that there are NOT more sardines in the ocean than can ever be caught.

The finny tidbits have all but disappeared from northern waters and a greatly expanded fleet off San Pedro—last haunt of the elusive sardine—has fished itself into the scuppers and caught a load of bad news.

Even here, where invading boats from as far away as Seattle have doubled the usual fleet, the catch for the first month of the new season yesterday chalked up a 25 per cent dip from last year's already sagging figure.

No sardines are being taken off British Columbia, Washington and Oregon and cannery operators in San Francisco and Monterey report they can't get enough to "dirty up the cannery line."

Everything from changing conditions in the ocean to piscatorial war nerves has been blamed, but one trim, energetic woman — Dr. Frances N. Clark, aquatic biologist for the Bureau of Marine Fisheries of the State Division of Fish and Game—disagrees.

She disputes with industry spokesmen and the United States Fish and Wildlife Service that billions of sardines have gone elsewhere because they don't like their historic haunts.

Dr. Clark — impressively bulwarked by charts, graphs and studies covering more than two decades — declares the sardines haven't gone anywhere except between crackers and into meal and oil.

To biologist Dr. Clark, the vanishing sardine is not a phenomenon—it's a simple case of the industry beheading and detailing the little fellows faster than nature can replace them.

As early as 1939, she warned yesterday, she warned that the catch must be regulated in proportion to the supply and spawning survival.

"You can't have your sardines and eat them," she observed.

Dr. Clark said she hasn't much hope for good sardine fishing off the Pacific Coast until there's realistic regulation or an exceptionally good spawning survival—and there hasn't been an outstanding hatch of sardines since 1939.

Dr. Clark's theory is based upon a study of the industry since its local inception during World War I.

From 1916, when 28,000 tons of sardines were taken from coastal waters, to the peak season of 1936-1937, the catch rose to 800,-000 tons, of which 726,000 tons came from offshore California.

Tremendous inroads were made during the depression years by offshore floating reduction plants, unrestricted by state limits, which

Dr. Frances N. Clark of the Bureau of Marine Fisheries for the California Division of Fish & Game, testifies in October 1947 on the dangers of over harvesting sardines off the California coast. This was the year of Ray's first trips to Baja, the very beginning of the Golden Age, and a time when the California sardine was already in deep trouble. The first California sardine cannery opened in Monterey in 1901. — COURTESY LOS ANGELES DAILY NEWS

a comeback would be close to impossible, as most all sizable sea creatures eat anchovy and would keep them cleaned out.

There is a general feeling among California anglers that the anchovy grab is on and that there is something rotten, or at least very fishy, in the latest opening of the anchovy flood gates.

There is much more hope south of the border where the anchovy has already faltered. Mexican authorities become greatly concerned when tourism is threatened or when the people's food supply is in danger. — RAY CANNON

BAJA RESEARCH DESPERATELY NEEDED

[Ray's first known column on Baja California conservation focuses on the immediate need for scientific research and proactive environmental advocacy. Also mentioned, the vulnerability and the pending collapse of the totuava fishery of the northern Cortez.]

JULY 19, 1956—A scientific research program in the Gulf of California is desperately needed—now. We must not wait 50 years as we have done on the Pacific Coast before starting the required vital studies.

The Gulf will soon become our fishing hole. A half-million Californians will be driving and flying to that region of abundances within the next two or three years, if not sooner.

When a spawning population is fished below the level where its young will not supply the predator demand, it cannot come back and there is no magic formula in nature to remedy the condition.

I have heard theories that when man reduces a fish population down to the point where it no longer interests him, nature will see to it that the species regains its former numbers. I have not yet found any proof of such opinions. Fossil skeletons of numerous species now extinct prove that whole fish populations can be wiped out completely and that nature showed no inclination to restore them.

The totuava in the Gulf is apparently vulnerable to overfishing and other acts of man, principally because of its very limited spawning area and range. It seems to be confined to the north end of the Gulf and is found no other place.

If we had certain scientific facts, Mexico, a very conservation-minded country, would move quickly to save this important species. With little more than a suspicion of depletion, the Secretary of Marine Affairs of the state of Baja California has succeeded in establishing a regulation prohibiting anglers from taking more than one totuava across the border.

But there are other correctable problems. Among them, the possibility that not enough fresh water will be flowing into the Colorado River estuary to support the spawning grounds. This condition may also effect the spawning of two or three species of corvina.

Other fish populations in the Gulf may be limited in their range to a single rocky area and if fished out would not be repopulated for years. Signs of this have already appeared.

Every attempt should be made at once to stimulate our state and federal governments to get a well-calculated program going.

Fishing in the Gulf is wonderful. Let's plan to help keep it that way. — RAY CANNON

SPEAR FISHING TOURNAMENT CONCERNS

[Ray speaks out strongly against killing large resident bass-like fish in this article, c. 1961, about a spear fishing tournament proposed in Mexico.]

In a recent report, Ralph Davis, representing the Inter-American Diving Championship Meet for 1962, is quoted as stating that the competition will be held at Guaymas, Sonora, Mexico. But according to a Mexican official concerned with fisheries, the meet may run into legal problems.

Expressing his personal opinion, he fears the very purpose of the meet will create ill-will against divers in general.

"With awards to be given to the team bringing in the greatest number of pounds of fish, there could be a considerable slaughter, especially of the more or less helpless groupers, cabrillas and black sea bass, which are trapped in caves and holes by divers.

"Being an amateur diver myself, I consider spearing these giant basses about as sportsmanlike as shooting fat hogs in a pig sty. If these professional divers are as heroic as their posed pictures and stories indicate, they should contest for the more worthy opponents, the sharks. Then they would be appreciated and praised by others than their own group."

Certainly the good official's opinions are worth some serious discussions. Seeing a diving team bring in 400 pounds of fish in a championship meet at Guaymas a few years ago, and having reports of divers taking carloads of fish to sell in the U.S., the Mexican government's Fisheries Department became concerned. A law prohibiting divers from taking any basses or other native fishes, such as snappers, was enacted. This was partially relaxed, but another massive haul could trigger legal action that would deprive thousands of individual amateur divers from enjoying the fine sport the Sea of Cortez provides.

The wisdom of contesting for highly-prized food fishes is being questioned wherever it is practiced, more especially when the largest number of pounds of fish determines the winner. I have not heretofore entered this debate but I certainly will when the giant basses of the Cortez become the object of such contests.

Because these fish seldom migrate from the small area of their habitats, and because these giants require 50 to 75 years to grow to a hundred or so pounds, they are depletable by overfishing. This has already been proved in some isolated spots.

Regulations on commercial fishing for the larger bass species has already been enacted and discussions now going on may place stricter limits on angler and diver catches.

A thorough classification of the present laws should be requested and rules revised accordingly before any diver or angler derbies or tournaments are planned in the Cortez.

— RAY CANNON

LETTER TO PESCA

[In a prescient letter written in 1963 to the Mexican Department of Fisheries, Ray foresees coming problems and proposes solutions. The correctness of Ray's analysis of the relative value to the Mexican economy of a sport-caught fish—as compared to the same fish caught for commercial purposes—is a key factor in the development of Baja California's modern tourist industry, especially when it is applied not only to sport fishing but to all forms of ecotourism. Ray's use of the term "albacora" in this letter is a reference to the Spanish term for the yellowfin tuna, not the long-finned tuna called "albacore" by English-speakers.]

March 19, 1963
Oficina de Pesca
San Pedro, California

After a ten-year, full-time study of the fishes and fishing in the Gulf of California (Sea of Cortez), more especially along the little-known coast and coastal islands of Baja California, I have found some few problems that may interest your governmental department.

Because of the productivity of enormous food supplies for the fishes and highly suitable environment for spawning, very few fish populations will ever be overfished by hook-and-line anglers. They catch only a small percentage from a school. Netters are likely to capture the whole school.

There are, however, some native fish populations that could be depleted by anglers and divers in localized isolated areas. Certain members of the bass family, *Serranidae*, especially groupers, cabrillas, black sea bass and mero (jewfish), and a few members of the (pargo) snapper family, *Lutjanidae*, because of their habit of remaining in very small and limited habitats.

A bag limit of five of all species in the aggregate of these two families seems appropriate; but a bag limit of one only, for those basses or snappers weighing more than 40 pounds. None should be netted.

Yellowfin tuna (albacora), *Neothunnus macropterus*:
The present pressure on the migrating yellowfin tuna by purse seiners appears close to the limit. Additional tuna boats licensed to fish Mexican waters seems unadvisable. For two good reasons none should be allowed in bays or within three miles of a line between outer points. These are: the destruction of near-shore fishes, and for protection of tuna schools that have taken up permanent habitat, remaining near shore the year round. This prohibition should be especially applied to Los Muertos and Las Palmas Bays. These bays should be reserved for anglers and small hook-and-line commercials out of La Paz and the resorts and villages around these bays.

The totuava population seems to be rapidly declining and may not survive many years of net fishing. If strictly regulated, I do not believe it would be depleted if caught only by hook and line. This species rarely feeds, if at all, during the migration before spawning in the Colorado River mouth. Thus, hook-and-line fishermen are unable to catch them during these critical runs northward, but only after the fish is spent. There would be no reason to have closed seasons for hook-and-line fishermen but anglers should be limited to one totuava (regardless of size) per day, and allowed to take no more than one back across the border. This because there is an increasing number of U.S. anglers fishing the region.

There may be one or two other reasons than netting for the totuava decline. The most likely is overfishing shrimp (food for young fish) near the Colorado. The other is the reduction of fresh water in the lower Colorado, which seems essential in early stages of the very young totuava.

These same influences may also be affecting the orangemouth and shortfin corvinas, which appear to have similar spawning habits. It seems wise to sustain an angler bag limit of five in the aggregate of these two species.

No fish should be taken across the border without the head and tail attached, by anglers, commercials, or anyone else. Only by this procedure can border inspectors recognize species. Exceptions for smoked or canned fish only. This to encourage native processing for anglers, as is now done successfully in most U.S. shore towns.

Concentrated or expanded commercial fishing for all species mentioned should not be encouraged. Contests, derbies, or tournaments which include any of these native species should be prohibited, especially when awards are based on the largest fish, number of fish, or number of pounds. Additional and special regulations should be set for scuba divers.

The economy of Mexico is benefited much more by having a U.S. angler catch a fish than by a commercial fisherman. Even in the north end of the Gulf the angler will spend (in Mexico) from $15 to $40 to catch one totuava or large bass, many times more than a commercial fisherman would receive. Therefore, angling should be welcomed and encouraged, especially in the south, where they spend hundreds of dollars.

The most destructive dynamiting of fish should be discouraged by heavy jail sentence penalties. Vast areas around La Paz and other resort cities have destroyed feeding grounds for large fish and now remain almost deserted. — RAY CANNON

SAVE THE TOTUAVA

[A year before the collapse, Ray warns that gill netting of totuava in the extreme northern Cortez will soon wipe out the once-enormous schools of the giant croaker that is capable of growing as large as a marlin. Dynamiting is often cited as a reason the totuava were wiped out, but the gill net was the primary method. Today, totuava survive in small pods of fish to about 30 pounds, and although protected, some are still killed illegally by both sport anglers and commercial fishermen.]

JULY 3, 1964—Many anglers who have fished totuava over a period of years are convinced that San Felipe is on a suicide course, and they predict that within another three or four years, buzzards will be occupying the main buildings.

The decline may not happen quite that fast but unless some drastic regulations on netting the popular king-size croakers are established by next year, both the angler and netter will likely find the fishing so poor and unprofitable, they will all be out of business and bring misery to the local population.

There are clear indications that the introduction of large nets in the totuava fishery has reduced the early February spawners to almost zero, and cut down the March migrators (once super-abundant) to a few thin schools. In the last year or so, the netting pressure has raised havoc with the April and May runs.

Up to the past two years, the lack of flooding fresh water from the Colorado River was thought to have cut down the totuava spawning success, but this would not have reduced the number of February and March spawners any more than in the following months.

I doubt that hand-line fishing, as done before nets were used, would have much, if any, effect on the totuava population. Since the migrators refuse baits on their way up the Colorado River, they would at least get a chance to spawn before being caught.

Although the net is more efficient, more natives could make a living if they go back to the old hook-and-line method.

Discussions of the vanishing totuava at this time of year is of the utmost importance if something is to be done. Mexican officials are as responsive to pressure letters as are our own, but they have more effect if sent in by Mexican nationals. U.S. anglers can help by sending this—

Frigate birds searching for forage fish on the Sea of Cortez. — PHOTO BY AL TETZLAFF

"Save the Totuava" message to a Mexican friend.

The officials must be made aware of the loss to the economy if the tens of thousands of anglers quit going to San Felipe and how a far greater number would go if they heard that netting was prohibited.

A crash campaign should rightly be conducted by the Mexican Bureau of Tourism, which is well aware of the incentive stimulated by angling in the Cortez, and of the far greater value to the Mexican economy of an angler-caught totuava above one taken commercially. — RAY CANNON

TOTUAVA DISASTER

[A year later, the predicted totuava collapse materializes as San Felipe experiences the near-disappearance of a once-thriving sport fishery.]

JUNE 4, 1965—As a great commercial and game fish, the giant, up to 300-pound totuava seems close to losing its popularity, if not its very existence.

The once enormous migrating schools have now been reduced to a scattered few, which because of their peculiar spawning habit, may now be too depleted to reproduce a sustaining number.

This great croaker which once drew as many as 10,000 people for an Easter weekend to San Felipe, will cease to attract any visiting anglers unless drastic action is taken to halt gill netting.

Like many other saltwater fishes the totuava broadcast their eggs and milt in open water. Unless the school is large and compact, the eggs are not so likely to get fertilized. Therefore, the thinner and smaller the schools—as totuava schools have become—the less chance there is for a successful spawn.

The rapid decline of the totuava population started with the introduction of the gill net in numbers about eight years ago, and all too often whole schools were netted before they spawned. This was not possible when commercial fishing was done with hooks and hand-lines, as the egg and milt-filled fish would not eat. Even after spawning, only a few out of each school were taken by hook and line.

It may take a half century or more for a totuava to grow to 200 or 300 pounds, and these large fish are going rapidly. Even more tragic is the lessening number of very young fish, which suggests spawning failures.

Now comes another threat, *i.e.*, an almost complete blocking of fresh water from the lower Colorado River. Brackish water is believed to be essential to totuava spawning success. A crash scientific study program of this should be started before it is too late for natural research.

A complete breakdown of the economy of San Felipe and the halting of a promising growth of El Golfo de Santa

Ray, c. 1972, with National Marine Fisheries biologist James L. Squire Jr., right, and Jesús Araiza, then a skipper at Rancho Buena Vista, whom Squire called the "kingpin" of the billfish tag-and-release program.

Clara seems certain unless the totuava fishery can be saved. I believe a four or five-year moratorium on gill netting could halt the decline and give scientists time to plan a sustaining management. — RAY CANNON

TOURISM A VIABLE, LONG-TERM ALTERNATIVE TO COMMERCIAL FISHING

SEPTEMBER 29, 1970—Often, when I write of a fish species as being super-abundant, commercial fishermen mistakenly think I am saying that there is a vast fish population that could hold out against purse seiners and other netters indefinitely. Then, after a superficial examination and finding fish plentiful in the spot at the time I mentioned, they go overboard investing considerable sums in establishing a large enterprise, then go for a bust.

Having heard of my repeated reference to the massive quantity of round herring and sardine in the waters of the Midriff, a sizable Mexican (or Portuguese) firm is said to have dropped $100,000 in a sardine packing plant just below Bahía Kino, only to discover that the canable sardine in the Cortez was limited in range to the cool waters of the Midriff, a belt averaging 60 miles in width and length. Or just about enough to support ten percent of Mexico City's cats, on a sustaining basis.

A second enterprise is catching all kinds of fish and sea creatures, principally for fish meal for chicken food and liquid fertilizer. Both factories were doing a thorough job of destroying the great sport fishing potential, which would bring in $1,000 for every $1 produced by commercials.

Tourism is the big business of Mexico, and it is not chicken feed.

Puerto Kino has had a history of disastrous failures due to poor planning. I don't know how many times sea product enterprises went from boom to poof. But when I arrived there for the first time in 1957, it had become a ghost town for the fifth time.

Since then I have written several hundred columns and feature articles on the several advantages of launching small boats to cruise and fish the Midriff and down the fantastic coastline of the Baja California Territory. These and other favorable publicity have encouraged a gradual development far larger and more important than ever before.

The future benefit to Mexico in keeping Kino Bay as a sport fishing and small craft port is immense. Five to ten-thousand small boats from everywhere west of Chicago and Dallas can be expected, with families spending their vacation time and money around the Sea of Cortez.

The success of Kino Bay as a small craft port will encourage development of others.

I am confident that the new President-elect, Luis Echeverría, and his cabinet members concerned will give Puerto Kino much profound thought and make it an example to follow in developing the economy of Mexico.

— RAY CANNON

BAN COMMERCIAL FISHING IN THE CORTEZ?

OCTOBER 22, 1970—The several million anglers who hope to get in on some of the great fishing in the Sea of Cortez will be especially interested in a discussion now getting concerned attention all around the sea. Realizing that tourists are attracted to the resorts almost exclusively by the greatest-in-the-world angling, and that any serious depletion of the fishes by commercial fishing would prove a total disaster for the resorts, government officials and others involved are shaken by reports of several fish meal and cannery enterprisers planning Cortez locations, and officials are talking of halting them until a scientific study proves that present fish abundances will not be disturbed.

If there is any chance of sport and edible fish numbers being reduced, as was the totuava in the north end following the introduction of gill nets, then they would move to shift all commercial fishing, canning, and processing to the Pacific side of Baja California south of San Quintín, leaving the Cortez to anglers.

Some of the top men are suggesting that such a division now would be the wiser plan, calling in commercial netters to fish the Cortez when scientists find a real surplus of a species that should be reduced.

The local market hook-and-line fishermen (not long-line) and the resorts' surplus catches could well supply local markets.

More scientific knowledge of the life history of the migratory fishes and their relationship to the environment and to other species may show that the Cortez is one of the most valuable habitats for increasing abundances to be found, as well as an essential sanctuary from overfishing by long-liners, blasting, and commercial nets.

Man does not have to catch the last fish in a population to wipe out that species. The natural predator demand on it may be greater than the population after over-commercial fishing has reduced it.

Little or nothing is known about the size of fish predation in the ocean and nothing about predator demand in the Cortez. So there is much logic to back those who would shift commercials to the Pacific. When ocean anglers take a few fish out of a vast school the adverse effect on the population is nil. But the very efficient commercial netter takes the whole school, leaving none for spawning. Even the few that occasionally escape may not be able to produce a successful spawn. Contact of eggs and milt may require clouds to insure fertilizing contact in open water, and those fish that do develop are preyed upon by every size creature from bacteria to finback whales, in a world where survival depends on the numbers. — RAY CANNON

FISH TAGGING WELL-TOLERATED AND USEFUL TO SCIENCE

[For many years, beginning in the mid-1960s, Fisheries Research Biologist James L. Squire Jr. was an important proponent of fish tagging programs in southern Baja California. According to Squire, the biggest supporter of fish tagging in those days was Colonel Eugene Walters of Rancho Buena Vista, and the Ranch's Jesús Araiza was the top skipper of the program. Fish tagging originated on the Atlantic coast in 1957-58, and Squire brought the program with him when he was transferred to the National Marine Fisheries Lab at Tiburon, California in 1963. He later worked out of the facility located at La Jolla, California. Among the program's discoveries were billfish migration patterns from southern Baja to Hawaii and Southern California.]

NOVEMBER 30, 1972—A brief report from James L. Squire Jr., Fishery Biologist (Research) Southwest Fisheries Center (U.S. Department of Commerce), La Jolla, California, included some very interesting incidents in the center's fish tagging program. Among them were several tag returns from fish that were tagged in the same region or an adjoining area.

The fact that the tagged fish remained in the area, or returned to it in a short period of time, backs up the notion of scientists that fish are not overly fearful or even concerned about the tag they bear. Some of the game fish skippers have erroneously thought that the fish were being driven away by the tags.

In the report, Squire expressed enthusiasm for the cooperation given by crews of the long range (Pacific side) angling boats out of San Diego, especially with the results of their tagging for science and for real conservation.

Anglers on week-long fishing voyages aboard one of the lux boats, the *Qualifier 105,* caught, tagged, and released a great many California yellowtail. Five of their tagged fish were recaught and tags recovered and sent to the Southwest Fisheries Center. This same boat recaught one of the tagged fish. A sister ship, the 85-foot *Red Rooster,* decked three of the tagged yellows, and a purse seiner got the fifth.

(According to the Squire report, all of the recovered fish were tagged and recaught close around the Escollas Alijos (Alijos Rocks). These three prominent, up to 112-foot-high rocks are about 150 miles southwesterly from Punta San Roque.)

Another interesting recovery was a roosterfish tagged right at Bobby Van Wormer's resort, Punta Colorada, in the Sea of Cortez near Rancho Buena Vista. Bobby said

Forage fish take to the air as they flee from a slashing predator at Buena Vista.

that the rooster barely had time to catch his breath before another angler caught him. But actually, it was caught less than ten miles from the spot, at Punta Arena, 17 days later.

Buena Vista's Chuck Walters reported that their crews had tagged several dolphinfish. One was caught 19 days later, near where it was tagged. But a roosterfish tagged near Rancho Buena Vista kept away from other anglers' hooks for slightly more than a year before getting careless. He was estimated to have gained 7 pounds in the 12 1/2-month period.

To the beginner or the old-timer who enjoys the primitive set of thrills that starts when he begins to prepare for the fishing trip, then on through the whole process, to taking his catch out of the frying pan and eating the fresh

and delicious food, seeing his first hard-fought fish brought alongside the boat and tagged, cut loose, then swim away, brings some deep but silent pangs of regret. But to the dedicated conservationist there is a feeling of real elation and satisfaction, for he knows he has made a valuable contribution to science.

Such a man is Fred Harleman, board of directors member of the Vagabundos Del Mar Club. At the annual Guaymas Fishing Tournament in July 1971, Fred won the Ray Cannon Cup for most billfish tagged. In 1972 he scored by having one of his sailfish recaught 20 days later and the tag recovered, showing that billfish, like others, may not be too spooked by the tag or tagging process.

The Southwest Fisheries Center has lots of records of

long trips made by tagged billfish. Most of the tags and recoveries were made by Japanese long-line fishermen in the tropical Pacific. They have been very cooperative in returning the tags and in making good reports.

Getting more data on fishes' apparent lack of concern with bearing the tag will help convince everyone fishing the Cortez that tagging does not disturb the fishing. This is only a minor objective. There are many more and they are vital in the pursuit of scientific knowledge on the habits of game fishes. To save any abundance of them we need much info as soon as possible, so that wise and legal management can be established before the populations are reduced below that point of no return. — RAY CANNON

AT THE HOTEL LOS ARCOS—THE FIRST TAG-AND-RELEASE TOURNAMENT

[According to Tuna Club of Avalon historian, Mike Farrior, the first known tag-and-release fishing tournament was hosted by the club at the Hotel Los Arcos in La Paz, May 19-26, 1957, the same year in which the Tuna Club began issuing tag-and-release certificates. Forty-four Tuna Club members and their wives attended the tournament and a total of 58 marlin and sailfish were caught. The Ben Meyer Memorial Trophy was presented by the Ruffo Brothers of La Paz to tournament winners, Wayne Jenkins and Club President Hugh Wright.]

JUNE 10, 1957—A couple of days of seeing all the fish released just as they were ready to be gaffed and boated had the boat crews at La Paz muttering such questions as, "Has a fish millennium set in, a pescado holiday?" and, "Was this group of anglers all vegetarians?"

It was difficult to explain that these members of the venerated Tuna Club of Avalon were conservationists— when there was an ocean full of marlin and sailfish extending to the far warm seas of the earth.

Before the Club's big tournament was over, the crews were paying the members their highest respect. The spirited gaiety and wholesome fun exhibited by the contestants and their wives aboard and ashore was the talk of the town. As a result, the Club can expect the royal carpet treatment next year.

Billfish were so plentiful the Club was forced to change their rules the second day. It seemed that the ladies were catching as many big marlin as the men. President Hugh Wright said that they had never had finer fishing. He also expressed great enthusiasm for the facilities, climate and hospitality on this, the first meet in La Paz.

Members new to the area were surprised to find the simplified technique employed no teaser lure or repeatedly circling the marlin to entice it to take the bait. The marlin seemed more often to come up out of nowhere to take the hook when trolled 30 to 50 feet astern. At the end of the meet all voted the Catalina flyingfish the best bait for

billfish. Three were caught on chrome waffle-iron lures, while trolling for other species. Quite a number agreed with me that the dolphinfish taken on light tackle was a magnificent game fish.

Robson English, La Paz Tournament chairman, reported more than 20 game species caught when all hands broke out their spinning gear and started spending a good part of their time in diversified fishing.

Humor dominated the evening meeting around the fiesta board in the floral patio of the Los Arcos Hotel. One contestant won a cup for catching a shark with two heads—its own, and the other the head of a hooked amberjack.

A book should be published on the history and events of the Tuna Club. It would certainly be an inspiration to anglers of today, more especially to members of the hundreds of newly organized fishing clubs in California.

— RAY CANNON

CORTEZ DISASTER AREAS CONNECTED TO EACH OTHER

[Ray describes the chain of events whereby the decimation of the yellowfin tuna population in the extreme southern end of the Cortez eventually threatens the sardines in the Midriff area.]

SEPTEMBER 5, 1973—All anglers who know the Sea of Cortez well rightly claim it has the greatest year-round big game fishing waters yet known. But they often forget that there are areas in this vast sea where fish seem to be absent entirely, and seasons when a plentiful and favorable species becomes quite rare.

In the past few years I have had to backtrack or tone down my enthusiasm for a certain small area, after finding the once super-abundance of fish there had suddenly disappeared after many seasons when I had observed massive schools swarming around the boat.

There are numerous ideas on the subject. Some suggest that the area's environment has been destroyed by explosives, such as the La Paz bay and other places, where fish will remain away for many years and may never be able to regain their former numbers due to the increase in human activities, or to predator threat to their young, as when the newly-hatched hake larvae devoured the sardine eggs spawned in the same waters, in Southern California, or as the frigate mackerel now are cleaning out the young sardine in the Midriff of the Cortez. It was no doubt that the sardine was the main attraction for large gamesters' visits to these areas.

In both cases, commercial purse seiners triggered the disasters by taking more than the ordinary surplus of the sardines, leaving less than the predators demanded.

There are times when the commercial overfishing of one large species can upset the whole environment. For example, the time seven years ago when 50 U.S. purse seiners hit the whole yellowfin tuna migration as the immense fish army entered the mouth of the Cortez. Under the watchful guidance and highly efficient air-spotter, every boat loaded and broke the back of that population of tuna, which had returned every year for centuries to feed and fatten on the sea's abounding supply of forage.

The frigate mackerel was a favorite item in the diet of the yellowfin, so when the tuna got knocked off there was a repeated explosion in the mackerel population. Last year an enormous number of the frigates had shifted to the Midriff more than 200 miles north of stretches I had seen them schooling in before.

If these small but ravenous feeders clean up the remaining sardine and round herring, then turn on the young of other inhabitants of the Midriff, that rich environment could be reduced from one of the finest angling regions to a near desert for anglers. — RAY CANNON

MORE BAD NEWS FOR THE ANCHOVY

JANUARY 1, 1976—The new year had barely started when in came word of a lot of good news and bad news, mostly rumors but with enough facts to alert all saltwater anglers. The subject is forage fish, the food supply of most game and edible fishes.

In the Cortez the sardine and round herring have been hit hard. So have the smaller near shore anchovy schools. The good news rumor is that the boats fishing them are to be shifted to the Pacific. The follow-up is that a larger than usual fleet of purse seiners are gathering at Ensenada. If they are after anchovies and get 'em, that is bad news for California anglers and commercials alike.

In Mexico some herring fishes are canned for human consumption but the big demand is for anchovies and the young of other species which are made into fish meal as protein for the millions of chickens raised in recent years in the Guaymas-Kino region.

According to George Rees, Fisheries Attaché, U.S. Embassy, Mexico City, Mexico entered an agreement with a Peruvian group to explore the anchovy off the Pacific side of Baja California.

Mexico quickly chartered a couple of U.S. purse seiners with full crews who had fished off Baja. They had no trouble in locating the fish and making sizable hauls. So did the Peruvians, who joined in. Mexico had already been convinced by the propaganda of the various State of California and U.S. Federal Commissions and Departments that the anchovy population off California and Baja coasts was enormous and that there was a half-million ton surplus off Baja to be taken annually.

Predicting the size of the California anchovy populations is based on batting average counts or more like taking a political poll. Both are hazardous. A weak spawning season, followed by a warm year that usually causes large migrations of bonito and numerous other warm-water predators to move in, and the anchovy population, especially that off Baja California, could be decimated to the point where it could not recover, just as the California population of the Pacific sardine was wiped out. It never returned.

According to the Department of Fish & Game "Cruise Report 75-A-7" of October 23 to November 12, "Purpose: To assess year-class strength of the Pacific sardine, *Sardinops caeruleaus*," the report's summary states: "Both the adult and juvenile populations of this species appear to remain at a very low level as indicated by the catch of only a single fish during this survey." This specimen was taken below Ensenada.

Anglers and commercial fishermen should be greatly concerned with the increase in the annual allotment of anchovy by the California Fish & Game Commission and Mexico's move to enter the fishery with a dozen or more boats and an increase of 30 more now under construction.

Crews of two West German boats have an agreement to make an 18-month study of the merluza (hake) abundance. Several years ago I quoted a Dr. Elbert Ahlstrom, U.S. Fisheries Service scientist, paper on the enormous numbers of eggs and larvae of the hake taken off Baja and California coasts. It suggested that there was a large commercial fishery possible in deep waters. I am hoping that hake will supply the demand for easy to get protein. The paper also disclosed that hake larvae fed principally on anchovy eggs and larvae. — RAY CANNON

WHITE SEABASS AND CROAKER WIPEOUT

[Of note in this column are the early dates cited for the decimation of white seabass and other croaker populations off California.]

MARCH 3, 1976—There are 40 species listed in the croaker family, *Sciaenidae*, along the coast of California and the Sea of Cortez, plus another half-dozen down the Mexican and Central American coasts and around offshore islands. All except some few small species are rapidly disappearing from this earth.

In our intense worship of the term "efficiency," we have allowed it to smother "common sense." At least until the rape and ruin of our natural resources and birthrights have been completed. The abundances of the croaker populations have been victims and are all but depleted by the highly efficient gill nets, beach seines and round-haul purse seines. Overfished down to the point of no return.

We can assume that along with the early development of croaker abundances, a balance was established. Even when a disaster or spawning failure occurred to a species, there were enough surplus survivors in the breeding stock to produce a successful spawn.

But much of that is now being destroyed by the hand

At Cabo Pulmo, 1964. "Even in those days, Ray feared for the fish."—Mark Walters, Rancho Buena Vista

of man. He is rapidly making the land and sea hostile environments for nature's animal world.

In 1922 the commercial catch of white seabass (member of the croaker family and not a bass) was close to 3,000,000 pounds from California and northern Baja California waters. That and the following three years broke the back of that population. The decline has continued regardless of "letup" in fishing pressure. Netting of the one to one-half-foot-long young this past year on their spawning grounds near Ensenada had made the Pacific white seabass a candidate for the endangered species list. Another race of this species is taking a beating in the north end of the Cortez.

All other species of croaker, the spotfin, black, yellowfin and (California) corbina, were netted down to bare survival stocks before laws removing them from commercial sale or capture were enacted in 1915. From ample abundances they are now considered rare, at least north of Ensenada.

There is a great threat to all of these fine food or game fishes. Again it is the commercial seiners, not for market

fish but for protein for the millions of chickens along the Mexican mainland. The great danger is not only in wiping out vast schools of sardines and other herrings but cutting down on this supply of forage will force other predators to devastate the offspring of the croaker and other fishes needed directly for human consumption. — RAY CANNON

SHARK STEAKS VS. "JAWS"

[Ray's column from about 1975 describes the large Cortez shark fishery that would eventually result in widespread depletion of this slow-reproducing group of fishes.]

There is widespread fear that the super-villainous role played by the shark in the very popular movie *Jaws* aroused so much emotion among psychos and the weak-minded, people will start on a shark slaughtering binge and be applauded by a vast segment of our thoughtless citizenry.

Those who have learned something of the great value of these fine food and game fishes believe that killing sharks without making use of the meat would be a criminal offense. The flesh of all members in the primitive class of fishes, *Elasmobranchii*, including sharks, rays, and skates within our section of the northeast Pacific and the Sea of Cortez, is considered wholesome. The exceptions are the 60-foot-long whale shark, *Rhincodon typus*, and the 40-foot-long basking shark, *Cetorhinus maximus*, which are no doubt edible but I have little info as to quality and no contradictions to the few reports that the cross-cut steaks broiled were delicious.

My favorites are a broiled or fried steak of bonito (mako) shark, *Isarus oxyrinchus*, or salmon shark, *Lamna ditropis*. The most abundant in the Cortez and up the Pacific to Point Conception, California is believed to be the blue shark, *Prionace glauca*. It is the one most often seen by anglers but may be outnumbered by the smaller, bottom-feeding smooth hounds, or Pacific dogfish, sold in markets as "gray fish" since the World War II meat shortage. Surprisingly, the wings or pectoral fins of skates and rays make good substitutes for scallops and are sometimes served as such in rating restaurants.

Blues and a few other common species are especially suitable for smoked fish. These and all others are excellent when brined, dried, and packed codfish-style. In Mexico a large industry of harvesting, curing, and packing Mexican "bacalao" has grown up and is flourishing, especially around the Baja coastlines.

The shark fishing industry was triggered by the demand for cod liver oil, or rather the vitamin found in the age-old remedy for "tired blood" due to a lack of red corpuscles. U.S. merchants were paying Baja ranch hands and goat herders upward of $2 per pound for the livers, and a very large part of the shark body is liver. Added to this, a Mexican-Chinese paid nearly as much for the fins—for the San Francisco gourmets' shark fin soup. Baja's shore ranchers had been salt-curing fish for more than a century. So when the Federal Government developed a market and provided factories for packaging and shipping the fancy bacalao fillets, they quickly got with it.

Everyone with a dugout, skiff, or other floatable craft had joined the bacalao rush. Every island near Baja's Cortez coast had a brush lean-to for sleeping and for a salting table canopy.

A sizable shark migration now moving up the Cortez may develop into another sea rush of happy days for shark men and the bacalao factory. — RAY CANNON

A NATIONAL PARK FOR JUANALOA

[Beginning about 1970, Ray wrote several articles promoting the idea of a national wilderness park in the area between Loreto and La Paz, which he had begun calling "Juanaloa" in 1961. This part of the Baja coast remains undeveloped to the present day and might still be considered a likely candidate for such preservation.

At the end of this article, Ray refers to a Vagabundo club cruise the following June. He did go on that voyage—aboard the boat *Gypsy*, owned by Bam and Jerry Heiner—and as it turned out, it would be his last cruise down the Sea of Cortez.]

MARCH 19, 1976—As Mexico emerges from a country of vast haciendas of farms and ranches to a member of the world's industrial nations, its statesmen are kept concernedly occupied with developing the Republic's natural resources—hence, very little attention to preserving large areas for national or regional parks and environmental sanctuaries.

A good start was made toward establishing sanctuaries for birds and animals and stronger regulations for the conservation of fish and other seafoods, and I found keen and sincere interest in changing the status of the Region of Juanaloa (Puerto Escondido to Bahía de la Paz at Cabeza Mechudo) into a Yellowstone National Park kind of region. An area 70 by 70 miles which includes that section of the Sierra de la Giganta mountains and all islands as far out as Las Animas and Catalán. You can be sure that I will try it out on the new administration to be elected this coming July.

In the document submitted I suggested that no motor-powered vehicle be allowed in the park and no roads be constructed except for bridal paths, hiking, and bicycle trails. A small fee would be charged to all except school students and teachers, to pay for road maintenance and water guzzlers' upkeep.

Yachts, resort cruisers, charter craft and trailerable boats could, however, use the coves, bays, and beaches but under strict sanitary and no-litter regulations. All litter to be buried. Fish could be caught only when eaten in the area or tagged and released. No land nor sea life could be removed; no plant nor part of a plant could be removed.

There are numerous small springs that could be developed for a great number of creatures. No cattle or domestic stock would be permitted.

The present small herds of goats and the few head of cattle there now would be removed and their owners be given training and jobs of developing trails and watering places from present drip springs, and as trails are cleared, they could act as guides for large hiking groups, also for those who may fear the pumas. As wildlife multiplies a couple of small dams could hold sizable ponds year round. After the first year the park would be completely self-supporting.

Some western flying clubs and conservation groups have shown great interest in helping to develop this immense wilderness territory and have expressed their enthusiasm in air-planting suitable grasses and other vegetation for free. Others would help in introducing Mexican game fowl and grazing animals, according to

A small hammerhead shark caught off Ensenada de los Muertos, 1965. — PHOTO BY AL TETZLAFF

success of planted foodstuffs. Limited hunts would be held only when overcrowding occurs.

In the beginning the big tourist and visitor center would be along the new highway near Puerto Escondido, where there is enough potable water available to support an enormous enterprise, *i.e.*, motel-resort, trailer park, bicycle shop and rental station, snack bar, cocktail room and discotheque, swimming pools, tennis courts, angling and snorkeling, boats and supplies, stables and corrals for horses, and a general store and fuel station for land and sea conveyances. All to be constructed gradually as demand requires.

From this center, tourists from Mexico's mainland and Baja Norte and from the U.S. would arrive by all kinds of air, overland, and sea carriers, both privately-owned and commercial. People from La Paz could come for a picnic by excursion boat to Rancho and Misión Dolores, which should be allowed to continue as is. All visitors could find deluxe accommodations, or very inexpensive quarters, as they would require, and be encouraged to spend their whole vacation there. Everyone should also be encouraged to photograph, in every way possible.

The bicycle road would run along the lower rim of shore; the bridal path along upper stretches of bench and up hills to mines and caves and down to the beach at one or two places. The hikers' trails would work toward high ground to other caves and vista points over terrain too steep and rough for horses. All three trails selected to fit their purpose.

An overnight camp-out and light meals cafe could be maintained at Bahía Agua Verde for cyclists, horseback riders, and boaters. A bike trail could be made to branch off from the highway to wind through the west side of the mountains then back through to the Dolores valley and on down to the rancho.

The whole region of Juanaloa is a fantastic wilderness. I became fascinated with it more than 20 years ago while flying at low altitudes in small slow planes. Pedro Mahieux, a prospector who made good, really turned me on for the place when he described its many points of attraction as he climbed over every mile of it and came out owning a sizable chunk.

I have made two-dozen trips into various parts of the region, repeating in several of them but always seeing something exciting, beautiful and new. Chances are good that I will get another look about the second week of June on another Vagabundo club voyage. — RAY CANNON

PURSE SEINE FLEET PUTS ITSELF OUT OF BUSINESS

[Ray wrote this strident column in the late spring of 1976 about an event that took place many years before— in 1959—when, he asserts, the purse seine fleet "broke the back" of the great annual yellowfin tuna migration into the Sea of Cortez.]

MAY 21, 1976—No Karl Marx philosophy was needed to halt the greed of the immensely rich commercial fishing purse seiners. Some say they are so avaricious that "they will catch the last fish in a population if they can get a net around it."

There are 130 boats in the Southern California purse seine fleets. Many of them are worth $3 million each. Some say that these vessels equipped with modern nets and machinery to work them are the most efficient food-harvesting tools ever produced.

Up to 1959 most of the U.S. tuna purse seiners working Mexican and California waters were doing very well with their enormous nylon nets and an airplane spotter to locate the great migrating schools of yellowfin tuna. In June of that year the rich hauls came to an abrupt halt.

I was working out of Rancho Buena Vista developing techniques for catching oddball fish in the list of 350 game fish species of the Cortez, when I met the spotter for the pursers.

For about six weeks he had flown in to the resort's airstrip to spend the night and each evening he would give me an account of his observations of sea life. He explained his method of looking for large pods of spinner, *Stenella microps*, or spotted dolphin, *S. graffmani*, which can be seen for many miles barreling on the surface. And if they are traveling northward, an enormous school of yellowfin tuna will be swimming under or following the dolphin (not to be mistaken for dolphinfish, or dorado in Spanish).

When the travelers hesitate or stop and surface to feed, the spotter can then see and estimate the size of the tuna school, then radio the nearest purse seiner in his contracted fleet to "come and get 'em."

This spotter located several schools approaching the entrance to the Cortez and alerted his fleet. But there was a vast over-abundance of frigate mackerel which kept the tuna and dolphin busy day after day, with new schools arriving to join in on the grand fiesta.

By the time the mass migration started to stretch out and become available for netting, the spotter had 50 boats standing ready. He estimated that the armies of migrators stretched out to form a school 100 miles long. (I published an account of it in this column at that time.)

I saw and photographed some of the purse seine boats in the big haul. It was the greatest one-day catch ever made to that date. Every boat in the fleet loaded.

That devastating raid on the population "broke its back," and despite moratoriums and commercial associations' restrictions of bag limits, that population could not make a comeback to compare with their abundance prior to 1959. Since then very small schools are occasionally found by anglers out of resorts. The vast pods of spinner dolphin have been greatly diminished. The present day tuna schools are more often found by anglers while observing working frigate birds or fast-shifting white terns.

The greed of commercial pursers was never shown more clearly than when the facts of the unnecessary slaughter of spinner and spotted dolphin came out.

If these mammals are destroyed, spotters will need a hell of a lot of time to locate yellowfin schools. They claim that the U.S. is the only nation forbidding the netting of dolphin, but the Latin American people are very fond of their romantic sea creatures and have many sentimental stories about them, and once they get the full story of the slaughter of dolphin they will move quickly to halt the killing of their Flippers.

Unless the commercial fishing industry can quickly develop safeguards against destroying dolphin and still protect young tuna and other fish, fishing will have to be done away from the Americas. Even then laws and regulations will be enacted to prohibit the sale of any product unless proof shows that no dolphin were killed or

A pelican diving for food on the Sea of Cortez. — PHOTO BY AL TETZLAFF

injured in harvesting the tunas.

The U.S. conservation groups (environmentalists) have become powerful and they are not about to be taken-in by pleas of poverty by millionaire owners of fishing vessels; or that they, like farmers, are striving mightily to help feed the public, when the truth is that they are quite the opposite in that they never plant seed, cultivate, nor enrich. The market fishermen do nothing but harvest and rob that part of the earth they claim as their oyster, to mismanage as they like. Most all of the world's fisheries are dying from mismanagement and greed. — RAY CANNON

CHUCK WALTERS—FIGHTER PILOT

[In a letter written to *Field & Stream* associate editor C. E. Gillham, Ray analyzes tuna purse seining operations in the Sea of Cortez and describes an adventurous incident involving former World War II Navy fighter pilot Chuck Walters of Rancho Buena Vista.]

JULY 28, 1963—There was little fear, if any, that the hook and jack-pole fishermen on the tuna clippers could possibly deplete the vast Pacific yellowfin population. But with the introduction of the synthetic fiber purse seine, and with most tuna boats completely converting to it by 1959, fears were aroused.

The jump in the commercial take of this population in Mexican waters, from 61,680 pounds in 1957, to 10,895,808 pounds in 1960, plus a jump from 4,000,000 to 12,000,000 pounds in South America, caused even the commercials to shudder.

Of even more concern to Baja California resort owners and to all anglers visiting this booming region, is the enormous destruction of other game fishes when purse seining is practiced in bays or close to any shore. Tons of highly prized roosterfish and dozens of other favorite species, being unwanted by commercials, are dumped overboard dead, from each haul.

The purse seine, half-a-mile in length and 250 feet deep, often encircles a whole school of tuna, leaving no escapement for reproduction, while hook-and-line fishermen take only a small portion, at most.

The ever increasing efficiency of the purser is likely to put him out of business. Airplane spotters for the U.S. fleets are now able to locate the schools easily by large pods of the telltale spinner dolphin, which for some unknown reason, travels in company with tuna schools and discloses their position by jumping, turning, and splashing. From the air this activity can be seen for many miles.

Chuck Walters, son of the Colonel, recently dramatized the anglers' and resort owners' resentment at having spotters direct the tuna fleet right into the favored angling bay, by buzzing a spotter's plane, forcing it to land, then giving the villain a good mauling. Chuck paid a sizable fine but won by creating a widespread interest.

I followed it up with a series of articles in a La Paz paper, pointing out that a tuna caught by a visiting angler was worth $100 to the local economy but only a few centavos (in permit fees) if taken commercially. I also suggest that all boats with a purse seine on board be prohibited within three miles of a line drawn from land head or point to point.

The purse seine reduced the Pacific Coast sardine (the major forage fish) below the point of no return. A number of years ago they netted half-a-million tons annually; this past year a little over three-thousand. This and other depletions reduced all big game fish except those surviving on anchovy. Pursers now threaten anchovy, the major forage fish. The purse seine replaced clippers because of efficiency, not for lack of bait, still plentiful south of the border. Japan, exporter of the big synthetic fiber purse seine, has curtailed their own use of them in favor of long-line fishing, especially for tuna. — RAY CANNON

SMASHING TERN EGGS ON ISLA LA RAZA

[Ray describes a fantastically destructive and wasteful egg-harvesting practice on now-protected Isla la Raza.]

The numerous, pure white islands strung out near the Peninsula's coast are nicely white-washed or plastered with guano (bird droppings).

But when you approach Isla la Raza, a dozen miles south of Isla Angel de la Guarda, from mid-March to mid-July, you will see the most immaculate field of white imaginable.

For there, occupying a large section of the 1/2 by 3/4-mile Isla la Raza, is the most dazzling of the Cortez sea birds, the immaculate white elegant tern, *Thalasseus elegans*, by the thousands. Their black caps and yellow beaks add a touch of jewel and ermine to the pure snowy background. They nest only on this and one other island.

The serious threat to the elegant tern's survival came from human commercial egg harvesters, who, preferring tern eggs, destroyed the first crop so that the next and following mornings, all of the eggs would be fresh.

Before they were banished, Indians harvested these eggs for centuries, selecting the fresh ones by touch (the developing eggs are slightly slick). The commercials learned this but not in time to influence President López Mateos, who by decree made La Raza a wildfowl sanctuary in May, 1964. — RAY CANNON

SAVE THE CENTURY-OLD GIANTS

[As late as the mid-1960s, Ray's published writing communicated a conviction that the large, slow-growing bass-like fish of the Cortez were so numerous they could never be depleted, except in localized areas. However, his personal correspondence shows that he had already begun to have second thoughts as early as 1957. The following three fragments track Ray's conversion from an all-out "meat fisherman" to a dedicated conservationist.]

"SOME SLIGHT CONFLICT OF EMOTIONS"

[In a letter to fishing pal and *Field & Stream* editor Frank Dufresne written about 1957, Ray tells of his personal intention to continue taking large bass-like fish, despite his concern for their safety:]

Since learning of the great ages of these fishes my conscience is beginning to choke my enthusiasm for pursuing them. I am developing an admiration for a creature that has escaped the many enemies for a century. Is it possible, that I, a salt-hardened scourge of the fishes, am endowing these sea monsters with admirable heroic personalities and becoming hypnotically thawed out by their fierce and formidable facial expressions?

I have not yet been overcome by grief, but there is some slight conflict of emotions. However, I shall clinch my store "uppers" and charge on. — RAY CANNON

GROUPER OVERFISHED?

[In 1961, Ray still argues that the large bass and groupers are so plentiful in the Sea of Cortez that they can never be depleted.]

AUGUST 24, 1961—Considerable fear has been expressed that the great 50 to 100-year-old basses in the Cortez will be fished down, and that anglers would have to wait another half-century or so for replacements to grow up.

The more I get around in this bountiful Sea, the more I doubt the pessimistic concern. There seem to be too many kinds, in too many places and too great abundances for anything near depletion for the next dozen decades. The exception being near cities and resorts, where few grand daddies will survive the fishing pressure. But such places now operating, and those to come in the foreseeable future, will cover a small fraction of the 6,000 miles of fishable shoreline around islands, in bays and along the coasts of this Sea and the Pacific side of Baja California.

Take Cabo Vírgenes as an example of way-out places. It is doubtful that the area around it was ever fished by an angler prior to the Ryan Expedition. Before anchoring for the night we spent part of an hour trolling large, white feathers. There seemed to be little difference along the cliffs and over reefs—whenever we let out a lure a large grouper would latch on. On John Rowan's boat a try was made for a monster, using a live skipjack for bait. But as soon as the baits cleared the boat they were nailed by huge, 40-pound dog snappers.

Vírgenes is only one of hundreds of isolated regions that will rarely be visited by fishermen, and its enormous bass and snapper population will go on growing old.

There are 36 or more members of the true bass family, *Serranidae*, in the Cortez. Half-a-dozen of these achieve weights above 100 pounds. The leopard grouper, *Mycteroperca rosacea*, called "pinta cabrilla" by natives in some areas, appears to be the most abundant and widespread in range. It is believed to run above 80 pounds. This species includes the golden grouper, which you will soon be hearing a lot about.

The real pinta cabrilla, *Epinephalus analogus*, have been weighed at 56 pounds and may go well above that. A 30-pound, deep-water cabrilla, not yet described or named, was caught off Rancho Buena Vista. Local natives claim they have caught them twice that size! Anglers fishing on 50-fathom reefs may find species plentiful in isolated spots.

After my second trip to Isla Catalán and rechecking my notes on the fish seen there, I feel that all tales I have heretofore thought exaggerations of the number and sizes of basses seen, were in reality understatements. A fisherman would have to stretch his imagination to the breaking point to visualize the quantity, sizes, and number of species of basses we saw on the submerged shelves of Catalán. — RAY CANNON

GIANT BASSES SHOULD NOT BE CAUGHT

[By the time he wrote the following column, Ray had become convinced of the need to conserve the giant bass species. The prohibition against taking large bass-like fish mentioned in this column was never enforced, and large sizes of these species have become very rare.]

SEPTEMBER 21, 1973—Several years ago, John Fitch of California Fish & Game, Marine Division, developed a remarkable method of aging many large fish by counting the rings on the ear bone (otolith). I remember he aged a 450-pound black sea bass as being 60 to 75 years old. With each year their growth slows down, thus a 550 to 600-pounder could be estimated to be well over a century, perhaps two. Other large basses may also live as long.

When Mexican marine biologists informed their Government that these old native fishes became more prolific with age; that a jewfish weighing close to 1,000 pounds contained and could have spawned millions of eggs, a law was passed prohibiting their capture by any means. They may not be taken or killed for any purpose. This is a serious law and carries a lengthy prison sentence. Like the no-gambling law that was suddenly enforced several years after its enactment, the same can be expected in killing the aged fish.

Mexicans can get just as sentimental about these harmless, old creatures as our ecologists do about shooting endangered birds or animal species in the U.S. There is, however, a lingering Daniel Boone spirit in most all of us old rod-and-gun-club members, and the "bar" we kill has to be the biggest, even if others do call us hard-hearted heathens.

Interested Mexicans have one point for their law that cannot be refuted, *i.e.*, the over-50-year-old fish is not replaceable, not ever. No replacement would get a chance to grow that long before being caught. So when they think of a century, or even half-century old fish that lives in a single cave or its vicinity, and escapes all kinds of predators for that many years only to be killed by a diver or fisherman, the act seems criminal.

Realizing the great length of time needed for a replacement to grow up, I will release every bass that looks like a 30-pounder. I will also include those big snappers and totuava above that weight.

Tuna, billfish and dolphinfish are short-lived and migrators. None of these entering the Cortez live more than seven years. I will be catching 'em, tagging 'em, and releasing 'em and getting the extra fun of making a contribution to the scientific knowledge of them, needed greatly now. — RAY CANNON

An enormous jewfish caught at Mulegé. The fish's characteristic rounded anal fin has been retouched in the original photo, dated March 16, 1957, but is still discernible.

The original Hotel Bajo Colorado, c. 1970, near Bahía Santa María, about 12 kilometers west of Cabo San Lucas. This facility was acquired by David J. Halliburton Sr., greatly expanded, and reopened as the Hotel Twin Dolphin in 1977. (See lower photo.) The wreck of the *Inari Maru No. 10* on "Shipwreck Beach" is just visible in the distance, in front of the coastal hill, Cabeza de Ballena. The wreck was about five years old and still fairly intact when this photograph was taken.

The Hotel Twin Dolphin, as it opened on the same site in 1977. The wreck of the *Inari Maru No. 10*, greatly reduced in bulk, is still just visible below the rise of Cabeza de Ballena. The Hotel Twin Dolphin was the final great resort to be built during the Golden Age. It was the personal dream and pet project of Texas-Oklahoma oilman, David J. Halliburton Sr., who first visited Cabo San Lucas in 1939 aboard the family yacht, *Twin Dolphin*. True to its Golden Age heritage, the Hotel Twin Dolphin has remained a luxurious and reserved, family-run operation, managed today by Halliburton's children, David Jr., Donald and Elizabeth.

— COURTESY NANCY DILLMAN

MODERN BAJA

END OF THE GOLDEN AGE

As BAJA CALIFORNIA entered the mid-1970s, there were three closely-spaced developments that signaled the advent of the modern era: the completion of the full-length Transpeninsular Highway in 1973; the dredging of the Cabo San Lucas inner harbor from 1973 to 1975; and the opening of the new International Airport at San José del Cabo in 1977.

—The completion and paving of the Transpeninsular Highway, or "Mex 1," in October 1973 signaled—more than any other event—the end of Baja California's Golden Age. The Transpeninsular Highway and the southern Transterritorial Highway that preceded it were built for general business purposes, but they also happened to coincide perfectly with the camping and recreational vehicle boom going on in the U.S., fostering a new industry of campgrounds, motels and "RV parks" distributed throughout Baja California. The old emphasis on small, exclusive, fly-in resorts disappeared the moment the first wave of campers and recreational vehicles crossed the border. For better or worse, the peninsula was open for the first time to the general public rather than just small groups of wealthy or adventurous travelers.

—The dredging of the Cabo San Lucas harbor transformed that small, sleepy cannery village into an internationally-known hotel and marina complex and touched off a real estate boom that eventually engulfed the entire south end of the peninsula.

—And in 1977, the opening of Los Cabos International Airport at San José del Cabo—with a capacity of bringing upwards of 3,000 tourists a day to the southern end—transformed the Baja California Sur tourist economy from one relying almost solely on hard-core sport fishing, into a mass market resort destination with a broad variety of attractions.

For Ray Cannon, these massive, fast-paced changes surely signaled the ending not only of Baja California's Golden Age, but of his own time as well. He was 81 years old when the official opening ceremonies were held for the Transpeninsular Highway, an event to which he had been strongly, even bitterly, opposed. That idyllic vision of a remote unspoiled paradise, first conceived on the beaches of San Felipe a quarter-century before, had been realized, and now, so quickly, had passed into history.

In the three-and-a-half years left to him after the opening of the Transpeninsular Highway, Ray's columns and articles become more and more a record of the Baja California that was growing rapidly away from the land that he had loved and helped to build. Following are some of his observations of this time of change—the end of the Golden Age.

FIRST ANNOUNCEMENT OF THE TRANSPENINSULAR HIGHWAY

[Ray's earliest known reference to the idea of a highway running the full length of the Baja California peninsula—made 15 years before "Mex 1" was actually graded and paved. In this initial announcement, Ray wastes no time in expressing his doubts about the opening up of coastal areas to mass tourism. The coastline of "a hundred bays, coves and grottoes" in Juanaloa was eventually bypassed by a more traditional route south from Loreto that crossed the mountains almost to the Pacific coast before recrossing again to La Paz.]

SEPTEMBER 25, 1958—A highway from Tijuana to La Paz and on down to the tip of the Baja California Peninsula is now being surveyed, and according to reliable reports from the resort metropolis, confirmation has been received on the newly elected president's determination to spare no expense in rushing the construction.

As Steinbeck found it. The outer harbor of Cabo San Lucas in 1960, when the population of the village was about 350 people.

— PHOTO BY RALPH POOLE

This new paved road will open vast stretches of coastline on the gulf side. South of San Quintín Bay it will follow the gradual slope across the peninsula from the Pacific to the gulf, at Santa Rosalía. Then down to Mulegé and on around Bahía Concepción to Loreto.

This first stretch follows a hazardous road now existing. But from Loreto to within a few miles of La Paz, it will be carved through a virgin country.

I have fished past much of this rugged wilderness and flown over it dozens of times and wondered how many Acapulcos would be built if this fabulously beautiful coast, heaven forbid, was in the U.S.

From Loreto the highway will run straight to Nopoló Cove, then through a beautiful bay-side ranch, and on past the hidden Puerto Escondido where the overland trails end.

From there on, no trails have ever followed this coast. Heretofore, all overland travel to and from the south end was done over a tortuous el camino that crossed back to the Pacific Coast and back again.

The new highway will bring anglers down to a hundred bays, coves and grottoes carved out of mountains that broke off and dropped into the great submerged chasms, brought on when the earth split during the early San Andreas faulting.

The peaks of toppled mountains are now seen as a chain of islands close up to channels too deep for early explorers to accurately chart. Except for the back bay beaches and washes, the shore islands are composed of solid or crumbling rock. Estimating the swarming fish populations in such ideal habitats would require an electric brain computer using astronomical figures.

Those of us who have deplored the very idea of building this road and opening our heavenly wilderness to all and sundry, will still have about four or five years to be shed of the maddening traffic and enjoy our primitive world of fishing.

We will have to race against time and progress to fill a lifetime with the joy found only in fishing the remote corners still left untouched. — RAY CANNON

TIME RUNNING OUT FOR PRIMITIVE BAJA

[As early as 1966, Ray foresaw how the rush of progress would soon obliterate a way of life that had been preserved—as though in a time-capsule—since the days of the padres. Although he expresses a desire to preserve interesting relics of the past in museums, Ray distances himself from the social, aesthetic and philosophical consequences of modernization, never indicating if he is in favor of it or not.]

MAY 13, 1966—The solemn thought suddenly struck me that time is running out for people who would like to see the primitive side of Baja California Sur, for modern machinery and modern ways are sure to replace the old— and very pronto. Then I wondered whether people had ever heard of the centuries-old hand-carved mills, machinery, and contrivances that are still to be seen in operation a short ways from the main highways.

I was fortunate in having Bill Escudero drive me to the ends of most all roads in the region. He knew most anyone and the location of the oddities.

The most elaborate were the sprawling sugar mills covering an area of half a city block and all made of wood. There were cheese presses, bake-ovens ten feet in diameter, stone cook stoves, brandy stills, and crude wineries, grain grinders, ash hoppers for making lye soap; strange also were old leather, hammock, and leather hat manufacturing works.

Bill took me to some crumbling haciendas that had been castles of rich plantation ranch owners—to isolated

Cabo San Lucas, c. 1970, from the construction site of the Hotel Finisterra, before the inner harbor was created by dredging. Note the cannery at far right. A road crosses what is now the mouth of the harbor. The Hotel Hacienda sits atop a large sand dune. At left, the cannery pier, 1960. The buildings and high sand bar to the right of the boat were removed during the creation of the inner harbor. At lower left and right, scenes from the old sand-filled area across what is now the inner harbor and commercial marina. — LOWER THREE PHOTOS BY RALPH POOLE

"One of the first effects of the opening of Mex 1 was that there were dead and maimed people all over Baja." Mark Walters, Rancho Buena Vista, 1998 — PHOTO BY GENE KIRA

May 13, 1974, Mike Bales' camper on the newly-graded road from Punta Prieta to Bahía de los Angeles. Paving of the road was completed by October of that year. — PHOTO BY MIKE BALES

Shirley and Tom Miller at Cabo San Lucas, c. 1977. After the opening of the Transpeninsular Highway, their *Baja Book* series and Mexico West Travel Club brought many thousands of new tourists to Baja California and helped bring about a mini-industry of tourism-oriented service clubs, most notably today's greatly expanded Vagabundos Del Mar Boat & Travel Club, and the Discover Baja Travel Club. — PHOTO BY ELMAR BAXTER

cattle ranches where a mule pulling a 200-foot rope brought water up from that depth in a cowhide bucket.

There were fossil deposits dating back for millions of years that included bones of great whales, Indian middens (ancient kitchens) of a few thousand years back, and ruins of missions and other historical spots of 200 or 300 years ago.

But none of the handmade furniture, carts, or implements seemed more quaint than the dugout canoas, chopped out of an unsplit tree trunk, seen high on the beaches of most every waterfront ranch.

The big concern about all this is that the time is almost at hand for collecting all of this handiwork for the museums. Transportation and communication lines are spreading like spider webs, and no matter how much the isolated people resist, our hectic civilization will be spun over them. The countryside, the resorts and the people will be as attractive as ever; only the antiqueness will be missing.

Two roads now being rushed to completion will hasten the change. One heading south for Cabo San Lucas from La Paz, the other from Puerto Escondido near Loreto, to connect with the La Paz paved highway north.

— RAY CANNON

RAY'S RESERVATIONS ABOUT MEX 1

[Ray's clearest statement of opposition to the Transpeninsular Highway. Once completion was accomplished in 1973, he would gradually reverse his opinion when the unruly hordes he feared never materialized. The Santa Rosalía-Guaymas ferry was put into operation in 1973. The resort of Dr. Enoch Arias described as being near Isla Coronado in Loreto was never opened.]

GUAYMAS, MAY 15, 1971—For several years, this column has advocated for large ferryboats—first, from Mazatlán and Topolobampo to La Paz. These were put into operation, and now word comes from Mexico City stating that the ferry to run between Guaymas and Santa Rosalía has been purchased and will start hauling cars, trucks, and campers in November of this year. The dock here is now being constructed.

This will do much for resorts now operating. I have seen an average of two to five ferry-transported cars and campers at the most popular hotels in the Baja Territory.

If publicized properly, the Guaymas ferry would stimulate the building of trailer parks and inexpensive accommodations—especially near clean beaches, where camper-top skiffs could be launched for close to shore fishing, clamming, etc. The principle reason why a few such facilities would succeed is that Santa Rosalía is at the north end of the Territory's fine scenic highway that runs past nearly all of the most interesting things to see on the peninsula, and it stretches all the way to Cabo San Lucas, the land's tip end.

Just imagine the good clean outdoor vacation a family could have campering at San Lucas Cove, 11 miles down the highway from Santa Rosalía. It has a farming village nearby, lots of good, clean water, and clams and fish in abundance. There is a fresh to brackish inner lagoon with interesting wildlife, unique rock, shell, cactus, and fossil collecting. There is a large airstrip here and it is only 29 miles, on a level-paved road, to Mulegé.

There would surely be another such park alongside of, or at the back of Bahía Coyote, halfway into Bahía Concepción. This would be about 15 or 20 miles below Mulegé. Another, about 12 miles above Loreto just opposite Isla Coronado. I believe that Dr. Enoch Arias, operator of the Hotel Misión de Loreto, already has a fine building already finished at this spot.

All these locations could make delightful mini resorts for self-sufficient camper-driving people, and there are more in out-of-the-way places.

You may notice that I am suggesting keeping them a good distance away from the towns and resorts, to enhance the value of remoteness and calm tranquility.

One of the principle reasons I plug for ferryboats is my belief that a daily, or tri-weekly, ferry crossing the Cortez at Guaymas would help to hold back, if not halt, the proposed highway from the border to Santa Rosalía, which I think would do more harm than good. It would definitely open the floodgates to the hordes of cheap, illicit-thrill-seekers from the U.S.

I am no nut on moral behavior, nor am I any kind of a snob, but I would hate to see the sweet and gentle people of the Territory subjected to the degrading influences that turn border towns into places of misery.

So far the people who are willing to pay the extra ferry fee and drive the extra distance have proven to be splendid representatives of the U.S. and have done nothing but add happiness to the Baja Californian's quiet way of life, and are in turn appreciated. — RAY CANNON

for U.S. tourists in Baja California. Miller's *Western Outdoor News* announcement of dedication ceremonies for the Transpeninsular Highway:]

NOVEMBER 30, 1973—This Saturday, December 1, the new $80 million highway, Mexico 1, will be dedicated by President Luis Echeverría Alvarez at the point where the highway passes from the State of Baja California into the Territory of Baja California Sur, just north of Guererro Negro.

A modernistic monument of a giant eagle has been erected here as part of a modern tourist complex which includes a 60-room hotel, rest stop or parador, gas station and trailer camp. The 135-foot-high "Monumento Aguila" will be visible from many miles as you approach the border between the two parts of Baja. Artfully landscaped with the cactus and the strange cirios that are typically Baja, it symbolizes the new growth that is finally coming to the peninsula, over 400 years after its discovery in 1533.

Named in honor of Benito Juárez, the father of the modern Republic of Mexico, the highway "Numero Uno" will open the entire length of the peninsula to hundreds of thousands of visitors each year.

Many Mexicans and Americans alike are fearful of the possible chaos that great numbers of tourists may cause because facilities are not yet capable of handling them. There have been a number of new gas stations, in addition to those at the five new paradors that are being built, but they may not be enough. Hotel space will surely be at a premium even though the Mexican Government and private companies alike have been building new overnight lodgings. Reservations will surely be a must for a long time to come.

It will take some time, maybe years, before the several thousand rooms and other services can be built to meet the demand. If, however, you are willing to plan ahead and maybe take along a sleeping bag you can have one of the greatest experiences of your life.

— TOM MILLER, COURTESY WESTERN OUTDOOR NEWS

THE OPENING OF MEX 1

[*Western Outdoor News* staff writer Tom Miller announces dedication ceremonies for the Transpeninsular Highway at Guererro Negro, December 1, 1973. Miller, who would assume responsibilities for *Western Outdoor News*' Baja column after Ray's death in 1977, wrote extensively about the new tourism opened up by Mex 1. His innovative and very successful *The Baja Book* series (coauthored with Elmar Baxter) used satellite photographs and road logs to introduce overland visitors to the peninsula in a way that had never been done before, and in the spring of 1975 he and wife Shirley Miller would launch the pioneering Mexico West Travel Club, whose newsletter was for many years the leading informational publication

CHET SHERMAN'S
FIRST REPORT ON MEX 1

[The opening of the Transpeninsular Highway effectively ended the era of Kino Bay launching for Southern California small boaters cruising the "Baja side" of the southern Sea of Cortez. No longer was it necessary to risk the difficult and long boat trip south from San Felipe, or to reach the Baja peninsula by island-hopping across the Midriff archipelago. With the opening of Mex 1, boats could be trailered directly to launch points in Mulegé, Loreto, or La Paz, and the standard Kino Bay seaway explored by Ray in the late 1950s quickly became outmoded.

Only a few months after its completion, the

Transpeninsular Highway received its first major paved side road—the 40-mile link to Bahía de los Angeles which was completed between May and October of 1974. This opened up an attractive launch point within a one-day drive of the border, and "L.A. Bay" quickly became the most popular trailer boat destination in Baja.

In the following column, Vagabundos Del Mar president Chet Sherman has just returned from a survey trip down Mex 1, undoubtedly in preparation for the trailer boat trip he would lead that summer. The new highway had just been dedicated the preceding month.]

JANUARY 17, 1974—The advice is still to wait for another couple of months for a more enjoyable trip down Baja California's new Trans-Peninsula Highway.

According to Chet Sherman, President of the Vagabundos Del Mar club, who has just returned from a drive to Cabo San Lucas and back—"It is wall-to-wall campers around Coyote Bay and other accessible stretches along that side of the 25-mile-long Concepción Bay, and the side streets of La Paz resemble the aimless scattering of a disturbed ant hill. Except for these, and the mud around Santa Rosalía, the Highway and arrangements throughout the Territory from Laguna Guererro Negro to Cabo San Lucas are well ahead of that long and narrow (only 19 feet wide in places) strip running northward from the Territory and State border line to El Rosario. Coming down it, a heavy rainstorm turned bitter cold at night— ice covered our windshield. Strangers to the area wondered if they were headed in the wrong direction. At best, this wind through the high and barren mountains and monotonous wasteland didn't seem to inspire the travelers I talked with along it."

Chet continued—"Several large work crews are striving to make shoulders and blacktop off-ramps to areas cleared for rest stops, and progress is being made on roadside stations, auto courts, and restrooms. Water will be hauled in. Emergency gasoline is available in drums at ranches. Even in the Territory, gas station tanks were too small to supply the after New Year's rush of campers and motor homes (about 50-50).

"The self-sufficient mobile homes are having far less trouble at present but new trailer parks to be ready by late spring will bring convenience for all recreational vehicles. Those that are in operation are very convenient and have started expanding.

"There is a lot of litter in spots but to everyone's surprise most U.S. vehicle visitors are doing a good job policing the camp areas. Litter and garbage is being buried."

"One of the best proposals yet was suggested by Carlos Riva Palacio, head of the Territory's Department of Tourism, *i.e.*, that all overnight motoring visitors to open shore or other allotted areas pay a $1 maintenance and litter collection fee—with a motto such as "Clean and Happy Baja."

When Mex 1 was young. One of several "not for high speed driving" signs, this one just south of Punta Prieta, in 1974.

— PHOTO BY MIKE BALES

The same sign, just before it was demolished in 1996.

— PHOTO BY MIKE BALES

Sherman made extra use of his look-see overland tour. The resulting slides and film will be projected at the Vagabundos Del Mar big Annual Fiesta at the Hotel Islandia, San Diego, February 2.

Plenty of fuel will be available by February 1, except along the new Trans-Peninsula Santa Rosalía–El Rosario stretch. In another month or so, gas tanks large enough to supply the Easter Week traffic will be installed, according to the various Mexican tourist offices. — RAY CANNON

THIS ONE DIDN'T FLY

OCTOBER 31, 1974—Ed Tabor, of Flying Sportsmen Lodge, Loreto, has started a new one for Baja 1. He says it's a "Seven-Day Trip" on a luxury cruise on a deluxe passenger motor coach, down the Highway, departing from San Diego.

Four days of seeing Baja and four nights at the Flying Sportsmen Lodge, where they can booze it up, hunt for shells, go fishing—or whatever. The driver-guide is an expert and knows the road and points of interest. Also on board will be a bilingual "steward." — RAY CANNON

LAW SOUTH OF THE PECOS

[A few months after the opening of the Transpeninsular Highway, Ray expresses satisfaction at the beginnings of the recreational vehicle revolution, as Loreto's Ed Tabor opens up one of Baja's first RV parks, and many RVs are among the first waves of vehicles to travel south.

Also recalled, a Judge Roy Bean-style courthouse session in Loreto involving Al Green's father. The territory of Baja California Sur would become a Mexican state on October 8, 1974.

The Guaymas fishing tournament referred to was heavily attended during the period by the members of the Vagabundos Del Mar club.]

JULY 17, 1974—Very soon the last of the Western Territories will be no more. Baja California Sur, having gained enough human population, is about to achieve the status of statehood, and the exciting days of the Old West will pass into history.

For the past 21 years I have been in on a lot of happenings that cannot return. Some were humorous and romantic despite their tragic beginning. I can never forget such events as the day Al Green (said to be a descendant of the noted British pirate, Captain Henry Green) rushed me to the Loreto courthouse to hear his father being convicted and sentenced in an 1849-style court for moonshining.

After an awful berating by the judge, which was interrupted every few minutes by uproarious laughter by an audience of friends and customers of the old man, the sentence laid on him was a fine of 2,500 pesos (or $200 U.S. dollars). The Judge then ordered the Clerk to write out a paper or license, making old Green a legitimate distiller, to be included in the 2,500-peso penalty.

Loreto should have a Grand Fiesta to celebrate statehood, for it was the first Capital of all of the Californias (Territories) in the beginning, and Loreto loves a rousing holiday. I have been in on some dillies there. Ed Tabor, operator of the Flying Sportsmen, has been throwing a clambake on the occasion of our Vagabundos Del Mar club's June arrival at his popular resort.

Tabor had a unique idea for a trailer park and cabaña combination under a canopy of huge palms. The first section is now open and getting a goodly number of campers and other recreational vehicles. They pay the standard price for space and services, then get dining room, bar, swimming pool and access to pier and beach privileges. Some smaller vehicle people take a cabaña and park next to it for convenience. All are within the confines of the resort's fenced-in area and are well protected. The resort maintains a sizable machine shop and good mechanics, also supplies of gas and oil. I have tried to encourage all resorts to get into the trailer park business in a big way, pointing out that a glance at the growth of this business at San Carlos Bay, a dozen miles above Guaymas, will quickly convince anyone of the importance of such enterprises. The rapid growth at San Carlos with very little overhead is astonishing, and I expect to be reporting on it within a few weeks if all goes well during my trip there for the Guaymas Billfish Tournament.

I was surprised to find no more than about 15 campers around Escondido and half of them were Vagabundos who had trailered all the way down the new highway, with stops all along the way. They will be shipping over to Guaymas on the Santa Rosalía ferry and rendezvousing at Hotel Las Playitas for the Tournament. They are certainly getting a lot of overland cruising experience to add to that of their several voyages on the Cortez Sea.

The settling down of the new highway traffic into an orderly number of campers with an increase of more affluent visitors in them will need to be given some wise thought and wise management. This new mode of recreation vehicle will then contribute its share to maintaining the new road and to the economy of the new State of Baja California, South. — RAY CANNON

DON JOHNSON—TRAFFIC DIRECTOR

[Mulegé's Don Johnson learns shortly after the opening of the Transpeninsular Highway that accommodating RV business at his Hotel Serenidad was a little tricky at first. Prior to the pavement, the hotel catered mostly to fly-in clients and the very few that arrived by boat. Similar "learning experiences" were occurring throughout Baja California during the period.]

JULY 12, 1974—To say that there was a state of confusion is misleading. It was more like chaos, and Don Johnson, with full responsibility of the heretofore quiet Hotel Serenidad, was the central figure in the town's most disturbing time since the night a snook so shook the ghost town pueblo, its few dozen citizens panicked. Some say that was the date when the town's 36-year siesta ended, and triggered a stir that turned it toward a favored angling resort city.

But this year's last week of June found delightful old Mulegé the bull's-eye target for hundreds of campers loaded with school kids on vacation mostly bugging parents to get with the fishing long before a place to park was found, hence the great crunch.

I am not against kids, parents, or campers as such, but I must admit that there comes a time when they form in swarms and the leaders lose their polite and good natures.

When Mex 1 was young. A trailer boat convoy, c. 1974.

I feel that getting to sea and off to an isolated cove is more to my liking.

Don Johnson couldn't escape for he is totally involved in the Serenidad, and the day I arrived climaxed the camper, small boat, and private plane push down the air lanes, seaways, and the new Transpeninsular Highway, which passes the hidden Mulegé before the land drivers realize that they have arrived.

The clear turnoff and sign "To Serenidad" is down river (2 1/2 miles) and vacationists see water, planes, vehicles, and boats congregated around the spreading resort, and head for it down a roughish dirt road that runs parallel to the Serenidad's smoother airstrip.

Into the night, overland travelers kept coming. Fernando del Moral, Johnson's partner, had suffered a heart attack at daybreak. Everything fell on Johnson. First—to get a plane among the flying guests to rush the stricken partner to La Paz. But before he could get anyone, all hell broke loose! The city power had blacked out; seven Vagabundos Del Mar camper-trailered boats had pulled in along the river, cutting off all view from the better class bungalows; a row of other recreational vehicles followed and made it a double row. One light

camper had parked across in front of a twin engine plane, which was due to take off. That one cleared in 30 seconds after the plane started two motors!

Don was going nuts from the questions hurled at him—all yelling dire emergency—from the kitchen, the bar, the boat desk, gas pumper, and the dozens of visitor tourists demanding rooms. But topping them all was a radio call from an overhead customer saying that he was ready to land but that there was an obstruction as big as a haystack right in the middle of the runway.

Don dashed to his car and up the airstrip, to find that a family had pitched a large tent dead center on the strip and was enjoying a leisurely breakfast and no doubt congratulating themselves on finding such a nice clearing. The usually serene Johnson came close to joining his partner in the hospital trip in a gasket-blowing exasperation.

He pointed to the overhead plane and effectively exaggerated by telling the family that the plane was so low on gas that he would have to land in exactly 1 1/4 minutes. He joined in throwing breakfast, kids, dogs, and equipment into the family pickup and clearing the runway.

Back in his office another plane was calling in for

accommodations. The flier asked, "Is this Hotel Serenidad?" Don answered, "It was yesterday, but I am about to rename it 'Grand Central Station.'"

Before the day was over, Johnson brought order out of the crunch and had developed a lot of new ideas on how to direct the new summer vacationers in a pleasant and orderly manner, such as larger signs, and others that give the driver a chance to anticipate with wording such as, "1 mile to the Mulegé turnoff." He also plans a large, well-equipped trailer park to keep vehicles off of the beaches and from choking resort areas.

After this early summer vacationing rush is over and people learn that littering is a jail offense in Mexico, I believe that Mulegé and other crowded places will settle back to their quiet ways, and Hotel Serenidad will again be a serene place to relax and go fishing. — RAY CANNON

FAREWELL CEREMONY IN SANTIAGO

[A celebration in the quiet town of Santiago for departing governor of Baja California Sur, Hugo Cervantes del Río, during whose administration much of the infrastructure for modern Baja was initiated.]

NOVEMBER 18, 1970—When we have spent many years in cities we are apt to forget the deep and lasting joy of simple small town pleasures, and the fun of preparing for special events.

At an elaborate farewell fiesta at Santiago, honoring Governor Hugo Cervantes del Río, I was pleasantly reminded of my own village school days in Tennessee, and the happy rehearsals of folk dances and musical numbers for our festivals.

I have mentioned before that Santiago (12 miles inland and south of Buena Vista) looks about like a California pueblo of 1849, and at the gay, yet sad, celebration, I was greatly surprised when the first native folk dance was performed much like our Tennessee mountain hoedown, to the tune of "Turkey in the Straw." After the first few well rehearsed movements and the dancers gained confidence, their smiles exposed their exhilaration, an emotion far deeper than we city people seem to feel anymore.

The occasion was repeated as the great Governor of the Territory made a last tour as reigning local official of the region. He will definitely go into the new President's Cabinet, December 3, according to authorities.

Señor Cirilo Gómez, owner of Santiago's new Hotel Palomar, where the banquet for 350 guests was held, said that Cervantes del Río had done more for the Territory of Baja California than all previous governors together.

Among the hundreds of important projects begun and completed by this knowledgeable and energetic Governor are the following: the vast, modern Territorial highway, now within a few miles of being completed; the

electrification of the villages by a network extending from La Paz to San José del Cabo; new ferryboats (two, with a third just begun and another expected soon); extension of schools, hospitals, and airports, including the big, modern jet structure at La Paz.

Cervantes is one of the few men in politics I have known who really thinks out problems with profound thought but he also proved that he has not lost the common touch in his contact with the citizenry of Santiago.

— RAY CANNON

FIRST VAGABUNDOS CARAVAN DOWN MEX 1

[Less than six months after the opening ceremonies for Mex 1, the Vagabundos Del Mar club sent its first trailer boat caravan south. In the following column, announcing the club's 1974 cruise, Kino Bay is still cited as the main launch point.

However, almost as an afterthought, Ray mentions a splinter group, led by club President Chet Sherman, that will trailer down the brand new Transpeninsular Highway and launch at Mulegé.

At the conclusion of this cruise, Sherman's group returned to the U.S. via the Santa Rosalía-Guaymas ferryboat, which had begun service the preceding year.]

MAY 16, 1974—This is the final notice to all trailerable, seaworthy power boat owners who wish to join our Vagabundos Del Mar's Cortez Cruise for the finest saltwater sport of them all. On this voyage we will be launched (June 15) at Old Kino by Tiburcio Saucedo who takes good care of vehicles and trailers in a large, private and protected area.

We will be island-hopping across to Bahía San Francisquito for some fishing and topping off, and a visit to the new resort at Punta San Francisquito adjoining Bahía Santa Teresa. Next morning to Mulegé. Dock in river. At the river's mouth Hotel Serenidad will meet the Chet Shermans with a small group trailering their boats down the new Transpeninsular Highway to launch there.

— RAY CANNON

ROAD BUILDING IN BAJA CALIFORNIA FROM THE BEGINNING

[The following section is adapted from a paper written by Homer Aschmann, University of California at Riverside Department of Geography (courtesy Fred Metcalf).]

EARLY ROADS AND TRAILS

Until after the middle of the 19th Century there is no record of roads for wheeled vehicles anywhere in the peninsula. Transport was exclusively along mule trails connecting widely-spaced missions, settlements and ranches. By 1870 gold, silver, and copper mines had been developed, and wagon roads were built from the mines to various points on the coast. By 1910 the peninsula had a disconnected network of these mine roads.

ROAD BUILDING IN THE NORTH

The development of agriculture in the Mexicali Valley and the advent of Prohibition in the U.S. accelerated economic development in northern Baja California. Governor Esteban Cantú (1915-20) constructed dirt roads from Tijuana to Mexicali and Ensenada. The Ensenada road was paved by General Abelardo L. Rodríguez, who became governor of the Northern Territory in 1923, and President of Mexico in 1932.

In 1927 a combined overland expedition of the Mexican military and the Automobile Club of Southern California reached Mulegé.

In 1929, Joaquin Sagrista became possibly the first traveling salesman in southern Baja California when he drove his Ford truck from Los Angeles to Cabo San Lucas, selling miscellaneous merchandise. He returned to Los Angeles and restocked at Sears, Roebuck and Company for the return trip. Sagrista was the uncle of Doris Ortega, who with her husband, Enrique, would found Baja's first travel agency, International Travel Services, in 1946. Sagrista and Doris Ortega's grandfather also drove the first wine grape plants to begin the Santo Tomás winery industry in 1929.

During World War II, the Ensenada road was extended and paved south to Santo Tomás.

In the late 1940's out-of-season tomatoes were trucked from the Cape Region to the U.S. border. A 1932 Cadillac limousine carried mail and passengers from Tijuana to Santa Rosalía on a weekly schedule.

In 1948, grading was accomplished to San Quintín, but funds for asphalt pavement were exhausted at San Telmo, some 75 kilometers short. Twenty years later, in 1968, work was resumed, but it had progressed only 40 kilometers by 1972.

On the northern Cortez coast, the road from Mexicali south to San Felipe had been paved in 1950, and six years later, in 1956, Arturo Grosso collected a 10,000 peso ($800) reward offered by the state government if he could drive his truck north from Calamajué to San Felipe, which he did with the aid of explosives. Within weeks tourists followed in four-wheel-drive vehicles.

THE SOUTHERN TERRITORY

In the south, the most extensive set of early roads had been built to connect the El Boleo copper mine of Santa Rosalía with Mulegé and San Ignacio. In 1927, the Mulegé road was extended south and into the mountains at Comondú.

About 1950, a separate road was pushed from Loreto over the mountains to join the main peninsular road at Santo Domingo. However this route was soon abandoned as a completely new road was gradually extended north from La Paz, beginning in 1954. By 1961 the pavement had reached north to Santo Domingo.

In 1968, the south end road between San José del Cabo and La Paz was paved, and in 1972 the Transterritorial Highway was completed with the paving of the final link between Santa Rosalía and San Ignacio.

THE TRANSPENINSULAR HIGHWAY

In 1972, road building was suddenly accelerated. Federal money became available and two major contracts were let to grade and pave the final 600-kilometer gap between San Telmo and San Ignacio. Working from each end, hundreds of trucks and graders and thousands of laborers were employed. Various stages of construction were carried on simultaneously over one-hundred-kilometer stretches to hasten completion of the highway by the end of 1973, including a second major realignment of the road as the mining town of El Arco was bypassed in favor of Guererro Negro. Dedication ceremonies were held at the 28th Parallel monument at Guererro Negro on December 1, 1973.

THE FIRST VAG CRUISE LAUNCH AT BAHIA DE LOS ANGELES

[In 1975, the Vagabundos Del Mar club scheduled its annual cruise for launching at Bahía de los Angeles, signaling the end of the Kino Bay era for boaters from Southern California.]

FEBRUARY 19, 1975—An invasion of the Cortez by a fleet of vessels from a new direction can be expected the latter part of May. The trailerable small boats, 18 to 28 feet, will be launched at Bahía de los Angeles (called L.A. Bay for short). More than half the fleet will be owned and skippered by experienced members of the Vagabundos Del Mar Club. I'll be with them—photographing, looking for exciting fun events for mag features, and having some of the finest hours and days of my life.

The best dates this year for launching (to avoid swift currents and upwelling) are between May 15 and 21st.

There will be two groups. One will confine its cruising to the Midriff, principally between L.A. and San Francisquito Bays. The other flotilla of boats with well over 100-mile range, will top off at San Francisquito and head for Mulegé, with a few highly interesting spots to re-explore on the way. After two nights in Mulegé we will proceed down the coast to the back of Bahía San Nicolas, then down for a night in Ensenada San Juanico and some special fishing and exploring.

We expect to fit out again in Loreto for the long hop to La Paz, with a stopover at Puerto Gatos for a try at the big game fishing there. Whitey Whitestine of

Oakland, an old sailing partner of mine, definitely plans to go on to Rancho Buena Vista. Three other boat owners expect to cruise with him.

The Midriff fleet, coordinated by Vagabundos club president Chet Sherman, will likely get into the craziest yellowtail fishing they have ever been mixed up in, and may be fortunate enough to get movies of a fish pileup. I have seen two of these terrifying carnages occur just north of Isla Salsipuedes, both in late May. I have witnessed several other fish pileups in which every fish-eating creature around chomped each other up, with total disregard for their own personal safety.

This Sherman fleet will have a chance to run over to the S.W. corner of Isla San Esteban and from there to Isla San Pedro Mártir for the arrival of striped marlin, dorado (dolphinfish) and yellowfin tuna.

There is a general opinion that this cruise is less expensive and less time consuming than going from Southern California to Kino, then across. The Baja 1 from Tijuana to the Parador Punta Prieta turnoff to L.A. Bay is about 372 miles, and 43 more or less down to the Casa Díaz, where a gas supply for boats and aircraft is maintained. Good launching, $3 round trip, and protection is provided by a high rock wharf.

Boats trailering from east of Imperial Valley will continue to launch at Kino. — RAY CANNON

THE FIRST L.A. BAY LAUNCH PARTY

[The 1975 Bahía de los Angeles launch of the Vagabundos Del Mar cruise proved to be a memorable one, not only because it was the first major club cruise from this well-known spot, but because of Fred Harleman's wedding by "Padre" Ralph Lucas, a title by which he is known to the present day.

This trip was most likely Ray's first drive down the Transpeninsular Highway south of San Quintín and he expresses little enthusiasm for the long, hot desert drive. He picks up the story from his departure at Los Angeles.]

JUNE 20, 1975—I was aboard "Whitey" Whitestine's camper with his traveling buddy, Ken Mullins, headed for L.A. Bay and the Vagabundos' annual small boat cruise down the Cortez. We were trailering Whitey's 22-foot Owens when we left my home and choked our way through a hellfire and brimstone smog.

Our first rendezvous point was the village of San Miguel (six miles above Ensenada). Sixteen boats showed up. Five had gone ahead and a dozen had headed down to Kino Bay from Arizona and points east. On our way to L.A. Bay, Ralph Lucas, our trip coordinator, with a couple of assistants, proved their sportsmanship when they drove back 40 miles to tow the crippled camper and boat of Cap. Jack Arnold all the way in.

After a rousing evening of cookouts and fun despite the seasonal cold fog, we pulled out to meet at the San Quintín Hotel (Parador) so we could hold the fleet together for picture making. Mark Pew of Hollywood would drive Marie La Bar of the *L.A. Times* and me ahead so we could shoot the fleet as it navigated the curves up cirio cactus-covered mountain and canyon sides.

This cactus dominates the landscape's vegetation from the mountain top above El Rosario to L.A. Bay and beyond.

I was surprised to see wolf-size coyotes, a kind that is more often seen near rocky shores, feeding on small sea animals (such as sea cucumbers) at low tide. Night driven vehicles inevitably leave a lot of rabbits, field mice and the like, for a morning fiesta for the several varmints, ravens, vultures, and eagles. All help to break the quiet and otherwise motionless vistas for people not used to observing closely and constantly. Those that do are forever stopping to have a closer look or get a close-up picture of things unique.

We halted for lunch at the Punta Prieta Presidente Hotel and found it expensive but with good food. This is the junction turnoff for L.A. Bay. It is actually eight miles or more north of the old village of Punta Prieta.

After several more miles of the same kinds of cacti, newcomers getting their first glance of the Cortez usually let out a "Eureka!" yell. Club member Roy Wickline and our old friend Antero Díaz, L.A. Bay Hotel owner-operator, were out front of the greeters waiting for us.

Wickline, a San Diego furniture manufacturer, announced a clambake at his bay shore home for the meet. Díaz was not unhappy when half-a-dozen of us decided to sleep there, as every room in the hotel was jammed. Several relinquished reservations and slept in their boats.

The lengthy drive had developed lengthy and broad appetites that couldn't be filled with less than two heaping plates of "chocolate" clams and cockles, and the 60 or more members and their families took care of the several gunnysacks full.

Next a.m. we were greeted by a delightful clear, warm and windless day. The first for the past week. Fishing was spotty—a few averaged four yellowtail and as many oddballs.

That evening we were surprised to suddenly feel a wind that felt like a blast of heat downwind from a blast furnace. Summer had arrived at the Midriff, timed exactly to the pleasure of the Vagabundo activities. All hands planned to get with it at daylight.

That morning there was an increase in bird works and surface breaking forage fish, pushed up principally by sizable yellowtail. The day's catches were much better.

That night Papa and Mama Díaz threw a turtle steak fiesta with all the margaritas every indulging Vagabundo could hold, and to the rhythm of good Baja California music. There was dancing 'til the morning hours. The "ball" also celebrated a wedding—the strangest I can remember. Fred Harleman, an officer and charter member in our Club, was determined to join our good friend Ginger in a lifetime partnership.

The title of Ralph Lucas was changed officially from "fleet coordinator" to "wagon master," allowing him to perform the ceremony. I gave the bride away. There was a due amount of solemnity with plenty of room for a little X-rated humor.

There were some problems getting everyone up and off on the planned cruise. — RAY CANNON

DREDGING THE CABO INNER HARBOR

[Concurrently with the opening of the Transpeninsular Highway, work was begun on construction of the crown jewel at its southern terminus: the man-made inner harbor of Cabo San Lucas.

The success of these projects—along with the opening of the Los Cabos International Airport a few years later—confirmed that the industry of tourism pioneered 25 years earlier by Abelardo L. "Rod" Rodríguez at Rancho las Cruces was something upon which a modern economy could be built.

Ray's 1973 report on black marlin fishing makes his earliest reference to the dredging of the new Cabo San Lucas inner harbor.

The "Camino Real" referred to was originally built as the Hacienda Cabo San Lucas by Rodríguez in 1963, taken over by Western Hotels as the Camino Real de Cabo San Lucas in 1970, and bought by Bud Parr in 1977 as the Hotel Hacienda. The Hotel Finisterra was opened by Luis Cóppola Bonillas and Luis Bulnes Molleda in 1971, and the Hotel Solmar would be opened by Bulnes in 1974.]

NOVEMBER 11, 1973—The news I have been expecting occurred yesterday—black marlin broke out all over. From Cabo San Lucas to Buena Vista, reports coming in suggest that the fall run is on. Three boats out of this port ran into a sea crowded with big blacks and there were half-a-dozen hookups but all were too big to handle. Anglers hoping to catch sailfish, wahoo, or dolphinfish were not prepared to cope with the monsters. Two large teasers were grabbed and broken off—both from the same boat. At Buena Vista, where a couple of blacks had been popped off the day before, anglers of four of the boats successfully hooked and fought it out and decked four huge blacks.

Sailfish and striped marlin fins are being seen over a large area straight out from Camino Real, but all skippers here at the Finisterra say they will not take bait or lures.

You who have seen this area will be surprised at the changes. The recent storm wiped out a lot of old shacks and the town is getting a fresh new look. The roads to Hotels Finisterra and the fine new Solmar on the Pacific side of the Cape have been rerouted and improved. A big old dredge is chewing out the floor of the old, ugly slough and disgorging its centuries of refuse and sand into the 500-fathom trench which extends up from the abysmal depths to the center of the bay. This to make way for a fine harbor and dock for a large, new seagoing ferryboat to run to Puerto Vallarta, plus a few visiting yachts. — RAY CANNON

CABO SAN LUCAS FERRY TERMINAL AND HARBOR DREDGING

[In 1974, Ray describes the continuing work and general panorama from his room at the three-year-old Hotel Finisterra, built on a high ridge near land's end, overlooking both sides of the Baja peninsula. The 1,070-mile Transpeninsular Highway to the U.S. border at Tijuana had been completed a few months earlier.

Luis Bulnes Molleda recounts the story of Ray sitting in the lobby of his Hotel Solmar and telling guests about the "trained" grey whales that would appear right at the beach in front of the hotel each afternoon at three o'clock. At the appointed hour, the guests would run out to look, and sure enough, if they waited for just a few minutes, whales would appear—just as they did every few minutes during the height of the annual migration.

Mario Cóppola, described here as manager of the Hotel Finisterra, today operates the Hotel Los Arcos in La Paz, and the Finisterra is operated by his brothers, Alberto and Luis Cóppola Jr.]

MARCH 16, 1974—From the balcony of deluxe suite B-24, looking out over the Pacific side of the Finisterra at the grey whales migrating back from the mainland calving grounds in the mangrove flats, my attention is attracted to a small marlin cruiser. The attention-grabber is a hooked and jumping billfish no more than 2 1/2 miles off shore.

As the fight goes on, my gaze shifts to a pod of four or five baleens, a mile or more off shore. A week ago other arctic-bound pods were within 100 yards of shore, lunching on a massive school of deep-bodied anchovy.

A couple of days ago one boat with two anglers caught and tagged seven marlin, but the general take here and all around the south end of the peninsula has averaged less than five per fleet.

At Cabo the lack of live bait was blamed for so few being hooked, according to Finisterra boat skippers. They are putting up a roar because the district fisheries official established a temporary ban on catching live bait around the cannery pier, where it has been taken for several years. Then came the harbor builders who used dynamite to blast out a rock formation in the entrance to the future harbor and slaughtered several tons of the favorite bait fish, caballito (big-eyed jack). Boat owners say that they will appeal to the Governor's office.

There have been great improvements in the operation of the Finisterra since young and energetic Mario Cóppola took over. He is the brother of Luis Cóppola Jr., the very

Scenes from the dredging of the Cabo San Lucas inner harbor in 1973-1975, here viewed from the Hotel Finisterra, which had opened in 1971.

The Hotel Hacienda across the newly-created channel. Opened by Abelardo L. "Rod" Rodríguez in 1963, it would be bought in 1977 by Bud Parr.

The dredging machine pumped sand out the harbor mouth and into the deep underwater canyon that comes close to shore there.

From near the Hotel Hacienda, looking north at the site of the future city of Cabo San Lucas.

The outfall pipe exiting the newly-created harbor.

The end of the outfall pipe, just outside the new harbor mouth.

popular manager of the Hotel Los Arcos in La Paz.

Mario has been pointing out the many developments being planned for this fantastic ridge-top hotel. On the Pacific side beach, about 100 feet straight down from my balcony, a large saltwater swimming pool is to be constructed. To the right of it, a walk will extend to the surf and surf side palapas. A row of tennis courts will extend along cliffs from a pool side bar. A perpendicular lift or slanting elevator will transport guests from this lower level up to the desk and rooms.

With the opening of the seagoing ferry slated for May, to run from its dock close by to Puerto Vallarta, the Finisterra can expect a considerable carriage trade from people driving down the new highway.

Just learned yesterday that the work on the ferry dock, at the foot of the Finisterra's hill, is progressing so rapidly the heavy excavating machines will continue in expanding the harbor to include twice as great an area as needed for the huge ferry ship.

The supervisor told me that the dredge will cut right up to Alonso Fisher's trailer park, giving him a large slice of the bay front. It is hoped that the port will include landings for hotel fishing fleets. — RAY CANNON

LUIS BULNES ON THE OPENING OF MEX 1

[Luis Bulnes Molleda, on life in early Cabo San Lucas and the effects of the opening of the Transpeninsular Highway in 1973. Bulnes was born in Ribadesella, state of Asturias, Spain, came to Mexico in 1948, and in 1955 became manager of the cannery at Cabo San Lucas for Impresas Pando. At that time, the population of the town was about 300 people. In 1973 Bulnes opened the Hotel Solmar, Baja's "last resort" built into the living rock at the extreme tip of the peninsula.]

"Our people were more happy then. Maybe they eat three times a day now but they have to work. Before, maybe they ate only once a day, but all they had to do

Below left, pioneering hotelier Luis Bulnes Molleda at his Hotel Solmar, located at land's end on the very tip of the Baja California peninsula. He is standing at the door to the southerly-most room of the hotel, a magnificent apartment built into the living rock of the cliff called the "Ray Cannon Suite" in honor of the man Bulnes regards as "the most important single person in the development of Baja California." However, Ray never stayed in the "Ray Cannon Suite," which did not exist during his lifetime. Instead, he stayed three doors north, in Room 1121. Top left, the hotel under construction in 1972. The large rock at left center is now part of the outside dining area of the hotel's main building. Center left, the hotel's southern wing as it appears today. The last two windows on the right belong to the Ray Cannon Suite.

— CENTER AND LOWER PHOTOS BY GENE KIRA

was go down to the pier and catch fish. We are going to lose the tranquility, but are going to make a lot of money. Civilization has a price." — LUIS BULNES MOLLEDA

BAJA IN THE MODERN AGE—1975

[By late 1975 most of the basic elements of the modern era were in place and jet air travel had become the primary means for tourists to reach Baja California Sur; the quaint exclusiveness and exotic atmosphere of the early sport fishing resorts was being superseded by mass-market tourism.

Two years before his death, Ray describes a Baja California that in many ways had already left the Golden Age behind. As he did throughout his long career, Ray emphasizes the positive aspects of progress, but by 1975 the tranquil, tradition-steeped Baja California of the Ray Cannon era had been lost.

The portrait of Baja that emerges from this report is remarkable for the great change it reflects from the beginning of the Golden Age—only a quarter-century before—and for Ray's hope that further progress will come "very gradually and with much profound thought."

Overdevelopment has, in fact, occurred in the dense Los Cabos corridor, but in most areas of Baja California vast open spaces still dominate and there is still opportunity for orderly planning. Also notable in this recap of infrastructure development at the end of the Golden Age is Ray's astonished observation that—once the initial rush had passed—the Transpeninsular Highway did not bring a crush of "illicit thrill seekers" to Baja after all. From combined articles written in 1974 and 1975:]

The destructive impact expected on Baja California's vast primeval environment—didn't happen!

The completion of the new Transpeninsular Highway (already called "Baja 1" in U.S. vernacular); the dredging of the Harbor at Cabo San Lucas; construction of deluxe airports at La Paz, Mulegé, and Loreto; expansions of hotels and resorts and their airstrips; addition of several ship-size ferries crossing the Sea of Cortez (formerly known as the Gulf of California); the home-building craze in La Paz, and addition of a few small brand new hotels at Cabo San Lucas, Loreto, and along Baja 1—have in no way destroyed any of the beauty of the thousands of miles of open wilderness, nor fouled the very clean sea water. Nor are any of the planned future improvements likely to for the next several decades.

There were times, however, during the early recreational vehicle (RV) influx when we lovers of nature in the nude got ready to start gagging—as when the hordes rushed down Baja 1 the week it first opened, and again for the Easter holiday, and a short-lived run during school vacation in mid-June.

Among that first group were many who did everything we feared—clutter the beaches and coves, and drive as if

East Cape's Felipe Jesús "Chuy" Valdéz Vásques on the tropically-landscaped grounds of his Hotel Buena Vista Beach Resort—usually referred to by locals as "Spa." Valdéz, originally from Guaymas, managed the Hotel Los Cocos in La Paz in the early 1970s, and opened his hotel with 12 rooms in 1976 as "Club Spa Buena Vista." The original buildings were built in the 1940s as a residence and servants' quarters for Territorial Governor Agustín Olachea. The greatly-expanded hotel today operates a large sport fishing fleet and is still a family-run business.

— PHOTO BY GENE KIRA

they were on a no-speed-limit freeway instead of a 19-foot road with no shoulders. Some say that there were 30 fatalities in collisions or in efforts to avoid them. A few carried no Mexican insurance and could have gone (or did go) to Mexican jails, where cash bail bonds come high.

But each in turn of the three large waves of RV travelers seemed to have learned to behave better, and Mexican authorities soon had men in charge of the beaches who collected a couple of U.S. bucks and guarded against littering.

We are pushing for the construction of independent trailer parks, or in connection with hotels or resorts already established, such as the one presently in operation by Ed Tabor at his Flying Sportsmen Lodge in Loreto.

Despite their isolation, the people of the Territory (southern half of Baja) did not suddenly jump from a sleeping-peon period into the 20th Century with the opening up of the Peninsula, as a lot of city-bred foreigners had thought. Those who came down the new Camino soon learned that the village and backcountry people of Baja are blessed with an unusual amount of native wisdom, and they proved it in adjusting to the problems following the opening of Baja 1.

Little time was lost in starting highway safety measures. First off—signs. Highly effective was one erected at intervals stating that the Highway was constructed for commercial carriers and not as a speedway for other vehicles. Half of the numerous roadside signs illustrate the danger or hazards ahead (see *The Baja Book*, by Tom Miller and Elmar Baxter). Memorizing the signs

is not difficult. Among the hundred other emergencies to be met were plans for keeping the 1,000-mile-long Highway clear of loosened hillside rocks, and most important, constructing shoulders in some of the more hazardous sectors.

An explosion in land subdivision and hotel building, expected by many, was checked. Most everyone thought they would see a rash of motel and hot dog stands all around Cabo San Lucas as soon as its harbor was dredged out and work on a paved, jet-size airstrip there was begun. Boom conditions were anticipated at the new airports and airstrips that have already been completed. But none jelled. However, extensive developments in this place, and to a greater extent in La Paz, are sure to come. But very gradually and with much profound thought.

There is going to be considerable change in air travel to the south end of the Baja California peninsula, and according to an official involved in the development "there will be another (the third) major airline joining the existing companies—Aeroméxico and Hughes Airwest—in carrying passengers here from the U.S. One other, and perhaps two, lines will be stopping at the extensive new international airport now being fashioned by day and night crews near San José Viejo, four miles north of the city of San José del Cabo.

With all of the recent developments in the Territory— the paved highway the full length of it; electric power, telephones, and potable water to towns and villages; the building and expansion of large resorts—you would think the boom was on. Then add the lengthening and improving of most all resort airstrips, the new, elaborate airports, the resurfacing now in progress at Cabo San Lucas. Also there are the ferry ships—Guaymas to Santa Rosalía, La Paz to Guaymas, to Topolobampo, to Mazatlán, and now from the new man-made harbor at Cabo San Lucas, to Puerto Vallarta.

Perhaps the most valuable of all additions to the Territory's orderly development and future welfare was the construction of schools and the staffing of them with highly qualified instructors.

All of this may seem like a giant leap into the 20th Century and readying to welcome the bulldozing subdividers. But there are safeguards and limiting factors against the spoilers. More than 95% of this half of the peninsula is still wilderness and the changes to come will not bring smog or other pollutions for another century.

Sí, the Baja California as we have known it looks better now than ever before. — RAY CANNON

CONDOR II "OVERLAND YACHT" TRIP BEGINNINGS OF THE RV ERA

Ray's 1973 trip around southern Baja aboard a Condor II recreational vehicle foreshadowed the RV revolution that would begin with the opening of the Transpeninsular Highway less than a year later.

This "overland yacht cruise" was sponsored by the Condor Coach Corporation of El Monte, California. Ray was escorted by photographer, Ted Hall, and Condor plant manager, Wesley Thomas, for the drive down the Mexican mainland; crossing of the Cortez on the Guaymas–Santa Rosalía ferry; an exploratory run through La Paz, Cabo San Lucas and up the Pacific coast to Bahía Magdalena; and a return to the mainland on the ferryboat from La Paz.

This route was similar to the one Ray had followed on his El Dorado pickup camper trip of 1961, but through a completely different world of new fishing lodges, paved roads, new airports, and grand resorts recently completed or under construction.

In 1973, the sight of the enormous Condor II recreational vehicle on the roads of southern Baja California

Clockwise from opposite page left, scenes from Ray's pioneering 1973 tour of southern Baja in the Condor II recreational vehicle: debarking the Mazatlán–La Paz ferryboat; on the Transterritorial Highway at El Triunfo; climbing the hill to the recently-opened Hotel Finisterra in Cabo San Lucas; going overland at Matancitas (Puerto López Mateos); and departing the Hotel Cabo San Lucas.

would have caused a sensation among the local people. It was one of their first experiences with a form of tourism that would become very familiar during the next quarter-century as RV parks and facilities were built all around the peninsula.

LOOKING BACK AT LA PAZ

[Ray reminisces about city he had loved and watched grow up from little more than a village. The dredging of the inner bay and the filling of El Mogote, the sandy finger of land forming its northern boundary, had occurred in the 1960s. Ray writes of cutting a canal through the blockage to restore the fishery of the inner bay, which had held quantities of snook and bonefish until about that time.

The great increase in vehicular traffic that Ray mentions here occurred during the same period, with the extensive development of agriculture in the Santo Domingo valley area, and especially with the paving of the Transterritorial Highway from Cabo San Lucas to Santa Rosalía in 1971. The federal territory of Baja California Sur had become a state on October 8, 1974. From combined columns written in July 1975:]

"What changes have you seen in your 20 years of observing this area? What happened to the abounding fish populations in the La Paz inner bay? What happened to those very "simpatico" girls of La Paz you wrote so much about in your early-day columns? Do they still have the slow-paced Sunday and Thursday evening promenades

The Puerto Vallarta ferry in the recently-dredged inner harbor of Cabo San Lucas, 1975. In two years, the Los Cabos International Airport at San José del Cabo would open, ushering in the modern era for the southern peninsula.

around the plaza? What about the old and quaint dwellings with expansive patios covered with a canopy of tropical fruit and flowering vines? Did Mrs. Murphy's Riding Academy ever reopen?"

Yes, it did, relocated under the new name of "Ranchita." But its occupants are no longer referred to as "fillies." You are more likely to hear them called "tomatoes," "chickens," or "chickadees."

Altogether, the changes here appear to have been slow and somewhat orderly to residents or visitors who come and go often. However, to those who have spanned a decade or so between visits, the changes may be shocking. For there are now a thousand cars, taxies, and trucks to one of 20 years ago.

Many old homes have disappeared, but behind modern store structures.

Most young ladies above high school age have retreated behind their patio walls and they don't walk to go shopping. They drive.

And now with jobs for the men folks, marriage has become popular again, reversing the trend that started with the successful 1910 Madero revolution, and resulting in an almost absence of the practice, up to a few years ago. So many men had gone to the mainland for work, Baja South was left populated with seven women to one man at the low period. Today it is claimed that there are less than five to one.

There are still enough girls to outnumber the men in the promenades, especially along the malecón, during the balmy evenings when the cooling Coromuel breezes balance the sultry sounds of Mexican love songs. Nor have the ladies forgotten how to throw a compelling pitch with a lingering glance. They are just as "simpatica" as ever.

There have been losses in the fish abundances. La Paz people say the depletion was caused by fishing with dynamite and systemic destruction of the basic food supply. Finding little or no food, the game fish gave the inner bay a wide berth. Now to get to the good fishing grounds, boats go out to Isla Espíritu Santo, or beyond, for billfish. Yellowtail are becoming the winter fish and may prove a good fishery within a year or so.

There is some renewed talk about cutting the Mogote to allow a sweep of fresh sea water into the back bay. I believe that the whole food supply for gamesters would be revived at once and bay fishing would be great again for snook, snapper, cabrilla, and pompano. And sierra could be restored if a strict bag limit was enforced. Commercial bay fishing would have to be barred for a couple or more years, or until signs of recovery had been proven.

The City of Peace is many things to this brand new "State of Baja California South." (To avoid confusion we use the English "South" instead of the more proper Spanish "Sur.")

La Paz is the capitol city of the state, as it was of the Territory. It is the junction for the sunburst of gravel and graded highways, old, rough dirt caminos, the paved Baja One, and trails to farms, ranches and mountainous back country.

It is a port for ferries and shipping, for yachts and small craft, a terminal or port of call for two or three or more flights of commercial airlines from the U.S., Mexican cities, Europe and South America. Also, the major airport for the Servicios Aéreos de la Paz planes serving resorts and towns in daily or multiple daily scheduled flights and charters.

Motor vehicles have taken over, except on special holidays when vaqueros (cowboys) on their single-foot-gated mules, and caballeros (horsemen) on their spirited high-steppers parade in full costume befitting their titles. Horse-pulled wagons and some pack burros were in the majority for overland transportation when I first arrived here.

Ten years later, the change over to cars and trucks was already moving rapidly. Anticipating a great increase in farm production in the Santo Domingo-Magdalena Plains region, the federal government was grading roads and financing trucks and farm machinery for agrarian and ejido farmers.

Paving of the first main highway was rushed, with a super boom in La Paz street traffic. This was perhaps the most noticeable abrupt change of all.

The chubasco (hurricane) of 1959 wrought considerable havoc among the tall palms and very large and spreading India laurel trees. Several of the narrow and winding streets leading up to the central plaza were completely covered with the converging limbs of the

The Puerto Vallarta ferry leaving Cabo San Lucas, c. 1975. Ferry service would continue until 1986.

evergreen laurels. Half of the palms were broken off and the laurels were toppled along the malecón. Most of the latter, trimmed and righted, made out with renewed vigor and growth. Within another decade we can expect that most of the former beauty will be restored.

I will not attempt to describe the buildings constructed during this period other than to mention that generally they were more pioneering than primitive efforts. Although I prefer the old La Paz-Spanish architecture to boxy modern structuring, I must admit that the additions have come gradually and orderly.

Most important innovations were completed or launched during the administration of the territory's foremost governor, Ing. Hugo Cervantes del Río, now Secretaria de Presidencia and Presiding Officer of the Cabinet of President Luis Echeverría.

When I asked Cervantes del Río which of these numerous accomplishments he considered the most beneficial, he seemed to weigh each with profound thought, then confidently replied—"Communication." When he noticed that I was puzzled, he added—"Not mechanical, but face-to-face discussions with the many factions settling their differences and thus breaking the barriers that separated them." — RAY CANNON

Ray aboard the *Gypsy*, 1976. — PHOTO BY ALIX LAFONTANT

RAY'S LAST CRUISE
VOYAGE OF THE "GYPSY" 1976

IN JUNE 1976, Ray departed Bahía de los Angeles aboard the boat, *Gypsy*, owned by Vagabundos Del Mar club members Bam and Jerry Heiner, for what would be his last cruise down the Sea of Cortez.

Ray was physically weakened by then, three months short of his 84th birthday, and had to be helped in and out of the boat. His columns from this final voyage are positive in tone—as always—but nevertheless betray an unmistakable undercurrent of weariness.

The Vagabundos "Secret Cove" features prominently on this trip and seems to have been Ray's main objective. The cove, called Ensenada Puerto Almeja in Jack Williams' *Baja Boater's Guide*, is a small pocket located on the north side of Punta San Basilio, between Mulegé and Loreto. Ray's sailing directions to find this spot were to go about nine miles south of Punta Púlpito on heading 168. He had visited this cove many times before, but he seems to have become fascinated by it late in life, and he made it a feature of this, his last trip down the Cortez in "little ships."

TO THE SECRET COVE

[The initial announcement of the Vagabundos Del Mar cruise of 1975. The passenger list for this cruise included photographer Jack Barcus, who was filming a movie.]

DECEMBER 12, 1975—You can get in on this only if you have a trailerable, 18 to 26-foot stern-drive boat with a fuel range of 150 miles or more. Or if you wish to charter a similar craft at La Paz or Loreto for the voyage.

There is no highway or byway within 50 miles of this secret hideout of several great game species, the largest ever to enter such a shallow cove in the Cortez Sea. I will advise fellow sportsman members of our Vagabundos Del Mar club on the location when they are ready to go for the voyage. I am not about to publish the name or location of the place for the simple reason that Mexican netters would be swarming all over the grounds where gigantic, up to 1,000-pound jewfish, *Promicrops itaiara* (not to be mistaken for the smaller California black sea bass, *Stereolepis gigas*) come to spawn.

On my first trip inside this cove we saw a jewfish in less than ten feet of water. We were trolling for sierra and hooked one when suddenly we saw the great bass heading for it. Knowing that our tackle was too light to even slow the big fish, we gave the boat full-throttle and circled the whole cove, barely keeping ahead of the monster. We did catch a couple of 60-pound yellowfin tuna, a larger baya grouper, a sizable dog snapper, and an amberjack that topped them all.

On a more recent trip we dropped in for just a quick look but ended by spending the afternoon and night in the rich cove. When we cut the motor our boat was engulfed in what seemed to be an enormous cauldron of boiling water. There were fleeting glances of yard-long flashes of silver. On the shaded, less active side of the boat we saw the reason for the frantic commotion. A whole army of half-grown roosterfish were milling around inhaling wounded anchoveta as fast as their brothers and sisters could maim them. Half the cove was jam-packed with the little forage fish and the roosters were harvesting.

If you would like to have the hair on the back of your neck stand up permanently like bristles on a razorback hog, just get into snorkeling togs and quietly slide down beside your boat during such a fish feeding binge and get a long look at the raw gluttony, which is exceeded only by man's greed.

We will have the date set for our annual June launching at Bahías de los Angeles and Kino. The plan will include a lengthy happy adventure fleet voyage to some very exciting islands and Baja coastlines. — RAY CANNON

Aboard the *Gypsy* in the summer of 1976. At Caleta San Francisquito, Ray is greeted by his friend of 18 years, José Villavicencio of Rancho el Barril. — PHOTO BY BAM AND JERRY HEINER

OVERNIGHT CARAVAN STOP AT SAN QUINTIN

[On his second caravan down Mex 1, Ray's spirits once again seem constricted by the long drive, but he expresses his joy and release when, for the final time, he is cruising down his beloved Sea of Cortez.]

Our Vagabundo club's qualified wagon master, Ralph Lucas, showed his leadership in reserving the whole trailer park, and we filled it. Our 20 to 27-foot-long boats and campers to match somehow looked larger than ever individually as well as collectively.

Due to the early morning seasonal fog which usually burns out at about 10:30 a.m., all units were asked to hold back on an 8 a.m. hit-the-road takeoff, so that photographing the hill climb of the long line of trailered boats would get good sunlight all the way up the climb.

The movies of that climb should provide a spectacular segment of the documentaries. Seen along the way were blooming cirio cactus, and a fantasyland section of great weird and grotesque rocks shaped like toadstools, and skull heads, with gigantic cardón and barrel cactus growing out of dome cracks and eroded holes. Yet all of this was made beautiful by a carpet of many colored blossoms to those who loved nature enough to stop and examine the minute flowering plants.

After a gas top-off and beer break at Parador Punta Prieta and finding no mechanical or other problems, Lucas led us down from the mountain crest to Los Angeles Bay. Like a miracle, the three-day blow that had kept early arrival boats from getting out of the bay, or Kino, subsided and some got out and into the super-abundant yellowtail.

A boat from Kino reported that sailfish and dorado (dolphinfish) were arriving and being caught above Isla San Pedro Mártir.

Once again Ralph "Padre" Lucas had trouble holding the eager beaver Vagabundos for the big turtle steak fiesta and ball, and more so the next morning when just about everyone was in a mood to make the big plunge a day ahead of schedule. But he managed to get a review parade past the outer end of the breakwater, for the take-off filming. Ralph came near losing control of half of his boats.

All little ships' skippers still had those racetrack starting jitters and kicked up great white breaker wakes as they zipped up to the Barcus camera and squeezed between it and Roca Blanca and then into a long line right into the early morning sun.

Free of the filming for an hour or so, I, and no doubt most of the others, settled down to enjoying some of life's finest intoxications. The salty morning spray is cool and embracing, but the deeper joy is the unexplainable thrill of the spirit experienced at the instant when the reveries' anticipation becomes reality. — RAY CANNON

ANCHORAGE AT BAHIA SAN FRANCISQUITO

[Ray returns to the scene of his favorite of all cruises— the 1958 "Kids' Trip" taken 18 years earlier—and a final reunion with José Villavicencio of Rancho el Barril.]

We got our bearing on a 450-foot-high land head just back of Punta San Gabriel, eastern perimeter of Bahía San Francisquito, as we headed out across Canal Salsipuedes.

Newcomers, making this simple crossing for the first time, will learn the importance of a charted course in trying to locate the outer San Francisquito Bay. Some fail completely to locate the landlocked inner baylet.

Among the good fun activities was the reminiscing with José Villavicencio. How, with a group of Hughes Aircraft Company executives, I met his family and visited their old-style ranch house, about 19 years ago. We had come across from the then ghost town of Kino Bay in 18-foot outboard cabin cruisers, the first such boats José's family had ever seen.

Prompted by Ralph "Padre" Lucas, we ceremoniously made José an honorary member of the Vagabundos Del Mar club. He had given a lot of extra energy to supplying our boats with fuel for more than 16 years.

We seemed to get across the lee of Cabo Vírgenes in fairly calm water. It's usually turbulent.

Bam and Jerry Heiner of Hidden Hills, California, proved to be par excellent sailors and fine sportsmen, despite our overloading and overcrowding their boat with an extra ton of movie equipment and fishing gear. They maintained a grand sense of humor in spite of all the restrictions our filming on their boat entailed. Both Jerry and Bam have been added to my list of "my kind of people." — RAY CANNON

LAST STOP AT MULEGE

Hotel Serenidad is booming, a popularity created by its new and complete facilities, trailer park, boat launching ramp, and new very hospitable and efficient manager-operator, Fernando del Moral, son of the late co-owner of the hotel, with Don Johnson, now retired and taking a long-deserved rest and getting in some of that fabulous Mulegé small game fishing. — RAY CANNON

RETURN TO VAGABUNDO COVE

[The visit to the secret cove is anticlimactic; Ray seems played out at this point.]

Having replenished our fuel and supplies the day before, and shifted photographer Jack Barcus and equipment to Whitey Whitestine's boat, we sailed at dawn for our regular meeting spot of Punta Púlpito.

Actor John Wayne at a family gathering with Don Johnson (standing), owner of the Hotel Serenidad, at the Johnson home in downtown Mulegé. Photo taken in 1975, about a year and a half after the opening of the Transpeninsular Highway. To right of Wayne is Nancy Johnson, Don's wife; then her sister Martha Ugalde. At left are brother, Alfonso Ugalde; and the Johnson's daughter, Nancy. — COURTESY DON JOHNSON

Johnson, at the "Saturday Night Pig Roast" that has been held at his Hotel Serenidad since the early 1970s. — PHOTO BY GENE KIRA

Whitey was given the honor of taking the point for the next hop to Vagabundo Bay. I knew he would never forget that course, since last year when he tried it he found he would have to sail straight up a high cliff to stay on 168. His unchecked compass had been about 45 degrees off. But this time, with a new Reinell boat and expensive compass, he didn't veer a second.

Despite the long dry season, our cove was a place of special isolated beauty. It was as if we had arrived in the classical Elysian Gardens on the day before all plant and animal life was reincarnated, as in the dawn of new life.

While the hills look barren, as in stateside winter months, the peninsula that land-locks the cove was bright green.

A cookout on the very white and clean beach is preceded by a nip of grog. Then a ceviche appetizer, and a nip. Followed by several broiled (over coals) fish fillets and a nip. Somewhere among the courses of a couple of huge bowls of mixed salad, I think the next grog intake was more of a swack and a guzzle. Anyway it was a most pleasant evening. — RAY CANNON

LORETO

[Ray's participation in the cruise ended in Loreto, as he and photographer Jack Barcus flew from there to La Paz, and then traveled overland to Buena Vista with Alix Lafontant and his wife, Patricia, in their RV.]

Due to the convenience for taking on fuel and supplies and easy access to good hotel accommodations, the Flying Sportsmen Lodge usually gets the Vagabundo boaters. The attractions include the hotel's new ramp and several special privileges extended to motor home and camper visitors to its new palm-shaded trailer park.

My dear and longtime friend Gloria Davis Benziger, co-owner of the Hotel Oasis, has been elected State Representative for Loreto. Her husband and partner, Bill Benziger, who got shipwrecked in a chubasco trying to get into Tambobiche Bay, was honored recently by having a large hidden lagoon there officially named for him.

With our cameramen, we enjoyed a very pleasant visit to the new Hotel Presidente Loreto. Another old and dear friend, Al Green, a man you should get to know when you go to Loreto, was our host. — RAY CANNON

FLIGHT TO LA PAZ

[Ray's description of Islas San José and Espíritu Santo was perhaps inspired by the view from his Aeroméxico airliner as it flew down Canal de San José and over Bahía de La Paz. He revisits the recently expanded Hotel Los Arcos—scene of his meeting 22 years earlier with Mayo Obregón, Guillermo "Bill" Escudero, and Luis Cóppola Bonillas—and, as always, he is enthusiastic for the economic growth and development of Baja California.]

No matter what direction you go out from La Paz by land or sea there are unique and strange vistas, such as the islands of Espíritu Santo and Partida, encompassing almost as much water in their baylets, coves, and straits as in their land areas. Farther northwestward are the even stranger cluster of small islands at the south end of Isla San José, with snook and clams in and just out of its mangrove labyrinth.

The first day I arrived in La Paz I wrote—"If I ever retire, then this is the place," and that was written close to a quarter of a century ago. Now, after more than a hundred

Ray's "Vagabundo Secret Cove" in foreground, with white, sandy beach, is located on the north side of Punta San Basilio, about 30 miles north of Loreto. — PHOTO COURTESY JACK WILLIAMS

Last cruise, aboard the *Gypsy*, 1976. — PHOTO BY ALIX LAFONTANT

visits over these many years I am more sold on this grand mixture of the old and the modern than ever before.

There are the gardened patios that matured in the 17th and 18th centuries, still being loved and nurtured by the descendants of the planters; old warehouse stores hidden behind towering spreading India laurel trees, and a few hundred other structures and ancient transplants, as well as aging things to see, in contrast to the two new elegant and deluxe hotels—the Los Arcos and El Presidente La Paz. I did get a good look at the Los Arcos and was astonished at the magnificent work of the architect.

As you approach the desk to sign in for an overnight stop, you see beyond a modern facade designed to give full view between the flying buttress columns of a most inviting open area with swimming pool and ramadas—all being patronized by shapely and otherwise beautiful girls, ladies, women, girls.

You hesitate to sign the register for one day only. Perhaps your thoughts drift or snap back to the old novel, *Ten Nights In a Moorish Harem.*

Everything about the new rooms and suites is comfortable and as plush as you would wish for.

La Paz today is no longer an old town but with its new, 200-room hotels, the Ruffo Brothers department store, and large supermarket, several hundred new homes, apartments, stores, modern schools and playgrounds, plus a population to match, La Paz is now a first-rate city.

— RAY CANNON

BUENA VISTA

[Ray reaches Rancho Buena Vista. He would return to the Ranch one more time, on his final trip to Baja, five months later, in November 1976.]

News of the fine fishing in the Buena Vista area and knowledge that our boats would be there caused us to shorten our further sight-seeing and head over the hills and the pass through the Sierra de la Laguna, 2,000 feet high, and on up to more than 3,000 feet due west of Rancho Buena Vista.

We couldn't resist a photographing stop at the semi-ghost town of El Triunfo to get shots of the arches of the ruins of the old opera house, honky-tonk and public houses, and the tall smoke stacks of gold, silver, and copper smelters which flourished a century ago.

Arriving at Rancho Buena Vista is always like college homecoming week.

There are the happy workers, all of whom I call "cousins." After I had spent most of my time at the resort getting material for close to ten years, I returned with a copy of *The Sea Of Cortez* and showed it around. Thinking that I had done the whole book during my absence for six months, one of the waiters said seriously—"Our cousin has gone to the big city and made good."

The feeling for that title stuck 'till this day.

— RAY CANNON

Ray and Matador, Rancho Buena Vista, 1964. — PHOTO BY HARRY MERRICK

FAREWELL TO A VAGABUNDO

RAY'S FINAL TRIP TO BAJA

RAY—THAT OLD Hollywood showman—made his last exit from the grand stage of Baja California's Golden Age in typically dramatic fashion.

The final act of Ray's 30-year run in Baja featured a large, fly-down Vagabundo club birthday party in La Paz; its dramatic cancellation; a true-to-life natural disaster and tragedy; the death of one of his closest friends; and some of his best writing—a fitting farewell and celebration of the perpetual process of rebirth and the Taoist philosophy by which he had lived his life.

The story begins in the summer of 1976, when the Vagabundos Del Mar club announced plans for its most ambitious event ever—a Ray Cannon "79th Birthday Party" to be held at the Hotel Los Arcos in La Paz on October 29-31. The inside joke was that this was to be the fifth celebration of Ray's 79th birthday; he would be 84 years old on September 1st.

For the elaborate party—actually a series of them—170 seats were reserved on Aeroméxico and hotel space was taken for 85 couples, at a time when the "Vags" club numbered only about 475 members.

But that celebration was never held. On September 30—a month before the party—Hurricane Liza struck southern Baja, causing tremendous damage and hundreds of deaths in La Paz when an earthen dam collapsed on October 1, sending a wall of water through the city. It was the worst hurricane to hit Baja since 1959. Shortly after the storm, the terrifying damage to the city was recorded from the air by photographer/pilot Harry Merrick.

Because of the tragedy, Ray's "Fifth 79th Birthday Party" was rescheduled and held in San Diego the following February.

Immediately after the storm, Ray wrote columns from dispatches that had reached him in Los Angeles, minimizing the extent of the damage in an effort to calm public fears that might result in the cancellation of travel plans. But as

more information arrived—all of it bad—he decided to go down for a look himself.

On November 9, 1976 Ray made that final trip to Baja—visiting once more his beloved Rancho Buena Vista. As it turned out, he would never see Baja or his good friend Colonel Eugene Walters again. Seven months after that final trip—on June 7, 1977—Ray died of complications from lung cancer in Los Angeles. Only a few weeks later, Colonel Walters was also gone, and with them a chapter of the Golden Age passed into history.

FIRST REPORTS OF HURRICANE LIZA

[From the *Los Angeles Times*, October 10, 1976.]

"Three truckloads of emergency housing materials and milk left Glendale Saturday bound for hurricane-stricken La Paz in Baja California…

The shipment… is expected to arrive by Monday in La Paz—hit by Hurricane Liza Sept. 30, leaving at least 750 dead and 40,000 persons homeless…"

MINIMIZING THE EXTENT OF THE DAMAGE

[From combined columns in *Western Outdoor News*, Ray—as always—attempts to aid tourism in Baja California, here by calming public fears of the hurricane. Later, the early reports of tremendous fatalities and damage would be confirmed.]

OCTOBER 15, 1976—Last week a Baja official who was sincerely mourning for the living workers of the peninsula as well as the dead, said that he had helped bury the last of those that got caught in the flood. He added that

Aboard the *Gypsy*. One of the last photos of Ray taken, in the summer of 1976. — PHOTO BY ALIX LAFONTANT

the living would now suffer from a lack of work due to a big drop in the tourist business, which he claims was caused in part by the exaggerations in the media. The horrible deaths, he says, were caused by a broken earth-filled dam flooding an arroyo where squatters had thrown up temporary expendable shacks of palm leaves and cardboard.

Except for the dam breaking, less material damage was done to Baja by this storm than during the 1959 chubasco.

As an example of press news distortion one of the great international news gathering and distributing agencies as late as October 7, released a story still claiming that 40,000 people were homeless in La Paz as a result of Hurricane Liza. This would be two-thirds of the whole population of a town of 60,000, and that during the tourist season, October 15 through July.

I have just heard that Bing Crosby is flying down to get movie shots of the damaged area around La Paz. I, too, will likely be going for a full roundup of the real harm done to the peninsula and the people still missing.

— RAY CANNON

REPORTS STILL CONFUSING

OCTOBER 22, 1976—Reports from Baja's late chubasco "Liza" are still confusing. Some reporters write of the damage done by the great storm that came from the sea doing a lot of minor damage to sea walls and water edge structures. None mentioned a single life lost in the resort areas or elsewhere, except for those caught in the palm leaf cardboard shacks in the arroyo when the dirt-fill dam broke in La Paz.

Other news tells of flooding from the chubasco. If it did as much or more damage than the 1959 storm it was because more of the expansion in major buildings in the region had been done in that 17-year period than in the past century or so. All structures are expected to be repaired by the October 16 opening season.

Some damage was done by the fierce winds, principally to very old palm leaf roofs and some few old palm frond palapas. Winds and waves combined to flip several commercial fishing and shrimp boats. Small craft that made up the resort fleets had advance warning in time to get the boats high enough on the shore to save them. A few may have been tardy.

When the 1959 blow came roaring up the Cortez I was with UCLA's Dr. Boyd Walker in Puerto Escondido. We saw no signs of a raging storm, much less a chubasco. But when we arrived at the Flying Sportsmen Lodge expecting to devour a hearty meal, we found that they didn't even have a cup of coffee. Most of the town was like that.

It seems that the flood waters from Loreto's spreading mountainous watershed had piled up at the arroyo forks, and for the first time in 50 years, tore down the main half-mile-wide wash, uprooted large trees of that age and transported them down to a thicket of big trees growing all across the dry gulch bottom just above the town. The pileup created a dam across the arroyo and diverted the water so it would come screaming down the main street of the ancient pueblo.

I have often said that I thoroughly disliked the whole pre-1959 Loreto except for the beauty queen, 16-year-old Gloria Davis (Benziger), who appointed herself my guide and social mentor. Today she is a member of State Congress. I remember her apologies for all of the fallen palm fronds and whole trees that no one could or would remove. Each house and old hovel had its share of pigs and chickens which roamed the streets. That is, until the '59 chubasco sent the wall of purging water sweeping down and pushed everything that was loose out into the sea, including the pigs and chickens, where they were rescued later.

No people were killed in Loreto and only two in the whole Territory. The governor rushed food and drinking water and put every able man to work building real homes or repairing and painting old ones, and within a few months flower gardens and fruit trees had replaced the trash, and Loreto, with its towering palms, was turned into

a "Garden of Allah." I have loved it ever since.

As of this day, reports from Loreto state "no damage from the recent chubasco "Liza."

A late report from the Buena Vista region resorts gives some details on the damage done in the area by high wind tides during Liza. There was not enough damage, however, to hinder or delay the October 16 opening of Rancho Buena Vista and Palmas de Cortez. Bobby Van Wormer sends word that his Punta Colorada resort will open October 20. His place lost a couple of palm-thatched roofs (easy to replace).

The flooding from the resort's watershed did fill Buena Vista's airstrip with gravel and sand, and while it is being reconditioned the nearby strip of the Palmas de Cortez will be used. It was a lake but easy to drain. The sea action also came up and tore at the Buena Vista veranda and bar, and dumped sand into the swimming pool.

A few rooms were flooded at the Palmas de Cortez and the road to Punta Pescadero was filled with boulders

Massive damage through the city of La Paz caused by Hurricane Liza in the fall of 1976. The shock of the storm and the many fatalities caused by it resulted in the cancellation of a large birthday party planned for Ray at the Hotel Los Arcos. — PHOTO BY HARRY MERRICK

Ray at Puerto Escondido. — PHOTO BY MIKE RYAN

from hillsides, where cuts were made.

I expect to go down shortly and get a firsthand account of the whole tragic business and see how things are being rebuilt. — RAY CANNON

GREAT STORMS AND
THE PHENOMENON OF RENEWAL

[Ray recalls the post-storm sea changes after the Benziger-Tambobiche shipwreck of 1964 and the great hurricane of 1959, and he muses on the enriching effect of severe storms on the coastal waters of Baja California. Just below the surface of this thoughtful column is Ray's lifelong belief in the concepts of regeneration and reincarnation.]

OCTOBER 29, 1976—For many years I have kept track of the effects of the mountain-scouring flood waters on fish life in the Cortez and am convinced that the richness transported helps to produce great abundances of marine life from the smallest entity right on up to the enormous marlins.

If this theory is correct, then there is a small measure

of good done by the big 15 to 20-year type chubasco that took such a heavy, tragic toll on one of its rare visits to Baja California's south recently.

The scenario of the good phenomenon begins with the 15-year accumulation of leaves, deadwood, and remains of massive populations of minute insects and other animals. It is only the sudden cloudburst downpour of rain that comes with the hurricane-like storm that floods all of the arroyos (washes) in its path. Other seasonal rains seep into the soil gradually, and slowly flow down to the bottom of the boulder-filled gulches and canyons. But the chubasco quickly fills the gullies, then moves tens of thousands of tons of the organic material all the way into the sea. There it is devoured by bacteria and other small sea creatures and secreted as fertilizing chemicals such as phosphates, nitrates, and potash. With the almost constant daylight sunshine, phytoplankton (vegetable plankton) organisms get the needed stimulation to absorb the fertilizers, which triggers and maintains a multiplying of the minute algae.

Zooplankton includes animals from the size of great jellyfish down to microscopic creatures so small that several million can live in one cubic foot of water, providing nobody else is in it. As soon as the phytoplankton start a "bloom" (splitting), so do the zooplankton after a heavy meal of grazing on the vegetables.

I recall that shortly after sunup on the day following the chubasco in which I was shipwrecked in Tambobiche Bay some years back, I saw the water become like buttermilk in color and thickness. The next day there occurred a massive population explosion of the tiny, 1/4-inch long opossum shrimp, thickening the water to the consistency of oatmeal. Inch-long fish were already feeding on the crustaceans.

It seems that several hundred-thousand tons of this nourishing protein is produced twice a month and provides bountiful slurping material for the great 60 to 70-ton finback whales, second only to the blue whale in size.

All of the sea's creatures depend upon plankton for their food supply in one way or another and a majority of the fishes thrive on the shrimp as their main entree, especially along rock walls of submerged canyons and around rock islands.

A year after the 1959 flooding chubasco, the Cortez was literally swarming with big fish. How they got the message of the abundant harvest I have no idea but the water was alive with them. Dorado (dolphinfish) by the thousands came within a hundred yards of shore near the mouth of the large arroyos. I noted also immense populations of ladyfish and pargo mulatto (a striped snapper). Several other snappers joined those species and took up residence among the three or four-foot boulders forming the arroyo expanses on down to 60 feet deep. All big gamesters selected their favorite foods.

There was a time when the Colorado River supplied

more than enough enrichening silts to keep the north end of the Cortez flourishing with all that nature could use. But then came the river-diverting dams that shut off all transporting of the basic food supplies, but the deposits of silts may continue to keep the breakdown bacteria busy for another half-century or so. — RAY CANNON

RANCHO BUENA VISTA
RAY'S LAST BAJA COLUMNS

[Ray came to his Round House at Rancho Buena Vista as often as he could, and it was to this place that he made his last pilgrimage to Baja, when he knew that he was dying. During that visit, in the aftermath of Hurricane Liza, he took pictures of the Round House in disrepair, with its roof gone and its glass doors broken out by flying wood.

But his writing from that trip reflects not the destruction, but his love of the natural beauty of Rancho Buena Vista and his faith in the power of living things to renew themselves.

This column is rich with references to plants and nature, as Ray returned one last time to the theme of natural beauty that he found so personally moving. The tone is reminiscent of the letters he wrote to Carla as he recovered from surgery in the garden that he had planted behind the house in the summer of 1949. Ray had tended his beloved plants and flowers all the years since, and according to Carla, the last thing he did at the house before leaving for the hospital in June of the following year, was to take a walk through the garden.

Ray's column from Baja, written on the day he arrived at Rancho Buena Vista for the last time.]

NOVEMBER 9, 1976—The dishwashers and chefs and all other kitchen workers were singing again. Glory had returned to the earth and its heavens. The light spectrum from the sun was again painting the Sea a royal blue. The valleys, hillsides, and mountaintops reflected all of the polished shades of green the spectrum provides. Hibiscus, bougainvillea, and numerous other blossoms were putting out their spring-like adornment in multicolor.

The long period of mourning was over for the unfortunate storm-belabored people of Obregón, La Paz, and Culiacán regions. No one in the area of Buena Vista, said to be the eye of the storm Liza, was so much as scratched and the damages to resorts were considered minor in comparison to the great good of a wide strip of white sand beach brought in by big waves. Hundreds of tons and miles of driftwood (considered so precious in the U.S.) were washed high up on the shore between the resorts of Palmas de Cortez and Punta Pescadero.

Several people here and elsewhere agreed that the eye or main thrust of the chubasco that tore across the peninsula hit this particular region. The strongest winds, largest waves and heaviest rains did little more here than

Ray's "Fifth 79th Birthday." The Vagabundos Del Mar club announcement for his last birthday party, at the Islandia Hotel in San Diego, February 4-6, 1977. The fiesta was held in lieu of a fly-in party in La Paz that had been canceled the previous October because of Hurricane Liza.

— COURTESY VAGABUNDOS DEL MAR

blow away palm leaf palapas and corners of palm leaf roofs. Several glass windows are broken—three of them and two glass doors in Casa Cannon were smashed by wind-borne driftwood.

A few days later, from a cozy cabaña, I can see through a plate glass window and door one of the most delightful landscapes to be found anywhere. I gaze across an artistic thatch-covered veranda. Beyond it is a corridor of freshly bathed coconut and royal palms that runs down the sides of formally cropped lawns, crisscrossed with curving flagstone walks and on to a swimming pool in blue tile.

Beyond it comes the newly replenished beach down to the edge of the royal blue Cortez.

As I write this a couple of marlin cruisers from the resort's fleet of 22 are edged in just below the sunset's orange haze lingering just above the sharp line of the horizon. My esthetic sense is appeased by all of this, but seeing all of those shapely ladies lolling around the pool, I must admit I am still afflicted with that Jimmie Carter rash of "lust in the chest."

Except for one boat with a big marlin hookup, all cruisers are in. Most of them look as if they had been decorated for Christmas, with outrigger poles bearing pennants of many colors. Most of them indicate dorado (dolphinfish), half-a-dozen sailfish flags, one for striped marlin, also one for a yellowfin tuna, a roosterfish, jack crevalle, threadfin pompano and several for sierra.

I am meeting a great many old friends and fellow anglers who are just arriving for the Bill Gallagher "World Festival of Fishing," a tournament honoring Colonel Eugene Walters, pioneer operator of Rancho Buena Vista and which will signal the beginning of the festive fall-winter angling season in this part of the big game fishing world. This contest starts off with a sea-plowing roar. All boats are loaded but stand by until the "GO" signal is given, when all peel off full-bore and fan out toward the skipper's favorite spot.

The musicians who will play for the Festival have arrived and are starting rehearsals of their native Baja California songs and dances. The rhythm, sounds, and fast tempo are so rousing that everyone feels a compelling urge to get up and start dancing, prancing, or whatever seems to fit the individual mode of expression.

When I arrived here there were a few "no-see-'em" gnats in the lush growth of grass, and seeing no birds around I was concerned.

But today I saw at least 20 species of birds, first in small groups then by flocks. There were many orioles and sparrows (the kinds that specialize in eating gnats). Among the returners were doves, finches, cardinals, hummingbirds, and a host of other species of which I am not sure. And thanks to Mother Nature, or someone, there are no cats around to change the melodious songs to squawking warning calls.

I asked some of the Tournament participants their opinions on starting a crusade to more quickly get Baja people singing again, and enlisting all of the anglers who may be visiting our favorite grounds to help banish the effects of the state's overpublicized misfortune. To a man they were more than anxious to join us by word of mouth, or whatever way possible. — RAY CANNON

TRUE EXTENT OF HURRICANE LIZA DAMAGE

[After his return to Los Angeles, Ray reveals the severity of the damage from Hurricane Liza.]

JANUARY 12, 1977—My superficial accounts in this column some few weeks ago of damage done to the La Ribera village by the October chubasco Liza, especially the emotional effect on old residents at seeing their homes or at least the roofs blown away by the raging winds, were understatements of the facts.

La Ribera, seven or eight miles below Rancho Buena Vista, is a town of 200 or so farmers and shark fishermen, and an extra hundred young crewmen working on marlin cruisers owned by the four main resorts in the region. All were striving to get small survival patches planted where floods had completely destroyed the farmers' marketable produce.

At 80 years old, the self-styled vagabundo and "Old Man of the Sea." — ARIZONA DAILY STAR PHOTO BY ALEX DRESHLER

An old native described the storm as the worst in the peninsula's history. He told of everything hitting at one time, of how the cyclonic tornado lifted roofs and things and sent them spinning over the tree tops and how the great arroyo flood made him wish he had an ark like Noah. The sea was rolling inland and the winds were strong enough to blow a child away. But parents had kept them crouching in corners that were partially sheltered. The old timers also told of century-old trees being dug up by the arroyo flooding and transported by it to the beach from as far as Las Cuevas village (which also took a beating).

I was happy to hear from Bobby Van Wormer, operator of the Hotel Punta Colorada resort, and get his note on the La Ribera damage. Also one from Pat Snyder re: the worthwhile work she and husband Tom are doing in their Hurricane Relief Fund. She writes: "Many, many thanks for your generous mention of the 'La Ribera Relief Fund' in your *Western Outdoor News* column. So far we've received almost $1,500."

The note from Bob Van Wormer reads: "We are back in our house and have the roof replaced on the two-story units so we have things pretty well back in order. Also we have helped over 15 families in La Ribera with the money from Pat Snyder's Hurricane Relief Fund. In another month things will be pretty well reconstructed again. This area was hit harder than ever known in history. Drop by when you can."

Roberto, as his Mexican neighbors affectionately call

him, is always first to volunteer to go to the assistance of anyone in trouble. We had some happy years in learning the way of the sea and the creatures in it. He was working half-days at Rancho Buena Vista wiring the place for lights. The other half was spent diving, mostly in observing fish and baits and refining angling techniques. — RAY CANNON

THE BEST AND MOST DELIGHTFUL MEMORIES

[A month before his death, Ray recalls the thrills and lessons of the Benziger shipwreck at Tambobiche in October 1964.]

MAY 6, 1977—Tambobiche taught me much by hurling wind and rainstorms, hurricanes, and tumultuous sea swells and breakers that crashed over 40-foot headlands. Yet through all of them I repeatedly said and wrote that I enjoyed those hours like few others. Now I consider those hours of striving my best to survive in nature's crucible as the best and most delightful memories.

— RAY CANNON

RAY'S LAST DAYS

[Carla describes Ray's final days, after he returned from Rancho Buena Vista.]

Months before Ray's death I had a strong premonition that he would be leaving this earthly plane soon. I felt it so strongly it cast a dark shadow over every waking moment of my life. My heart was breaking. I knew Ray was going to leave me. I wanted to be with him all the time—I wanted to hold him here.

It was in the fall of 1976, when Ray returned from his last trip to Baja California that I first knew that he was gravely ill. He seemed weak and exhausted and his skin had an unhealthy sallow look. He told me he had not been feeling well, that he'd had some bad headaches and that he'd had a sunstroke. That was all he told me. Ray died seven months later, June 7, 1977.

I found out much later that Ray had seen a doctor in La Paz. It seems that while he was at Rancho Buena Vista he confided to Colonel Walters' sister, Monta Chamberlin, that the doctor had told him he had cancer.

I was shocked when she told me this. Ray had never said anything to me about it. Long before I knew him and for many years afterward, Ray was a heavy smoker—a chain-smoker, in fact. Back then he rolled his own. Store-bought, packaged cigarettes were too expensive.

Ray said he had to have a cigarette before he could write anything. He was addicted.

Years later, when Ray became critically ill with a severe bronchial infection, his doctor told him point blank that if he did not quit smoking it would kill him.

Ray did quit smoking then and there, cold turkey. But it appears it was too late. Although he didn't know it at the time, the damage to his lungs had already been done, and while it was a good many years later, Ray developed lung cancer. Although the cancer was surgically removed from his lungs, it had already metastasized and spread to his brain. Tragically the tumors were inoperable.

Ray never talked to me about dying. Whether he knew that his earthly time was at hand he never gave any intimation of it. But I knew it and I'm sure he must have known it too. Ray would not have feared death, as he believed in the immortality of the spirit. I believe in that too, but I still miss Ray's presence more than anything in the world. Ray embraced life with gusto and instilled in others his zest and enthusiasm for living it to the fullest.

— CARLA LAEMMLE

LETTERS FROM COLONEL WALTERS

[Two days before Ray died in Los Angeles, Colonel Eugene Walters expresses the concern and intimacy of an old friend and kindred spirit.]

Rancho Buena Vista, June 5, 1977—Dear Ray, I hear you are in the hospital? I'm sending this to your sweet fine Secretary knowing she'll have the latest dope on you and pray it is nothing too serious!

You've got to lay off all those big banquets for you—

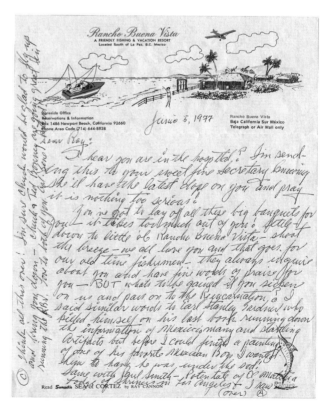

The letter from Colonel Walters.

Fishing pals, Colonel Eugene Walters and Ray during a trip to visit Ed Tabor's Flying Sportsmen Lodge in Loreto, c. 1960.

November 1976, Ray's damaged Round House at Rancho Buena Vista, as he photographed it on his last trip to Baja.

The Round House, 1997. — PHOTO BY GENE KIRA

it takes too much out of you! Settle down to little ol' Rancho Buena Vista—shoot the breeze—we all love you and that goes for our old-time fishermen. They always inquire about you and have fine words of praise for you. BUT what's to be gained if you sicken on us and pass on to the reincarnation? I said similar words to Erle Stanley Gardner who killed himself on his last book running down the information on Mexico's many and startling artifacts but before I could finish a painting of one of his favorite Mexican Boys I wanted him to have he was under the sod!…

Come on down here before it is too late and enjoy the sun and beach and fishing—and get some use in your declining years on that 12-foot bed of yours. The weather is great. Fishing fine too. We're over-booked notwithstanding the terrible hurricane!

That's no way to live your retirement up there in Hollywood. No expense for you whatsoever down here!

Everyone sends their love and wishes for an early recovery. Of course bring Carla to take care of you…

Think all this over! I'm sure Chuck would be glad to fly up and bring you down. Chuck and Ted Bonney are going great in running the R.B.V. Love to both of you."

*****

[Colonel Walters, only a few weeks from his own passing, writes to Carla after hearing the news of Ray's death:]

My Dear Carla, The sad news about dear "ole" Ray reached me this morning—I knew it was coming… and Ray never drank or smoked—does not seem fair somehow!

Now Honey Chile my own health is so jittery that I can't make it for the funeral! I'm too weak as it is but steadily growing stronger. But I've had to give up all activities where there is a strain on my mental and physical powers. BUT CHUCK my son is flying up to represent Rancho Buena Vista—and ole Colonel Gene Walters, Bonney and many others who always enjoyed Ray so much!

How well I enjoyed my first trip to Baja Sur when Ray brought me down for the first time!

Now Carla I know the strain has been terrible for you—so you'd better come down and rest a bit—lie in the sunshine by the pool. Speak to Chuck about this and he may have room in his plane…

I'll probably be next in line—except for the saying—OLD SOLDIERS NEVER DIE—they just fade away! I've been fading for some time now but recently got a hold of myself—getting stronger every day.

Time to fold up for the night so I can get this in the early mail tomorrow. God bless Ray's soul. Now take care of yourself. You are not completely out of the woods after all this strain.

Love, Col. Gene Paul Walters

FAREWELL TO LA PAZ

[On June 25, 1977, Ray Cannon's ashes were scattered on the Sea of Cortez, at Canal de San Lorenzo, near La Paz. The boat used for the ceremony was the 56-foot *Pachanga* of Bob Butler, and Ray's ashes were scattered on the outgoing tide, in mid-channel between Playa Tecolote and Isla Espíritu Santo, by Carla Laemmle, assisted by Ricardo García Soto. In this final tribute, Carla describes the trip on which Ray joined forever that spiritual fraternity of the wandering canoe fishermen he so admired, the *vagabundos del mar.*]

I agonized over the thought of carrying Ray's ashes on the plane with me. Could I possibly do it and still retain my composure? No, I knew I could not.

I called my good friend, Doris Ortega, to ask her if she would, por favor, be their custodian on the flight to La Paz. Yes, of course, she would. Other friends going with us were photographer Jack Barcus and his wife, Lucille, and Bob and Rosamond Durnall.

As I boarded the plane, a feeling of utter emptiness swept over me. I had never traveled to Baja without Ray beside me. My whole world had revolved around him, his projects and activities. I knew that nothing would ever be the same again.

It was shortly after midday when our DC-9 touched down in La Paz. We were asked to remain on the plane until all the other passengers had taken their leave.

I could hardly hold back my tears as I stepped off the plane. An official welcoming party was there to greet us, among them a deputy representing the governor, officials of the Department of Tourism, the National Archives, Aeroméxico Airlines, and other friends of Ray's.

Their warm and meaningful words touched me deeply. I am sure I responded emotionally to them. I must have. And yet, somehow I wasn't there. Much of it is a blur to me now.

The urn containing Ray's ashes was carried to a waiting hearse and we were escorted to the procession of cars. I was weeping inside as I seated myself in the car. I wanted to jump out and run away and shout that it wasn't so. Our funeral procession moved over the hot pavement at what seemed like a snail's pace. It was as if we were traversing the same ground over and over. I longed for it to move faster.

I was mystified to see people along the way stop, remove their hats, and bow their heads as the procession passed by. They knew that it was Señor Cannon.

At last we arrived at the chapel in La Paz.

Upon entering, our eyes beheld a magnificent floral display. Nestled in the midst of these floral tributes was a portrait of Ray. The sweet, heavy scent emanating from the profusion of blossoms was almost intoxicating. It was—to quote one of Ray's lines from his Chinese play, *Her Majesty the Prince*—"like the perfume of the rainbow."

RAY CANNON
1893-1977
HAPPIER DAYS—WON Columnist Ray Cannon, who died last week in Los Angeles, is shown helping board 200-pound baya grouper during one of his numerous fishing trips to Mulege in Baja California.   See Page 1

Photo Courtesy THE SEA OF CORTEZ

— COURTESY WESTERN OUTDOOR NEWS

Ray's ashes were brought into the chapel and placed on the platform. The service was a Mexican wake, in which friends of the deceased take turns "standing watch" in silent and loving remembrance. It is a simple, very personal and moving ceremony. My turn was not easy for me.

Doris and I stayed at the Hotel Los Arcos. From the time of his first visit to La Paz and his meeting with hotel owner, Luis Cóppola Bonillas, it had always been one of Ray's favorite places. Visiting the hotel again brought back bittersweet memories.

As difficult as the Mexican wake had been, I knew that the hardest task was yet to come—the final scattering of Ray's ashes into the Sea of Cortez.

Early Saturday morning we were driven back to the chapel, where our procession began its final journey to the pier with a police escort.

An overwhelming sense of sadness came over me as our procession slowly made its way through the city streets. It would be—perhaps—the last time I would ever see them. People were gathered all along the route of our procession to pay a last farewell to their Señor Cannon. Their sorrow and loss was reflected in their faces. It was like the city of La Paz was in mourning.

At the pier, the container with Ray's ashes, along

Promise of the Golden Age—A calm sea and a glorious dawn at Rancho Buena Vista, c. 1966.

with all of the floral tributes, was transferred onto the boat, after which our party boarded it.

It was a gorgeous day for Ray's farewell voyage. The Sea of Cortez had a translucent glow. I was in a strange state that morning, not wholly of this world. I was hoping that Ray's spirit was there with us.

As our boat reached the middle of the channel near the island of Espíritu Santo, the captain maneuvered it so as to be in right relation to the tide when the ashes were scattered into the sea. We were in readiness now for the dramatic and emotionally charged event that was about to take place.

A memorial service was conducted in Spanish with great warmth and feeling by Doctor FCO Javier Carballo, Chronicler and Historian of Baja California Sur. It was then translated into English by Lic. Ricardo García Soto, Delegado de Codibac, Baja California Sur. At that point the floral tributes were cast overboard and the container with Ray's ashes was solemnly handed over to Ricardo.

My heart was pounding and I was trembling. I held Ricardo's arm as we jointly scattered Ray's ashes into the Sea of Cortez, to be carried by the tide to the shores of Isla Cerralvo—a moment in my life indelibly engraved on my heart. — CARLA LAEMMLE

THE PURSUIT OF LIFE

MAY 31, 1963—There is an area in the brain that functions as the seat and control center of pleasure. According to scientists, the responses from cells in this area are more compelling than the reactions from cells that have to do with satisfying appetites and physical desires.

When this pleasure area was kept constantly stimulated in a subject for months, there was no sign of physical or mental loss but a general improvement was shown while in this high state of happiness.

You have, no doubt, already guessed my interpretation of this.

For if you have read this column for some length of time, you have noted that I have repeatedly urged people to get out of the rat-race our highly mechanized civilization has imposed, and get into the region of near total pleasure I have found, where the philosophy of "there is no pleasure without pain" is proven false, and where the pendulum need not swing back from its high point of joy to its opposite—despair.

Enduring pleasure is not only possible but highly beneficial to physical and mental stability and well-being, especially in escaping from the ravages of tensions and stress.

Although thousands of people may find as many ways to fulfill the pursuit of happiness, there is one simple rule that allows a great measure of freedom in the search. That is, "Harm no one, especially yourself." And another Oriental proverb that promises the greatest reward, "Make the many happy, expecting no reward."

All of us cannot find the same degree of happiness or fun in the same kind of experiences, but except for those who like living in a frigid climate or an icehouse, I am sure most normal humans will find more things to enjoy around the Cortez than they have experienced elsewhere on earth.

Then there are always those who prefer living fictitious lives, ridiculously striving to impress other phonies, regardless of the anguish it produces. But most pathetic is the intelligent but procrastinating man who sticks to the grind, putting off "till next year" that long vacation trip, then being forced to take it in a hospital.

I have a sizable list of correspondents who write me from their beds, always asking me to warn others. But I also have an enormous list of people, thousands of them, who know they have escaped and know they have gained health, tranquility, and a life full of fun. From their repeated sign-off phrase—"Keep up the good work"—I know I have made some contribution to their happiness.

This quoted phrase is the most satisfying paycheck I receive.

You may now have guessed that in the dim and distant ages ago I studied to be a preacher, but reversed the scheme of fishing for man, to fishing for fish. — RAY CANNON

1535

Hernán Cortés lands in Baja California, possibly near site of present Rancho Las Cruces resort, outside of La Paz.

1861

Silver is discovered at San Antonio, south of La Paz.

La Paz pearl industry reaching its height.

1863

La Paz population: 1,500

Mines established at El Triunfo.

Hotel Americano and Hotel Progreso open in La Paz.

1884

La Paz population: 4,000

1885

El Boleo mines established at Santa Rosalía.

1892

Ray Cannon born in Tennessee (September 1).

1895

Loreto population: 322

1900

Baja California population (north and south): 47,624

Hotel Frances opens in Santa Rosalía (approximate date). Burns in 1911 or 1917; reconstructed in 1920 with wood brought from Oregon.

1907

La Perla de la Paz mercantile company established by Antonio Ruffo.

1909

Carla Laemmle born in Chicago (October 20).

1910

Mexican Revolution begins.

1912

Ray lured to California by articles in *Sunset Magazine*.

1913

Ray acting at the Bentley Grand Theater in Long Beach, California; begins shore fishing near Malibu.

First cannery ship stationed at Cabo San Lucas.

1915

Ray's first named movie roll, "The Beggar" in *The Garden of Allah*.

1916

Carla's uncle, Carl Laemmle, founds Universal Studios.

Ray works with D. W. Griffith in *Intolerance*.

1920

Ray marries Fanchon Royer.

1921

Carla and family move to Universal Studios movie lot.

1923

Baja's first paved road constructed, Tijuana to Ensenada.

1925

Carla featured as prima ballerina in *Phantom Of The Opera*, with Lon Chaney.

1926

First postal service established between Santa Rosalía and Mulegé, contracted by Anselmo Zúñiga, later by his son Antonio "El Tobaco" Zúñiga Meza, for whom the Mulegé bridge is named.

1928

Southern California Automobile Club overland expedition reaches Mulegé.

Carla is prima ballerina at Shrine Light Opera Season.

Over 1.8 million pounds of totuava exported to U.S. from San Felipe.

Ray wins critical kudos for directing, *Life's Like That*, produced by Fanchon Royer; writes and directs *Red Wine*, with Conrad Nagle.

1929

Ray and Fanchon Royer divorce in Los Angeles.

Ray credited with developing several innovative movie camera techniques.

Carla dances in *Broadway Melody*, named Best Picture of 1930.

1930

Population of Baja California Sur: 47,089.

Carla dances on giant piano for George Gershwin in *The King of Jazz*.

Ray working in public relations for Chinese business community in Los Angeles.

1931

Carla has first speaking part in world's first supernatural "talkie" horror movie, *Dracula*, with Bela Lugosi.

1932

Cabo San Lucas cannery built.

1935

Ray and Carla meet while working on movie at Universal Studios.

Ray writes the play *Her Majesty The Prince* for Carla (opens at Music Box Theater, May 10, 1936).

1936

Carla's uncle, Carl Laemmle (deceased 1939), sells Universal Studios.

Ray leaves on film-making trip, writes letters to Carla from Mexico City.

1939

Ray organizes King Cotton Ball and Cotton Co-Action Committee, advocates boycotts of Japanese silk products.

Antero and Cruz Díaz leave Mexico City, arrive at Calmallí mine, east of Guererro Negro.

1940

Baja California Sur population: 51,471

Ray declares bankruptcy.

John Steinbeck cruises around tip of Baja with Edward F. "Doc" Ricketts, encounters fly-in anglers at Bahía de los Angeles.

Hotel Perla de la Paz opens in La Paz as the territory's first modern hotel. Sponsored by Territorial Governor Rafael M. Pedrajo, a semipublic corporation is formed and shares are sold to leading citizens throughout the territory. The shares are gradually bought by the Castro and Ruffo families, and later the Coronado family.

First air service for La Paz opened briefly by Líneas Aéreas Mineras, S.A. (LAMSA). Discontinued the following year.

1941

Aeronaves de México establishes air service between La Paz and Mazatlán. Service is extended on an as-needed basis to Santa Rosalía in 1942, Loreto and Mulegé in 1944.

1942

First Lieutenant Ronald Reagan rejects Ray's application for commission in Army Motion Picture Unit.

1945

Ray develops severe stomach ulcers, directs last movie, *Samurai*, and leaves Hollywood movie industry.

1946

Doña Blanca Verdugo and Juan "Juanito" José Garayzar open first guest house in Loreto.

1947

Ray catches the "opaleye that changes his life"; makes first trip to Baja (San Felipe) with Eddie Urban (possibly 1948).

1948

Ray begins research and writing for *How To Fish The Pacific Coast.*

Ensenada highway pavement extended to San Telmo.

1949

Cora Galenti saves Ray's life by raising money for ulcer operation.

Mayo Obregón establishes Trans Mar de Cortés airline with war surplus DC-3s and Luis Cóppola Bonillas as his first pilot. Service begins to La Paz, Loreto, Puerto Cortés (Bahía Magdalena). Aeronaves de México also servicing La Paz.

1950

Population of Baja California Sur: 60,684

Mexicali to San Felipe road paved.

Servicios Aéreos de La Paz (later, Aerocalifornia) and Líneas Aéreas del Pacífico airlines begin air taxi service (approximate date).

Hotel California opened in Todos Santos by Antonio "El Chino" Tobasco.

Rancho Las Cruces opens near La Paz, Baja's first fishing resort.

1951

Herb Tansey's first trip to Rancho Buena Vista, with Joe García and Olen Burger.

Fisher House opens in San José del Cabo.

1952

Northern Territory of Baja California becomes a state.

Southern half of Baja California becomes a territory.

Hotel Los Arcos in La Paz bought by Luis Cóppola Bonillas and Evangelina Joffroy. Original 12-room hotel constructed in 1950 by Casto Verdayes Piñera and managed by Sabino and Antonio Pereda; expanded in 1956 (32 rooms); expanded and remodeled in 1956; expanded in 1976 (182 rooms).

Flying Sportsmen Lodge opens in Loreto.

Rancho Buena Vista opens in East Cape area with 12 rooms.

1953

How To Fish The Pacific Coast published.

Western Outdoor News launched by Burt Twilegar and Earl H. "Tex" Hardage (December 4).

Rudy Vélez managing Ruffo Brothers marlin sport fishing fleet.

1954

Ray's first Charlie Rucker Midriff trips; he makes first use of the term "Midriff" in his field notes.

Ray's first visit to La Paz; he is given free transportation privileges during meeting at Hotel Los Arcos with Trans Mar de Cortés' Mayo Obregón, Luis Cóppola Bonillas, and Guillermo "Bill" Escudero.

El Boleo mines closed in Santa Rosalía.

Guererro Negro salt plant opened by Daniel K. Ludwig. Population shifts from Santa Rosalía to Guererro Negro.

Highway construction begins between La Paz and agricultural area of Santo Domingo Valley (Ciudad Insurgentes and Ciudad Constitución).

1955

Cabo San Lucas population: c. 300

Luis Bulnes Molleda managing Cabo San Lucas cannery.

Beginning of significant tourism in Baja California Sur during governorship of Agustín Olachea. La Paz lists about a dozen hotels, led by the Hotel Perla and Hotel Los Arcos.

Club Mulegé opened by Octavio "Sal" Salazar. Later becomes Hacienda de Mulegé, then Old Hacienda de Mulegé under Alfonso Cuesta and Roberto Real in 1969.

1956

Arturo Grosso establishes road from Laguna Chapala to San Felipe.

Giant snook "discovered" at Mulegé.

"Gene Perry Trip" down Colorado River fails to reach Sea of Cortez.

Ray assigned by *Western Outdoor News* to write full-time about Baja.

"Bob Francis Cruise" (non-Cannon), San Felipe to La Paz, first known full-length trailer boat cruise of Cortez.

Carla retires from stage and movies (approximate date).

Radio station XENT opens in La Paz.

Loreto Mission reconstructed.

Hotel Las Cruces Palmilla (later, Hotel Palmilla) opened in Los Cabos area by Abelardo L. "Rod" Rodríguez and William Matthew "Bud" Parr.

1957

Ray's first visit to Rancho Buena Vista, with Frank Dufresne and Guillermo "Bill" Escudero.

"Gene Perry Cruise," Ray's first down the Cortez, San Felipe to Isla San Lorenzo.

"Hurricane Cruise," Kino Bay to Isla San Esteban.

Comité Pro-Turismo de La Paz established.

Hotel Los Cocos opens in La Paz as an expansion of "Quinta Los Cocos," a residence owned by Antonio Navarro Encinas and his wife Rosa María Almada. After passing though the

ownership of Abe Kookish and Arthur Froelish, it was acquired by the family of Miguel Alemán and became the Hotel Continental in 1969. In 1974, it was converted to workers' quarters for construction of the adjacent 250-room high-rise Hotel Presidente (later, Gran Baja), which was closed in 1994. Both structures are now abandoned.

Hotel Vista Hermosa opened in Mulegé by Jean Bonfantes, Luis Frederico, Don Johnson, and a partner named Ortiz. Later, owned variously by Richard Stockton, David Galloway, and Alejandro Arcos under several names including Club Aéro Mulegé, Loma Linda, and Vista Hermosa. Closed in 1993, due to problems with property title.

1958

"Kids' Trip," Kino Bay to Bahía San Francisquito.

Hotel Guaycura opened in La Paz by Sabino Pereda (closed 1991).

1959

Herb Tansey and Arthur Young of Rancho Buena Vista die in plane crash near El Triunfo.

Colonel Eugene Waters buys Rancho Buena Vista.

"Shipwreck Charlie" Cohen cruise, San Felipe to La Paz.

Severe chubasco strikes southern Baja California.

Bahía de Palmas Lodge opens in East Cape area with seven rooms. Property reverts to Ruiz family in 1973, and becomes the Hotel Palmas de Cortez, operated by Bobby and Cha Cha Van Wormer.

1960

Population of Baja California Sur: 81,594.

Hotel rooms in Baja California Sur: 324

Mulegé Beach Lodge (later, Playas de Mulegé Lodge) opens on Playa Equipalito just south of river mouth (closed, c. 1966).

Ray's *Peggy Sue* trip to Isla Cerralvo.

1961

Ray's El Dorado camper trip around southern end.

Herb Holland "Live Bait Cruise," Kino Bay to Rancho Buena Vista.

Ray names "Juanaloa" area south of Loreto.

Hotel Cabo San Lucas opens in Los Cabos area.

Hotel Serenidad opened in Mulegé by Leroy Center. In 1968, bought by Don Johnson and his wife Nancy Ugalde Gorosalve.

Las Casitas lodge (later, Hotel Las Casitas) opened in Mulegé by Cuca Woodworth (approximate date).

1962

Trans Mar de Cortés airline taken over by Aeronaves de México.

DC-6 propeller airliners begin direct flights from Los Angeles to La Paz.

1963

Hotel Oasis opened in Loreto by Bill and Gloria Benziger with two (2) rooms.

Hacienda Cabo San Lucas opened in Cabo San Lucas by Abelardo L. "Rod" Rodríguez. Acquired by Western International Hotels of Mexico, S.A., 1970, as Camino Real de Cabo San Lucas; bought by Bud Parr in 1977 as Hotel Hacienda Beach Resort.

1964

"Tambobiche Shipwreck," Punta San Telmo.

1965

Baja's first ferryboat service opens, La Paz to Mazatlán. A commercial boom in La Paz is created by mainland visitors patronizing duty-free shops.

1966

The Sea Of Cortez published by Lane Magazine and Book Company.

First cruise of Vagabundos Del Mar Boat & Travel Club, Kino Bay to La Paz (December 4).

La Paz to Cabo San Lucas road graded.

Aeronaves de México begins jet airliner service to La Paz.

Hotel Punta Colorada opened in East Cape area by Bobby and Cha Cha Van Wormer.

Hotel Borrego de Oro (later, Punta Chivato) opens near Mulegé. Acquired by Bill Alvarado in 1980; later taken over by the ejido of San Bruno.

Round House construction begins at Rancho Buena Vista.

Hotel Palomar opened in Santiago by Cirilo and Virginia Gómez.

Hotel La Posada opened in La Paz just south of Hotel Los Cocos. After several changes in ownership, acquired by singer Engelbert Humperdinck and renamed La Posada de Engelbert.

1967

Ray's trip to El Salvador.

Rancho Leonero name used by Gil Powell for his private guesthouse on the south shore of Bahía de Palmas. Later becomes Hotel Rancho Leonero under ownership of John Ireland.

1968

Sport fishing fleets expanding rapidly in Baja California Sur.

Tourism recognized by federal and state governments as a major area of future economic growth.

Hotel Punta Pescadero opened in East Cape area by Jorge Escudero Luján and Johnny Mitre.

1969

Round House completed at Rancho Buena Vista.

Hotel Misión de Loreto opened by Dr. Enoch Arias.

Hotel Playa Hermosa opened in East Cape area. Sold to Bobby and Cha Cha Van Wormer in 1994 and renamed the Hotel Playa del Sol.

1970

Population of Baja California Sur: 128,019.

Ferry service begins, La Paz to Topolobampo.

New airport opens at La Paz.

Hotel Bajo Colorado (later, Hotel Twin Dolphin, 1977) opens in Los Cabos area.

1971

Transterritorial Highway paved from Cabo San Lucas to Santa Rosalía.

1972

Ray hospitalized for prostate surgery.

Transterritorial Highway pavement extended to San Ignacio.

Planning for future system of paradores established for peninsula.

Hotel Finisterra opened in Cabo San Lucas by Luis Bulnes Molleda and Luis Cóppola Bonillas.

Hotel Mar de Cortés opens in Cabo San Lucas.

Hotel Playas de Loreto opened by Ildefonso "Al" Green Garayzar, and other investors (later, Hotel Presidente Loreto; then Hotel La Pinta).

1973

Ray's Condor II motor home trip.

Mulegé bridge constructed.

Loreto International Airport opens.

Ferry service begins, Santa Rosalía to Guaymas.

Transpeninsular Highway inaugurated at Guerrero Negro (December 1).

San Francisquito resort opens on Punta Santa Teresa.

Cabo San Lucas harbor dredging begins.

1974

Ferry service begins, Cabo San Lucas to Puerto Vallarta (ends, 1986).

Road to Bahía de los Angeles paved between May and October.

Baja California Sur becomes a state (October 8).

Fondo Nacional de Fomento al Turismo (FONATUR, National Fund for the Promotion of Tourism) established to plan and finance tourist facilities. Loreto and Cabo San Lucas designated as future centers of tourism.

Hotel Solmar opens at Cabo San Lucas.

Motel Dunas opens in Guererro Negro.

1975

Cabo San Lucas Harbor dredging completed.

Hotel Escuela de la Paz opens at Kilometer 5 on Pichilingüe highway, later becomes Hotel Presidente; then the La Concha Beach Resort Hotel in 1988.

Baja Sur Motel opened in Guererro Negro by Dr. Sergio Noyola; becomes Hotel El Morro in 1985.

Hotel Las Brisas opens in San Carlos (Bahía Magdalena).

1976

Ray's last cruise, aboard Bam and Jerry Heiner's boat, Gypsy, Bahía de los Angeles to Loreto; later, rendezvous at Rancho Buena Vista.

Hurricane Liza strikes La Paz (September 30).

Ray's "Fifth 79th Birthday" party canceled in La Paz (October 29).

Ray's last trip to Baja California, Rancho Buena Vista (November 9).

Club Spa Buena Vista (later, Hotel Buena Vista Beach Resort) opened in East Cape area by Felipe Jesús "Chuy" Valdéz Vásques.

Hyatt Cabo Baja opens near Cabo San Lucas; becomes Calinda Beach Resort in 1985.

1977

Ray's postponed "Fifth 79th Birthday" party celebrated at Islandia Hotel, San Diego (February 4–6).

San José del Cabo International Airport opens.

Ray dies in Los Angeles (June 7).

Ray's ashes scattered on the Sea of Cortez near La Paz (June 25).

Hotel Twin Dolphin (formerly Bajo Colorado, 1970) opens in Los Cabos area.

1979

The Sea Of Cortez goes out of print after 12 years of publication and 280,000 copies sold

1980

Hotel Rooms in Baja California Sur: 3,581

1997

Hotel Rooms in Baja California Sur: 7,829

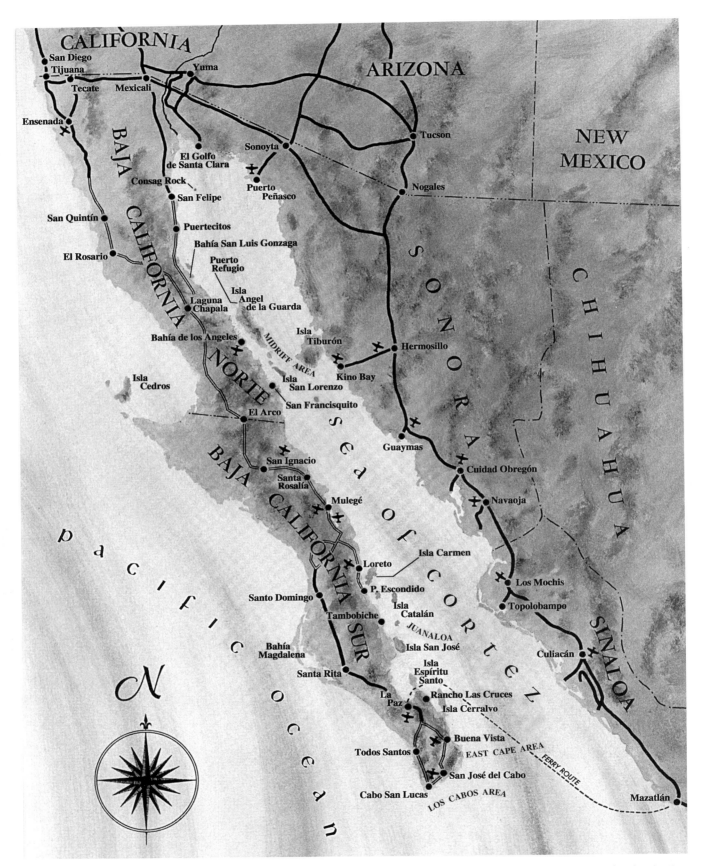

Baja California of the Golden Age, adapted from the end paper illustration by Joe Seney for Ray Cannon's 1966 book, *The Sea Of Cortez*. Solid lines indicate paved roads. Double lines indicate unimproved roads. The full-length overland route shown, from the U.S. border at Tijuana, to Cabo San Lucas at the tip of the peninsula, is slightly more than 1,000 miles in length.